Organizing Crime: Mafias, Markets, and Networks

Associate Editors
Philip J. Cook
Francis T. Cullen
Anthony N. Doob
Jeffrey A. Fagan
Daniel S. Nagin

Organizing Crime: Mafias, Markets, and Networks

Edited by Michael Tonry and Peter Reuter

VOLUME 49

The University of Chicago Press, Chicago and London

The University of Chicago Press, Chicago 60637
The University of Chicago Press, Ltd., London

© 2020 by The University of Chicago
All rights reserved.
Printed in the United States of America

ISSN: 0192-3234

ISBN-13: 978-0-226-70839-3 (cloth)
ISBN-13: 978-0-226-72283-2 (paper)
ISBN-13: 978-0-226-70842-3 (e-book)

LCCN: 2020026837

Library of Congress Cataloging-in-Publication Data

Names: Tonry, Michael H., editor. | Reuter, Peter, editor.
Title: Organizing crime : mafias, markets, and networks / edited by Michael Tonry
   and Peter Reuter.
Other titles: Crime and justice (Chicago, Ill.) ; c. 49.
Description: Chicago : The University of Chicago Press, 2020. | Series: Crime and
   justice: a review of research ; volume 49 | Includes bibliographical references. |
   Summary: "Organizing Crime: Mafias, Markets, and Networks provides the most
   exhaustive overview ever published of knowledge about organized crime. It provides
   intensive accounts of American, Italian, and Dutch developments, covers both
   national mafias and transnational criminality, and delves in depth into gender,
   human capital, and money laundering issues. The writers are based in seven countries.
   To a person they are, or are among, the world's most distinguished specialists in their
   subjects. At last, credible explanations and testable hypotheses are available concerning
   when, why, and under what circumstances mafias and other organized crime
   organizations come into being, what makes them distinctive, what they do and with
   what effects, and how to contain them"—Provided by publisher.
Identifiers: LCCN 2020026837 | ISBN 9780226708393 (cloth) |
   ISBN 9780226722832 (paperback) | ISBN 9780226708423 (ebook)
Subjects: LCSH: Organized crime. | Mafia.
Classification: LCC HV6441 .O77 2020 | DDC 364.106–dc23
LC record available at https://lccn.loc.gov/2020026837

The paper used in this publication meets the minimum requirements of American
National Standard for Information Sciences—Permanence of Paper for Printed
Library Materials, ANSI Z39.48-1984. ♾

Contents

Dedication

To James B. Jacobs (1947–2020), long America's most distinguished organized crime scholar, whose essays appear in volume 1 of *Crime and Justice* and in this one. He is sorely missed.

Preface

The Godfather, *The Sopranos*, and La Cosa Nostra exemplify organized crime for most Americans. In Asia the term conjures up images of Japanese yakuza and Chinese triads, in Italy the Cosa Nostra and 'Ndrangheta, in Latin America Mexican narco-gangs and Colombian drug cartels, in the Netherlands transnational drug and human trafficking, and in Scandinavia outlaw motorcycle gangs. Some but not all those organizations are "mafias" with centuries-long histories, distinctive cultures, and complicated relationships with local communities and governments. Others are new, large but transitory, and with no purpose other than maximizing profits from illegal markets.

The phenomena have existed for centuries but serious scholarly, as opposed to journalistic or law enforcement, efforts to understand them date back only a few decades. In *Crime and Justice*'s early days, we several times commissioned organized crime essays. That was almost inevitable. The series' mission, after all, is to publish state-of-the-art surveys of knowledge about topical subjects. The federal government during the 1970s through the 1990s fiercely challenged and fundamentally weakened American mafia organizations. Few subjects were more topical. Unfortunately, the editors and outside referees at the time agreed, only one of those early commissioned papers, by Peter Reuter on mafia involvement in New York City's waste management industry, worked out. The rest failed not from insufficient authorial effort, but because rigorous, analytically acute, and methodologically sophisticated scholarly literatures on organized crime did not exist.

Impressive and useful scholarly literatures have, however, begun to emerge, mostly outside the United States. They have developed in different countries, involve work in different languages and disciplines, and deploy a wide range of methods. *Organizing Crime: Mafias, Markets, and Networks* provides the most exhaustive overview ever published of knowledge about organized crime. The writers to a person are, or are among, the world's most distinguished specialists in their subjects. At last, credible explanations and testable hypotheses are available concerning when, why, and under what circumstances mafias and other organized crime organizations come into being, what makes them distinctive, what they do and with what effects, and how to contain them.

We followed the standard *Crime and Justice* developmental process. Essays were commissioned from well-known, widely respected scholars. The writers, the editors, and other specialists from the United States and Europe attended a May 2019 conference in Bologna, Italy, to illuminate and deconstruct initial drafts. Each essay was rewritten after the conference and distributed to paid referees for critical reactions and suggestions for improvement. Peter Reuter and I then provided our own questions, comments, and suggestions.

Many people have served as coeditors of *Crime and Justice* thematic volumes. Some extensively participated in developing the volumes their names adorn; some did not. Peter is among the heavy lifters. He and I have been partners in organized crime since the outset. He proposed the volume. We lengthily discussed topics and writers and referees and drafts. He read and commented on initial and revised drafts, wrote the introduction with me, and advised on the dust jacket and this preface. I am in his debt.

The volume would not exist save for many people's efforts. The indefatigable Su Love coordinated and managed the Bologna conference. The attendees, besides the writers, were Hans-Jörg Albrecht (Max Planck Institute, Freiburg), Francesco Calderoni (Universita Cattolica, Milan), Philip J. Cook (Duke University), Manuel Eisner (University of Cambridge), Vanda Felbab-Brown (Brookings Institution), Lars Korsell (Swedish National Council for Crime Prevention), Gianguido Nobili (Department of Police and Urban Security, Regional Government, Emilia-Romagna), and Tom Vander Beken (Ghent University). Some attendees, and some of the writers, also served as anonymous referees for particular essays. Other referees were Peter Andreas, Gerben Bruinsma, Scott Decker, Ombretta Ingrascì, Monica Massari, Francesco-Niccolò Moro, Andrew Papachristos, Stephan Parmentier, Alex Piquero, Michele Riccardi, and Jason Sharman.

The writers endured a long, arduous process with remarkable patience and goodwill. Meeting participants did their reading ahead of time and offered helpful advice and challenging criticism. Referees prepared reports substantially more detailed and reflective than is common;

writers took the reports seriously. Su Love provided painstaking, indispensable help behind the scenes. Peter and I are enormously grateful to them all. Readers will decide for themselves whether the effort was worthwhile.

Michael Tonry
Bagnaia, Isola d'Elba, April 2020

Peter Reuter and Michael Tonry

Organized Crime: Less Than Meets the Eye

"Less here than meets the eye," a Venusian documentary maker calling home might say. Books, films, and mass media portray organized crime as larger than life, a fearsome monster among us, an awesome money-making machine. Reality is different. Organized crime organizations are life-size, understandable outgrowths of local cultures, political systems, and markets. In some times and places, they control markets and peoples' lives, just as state institutions do in other times and places, but that too is understandable and can be explained. Organized crime organizations are not enormously profitable. Frightening, malevolent, and lethal, sometimes yes. Practically useful to ordinary law-abiding people, sometimes also yes. Economically important in any larger scheme of things, almost never.

Novelists, filmmakers, journalists, law enforcement officials, and policy makers have long paid attention to organized crime; scholars not so much. Mario Puzo's novel *The Godfather* and Francis Ford Coppola's follow-up films on the American Cosa Nostra exemplify long lines of popular novels and films in many languages and countries. Organized crime is a regular topic on the front pages of newspapers and a recurring subject of in-depth investigative reporting, exemplified by Roberto Saviano's *Gomorrah* on the Campanian Camorra and its eponymous film version. Organized crime is blamed for many modern ills, ranging from contraband cigarettes in Britain, high condominium prices in Miami, and the impossibility of conducting business honestly in Albania, to human smuggling, drug epidemics, and destabilization of communities and countries.

Organized crime has not, however, been a longtime, mainstream subject of research by social scientists. Part of the explanation is intellectual fashion. Criminologists traditionally focused on understanding crimes by

Electronically published May 19, 2020

individuals, especially young ones, and operations of the criminal justice system. Other subjects including organized and white-collar crime received and receive shorter shrift, as contents pages of criminology journals attest.

Several things contribute to the dearth of scholarly work. One is the increasingly quantitative character of contemporary social sciences, including criminology. Until recently, little research on organized crime was quantitative or easily could have been. Few numerical data sets provide much insight into its origins, operation, or effects. Important scholarly works were mostly qualitative. That is beginning to change, but mainstream statistical data on crime and victimization continue to shed comparatively little light.

A second is that there are only two quality journals, *Global Crime* and *Trends in Organized Crime*. Because tenure-seeking academics need and established scholars want their writings to be published in refereed journals, important work appears in a wide range of disciplinary and professional journals. Much important work is self-published by government and international organizations and research institutes. As a result, much of the literature is fugitive. No one purposely hides important work, but it is often hard to find.

A third, far from least important, is that research on organized crime presents special challenges. Participant observation or ethnographic study of transnational drug, human smuggling, and other markets, or of deliberations and activities of organized crime leaders, for example, are neither welcomed nor feasible. Representative surveys of participants in illegal markets or of members of organized crime groups are unsurprisingly rare. These are among the reasons why much writing on organized crime continues to draw heavily on journalistic sources, courtroom testimony, surveillance transcripts, biographies and autobiographies of offenders, and law enforcement officials' reflections.

Despite those challenges, comparatively rich literatures are beginning to emerge, especially in the Netherlands and Italy. Notorious events in those countries focused attention. A huge uproar occurred in the Netherlands when it became known that a police team had facilitated import of several tons of drugs, reportedly in order to help informers move up in trafficking organizations (Kleemans 2014). A parliamentary inquiry, charged to investigate the nature, seriousness, and scale of organized crime in the Netherlands, appointed an academic study group, chaired by Cyrille Fijnault, to establish what was known and knowable (Fijnault et al. 1996, 1998). A key finding was that remarkably little was known. The then minister of justice undertook to remedy this by promising regular reports on Dutch organized crime; the ministry's Research and Documentation Centre has continually followed up. The Dutch Organized Crime Monitor was established to support and conduct an ongoing program of research and to create new, cumulative, databases on organized crime activities and participants. Essays in *Organizing Crime: Mafias, Markets, and Networks* draw on their fruits (e.g., Kleemans and Van Koppen 2020; Selmini 2020; von Lampe and Blokland 2020).

In the late 1980s and early 1990s, a wave of assassinations of police officers, prosecutors, judges, and other public officials in Italy culminated in the 1992 bombing deaths of judges Paolo Borsellino and Giovanne Falcone, joint leaders of an antimafia task force (Catino 2020). Their deaths precipitated enactment of unprecedentedly severe antimafia laws; a relentless series of investigations, prosecutions, convictions, and imprisonments; and an explosion of interest among Italian scholars. Researchers gained access to hundreds of thousands of pages of wiretap transcripts and the testimony of hundreds of mafiosi who changed sides.[1] Over time these records have been mined to create new databases on organized crime activities, participants, and revenues and to develop large and growing literatures. Essays in *Organizing Crime: Mafias, Markets, and Networks* draw on them (e.g., Catino 2020; Paoli 2020; Reuter and Paoli 2020; Selmini 2020; Varese 2020).

Those Dutch and Italian developments, and an international diaspora of Italian organized crime researchers, may have catalyzed work in other countries, though that would be difficult to prove. In any case, new literatures emerged, old ones adapted, and Dutch and Italian scholars played major roles. Specialists in network analysis explore webs of relationships and activities among organized crime members and between them and outsiders (Bouchard 2020). Criminologists explore similarities and differences between youth gangs, outlaw motorcycle gangs, and organized crime organizations, and interactions among them (Selmini 2020; von Lampe and Blokland 2020). They draw on criminal careers, developmental psychology, and life-course research traditions to learn about initiation, continuation, and desistance in crime involvement of participants in organized crime organizations and transnational criminal activities

---

[1] Similar sources generated by unprecedented federal antimafia efforts in the 1970s, 1980s, and 1990s have enriched understanding of the operations, organization, and effects of American organized crime (Jacobs 2020).

(Kleemans and van Koppen 2020). Economists and others develop and test theories about operations of and changes in illegal markets (Levitt and Venkatesh 2000; Cook et al. 2007). Traditional small-scale qualitative studies and journalists' investigations continue, as has publication of biographies, autobiographies, and professionals' reflections.

Much more is known than even a decade ago and incomparably more than 20, 30, or 40 years ago. The essays in this volume speak for themselves so we neither describe nor summarize them. Instead, we identify a few important lessons that have been learned.

Every society gets the kind of criminal it deserves.
(—John F. Kennedy)

Research on organized crime has long faced the difficulty that its conceptualization is contested. Definitions vary widely and no widespread agreement is in sight. There is agreement that transnational organized crime and long-enduring organized crime organizations, usually shorthanded as mafias, are distinguishable albeit overlapping phenomena. Illegal markets, ubiquitous in modern societies and present in many premodern ones, generate a wide variety of organizational forms. Some are evanescent, a couple of people seizing a tempting opportunity. Others that last longer as small change—three students selling marijuana in a college dormitory—fall within formalistic organized crime definitions set out in criminal codes and international agreements. Still others are more and less stable networks in which individuals collaborate opportunistically over time, switching partners as market conditions change. Occasionally, but not often, large and enduring organizations emerge.

"Mafias" are large, enduring criminal organizations that serve multiple functions. Japanese yakuza, Chinese triads, and the Italian 'Ndrangheta and Cosa Nostra are prominent examples. These exist only in a few countries and are in sharp decline. Illegal markets and social disruption have precipitated criminal organizations in other countries, particularly in Russia and Eastern Europe, that acquire mafia-like reputations, but they have typically proven to be short-lived. In still other countries, typically in South and Central America, combinations of lucrative illegal markets and weak governments have fostered large, conspicuously violent, criminal organizations that may or may not prove long-lived.

Societies get the crime they deserve, President Kennedy observed. That appears to be true of criminal organizations. Violent crime represents a failure of social control, but is rooted in human behavior; the impulse to violence is universal and manifests itself everywhere. So do the impulses to steal and defraud. Organized crime in various of its nontrivial senses is, by contrast, a response to a specific kind of governmental failure—inability to prevent ongoing coordinated actions to earn money from predation or illegal markets. The emergence of powerful organized crime groups in the Northern Triangle of Central America (El Salvador, Guatemala, and Honduras), for example, is indicative of weak, almost failed, states. The emergence of similar groups in Venezuela and Brazil is associated with state failures to provide security in prisons and urban ghettos. The influence and power of mafia groups in the United States through much of the twentieth century was attributable in part to their successful, long-term accommodations with urban political machines. Similar accommodations in Mexico during the long reign of the Partido Revolucionario Institucional (PRI) broke down when the PRI lost its political monopoly; this and fundamental state weakness are among the reasons why violent drug gangs have since 2007 seemed beyond the reach of state control. By contrast, the Netherlands' modest organized crime problem, despite being the principal entry point for cocaine and heroin into Europe because of the importance of the Port of Rotterdam and Schiphol Airport, shows that a well-run democratic state can maintain order and provide adequate services even in the presence of large-scale drug trafficking. Similarly, the Scandinavian countries in which quasi-legal motorcycle gangs have in recent decades symbolized organized crime have experienced only modest violence.

Every community gets the kind of law enforcement it insists on.
(—John F. Kennedy)

Violence, theft, and fraud are parts of the human condition. So, *Homo sapiens* being social animals, are collaborative efforts to commit them. Neither individual nor collaborative crimes will ever cease, but both can be contained, and more elaborate forms of collaborative crime can be weakened and controlled.[2] Enforcement campaigns against mafias have been unexpectedly successful. Unceasing law enforcement attacks

---

[2] Though the matter is not free from controversy, the prevalence of individual crimes also can be contained, though more effectively through the delivery of social welfare programs and services than through law enforcement efforts.

by local US Attorneys' offices, the US Department of Justice, and the FBI greatly weakened the American Cosa Nostra and eliminated it in some US cities. Italian campaigns against the Sicilian Cosa Nostra and the Campanian Camorra have resulted in imprisonment of generations of their leaders, largely dissuaded them from the use of lethal violence, and greatly reduced their power and influence. Similar stories can be told about the Japanese yakuza and Chinese triads in China, Hong Kong, Taiwan, and Southeast Asian countries. The organizations endure but wield much less power than they once had. Essays in *Organizing Crime: Mafias, Markets, and Networks* tell some of these stories and other similar ones (e.g., Catino 2020; Jacobs 2020; Paoli 2020; Reuter and Paoli 2020).

Each of these stories needs to be understood in its own terms. In the United States, for example, important contextual changes coincided with law enforcement attacks on organized crime. These included the declining power of labor unions after 1970, the breakdown of urban political machines in the Northeast and Midwest, and increasing professionalism of policing in large cities. The Borsellino and Falcone assassinations prompted not only a massive and ongoing law enforcement response in Italy but also a change in national consciousness evidenced by the formation of countless local antimafia civic associations, large-scale asset forfeiture programs, and dissolution of hundreds of mafia-influenced local governments. The weakening of the yakuza and triads is partly a by-product of development of more effective centralized states. The elimination of the Medellin drug cartel in Colombia resulted not only from US pressures, a law enforcement crackdown, and government resolve, but also from active involvement of the military, responding to the cartel's challenges to the central government. The failures of weak states to control and diminish the power of organized crime organizations in Mexico, Argentina, Brazil, and the Northern Triangle of Central America each involve different kinds of stories. The bottom line nonetheless is that at least the more visible forms of organized crime can be suppressed by effective modern states.

Organized crime is the dirty side of the sharp dollar.
(—Raymond Chandler)

Cupidity and stupidity are, alas, also part of the human condition. Most people, probably all of us, want to enjoy pleasures, benefits, and resources beyond their means. Efforts to obtain them unlawfully lead to both creation of organized crime organizations and individuals' willingness to collaborate with them.

Markets distribute goods and services. Most illegal markets operate without generating large criminal enterprises. One of us (Reuter 1983) offered an early theoretical explanation, focusing on the structural consequences of product illegality, which limits criminal entrepreneurs' and managers' use of many features of modern commerce, including advertising, open communication, systematic research and development, and access to legitimate forms of dispute resolution such as courts, mediation, and arbitration. Criminal entrepreneurs need to get jobs done, but many must do them on their own in unstable collaborations in chaotic settings. The optimal configuration of human smuggling, among the largest illegal markets, for example, is of small adaptive enterprises that specialize in specific market segments (Campana 2020). This is true even in regions with sizable criminal enterprises, such as the US-Mexico border, where large drug-trafficking organizations operate, and in Sicily where Cosa Nostra remains powerful and active albeit diminished.

Some large criminal enterprises employ thousands of individuals and create barriers to entry by other criminal entrepreneurs but lack access to facilities and services that empower legal enterprises. The traditional way to solve this problem is to collaborate with willing entrepreneurs, politicians, and governments. A major obstacle to effective antimafia efforts in Italy, wiretaps and court cases show, is that otherwise legitimate entrepreneurs are attracted by moneymaking opportunities mafias can provide, either earnings from providing noncriminal services to criminal actors, or purchase of mafia services such as debt collection that are faster, cheaper, and more effective than courts can achieve. Outlaw motorcycle gangs, which share many characteristics with mafias, typically achieve a borderline status in which clubs are legally chartered organizations, copyrighting symbols and suing infringers, while many members engage in active criminal careers. Drug markets in Brazil and Mexico have long been dominated by organizations that reached live-and-let-live accommodations with corrupt police, politicians, and armies. Illegal gambling in Rio de Janeiro led in the twentieth century to the emergence of a large criminal federation that became tightly bound to the city's politics; the federation was a major player in the operation of Rio's famous Carnivale celebrations (Misse 2007). However, like mafias, these are not the norm.

Illegal markets and legitimate institutions are often intertwined, particularly conspicuously in money laundering. Major international banks in Denmark, the Netherlands, Switzerland, the United Kingdom, and the United States[3] have paid billions of dollars in fines for knowingly accepting and transferring money that originated in illegal market activity (Levi and Soudijn 2020). Compelling evidence in all these cases showed that senior bank managers, often including boards of directors, knew or willfully disregarded the likelihood that transactions flowed from drug traffickers or mafias. Despite making large investments in money-laundering controls, in the hundreds of millions of dollars for large banks,[4] directors often have few scruples about banks accepting such money.

Such connections have not been unique to money laundering. Major tobacco companies have been shown to have collaborated with mafias in smuggling their products into high tax markets, thus avoiding local taxes and boosting cigarette sales (Beare 2003). The yakuza over many decades provided important services to the ruling Liberal Democratic Party in Japan (Kaplan and Dubro 1987). Long-term connections between American labor unions and American mafias have been well documented (Jacobs 2020).

Organized crime in America takes in over forty billion dollars a year. This is quite a profitable sum, especially when one considers that the Mafia spends very little for office supplies.
(—Woody Allen)

Office supply budgets are no doubt comparatively small, partly because organized crime organizations do not pay taxes, comply with administrative regulatory regimes, or file lawsuits to settle commercial disputes or collect debts. However, although Woody Allen's $40 billion was probably meant to show that mafia revenues are enormous, in any big picture perspective they are small. In 2018, the gross revenues of 17 companies exceeded $200 billion each. Of the 50 companies with highest revenues, the smallest took in $119 billion. The United Nations Office

---

[3] The list includes HSBC, ING, Wachovia, Credit Suisse, Danskbank, and Wells Fargo. The 10 largest European banks have all been fined for money-laundering violations.

[4] HSBC, following a then record fine of $1.9 billion, reported that its annual expenditures on anti-money-laundering efforts (AML) exceeded $750 million (Arnold 2014). LexisNexis Risk Solutions (2017) estimated that the average bank in five European countries spent about $20 million on AML activities and that the European total exceeded $83 billion.

on Drugs and Crime (2012) estimated that global revenues from a very broad definition of organized crime amounted to $900 billion, but that constituted just 1.5 percent of global GDP. A European Commission–sponsored study of organized crime revenues produced an estimate of about 1 percent of the European Union's GDP (Savona and Riccardi 2015). Both studies erred on the side of generosity in their estimates.

Extraordinary powers are often ascribed to organized crime, particularly in the United States. Donald Cressey's *Theft of a Nation* (1969) described a criminal conspiracy that embraced every level of government and caused enormous damage. Cressey seemingly seriously quoted the famous claim of Meyer Lansky, a well-known mafia figure, that "We're bigger than General Motors." This is a perfect illustration of a taste for uncritical exaggeration that once characterized organized crime research. Estimates of the revenues of Italian mafias suggest that they have imposed a massive tax on business in Sicily and southern Italy in addition to corrupting many municipal governments (Calderoni 2014). Government agencies occasionally produce social cost estimates of the harms from organized crime that point to it as a major social problem (Fell et al. 2019; National Audit Office 2019).

None of these estimates have a sound conceptual basis or a strong empirical base. Part of the problem is empirical; the activities of organized crime are clandestine, and its finances are hidden. The conceptual problem is to define the counterfactual; what does Sicily look like without the Cosa Nostra? Corruption will be less serious. The Cosa Nostra is efficient in its subversion of government at every level, but how much will corruption decline? Drug markets may be less efficient and more violent; how does one value that? The data in support of the estimates are fragmentary and require what economists unblushingly call "heroic assumptions." This is illustrated by Pinotti (2015), who used sophisticated modeling techniques to estimate that the presence of 'Ndrangheta in two southern Italian provinces reduced per capita income by about one-sixth but with a long list of arguable assumptions.

Arguments are made that organized crime provides some social benefits. Fifty years ago, James Buchanan, a Nobel laureate economist, suggested that organized crime, by monopolizing illegal markets, reduced the cost of crime since a rational monopolist would raise the prices of illegal goods whose consumption produced harms (Buchanan 1973). Studies of Italian mafias that operate mechanisms to resolve internal conflicts, the true mafias, show that historically they have lower homicide rates than other organized crime organizations (Catino 2020).

Organized crime organizations can cause still other harms, such as threats to the state, that are impossible to value in monetary terms; rare but important. The provision of a criminal infrastructure may serve to expand the supply of illegal goods. Effective dispute settlement services, for example, allow for lower cost provision of goods and services. Similarly, organized crime can connect criminals with complementary skills more efficiently.

Nonetheless, it is hard to imagine that the harms of organized crime, net of any improvements in societal well-being à la Buchanan, are comparable to those resulting from violent or property crime. Credible estimates of the latter for the United States are in the many hundreds of billions of dollars per year (Miller et al. 2020).

In the broader context of important societal problems, organized crime is a minor one. Consider by contrast the apparently unending line of banking industry schemes that rake money from vast numbers of their customers. In the last decade alone that list includes the subprime mortgage scandals in the United States (Sorkin 2010) that precipitated a global recession, the Personal Protection Insurance scheme in the United Kingdom (Ferran 2012), bank scandals uncovered by the 2018 Royal Banking Commission in Australia (e.g., charging customers for services not provided; Hayne 2019), and similar frauds committed by Wells Fargo Bank against its customers. The LIBOR (London Interbank Overnight Rate) scandal is another instance of financial fraud with large-scale consequences, conducted by employees of the most respectable of City of London financial institutions (Bryan and Rafferty 2016).

Power tends to corrupt and absolute power corrupts absolutely.
(—Lord Acton)

Mafias may be less common than some might expect, organized crime may take many forms, and its economic consequences may be less than many believe, but none of that gainsays the reality that impunity empowers and sometimes has massive human costs. Living outside the law can mean living beyond reach of the law. Italian mafias, South American urban and prison-based gangs, and Colombian and Mexican narcogangs have at times been extravagantly violent (Reuter and Paoli 2020). So have gangs in the Northern Triangle of Central America. Much violence by Italian mafias has been intragroup, but not always as the 1980s and early

1990s spasms of the Sicilian Cosa Nostra demonstrate. Violence by South and Central American gangs has been mostly intragroup, in Mexico it has been both intra- and intergroup, and some in all these places, especially in Mexico, has targeted state employees and ordinary citizens. National homicide rates in many of these places (but not Italy) have at times as a result been among the world's highest. Within Italy, homicide rates are highest in Sicily, Campania, and Calabria, home bases of the three major mafias.

However, at least in effective modern states, extreme violence does not inexorably accompany the presence of mafias and other organized crime organizations. The American Cosa Nostra traditionally used violence instrumentally; murders usually occurred within or between mafia families, at least in part because of anticipated repercussions if law enforcement and other government personnel or ordinary citizens were often targeted (Jacobs 2020). The antimafia crackdown after the Borsallino and Falcone assassinations appears greatly to have suppressed killings by the Italian mafias (Catino 2020). Neither the yakuza nor the triads were historically or are now known for violence against outsiders.

It thus appears that effective modern and centralized states can restrain violence, especially against outsiders, by mafias and other organized crime organizations. Prospects in failed and demonstrably weak states are not reassuring.

There is always a well-known solution to every human problem—neat, plausible, and wrong.
(—H. L. Mencken)

Organized crime in some form is surely a permanent feature of modern societies. The most prominent new form, or at least new label, is transnational organized crime, invoked by many scholars and governments as the source of manifold evils. Twenty-five years ago Louise Shelley (1995, p. 463) warned, "Transnational organized crime has been a serious problem for most of the 20th century but it has only recently been recognized as a threat to the world order. This criminality undermines the integrity of individual countries but it is not yet a threat to the nation-state."[5] Similar sentiments are echoed in books from distinguished

---

[5] A quarter-century later she added, "What has changed from the earlier decades of transnational crime is the speed, extent and the diversity of the actors involved" (Shelley 2019, p. 223).

policy commentators (e.g., Naim 2010) and in countless government documents (e.g., Executive Office of the President 2011; Council of Europe 2014).

The definition of transnational organized crime offered by the US Department of Justice (no date) is broad indeed:

> Transnational Organized Crime refers to those self-perpetuating associations of individuals who operate internationally for the purpose of obtaining power, influence, monetary and/or commercial gains, wholly or in part by illegal means, while protecting their activities through a pattern of corruption or violence. There is no single structure under which international organized crime groups operate; they vary from hierarchies to clans, networks and cells, and may evolve to other structures. The crimes they commit also vary.[6]

It may be unfair to mock the vagueness of this definition—the phenomenon is widespread—but it is fair to ask whether putting a label on something as amorphous as this serves a useful purpose. How can organized crime not be affected by globalization as crime more generally is transformed by technology and social change? Criminal organizations are no less likely than auto makers, oil companies, and IT companies to become more international. Whether that importantly changes organized crime and justifies new laws and controls is a question, not a conclusion.

There is no answer to the problems posed by organized crime. There are many answers. They are as diverse as the separate problems they address. Italians and Americans have shown that the activities, powers, effects, and social influence of mafias can be curtailed. Dutch and Scandinavian experience shows that mafias are not an inevitable feature of modern states. More narrowly focused problems can be attacked in various ways, some more effective than others. Continued construction of effective modern states governed largely by rule-of-law values will help, as will growth of modern welfare states that improve human life chances and diminish the allure of lives in crime. Organized crime, including in its nontrivial forms, will always be with us, just as individual crimes of violence, property, and fraud always will be.

Organized crime organizations, including mafias, and the less dramatic types of criminal collaboration come in many forms. *Organizing Crime:*

---

[6] See https://www.justice.gov/criminal-ocgs/international-organized-crime.

Mafias, Markets, and Networks offers insights into many. It also demonstrates major advances in understanding of the diversity, organization, operations, and effects of organized crime. It shows that mafias such as the American and Italian Cosa Nostras, the Chinese triads, and the Japanese yakuzas are more controllable and containable than fatalists expected. Those successes will not prevent criminals from finding new ways of organizing to execute complex and profitable crimes. The beat will go on.

REFERENCES

Acton, Lord (John Emerich Edward Dalberg-Acton). 1907. Letter to Mandell Creighton (April 5, 1887). In *Historical Essays and Studies*, edited by John Neville Figgis and Reginald Vere Laurence. London: Macmillan.
Allen, Woody. 2007. *The Insanity Defense: The Complete Prose*. New York: Random House.
Arnold, Martin. 2014. "HSBC Wrestles with Soaring Costs of Compliance." *Financial Times*, August 4. https://www.ft.com/content/0e3f0760-1bef-11e4-9666-00144feabdc0.
Beare, Margaret E. 2003. "Organized Corporate Criminality: Corporate Complicity in Tobacco Smuggling." In *Critical Reflection on Transnational Organised Crime, Money Laundering, and Corruption*, edited by Margaret Beare. Toronto: University of Toronto Press.
Bouchard, Martin. 2020. "Collaboration and Boundaries in Organized Crime: A Network Perspective." In *Organizing Crime: Mafias, Markets, and Networks*, edited by Michael Tonry and Peter Reuter. Chicago: University of Chicago Press.
Bryan, Dick, and Michael Rafferty. 2016. "The Unaccountable Risks of LIBOR." *British Journal of Sociology* 67(1):71–96.
Buchanan, James. 1973. "A Defense of Organized Crime." In *The Economics of Crime and Punishment*, edited by Simon Rottenberg. Washington, DC: American Enterprise Institute.
Calderoni, Francesco. 2014. "Measuring the Presence of the Mafias in Italy." In *Organized Crime, Corruption, and Crime Prevention*, edited by Stefano Caneppele and Francesco Calderoni. New York: Springer.
Campana, Paolo. 2020. "Human Smuggling: Structure and Mechanisms." In *Organizing Crime: Mafias, Markets, and Networks*, edited by Michael Tonry and Peter Reuter. Chicago: University of Chicago Press.
Catino, Maurizio. 2020. "Italian Organized Crime since 1950." In *Organizing Crime: Mafias, Markets, and Networks*, edited by Michael Tonry and Peter Reuter. Chicago: University of Chicago Press.

Chandler, Raymond. 1959. *The Long Goodbye*. Harmondsworth: Penguin.

Cook, Philip J., Jens Ludwig, Sudhir Venkatesh, and Anthony A. Braga. 2007. "Underground Gun Markets." *Economic Journal* 117(524):F588–F618.

Council of Europe. 2014. *White Paper on Transnational Organized Crime*. Strasbourg: Council of Europe.

Cressey, Donald R. 1969. *Theft of a Nation: The Structure and Operations of Organized Crime in America*. New York: Harper & Row.

Executive Office of the President. 2011. *Strategy to Combat Transnational Organized Crime: Addressing Converging Threats to National Security*. Washington, DC: White House.

Fell, Emily, Owen James, Harry Dienes, Neil Shah, and James Grimshaw. 2019. "Understanding Organized Crime 2015/16: Estimating the Scale and the Social and Economic Costs." Research Report 103. London: Home Office.

Ferran, Eilis. 2012. "Regulatory Lessons from the Payment Protection Insurance Mis-Selling Scandal in the UK." *European Business Organization Law Review (EBOR)* 13(2):247–70.

Fijnault, Cyrille, Frank Bovenkerk, Gerben J. N. Bruinsma, and Henk G. van de Brunt. 1996. "Bijlage VII: Eindrapport Onderzoeksgroep Fijnaut." In *Parementaire Enquêtecommissie-Opsporingsmethoden, Inzake opsporing: Enquête opsporingsmethoden*. Den Haag: Sdu Uitgevers.

———. 1998. *Organized Crime in the Netherlands*. Boston: Kluwer Law International.

Hayne, K. M. 2019. *Royal Commission into Misconduct in the Banking, Superannuation, and Financial Services Industry: Final Report*. Canberra: Commonwealth of Australia.

Jacobs, James B. 2020. "The Rise and Fall of Organized Crime in the United States." In *Organizing Crime: Mafias, Markets, and Networks*, edited by Michael Tonry and Peter Reuter. Chicago: University of Chicago Press.

Kaplan, David E., and Alec Dubro. 1987. *Yakuza: The Explosive Account of Japan's Criminal Underworld*. London: Futura.

Kennedy, John F. 1964. *The Pursuit of Justice*. New York: Harper & Row.

Kleemans, Edward. 2014. "Organized Crime Research: Challenging Assumptions and Informing Policy." In *Applied Police Research: Challenges and Opportunities*, edited by Ella Cockbain and Johannes Knutsson. London: Routledge.

Kleemans, Edward, and Vere van Koppen. 2020. "Organized Crime and Criminal Careers." In *Organizing Crime: Mafias, Markets, and Networks*, edited by Michael Tonry and Peter Reuter. Chicago: University of Chicago Press.

Levi, Mike, and Melvin Soudijn. 2020. "Understanding the Laundering of Organized Crime Money." In *Organizing Crime: Mafias, Markets, and Networks*, edited by Michael Tonry and Peter Reuter. Chicago: University of Chicago Press.

Levitt, Steven D., and Sudhir Alladi Venkatesh. 2000. "An Economic Analysis of a Drug-Selling Gang's Finances." *Quarterly Journal of Economics* 115(3):755–89.

LexisNexis Risk Solutions. 2017 *The True Cost of Anti Money Laundering Compliance: European Edition*. https://risk.lexisnexis.com/global/-/media/files/corporations

%20and%20non%20profits/research/true%20cost%20of%20aml%20compliance %20europe%20survey%20report%20.pdf.pdf.

Mencken, H. L. 1920. "The Divine Afflatus." In *Prejudices: Second Series*. New York: Knopf.

Miller, Ted R., Mark A. Cohen, David Swedler, Bina Ali, and Delia Hendrie. 2020. "Incidence and Costs of Personal and Property Crimes in the United States, 2017." *SSRN Electronic Journal*. https://doi.org/10.2139/ssrn.3514296.

Misse, Michel. 2007. "Illegal Markets, Protection Rackets, and Organized Crime in Rio de Janeiro." *Estudos Avancados* 21(61):139–57.

Naim, Moises. 2010. *Illicit: How Smugglers, Traffickers, and Copycats Are Hijacking the Global Economy*. New York: Random House.

National Audit Office. 2019. *Tackling Serious and Organised Crime*. London: National Audit Office.

Paoli, Letizia. 2020. "What Makes Mafias Different?" In *Organizing Crime: Mafias, Markets, and Networks*, edited by Michael Tonry and Peter Reuter. Chicago: University of Chicago Press.

Pinotti, Paolo. 2015. "The Economic Costs of Organised Crime: Evidence from Southern Italy." *Economic Journal* 125(586):F203–F232.

Puzo, Mario. 1969. *The Godfather*. New York: Putnam.

Reuter, Peter. 1983. *Disorganized Crime: The Economics of the Visible Hand*. Cambridge, MA: MIT Press.

Reuter, Peter, and Letizia Paoli. 2020. "How Similar Are Modern Criminal Organizations to Traditional Mafias?" In *Organizing Crime: Mafias, Markets, and Networks*, edited by Michael Tonry and Peter Reuter. Chicago: University of Chicago Press.

Saviano, Roberto. 2008. *Gomorrah: Italy's Other Mafia*. New York: Macmillan.

Savona, Ernesto U., and Michele Riccardi, eds. 2015. *From Illegal Markets to Legitimate Businesses: The Portfolio of Organised Crime in Europe*. Final Report of Project OCP [Organised Crime Portfolio]. Trento: Transcrime, Università degli Studi di Trento.

Selmini, Rossella. 2020. "Women in Organized Crime." In *Organizing Crime: Mafias, Markets, and Networks*, edited by Michael Tonry and Peter Reuter. Chicago: University of Chicago Press.

Shelley, Louise. 1995. "Transnational Organized Crime: An Imminent Threat to the Nation-State?" *Journal of International Affairs* 48(2):463–89.

———. 2019. "The Globalization of Crime." In *International and Transnational Crime and Justice*, edited by Mangai Natarajan. New York: Cambridge University Press.

Sorkin, Andrew Ross. 2010. *Too Big to Fail: The Inside Story of How Wall Street and Washington Fought to Save the Financial System—and Themselves*. New York: Penguin.

United Nations Office on Drugs and Crime. 2012. *World Drug Report 2012*. Vienna: United Nations.

Varese, Federico. 2020. "How Mafias Migrate: Transplantation, Functional Diversification, and Separation." In *Organizing Crime: Mafias, Markets, and*

Networks, edited by Michael Tonry and Peter Reuter. Chicago: University of Chicago Press.

von Lampe, Klaus, and Arjan Blokland. 2020. "Outlaw Motorcycle Clubs and Organized Crime." In *Organizing Crime: Mafias, Markets, and Networks*, edited by Michael Tonry and Peter Reuter. Chicago: University of Chicago Press.

James B. Jacobs

The Rise and Fall of Organized Crime in the United States

ABSTRACT

The Italian American Cosa Nostra crime families are the longest-lived and most successful organized crime organizations in US history, achieving their pinnacle of power in the 1970s and 1980s. The families seized opportunities during the early twentieth-century labor wars and under national alcohol prohibition from 1919 to 1933. Control of labor unions gave them power to determine the companies that could operate in various sectors and enabled them to establish employer cartels that rigged bids and fixed prices, and provided opportunity to exploit pension and welfare funds. The racketeers were urban power brokers. The families also profited from gambling, illicit drugs, loan-sharking, prostitution, and pornography, and they extorted protection payments from other black marketeers. For decades they faced little risk from law enforcement. FBI Director Hoover denied the existence of a national organized crime threat. Local police were corrupted. After Hoover's death, the FBI made eradicating organized crime a top priority. Relentless law enforcement coincided with socioeconomic and political changes that greatly weakened the Cosa Nostra families.

As the second decade of the twenty-first century draws to a close, the Cosa Nostra crime families are shadows of their former selves. Relentless investigation and prosecution of Cosa Nostra members and associates, legalization of gambling, increased competition in other black markets,

Electronically published November 18, 2019
   James B. Jacobs (1947–2020) was Chief Justice Warren E. Burger Professor of Constitutional Law and the Courts, New York University.

17

dramatic decline of private sector unions, waning influence of urban political machines, disappearance of Italian neighborhoods, and emergence of new organized crime groups have all contributed to the decline of the Cosa Nostra families. In this essay I describe their rise and fall.

The academic and popular treatment of organized crime in the United States, including in this essay, overwhelmingly focuses on Italian American Mafia or Cosa Nostra "families." This is justified by their longevity; alliances with political, business, and law enforcement elites in numerous cities; political and economic power; headline-making assassinations; and colorful depictions in print, movies, and television series. There is no denying Italian American dominance among organized crime groups, at least since the late 1930s, although non–Italian American groups have sometimes competed and sometimes cooperated with a Cosa Nostra family. The mostly Irish American Winter Hill Gang in Boston, which flourished from the 1960s to the 1980s, is a good example (Lehr and O'Neill 2001). During roughly that same period, the Westies, an Irish American New York City gang, engaged in extreme violence, sometimes at the behest of one of the Cosa Nostra families, often in furtherance of drug trafficking (English 1990). Throughout the twentieth century, black organized crime groups have been active in gambling, prostitution, and other rackets (Schatzberg 1993). In the 1970s, for example, Nikki Barnes established a seven-man African American syndicate to control heroin distribution in Harlem (Barnes and Folsom 2007). Russian and Russian American crime groups rose to prominence in the 1990s (Finckenauer 1994; Handelman 1995). Vyacheslav Ivankov built an international operation that included narcotics, money laundering, and prostitution. He forged ties with Cosa Nostra groups and Colombian drug lords in Boston, Los Angeles, Miami, and New York. Chinese triads or tongs have long operated in Chinese American neighborhoods of some American cities (Chin 1990, 1994).

Colombian drug traffickers, Jamaican posses, and Central American gangs are well-entrenched in many parts of the United States (Kenny and Finckenauer 1995). In the twenty-first century, MS-13, a gang with one foot in the United States and the other in Central America, has been heavily involved in drug trafficking and extortion (Progressive Management 2017). In the 1990s and 2000s, Armenian Power attracted major law-enforcement attention, at least in Los Angeles. In 2011, a hundred people associated with Armenian Power were charged with crimes ranging from identity theft to kidnapping, fraud, extortion, loan-sharking, robbery, witness intimidation, and drug trafficking. In 2015, a shootout in Waco, Texas, between the Bandidos Motorcycle Club and Cossacks Motorcycle Club left nine dead. In its wake, the US Department of Justice (DOJ) labeled seven motorcycle gangs as highly structured criminal enterprises (Duara 2015). Despite recognizing all this organized crime diversity, I deal exclusively with the Cosa Nostra crime families, no small challenge given their long history and their presence in at least 24 cities.

The families operate independently, but often cooperate, especially in "open cities" like Miami and Las Vegas. Since 1950, there have been no wars between the families, each being recognized as having exclusive jurisdiction in its city except New York City. Relations are more complex for the five New York City families, but they too have largely respected one another's territory, interests, and operations. There is no national body that governs all the families.

The families are organized similarly. A boss or "godfather" dominates each. The boss appoints an underboss, the *consiglieri* (counselors), and a number of *capos* (captains). Each captain oversees a crew of soldiers and associates. Soldiers are full members of the family ("made men"), but associates are not. The capos and soldiers pursue their own underworld and upperworld opportunities. They are entrepreneurs in crime. The boss is entitled to a percentage of each subordinate's earnings.

Members of Cosa Nostra have been involved in myriad schemes and businesses. Labor racketeering has been especially important. Control of a union makes possible extortion of employers and employees and establishment of employer cartels that rig bids and fix prices. Cosa Nostra members have or have had ownership interests in all sorts of companies. They are active in black markets in drugs, gambling, prostitution, pornography, and loan-sharking.

Until the 1970s, the Cosa Nostra families were not seriously threatened by federal, state, and local law enforcement. The Federal Bureau of Investigation (FBI) under J. Edgar Hoover did not regard the local families as a federal problem. Local police did not have the resources or expertise to support systematic investigations and make cases against members of the families. Besides and importantly, many urban police departments were corrupted by the crime families. The occasional successful prosecution had little, if any, effect on the families' businesses and operations. New members could easily be recruited to replace imprisoned colleagues.

Federal law enforcement's view of Italian American organized crime changed radically in the 1960s. Cosa Nostra attracted the attention of powerful congresspersons who warned especially of organized crime's role in unions and the legitimate economy. Consequently in 1968, Congress enacted the Omnibus Crime Control and Safe Streets Act of 1968. Title III provided for electronic eavesdropping pursuant to court orders. Wiretaps and bugs became the most important investigatory tools for combatting organized crime. In 1970, Congress passed the Racketeer Influenced and Corrupt Organizations (RICO) Act, which facilitated organized crime investigations and made possible the simultaneous prosecution of multiple members of each crime family. It made membership in an organized crime group an offense and authorized lengthy prison terms and substantial financial penalties. In 1970, Congress created the Witness Security Program, which offered protection and relocation with a new identity to Cosa Nostra defendants who became cooperating government witnesses.

More importantly, the FBI reinvented itself after Hoover's death in 1972. Hoover defined the FBI's top priority as internal subversion by Communists, socialists, and other left-wingers. His successors and the Criminal Division of the DOJ made organized crime control a top priority. In 1968, the DOJ established more than a dozen organized crime strike forces in jurisdictions where Cosa Nostra was thought to be strongest. The strike forces, reporting directly to the DOJ headquarters, were independent of the US Attorneys' offices in those jurisdictions. Thus, they focused full time on investigating and prosecuting organized crime without responsibility for dealing with other crime problems.

In 1975, after Cosa Nostra's assassination of former Teamsters Union president Jimmy Hoffa, labor racketeering became the principal focus of the federal effort. A few important prosecutions were brought in the 1970s, followed by a torrent in the 1980s. Practically every Cosa Nostra boss, and usually their successors, were convicted. Hundreds of Cosa Nostra members were imprisoned. In addition, a civil remedy, wielded by federal prosecutors, enabled lawsuits to bring organized-crime-dominated unions under the remedial authority of federal courts. By 2000 Cosa Nostra was severely weakened everywhere and in several cities eradicated.

Here is how this essay is organized. Section I describes in more detail the inter- and intra-organization of Cosa Nostra families. Section II describes their infiltration and exploitation of unions, business, and politics. Section III examines the Cosa Nostra crime families' black market operations. Section IV focuses on their political influence and role as a power broker in urban America. Section V sketches the evolution of the federal, state, and local organized crime control campaign. Section VI surveys the law enforcement strategies wielded by federal, state, and local law enforcement and by local governments. Section VII reviews the reasons for Cosa Nostra's decline and speculates on its current and future prospects.

I. The Organization of Italian American Organized Crime
The origins of Cosa Nostra date from the nineteenth century in Italy and later in the United States. Its prominence, visibility, and a widely shared organizational structure date from the twentieth century.

A. Cosa Nostra Families

Each family is headed by a boss, sometimes called the "godfather." How bosses are chosen or choose themselves is not clear. There is most likely no single method. Perhaps in some cases, as in the *Godfather* movies, the incumbent boss chose his successor. This would have required acquiescence by at least a substantial proportion of the family's membership. Perhaps in other cases the underboss, consiglieri, and capos, after negotiation and deal making, reached a consensus. Leadership succession is sometimes determined by intrafamily warfare as occurred in the Bonanno wars of the 1960s in New York City (DeStefano 2006). In theory, the boss exercises nearly absolute authority over the family; receives a share of his subordinates' revenues; oversees payoffs to politicians, police, and other officials; and takes care of the families of imprisoned (and sometimes deceased) members. Reality often differed. Imprisoned members' families were frequently not provided for adequately, if at all. Ambitious subordinates disagreed with a boss's policies or appointments and otherwise felt mistreated or disrespected.

Bosses of two dozen Cosa Nostra families operating over three-quarters of a century necessarily varied greatly in intelligence, energy, competence, and ambition. Since the mid-1970s, bosses have faced significant threats of arrest and prosecution. It would have been challenging for bosses tied up in criminal litigation to effectively govern their families. That challenge would have been even greater after conviction and during a lengthy imprisonment. There appears to be no standard practice or rule about when leadership must be relinquished.

Each family has an underboss, consiglieri, and several capos. The boss appoints this leadership team without the need for advice and consent, but subordinates' approval or at least respect for the underboss, consiglieri, and capos would likely be important. Each capo has authority over a "crew" comprising soldiers, sometimes called "good fellows" or "wise guys." All members must be males of Italian descent (Sicilian according to some writers). The consanguine definition of "Italian descent" is not clear. Are two "full-blooded" Italian parents required? John Gotti's wife, Victoria, had a Russian mother and an Italian father, so her son John Gotti Jr., Gambino boss for several years, was not full-blooded Italian. What counts as qualifying Italian lineage—"fully" Italian mother, father, or both—is not clear and probably varies between families and over time.

An individual must be invited to become a made member, almost always after years of being associated with the family. Prominent defector Joseph Valachi, a member of the predecessor of New York City's Lucchese family, testifying before Senator McClellan's Permanent Subcommittee on Investigations, described the secret Cosa Nostra induction ceremony. It included an oath of fealty to the family and its code of *omerta* that requires silence about the family's organization, membership, and activities (McClellan 1962). Blood is drawn from the initiate's hand (usually the trigger finger). Then a picture of a saint is burned in that hand (Fresolone and Wagman 1994; Maas 1997). Subsequent defectors confirmed Valachi's description of the ceremony. FBI agents, using an eavesdropping device, in 1989 recorded the initiation of four men into New England's Patriarca family (*United States v. Bianco*[1]). The following year, George Fresolone, cooperating with the FBI, recorded his initiation into the Bruno-Scarfo family (Fresolone and Wagman 1994). Fresolone claimed in his autobiography that the Philadelphia family's failure to provide financial assistance to his family when he was incarcerated led to his disillusionment with Cosa Nostra and ultimately to his violation of *omerta* (Fresolone and Wagman 1994). His information contributed to racketeering indictments in 1991 against 38 reputed mobsters, including Nicodemo Scarfo, the Philadelphia–Atlantic City boss (Cox 1989).

Cosa Nostra crews include "associates" who work for and with made members. A 1998 estimate of the size and composition of New York's Genovese family calculated that there were four or five associates for

---

[1] See the appendix for full citations of all cases cited in this essay.

every made member, of whom there were approximately 250 (Raab 1998c). Associates need not be Italian.

A high-earning associate can be highly influential within the family leadership. Meyer Lansky, a principal in the development of Las Vegas as a gambling center, became one of Cosa Nostra's most powerful figures, although he himself could never become a made man. Nor could Murray Humphries, Red Dorfman, and Stanley Korshak, major figures in the Chicago family in the 1950s, 1960s, and into the 1970s. Nor was Moe Dalitz in Cleveland. Benjamin Siegel played a key figure in establishing Cosa Nostra's Las Vegas gambling empire.

Cosa Nostra members and associates function as criminal entrepreneurs, seeking out profitable legal and illegal opportunities; the legal businesses were typically run in illegal ways (Jacobs and Panarella 1998). Members and associates must share revenues with the family's leaders, but there are no hard-and-fast accounting rules or fixed percentages. Presumably, the sizes of payments to capos, consiglieri, underbosses, and bosses are individually negotiated. Financial disputes are not litigated in lawsuits; a subordinate suspected of cheating the boss can be assaulted or killed.

B. Relations among Families

Despite the late Donald Cressey's (1969) assertion that Italian American organized crime constituted a nationwide conspiracy, Cosa Nostra has never been a single organization. Since the 1930s, at least 24 Italian American crime families have operated independently, each with exclusive jurisdiction in its own geographic area (except in New York City, where five families operate). Each family chooses its own leaders, members, and associates; launches and conducts its own criminal enterprises; invests in legitimate enterprises; and divvies up revenues. Retired Bonanno family boss Joseph Bonanno claimed in his autobiography that the families were governed by a nationwide Cosa Nostra "commission" established in the 1930s by Charles Luciano (Bonanno and Lalli 1983). However, other than a bungled 1957 conclave in Apalachin, New York, attended by dozens of Cosa Nostra figures from all over the country, there is little evidence to support the existence of a national governing body (*United States v. Bufalino*). A nominal commission with representatives from some families may have met occasionally to discuss mutual interests and inter- and intrafamily disputes, but if so it did not in any meaningful sense "govern" the organized crime families.

Cosa Nostra families sometimes cooperated on ventures. Several families, for example, cooperated in skimming from Las Vegas casinos in order to avoid taxes. Several families operated in Miami, which apparently was considered "an open city."

Indictments in the 1986 "commission case," which brought charges against the leaders of four of the five Cosa Nostra families in New York City, charged the existence of a commission comprised of the heads of the five families (Bonanno, Columbo, Gambino, Genovese, and Lucchese). According to the prosecutors, this commission "regulated and facilitated the families' interrelationships, promoted and carried out joint ventures, resolved actual and potential disputes, extended formal recognition to new bosses and, from time to time, resolved leadership disputes within a family, approving the initiation or 'making' of new members or soldiers, keeping persons inside and outside La Cosa Nostra in fear of the commission with threats, violence, and murder" (*United States v. Salerno*, indictment; see Jacobs, Panarella, and Worthington 1994). To the extent that the commission existed, it is not clear how it enforced its decisions. Most likely, the New York City bosses met from time to time on an ad hoc basis to discuss issues of common concern, for example, the 1960s warfare within the Bonanno family. There was no commission office, no staff, no budget. We know nothing about the alleged commission's decision-making procedures. Was unanimity required? If not, did bosses in the minority acquiesce to the will of majority?

There is lore that commission approval was needed before members of a family could depose (assassinate) their boss. However, no information has surfaced that John Gotti, a Gambino family capo, sought, much less received, commission approval to assassinate Gambino boss Paul Castellano. Surely Gotti would not have risked disclosing his plot to the other families' bosses lest information be leaked to Castellano. It is hard to imagine Gotti having been able to arrange a confidential meeting with the bosses minus Castellano. And if Gotti had appeared before the commission, would his anti-Castellano allegations have been accepted at face value, or would the bosses have wanted to hear what Castellano or any defenders of his leadership had to say? Without some kind of fact-finding, it would have been hard for a commission to anticipate the ramifications of an unsuccessful or even a successful assassination attempt. Finally, might not the other bosses have been reluctant to approve a capo's assassination of a boss in light of their own vulnerability to subordinates?

Families are better conceptualized as franchises than as formal bureaucratic organizations. A made member or associate derives power and economic benefit from being recognized by the family. Businessmen, union officers, and politicians are likely to comply with a family member's "requests" because of the family's reputation for wielding power through violence and other means.

II. Labor and Business Racketeering

The Cosa Nostra families' success over much of the twentieth century results from seeking out, developing, and exploiting a range of criminal and noncriminal opportunities including corruption of national and local labor unions; creation and enforcement of employer cartels; supplying illicit goods and services; and carrying out thefts, hijackings, frauds, and arson. At the same time, members often own and sometimes run ostensibly legitimate businesses, such as clubs, restaurants, trucking companies, linen suppliers, and concrete plants, and routinely violate antitrust, tax, and other laws. Cosa Nostra's footholds in both the criminal underworld and the world of legitimate businesses, unions, and politics distinguish it from other organized crime groups active in US black markets (Jacobs 1999).

A. Labor Racketeering

Since the beginning of the twentieth century, labor racketeering has provided Cosa Nostra with power, status, legitimacy, and financial reward (Seidman 1938; Taft 1958; Hutchinson 1969; Jacobs 2006). Infiltration of unions began in the 1910s and 1920s when companies recruited gangsters to break strikes, and unions recruited them to fight the strike breakers. With a foot in the door, organized crime families took over unions by replacing their officers by force or election fraud (Jacobs and Panarella 1998; Jacobs 2006). In some cases, they parlayed control of locals into influence and sometimes control of the national union (international if there were locals in Canada). For decades, Cosa Nostra wielded significant influence in the International Longshoremen's Association, the Laborers Union, the Hotel Employees and Restaurant Employees Union, and the International Brotherhood of Teamsters.

Cosa Nostra turned union power into profit by extortion (selling labor peace to employers), embezzling from and defrauding pension and welfare funds, taking employer payoffs in exchange for sweetheart contracts or ignoring violations of collective bargaining agreements, paying union officers bloated salaries, and forcing employers to hire no-shows (Reuter 1985, p. 56). The Cosa Nostra crime families also used their union power to acquire ownership interests in businesses; a business could not operate if the union would not allow its members to work for it. Organized crime figures could easily put an employer out of business or take an ownership interest. Moreover, by controlling which businesses could operate in a particular sector, they were able to establish employer associations (cartels) in waste hauling, construction, seaborne and air cargo, and other business sectors (New York State Organized Crime Task Force 1990; Jacobs 2006). The cartels set prices and decided which companies could bid on contracts and how much they could bid. In short, they designated who would win contracts.

Beginning in the 1950s, Cosa Nostra's influence in the International Longshoremen's Union enabled the Gambino (Brooklyn and New Jersey) and Genovese (Manhattan) families to exploit many of the port's operations. Cosa Nostra determined who worked on the docks and decided when cargo ships would be unloaded. They solicited bribes from or extorted shippers by determining which cargo was loaded and unloaded and when (Bell 1960; Abadinsky 1994). In the 1970s, the FBI's massive Operation UNIRAC (*Uni*on *Rac*keteering) investigation revealed that the Gambino and Genovese families' influence in the Longshoremen's Union extended from New York to Miami (*United States v. Local 1804-1, International Longshoremen's Association*). Shippers paid off the families to avoid harm, to gain advantage, or both.

Cosa Nostra wielded extraordinary influence in the International Brotherhood of Teamsters (IBT). It was the nation's largest private sector labor union, with 2.3 million members at its height. Jimmy Hoffa attained the presidency with the assistance of Cosa Nostra and, in return, deferred to their wishes. However, Hoffa was convicted of jury tampering, attempted bribery, and fraud and sent to prison in 1967. Frank Fitzsimmons served as acting president. President Richard Nixon pardoned Hoffa in December 1971 on condition that he not participate in union activities. Hoffa immediately repudiated that condition and sought to regain his old position. Cosa Nostra bosses, however, preferred Fitzsimmons and, after warning Hoffa to desist, assassinated him (Brandt 2004). Fitzsimmons served as IBT president from 1971 to 1981.

By the late 1980s, organized crime was entrenched in at least 38 of the largest Teamster locals (PCOC 1986*a*; Jacobs and Cooperman 2011). Cosa Nostra bosses promoted their favored candidates for the IBT presidency and other top positions. For example, the Kansas City family successfully lobbied for Roy Williams's candidacy to succeed Fitzsimmons. Williams resigned after conviction for conspiracy to bribe a US senator. The Cleveland family then promoted Jackie Presser's successful candidacy (Brill 1978; Moldea 1978; Crowe 1993; Jacobs 2006; Jacobs and Cooperman 2011).

Cosa Nostra's influence in the Laborer's International Union of North America guaranteed a powerful presence in the construction industries in many cities. Extensively recorded conversations of Sam DeCavalcante (New Jersey family) detailed his family's control of a laborer's union local (Zeiger 1970). For years, the "Outfit" (the Chicago family) strategically positioned Cosa Nostra members in the Laborers Union's locals in that city (Abadinsky 1994). The President's Commission on Organized Crime (PCOC 1986*a*) and several civil federal lawsuits documented the Lucchese and Genovese families' influence in New York's Laborers Local 6A and the Eastern District Council (New York State Organized Crime Task Force 1990).

Cosa Nostra, especially the Lucchese crime family, has been firmly entrenched in many New York City local building trades' unions, including painters, carpenters, mason tenders, and plumbers (New York State Organized Crime Task Force 1990). The "mobbed-up" unions crushed opposition by means of blacklisting and personal violence. Union officials who were members or associates of Cosa Nostra ran patronage systems in their locals.

Cosa Nostra has had a strong presence in the Hotel Employees and Restaurant Employees International Union (HEREIU). Control of HEREIU Local 54 enabled Philadelphia's Bruno-Scarfo family to direct the purchasing decisions of Atlantic City hotels (Abadinsky 1994). In Chicago, the Outfit's control of an HEREIU local gave it power over the restaurant industry (McClellan 1962). In New York City, the Colombo and Gambino families for many years dominated HEREIU Locals 6 and 100 (PCOC 1986*a*).

Cosa Nostra benefited enormously from its union influence (New York State Organized Crime Task Force 1990). John Cody (Teamsters), Ralph Scopo (Laborers), Albert Anastasio and Anthony Scotto (Longshoremen), and Harry Davidoff (Teamsters) were among the most powerful New York City labor figures in the second half of the twentieth century. Red Dorfman was president of Chicago's Waste Handler's Union and a key figure in Chicago's Outfit. Murray Humphries, another top Outfit figure, though not a union official himself, wielded enormous influence over several Chicago unions.

As joint employer/union pension and welfare funds grew, Cosa Nostra members and associates, serving as fund trustees, treated the funds as piggy banks. The most notorious example was the Chicago, Kansas City, Milwaukee, and Cleveland bosses' exploitation of the massive Teamsters Central States Pension and Welfare Fund (*United States v. Dorfman*). Generous loans from this fund (controlled by the Chicago Cosa Nostra family through Allen Dorfman, who approved loans) financed Cosa Nostra's operations in Las Vegas (Skolnick 1978).

Control over unions enabled Cosa Nostra members to extort labor peace payoffs from businesses and to solicit bribes in exchange for sweetheart collective bargaining contracts (Jacobs and Panarella 1998; Jacobs 2006). Cosa Nostra–dominated unions turned a blind eye to employers' failures to make required payments to pension and welfare funds by overlooking "double-breasted" shops (staffed by both union and non-union workers) and by facilitating other employer practices that violated contractual obligations. In some jurisdictions, a mobbed-up union maintained two locals, one with a strong collective bargaining agreement and the other with a weak one. Employers who paid bribes to the union bosses and their Cosa Nostra allies were permitted to contract with the low-cost union. Employers were also induced to put no-show Cosa Nostra members, friends, or associates on their payrolls.

Influence over unions and pension funds enabled Cosa Nostra to direct union contracts for dental and medical providers, legal services, and other goods and services (New York State Organized Crime Task Force 1990). Sometimes firms owned by Cosa Nostra members or associates were the chosen contractors; other times, contracts went to legitimate contractors who paid kickbacks. For example, contracts for maintaining the heavy equipment for unloading seaborne cargo in New Jersey have for decades been controlled by Cosa Nostra labor racketeers (Stewart 2019).

Cosa Nostra racketeers also extorted kickbacks from rank and file union members. A worker had to pay part of his salary to an organized crime-controlled union boss in order to get a desirable assignment and even to work at all, especially on the New Jersey side of the Port of New York. These kickbacks were, among other ploys, sometimes called "Christmas gifts" from the union member to the boss (Stewart 2019).

B. Business Racketeering and Cartels

From the early twentieth century, New York City mobsters exerted strong influence in the construction industry, the garment center, the Fulton Fish Market, and sea cargo operations in the Port of New York and New Jersey (Hortis 2014). From the 1950s to the 1990s, based on their influence in unions, the New York City Cosa Nostra families were deeply entrenched at the Javits Exhibition Center, in John F. Kennedy Airport's air cargo operations, and in commercial waste hauling and disposal. They were also involved in moving and storage, securities, linen supplies, food processing, importation, and retail distribution (Kwitny 1979; Jacobs and Hortis 1998; Jacobs 1999). The Genovese, Gambino, Colombo, and Lucchese families made millions from a monopoly over window replacement in all public housing and much private housing in New York City.

Gambino family boss Paul Castellano owned Dial Meat Purveyors, which distributed poultry to 300 butchers, grocers, and supermarkets in the New York City metropolitan area and, ultimately, to two national supermarket chains (Maas 1997). Chicken magnate Frank Perdue found that getting supermarkets to purchase his chickens required paying off Castellano (PCOC 1986a; O'Brien and Kurins 1991; Maas 1997). Small butchers could not obtain poultry from anyone other than Dial (Maas 1997). If a business complained, Castellano orchestrated union problems.

Control over a union allowed Cosa Nostra to determine which companies could do business in a sector whose workers that union represented. The cartels allocated contracts and fixed prices. The cartels' members inflated prices, in effect imposing a "cartel tax" or "mob tax" on consumers (Jacobs and Hortis 1998). Businesses that were not members could neither get union labor nor operate with nonunion labor. A business that tried to operate with nonunion labor would be picketed, disrupted, and ultimately shut down.

In the "commission case," *United States v. Salerno*, federal prosecutors proved that four of New York City's five Cosa Nostra crime families controlled a concrete contractors cartel. S&A Concrete, owned in part by Anthony Salerno ("front" boss[2] of the Genovese family) and Paul Castellano (boss of the Gambino family), was the only company permitted to bid on poured concrete contracts in excess of $5 million (Jacobs, Panarella, and Worthington 1994). The cartel assigned middle-sized contracts (i.e., $2–$5 million) to one of a half-dozen contractors in which Cosa Nostra families held interests. Other companies could bid on and carry out smaller contracts, as long as they kicked back 2 percent of the contract price to the Colombo family (*United States v. Salerno*). The Cosa Nostra families also had a monopoly over concrete manufacturing in New York City, owning the only two plants in that business. These companies were forfeited to the government in the prosecution of Cosa Nostra front man Edward Halloran, who was subsequently assassinated by his former sponsors.

Cosa Nostra exerted similar influence in the New York City drywall industry through Vincent DiNapoli, a Genovese capo. Through its control of the Carpenters Union, the Genovese family held ownership interests in several drywall contractors and ran the Metropolitan New York Drywall Contractors Association (Jacobs 1999). Much like its concrete counterpart, the drywall cartel allocated bids and took 2 percent of contracts as a kickback. Firms that were not members of DiNapoli's cartel paid an additional $1,000 per week to ensure labor peace. The association's district council was placed under a federal trusteeship in 1990, but Cosa Nostra's control of the union was not broken (Jacobs 1999). The government brought a new round of charges against the union's leadership in 2010.

For at least two decades, two powerful Cosa Nostra–sponsored cartels allocated contracts and fixed prices in the New York City and Long Island waste hauling industry (Jacobs and Hortis 1998; Cowan and Century 2002). Peter Reuter (1993) explains that these cartels operated smoothly because a Cosa Nostra member sat on the grievance committee of the employers' association, the New York Trade Waste Association. Consequently, no carting company ever refused to accept the committee's resolution of a dispute over "ownership" of routes and customers (Jacobs 1999). Similar waste hauling cartels operated in Chicago, Los Angeles, Philadelphia, Long Island, and many other northeastern and Midwest cities and counties (Russo 2001).

---

[2] Vincent Gigante was the actual boss of the Genovese family but preferred that Salerno appear to be the boss in order to divert law enforcement attention from himself.

The Chicago family's Murray Humphries parlayed his control of unions into a dry cleaning and laundry empire. He also achieved a monopoly on supplying ice to Las Vegas casinos (Russo 2006).

Brothers Thomas and Joseph Gambino gained control of New York City's garment district through their domination of International Ladies Garment Workers Union Local 102 (Jacobs 1999) and ownership of several trucking companies. Thomas Gambino (a capo in the Gambino family) amassed a $100 million fortune, mostly through ownership of trucking companies operating in the garment center. In 1981, the garment industry honored Gambino as its Man of the Year. The Lucchese family operated similar schemes in painting and window replacement.

Cosa Nostra members and associates owned and invested in myriad other businesses, particularly nightclubs and restaurants. In the mid-twentieth century, Stefano Magaddino, boss of the Buffalo family, owned the Magaddino Funeral Parlor, the Camellia Linen Supply Co., and Pandoro Exterminators, Inc. *Wall Street Journal* investigative journalist Jonathan Kwitny (1979) documented Cosa Nostra's ownership or control of meat and cheese processing firms in New York City.

III. Black Markets

Cosa Nostra members and associates have, since at least national alcohol prohibition in 1919–33, provided illegal goods and services including gambling, loan-sharking, prostitution, pornography, and drugs (Haller 1990).

A. Gambling

Gambling has always been an important source of revenue for Cosa Nostra families. The 1967 President's Commission's Task Force on Organized Crime identified gambling as Cosa Nostra's main moneymaker. The 1985 President's Commission on Organized Crime (PCOC) focused much of its attention on Cosa Nostra's gambling operations. FBI agent Frank Storey Jr. told the later commission that by a conservative estimate (for which he did not provide a source) more than half of Cosa Nostra revenues came from gambling (PCOC 1985, p. 57).

The Cosa Nostra families thrived on bookmaking for numbers, horse races, and sporting events (Liddick 1998). Some of the midcentury titans of organized crime, such as Frank Costello, became rich via slot machines and other gambling rackets. The PCOC (1985) concluded that sports betting provided the largest proportion of gambling revenue, but they presented no reliable data, nor are any likely to become available.

Las Vegas's development as a gambling mecca is a critical chapter in Cosa Nostra's history. With financial backing from Meyer Lansky, Frank Costello, Bugsy Siegel, and other Cosa Nostra figures projected its influence in Las Vegas just as they had previously done in Havana (Colhoun 2013). With organized crime financing, Siegel built the Flamingo, the first huge Las Vegas casino hotel. Over time, Cosa Nostra bosses obtained ownership interests in many Las Vegas hotels and casinos (Skolnick 1978). At one point, the Teamsters Central States Pension lent approximately a quarter of a billion dollars secured by mortgages on those properties (PCOC 1985). Even more important than mob ownership of the casinos was control over their operation. This enabled the Cosa Nostra bosses to skim money, thereby avoiding taxes (Skolnick 1978; PCOC 1983). In 1986, with the aid of testimony from Angelo Lonardo, Cleveland underboss turned government witness, federal prosecutors convicted a number of those involved in skimming (e.g., *United States v. Spinale*).

The PCOC explained that the Outfit, which controlled gambling in Chicago, imposed a 50 percent tax on bookmakers. The Outfit supplied wire rooms, clerks, and telephones. The bookmaker had to attract his own clients. Government telephone intercepts exposed a Milwaukee-based sports bookmaking operation headed by Frank Balistrieri (boss), Steve DiSalvo (underboss), and Balistrieri's sons (PCOC 1985). "Writers" answered phones and dealt with customers.

Cosa Nostra members also profited by fixing sports contests that made their bets a sure thing. Cosa Nostra families fixed boxing and jai alai matches and dog and horse racing. It is easier to fix contests in individual sports where just one contestant has to be corrupted, but team sport contests could also be fixed. The notorious Boston College basketball fix began with a small-time bookie, Tony Perla, who was friendly with Rick Kuhn, a member of the Boston College basketball team. Perla bribed Kuhn to keep Boston College's margins of victory within the point spread. In order to increase profits, Perla needed a multicity bookmaking network. This led him to the Lucchese family. Ultimately, the Luccheses paid Kuhn and one other player $2,500 (and drugs) per game (PCOC 1985).

The PCOC reported that Cosa Nostra placed illegal gambling devices in restaurants, clubs, and stores and shared revenue with those businesses. If a player won, the business paid out. Cosa Nostra members picked up its share of the profits on a weekly basis.

B. Loan-Sharking

Loan-sharking, which involves usurious loans backed up by intimidation and threats of force to obtain repayment, has been a Cosa Nostra mainstay (Goldstock and Coenen 1978). Organized crime members loaned money to their own associates, gamblers, and individuals who could not or would not obtain bank loans (Kenney and Finckenauer 1995). Estimates of interest rates range as high as 250 to 1,000 percent per annum (Kenney and Finckenauer 1995).

One of the predicate racketeering offenses charged in the 1986 commission case (*United States v. Salerno*) was conspiracy to allocate loan-sharking territories on Long Island. The indictment charged the defendants facilitated loan-sharking by resolving a territorial dispute between the Lucchese and Gambino crime families (Jacobs, Panarella, and Worthington 1994). Gambino family boss John Gotti was convicted of loan-sharking, among other offenses (*United States v. Gotti*, aff'd, *United States v. Locascio*).

In *United States v. DiSalvo*, federal prosecutors in Philadelphia convicted two Scarfo family associates of loan-sharking offenses. Former underboss Philip Leonetti, testifying as a cooperating witness, described how intra-family lending worked. When Scarfo became boss, he agreed temporarily to exempt DiSalvo's loan-sharking operations from having to kick back to him. However, when Scarfo assisted DiSalvo in collecting on a $200,000 loan, DiSalvo was required to share the money with Scarfo.

Loan-sharking continued into the twenty-first century. In 2009, the New York Police Department arrested 22 Lucchese and Gambino members and associates for loan-sharking and sports gambling. However, it seems likely that the vast expansion of consumer credit options in the last several decades diminished Cosa Nostra's loan-sharking business. Bank of America launched the first bank credit card, which eventually became Visa, in the mid-1950s, American Express followed in 1959, and Mastercard in the mid-1960s. More than 80 percent of American households have at least one credit card.

C. Prostitution and Pornography

In 1936, Lucky Luciano and several codefendants, targeted by investigators for their efforts to centralize control of New York City brothels, were successfully prosecuted for 62 counts of compulsory prostitution (Block 1983). Governor Thomas Dewey granted Luciano clemency in exchange for his assistance in keeping East Coast ports free of labor unrest during World War II (Kenney and Finckenauer 1995). Beginning in the 1960s, the sexual revolution likely reduced the demand for paid sex. In any case, by the 1970s and 1980s the Cosa Nostra families had largely ceased to operate brothels, although some organized crime figures continued to extort protection payoffs from independent brothel owners (Abadinsky 1994).

Historically, Cosa Nostra members actively trafficked in pornography. According to the FBI, Cosa Nostra families controlled the pornography industry through threats and use of force. In the 1960s, the Colombo family ran coin-operated machines showing 8-millimeter pornography films in New York's then seedy Times Square. In the 1970s, Matthew Ianniello, boss of the Genovese family, amassed an empire of topless bars, porn shops, and sex shows centered in Times Square (Raab 2005). A mobster affiliated with the Colombo family financed the breakout 1972 porn movie *Deep Throat*. The Bonanno family's Mickey Zaffarano owned Pussycat Cinemas, a chain of movie theaters that specialized in porn. In 1980, a two-and-a-half-year FBI investigation resulted in 45 pornography indictments that included Cosa Nostra figures. A 2002 indictment charged the Chicago Outfit with extorting payments from adult entertainment businesses (*United States v. Calabrese*).

In recent years, the availability of so much explicit sexual material in print, films, and over the internet has likely diminished Cosa Nostra's role in the pornography market. However, that does not mean that entrepreneurial mobsters haven't found ways to continue to profit. In 2005, prosecutors charged Gambino family members with fraud for offering free tours of adult websites and then extravagantly billing customers' credit cards. The Gambinos, as individuals, invested profits in a phone company, bank, and more than 64 shell companies and foreign bank accounts.

D. Drug Trafficking

Italian American organized crime figures have been heavily involved in drug trafficking since the early twentieth century (Hortis 2014). For example, Lucky Luciano was arrested for transporting heroin (Kenney and Finckenauer 1995). Vito Genovese, "boss of bosses" in the late 1950s, was ultimately convicted of drug trafficking (Hanna 1974). The infamous "French Connection" case revealed Lucchese family dominance and Bonanno family involvement in importing heroin from France to New York City in the 1950s. In the 1980s, prosecutors proved extensive Bonanno family drug trafficking in *United States v. Badalamenti* (known as the "pizza connection" case because several defendants used pizzerias as fronts). The federal government exposed an international drug-trafficking network, with over 200 participants, coordinated primarily by the Bonanno family and a Sicilian Mafia group (Jacobs, Panarella, and Worthington 1994).

Some Cosa Nostra members (and the fictional Don Corleone in the 1972 *Godfather* movie) claimed to oppose drug trafficking for moral reasons and because of the risk of provoking law enforcement crackdowns (Bonanno and Lalli 1983; Maas 1997). If such a no-drugs edict existed, it was routinely violated (Jacobs, Panarella, and Worthington 1994; Hortis 2014). Gambino family boss Paul Castellano allegedly prohibited members of his family from participating in drug trafficking, but demanded a cut of Sonny Black Napolitano's (Bonanno family) heroin business in exchange for supporting Napolitano in the Bonanno intrafamily conflict (Bonavolonta and Duffy 1996). In addition, the Gambino family's capos and soldiers were heavily involved. Castellano's inconsistent drug policy is one reason John Gotti arranged his assassination in 1985 (Bonavolonta and Duffy 1996).

Many members of the Genovese family have been convicted of drug trafficking offenses (Peterson 1983). Alphonse D'Arco, cooperating with the government, testified that he did not directly sell drugs while serving as acting Lucchese family boss but that subordinates did (*United States v. Avellino*). Angelo Bruno, head of the Philadelphia crime family, adopted a similarly hypocritical approach (Fresolone and Wagman 1994). While many Cosa Nostra individuals and crews participated in drug trafficking, they could not dominate the market. There are just too many traffickers, some as violent and ruthless as Cosa Nostra.

E. Thefts and Frauds

Cosa Nostra families did not and do not limit themselves to activities stereotypically associated with organized crime. They also sponsor and engage in garden-variety crimes.

1. *Thefts.* Cosa Nostra members engaged in all manner of acquisitive crimes. For example, because of its entrenched position on the waterfront

and in the construction industry, and through its influence over cargo operations at Kennedy Airport, Cosa Nostra members and associates carried out truck hijackings and other thefts (Jensen 1974; Kwitny 1979; New York State Organized Crime Task Force 1990). The Lucchese family's control of two Teamsters locals enabled systematic thefts from air cargo at John F. Kennedy Airport. Dispatchers provided information about the arrival of valuable shipments, shipping times, and delivery routes. Trucks leaving the airport could then be intercepted by a Lucchese operative, sometimes with the driver's cooperation (Jacobs 1999). The most ambitious such theft, the basis for the movie *Goodfellas*, was a $5 million heist from the Lufthansa cargo hangar in 1978 (Jacobs and Panarella 1998).

Thefts of equipment and materials were so predictable on some construction projects that contractors incorporated the anticipated losses into their bids. Sometimes contractors repurchased their stolen equipment from the thieves. Sometimes Cosa Nostra destroyed materials and equipment to generate more business for their suppliers and construction companies (New York State Organized Crime Task Force 1990).

2. *Frauds.* Cosa Nostra members did and do perpetrate all kinds of frauds. They have sold shares in sham corporations, counterfeited stock certificates, and controlled small brokerage houses that raised money from unsuspecting investors. Thefts by Joey Franzese, whose uncle was a member of the Colombo family, from Dean Witter investment bank provide a notorious example. Franzese, a Dean Witter employee, created phony accounts on which he wrote checks to himself (Kwitny 1979).

In 1997, a grand jury indicted a dozen Genovese and Bonanno members for securities fraud, bank fraud, and extortion (Jacobs 1999). The indictments charged a classic "pump and dump" scheme. The defendants pressured employees of a small brokerage firm to acquire shares of HealthTech. With cooperation from HealthTech's CEO, the defendants then sold the company's inflated shares to unsuspecting customers (Jacobs 1999). In 2006, federal prosecutors in the Southern District of Florida brought one of the largest internet fraud prosecutions in history; 46,000 victims lost more than $16 million. Investigators discovered the fraud in the course of an investigation of Colombo family associates' control over a Pennsylvania internet company and its South Florida–based marketing partners.

Bankruptcy fraud has long been popular with Cosa Nostra soldiers and associates. They take over a legitimate company and loot its assets, leaving creditors high and dry. A variation involves creating a company for the purpose of bankrupting it (Hanna 1974; Kwitny 1979). Tax fraud has also been routine (*United States v. Ianniello*).

F. Violence

Cosa Nostra's power derives from its reputation for ruthless violence. Peter Reuter (1987) explains that Cosa Nostra members rely on and exploit Cosa Nostra's violent reputation. However, "because organized crime figures have a reputation for being able to execute threats of violence ... and to suppress the course of justice when complaints are brought against them means that actual violence is rarely necessary" (Reuter 1985, p. 56). This explains why Cosa Nostra members signal their family ties through dress and comportment (Gambetta 2009).

By far, most Cosa Nostra murder victims have themselves been Cosa Nostra members and associates. In his testimony against Gambino family boss John Gotti, Sammy Gravano explained that murder is employed as a tool for maintaining family discipline (Jacobs, Panarella, and Worthington 1994). Gravano admitted to participating in 19 murders. Gotti was convicted of murdering Paul Castellano and several of Castellano's henchmen. Defendants in the commission case, *United States v. Salerno*, were convicted of ordering the murder of Carmine Galante (Bonanno family boss) and two of his associates. The discovery of the remains of two murdered mob members below the Arista windows factory in Brooklyn (owned by Pete Savino, the leader of the Cosa Nostra window replacement scam) enabled the government to recruit Savino as a cooperating witness (Bonavolonta and Duffy 1996).

In Cosa Nostra's long history there are practically no examples of violence against police, prosecutors, judges, or jurors, which is not uncommon in Italy. It is puzzling why the extraordinary post-1970s government campaign against Cosa Nostra did not degenerate into the kind of violent conflict between gangsters and law enforcement agents that occurs in Mexico, Central and South America, and elsewhere. Investigators and prosecutors say that Cosa Nostra feared all-out repression would result from assassinating government personnel or jurors. Perhaps, but since the mid-1970s, the FBI and the DOJ have engaged in all-out suppression of Cosa Nostra, albeit using legal strategies, not assassinations (Jacobs, Panarella, and Worthington 1994). It does not seem likely that federal, state, and local law enforcement agencies would have engaged in a campaign of assassinations against Cosa Nostra even if Cosa Nostra had targeted law enforcement, prosecutors, court personnel, and jurors.

IV. Local Government

Cosa Nostra bosses have functioned as fixers to whom businessmen, politicians, and criminals reach out to resolve disputes with labor organizations, law enforcement agencies, and government regulators (Jacobs, Panarella, and Worthington 1994). They sometimes played a stabilizing role in what otherwise would have been chaotic black markets (Bell 1960). However, in order to advance their interests, organized crime bosses routinely corrupted local politicians.

In many cities, Cosa Nostra bribed police to turn a blind eye to gambling and other black market activities. In addition, organized crime bosses functioned as power brokers, supporting and promoting their favored political candidates with funds and get-out-the-vote assistance. In return, politicians gave Cosa Nostra protection from apprehension and prosecution. Cosa Nostra also benefited from corrupt contract letting and land deals.

In the early 1950s, the Senate Special Committee to Investigate Crime in Interstate Commerce—often called the Kefauver Committee after its chairman, Senator Estes Kefauver—investigated the symbiotic relationship between Cosa Nostra families and big city politicians. The committee focused on William O'Dwyer, Brooklyn district attorney from January through August 1945 and New York City's mayor from 1946 until his resignation in 1950 (Block 1983). Members of the committee suspected that, as Brooklyn district attorney, O'Dwyer protected organized crime figures from prosecution. Frank Costello, New York City's "boss of bosses," who had strong ties to Tammany Hall, New York City's dominant Democratic club, helped O'Dwyer win the mayoralty in 1945 (Block 1983). O'Dwyer's 1950 resignation did not end Cosa Nostra's city hall influence. His successor, Vincent Impellitteri (1950–54), also had close ties to Costello and to the Lucchese family (Peterson 1983). In Kansas City, there was a working relationship between the Pendergast political machine and Cosa Nostra. The police protected organized crimes's gambling enterprises (Abadinsky 1994).

Formal position as labor officials gave Cosa Nostra members and associates reason and right to participate in mainstream metropolitan politics. For four decades Harry Davidoff, president of IBT Local 295, whose jurisdiction included John F. Kennedy Airport, was an important New York City power broker. When Anthony Scotto, a Gambino family capo and third highest ranking official in the International Longshoremen's Association, was tried for bribery and racketeering, New York Governor Hugh Carey testified as a character witness for him. Former New York City mayors Robert Wagner and John Lindsay submitted letters to the sentencing judge on Scotto's behalf. In the 1970s, John Cody, president of Teamsters Local 282, was the most powerful labor official in New York City's construction industry. In 1982, he was convicted of racketeering and sentenced to 5 years. Ralph Scopo, Colombo crime family capo, served as president of a local of the Laborer's International Union of North America and as an official of the Concrete Workers District Council until, after indictment in the commission case, he was forced to resign from the District Council. He was convicted and sentenced to a 100-year prison term.

Cosa Nostra's influence with city officials proved advantageous in steering government contracts to Cosa Nostra–connected firms. In 1967, Lucchese family boss Antonio Corallo and Daniel Motto were indicted with James Marcus, commissioner of New York City's Water Department, for bribery in connection with awarding a multimillion-dollar water reservoir rehabilitation contract to a company controlled by the Lucchese family (*United States v. Corallo*; Jacobs 1999). In 1983, Teamsters president Roy Williams, Teamsters Central States Pension Fund broker Allen Dorfman, and Joseph Lombardo (Chicago Outfit) were convicted of conspiring to bribe US Senator Howard S. Cannon to help shelve a trucking deregulation bill (PCOC 1983; *United States v. Williams*). The New Orleans crime family, during Carlos Marcello's reign from 1947 to the late 1980s, exerted enormous influence in Louisiana politics. For decades, the Outfit controlled the First Ward in downtown Chicago. In the 1980s and 1990s, the Patriarca family exercised strong influence over politics and government operations in New England. Buddy Cianci, who was mayor of Providence, Rhode Island, from 1975 to 1984, when he was sent to prison, and again from 1991 to 2002, when he was again sent to prison, had a close relationship with the Patriarcas (Trotter 2014). Cosa Nostra had a strong presence in New Haven from the 1950s to the 1980s. First, the Colombo family was dominant and then the Patriarcas. Youngstown, Ohio, was notoriously entangled with Cosa Nostra from the 1950s to the 1990s; there was a close relationship between organized crime figures and city politicians.

Philadelphia's Bruno-Scarfo family thoroughly corrupted Philadelphia city government and politics in the 1980s (Cox 1989). *United States v. DiSalvo* exposed Cosa Nostra's influence on a Philadelphia councilman. Testimony from Philip Leonetti, former Bruno-Scarfo underboss, and Nicholas Caramandi led to conspiracy convictions for several Bruno-Scarfo family members, Philadelphia councilman Leland Beloff, and Beloff's legislative aide Robert Rego. At the 1992 trial, prosecutors proved that Beloff and Rego conspired with boss Nicodemo Scarfo to move a multimillion-dollar construction project bill through the council and share the developer's $100,000 kickback (*United States v. DiSalvo*). Cosa Nostra was closely allied with Newark Mayor Hugh Addonizio's administration (1962–70); after Addonizio's 1970 conviction for racketeering, federal prosecutors observed that the conviction demonstrated for the first time how a municipal administration could be taken over by organized crime (Barbanel 1981).

V. The Evolution of Effective Organized Crime Control

Government success against Cosa Nostra is attributable to a change in the FBI's and the DOJ's commitments and strategies, political support at the highest governmental level, the use of extensive electronic surveillance, the ability to protect cooperating witnesses, powerful new criminal and civil law tools, and innovative administrative strategies.

A. Early Days of Organized Crime Control

J. Edgar Hoover became director of the Bureau of Investigation, the FBI's predecessor, in 1924 and became first director of the FBI in 1935. He remained director until his death in 1972. During that long period, communists and other "subversives" were his top priority. Hoover denied the existence of nationwide organized crime, arguing that city police and county prosecutors were responsible for investigating local criminal groups. The FBI decimated communist and left-wing involvement in the fledgling labor movement but left organized crime's labor racketeering untouched. Cosa Nostra bribery and intimidation neutralized local law enforcement.

Congressional attention to organized crime dates to 1950, when a Special Senate Committee, chaired by Tennessee Senator Estes Kefauver, exposed ties between organized crime and local government in several

US cities (Kefauver 1951). Unfortunately, there was no follow-up. In 1956, Arkansas Senator John McClellan initiated hearings for the Senate Select Committee on Improper Activities in the Labor or Management Field that extended for 15 years (McClellan 1962). During Robert F. Kennedy's tenure as that committee's chief counsel, he engaged in acrimonious exchanges with IBT President Jimmy Hoffa (Kennedy 1960).

In 1957, a New York State police officer in rural Apalachin, New York, stumbled on what appeared to be a nationwide conclave of mob bosses. After Apalachin, an embarrassed Hoover launched the "Top Hoodlum Program," consisting of extensive intelligence gathering (electronic eavesdropping) on Cosa Nostra families around the country. However, the fruits of wiretaps and bugs were not admissible in federal court until 1968, when Congress authorized judicial supervision of electronic surveillance. When, in 1961, Robert Kennedy became attorney general, he revitalized the DOJ's Organized Crime and Racketeering Section. In 1964, federal prosecutors convicted IBT President Jimmy Hoffa of jury tampering, attempted bribery, and fraud. However, the DOJ's organized crime control effort withered after Kennedy's resignation in summer 1964. His successor, Ramsay Clark, was a critic of electronic surveillance.

B. Organized Crime Control Laws

In 1968, Congress authorized federal law enforcement agencies to conduct electronic surveillance subject to judicial supervision. The 1970, the RICO Act enabled law enforcement agents and prosecutors to target entire crime families and the New York families' commission, such as it was. Under RICO, defendants faced the prospect of lifetime imprisonment. The 1970 Witness Security Program enabled crime members to survive if they chose to cooperate with the government.

1. *Title III.* In 1968, Congress authorized use in federal courts of evidence obtained by electronic eavesdropping (Title III of the Omnibus Crime Control and Safe Streets Act of 1968, United States Code, vol. 18, secs. 2510–20 [1982]; Goldsmith 1983). Title III permits electronic eavesdropping with a judicial warrant issued on a showing of probable cause of past or ongoing criminality and the unavailability of viable alternative investigatory means. Eavesdropping is limited to a duration of 30 days, although a judge may grant extensions. The law requires "minimization," that is, the eavesdropping device must be turned off if, after a brief period

of listening, it is apparent that the intercepted conversation is not relevant to the matter underlying the warrant. Amendments in 1986 authorized "roving surveillance" involving different phones or sites at which the investigative target conducts criminal business (Goldsmith 1987; Jacobs, Panarella, and Worthington 1994). Subsequent amendments extended legal eavesdropping to computer and mobile phone communication. The number of state and federal electronic eavesdropping orders increased from 564 in 1980 to 801 in 1984, 900 in 1992, and more than 1,000 every year after 1994, reaching 2,000 in 2007 and over 4,000 in 2015 (US Administrative Office of the Courts 2015). The absolute number of authorizations, however, is an imperfect indicator of surveillance activity, because some interceptions last many months, cover multiple phones and locations, and intercept thousands of conversations.

The listening device that the FBI placed in Gambino family boss Paul Castellano's kitchen produced information that led to the indictment of Castellano and cronies. A device in East Harlem's Palma Boys Social Club recorded Genovese family "front boss" Anthony Salerno discussing commission business and Teamsters politics (Bonavolonta and Duffy 1996). Vincent Gigante, the actual Genovese boss, preferred to remain in the background. These intercepted conversations provided critical evidence for the commission case, *United States v. Salerno*, and for the government's complaint in the civil RICO suit against the General Executive Board of the Teamsters Union and organized crime bosses (*United States v. International Brotherhood of Teamsters*).

Listening devices in the Ravenite Social Club and an apartment above the club recorded conversations that led to the successful prosecution of Gambino boss John Gotti, the most flamboyant mob figure of modern times. Gotti's conviction shattered Cosa Nostra's aura of invincibility and gave a boost to law enforcement morale. Devices in acting Colombo boss Tommy DiBella's home, the Maniac Club, and the Casa Storta Restaurant provided important evidence against several dozen Colombo members (Bonavolonta and Duffy 1996). Philadelphia's Bruno family boss John Stanfa (Scarfo's successor) tried to protect himself from eavesdroppers by holding meetings in his lawyer's office. Unfortunately for Stanfa (and for his attorney), the government persuaded a judge to issue an eavesdropping warrant upon finding probable cause to believe that the attorney was participating in organized crime activities (Goldstock and Chananie 1988; Fresolone and Wagman 1994). By the end of the decade, Cosa Nostra members could hardly converse without risking being overheard. As the government's cases against Cosa Nostra members and associates became more numerous and stronger, more defendants agreed to cooperate in exchange for admission to the Witness Security Program (Earley and Shur 2002).

2. *Witness Security Program.* Historically, from fear of retribution, victims, witnesses, and mob members themselves typically refused to testify for the government in organized crime prosecutions. The Witness Security Program (WITSEC), authorized by the Organized Crime Control Act of 1970, sought to protect witnesses who cooperate with the government (Earley and Shur 2002). Operated by the US Marshalls Service, WITSEC protects cooperators before, during, and after trial. After release from prison, the protected witness was relocated with a new identity, residence, and job.

Until the 1980s, few Cosa Nostra members had testified against fellow Cosa Nostra members. In the late 1980s and early 1990s, in exchange for sentencing leniency and admission into WITSEC, many agreed to testify (Pileggi and Hill 1985). Over the years, at least 100 Cosa Nostra members have been admitted to WITSEC. In 1980, acting Los Angeles crime family boss Jimmy Fratianno became the most important cooperating witness against organized crime since Joseph Valachi (Demaris and Sloan 2010). His testimony contributed to the conviction of Genovese boss Funzi Tieri and later the defendants in the commission case. A few years later, Angelo Lonardo, acting boss of the Cleveland crime family, provided extraordinary information about Cosa Nostra's influence in the International Brotherhood of Teamsters, at that time the largest private sector labor union in North America (Porrello 2004). He also provided important testimony in the commission case. Tomasso Buscetta, a former high-ranking member of the Sicilian mafia, testified for Italian and American prosecutors after his two sons and son-in-law were murdered by a rival Sicilian mafia faction. Facing labor racketeering charges, Vincent Cafaro of the Genovese family assisted the FBI, even wearing a wire to obtain evidence. He testified against Gambino family boss John Gotti, Bruno-Scarfo family underboss Philip Leonetti, and others. After being implicated in a construction industry sting operation (*United States v. DiSalvo*), Nicholas Caramandi contributed to successful prosecutions of leaders of the Bruno-Scarfo family (Abadinsky 1994).

In 1991, Alphonse D'Arco, acting boss of the Lucchese crime family, became the highest ranking member of New York City's five Cosa Nostra crime families to become a cooperating government witness; he assisted in the prosecution of dozens of organized crime members and associates (Capeci and Robbins 2013). By the mid-1990s, there was a steady stream of Cosa Nostra members and associates, including Dominick LoFaro (Gambino family associate), Peter Chiodo (Lucchese family capo), Peter Savino (Genovese family associate), John Pate (Colombo family capo), Carmine Sessa (Colombo family consigliere), Anthony Accetturo (New Jersey Lucchese family), Anthony Casso (Lucchese family underboss), and William Raymond Marshall (Gambino family associate). The code of *omerta* was evaporating.

In 2001, Sammy Gravano, Gambino crime family underboss, became one of history's most productive cooperating witnesses. His testimony was crucial to convicting Gambino family boss John Gotti of five murders, racketeering, obstruction of justice, tax evasion, gambling, extortion, and loan-sharking. In 2004, Bonanno family boss Joseph Massino was convicted of murders, loan-sharking, arson, gambling, money laundering, and extortion; the government threatened to seek the death penalty in still another murder case. In 2011, he became the first boss of a New York City Cosa Nostra family to defect to the government. In April 2011, Massino testified against acting Bonanno boss Vincent Basciano and revealed to federal investigators the names of hundreds of people associated with organized crime. A federal judge reduced his sentence to 10 years, in effect time served. Upon release, he entered WITSEC.

3. *Racketeer Influenced and Corrupt Organizations Act.* RICO made it a crime to acquire an interest in an enterprise with proceeds of a pattern of racketeering activity (e.g., drug proceeds) or collection of an unlawful debt; acquire an interest in an enterprise through a pattern of racketeering activity (e.g., extortion); conduct the affairs of an enterprise through a pattern of racketeering activity (e.g., violating antitrust law or violating the rights of union members); or conspire to commit a substantive RICO offense.[3] RICO's severe authorized punishments include a maximum 20-year prison term for each substantive violation plus an additional 20-year maximum for RICO conspiracy. The convicted RICO defendant is also subject to mandatory forfeiture of the proceeds of his RICO offense and to a substantial monetary fine. In addition, the defendant

[3] For a comprehensive discussion of RICO, see Lynch (1987).

may be sentenced for each of the predicate offenses that constituted the pattern of criminal activity.

RICO also contains two civil remedial provisions. One authorizes victims to sue their offenders for treble damages. For obvious reasons, RICO victims have not used this provision against Cosa Nostra defendants. However, the second civil RICO provision, which authorizes the government to obtain restraining orders, injunctions, and other equitable remedies to prevent further racketeering, has been an effective tool for purging labor unions and industries of organized crime influence (Jacobs 2006; Jacobs and Cooperman 2011). Civil RICO cases are governed by civil discovery rules and the civil preponderance of evidence burden of proof.

A successful government-initiated civil RICO suit usually results via a negotiated consent decree in appointment of a monitor or trustee tasked with reforming the union, business, or employer association. Some of these monitors have been successful, others not. Much depends on the commitment and competence of the monitor and the degree of support the monitor receives from the court and the US attorney's office. The tenacity of the monitored entity's organizational, legal, and political resistance to the monitor's role is also important.

VI. Implementation of the Modern Organized Crime Control Program

The beginnings of effective federal government attacks on Cosa Nostra date from the 1960s, beginning with greatly increased efforts by the DOJ. The FBI became seriously and extensively involved after Hoover's departure. Since then law enforcement attention to organized crime, peaking in the 1980s and 1990s, has been relentless.

A. FBI Top Priority

Italian American organized crime became the FBI's number one priority after the death of J. Edgar Hoover and the presidential election of Richard Nixon (Nash 1972; Schlesinger 1978; Powers 1986). Initially, the strategy focused on disrupting Cosa Nostra's gambling operations. But the gambling investigations and prosecutions were not notably successful. Prosecutions faltered, but even when they were successful, sentences were light. Juries and judges did not see mostly low-level gambling figures as a serious threat to American society (US General Accounting Office

1976). Former IBT President Jimmy Hoffa's 1975 disappearance and death touched off a major investigation of the relationship between the Teamsters and organized crime.

The FBI promoted its attack on labor racketeering to the top of its organized crime control agenda. The Miami Organized Crime Strike Force's Operation UNIRAC (for *uni*on *rac*keteering) targeted organized crime's influence in the International Longshoremen's Association. Eventually, the investigation expanded across the whole East Coast; more than a hundred individuals, including labor and Cosa Nostra leaders, were convicted of embezzlement, taking kickbacks, and other offenses. Operation BRILAB (for *bri*bery/*lab*or) resulted in bribery, corruption, and racketeering convictions of New Orleans Cosa Nostra boss Carlos Marcello, other organized crime members and associates, and Louisiana politicians. The Operation PENDORF (for *pen*etration of Allen *Dorf*man) investigation, focusing on Cosa Nostra's corruption of Teamsters Central States Pension and Welfare Fund, resulted in convictions of Teamsters President Roy Williams and Cosa Nostra figures in Chicago, Milwaukee, Cleveland, Las Vegas, and Kansas City (Jacobs, Panarella, and Worthington 1994).

B. Donnie Brasco

The undercover infiltration of the Bonanno, and to a lesser extent the Colombo, families in 1976–82 by FBI agent Joe Pistone (aka "Donnie Brasco") provided invaluable information that led to the conviction of more than 100 Cosa Nostra members and associates (Pistone and Woodley 1987; Bonavolonta and Duffy 1996). Posing as a jewel thief and burglar, Pistone made contact with organized crime members and associates at bars and restaurants. That the FBI would attempt to place an undercover agent inside a Cosa Nostra family reveals how committed, confident, and creative the agency had become since the days when undercover operations were prohibited (Nash 1972; Schlesinger 1978). Pistone was eventually befriended by a Bonanno soldier whom he cut in on a number of apparent jewel thefts. He eventually became a full-fledged Bonanno family associate. After his undercover operation ended, he testified in dozens of Cosa Nostra trials, including the commission case, *United States v. Salerno*. His infiltration of the Bonanno family resulted in that family's expulsion from the New York City commission (DeStefano 2006). His undercover work generated a mountain of intelligence material that supported other indictments in Milwaukee and Tampa (Bonavolonta and Duffy 1996).

C. Department of Justice's Initiatives

In 1967, the US DOJ established Organized Crime Strike Forces in 14 cities (Ryan 1994). Comprised of prosecutors and investigators, the strike forces reported to the Organized Crime and Racketeering Section at the DOJ headquarters in Washington, DC, not to the US Attorneys in the strike forces' jurisdictions. They played an important role in bringing federal, state, and local agencies together in well-designed and well-executed investigations. According to supporters, the strike force prosecutors developed specialized expertise, achieved close working relationships with state and local law enforcement agencies, and stayed in their jobs longer than other federal prosecutors (Jacobs, Panarella, and Worthington 1994). However, many US attorneys resented the strike forces' independence. When Richard Thornburgh, a former US Attorney and a strike force opponent, became US Attorney General in 1988, he disbanded the strike forces, transferring their mission and personnel back to the US Attorneys (Jacobs, Panarella, and Worthington 1994). In 2010, the DOJ's Organized Crime and Racketeering Section merged with the Gang Unit and the National Gang Targeting, Enforcement and Coordination Center to become the Organized Crime and Gang Section within the Criminal Division. In the last decade, the Organized Crime and Gang Section has targeted diverse organize crime groups, not only or primarily Cosa Nostra.

D. Federal, State, and Local Law Enforcement Cooperation

In 1970, President Richard Nixon established the National Council on Organized Crime and tasked it with formulating a strategy to eliminate organized crime. The council, composed of representatives of all federal agencies whose work or responsibilities touch on organized crime, mainly addressed the rivalries that undermine interagency cooperation; it did not formulate an organized crime control strategy. The Executive Working Group for Federal-State-Local Prosecutorial Relations, established in 1980, was another attempt to coordinate efforts.

Informal multiagency agreements supplemented and reinforced formal coordinating efforts (Jacobs, Panarella, and Worthington 1994). For example, the FBI and the New York City Police Department effectively cooperated in numerous organized crime investigations. Former FBI organized crime supervisor Jules Bonavolonta estimates that the New York City FBI office's organized crime division by the mid-1980s had 350 agents, supplemented by more than 100 police officers (Bonavolonta and Duffy 1996). This formidable task force supported round-the-clock investigations, particularly labor-intensive electronic surveillance, of the five Cosa Nostra crime families (Jacobs, Panarella, and Worthington 1994).

E. Political Support from Washington

The federal focus on Cosa Nostra waned after Robert Kennedy resigned his position as attorney general in 1964. His successor, Ramsey Clark, President Lyndon Johnson's attorney general, viewed electronic eavesdropping as a threat to civil liberties. The Nixon administration revitalized the attack on Cosa Nostra; it reached its pinnacle during Ronald Reagan's presidency. Due to his involvement with the Cosa Nostra–influenced International Alliance of Theatrical Stage Employees, President Ronald Reagan was aware of Cosa Nostra's labor racketeering. He appointed the PCOC, which, from 1983 to 1987, issued 12 reports documenting Cosa Nostra's organization, drug trafficking, gambling, and labor racketeering (PCOC 1983, 1985, 1986a, 1986b). It recommended that the DOJ bring a civil RICO suit against the International Brotherhood of Teamsters with the goal of court appointment of a trustee charged to purge the union.

The US Senate's Permanent Subcommittee on Investigations, under the leadership of Georgia Senator Sam Nunn, kept the spotlight on organized crime. The subcommittee held hearings on Cosa Nostra's role in illicit rackets and in the legitimate economy (US Senate Permanent Subcommittee on Investigations 1981, 1983; Jacobs and Mullin 2003). Cosa Nostra defectors and other witnesses testified about Cosa Nostra's structure and operations.

1. *Criminal RICO.* Because of the complexity of the RICO statute and federal prosecutors' long experience using conspiracy and other offenses, it took a decade for federal prosecutors to begin using RICO. Eventually, significantly due to proselytizing by law professor and RICO drafter G. Robert Blakey, the FBI began using RICO to target entire crime families. This facilitated drafting probable cause applications for wide-ranging electronic surveillance against each family's leadership

cadre. In 1981, Genovese family boss Frank Tieri became the first Cosa Nostra boss to be convicted of a RICO offense.

Since then, practically every significant organized crime prosecution has included a RICO count. Several cases charged members of a Cosa Nostra family with participating in the affairs of an enterprise (the family) through a pattern of racketeering activity (e.g., murder, extortion, obstruction of justice, gambling, drug trafficking). Rudolph Giuliani, then US Attorney for the Southern District of New York, obtained grand jury indictments against the bosses of four of the five New York City families, alleging their participation in the affairs of an enterprise (the Cosa Nostra New York City commission) through a pattern of racketeering activity, including directing the 1979 assassination of Bonanno family boss Carmine Galante and two Bonanno associates, and with operating a poured concrete contractors' cartel.

Many RICO defendants chose to cooperate with the government in order to avoid an almost certain life sentence. There have also been dozens of RICO jury trials. For example, in *United States v. Badalamenti*, investigation of an international heroin-trafficking operation involving over 200 members and associates of a Sicilian Mafia faction, led to a RICO "mega-trial" involving numerous Bonanno family members and associates. Some pled guilty, some died, and some fled. However, 22 individuals went to trial together. Louis Freeh, later a federal judge and FBI director, was lead prosecutor. The trial lasted 3 years. All but one defendant was convicted (Jacobs, Panarella, and Worthington 1994). To prove the existence of an "enterprise," a formal organization or "an association in fact," prosecutors introduced evidence on the history, structure, and operations of the Cosa Nostra crime families and the commission (Jacobs, Panarella, and Worthington 1994). This provided an exquisite opportunity to place a Cosa Nostra defendant in the context of a long and frightening organized crime history.

In 1992, after several failed attempts, federal prosecutors convicted Gambino family boss John J. Gotti of RICO offenses and five murders, conspiracy to commit murder, obstruction of justice, tax evasion, illegal gambling, extortion, and loan-sharking. After Gotti's imprisonment, his son, John A. Gotti Jr., served as acting Gambino boss. In 1998, federal prosecutors obtained an indictment against Gotti Jr., alleging that, among other crimes, he extorted over $1 million from the owners and employees of an upscale Manhattan strip club. Gotti Jr. pled guilty to loan-sharking, bookmaking, and extortion. He was sentenced to 77 months in prison.

His uncle, Peter Gotti, became acting boss. He was indicted in 2001, convicted in 2003 (and, on separate charges, in 2004), and sentenced to 25 years imprisonment.

In 1997, federal prosecutors successfully prosecuted Genovese crime family boss and commission head Vincent Gigante (*United States v. Gigante*; McShane 2016). Prosecutors alleged that Gigante and his subordinates held interests in numerous businesses, including window replacement, mixed concrete, trucking, waste hauling, painting, and operation of the Javitz Convention Center. Rejecting Gigante's defense of mental incompetence, the jury convicted him of RICO conspiracy, extortion conspiracy, labor payoff conspiracy, and two counts of conspiring to murder in aid of racketeering. At sentencing, the court stated that Gigante earned millions of dollars from his business interests plus loan-sharking, hijacking, gambling, and other criminal conduct.

Liborio Bellomo served as acting Genovese boss until he was indicted in 1997 and, while serving that sentence, was indicted again in 2001 and, for a third time in 2006 along with 30 other Genovese members. Daniel Leo succeeded him as boss and was sent to prison in 2008. In 2018, five Genovese members and associates, including Vincent Gigante's son, were charged with racketeering, conspiracy, extortion, labor racketeering conspiracy, fraud, and bribery (*United States v. Esposito*). These bare-bones facts illuminate the relentless pressure that the government applied to the Cosa Nostra families in the 1990s, 2000s, and 2010s.

2. *Civil RICO.* Cosa Nostra's labor and business racketeering have been seriously disrupted by successful civil RICO suits. These lawsuits ask for a judicial remedy to prevent present and future use of an enterprise (union or business) for racketeering. Many have been resolved by negotiated consent decrees tasking approved monitors or trustees (usually former federal prosecutors), paid for by the monitored entity, with reforming organized-crime-influenced union or business. The monitor's powers are specified in the decree or settlement. The trustees have expelled organized crime members and their associates from unions, companies, and other organizations (Jacobs, Worthington, and Panarella 1994). They have conducted elections, required the hiring of auditors and other professionals, imposed operational procedures, and mandated transparency. The court can punish a defendant's lack of compliance as contempt. Typically, a monitor's service continues for years, in part due to litigation over the monitor's powers and the monitored entity's compliance.

3. *Labor Racketeering Cases.* US organized crime is unique with respect to its influence over labor unions. Labor racketeering predates Italian American organized crime, dating back to the labor wars of the late nineteenth and early twentieth centuries. In 1982, the DOJ's Newark Organized Crime Strike Force filed the first civil RICO lawsuit against a labor union, Teamsters Local 560 (*United States v. Local 560, International Brotherhood of Teamsters*). Local 560 had been dominated by Anthony Provenzano, a Genovese crime family, a soldier, and his brothers since the 1950s (Goldberg 1989). The litigation resulted in a court-imposed trusteeship that empowered the trustee to run the union until organized crime figures were purged and fair elections held. After 10 years, the court determined that Local 560 was reformed and dissolved the trusteeship (Jacobs and Santore 2001). By that time, the IBT union was subject to court-approved monitoring.

In 1988, the US Attorney's Office for the Southern District of New York filed a civil RICO suit against the IBT, its general executive board, and a number of Cosa Nostra members, alleging that the defendants were involved in racketeering (Jacobs and Cooperman 2011). It charged the defendants with conspiring to conduct the affairs of the IBT through such offenses as conspiracy to defraud union members of their union membership rights (Jacobs and Cooperman 2011). The entire general executive board resigned pursuant to the 1989 consent decree that settled the case. The Teamsters agreed to appointment of a three-person monitoring team whose goals were to purge corruption and racketeering from the union and supervise a direct election (a first for any international union) for president and general executive board members. The rationale was that a democratically operated union would be less vulnerable to organized crime influence and corruption.

The monitoring continued for almost 30 years. One of the monitors, the investigations officer, brought disciplinary actions that resulted in expulsion or resignation of more than 500 Teamster officials and members from locals because of organized crime ties or toleration of organized crime influence. In the first rank-and-file general election, an insurgent reformer, Ron Carey, won the presidency (Crowe 1993). He sought to purge mobsters and corrupt officials from IBT locals around the country (Jacobs and Panarella 1998). Ironically, however, in 1997 the monitors expelled Carey because he had diverted Teamster funds to his election campaign. Former president Jimmy Hoffa's son, James Hoffa Jr., was elected president and has held that office until the time this was written (Jacobs and Cooperman 2011). On January 14, 2015, the Teamsters and the Justice Department announced an agreement, to be phased in over 5 years, to terminate monitoring.

The DOJ also focused on reforming the three other international unions that the PCOC identified as organized crime influenced. In November 1994, the DOJ warned the Laborers International Union of North America (membership 800,000) that a civil RICO lawsuit was imminent because of credible evidence of Cosa Nostra influence over the union's leadership (*Serpico v. Laborers' International Union of North America*). This prompted a negotiated agreement requiring removal of high-level union officers and appointment of a disciplinary officer acceptable to the DOJ who was responsible for administratively investigating and prosecuting organized crime members, associates, and their allies. The disciplinary officer has always been a former federal prosecutor. Many officers of the Laborer's International Union of North America have been expelled or forced to resign, including, in 2001, three officers alleged to have had longtime ties to the Chicago Outfit.

In 1995, the HEREIU entered into a consent decree with the DOJ to resolve a civil RICO suit (alleging over 25 years of Cosa Nostra influence) (*United States v. Hotel Employees and Restaurant Employees International Union*). The consent decree specified that Kurt Muellenberg, former chief of the DOJ's Organized Crime and Racketeering Section, would serve as monitor with power to investigate the international union, to review union actions and operations, and to bar individuals from union office. In May 1998, as a result of Muellenberg's prodding, HEREIU President Edward T. Hanley retired from the office he had held for 25 years (Crowe 1998).

The decades-long effort to purge the International Longshoremen's Union of organized crime influence appears not to have been successful. Despite numerous convictions and trusteeships, organized crime figures have been able to hold onto power (Stewart 2019). Assistant monitor Robert Stewart describes the 12-year effort to purge Cosa Nostra's influence from New Jersey International Longshoremen's Association Local 1588 and thus from the New Jersey side of the Port of New York (Stewart 2019). According to Stewart, the Genovese and Gambino families exploited a "culture of corruption" to outmaneuver the court-appointed monitors and wear down the US Attorney. The New York–New Jersey Waterfront Commission, established in 1958 to combat racketeering in the port, was stymied by incompetence, endless litigation, and the opposition of some New Jersey politicians (Goldstock 2018).

US attorneys filed numerous civil RICO lawsuits against union locals (Jacobs 1999, chap. 15.) For example, the Southern District of New York office brought a civil RICO suit against Laborers Local 6A, long controlled by the Colombo family, for enforcing a cartel of poured concrete contractors (*United States v. Local 6A, Cement and Concrete Workers*). The consent judgment required removal of 16 of the union's 25 officers and appointment of a trustee to oversee union operations (Goldberg 1989).

In 1985, the Bonanno family's 25-year domination of Teamsters Local 14 served as the basis for a labor racketeering and conspiracy prosecution of the Bonanno family boss and other leaders, as well as Local 14 officials (*United States v. Rastelli*). Shortly thereafter, the government initiated a civil RICO action against numerous Bonanno family members, the Bonanno family itself, and IBT Local 14 (*United States v. Bonanno Organized Crime Family*). The consent judgment established an interim executive board to oversee the local's operations (Goldberg 1989).

Criminal investigations of Philadelphia's Bruno-Scarfo family provided grist for a civil RICO suit against the local roofers union (*United States v. Local 30, United Slate, Tile and Composition Roofers*). For more than two decades, the Bruno-Scarfo family had used its control of the roofers local to extort roofing contractors, embezzle pension and welfare funds, and bribe public officials (Goldberg 1989). Satisfying neither the government (seeking a trusteeship) nor the defendants (pressing for dismissal of the complaint), the judge imposed a "decreeship" that removed convicted defendants from the union but otherwise left the local's operations untouched (Goldberg 1989).

4. *State and Local Strategies.*   In 1992, the Manhattan District Attorney's Office brought a major criminal prosecution against Thomas and Joseph Gambino and several other Cosa Nostra defendants, alleging extortion and racketeering in the New York City garment district. The case ended midtrial with the defendants pleading guilty to a criminal antitrust count, agreeing to sell all their garment center–related trucking interests, and paying a $12 million fine (Jacobs 1999). The Gambinos are no longer a presence in the garment center; however, the garment center is only a shadow of its former self because the manufacturing of clothing has largely moved to China and other foreign countries.

A 1994 civil RICO settlement against 112 defendants (including 64 Gambino and Lucchese members and associates and several waste hauling companies) resulted in appointment of a monitor of Cosa Nostra's Long Island waste hauling cartel (*United States v. Private Sanitation Industry Association of Nassau/Suffolk*). Michael Cherkasky, a former prosecutor who previously led the Manhattan district attorney's successful prosecution of the Gambino brothers, oversaw compliance (Jacobs 1999). National waste hauling companies entered the Long Island market (Jacobs 1999).

F. State and Local Law Enforcement and Regulatory Initiatives

State and local law enforcement also contributed to the decimation of Cosa Nostra. The New York State Organized Crime Task Force, led by Ronald Goldstock, was particularly creative in the 1980s (Goldstock 1989). In 1983, the task force placed a listening device in Lucchese family boss Anthony Corallo's car. Over the course of 6 months, it intercepted incriminating conversations that led to the successful prosecution of Corallo, underboss Salvatore Santoro, and several others (Bonavolonta and Duffy 1996). It also provided evidence for the civil RICO suit that put an end to Cosa Nostra's Long Island waste hauling cartel (Abadinsky 1994). Goldstock encouraged use of civil remedies to purge Cosa Nostra from mob-influenced industries (Goldstock, n.d.; Jacobs 1999). He and his chief assistant, Martin Marcus, drafted and successfully promoted a "little-RICO law" in New York State (Jacobs 1999). Many other states followed suit. Besides purging the Gambino family from garment center trucking, its power base, Manhattan District Attorney Robert Morgenthau brought important cases against Cosa Nostra–controlled cartels of painting and window replacement (Jacobs 1999).

As New York City mayor (1994–2001), Rudy Giuliani continued the campaign against organized crime that he had aggressively waged as US Attorney. He launched an administrative strategy to continue purging organized crime from the city's economy. He required wholesalers at the Fulton Fish Market, which had been dominated by organized crime since the 1930s, to apply for city licenses; companies with organized crime ties were denied licenses (Jacobs and Hortis 1998). The Cosa Nostra–dominated organization that ran and profited from the annual Feast of San Gennaro street fair in Little Italy was replaced by an untainted organization and the Roman Catholic Archdiocese (Jacobs 1999). New York City's School Construction Authority used much the same strategy to deny contracts to construction contractors with organized crime ties.

In June 1996, the New York City Council, at Giuliani's urging, created the Trade Waste Commission (TWC) to use a licensing strategy to eliminate Cosa Nostra's domination of waste hauling (Jacobs and Hortis 1998). The TWC hired executive officers, attorneys, monitors, and police detectives with experience in organized crime investigations and prosecutions (Jacobs and Hortis 1998). It denied waste hauling licenses to companies operated by individuals in any way connected with the organized-crime-dominated waste hauling cartel (Jacobs and Hortis 1998). The TWC also set maximum rates and regulated the duration of waste hauling contracts. National waste-hauling companies began operating in New York City for the first time (Raab 1998*a*).

In 2001, the city merged the TWC and the Gambling Commission into an Organized Crime Control Commission and, a year later, into a general-jurisdiction Business Integrity Commission, with a mandate "to eliminate organized crime and other forms of corruption from the public wholesale markets, the trade waste and shipboard gambling industries." The Business Integrity Commission's goals are "to ensure that the regulated businesses are able to compete fairly; that the marketplaces remain free from violence, fraud, rackets and threats; that customers receive fair treatment; and that regulated businesses … conduct their affairs with honesty and integrity."[4]

VII. Cosa Nostra's Current and Future Prospects

The world in which Cosa Nostra became powerful is largely gone. No longer can they easily infiltrate labor unions or dominate cartels in local industries, and unions are themselves much less powerful. The political machines that gave Cosa Nostra entrée into the corridors of power and access to corruptible mayors, police, prosecutors, and judges are, if not entirely gone, vastly weaker. Many of the illicit markets Cosa Nostra long influenced or dominated—gambling, prostitution, pornography, drugs—have changed in ways that make their exploitation much more difficult. Law enforcement has gained and knows how to use enforcement tools that did not exist in early times. Cosa Nostra is down, though not out. Regaining more than a shadow of its former power will not be easy.

A. Legalization of Gambling

For decades, the Cosa Nostra crime families benefited from legal prohibition of most forms of gambling, much as they had in the early twentieth

---

[4] See https://www1.nyc.gov/site/bic/index.page.

century from national alcohol prohibition. They ran urban numbers games, sports betting, and local casinos and controlled the wire services that carried the results of horse racing and dominated local bookies. Cosa Nostra's legitimate and illegitimate gambling interests in Havana and Las Vegas generated vast revenue.

This gambling near-monopoly imploded. Lotteries are run by 47 jurisdictions: 44 states plus the District of Columbia, Puerto Rico, and the US Virgin Islands. The Supreme Court's decision in *California v. Cabazon Band of Mission Indians*, 480 U.S. 202 (1987), overturned prohibition of gambling on Native American territories. Congress responded by passing the 1988 Indian Gaming Regulatory Act; it expanded the kinds of games that tribal casinos can offer and provided a framework for regulating the industry. The act established the National Indian Gaming Commission and divided Indian gaming into three classes. Class I encompasses charitable and social gaming with nominal prizes; Class II includes bingo and other punch-board/pull-tab style games; and Class III includes high-stakes bingo, casinos, slot machines, and other commercial gaming.

In 1996, there were 184 tribes operating 281 gaming facilities in 24 states. After expenses, this amounted to $1.9 billion in net income, $1.6 billion of which went straight to the tribes. By 2007, the tribal gaming industry had become a $25 billion industry; there were 350 tribal casinos in 28 states.

In May 2018, the Supreme Court struck down a federal law that prevented states other than Nevada from authorizing sports betting (*Murphy v. National Collegiate Athletic Association*). That ruling means that individuals will be able to legally bet online on amateur and professional sports. Cosa Nostra members will probably not be wiped out since their bettors can more easily avoid taxes on winnings, but the legalization will take a large bite out of their sports gambling operations. Video poker machines are legal in Native American casinos. Online video poker betting is legal when played at licensed foreign casinos. Many foreign casinos welcome US players and offer secure, high-quality online video poker. Cosa Nostra members have an ownership interest in some legal gambling operations, but competition is fierce.

Despite the radically changed gambling business, Cosa Nostra families still profit from gambling operations (*Trends in Organized Crime* 1997). *State v. Taccetta* exposed Cosa Nostra's placement of Joker Poker video slot machines in New Jersey bars, restaurants, and other businesses. The Lucchese and Bruno-Scarfo crime families shared the revenue with the business owners and extorted the manufacturer. The 2002 indictment in *United States v Calabrese* alleged that several Chicago Outfit crews dominated video device gambling and sports gambling in Chicago suburbs and threatened and used violence to collect gambling debts.

B. Competitive Drug Markets

Cosa Nostra never had a monopoly or near-monopoly on drug importation and distribution, but in some places and times individual mobsters and their crews were major importers and wholesalers. Today, competitors can block opportunities that Cosa Nostra members covet and cooperate with government in investigation and prosecution of Cosa Nostra members (Reuter 1995). In states where marijuana is legal, Cosa Nostra's opportunity to profit from trafficking in the drug is much diminished.

C. Decline of Private Sector Unions

Much of Cosa Nostra's power derived from its influence in labor unions, but private sector labor unions have been on the decline for decades. In the mid-1950s, about 35 percent of US workers belonged to a union. In recent years, only 6.5 percent of private sector workers have been union members. The DOJ has used criminal and civil remedies to eliminate Cosa Nostra's presence and curb its influence in the big four unions in which it was ensconced for decades. Thus, labor racketeering opportunities are diminished. Jointly managed union pension and welfare funds are much better insulated from organized crime influence.

D. Italian Assimilation

Fifty years ago most big US cities had well-recognized working class Italian neighborhoods, often called Little Italy, where Cosa Nostra members maintained physical presence and exerted influence. They hired teenage boys, some of them Italian immigrants, for odd jobs and recruited the most promising into their operations. These neighborhoods have dramatically shrunken as Italian Americans have steadily assimilated into mainstream society, thereby radically diminishing the pool of tough teenagers with Cosa Nostra potential.

E. Criminal Prosecutions

There is no exact figure on the number of federal, state, and local criminal organized crime prosecutions over the past 40 years, but the number certainly exceeds 1,000. According to David Williams, director of the US Government Accounting Office's Office of Special Investigations, between 1983 and 1986 there were 2,500 indictments of Cosa Nostra members and associates (this does not mean 2,500 separate individuals). In 1988, FBI director William Sessions reported to the Senate Subcommittee on Investigations that federal prosecutors had since 1981 convicted 19 bosses, 13 underbosses, and 43 capos (Jacobs, Panarella, and Worthington 1994; US Senate Permanent Subcommittee 1988). Federal prosecutions, plus some state and local prosecutions, systematically decimated whole organized crime families. The incomplete list in table 1 of Cosa Nostra bosses and acting bosses convicted since 1980 illuminates the results.

The FBI's and the DOJ's priorities radically changed after the September 11, 2001, al-Qaeda attacks on the World Trade Center and Pentagon. The FBI shifted 2,000 agents from criminal investigations to counterterrorism, counterintelligence, and cybersecurity.

The successful law enforcement attack on Cosa Nostra in the 1980s and 1990s meant that there was less need, going forward, to devote so many resources to organized crime (Raab 1998b). The DOJ's organized crime control priority changed from Cosa Nostra to international organized crime groups. In April 2008, Attorney General Michael Mukasey announced a Law Enforcement Strategy to Combat International Organized Crime (IOC) "in order to address the growing threat to US security and stability posed by international organized crime groups." The strategy aims "to identify priority IOC groups and individuals for concerted, high-impact law enforcement action by domestic and international agencies to significantly disrupt and dismantle those targets" (US Department of Justice 2008). In November 2008, the DOJ's Organized Crime and Racketeering Section distributed the first Top International Criminal Organization Targets List to federal investigators and prosecutors. It also organized a special task force to break up MS-13, a Central American gang with a presence on both the West and East Coasts. *United States v. Dany Freedy Ramos Mejia et al.* (2007) involved charges against 50 MS-13 members, and *United States v. Manuel de Jesus Ayala et al.* (2008) charges against 26 MS-13 members.

Despite the reduction in resources aimed at Cosa Nostra, investigations and prosecutions continued into the twenty-first century. In 2004, the FBI arrested 27 Bonanno family members who were charged with racketeering, murders, attempted murders, and conspiracy to murder. That same

TABLE 1

Cosa Nostra Bosses and Acting Bosses Convicted since 1980

Boss/Acting Boss	Family	Location
Alphonse D'Arco	Lucchese	New York, NY
Anthony Corallo	Lucchese	New York, NY
Vittorio Amuso	Lucchese	New York, NY
Funzi Tieri	Genovese	New York, NY
Liborio Bellomo	Genovese	New York, NY
Dominick Cirillo	Genovese	New York, NY
Anthony Salerno	Genovese	New York, NY
Vincent Gigante	Genovese	New York, NY
Daniel Leo	Genovese	New York, NY
Carmine Persico	Colombo	New York, NY
Vittorio Orena	Colombo	New York, NY
Joseph Massino	Bonanno	New York, NY
Vincent Basciano	Bonanno	New York, NY
Philip Rastelli	Bonanno	New York, NY
John Gotti	Gambino	New York, NY
John Gotti Jr.	Gambino	New York, NY
Peter Gotti	Gambino	New York, NY
John Riggi	DeCavalcante	New Jersey
Raymond Patriarca	Patriarca	New England
Frank Balistrieri	Patriarca	New England
Gennaro Angiulo	Patriarca	New England
Nicodemo Scarfo	—	Philadelphia
John Stanfa	—	Philadelphia
Joseph Ligambi	—	Philadelphia
Russell Bufalino	—	Northeastern PA
William D'Elia	—	Northeastern PA
Carlos Marcello	—	New Orleans, LA
Eugene Smaldone	—	Denver, CO
Tony Accardo	—	Chicago, IL
Joseph Aiuppa	—	Chicago, IL
Michael Sarno	—	Chicago, IL
Salvatore DeLaurentis	—	Chicago, IL
Albert Vena	—	Chicago, IL
Nick Civella	—	Kansas City, KS
Carl Civella	—	Kansas City, KS
Dominic Brooklier	—	Los Angeles, CA
James Licavoli	—	Cleveland, OH
Michael Trupiano	—	St. Louis, MO
Sam Russotti	—	Buffalo, NY

year, 22 Genovese members and associates were charged with racketeering, extortion, fraud, and tax evasion related to bid rigging and price fixing in the New York City drywall industry.

In January 2011, a joint task force involving 800 federal, state, and local law enforcement officers arrested more than 120 defendants, including dozens of Cosa Nostra members. The defendants were charged by grand juries in New York, New Jersey, and Rhode Island with numerous violent and illegal acts—from murder and narcotics trafficking to extortion, illegal gambling, arson, loan-sharking, and labor racketeering. US Attorney General Eric Holder said:

> Today's arrests mark an important, and encouraging, step forward in disrupting La Cosa Nostra's operations. But our battle against organized crime enterprises is far from over. This is an ongoing effort and it must, and will, remain a top priority. Members and associates of La Cosa Nostra are among the most dangerous criminals in our country. The very oath of allegiance sworn by these mafia members during their initiation ceremony binds them to a life of crime.
>
> As we've seen for decades, criminal mafia operations can harm the American economy by means of a wide array of fraud schemes but also through illegal imposition of mob "taxes" at ports, on construction industries, and on small businesses. In some cases, Cosa Nostra members and associates seek to corrupt legitimate businesses and those who have sworn to uphold the public trust. And their methods often are lethal. Time and again, they have shown a willingness to kill—to make money, to eliminate rivals, and to silence witnesses.
>
> Past and present successful arrests and prosecutions in many cities and involving multiple mafia families send a clear message that the Justice Department is targeting federal resources and working with state and local law enforcement partners like never before. They are committed, and determined, to eradicate these criminal enterprises once and for all. (*Financial Times* 2011)

F. Cosa Nostra Dysfunction

The decades-long federal campaign against Cosa Nostra coincided with and no doubt reinforced Cosa Nostra's internal deterioration, most strongly evidenced by the number of its members who served as cooperating witnesses in exchange for leniency and protection. The breakdown of *omerta* in the 1980s and 1990s is attributable to more powerful and effective law enforcement and the possibility that defecting members will survive in the Witness Security Program. The current generation of members and associates may have less loyalty to the Cosa Nostra (Demaris 1980; Goldstock 1989).

Several families experienced violent conflict over leadership succession. The Persico and Orena factions' battle for control of the Colombo family (described in *United States v. Orena*) and bloody internecine conflicts in the Bonanno family following Carmine Galante's assassination are examples. Following Nicodemo Scarfo's incarceration, Philadelphia's Bruno-Scarfo family was wracked by intrafamily warfare (*United States v. Stanfa*).

G. Purging Cosa Nostra from the Legitimate Economy

The federal government, using criminal and civil forfeiture laws, has taken possession of forfeited Cosa Nostra businesses, including restaurants and a concrete manufacturing plant. The New York City poured concrete contractors and waste hauling company cartels no longer exist. The Fulton Fish Market has been moved to the Bronx and purged of mob influence. Cosa Nostra's presence at the Javits Exhibition Center has been eliminated. Organized crime has been purged from some union locals. Even those locals that have stubbornly resisted reform are far less easily dominated than they were decades ago.

H. A Caution

Cosa Nostra's involvement in the legitimate economy, black markets, and crimes like theft, extortion, and fraud significantly diminished in the first two decades of the twenty-first century, and economic and legal changes have reduced traditional targets and illicit opportunities. Cosa Nostra's resilience for more than a century nonetheless cautions against declaring its extinction inevitable.

APPENDIX 1
Cases Cited

Commission case: see *United States v. Salerno*
Murphy v. Nat'l Collegiate Athletic Ass'n, 138 S. Ct. 1461 (2018)
Serpico v. Laborers' Int'l Union of N. Am., 97 F.3d 995 (7th Cir. 1996)
State v. Taccetta, 301 N.J. Super. 227 (App. Div. 1997)
United States v. Avellino, 136 F.3d 249 (2d Cir. 1998)
United States v. Badalamenti, Crim. No. 84–236 (S.D.N.Y.1984), aff'd, *United States v. Casamento*, 887 F.2d 1141 (2d Cir. 1989)

United States v. Bonanno Organized Crime Family of La Cosa Nostra, 683 F. Supp 1411 (E.D.N.Y. 1998)

United States v. Bianco, 998 F.2d 1112 (2d Cir. 1993)

United States v. Bufalino, 285 F.2d 408 (2d Cir. 1960)

United States v. Calabrese, Nos. 07-1962, 07-1969 (7th Cir. 2007)

United States v. Corallo, 413 F.2d 1306 (2d Cir. 1969)

United States v. DiSalvo, 34 F.3d 1204 (3d Cir. 1994)

United States v. Dorfman, 470 F.2d 246 (2d Cir. 1996)

United States v. Esposito, 309 F. Supp.3d 24 (S.D.N.Y. 2018)

United States v. Gigante, 982 F. Supp 140 (E.D.N.Y. 1997)

United States v. Gotti, No. CR-90-1051(S-1), 1992 WL 12146729, at 1 (E.D.N.Y. June 23, 1992), aff'd, *United States v. Locascio*, 6 F.3d 924 (2d Cir. 1993)

United States v. Hotel Emp.'s & Rest. Emp.'s, Int'l Union, 974 F. Supp. 411 (D.N.J. 1997)

United States v. Ianniello, 808 F.2d 184 (2d Cir. 1986)

United States v. Int'l Bhd. of Teamsters, 708 F. Supp 1388 (S.D.N.Y. 1989)

United States v. Local 6A, Cement & Concrete Workers, Laborers Int'l Union of N. Am., 663 F. Supp 192 (S.D.N.Y. 1986)

United States v. Local 30, United Slate, Tile & Composition Roofers, Damp & Waterproof Workers Assoc. et al., 683 F. Supp 1139 (E.D.Pa. 1988)

United States v. Local 560 of Int'l Bhd. of Teamsters, 581 F. Supp 279 (D.N.J. 1984), aff'd, 780 F.2d 267 (3d Cir. 1985)

United States v. Local 1804-1, Int'l Longshoremen's Assoc., 812 F. Supp. 1303 (S.D.N.Y. 1993)

United States v. Locascio: see *United States v. Gotti*

United States v. Orena, 145 F.3d 551 (2d Cir. 1998)

United States v. Private Sanitation Indus. Assoc. of Nassau/Suffolk, Inc., et. al., F. Supp 1114 (S.D.N.Y. 1994)

United States v. Rastelli, 870 F.2d 822 (2d Cir. 1989)

United States v. Salerno, 868 F.2d 524 (2d Cir. 1989)

United States v. Spinale, Crim. No. 85–95 (D.Nev. 1986)

United States v. Stanfa, 685 F.2d 85 (2d Cir. 1982)

United States v. Williams, 737 F.2d 594 (7th Cir. 1984)

REFERENCES

Abadinsky, Howard. 1994. *Organized Crime*. 4th ed. Chicago: Nelson-Hall.

Barbanel, Josh. 1981. "Hugh J. Addonizio, 67, Ex-Mayor of Newark Jailed 5 Years, Dead." *New York Times*, February 2.

Barnes, Nicky, and Tom Folsom. 2007. *Mr. Untouchable: The Rise, Fall, and Resurrection of Heroin's Teflon Don*. New York: Rugged Land.

Bell, Daniel. 1960. *The End of Ideology*. Glencoe, IL: Free Press.

Block, Alan A. 1983. *East Side, West Side: Organizing Crime in New York 1930–1950*. New Brunswick, NJ: Transaction.

Bonanno, Joseph, with Sergio Lalli. 1983. *A Man of Honor: The Autobiography of Joseph Bonanno*. New York: Simon & Schuster.

Bonavolonta, Jules, and Brian Duffy. 1996. *The Good Guys: How We Turned the FBI 'Round and Finally Broke the Mob*. New York: Simon & Schuster.

Brandt, Charles. 2004. *"I Heard You Paint Houses": Frank "The Irishman" Sheeran and the Inside Story of the Mafia, the Teamsters, and the Last Ride of Jimmy Hoffa*. Hanover, NH: Steerforth.

Brill, Steven. 1978. *The Teamsters*. New York: Simon & Schuster.

Capeci, Jerry, and Tom Robbins. 2013. *Mob Boss: The Life of Little Al D'Arco: The Man Who Brought Down the Mafia*. New York: Thomas Dunne.

Chin, Ko-Lin. 1990. *Chinese Subculture and Criminality: Non-traditional Crime Groups in America*. New York: Greenwood.

———. 1994. "Chinese Organized Crime in America." In *Handbook of Organized Crime in the United States*, edited by Robert Kelly, Ko-Lin Chin, and Rufus Schatzberg. Westport, CT: Greenwood.

Colhoun, Jack. 2013. *Gangsterismo: The United States, Cuba, and the Mafia, 1933 to 1966*. New York: Orr.

Cowan, Rick, and Douglas Century. 2002. *Takedown: The Fall of the Last Mafia Empire*. New York: Putnam.

Cox, Donald. 1989. *Mafia Wipeout: How the Feds Put Away an Entire Mob Family*. New York: Shapolsky.

Cressey, Donald R. 1969. *Theft of the Nation: The Structure and Operations of Organized Crime in America*. New York: Harper & Row.

Crowe, Kenneth C. 1993. *Collision: How the Rank and File Took Back the Teamsters*. New York: Scribner's.

———. 1998. "Sealed Deal: Hotel Union Head Pushed to Retire." *Newsday*, May 21.

Demaris, Ovid. 1980. *The Last Mafioso: The Treacherous World of Jimmy Fratianno*. New York: Crown.

Demaris, Ovid, with Sam Sloan. 2010. *The Last Mafioso: The Treacherous World of Jimmy Fratianno*. Rev. ed. New York: Ishi.

DeStefano, Anthony M. 2006. *The Last Godfather: Joseph Massino and the Fall of the Bonanno Crime Family*. New York: Kensington.

Duara, Nigel. 2015. "7 Motorcycle Clubs the Feds Say Are Highly Structured Criminal Enterprises," *Los Angeles Times*, May 18.

Earley, Pete, and Gerald Shur. 2002. *WITSEC: Inside the Federal Witness Protection Program*. New York: Bantam.

English, Thomas J. 1990. *The Westies: Inside the Hell's Kitchen Irish Mob*. New York: Putnam.

Financial Times. 2011. "Remarks as Prepared for Delivery by Attorney General Eric Holder at the Press Conference on Organized Crime Arrests." *Financial Times*, January 20. https://www.ft.com/content/64718986-24be-11e0-a919-00144feab49a.

Finckenauer, James O. 1994. "Russian Organized Crime in America." In *Handbook of Organized Crime in the United States*, edited by Robert Kelly, Ko-Lin Chin, and Rufus Schatzberg. Westport, CT: Greenwood.

Fresolone, George, and Robert J. Wagman. 1994. *Blood Oath*. New York: Simon & Schuster.

Gambetta, Diego. 2009. *Codes of the Underworld: How Criminals Communicate*. Princeton, NJ: Princeton University Press.

Goldberg, Michael J. 1989. "Cleaning Labor's House: Institutional Reform Litigation in the Labor Movement." *Duke Law Journal* 38(4):903–1011.

Goldsmith, Michael. 1983. "The Supreme Court and Title III: Rewriting the Law of Electronic Surveillance." *Journal of Criminal Law and Criminology* 74:1–87.

———. 1987. "Eavesdropping Reform: The Legality of Roving Surveillance." *University of Illinois Law Review*, pp. 401–33.

Goldstock, Ronald. n.d. "Some Ruminations on the Current and Future Status of Organized Crime in the United States and on Efforts to Control Illicit Syndicates and Enterprises." Unpublished report for the New York State Organized Crime Task Force, Office of the Attorney General, White Plains, NY.

———. 1989. *Corruption and Racketeering in the New York City Construction Industry: The Final Report of the New York State Organized Crime Taskforce*. New York: New York University Press.

———. 2018. Unpublished and untitled report. "[Farewell Letter upon Stepping Down as New York Commissioner to the Waterfront Commission of New York Harbor]." Waterfront Commission of New York Harbor, New York, NY.

Goldstock, Ronald, and Steven Chananie. 1988. "'Criminal' Lawyers: The Use of Electronic Surveillance and Search Warrants in the Investigation and Prosecution of Attorneys Suspected of Criminal Wrongdoing." *University of Pennsylvania Law Review* 136:1855–77.

Goldstock, Ronald, and Dan T. Coenen. 1978. *Extortionate and Usurious Credit Transactions: Background Materials*. Ithaca, NY: Cornell Institute on Organized Crime.

Haller, Mark H. 1990. "Illegal Enterprise: A Theoretical and Historical Interpretation." *Criminology* 8:207–35.

Handelman, Stephen. 1995. *Comrade Criminal: Russia's New Mafiya*. New Haven, CT: Yale University Press.

Hanna, David. 1974. *Frank Costello: The Gangster with a Thousand Faces*. New York: Belmont Tower.

Hortis, C. Alexander. 2014. *The Mob and the City: The Hidden History of How the Mafia Captured New York*. Amherst, NY: Prometheus.

Hutchinson, John. 1969. "The Anatomy of Corruption in Trade Unions." *Industrial Relations* 8(2):135–50.

Jacobs, James B. 2006. *Mobsters, Unions and Feds: The Mafia and the American Labor Movement*. New York: New York University Press.

Jacobs, James B., and Kerry T. Cooperman. 2011. *Breaking the Devil's Pact: The Battle to Free the Teamsters from the Mob*. New York: New York University Press.

Jacobs, James B, with Coleen Friel, and Robert Radick. 1999. *Gotham Unbound: How New York City Was Liberated from the Grip of Organized Crime*. New York: New York University Press.

Jacobs, James B., and Alex Hortis. 1998. "New York City as Organized Crime Fighter." *New York Law School Law Review* 42(3/4):1069–92.

Jacobs, James B., and Elizabeth Mullin. 2003. "Congress' Role in the Defeat of Organized Crime." *Criminal Law Bulletin* 39:269–312.

Jacobs, James B., and Christopher Panarella. 1998. "Organized Crime." In *The Oxford Handbook of Crime and Punishment*, edited by Michael Tonry. New York: Oxford University Press.

Jacobs, James B., Christopher Panarella, and Jay Worthington III. 1994. *Busting the Mob: United States v. Cosa Nostra*. New York: New York University Press.

Jacobs, James B., and David Santore. 2001. "Liberation of IBT Local 560." *Criminal Law Bulletin* 37(2):125–58.

Jensen, Vernon. 1974. *Strife on the Waterfront: The Port of New York since 1945*. Ithaca, NY: Cornell University Press.

Kefauver, Estes. 1951. *Crime in America*. Garden City, NY: Doubleday.

Kennedy, Robert F. 1960. *The Enemy Within*. New York: Popular Library.

Kenney, Dennis, and James O. Finckenauer. 1995. *Organized Crime in America*. Belmont, CA: Wadsworth.

Kwitny, Jonathan. 1979. *Vicious Circles: The Mafia in the Marketplace*. New York: Norton.

Lehr, Dick, and Gerard O'Neill. 2001. *Black Mass: The True Story of an Unholy Alliance between the FBI and the Irish Mob*. New York: Perennial.

Liddick, Don. 1998. *The Mob's Daily Number: Organized Crime and the Numbers Gambling Industry*. Lanham, MD: University Press of America.

Lynch, Gerald E. 1987. "RICO: The Crime of Being a Criminal." *Columbia Law Review* 87:661–764, 920–84.

Maas, Peter. 1997. *Underboss: Sammy the Bull Gravano's Story of Life in the Mafia*. New York: HarperCollins.

McClellan, John. 1962. *Crime without Punishment*. New York: Duell, Sloane, & Pearce.

McShane, Larry. 2016. *Chin: The Life and Crimes of Mafia Boss Vincent Gigante*. New York: Kensington.

Moldea, Dan E. 1978. *The Hoffa Wars*. New York: Paddington.

Nash, Jay Robert. 1972. *Citizen Hoover: A Critical Study of the Life and Times of J. Edgar Hoover and His FBI*. Chicago: Nelson-Hall.

New York State Organized Crime Task Force. 1990. *Corruption and Racketeering in the New York City Construction Industry*. New York: New York University Press.

O'Brien, Joseph F., and Andris Kurins. 1991. *Boss of Bosses: The Fall of the Godfather: The FBI and Paul Castellano*. New York: Simon & Schuster.

PCOC (President's Commission on Organized Crime). 1983. *Organized Crime: Federal Law Enforcement Perspective*. November 29, Record of Hearing I. Washington, DC: US Government Printing Office.

————. 1985. *Organized Crime and Gambling.* Record of Hearing VII. Washington, DC: US Government Printing Office.

————. 1986*a. The Edge: Organized Crime, Business, and Labor Unions.* Washington, DC: US Government Printing Office.

————. 1986*b. The Impact: Organized Crime Today.* Washington, DC: US Government Printing Office.

Peterson, Virgil W. 1983. *The Mob: 200 Years of Organized Crime in New York.* Ottawa, IL: Green Hill.

Pileggi, Nicholas, and Henry Hill. 1985. *Wiseguy: Life in a Mafia Family.* New York: Simon & Schuster.

Pistone, Joseph D., and Richard Woodley. 1987. *Donnie Brasco.* New York: New American Library.

Porrello, Rick. 2004. *The Rise and Fall of the Cleveland Mafia: Corn, Sugar, and Blood.* New York: Barricade

Powers, Richard Gid. 1986. *Secrecy and Power: The Life of J. Edgar Hoover.* London: Collier Macmillan.

President's Commission on Law Enforcement and Administration of Justice. 1967. *Task Force Report: Organized Crime.* Washington, DC: US Government Printing Office.

Progressive Management Publications. 2017. *Complete Guide to the MS-13 Salvatrucha Central American Gang: Origins in El Salvador, National Security Threat, Los Zetas and 18th Street, Transnational Criminals, Possible Links to Terrorism.* Reports prepared by the Congressional Research Service. Los Gatos, CA: Progressive Management Publications.

Raab, Selwyn. 1998*a.* "Costs Plummet as City Breaks Trash Cartel." *New York Times,* May 11.

————. 1998*b.* "Mob's 'Commission' No Longer Meeting, as Families Weaken." *New York Times,* May 11.

————. 1998*c.* "A Who's Who and Who's Where, of Mafia Families." *New York Times,* April 27.

————. 2005. *Five Families: The Rise, Decline, and Resurgence of America's Most Powerful Mafia Empires.* New York: Thomas Dunne.

Reuter, Peter. 1985. "Racketeers as Cartel Organizers." In *The Politics and Economics of Organized Crime,* edited by Herbert E. Alexander and Gerald E. Caiden. Lanham, MD: Lexington.

————. 1987. *Racketeering in Legitimate Industries: A Study in the Economics of Intimidation:* Prepared for the National Institute of Justice (US). Santa Monica, CA: RAND.

————. 1993. "The Cartage Industry in New York." In *Beyond the Law: Crime in Complex Organizations,* edited by Michael Tonry and Albert J. Reiss Jr. Vol. 18 of *Crime and Justice: A Review of Research,* edited by Michael Tonry. Chicago: University of Chicago Press.

————. 1995. "The Decline of the American Mafia." *Public Interest* 40:89–99.

Russo, Gus. 2001. *The Outfit: The Role of Chicago's Underworld in the Shaping of Modern America.* New York: Bloomsbury.

———. 2006. *Supermob: How Sidney Korshak and His Criminal Associates Became America's Hidden Power Brokers*. New York: Bloomsbury.

Ryan, Patrick. 1994. "A History of Organized Crime Control: Federal Strike Forces." In *Handbook of Organized Crime in the United States*, edited by Robert Kelly, Ko-Lin Chin, and Rufus Schatzberg. Westport, CT: Greenwood.

Schatzberg, Rufus. 1993. *Black Organized Crime in Harlem: 1920–1930*. New York: Garland.

Schlesinger, Arthur M., Jr. 1978. *Robert Kennedy and His Times*. Boston: Houghton Mifflin.

Seidman, Harold. 1938. *Labor Czars: A History of Labor Racketeering*. New York: Liveright.

Skolnick, Jerome H. 1978. *House of Cards: Legalization and Control of Casino Gambling*. Boston: Little, Brown.

Stewart, Robert. 2019. "Eight Decades of Labor Racketeering on the New York–New Jersey Waterfront." Unpublished manuscript.

Taft, Philip. 1958. *Corruption and Racketeering in the Labor Movement*. Ithaca, NY: Cornell University, New York School of Industrial and Labor Relations.

Trends in Organized Crime. "Interview with Frederick T. Martens, Former Executive Director, Pennsylvania Crime Commission, October 1997." *Trends in Organized Crime* 3(2):28–29.

Trotter, Steven. 2014. "The Rise and Fall of the Patriarca Crime Family." *Global Mafia News*. https://globalmafianews.wordpress.com/2014/11/17/the-rise fall-of -the-patriarca-crime-family/.

US Administrative Office of the Courts. 2015. "Wire Tap Report, December 31, 2015." https://www.uscourts.gov/statistics-reports/wiretap-report-2015.

US Department of Justice. 2008. *Overview of the Law Enforcement Strategy to Combat International Organized Crime*. Washington, DC: US Department of Justice. https://www.justice.gov/sites/default/files/criminal-ocgs/legacy/2011 /05/20/04-08oic-strategy-english.pdf.

US General Accounting Office. 1976. *War on Organized Crime Faltering: Federal Strike Forces Not Getting the Job Done*. Washington, DC: US General Accounting Office.

US Senate Permanent Subcommittee on Investigations. 1981. *Waterfront Corruption*. Washington, DC: US Government Printing Office.

———. 1983. *Organized Crime in Chicago*. Washington, DC: US Government Printing Office.

US Senate Permanent Subcommittee on Investigations of the Committee on Governmental Affairs. 1988. *Twenty-Five Years after Valachi*. 100th Congress, 2nd Session. Washington, DC: United States Government Printing Office.

Zeiger, Henry A. 1970. *Sam the Plumber: One Year in the Life of a Cosa Nostra Boss*. New York: New American Library.

Maurizio Catino

Italian Organized Crime since 1950

ABSTRACT

Italian mafias—Cosa Nostra, Camorra, and 'Ndrangheta—are long-lived, resilient organizations that have evolved to adapt to environmental changes.
They have different organizational models. While Cosa Nostra (in the past) and
'Ndrangheta are characterized by a unitary, vertical structure and higher-level
coordination bodies, Camorra has a plurality of organizational models; the
majority of clans maintain a structure that is fluid, polycentric, and conflictual. In
general, mafias with a vertical organizational order have greater control over
conflict, and greater capacity to resist state power. The 'Ndrangheta has become
the richest and most powerful of the three, replacing Cosa Nostra in international drug trafficking. It is able to reproduce its organizational structures and
business model in new territories in Italy and elsewhere. In contrast, owing
to unprecedented law enforcement efforts in recent decades, Cosa Nostra is
weaker, down but not out. Camorra continues to be the most violent mafia,
committing more homicides than the other two combined. Consistent with their
adaptive capacity, mafias in new areas of expansion are treated as novel agents
that can provide extralegal services and business opportunities. They are sought
out by entrepreneurs, white-collar professionals, and local politicians to solve
problems such as debt collection, labor unrest, and disputes with suppliers.

The Italian mafias—the Cosa Nostra, Camorra, and 'Ndrangheta—are a
distinctive form of organized crime. Their existence in Italy is detrimental

Electronically published February 24, 2020
Maurizio Catino is professor of sociology of organizations in the Department of Sociology
and Social Research at the University of Milano–Bicocca. I am grateful to participants in the
Crime and Justice conference on organized crime in Bologna (May 16–18, 2019) for helpful
comments on an earlier version of this essay. I thank the editors Michael Tonry and Peter
Reuter, Francesco Calderoni, Anna Sergi, Paolo Storari, Federico Varese, and two anonymous reviewers for their comments and insights.

to economic growth and could reduce gross domestic product per capita (Pinotti 2015). For a long time, mafias (Cosa Nostra, in particular) were not considered to be either cohesive units or corporate groups. The mafia, claimed the ethnologist Pitrè (1889), is neither a sect nor an association and has neither regulations nor statutes. Scholars deemed mafias to be a cultural phenomenon (Hess 1973), a collective attitude (Hobsbawm 1959), a method (Albini 1971), a *forma mentis*, or a form of power with no corporate dimension. "The mafioso exists, but not the mafia," stated the magistrate Lestingi (1880, p. 292). Indeed, it was long regarded as a "mafioso spirit," a social practice, a behavior and a power, and not as a formal, secret organization (Blok 1974; Ianni 1972; Schneider and Schneider 1976).

This misperception lasted until the 1980s, when the focus shifted to entrepreneurial features of mafia actors (Arlacchi 1988) and to fundamental functions they performed as illegal economic enterprises engaged in production, promotion, and sale of private protection (Gambetta 1993). Mafias are formal organizations, although of a very different kind from a multinational company or from the rational and bureaucratic organizations that Max Weber described in 1922. Judicial investigations have helped reveal the complex and unitary organizational model of the Italian mafias. These include the 1986–92 Cosa Nostra maxi-trial in Palermo; the 2009–10 'Ndrangheta *Crimine-Infinito* investigation in Reggio Calabria and Milan; and the *Spartacus* trial in Santa Maria di Capua Vetere, Caserta, in 1998–2010 involving the Casalesi, an important cartel of Camorra clans.[1]

All three primary Italian mafias feature some form of origination myth, a kind of historical narrative that describes the unique exploits of a group and its leader, usually in epic terms. The 'Ndrangheta has the legend of *Osso* (bone), *Mastrosso* (masterbone), and *Carcagnosso* (heelbone), three legendary Spanish knights who created the three Italian mafias (Ciconte, Macrì, and Forgione 2010; Dickie 2012). The legend of the Beati Paoli sect relates to the Cosa Nostra and involves only Palermo. First described in 1909 (Natoli 1971), the story relates the adventures of an order of knights that fought to help the commoners and the poor. When the feudal system was introduced in Sicily, nobles began to exploit their advantages and, according to legend, in 1071 the Beati Paoli were founded to oppose the powers of the nobility and the church.

---

[1] Police commissioner Ermanno Sangiorgi provided evidence in 1898–1900 about the structures and activities of the Sicilian mafia (Lupo 2011*b*).

It is not important whether these stories are true. What is important is that the Italian mafias, like other similar organizations (e.g., the Yakuza, Triads), feel the need for a mythological origin, an aura of justice that surrounds their work—a false one, of course. In addition to their origin myths, the mafias are characterized by complex rituals that accompany the various events that make up organizational life, including initiation, integration, and promotion.

The three mafias have different organizational models. While the Cosa Nostra and the 'Ndrangheta are characterized by a unitary structure and higher-level coordination bodies, the Camorra clans are diverse, with the majority maintaining a fluid, polycentric, and conflictual structure. The Cosa Nostra and the Camorra have particularly strong roots in their places of origin, mostly carrying out trading activities when they move into new areas, while the 'Ndrangheta, in addition to its territorial roots, coordinates a multitude of organizational units in Italy, Europe, and elsewhere. Over time, relationships have existed among the three mafias, who have cooperated in some forms of trafficking, and there have been a limited number of cases of shared membership. No violent conflict has ever broken out among them.

The Italian mafias are long-lived and resilient, evolving organizations that can adapt to environmental changes. Changes may derive from internal dynamics, such as the organizational characteristics of each individual mafia, and from external factors related to changes in legal and illegal economic environments. These factors include opposition from or connivance with the political system, the role of law enforcement agencies (LEAs), and changing social contexts.

In this essay, I trace the organizational histories of the three main Italian mafias from 1950 to today. I discuss factors influencing their evolution over time, including successes and failures of the political system and LEAs in controlling and containing them. Mafia organizations are difficult to penetrate; they cannot be studied as easily as legitimate organizations can be. I draw on diverse qualitative and quantitative data. Many primary sources have been used in addition to historical accounts. These include documents from the Italian Parliamentary Anti-Mafia Commission; major judicial investigations into mafia organizations and mobster trials; accounts of cooperating witnesses, which constitute a fundamental source of evidence, in particular in order to obtain a detailed and accurate view from the inside of mafia organizational life; DIA (the anti-mafia direction investigation; see Sec. VI) biannual reports on the criminal activities and evolution of Italian mafia organizations; DNA (the anti-mafia national direction; see Sec. VI) annual reports; police and Italian Institute of Statistics data on homicides by mafia organizations; and data on high-profile assassinations. Integrating different sources, I have compiled an original data set on high-profile assassinations since the second half of the nineteenth century (Catino 2019).

This essay has seven sections. The first describes the different organizational orders that characterize the Italian mafias. Section II analyzes their main activities and extralegal services and how they have evolved over time. Section III examines the use of violence over time, particularly homicide. Section IV describes the different strategies employed by the three mafias in their expansion into new territories, and section V discusses other criminal organizations operating in Italy. Section VI discusses the evolution of anti-mafia policies and actions, and Section VII concludes with an analysis of the main changes in the strategies and structures of the mafia organizations.

Italian mafias belong to a single criminal category, although they differ in their behavior and have different organizational models. There are some reasons for optimism about future anti-mafia developments, and reasons to be worried (especially about the 'Ndrangheta). The main reasons for optimism:

- The effectiveness of state response and the growth of anti-mafia efforts, especially after 1992. More than 450 sentences to life imprisonment were imposed for mafia murders in the Palermo district between 1992 and 2006 (compared to only about 10 in the preceding 100 years). More than 200 municipal and provincial councils have been dissolved in recent decades because of mafia infiltration. New laws against mafia business have been enacted. All three mafias have been financially hit by continuous law enforcement activities.
- The general decline in the number of homicides, and the end of high-profile murders (e.g., magistrates, journalists, priests, politicians). Strong anti-mafia efforts by the state after the 1992 killings by Cosa Nostra of magistrates Giovanni Falcone and Paolo Borsellino made this practice extremely costly.[2] No high-profile people have been killed in the past 10 years.

---

[2] Judges Giovanni Falcone and Paolo Borsellino were two central figures in the fight against the mafia, Cosa Nostra in particular. They were killed in bomb attacks in 1992 in Palermo.

- The arrest of all the most important leaders of the Cosa Nostra "commission," and of many high-ranking members. Cosa Nostra is experiencing a leadership crisis without precedent in its 160-year history.
- The growing number of cooperating witnesses. Their role is fundamental to efforts to discover and contain mafia businesses and weaken the organizations' strength.
- Reactions against mafia in a large part of southern Italy, and the birth of many anti-mafia movements and associations.

Despite those significant successes, it would be a serious mistake to consider the battle over. Italian mafias are not yet a residual problem. Quite the contrary. Their resilience and adaptive capacities should not be underestimated. There are numerous reasons to worry:

- Cosa Nostra is down, but not out.
- The growth of the 'Ndrangheta: the 'Ndrangheta has replaced the Sicilian mafia as a main broker in international drug trafficking and has developed a privileged relationship with large South American and Mexican cocaine suppliers.
- 'Ndrangheta (and to a lesser extent other mafias') expansion in northern Italy, Europe, and elsewhere, and its growing role in some legitimate industries (e.g., construction, transportation).
- The demand for protection and extralegal services by entrepreneurs, professionals, and politicians. Civil justice in Italy is inefficient and extremely slow—matters on average take three times longer than in Germany, France, and the United Kingdom. Entrepreneurs increasingly turn to the mafia to solve important problems such as credit recovery, labor conflicts, and disputes with suppliers. Local politicians, professionals, and entrepreneurs increasingly seek out relationships with the mafia as an agency that can provide extralegal services and business opportunities.
- The persistent use of violence and murder by some Camorra clans.

I. The Organizational Orders

Two organizational levels can be distinguished in the mafias. The first is the basic organizational unit, which has different names in Italian mafias, such as the *family*, the *clan*, and the *'ndrina*, and is hierarchically based, with a boss in command and up to three or four subordinate levels. The second is the higher-level coordination bodies (HLCBs), organizational units above the families with functions of strategy, coordination, and conflict resolution. HLCBs are not hierarchically controlled, even though the Corleonesi clan dominated the HLCBs of the Cosa Nostra for about 20 years. The presence or absence of HLCBs makes it possible to distinguish two organizational schema: "clan-based federations" (with HLCBs) and "clan-based" (without HLCBs). The former have HLCBs, centralized coordination, and more systemic decision-making. The latter lacks HLCBs, favoring distributed power and clan-based decision-making. HLCBs coordinate but do not rule the families.

These organizational orders are not immutable over time but alter due to internal developments such as attempts by one or more clans to make a power play, and external factors such as pressures from law enforcement agencies (LEAs). Table 1 summarizes the main features of contemporary mafia organizations.

Description of mafias' organizational models is difficult and complex, owing to the characteristics of these secret organizations, their internal variety, and the reliability of available information. In what follows, I provide models that encompass the majority of the organizations analyzed. They do not exhaust the full variety of mafia organizational forms.

A. The Cosa Nostra

The Sicilian mafia, the Cosa Nostra ("Our Thing"), emerged in the mid-nineteenth century and has 2,000–3,000 members organized into 100–150 families active in Sicily (DIA 2017). Its basic unit is the "family,"

TABLE 1
Current Main Features of Mafia Groups

	Cosa Nostra	'Ndrangheta	Camorra
Approximate number of members	3,000	6,000	6,000
Approximate number of organizational units	100–150	150–70	100–130
Type of organizational units	Semi clan-based federation	Clan-based federation	Mostly clan-based
Higher-level coordination bodies	Present (weak)	Present	Absent
Decision-making processes	Partly systemic	Systemic	Clan-based
Strategy	Coordinated	Coordinated	Emergent

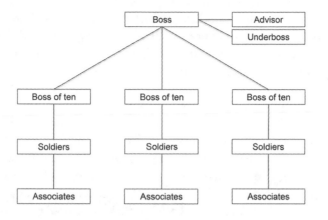

Fig. 1.—The organizational structure of a Cosa Nostra family (Catino 2019).

a criminal group controlling a specific territory. The term "family" denotes the fundamental importance of concepts of loyalty and honor. Recruitment is extremely limited and is not based on blood ties, although being the relative of a mafioso can be a positive element in terms of recruitment. Membership is not restricted to blood ties, but selection is very strict.[3]

The families are characterized by a hierarchy in which subdivision of power is well defined: from the *picciotto* (soldier) at the bottom to the family heads (fig. 1). The soldiers, also known as "men of honor," carry out operational orders. The *capodecina* ("head of ten") manages and oversees a crew of soldiers, ranging from 5 to 30 depending on the size of the family. The boss is elected by the soldiers and makes the decisions. The boss nominates an underboss who makes decisions in his absence. Advisors or counselors provide advice to the boss and serve as liaison with the soldiers. In the current period of Cosa Nostra crisis, the families have a simpler structure and fewer members.[4]

The Cosa Nostra tends to achieve complete control over the territory under its influence. All illegal activities must be agreed upon with the

[3] Members must come from a family with a respectable and untarnished reputation, and not have relatives who are members of the police forces or the judicial system. Illegitimate children, homosexuality, left-wing tendencies, and divorce are not tolerated.

[4] In Sicily alone, 557 fugitives were captured between 1992 and 2006 (La Spina 2014, p. 604).

boss, including matters of relationships between families.[5] The Sicilian mafia probably began to refer to itself as Cosa Nostra after the Second World War; the term was used in the United States to indicate that the organization was not open to membership from other ethnic groups (Lupo 2011a, 2015). Under the influence of the American Cosa Nostra, after a meeting held in Palermo in 1957 with Joe Bonanno, head of one of the five New York families, the Sicilian Cosa Nostra entered an agreement to become involved in heroin traffic. The Sicilians would supply the American distributors. At the same time, the Sicilian Cosa Nostra began to develop the structure of the organization, deploying HLCBs (Bonanno 1983; Arlacchi 1994; Lupo 2011a). It is likely that the opportunities provided by international drug trafficking favored the creation of HLCBs, in order to coordinate complex activities on an international scale and contain and regulate conflicts resulting from these new business opportunities.

The heads of families from a province nominate a boss for that province, called the "provincial representative." In the province of Palermo, and sporadically in other ones (e.g., Agrigento), three or more families with adjoining territories form a *mandamento* (district). When operations occur in the territories of more than one family, the head of the mandamento coordinates the families and resolves disputes. In the province of Palermo, a commission consisting of the province's district bosses elects a provincial representative for the entire province.[6] The provincial representative acts as a secretary or coordinator and has no power to command the district bosses.

According to the cooperating witness Tommaso Buscetta, the Cosa Nostra's Palermo provincial commission was dissolved as a result of increased law enforcement pressures following the first mafia war (1962–63), and was reestablished a few years later (Procura della Repubblica di Palermo 1989).[7] In 1974–75, the commission or regional *Cupola* was established at the regional level; it includes representatives of the six provinces

---

[5] The reconstruction of the organizational structure, regulations, and mechanisms derives from both the confessions and memories of mafiosi such as Leonardo Vitale (1973), Tommaso Buscetta (1984), Salvatore Contorno (1984–85), and Antonino Calderone (1987–88), and investigative work carried out by the anti-mafia team in Palermo.

[6] The provincial commission included 18 district bosses representing 54 families.

[7] There have been two wars within Cosa Nostra, both extremely violent conflicts between different family cartels. The first (1962–63) emerged from a drug trafficking dispute. The second (1981–82) was due mainly to the ascent of the Corleonesi to leadership.

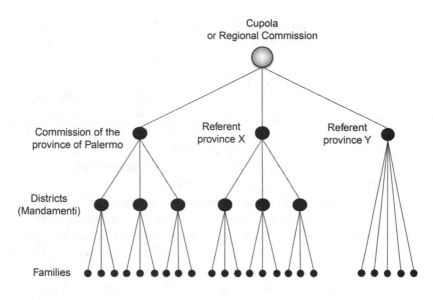

Fig. 2.—Cosa Nostra HLCBs (Catino 2019).

in which the Cosa Nostra operates (fig. 2). This coordination body was responsible for defining and monitoring compliance with the rules of the organization, resolving disputes between families from different provinces and authorizing the possible killing of men of honor and, above all, high-profile figures who posed a danger.

By developing HLCBs at local, provincial, and regional levels, the Cosa Nostra moved toward a clan-based federation structure. Notwithstanding the formal structure, however, its functioning has been always dominated by Palermo and its province. They have always exercised strategic leadership over the entire system.[8] Starting in the 1960s and 1970s, the top-down, vertical character was accentuated with progressive shifts of power from families to the *mandamenti* and the provincial and regional levels. At the same time, one branch of the Cosa Nostra, the Corleonesi, headed by Totò Riina, attempted to seize control of the whole organization.[9] The consequence was a significant increase in internal conflict.

[8] This dominance is a consequence of Cosa Nostra originating in this area of Sicily.

[9] The Corleonesi are the dominant coalition within Cosa Nostra and have tried to control most of the families and the organization's mandamenti. When the Corleonesi were running things, the family heads, rather than being elected by the soldiers, were nominated on the basis of loyalty to the Corleonese coalition (Polizia e Carabinieri di Palermo 1982).

After the 1992 maxi-trial that led to the final conviction of hundreds of mobsters and their bosses,[10] the Cosa Nostra leader, Totò Riina, adopted a strategy of frontal confrontation with the state that involved the killing of numerous high-profile figures. The new strategy was intended to pursue various aims: revenge against the decisions of the courts, destabilization of institutions, establishment of new political contacts given that previous ones had not prevented the convictions, and an easing of law enforcement pressures. The strategy led nowhere. In the end, law enforcement measures broke up the Cosa Nostra organization at the regional level and, in part, the provincial level.

With the arrest of Totò Riina and other bosses in January 1993, Riina's successor Bernardo Provenzano promoted a "submersion" strategy. Until his arrest in 2006, Provenzano preferred to do business quietly, minimizing homicides, in order to lessen attention from newspapers, the general public, the government, and the LEAs. Recent law enforcement efforts have undermined Cosa Nostra's efforts to reestablish itself at the provincial level, particularly in Palermo.[11]

B. The 'Ndrangheta

The Calabrian mafia, the 'Ndrangheta or "Honored Society," has become the most powerful mafia in Italy (CPA 2008; DIA 2017; DNA 2017). It has around 6,000 members, grouped into 150–70 gangs called 'ndrine; they also operate outside Calabria in many Italian regions, in Europe, and in other countries (CPA 2010; DIA 2017; DNA 2017).[12] The 'Ndrangheta is the only mafia whose membership relies on blood ties and strategic marriages between families.[13] Within each family there is a strong hierarchy based on doti (ranks) and cariche (offices), which are

[10] The Maxiprocesso (maxi-trial) of Palermo was one of the largest criminal prosecutions ever conducted against the mafia. There were 460 defendants. The trial ended with heavy sentences: 19 life sentences and prison sentences totaling 2,665 years. Almost all the convictions were confirmed by higher courts. This followed the Cosa Nostra massacres of judges Falcone and Borsellino and other important anti-mafia personalities.

[11] The district attorney's office of the Republic of Palermo, Gotha 2008 and Perseo 2008 operations.

[12] There are 160 'ndrine (clans) in Calabria, with a total of around 4,300 members, corresponding to 0.24 percent of the region's population. Approximately half are based in the province of Reggio Calabria; the rest are scattered throughout Calabria (Corte d'Appello di Catanzaro 2018).

[13] Marriage is used to settle violent feuds or to create stronger and more stable connections. Family relationships increase trust among members and reduce the risk of elimination.

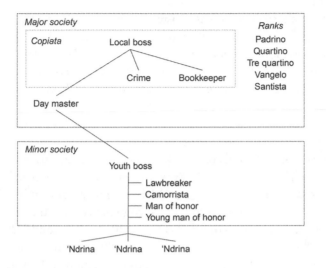

FIG. 3.—The organizational structure of the 'Ndrangheta Local (Catino 2019).

all awarded with specific ceremonies (fig. 3). The ranks represent the merit accumulated by members during their careers, which increases with crimes committed and can be awarded only with the approval of the Calabrian headquarters.

The nominal rank of *giovane d'onore* (young man of honor) is assigned by "blood right" at the birth of the sons of the *'ndranghetisti*. The first true rank is the *picciotto d'onore* (man of honor), who is designated merely to carry out orders. The most important universally recognized rank is *padrino*, "godfather," although recent surveys have reported new ranks at higher levels.[14]

The offices relating to the roles within the structural organization are temporary. The basic organizational level is the *'ndrina*, which gathers together members connected by blood ties (up to a few dozen) and has its own boss, the *capondrina* or *capobastone* (zone boss). Several 'ndrine operating in the same territorial district form a *locale* or *Società*, the boss of which, called the *capo locale* (local boss), manages both the criminal activities of that territory and all issues related to the locale's internal structure

[14] Before his murder in 2008, Carmine Novella, the boss of the Lombardy *locale*, created the ranks of *stella*, *bartolo*, *mammasantissima*, *infinito*, and *conte agadino*. It is generally believed that these ranks have been progressively introduced elsewhere in the organization, even if they are not always recognized by the Calabrian head office (Tribunale di Milano 2010, 2014; Tribunale di Reggio Calabria 2010).

and functioning.[15] The boss is assisted by the *contabile* (bookkeeper) and the *crimine* (crime), who deals with violent activities. These three roles form the *copiata*. In addition, the *mastro di giornata* (day master) circulates information and orders throughout the organization, connecting the two organizational groups within each locale, known as "the major society" and "the minor society."

The first attempts at creating a top-down structure through the establishment of HLCBs took shape at the end of the nineteenth century, when forms of territorial coordination between the various 'ndrine were created. In 1933, two HLCBs were formed, called "criminal," coordinating criminal groups in Reggio Calabria, and "great criminal," superior to the first and created to control compliance with the rules of association and manage conflicts (Dickie 2012; Truzzolillo 2013). In 1969, a meeting in Calabria of more than 100 participants highlighted the need for a structure that would coordinate action and resolve internal conflicts (Ciconte 1996; Tribunale di Reggio Calabria 2010).

Two modern-day HLCBs emerged only in 1991, at the end of violent conflict between two opposing clan cartels (Dickie 2012; fig. 4). The mandamenti gathered several locali together. There are three main mandamenti in Reggio Calabria (Ionian, Tyrrhenian, and Centre), and there are other coordinating structures known as "control rooms" throughout Italy and the world. At a regional level, the "Province" or "Crime" includes the three Reggio Calabria mandamenti. Headed by a crime boss assisted by the general master, day master, and bookkeeper, this supreme coordination body supervises the management of the locali, enforces shared rules, ratifies the most important decisions such as the opening of new locali and the awarding of new ranks and offices, and settles disputes between families. Its role is to ensure the harmony and organization necessary for carrying out criminal activities, making it possible for the 'Ndrangheta to survive over time and become increasingly "influential, functional, and recognizable" (Tribunale di Reggio Calabria 2010, p. 75).

This model represents almost the entirety of the *'ndranghetista* universe. However, in some provinces (e.g., Catanzaro), the organizational structure is more horizontal, based on 'ndrine and locali, and without HLCBs.

---

[15] All *locali* have the same power to rule over their territories, as long as they devolve some of their income to the headquarters, i.e., "alla mamma di San Luca," and respect other localis' territories and interests and the decisions of the coordination body called *Provincia*.

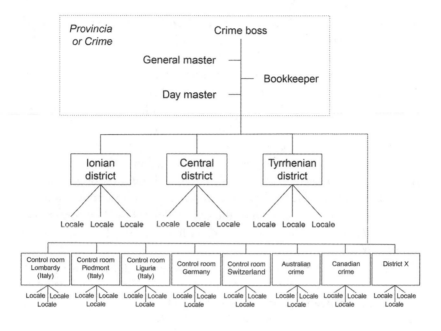

FIG. 4.—'Ndrangheta HLCBs (Catino 2019).

The two HLCBs, namely the mandamenti and the "Province" or "Crime," indicate the evolution of the 'Ndrangheta from a clan-based structure to a clan-based federation structure deploying various levels of HLCBs. This makes it the only Italian mafia with unified coordination of the whole organizational system. Since the 1970s, the 'Ndrangheta has also established a specific structure known as the *Santa*, dedicated to relationships with external groups such as politicians, freemasons, entrepreneurs, members of secret services, and other figures and bodies of interest.

C. The Camorra

The Camorra originated in the first half of the nineteenth century among people from lower social classes, particularly within prisons, in Naples, Caserta, and other areas in Campania (Paliotti 2007; Barbagallo 2010; Marmo 2011). It developed a written statute, called *Frieno* in 1842, and called itself the *Bella Società Riformata*—the "Excellent Reformed Society." The Camorra was initially organized into small, independent groups called *paranze* (*Memoria sulla consorteria* 1861, in Marmo 2011;

Monnier 1862; Alongi 1890; De Blasio 1897). These showed a high level of organized hierarchy, being subdivided into the minor society and the major society, with a fairly slow career path (Alongi 1890). In Naples, there were 12 paranze, one for every district in the city, whose heads, the *caposocietà*, gathered together to form the "great council." This was directed by a *capintesta*, the boss of bosses, who had absolute authority over the organization. These HLCBs provided quick responses to any emerging conflicts between groups.

This organizational model disappeared at the beginning of the twentieth century, following intense police and judicial attention after the Cuocolo trial (1911–12).[16] The contemporary Camorra is thus more a product of recent history than of the past (Sales 1988). The contemporary Camorra is fluid and polycentric, with a clan-based organizational configuration.

The clans, for the most part, operate independently. However, there may exist strong ties, giving rise to alliances, or weak ties, such as pacts of nonbelligerence or sporadic activities and relationships. Unlike the other Italian mafias, the Camorra lacks HLCBs that can potentially coordinate the entire system. Power is distributed among competing clans that can independently undertake strategies and criminal actions. Clan sizes range from 30 to 300 members and, depending on the activities to be implemented, possess organizational structures with different degrees of formalized roles and hierarchies. It is therefore more appropriate to refer to *Camorre*—the plural form of Camorra, rather than to a single mafia organization (Sales 1988; Tribunale di Napoli 2008, 2011; Tribunale di Santa Maria Capua Vetere 2013). At least three organizational models, with increasing levels of coordination, can therefore be distinguished (fig. 5).

1. *Gangs.* The gangs are criminal groups, mainly present in Naples, characterized by an elementary organizational structure and a low level of formalization and division of labor. The average age of members is low. Violence, to regulate continuous disputes and make the most of opportunities, is common. Examples are the D'Amico, De Micco, and Buonerba clans. The low levels of complexity and formalization cause the city clans to be highly unstable and conflictual, with a preference

---

[16] The Cuocolo trial was the first judicial proceeding against numerous defendants from the Neapolitan Camorra. It received wide media attention and resulted in convictions and heavy punishments.

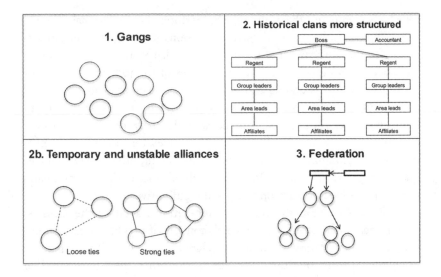

F IG . 5.—The various organizational orders of the Camorra.

for short-term gains from drug trafficking. Their behavior is more similar to that of some American urban gangs than to other Camorra families a few hundred meters away.

2. *Historical Clans.* There are also highly structured clans, such as the Contini, Di Lauro, Licciardi, Mallardo, Mazzarella, Moccia, Nuvoletta, Orlando, Polverino, and Vollaro. These are historical families with long traditions, characterized by greater levels of formalization and organizational complexity that produce less conflict and greater stability. This allows them to pursue medium- and long-term goals, thanks partly to infiltration into the public administration and to agreements between politicians and mafia regarding control over decision-making power in local government, and partly to access to public tenders and companies controlled through front men.[17] These clans are structured in a way similar to a Cosa Nostra family. The "regents," together with the boss, form the top management that defines the organization's strategies. Each regent oversees a number of group leaders, who in turn coordinate more than one "area lead."

---

[17] From Procurator General of Naples, Vincenzo Galgano, 2005, *Relazione annuale per l'anno giudiziario*, in Di Fiore (2016, pp. 318–19).

The latter command the affiliates, who perform the operational criminal roles. Regents and group leaders make decisions about investments, for example for the purchase of large quantities of drugs and weapons. Group and area leaders together decide the salaries of the various members of the organization, depending on roles performed, danger incurred, and seniority. The most important business is handled directly by people in higher roles (i.e., the regents). In some cases, the clans create tight alliances (e.g., military or economic alliances) or loose ones, for instance in the case of nonaggression pacts. These alliances are often unstable and exhibit frequent changes of affiliation. One of them, the alliance of the Secondigliano clans, has enjoyed greater longevity and is still active.

3. *Federations.* Finally, there are federations, such as the Casalesi clan in the province of Caserta, which consists of two historical families (the Bidognetti and Schiavone) and related allied clans. The organizational model resembles the Cosa Nostra more than the city gangs. The top organizational level defines organization strategy, settles internal disputes, and manages the common fund. This organizational model is capable of exercising widespread control over the territory, in terms of both economic and political activity, and is able to influence local election results by favoring candidates close to the clan.

Clans 2 and 3 present a more structured model of organization. The size of the groups varies from 30–40 members (the group of "secessionists") up to 200 in the Misso and Lo Russo clans, 250 for the Mazzarella clan, and 300 members for the Contini and Licciardi clans (Di Fiore 2016).

Clans have multiplied over time, from 16 in 1861[18] to more than 100 along with 28 minor groups today (DIA 2010).[19] The Camorra organizational order is clan-based. The only attempts to organize the various Camorra clans into a clan-based federation order were carried out at the beginning of the 1970s with Raffaele Cutolo's *Nuova Camorra Organizzata* (New Organized Camorra), which echoed the structure of the nineteenth-century Camorra. Cutolo designed a pyramidal and paramilitary organizational structure, based on the cult of personality of its

---

[18] From *La memoria sulla consorteria dei camorristi esistente nelle provincie napoletane* (Memoir regarding the groupings of camorristi in the Neapolitan province) 1861 (in Marmo [2011], p. 35).

[19] This includes the Casalesi cartel, composed of 10 groups with 9 other allied-federated groups.

creator (Tribunale di Roma 1985).[20] Not long after, a group of clans formed a temporary federation of families, called the New Family, to resist Cutolo's attempt to centralize power. This exacerbated the Camorra's "anarchic fragmentation" (CPA 2000) and led to a bloody conflict that, between 1978 and 1983, resulted in around 1,500 deaths. Internal conflict coupled with intense repressive measures from law enforcement agencies weakened the New Organized Camorra until it could no longer survive. In the 1980s, an attempt by Carmine Alfieri to adopt a similar hierarchical structure of coordination had a similar outcome.

The Camorra is thus characterized by a clan-based model. Except for the Casalesi clan cartel and other alliances between clans, however unstable and temporary, the Camorra has no HLBCs that are capable of coordinating the entire system (Catino 2019).

II. Activities and Markets

The main Italian mafias are active in legal and illegal markets. Drug trafficking and extortion are the most important sources of revenues, but their ranges of illegal activities are enormous and regularly change in response to new opportunities. Each maintains traditional dominance in its home territories. Elsewhere in Italy, they tend to invest in trading by legal businesses whose interests they pursue in illegal ways. The 'Ndrangheta are the most active and well-established outside Italy.

A. Activities and Extralegal Services

According to Diego Gambetta (1993), what distinguishes mafia organizations from other types of criminal organizations is that they supply private protection. While "an organized crime group attempts to regulate and control the production and distribution of a given commodity or service unlawfully ... a mafia group attempts to control the supply of protection" (Varese 2017b, pp. 45, 48). A criminal organization can operate in illegal markets by producing illegal goods (e.g., drugs) or

---

[20] Raffaele Cutolo himself was the boss of the organization, the *caposocietà*, or *vangelo*, and he made use of an advisory council led by certain trustworthy figures, known as *santisti*. Below these were the *capizona*, responsible for specific geographical areas that included the whole of Campania. Finally, there were members, with the ranks of *picciotto*, *camorrista*, or *sgarrista* (lawbreaker). Cutolo reintroduced the oath of membership, which had almost disappeared.

by trading such goods (e.g., human beings, information, drugs), but only mafias are able to provide governance and protection by eliminating competition; provide protection from thieves; intimidate customers, workers, and unions for the benefit of entrepreneurs; quell disputes; and obtain credit (Varese 2017*b*).

Decades of empirical and judicial evidence have shown that mafia protection in legal markets is not reducible only to protection from external threats. Rather, it consists of a set of extralegal services of value to entrepreneurs, with the mafia organization seen as a potential "business partner" for the legal enterprise. Mafia protection is split into activities that in turn are split into specific services, analytically distinct even if often empirically connected: business development of the client entrepreneur, limitation of competition to the advantage of certain entrepreneurs, enforcement of contracts and regulations, and dispute management (table 2).

B. Markets and Earnings

The economic activity of Italian mafia groups occurs in both illegal markets and legal markets, where they often operate illegally. In both legal and illegal markets, mafia groups can provide market protection and governance and become market players (table 3). This is referred to as mafia *trading*. Mafias in their territories of origin provide protection and governance of markets and territories, but in areas of more recent penetration they tend to limit themselves mainly to trading (Campana 2011). 'Ndrangheta in some areas is the exception; I discuss this in Section IV. This prevalence of trading is due to difficulties in replicating the

TABLE 2

Extralegal Services Offered by Mafias

Forms of mafia protection	Extralegal services (examples)
Business development	Access to markets
	New business opportunities
Limitation of competition	Creation of cartels
	Reduction of prices and costs
Enforcement	Protection from external threats
	Dispute resolution
	Worker control
	Credit recovery

SOURCE.—Moro and Catino (2016).

TABLE 3

Markets and Activities of Mafia Groups

	Markets	
Activities	Illegal	Legitimate business investments
Protection and "governance"	Protection and regulation of illegal businesses, e.g., illegal betting, drug trafficking	Protection and regulation of legal businesses, e.g., supply and control of the labor market, control of competition, cartel enforcement
Trading	For example, drug trafficking, arms trafficking	For example, construction, transport, bars and restaurants

SOURCE.—Moro and Catino (2016).

models of behavior and control that exist in home territories, given the constraints in terms of enforcement and limited ability to exert control over the nontraditional territory. In northern Italy especially, the mafias aim to invest and augment criminal assets by exploiting opportunities offered by legitimate markets (DIA 2017).

Illegal markets in the European Union produce about $127 billion a year, equal to 1 percent of gross domestic product (GDP) of the entire area (Savona and Riccardi 2015). Numerous estimates of mafia revenues have been made (e.g., Eurispes 2008; CENSIS 2009; CNEL 2010; Legambiente 2012). They vary widely. Large differences result from lack of reliable data and use of methodologies that often are not adequately specified. Many are "mythological numbers," meant to draw public attention to the subject. They gain prominence because they are repeated by the media, the general public, policy makers, and some scholars.[21]

Illicit annual mafia revenues in Italy are approximately €3.3 billion for the Camorra, nearly €3 billion for the 'Ndrangheta, and €1.87 billion for Cosa Nostra. The total represents 0.7 percent of national GDP (Calderoni 2014a). Approximately 75 percent of revenues are received by the Camorra and 'Ndrangheta.

Cooperating witness Antonino Calderone observed that drug trafficking made the Cosa Nostra very rich (Arlacchi 1993). The Cosa Nostra was already active in morphine trafficking in the 1920s. A major increase occurred between 1950 and 1963, when the Cosa Nostra became active

---

[21] For a critique, see Reuter (1984) and Calderoni (2014b).

in heroin refining and trafficking between Europe and the United States. Heroin-refining laboratories flourished in western Sicily in the 1970s (Lupo 2011*a*) but no longer exist. It has been estimated that the Sicilian mafia during some periods controlled refining, shipping, and a large part of the distribution of 80 percent of the heroin consumed in the northeastern United States.[22] Drug trafficking continues to generate the largest revenues of the three main Italian mafias (DIA 2017; DNA 2017), estimated at approximately $8.9 billion a year (Transcrime 2013).

The Camorra plays an important role in international drug trafficking, often in collaboration with Spanish and Dutch criminal groups. The 'Ndrangheta seems to dominate in the Italian market (DNA 2017). The huge quantity of cargo traffic at the port of Gioia Tauro (Reggio Calabria) has made Italy into a strategic center for cocaine trafficking in Europe. The US government has since 2008 included the 'Ndrangheta on the "blacklist" of foreign criminal organizations to be fought in the struggle against drug trafficking (i.e., the Foreign Narcotics Kingpin Designation Act).

The 'Ndrangheta has focused on cocaine trafficking. It deals directly with South American producers, thus reducing intermediation and transport costs. It also plays a significant role in the control of other ports such as Rotterdam in the Netherlands. The 'Ndrangheta has proved to be more reliable than the Cosa Nostra in management of the process from producer to consumer, of economic aspects and payments to suppliers, and, because there have been few significant cooperating witnesses, of security.

However, although the 'Ndrangheta plays an important role in drug trafficking, there is no empirical evidence that it has a monopoly in Italy on cocaine trafficking from Colombia (Paoli, Greenfield, and Zoutendijk 2013; Paoli 2014), as is frequently stated (CPA 2008). The 'Ndrangheta faces competition from Italian and foreign traffickers who have direct connections with drug-producing and transit countries (Paoli 2003). Despite this, the 'Ndrangheta is the Italian mafia organization most involved in drug trafficking.

Although drug trafficking revenues remain high, Italian mafias have lost the primary role they played at the end of the last century (Paoli 2004; EMCDDA 2014). This probably results from the emergence of new

---

[22] As came out of the "Pizza Connection" inquiry conducted in the 1980s in the United States.

criminal groups in the market (e.g., from Africa) and from law enforcement pressures (Savona and Riccardi 2015). Most families have delegated management of the most visible illicit activities, such as selling, to unaffiliated criminal groups and collect a percentage of the proceeds.

This is what happens with the so-called Camorra drug markets in Naples. The clan that controls the territory collects a fixed monthly amount, requires the sale of a certain amount, or finances the purchase of a certain quantity and collects shares of the income. Camorra clans mainly import cocaine and hashish, although some traffic in heroin. Spain and Netherlands are the major countries throughout which drugs enter Europe en route to Naples, but there are also direct routes to Naples from South America (Allum 2016, p. 55).

Extortion is the second most important source of revenue. Particularly in their home territories, the mafias organize structured and complex extortion systems (Asmundo and Lisciandra 2008; Savona and Riccardi 2015) that generate an estimated income of about $5.4 billion (Transcrime 2013). Extortion constitutes the most reliable way to meet the organization's economic needs, and functions as an instrument for achieving territorial control and asserting the organization's criminal authority. Intimidation and damage from fires affecting properties of merchants and entrepreneurs, mainly in the mafias' home territories, express their extortive pressures (DIA 2017; DNA 2017).

Sexual exploitation and counterfeiting also generate high illicit revenues (Transcrime 2013). The Camorra stands out for its know-how in creating fake products (from clothing to work tools such as drills, etc.), and in marketing. Large quantities of goods arrive in Naples from Asia through dense networks of contacts (DIA 2017). The Camorra also specializes in counterfeiting banknotes and documents. A cooperating witness recently declared that his clan provided fraudulent disability pensions and mobility allowances to individuals connected to the criminal group for about a decade. This was done by counterfeiting administrative rules and provisions and eliciting cooperation from corrupt public employees (DIA 2017).

The Camorra also manages numerous fuel distribution outlets. Its intimidating power in its home territory allows it to dominate the supply of fuel. This leads to market distortions and prices significantly higher than market rates in other territories.

Other illegal activities typical of mafia organizations include usury, arms trafficking, and cigarette smuggling, and low-profile crimes such as theft and robbery of credit institutions, post offices, jewelers, tobacconists, and tobacco carriers that provide quick sources of funds (DIA 2017). The illicit proceeds can then be invested in legal markets.

Studies on the emergence and development of Italian and North American mafias show that they tend to favor construction and cement production markets that are linked to public and residential building (Anderson 1995; Caneppele and Martocchia 2014; Dugato, Favarin, and Giommoni 2015), transport (Hess 1998; Riccardi 2014), and catering (Anderson 1979; Lombardo 2013). Legal activities offer advantages for criminal groups (Anderson 1979), including financial cover; support for illegal activities by providing a seemingly legitimate "front office"; provision of services to members of the criminal organization, such as salaries in legal sectors; diversification of investment and risk; and production of additional profits.

The main evidence of mafia infiltration of the legal economy in Italy is in sectors with low technological complexity and high levels of labor and cash intensity; these are mainly catering, trade, real estate, and construction (Gambetta and Reuter 1995; Transcrime 2013; Savona and Berlusconi 2015; Savona and Riccardi 2015). In construction, mafia corruption and infiltration of political and administrative networks generate lucrative revenues, especially through investments in public tenders (Savona 2010; Transcrime 2013; Caneppele 2014; Riccardi 2014). The 'Ndrangheta tends to move into firms in economic and financial distress. It prefers sectors that rely on public sector demand, such as utilities and construction, and are suitable for money laundering (Mirenda, Mocetti, and Rizzica 2017).

Mafia infiltration into the public tender sector, increasingly through collusion and corruption, is carried out not only to win the tenders or decide the winners, but above all to "fine tune" the entrepreneurs—in other words, manage the related subcontracts, supplies, labor, and resources (DIA 2017). Infiltration is often achieved by purported emergencies, often nonexistent, that provide justification for deviating from normal public tender processes (DIA 2017).

Italian mafias have specialized in supply of goods and services for local authorities and enterprises, mainly in waste disposal, green space conservation, school renovations, and road maintenance. Public funds have reinvigorated a historic interest, especially for the Cosa Nostra, in rural land management. This is done through extortion of and impositions on agricultural entrepreneurs and through destruction of cultivated fields, clandestine slaughter, and infiltration of the food supply chain (Transcrime 2013; Savona and Riccardi 2015; DIA 2017).

The Italian mafias have been diversifying by investing in emerging sectors such as renewable energy and gambling and betting, mainly online (Transcrime 2013; Savona and Berlusconi 2015). Mafia attention was attracted to renewable energy by public funding subsidies for alternative energy production plants (DNA 2017).

Gambling offers quick and substantial revenues. The mafia families, especially the Cosa Nostra and the Camorra, exerted pressure within their territories to open new agencies or to take control of well-established betting centers through extortion. The volume of business is multiplied thanks to virtual gambling platforms, often located abroad, that facilitate tax evasion concerning large sums of difficult-to-track money (DIA 2017; DNA 2017).

The 'Ndrangheta is the most active of the main Italian mafia organizations in legal markets and in diversifying its revenues geographically.[23] The Camorra is diversifying its investment strategy in a broadening range of economic sectors. The Cosa Nostra, although first to diversify, has been the most affected by law enforcement pressures (Transcrime 2013; Savona and Riccardi 2015).

That picture could soon change. Mafia organizations may have infiltrated other markets, thanks both to pressures arising from investigative activities and to the organizations' abilities to swiftly exploit new opportunities. One recent investigation, for example, highlighted an urgent need for new laws concerning maritime transport. The industry receives huge amounts of public funding and is economically important in the home territories of the main Italian mafias. Both characteristics provide inducements for corruption (DIA 2017).

The negative effects of mafia activities on markets and companies are evident. 'Ndrangheta infiltration generally displaces healthy businesses, which lose revenues when the 'Ndrangheta expands its market share (Mirenda, Mocetti, and Rizzica 2017). The 'Ndrangheta acquires a dominant position that makes it possible to remove its competitors.

---

[23] While about 60–65 percent of the total revenues of the Cosa Nostra and the Camorra are generated in their respective areas of origin, only 23 percent of the revenues of the 'Ndrangheta comes from Calabria and the rest is distributed throughout various Italian regions, including mainly Piedmont (21 percent), Lombardy (16 percent), Emilia-Romagna (8 percent), Lazio (8 percent), and Liguria (6 percent) (Transcrime 2013).

III. Violence and Conflict

Violence is not the objective of mafia organizations, but only an instrument, a resource of last resort (Gambetta 1993). Mafias may use it to establish their reputation and to defeat other criminal groups, enforce contractual agreements, and resolve disputes for which there can be no recourse to the legal system. However, they are obliged to limit its use in order to avoid destructive internal conflicts, forceful responses from law enforcement agencies, and the loss of social consensus.

The use of violence is difficult to measure. It begins with intimidation and threats, passes through arson and destruction of objects, may involve injuries, often through the use of weapons (kneecapping, for example), and can result in murders or massacres (such as the attacks on judges Falcone and Borsellino in 1992). Since few official complaints are made concerning threats, vandalism, and minor injuries, the low number of complaints is misleading. Homicide numbers are the only reasonably reliable data to measure the use of violence by Italian mafias. A challenge for mafias is to transform conflict systems, in which people have inconsistent objectives, into a cooperative system in which individuals act rationally to reach common objectives. The mafias must be able to control the use of violence within the different clans and against citizens and law enforcement agencies.

Mafias' use of violence varies with different factors, such as the nature and structure of markets in which they operate, political opportunities and incentives, and the role of LEAs (Catino and Moro 2018). There is a relationship between the organizational models mafias adopt and their use of violence in terms of frequency and targets (Catino 2014, 2019).

Hierarchy establishes a mechanism for dealing with disputes that cannot be resolved at lower levels, and whose resolution is required for the organization to act (Boulding 1964). HLCBs in mafia organizations manage internal conflict and provide stability. A clan-based federation organizational structure facilitates greater collusion between criminal groups; in a clan-based structure, there is instead competition and conflict.

Collusion and competition affect mafia organizations in different ways. Competition results in the massive use of violence within the organizational system. Collusion reduces internal conflict and related costs and maximizes business at the same time. HLCBs increase power within the organization by containing internal conflict (Ocasio 2005) and increase its power in relation to the external environment and other organizations (Mizruchi and Yoo 2005). A mafia organization based on a clan-based federation order has strong influence in its territory, which prevents competitors from providing services and "clients" from contacting other suppliers.

The number of major intra- and interconflicts in the three mafia organizations since the 1980s confirms the HLCBs' ability to control the use of violence. Intraclan conflicts may lead to an internal division of the organization. Interclan conflicts may result in conflicts for control of a specific territory. This in turn may bring about mafia wars. The Cosa Nostra experienced three mafia wars, in 1962–69, 1981–83, and 1991–92, and the 'Ndrangheta had two, in 1974–76 and 1985–91, before the establishment of HLCBs. There were a limited number of feuds and no major divisions. By contrast, the Camorra experienced one violent mafia war, causing around 1,500 deaths,[24] several feuds, and several major divisions.

Differences among the mafias in the use of violence can be seen in the frequency and types of homicides they commit. Ordinary and high-profile homicides should be distinguished. Ordinary victims are members of the organization or ordinary people outside. High-profile victims are figures from institutions,[25] politics, and the public sphere who, given their roles, can threaten the mafia organization's existence and interests.[26] Clan-based federation organizational systems, with common collusion between clans and the presence of HLCBs, commit more high-profile murders. They can coordinate strategic actions, identify and eliminate possible external enemies, and provide the organizational resilience to manage the consequences of LEA retaliation.

At the same time, such systems are more capable of controlling and settling internal conflicts and are therefore characterized by fewer ordinary murders. In contrast, clan-based organizational systems without HLCBs are less able to settle internal disputes and conflicts, which results in a greater number of ordinary murders. They cannot produce

[24] The Camorra war occurred in 1979–83 in reaction to Cutolo's attempt to centralize power.

[25] This group includes magistrates and legal professionals, people from law enforcement agencies, and institutional officials.

[26] Victims from institutions include magistrates, professionals in the legal world, law enforcement agents, and other officials; victims related to politics include politicians (activists and elected) and trade unionists; victims from the public sphere include journalists and priests.

organizational strategies and are less able to identify external enemies such as individual prosecutors, politicians, and journalists.

Figure 6 shows ordinary and high-profile homicides by the three mafias.[27] The Camorra killed 3,141 ordinary people in Italy in 1983–2018 (to July), almost as many as the Cosa Nostra (1,714) and 'Ndrangheta together (1,471). The Cosa Nostra, however, killed 237 high-profile people in the period 1861–2018, almost three times as many as the Camorra (49) and the 'Ndrangheta combined (31).

A. The Cosa Nostra

The average number of deaths per year is 48, with peaks at the beginning of the 1990s for two reasons (fig. 7). First, the Corleonesi attempt to control the organization resulted in an internal war with violent feuds, including the Partanna feud between 1987 and 1991. Second, the maxitrial against the Cosa Nostra involved the arrest of several bosses who were sentenced to life imprisonment. This led to internal conflicts to fill the power vacuum.

The subsequent decline in ordinary murders was influenced by severe law enforcement efforts, culminating in the 1993 arrest of the Corleonesi boss, Totò Riina, head of the Cosa Nostra's dominant coalition. At the same time, members tried to halt internal conflicts to prevent further weakening of the organization. Declarations by important Cosa Nostra bosses Bernardo Provenzano in 2001 and Matteo Messina Denaro in 2004 confirm that they suppressed internal conflicts because that was "good for all of us . . . and our cause" (Pignatone and Prestipino 2019, p. 20).

Career paths provide an additional explanation for the lower number of ordinary Cosa Nostra murders compared to the Camorra. The average ages of Cosa Nostra family heads are higher than in the Camorra because positions of power are acquired through a more organized selection process, discouraging younger members from challenging the internal hierarchy (Gambetta 1993). The HLCBs also reduce conflicts between and within clans. The resulting greater organizational stability

---

[27] The data refer to the period 1983–2016 for ordinary murders and 1861–2018 for high-profile murders. The original data set of high-profile assassinations triangulates information from historical records, official reports, and websites. The raw numbers of killings committed by the three organizations are comparable because of their similar number of members.

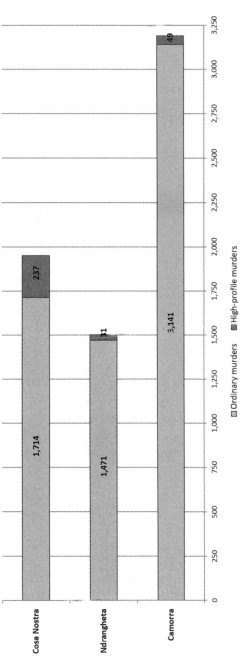

Fig. 6.—Ordinary (on the left) and high-profile murders (on the right) by Italian mafias (elaboration of data obtained from DIA, Ministry of the Interior, ISTAT, and other sources).

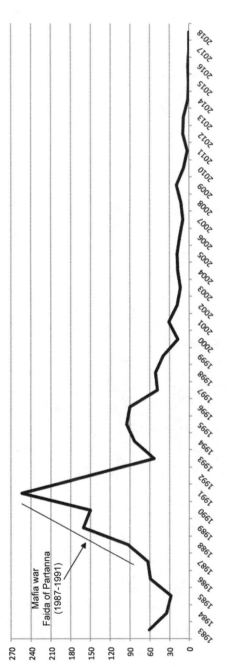

Fig. 7.—Cosa Nostra ordinary murders, 1983–2018 (to July, updated from Catino 2019; elaboration of data obtained from DIA, Ministry of the Interior, and ISTAT).

discourages intrafamily disputes and attempts to seize power. Informant Vincenzo Marsala explained that disputes that are hard to resolve or involve an entire family territory may ultimately be dealt with by an order issued by the provincial commission (OSPA and Stajano 2010).

The patterns of high-profile murders confirm the importance of the Cosa Nostra's organizational structure in managing violence. Cosa Nostra has killed 237 high-profile people, three times more than the other two mafias combined; the presence of the regional commission was a turning point in the escalation of murders. In 1965–75, the decade before the commission was created, there were 10 high-profile murders. In 1976–86, there were 56. Despite high media attention and very high costs in state retaliation, the Cosa Nostra mainly killed people working for state institutions (fig. 8).

These data, coupled with informants' accounts, show that an organizational model with HLCBs provides the coordination and abilities needed to reduce and contain internal conflict and to identify external enemies and act decisively. Informants Leonardo Messina and Antonino Calderone reported that the provincial boss could approve ordinary murders, but only the regional commission could approve high-profile homicides (CPA 1992; Arlacchi 1993). To decide whether to proceed, the mafia organization collects opinions of people such as politicians, freemasons, and entrepreneurs who have important roles in noncriminal environments but interact with criminals (Di Matteo and Palazzolo 2015; CPA 2017). If the commission decides to go ahead, informant Tommaso Buscetta testified, it decides who will carry out the murder (OSPA and Stajano 2010).

High-profile murders may, of course, result in significant disadvantages for the organization, as the crackdown after the 1992 killings of judges Falcone and Borsellino illustrates. This provoked law enforcement determination and severity that has no equal in the history of the Cosa Nostra. The post-1992 campaign was harsher than that carried out in Sicily under fascism by the prefect Cesare Mori in the years 1924–29.

The organization can opt for the opposite strategy, "submersion." This is what happened after the change of command in the Corleonesi. Toto Riina's frontal attack on the political system and law enforcement agencies focused LEA attention on the Cosa Nostra. This led to numerous arrests and stimulated activity of the other Italian mafias who received reduced attention. Riina's successor, Bernardo Provenzano, adopted a low profile strategy in order to diminish attention from the LEAs and avoid conflicts

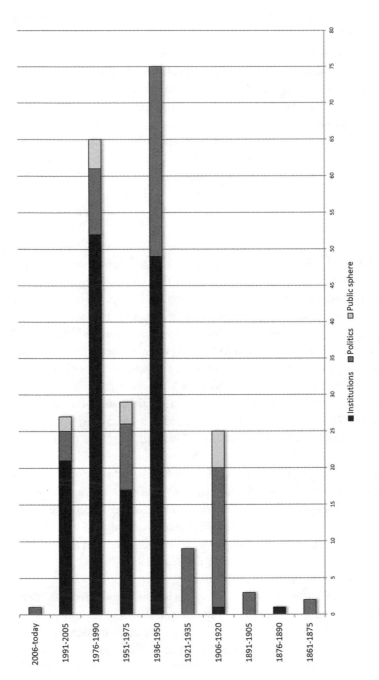

Fig. 8.—Cosa Nostra high-profile murders, 1861–2018 (updated from Catino 2019).

with them or prominent institutional figures, while restricting the number of ordinary murders. Informant Antonino Giuffrè, a member of the provincial commission of Cosa Nostra and head of the district mandamento, observed that "the process of submersion was launched, that is, making the Cosa Nostra invisible, so that we could reorganize calmly" (in Pignatone and Prestipino 2019, p. 29).

B. The 'Ndrangheta

Overall, the 'Ndrangheta has committed a lower number of ordinary murders than the Cosa Nostra or, above all, the Camorra. 'Ndrangheta relies on blood ties that dictate the chains of power. Dynastic male succession minimizes internal disputes relating to criminal careers, minimizing conflicts within the clan, if not between clans.

The trend of ordinary murders over time reflects the decline of internal conflict and the introduction of HLCBs. Even though they originated in the 1930s (Dickie 2012; Truzzolillo 2013), they were effectively institutionalized only in 1990–91, following a violent clash between clans. Attempts to control contracts and tenders related to a major public procurement triggered the second war between 'Ndrangheta clans in 1985.[28] The informant Giacomo Lauro reported that after the war it was established that every disagreement should be reported to the commission before violence was used (in Ciconte 1996, p. 151).

Thus began a process of verticalization and centralization, inside and outside Calabria, which resulted in establishment of the provincial *Cupola* (DIA 2010). The number of 'Ndrangheta feuds and homicides dropped sharply, and ordinary murders more than halved (680 between 1986 and 1991; 254 between 1992 and 1997) and then continued declining (fig. 9). On average, the 'Ndrangheta has committed 41 ordinary murders per year. Considering that the 'Ndrangheta has around 6,000 members, the number of homicides is small compared with the other mafias.

The 'Ndrangheta has been targeted by severe law enforcement actions only in recent decades. Not until early in this century was 'Ndrangheta recognized as a dangerous mafia organization in the Italian anti-mafia laws (CPA 2008; DNA 2010). In reaction to law enforcement attention, the

---

[28] A number of clans were keen to win public contracts in the area of Villa San Giovanni (Calabria) related to the construction of the bridge between Calabria and Sicily.

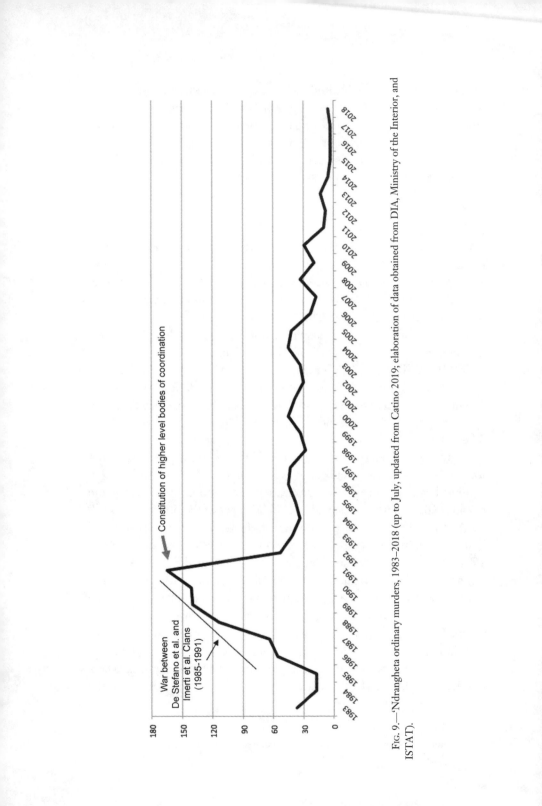

Fig. 9.—'Ndrangheta ordinary murders, 1983–2018 (up to July, updated from Catino 2019; elaboration of data obtained from DIA, Ministry of the Interior, and ISTAT).

'Ndrangheta launched a series of attacks on high-profile figures including killings (DNA 2010). This may explain why the 'Ndrangheta has killed only 31 high-profile people, nine since 1991 (fig. 10). Fourteen of the victims, almost half, were law enforcement agents; 11 were politicians.

The 'Ndrangheta, albeit rarely, commits homicides outside the regional borders of Calabria and also outside Italy. Ordinary murders include the Duisburg, Germany, massacre on August 15, 2007, when to settle accounts between 'ndrine, six 'Ndrangheta affiliates were killed leaving an Italian restaurant.[29]

C. The Camorra

The absence of HLCBs, the fragmentary nature of its clans, and the fluidity of alliances contribute to high levels of violent conflict within the Camorra—87 ordinary murders per year. These are mainly related to territorial disputes concerning a new form of violence, called *stesa* (knock out), which has recently emerged. In Naples and especially the provincial municipalities, groups of at least four, two riders on each of two motorcycles, break into the opposing clan's territory, firing wildly with pistols and machine guns against buildings, shops, and other casual objectives, sowing panic among residents and often creating innocent victims. The shooters are often minors known as the *paranza dei bambini* (the fleet of kids), trigger-happy youngsters, heavily influenced by violent TV dramas, without hierarchical form or medium-term strategies.[30]

The largest number of Camorra murders are committed by clans characterized by a low level of organizational structure; more structured clans use violence more sparingly. One destabilizing factor is the disappearance of a clan boss. This creates power play opportunities within the clan and in neighboring clans and, coupled with the lack of HLCBs, can result in violent conflict. In contrast, the more structured Casalesi federation committed just one murder between 2010 and 2015 (DNA 2017). Of course, when more structured groups experience conflict, the greater

---

[29] In 2018 the reporter Jàn Kuciak and his girlfriend were murdered in Slovakia. Kuciak was investigating 'Ndrangheta infiltration in the country, involving relations among 'Ndrangheta, entrepreneurs, and politicians concerning European Union funds (Slovakia was allocated about $17 billion). The investigation, still underway, highlights relations between the Calabrian 'ndrine and those in Slovakia (*Corriere della Sera*, March 3, 2018, p. 15; *Il Sole 24 Ore*, March 2, 2018, p. 9).

[30] The term *paranza*, borrowed from the maritime world, indicates a homogeneous group.

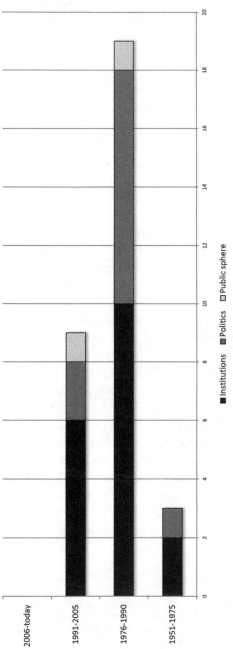

Fig. 10.—'Ndrangheta high-profile murders, 1861–2018 (updated from Catino 2019).

power available causes a high number of deaths. This happened during Cutolo's climb to power in the *Nuova Camorra Organizzata* (New Organized Camorra [NCO]; 1975–83) and during the conflict within the Casalesi federation (fig. 11).

The Camorra's fragmentary nature affects the number of high-profile murders. Lack of a unified strategy hinders identification of enemies, resulting in a limited number of high-profile assassinations (49). Almost 70 percent of them, 33, occurred when the Camorra was organized as a clan-based federation between 1975 and 1983.

The contemporary Casalesi cartel, composed of 10 clans, has an organizational structure that enables it to identify external enemies as potential targets for assassination. The informant Salvatore Venosa stated that Casalesi bosses Giuseppe Setola and Nicola Schiavone planned to murder several magistrates and law enforcement agents.[31] The latter group constituted the vast majority of high-profile victims (32) (fig. 12).

IV. Expansion

The three Italian mafias have expanded their economic activities, and in some cases their organizational structures, into new areas in their home regions and in central and northern Italy, Europe, and several other countries.[32] This takes different forms and is achieved within certain limits, given the difficulty of monitoring associates, gathering information, and advertising goods and services (Gambetta 1993). In Italy, the expansion began in the 1950s.[33]

The expansion suggests that mafia organizations have found "environmental host niches"; in other words, environmental conditions within which the mafia population can reproduce. The political system and law enforcement agencies realized what was happening surprisingly late, earlier considering mafias an exclusively southern Italian phenomenon. The first report on the expansion, from the Parliamentary Anti-Mafia Commission, was in 1994 (CPA 1994). It highlighted dispersion

---

[31] For more information, see *La Republica*, July 31, 2012: "Gomorrah. The campaign of violence plan. Targeting magistrates and carabinieri."

[32] See Massari 2001; Varese 2006, 2011; Kleemans 2007; Campana 2011; Von Lampe 2012; Calderoni 2014*a*; CROSS 2014; Sciarrone 2014; Allum 2016; Calderoni et al. 2016; Dalla Chiesa 2016; Moro and Catino 2016; Sergi and Lavorgna 2016.

[33] On mafia movement generally, see Varese (2011, 2020) and Campana (2011).

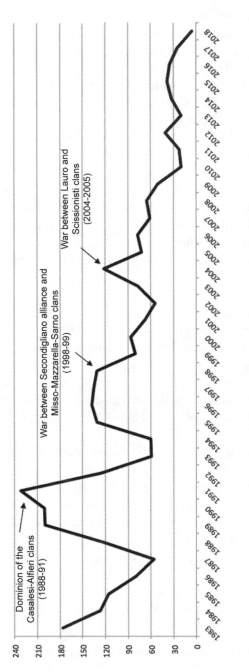

Fig. 11.—Camorra ordinary murders, 1983–2018 (up to July, updated from Catino 2019; elaboration of data obtained from DIA, Ministry of the Interior, and ISTAT).

104

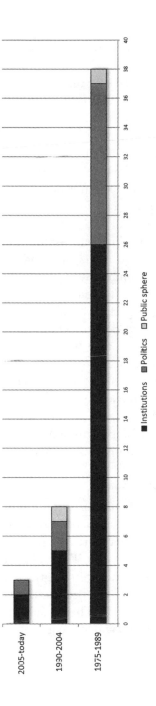

FIG. 12.—Camorra high-profile murders, 1861–2016 (updated from Catino 2019).

into almost every region even though, the commission emphasized, the north seemed to possess antibodies that hindered its expansion and consolidation.

The picture that has emerged over time is very different. The dissemination and establishment of mafia business relationships with companies, professionals, and politicians occurred quickly. In particular, following the 2008–10 economic crisis, the extralegal services offered by mafias (credit and credit recovery, business opportunities, construction of cartels, cheap labor, false invoices to create black funds) were welcomed by companies in central and northern Italy. There was a correspondence between the presence of mafiosi and demand for low-cost and extralegal services. According to Moro and Villa (2017), the presence of business sectors with low entry barriers significantly increases the probability of mafia activity. They also find that low levels of civic culture provide facilitating conditions.

The main mafia activities in nontraditional areas chiefly involve trafficking in valuable goods, especially drugs, and recycling and reinvestment of capital. Subsequently, kidnapping was added to their repertoire, initially by the Cosa Nostra and then above all by the 'Ndrangheta. Following a 1991 law that blocked access to the bank accounts of victims' families, kidnapping nearly disappeared.[34] This encouraged the 'Ndrangheta to move into new markets, both legal (the construction industry) and illegal (drug trafficking). The movement of Italian mafias into new territories, both in Italy and abroad, varied in terms of the kind of presence, the types of activity carried out, and relations with the home territory (Varese 2020).

A. Expansion Presence and Activity

Two different processes of mafia presence can be distinguished: "operational or organizational establishment" and "transplantation" (table 4). These are polar mechanisms, but there are few instances of mafia expansion that lie between these two poles. The mafia organizations are present with variable numbers of members, logistical bases, and operating structures but do not reproduce the organizational models and territorial control of the home territories. They mainly carry out trading activities, initially in illegal markets and subsequently in legal markets. The

---

[34] From 632 kidnappings in 1969–90 to 40 in 1991–97 (CPA 1998).

TABLE 4

The Present Situation of Italian Mafias in Nontraditional Areas

	Cosa Nostra	'Ndrangheta	Camorra
Operational or organizational establishment	*Italy*: Lazio, Tuscany, Lombardy	*Italy*: Abruzzo, Lazio, Umbria, Molise, Tuscany, Friuli, Trentino Alto-Adige, Veneto	*Italy*: Lazio, Marche, Tuscany, Emilia-Romagna, Veneto.
	Abroad: Belgium, Brazil, Germany, UK, US	*Abroad*: Argentina, Austria, Belgium, Brazil, Colombia, Costa Rica, France, Holland, Guyana, Malta, Dominican Republic, Romania, Slovakia, Spain, Switzerland, US, Venezuela.	*Abroad*: Germany, Netherlands, Holland, Romania, Spain, UK
Transplantation		*Italy*: Emilia-Romagna, Liguria, Lombardy, Piedmont, Valle d'Aosta	
		Abroad:[a] Australia, Canada, Germany	

SOURCE.—Elaboration of data obtained from DIA, DNA, and judicial investigations.

NOTE.—The degree of establishment and transplantation varies from territory to territory. The three mafias also have business relationships in other countries where they have not developed a structured presence. The Cosa Nostra has business relationships in Austria, Canada, Colombia, Costa Rica, Guyana, Malta, the Dominican Republic, and Venezuela; the Camorra, in Austria, Brazil, Colombia, Costa Rica, Malta, the Dominican Republic, the United States, and Venezuela. The table is based on information available in 2019.

[a] Some 'Ndrangheta groups in Australia and Canada are almost autonomous (Sergi and Lavorgna 2016).

revenues generated are mainly transferred to the home areas. Large networks of collaborators, knowledge brokers, and knowledge providers are employed in the new territories, but recruitment and membership are handled only in the areas of origin (Catino 2018).

A transplanting mafia group reproduces its organizational model, adapted and modified to address local circumstances, and is able to supply illegal protection for a substantial period outside the home territory (Varese 2011). In some cases, mafia groups carry out business activities and in some places provide governance and extralegal services. However, the protection and governance they can provide in new areas is not comparable to the protection provided in the home territory. They try to control particular businesses by providing extralegal services but cannot control the territory as in their home areas.

The 'Ndrangheta is the only mafia that reproduces its organizational model in many of its new territories, with adaptations to the local context. The importance of blood and kinship ties in 'Ndrangheta recruitment may be the reason. Family ties favor the maintenance of the network in the new territories. Members in the new territories often come from the same cities in Calabria (Tribunale di Milano 2010; Tribunale di Torino 2011, 2014). With 62 percent of its revenues coming from new territories in Italy and abroad, 'Ndrangheta has the most geographically diversified sources of income (Calderoni 2014a).

Transplantation is an evolutionary outcome of a long process of infiltration, particularly in small- and medium-sized municipalities. Mafias there benefit from less attention from LEAs and have easier access to public administrations because of the greater ease of influencing municipal elections with mafia contributions.

In some regions, one type of mafia has a prevailing presence; in others, different mafias are simultaneously present (Calderoni 2014a). Campana (2011, 2013) argues that mafias employ a strategy of "functional diversification." In traditional territories, they govern. In new territories, they trade in illegal goods.

The Cosa Nostra and the Camorra primarily carry out trading activities in new territories. The Cosa Nostra has been present in northern Italy since the 1960s and 1970s, allowing its members to operate transnational criminal activities without reproducing the organizational model. Instead, families send emissaries to areas of interest to set up illegal activities. Drug trafficking and money laundering are the principal criminal activities engaged in by Cosa Nostra members abroad (Europol 2013).

The 'Ndrangheta, by contrast, carries out both trading activities and, in some areas, protection and extortion, such as enforcement of cartel agreements to the advantage of entrepreneurs in particular markets—the cement sector, for instance (construction, earth moving). The protection activity and territorial control are not comparable to those in the home areas. Where they are newly established, the mafias have neither the same characteristics nor the same level of power as in the home areas.

They are able to exercise control of human resources, to gain visibility over time, and, through knowledge brokers and knowledge providers, to collect economically relevant information. However, governance in nontraditional areas is always limited to particular areas and markets and does not cover the territory's entire legal or illegal economy. This was, at least, the situation through 2019.

The presence of the 'Ndrangheta in the center north is not homogeneous. In Lombardy, Piedmont, and Liguria, it is more structured and over time has replaced other criminal organizations such as the Cosa Nostra, which was weakened by post-1992 LEA activity. In other regions, its presence is so far less structured, and mainly devoted to trading activities, reinvesting its capital, and operating in the real estate sector. The 'Ndrangheta is the only Italian or world mafia to reproduce its organizational model in North America, Australia, and Europe (DNA 2017).[35]

In this way, it has established logistical bases and operational structures that facilitate a continuous supply of drugs, cocaine especially, through the creation of safe transport, exploiting the movement of goods and foodstuffs destined for export to North America and Europe. A presence in those areas ensures an interface with the Colombian and Mexican narco-cartels. Recent investigations by the Italian police and the FBI have highlighted close links between the 'Ndrangheta and some Cosa Nostra families in New York (Gambino, Genovese, and Bonanno), particularly in drug trafficking.

Another investigation in New York showed that some clans procured in Costa Rica large quantities of Colombian cocaine destined for Calabria (Tribunale di Reggio Calabria 2015b). This confirms the 'Ndrangheta's leadership role in the management of drug trafficking and that, thanks to its reliability, it has replaced the Cosa Nostra in relations with American contacts (DNA 2017).[36]

The Camorra does not possess a presence or structure like those of the 'Ndrangheta. Clans operating outside their home territories mainly engage in drug trafficking, cigarette smuggling, illicit waste dumping, and sale of counterfeit products provided by allied Chinese groups or manufactured in clandestine factories near Naples (Europol 2013). They

[35] The 'Ndrangheta is active in at least seven US states: New York, New Jersey, Florida, Michigan, Pennsylvania, Connecticut, and California. In New York (Albany and New York City) there are some locali. In Canada there are 11 locali: 9 in Toronto, 1 in Thunder Bay, and 1 in Montréal (Gratteri and Nicaso 2018).

[36] Operations New Bridge, Columbus I, and Columbus II in Italy and New York City (Tribunale di Reggio Calabria 2014, 2015a, 2015b).

also deal in counterfeit currency, with many organized crime groups buying from them. Camorra clans in new areas also operate money-laundering activities, including for construction companies and real estate investments. Outside its home areas, the Camorra mainly carries out trading activities (Campana 2011). However, recent investigations have shown Camorra clans (especially Polverino) to be present in Spain.

B. Relationship with the Home Territory

Relations between clans in new territories and those in the home regions can assume three different organizational forms, depending on components of the mafia *technical core* (Thompson 1967): management of economic resources, recruitment and career paths, and use of violence.

1. *Low Autonomy.* The organizational units exercise predominantly an executive role, depending entirely on the headquarters both strategically and operationally. Revenues from the new areas are usually transferred to the headquarters. Human resources come from the home territories. Headquarters always have the last word on the use of violence, and the executors come from the home regions. This is mainly the Cosa Nostra and Camorra pattern and also characterizes some 'Ndrangheta clans in other Italian regions and countries.

2. *Partial Autonomy.* Organizational units in nontraditional areas are operationally autonomous but dependent strategically on the headquarters when matters of general interest are concerned. Revenues remain in the new area. Recruitment also occurs in the new area, but career management is controlled by the clans in the home areas. Headquarters always has the last word concerning the use of violence, but executors come from both the home and new areas. This is the 'Ndrangheta pattern in Piedmont, Lombardy, and Liguria.

3. *Full Autonomy.* This pattern characterizes some contemporary Camorra and 'Ndrangheta clans. For the Camorra, it is not an evolutionary phase but abandonment by some clans of their original areas and replication of mafia methods elsewhere. Other instances involve some 'Ndrangheta clans operating in Australia (Sergi 2018). In Italy, an attempt at full autonomy was attempted by 'Ndrangheta clans in Lombardy, but was blocked by the Calabrian headquarters with the killing of the boss Carmelo Novella in 2008 in Olona, Lombardy. Novella was accused of trying to give full autonomy to the Lombardy "control room," which grouped together all the locali in that region (Tribunale di Milano 2010). In the future, given greater economic profitability and autonomy in recruitment, full autonomy could also affect other 'Ndrangheta clans. The

classic case of complete autonomy is the separation in the 1930s and 1940s of the American Cosa Nostra from the Sicilian Cosa Nostra.

V. Other Criminal Organizations

Other criminal organizations of Italian and foreign origin exist in Italy. Of these, only the *Stidda*, a spinoff of Cosa Nostra in Sicily, and the *Sacra Corona Unita* (Sacred United Crown [SCU]) in Apulia can be linked to other mafia organizations.

The Apulian mafia was founded between 1981 and 1983 in local prisons to regulate issues arising between prisoners and to counteract the power of other mafias (Massari 2014). Currently, the SCU is confined to certain territories in the southern part of Apulia, in the Salento peninsula. Originally dedicated to tobacco trafficking, it has begun trafficking drugs from nearby Albania and protecting businesses from extortion, online gaming, public tenders, and recently, the tourism industry. The SCU experienced its maximum growth in the late 1980s and early 1990s, with a series of highs and lows that led to the birth of the *Nuova Sacra Corona Unita*, the "New Sacred United Crown." The SCU is facing current difficulties, due to pressure from LEAs and violent competition from other criminal organizations. This has led to a narrowing of its territory of reference and a change in behavior; it has become less violent and shows greater interest in the business world (DIA 2017; DNA 2017).

Other criminal organizations exist in Apulia, often extremely violent ones. They include the *Società Foggiana*, which has about 200 members; the *Mafia dei Montanari* in the Gargano area; and the *Mafia della Pianura* in the Capitana area. Fragmentation and the absence of a top management level and HLCBs prevent these organizations from containing internal conflict and developing medium- and long-term strategies.

In the adjacent region of Basilicata, the *Famiglia dei Basilischi* was founded in 1994, operating along mafia lines and characterized by methods, rites, and codes typical of other long-established mafias (P. Sergi 2003; A. Sergi 2016). The organization was nearly eradicated by LEAs in the late 1990s and early 2000s, as a result of collaboration by informants and competition from neighboring mafias.[37]

---

[37] Other Italian criminal organizations active in Rome and its province are the *Fasciani* operating in Ostia, the *Casamonica*, and the *Spada*. Of Romany origin, and interrelated with one other, these groups concentrate on drug trafficking, extortion, usury, and other crimes.

Albanian groups have a strong presence in Italy. They collaborate with Italian criminal organizations in drug trafficking, exploitation of prostitution, and crimes against property. Romanian criminals commit the same kinds of crime, competing with both Italian and Albanian organized crime, and, especially in northern Italy, have acquired expertise in credit-card cloning and tampering with ATMs.

Criminal groups from the former Soviet Union are also active (Varese 2011, 2012; Ingrascì 2015). They are active in the legal economy, through sophisticated financial operations, and in drug and weapons trafficking, smuggling of tobacco manufactured abroad, and predatory crimes. Ukrainian organizations are active in facilitation of illegal immigration and trafficking in human beings, especially for the purpose of sexual exploitation. Georgian groups, characterized by high internal cohesion and well-defined organizational structure, specialize in apartment and villa robberies, often employing exceedingly violent and brutal methods (DIA 2017).

Other foreign organizations, mainly from South America, North Africa, and Nigeria, collaborate with indigenous mafias in trafficking in drugs and in human beings for purposes of sexual and labor exploitation (Campana 2016). Nigerian groups have developed operational methods for human trafficking for trade, clandestine labor, and prostitution. They manage an entire supply chain for prostitution through the recruitment of Nigerian women, including the production of false documents to give the women legal status.[38] Organizations from the former Soviet Union, together with local groups, recruit women from Moldavia, Latvia, Estonia, and Belarus to work in street prostitution or nightclubs. These groups are also active in drug and weapons trafficking. Nigerian groups have replaced the Sicilian mafia in drug dealing. They control the prostitution market in Palermo (Varese 2017a).

Some foreign organizations have greater operational autonomy and are typically present in the north of the country. These include Chinese criminal groups, which have adopted hierarchically structured models and are active in illegal immigration, brand and document counterfeiting, cigarette smuggling, and, at a lesser level, gambling and drug trafficking. Their final aim is recycling and reuse of capital, carried out through relationships established with the professionals in areas in which the gangs are present, especially Tuscany and Lombardy.

---

[38] For more detail regarding this methodology, see Mancuso (2014) and Baarda (2015).

Recent mass immigration has highlighted the presence of Kurdish-Iraqi, Turkish, Middle Eastern, and Indian groups. They are particularly active in the recruitment and illegal transport of their compatriots and Afghan and Syrian refugees.

VI. Anti-mafia Control Efforts

The degree of consolidation of mafia organizations is influenced by the severity of laws and the legal system, the effectiveness of law enforcement agencies, and the mafias' perceived legitimacy in the social systems and environments in which they operate. Greater severity forces them to carry out their activities in different ways, increasing secrecy and internalizing or outsourcing critical activities, and to develop new areas of business and reduce their presence in high-risk markets.

There have been significant changes since the 1950s. Actions to combat the mafia can be divided into three different areas: greater severity through new laws, more arrests, and use of informers and municipal dissolution; institution building though the creation of law enforcement institutions and strengthening magistrates and the police; and social changes that transform perceptions of the mafias, the emergence of civil anti-mafia groups, and a changing role for the Catholic Church.

A. Greater Severity

Since 1982, there has been an expansion of anti-mafia laws without equal in the world. Frequently, they were enacted immediately after high-profile murders. For example, in 1982, immediately after the murders of member of parliament Pio La Torre and Prefect General Carlo Alberto Dalla Chiesa, article 416-bis was added to the Italian Criminal Code; it criminalizes participation in any association that uses "mafia methods." Three key elements characterize mafia methods: intimidation, subjugation, and *omertà* (criminal silence). Membership is a crime in itself. Mafia methods are used to pursue different goals, such as committing criminal offenses, controlling economic activities, acquiring unlawful advantages, or influencing voting. Article 416-bis was accompanied by antiracket legislation approved following the murder of the entrepreneur Libero Grassi in Palermo in 1991.

Article 7 of special law 203/1991 allows prosecutions for "external participation" in the criminal organization—this covers people who are not part of the organization but benefit from collaboration with it. Mafias are famous for achieving their goals through penetration of the social and economic fabric by means of collaborations with representatives of state agencies, entrepreneurs, and legal actors. Articles 418 and 416 *ter* criminalize assistance to mafia members and participation in mafia-connected voting schemes.

The increased severity resulted in 17,391 individuals being convicted of mafia association and involvement in mafia methods between 1982 and March 2017. There were 21,373 imprisonments; 20 percent of defendants were imprisoned more than once (Savona et al. 2018). Information on 9,141 convicted mafiosi showed that 36.6 percent were affiliated with the Camorra, 24.5 percent with the Cosa Nostra, and 18.8 percent with the 'Ndrangheta.

One mafia strength is their relationships with the world of politics. Mafias are interested in resources managed by local authorities. They attempt to influence local governments, especially small ones that are more easily penetrated by people friendly to the organization, or even by members (CPA 2018). Parliament in 1990 accordingly enacted law 55/1990 that provides for dissolution of municipal and provincial councils or the suspension of mayors. An agency can be dissolved even in the absence of illicit conduct if there are "concrete, univocal, and relevant" indications of organized crime influence.

Through August 2018, 221 municipalities have been dissolved, a quarter more than once (9 twice and 13 three times). Almost all (200) are in Sicily, Calabria, and Campania (fig. 13).[39]

Another important anti-mafia enforcement mechanism attacks mafia assets. Law 416-bis gave increased investigative powers to magistrates and LEAs (covering environmental and communication interception, covert operations, etc.) and authorized seizure and confiscation of assets.[40] These measures involve valuable properties (fig. 14). Law no. 109 of 1996 directed that confiscated real property be at the disposal of the state or distributed to municipalities. Since 2010, the *Agenzia nazionale per*

---

[39] These measures leave the administrative structure unchanged. Since procurement management is in the hands of technical officials, this is a serious problem in terms of introducing true change.

[40] Both measures can be enforced before the end of an investigation. Seizure is a temporary measure applied when there is a discrepancy between a suspect's assets and declared income; confiscation occurs when the suspect fails to explain the legitimate origin of the assets.

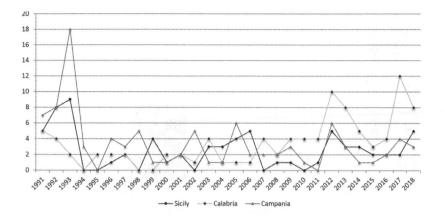

Fig. 13.—Municipal dissolution due to mafia infiltration in the three regions, 1991–2018 (up to August) (N = 264; elaboration of data obtained from http://www.avvisopubblico.it).

l'amministrazione e la destinazione dei beni sequestrati e confiscati alla criminalità organizzata (National Agency for the Confiscation and Management of Criminal Assets) has managed huge resources seized from the mafia in order to reallocate them for productive and social purposes. Measures to confiscate mafia assets, including from mafia heirs, are also being tightened.

Legislative decree 153/1997 requires banks and financial brokers to report suspicious transactions to the Bank of Italy. Legislative decree 231/2001 created criminal liability for companies for crimes perpetrated by company managers. Companies have developed control and monitoring departments to police their efforts to prevent economic crimes, avoid economic sanctions including confiscation of profits, and enforce the anti-mafia ban (*informazione antimafia interdittiva*).

A final fundamental element in the fight against mafias comes from the organizations themselves. Collaboration between former mafia members and LEAs dates from the nineteenth century, but only since 1991 has there been an organized system for protection of cooperating witnesses (improperly known as *pentiti*—"penitents").[41] There have been many

---

[41] The first cooperating witness was Salvatore D'Amico of the Cosa Nostra in 1878. On cooperating witnesses generally, see Dino (2006).

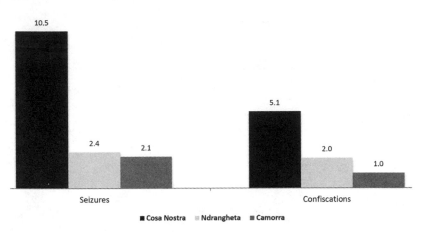

Fɪɢ. 14.—DIA patrimonial preventive measures, 2008–17 (in billions of dollars; elaboration of data obtained by the author from DIA).

cooperating witnesses who have brought mafia secrets to light (fig. 15).[42] Of 1,277 collaborators under protection in June 2016, 43.6 percent (557) were from the Camorra, 24.3 percent (310) from the Cosa Nostra, 18.7 percent (239) from other criminal organizations, and only 13.4 percent (171) from the 'Ndrangheta (Ministero dell'Interno 2017).[43] Collaboration with LEAs may be positively correlated with the vigor of law enforcement efforts and negatively with blood ties among mafia members.

B. Institution Building

New institutions have been created to provide deeper knowledge and ensure the availability of specialized anti-mafia magistrates and police

---

[42] The law provides for protection of cooperating witnesses (victims, witnesses, or mafiosi) and a series of penitentiary benefits for the *pentiti*. The 2001 reform brought some changes and restrictions: cooperating mafia witnesses must disclose illegally obtained earnings, undergo a minimum period of punishment, and cooperate within a maximum period of 6 months.

[43] Reports on collaborators have been issued biannually since the end of 1994 on the Italian Senate webpage (http://www.senato.it/Leg17/2880, last accessed on April 5, 2018). Each indicates the total number of collaborators, adding new collaborators to those already included in the protection program. Although this method prevents the identification of the number of collaborators by mafia per year, it allows comparisons across mafias.

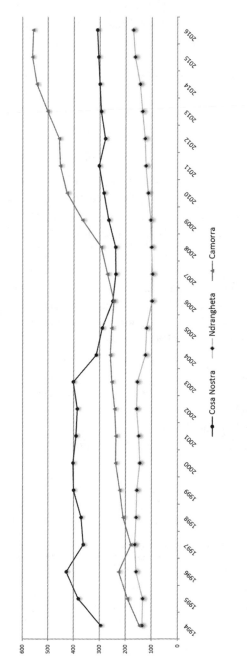

FIG. 15.—Cooperating witnesses per mafia, 1994–2016 (I semester) (N = 1,277; elaboration of data obtained from the Ministry of the Interior).

forces. Since 1962, the *Commissione Parlamentare Antimafia* (Italian Parliamentary Anti-Mafia Commission [CPA]) has produced important reports that have increased knowledge and awareness about mafias and shed light on their relationship to politics.[44]

Other critical sources of information are the *Direzione Nazionale Antimafia e Antiterrorismo* (National Anti-Mafia and Counterterrorism Directorate [DNA]) and the *Direzione Investigativa Antimafia* (Anti-mafia Investigative Directorate [DIA]) established in 1991. Equipped with new tools and expertise, they disseminate information about organized crime groups and activities.[45]

The DNA is a department of the Prosecutor's Office in the *Corte di Cassazione* (the highest court in Italy) consisting of 20 magistrates coordinating anti-mafia investigations in the *Direzione Distrettuale Antimafia* (Anti-mafia District Directorate [DDA]) in the 26 prosecutor's offices around Italy. The objective is to create an expert team of magistrates who handle mafia investigations full-time in a coordinated way.

The DIA is a specialized LEA that includes officers from various Italian police forces conducting anti-mafia investigations with the support of specialist groups and international cooperation. Over the past 10 years the DIA has carried out more than 500 operations.[46]

Operations are also conducted by the three main Italian law enforcement agencies, the *Guardia di Finanza*, *Carabinieri*, and *Polizia*. Each brings particular skills and methods to the battle. For example, Europol (2013, p. 18) recommends that "All criminal investigations on Families and Clans need to be accompanied by parallel financial investigations from an early stage." The *Guardia di Finanza* possesses the specialized skills to do this.

---

[44] This was proposed in 1948 after the mafia massacre of Portella della Ginestra in Piana degli Albanesi (Palermo). Eleven people were killed and 27 wounded by the band of Salvatore Giuliano during the workers' holiday against latifundism on May 1, 1947. The quality and caliber of the reports vary according to their historical contexts and the political parties leading the commission. In general, left-wing parties have paid more attention to the relationship between mafia and politics. Most reports are available on the institution's website at http://www.camera.it.

[45] Reports have been issued annually by the DNA since 1999 and biannually by the DIA since 1998. DIA reports are available on the institution's website at http://direzione investigativaantimafia.interno.gov.it. DNA reports are not indexed in any database but are downloadable from the internet.

[46] The DIA reports for the period 2008–17 describe the start of 524 operations against the three mafia organizations in Italy; 43 percent involve the Cosa Nostra, 26 percent the 'Ndrangheta, and 31 percent the Camorra.

However, the duplication of police agencies increases coordination costs and undermines their collective effectiveness and efficiency.

Other mafia-focused institutions include the National Agency for the Confiscation and Management of Criminal Assets (ANBSC), the agency responsible for management and disposal of seized and confiscated assets. An appointed legal administrator assesses the status of the seized assets, and the ANBSC preserves and manages them. In confiscation cases the ANBSC advises the judge on their disposition. Other processes screen companies with connections to the public sector to confirm that they have no mafia associations. The *Autorità Nazionale Anticorruzione* tries to ensure legality, transparency, and accountability by requiring documents and issuing sanctions.

C. Social Change

Social change plays a crucial role in the fight against mafias. Unlike in some earlier times, it is widely considered inappropriate to be seen in public with suspected mafiosi or have one serve as a godfather at a christening. Either could ruin a politician's career. Anti-mafia associations were formed after the murders of judges Falcone and Borsellino.[47] *Libera*, founded in 1995, consists of more than 1,200 associations, groups, and schools aiming at "involving and supporting all those who are interested in the fight against mafias and organized crime."[48] Other important associations are *Addiopizzo* ("Goodbye Extortion") and *Libero Futuro* ("Free Future") in Sicily, and *Ammazzateci Tutti* ("Kill us all") in Calabria.[49]

Study centers and institutions dedicated to the memory of important mafia victims[50] play important roles in providing information in schools, carrying out research, and maintaining a constant public focus on mafia issues. *Avviso Pubblico* (Public Notice), an organization composed of municipalities, provinces, and regions to oppose mafia infiltration in local authorities, was created in 1996.

[47] For greater detail, see Ramella and Trigilia (1997), Santino (2010), Mattioni (2013), and Dalla Chiesa (2014).

[48] For more details, see http://www.libera.it.

[49] See http://www.addiopizzo.org; http://www.liberofuturo.net; http://www.ammazzatecitutti.org.

[50] For example, the Centro Siciliano di Documentazione Giuseppe Impastato (http://www.centroimpastato.com).

The Catholic Church has long had an ambiguous relationship with the mafia, especially since the unification of Italy. This began to change in the 1970s, following the killing of several priests mostly by the Cosa Nostra but also by the Camorra, and culminated in Pope John Paul II's condemnation of the mafia in 1993. This was echoed by the Italian Episcopal Conference in 2010. In 2014, Pope Francis excommunicated the mafia (Dino 2008; Sales 2016). Church behavior remains nonetheless ambiguous, combining public condemnation with private service. Clergy, for example, sometimes celebrate functions for mafia families; this is probably due to donations mafia members often provide to local churches.

These anti-mafia efforts have significantly changed the mafias' environments, particularly in their traditional areas.[51] This has influenced their behavior, diminishing some activities and methods, such as use of violence, and catalyzing others, such as public corruption and entrepreneurial activity. Anti-mafia legislation has progressively targeted mafia assets. Entrepreneurs involved in collusion, originally viewed as victims, were often dealt with lightly. This has changed. There is now greater awareness of the facilitating roles of politicians, entrepreneurs, and white-collar workers; the character and consequences of their relationships with the mafia are often denounced.[52]

Although media often suggest that the government is always on the losing side, this is not, or no longer, true. The successes achieved and the constant pressures exerted by law enforcement agencies document effective opposition to mafia organizations. For example, since 2002, special prison conditions for mafia members, which were previously subject to annual renewal, have become permanent. More than 450 sentences to life imprisonment were imposed for mafia murders in the Palermo district from 1992 to 2006, 19 after the maxi-trial, compared with only about 10 in the preceding 100 years (Natoli 2006).

Since the beginning of the 1980s, the Cosa Nostra has been greatly weakened and deprived of leadership to deal effectively with law enforcement and civil society pressures. One of Giovanni Falcone's killers, highlighting the Cosa Nostra's strategic error in frontally attacking the

---

[51] For further information, see La Spina (2014).

[52] In Sec. VII, I discuss empirical evidence that shows that entrepreneurs continue to seek business relations with mafias. The slowness of civil court proceedings (514 days on average in Italy compared to a European average of 255) and economic problems often motivate entrepreneurs to look for faster and more effective, even if illegal, solutions to legal and labor problems.

state, observed, "Falcone has done more damage dead than alive" (Di Cagno and Natoli 2004, p. 49).

VII. Adaptive Organizations: Evolution and Change

Italian mafias are adaptive organizations dealing with changing environments. Changes are influenced by a mix of internal and external factors. Internal factors are organizational characteristics of each mafia and the dominant forces in it at any one time. External factors are actions of opposition or cooperation by the political system, LEAs, and the larger society.

These factors favor Lamarckian and Darwinian changes. Lamarckian changes are adaptations to environmental circumstances. Mafias show "absorptive capacity" (Cohen and Levinthal 1990), organizational capacity to acquire, adapt, and internally diffuse new knowledge and innovations. They adapt their "dynamic capabilities" (Teece, Pisano, and Shuen 1997) for survival, integrating, building, and reconfiguring internal and external competencies. Darwinian changes include elimination of organizational units less appropriate in changing times due to competition from other organizations and to challenges posed by law enforcement agencies. From a perspective of population ecology, the environment produces optimization (Hannan and Freeman 1977, 1989). The mafia organizational forms that best survive are those that adapt most effectively.

Successful LEA efforts produce transformation and adaptation in the system, and force mafia organizations to innovate and change. For example, in the Camorra, the arrest in 2002 of 70 members of the Di Lauro clan in Naples opened a breach within the clan, which resulted in generational conflict for leadership (Di Fiore 2016). The defeat of the Giuliano clan in Forcella (Naples) handed control of the territory to the Mazzarella clan. Kidnapping was a favorite 'Ndrangheta practice in the 1970s, particularly in northern Italy, but enactment of the law blocking the current bank accounts of the kidnap victim's family initially reduced and then eliminated kidnapping. Instead, mafia interest shifted toward new legal markets (the construction industry) and illegal ones (greater investment in drug trafficking).

Put differently, more effective law enforcement efforts and tighter regulations can transform criminal organizations and catalyze innovation. Naturally, the organizational responses depend on specific organizational circumstances.

It is important to recognize the difference between what we know and the limits of our information. In this section, I discuss some of the changes and trade-offs that characterize the three mafia organizations.

A. Structure: Between Centralization and Decentralization

Centralization helps the Italian mafias achieve better internal coordination and faster decision-making. Mafias characterized by a clan-based federation order can speak with one voice (Zuckerman 2010). Centralized organizations favor reduction in conflict, containment of violence, and strategic adaptations to environmental changes or changes in law enforcement methods.

Clan-based federation orders nonetheless have their own downsides. HLCBs increase the organization's vulnerability to law enforcement actions and collaboration by informants. Hierarchical organization makes it easier for LEAs to establish strategic priorities and target leaders. Informant collaboration can cause great damage. The construction of the Cosa Nostra organization chart, for example, based on information from co-operating witnesses, led to the arrest of all the members of the Cupola, effectively "beheading" the organization's HLCBs. Clan-based orders, by contrast, are more resilient in hostile environments. The arrests of any of their members, and informant collaboration, have limited consequences for the organization as a whole, as clans are independent and unable to devise complex, coordinated strategies.

The mafias, with the exception of the Camorra after the leadership phase of the boss Raffaele Cutolo (1975–83), are highly centralized organizations, both within individual units (cosche, families, clans), and overall, with the establishment of HLCBs (mandamenti, commissione provinciale, cupola, provincia). HLCBs based on consensus and without the atypical "boss of bosses" seem more likely to be successful and endure than when a single boss commands the whole organization. Extreme hierarchical centralization seems destined to fail. The "boss of bosses" is incompatible with an organizational order based on families, since it tends to compromise the interests of the many and provide advantages to the few, and to trigger attempts by other families and individuals to seize the position of leadership.[53]

---

[53] Raffaele Cutolo's attempt to impose a totally clan-based federation model on the Camorra, with himself as the "boss of bosses," triggered the opposition of many families, which formed a coalition against the change.

Italian mafias have to deal with an organizational dilemma, a "trade-off," between the benefits of both models (Catino 2019). The historical reconstruction of mafia organizational orders discussed earlier shows that mafias subsist in an unstable dynamic equilibrium, moving between clan-based federation model and a clan-based model.

Analytically, this dynamic equilibrium goes from individual organizational action (the family, clan, 'ndrina) toward greater coordination. This leads to the creation of HLCBs (based on the municipality, province, region), which facilitate reductions in conflict and seizure of greater opportunities for complex business. Clan-based federation coordination makes strategy development possible but also engenders greater visibility and vulnerability, which allows LEAs to focus their energies on higher-ranking members. Centralization also increases discontent and fosters centrifugal forces that generate clan conflicts (mafia wars). The HLCBs are thus delegitimized or undermined by LEAs, and individual organizational actions again predominate.

Cosa Nostra HLCBs have been dismantled twice. In 1963, the Palermo Provincial Commission was dismantled as a result of law enforcement efforts during the first mafia war (1962–63; OSPA and Stajano 2010). In 1995–96 the regional level and in some places the provincial level were abolished due to severe law enforcement measures and contrasting strategies within the Cupola. More recently, the organization features families and mandamenti, with no evidence of provincial (excepting perhaps Trapani) or regional levels (DIA 2017; DNA 2017). The Cosa Nostra may also suffer from increasing internal conflict. When leadership in clan-based federation orders is weakened, attempts to seize power proliferate.

B. Strategy: From Visible to Invisible

Italian mafias are adaptive and flexible organizations (Nelson and Winter 1982). It is necessary to distinguish between planned strategy and emerging strategy. Planned strategy is possible in mafia organizations equipped with HLCBs (the Cosa Nostra, a large part of the 'Ndrangheta, and some Camorra cartels). Emerging strategy characterizes mafias without HLCBs (most of the Camorra clans).

The Cosa Nostra for a time adopted a strategy of frontal confrontation with the state. Then, however, following the state response after 1992 and massive arrests at all levels, a radical change was made that encouraged the "camouflage and submersion" promoted by the boss Bernardo

Provenzano[54] (1995–2006). This entailed taking the organization out of public sight and discussion. This was more a process of adaptation rather than development of a deliberate strategy. The Cosa Nostra's common fund for prisoners was reactivated, sustained by a tax on the income of the entire organization. There was a change in relationship with the pentiti. Totò Riina issued death threats to the twentieth degree of kinship of the cooperating witness, including 6-year-old children. The subsequent approach, invoking the parable of the "prodigal son," aimed to return the informant back to the fold by use of economic incentives and reminders of a sense of belonging to the mafia community. The goal was for the witness to withdraw statements given to the magistrates.

As a result of the new strategy, high-profile murders greatly decreased. In the decade 1983–92, the Cosa Nostra killed 40 high-profile figures, the 'Ndrangheta 16, and the Camorra 15. In 1993–2002, there was a drastic reduction of 75 percent for each mafia: the Cosa Nostra, 10; the 'Ndrangheta, 4; and the Camorra, 4.

Integration with the business and professional worlds resumed. Michele Zagaria, boss of the Casalesi cartel (Campania), in the so-called "Zagaria theorem" (DNA 2017), observed that clan entry into the local economy should be as invisible as possible, thereby minimizing perception of problems of public order. One of today's most important Cosa Nostra bosses, Matteo Messina Denaro, supports this approach, encouraging a reduction in conflict, the development of business outside Sicily, and reductions in oppressive relationships and extortion.

If business relations are based on common interests between the mafia and white collar workers, violence becomes less necessary, even if remaining latent as a guarantee for criminal agreements.[55] For mafias, violence represents a means, not an end, the "second best solution" to resort to when collusion and threats fail (Gambetta 1993). The combination of constraints and opportunities, present above all in nontraditional areas,

---

[54] Report from the Palermo *Squadra Mobile* (Flying squad) in 2006, *Operazione Gotha*, April 21; DDA Palermo (*Direzione Distrettuale Antimafia*, Palermo Anti-mafia District Directorate) 2008.

[55] It should be emphasized that corruption has always been one of the mafia's methods of action. Although mafia and corruption are industries that deal with different assets, respectively private protection and property rights on political revenues (Gambetta 1993; Della Porta and Vannucci 2012; Vannucci 2012), often the two industries overlap. Given that it is difficult to measure corruption, especially given the presence of a high dark figure, it is not clear whether the corrupting phenomena are really increasing quantitatively, or becoming more evident due to greater media and judicial attention.

is a disincentive to the use of violence (Catino 2018, 2019; Moro and Sberna 2018). When it is employed, it more often involves damage to goods and productive instruments than to people, as is shown by the decline in mafia-style killings (fig. 16).

The decrease in the number of homicides is particularly marked in the Cosa Nostra, down by 50 percent in 1983–2002 and a further 77 percent in 2003–12. Over the same periods, the figures are 53 percent and 31 percent for the 'Ndrangheta and 34 percent and 35 percent for the Camorra. Figures for 2013–18 confirm this trend and highlight the differences between the mafias, with the Camorra killing about three times more people than the 'Ndrangheta and Cosa Nostra combined. Given its structure, some Camorra clans seem unable to deal with internal conflict in a nonviolent manner. Most of its murders are committed to control the drug-dealing areas of clans operating in the city and province of Naples. Competition over these important sites and maintenance of control favor a high level of conflict. The situation is exacerbated by the young age of the members of these metropolitan clans and the lack of strategic leadership.

Violence nonetheless remains in the background. The reduction in killings does not indicate that mafias are less present or less powerful, but that, in this period, violence presents more disadvantages than advantages. There thus emerges a form of organizational learning based on the consequences of excessive use of violence in 1992–93 and on benefits from the shift to collusion and corruption. Several investigations show the "the regression of the *action-centered* element—to be understood as activity classified according to the typical categories of mafia phenomenon: homicides, acts of violence, etc.—in favor of the *business-centered* element" (Tribunale di Bologna 2015, p. 191).

Some Italian magistrates and jurists, referring particularly to the expansion of the 'Ndrangheta in new territories, describe this behavior as "silent mafia." According to the Court of Cassation[56] this expression describes criminals employing mafia methods but without resorting to conspicuous forms such as homicide and massacre. Intimidation derives from hints, whispers, and the implication that it is vain to resist. The Italian mafias, given their past behavior and reputations, do not need to resort to violence. It has become superfluous and has negative effects.

---

[56] *Cassazione penale*, May 18, 2017. Also see Sparagna (2015) and Visconti (2015).

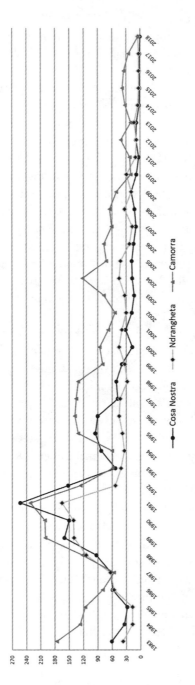

Fig. 16.—Homicide trend in the three mafias, 1983–2018 (N = 6,326; elaboration of data obtained from DIA, Ministry of the Interior, and ISTAT).

Today's mafias prefer to resort to corruption and collusion. Some scholars believe that mafias (and Cosa Nostra in particular) have lost their capacity to exert credible threats of violence, and widespread corruption is not a valid substitute for it.

In reality, common interests attract entrepreneurs and white-collar workers, as I discuss below. Collusion and corruption are widespread. In 2015–16, 200 cases of corruption involving mafias were prosecuted in Italy. There were 260 cases of mafia-related bid tampering.

Other changes concern secrecy and compartmentalization. Mafia organizations have enhanced their security systems, resorting to secret affiliations so that members do not always know their affiliates. Activities are highly compartmentalized so that no one has entire knowledge of a process. To make communications safer and more secret, particularly in the Cosa Nostra, epistolary means are employed, with several intermediate steps so that the final recipient is not known except in the very last stage. Information to be circulated within prisons is reduced. Particularly risky activities are often "outsourced" to nonmembers.

Cosa Nostra has been weakened, diminished, and fragmented. There have been a few attempts to rebuild the HLCBs, but they were unsuccessful. In sum, Cosa Nostra is down but not out. One option for overcoming the current crises would be to resume drug trafficking, by reestablishing its relationship with American Cosa Nostra families.[57] This was attempted in 2002–3 but failed (Tribunale di Palermo, Operation Old Bridge 2008; Varese 2017a).[58] The American Cosa Nostra, recognizing the weakness of the Sicilian Cosa Nostra, has in recent years preferred the 'Ndrangheta as a business partner (Operations New Bridge, Columbus I and II in both Italy and New York City; Tribunale di Reggio Calabria 2014, 2015a, 2015b).

C. The External Network: Entrepreneurs, Politicians, and White-Collar Workers

To understand the functioning of a company, analysis of a complex organization cannot be limited only to the *interna corporis*, the area within

---

[57] For instance, through the Inzerillo family, which fled Sicily and is now based in the United States.

[58] See also Tribunale of Palermo *Grande Mandamento* (2005) and *Gotha* (2008) operations.

its formal organizational boundaries. Broader networks need to be analyzed. Allocation of resources is mainly achieved through networks of organizations and individuals engaged in mutually cooperative actions. This is also true for criminal enterprises.

The strength of the mafia organizations depends not only on internal elements such as the quality of human resources, but above all on those outside who collaborate. They are not only clients or victims—though, of course, in many cases obviously they are. Their roles are increasingly more active, entrepreneurial, and creative. It is therefore essential to analyze mafia networks of entrepreneurs, white-collar workers, politicians, law enforcement officers, and members of public agencies without which mafia activities would be severely limited.

These figures constitute the social capital (Coleman 1988, 1990) of the criminal associations, in the sense of an "investment in social relations with expected returns in the marketplace" (Lin 2001, p. 19). External actors make their skills, relationship networks, and decision-making power available to mafias in exchange for economic interests. They are increasingly attracted by opportunities arising from collaboration with mafias, which are sometimes pragmatically considered as an element of the ecosystem, as extralegal service agencies that provide business opportunities. In turn, the mafias require outside expertise to develop business in the legal world, making use of external social capital to compensate for lacks in internal human capital.[59]

Exchange with the world of politics has always characterized mafias in Italy. The mafia has offered or, in some cases, sold votes. Each local Mafia family can count on several dozen votes, which can have important consequences in elections, especially at a local level. Sometimes mafias have elected members of their own organization. Mafias have benefited from tenders and other business opportunities at local and national levels, and been tolerated, particularly during particular periods and at least until the beginning of the 1980s.

Giulio Andreotti, a seven-time prime minister of Italy, was found guilty by the Court of Cassation of having favored Cosa Nostra interests until 1980, but the prosecution failed due to the expiration of the statute

---

[59] Eighty-two percent of those convicted in Italy for crimes linked to mafia methods from 1982 to 2017, whose education level is known ($n = 13,882$), had between 5 and 8 years of formal education (Savona et al. 2018).

of limitations. Marcello Dell'Utri, a cofounder of Forza Italia, the center-right party led by Silvio Berlusconi, which formed several governments over many years from 1994 to 2013, was sentenced to 7 years in prison for association with Cosa Nostra.

Several ministers and vice ministers have been considered close to mafia organizations and, in some cases, convicted for this. In April 2018 the Court of Palermo identified members of the Carabinieri and politicians (including Forza Italia's cofounder), and top level members of the Cosa Nostra who engaged in state-mafia "negotiations" between 1992 and 1994. The aim was to end the "massacre season" inaugurated by the Cosa Nostra with the Capaci attack in 1992, following the outcome of the maxi-trial that affected many of its members.[60] Relations today between the mafias and the central government's agents seem different from the recent past. There are, in contrast, still many cases of collusion at a local level among mafias, politicians, entrepreneurs, and white-collar workers in the south and in central-northern regions.

Beginning in the 1970s, the 'Ndrangheta created the *Santa*, an elite level of the organization dedicated to relationships with particular politicians, freemasons, entrepreneurs, members of the secret services, and others in roles relevant to the organization's interests. It is a private structure of command, with specific rites and oaths, whose existence has been kept hidden from most of the affiliates, even those of a high rank (DNA 2017).[61] It is the main operational tool for business development with entrepreneurs and politicians.

Magistrates have pointed out that the Santa was set up to define the strategic choices of the 'Ndrangheta, in particular the mandamento of the city of Reggio, in identifying economic sectors in which to invest, sectors of public administration in which to maintain stable relationships, territories in which public works should be carried out, and, consequently, the municipalities that would manage relevant contracts. Above all, it would indicate politicians to whom votes would be channeled at municipal and parliamentary levels, both national and European

[60] Tribunale di Palermo, Corte d'appello (2018). This is a judgment of first instance, subject to appeal. The offense is a crime of violence or threat to a political body of the state. There have been many opinions and arguments against this ruling.

[61] With regard to the Santa, see Tribunale di Reggio Calabria (2001). For relations between mafias and masonry, see CPA (2017).

(DNA 2017).[62] The case of *Mafia Capitale* highlights the close cooperation between criminal organization and corrupt public and private actors. It is the local level that today arouses the greatest interest in relations between mafias and politics.

Recent research shows that outsiders can connect mafia organizations to actors in the legal world, acting as knowledge brokers, and, acting as knowledge providers, make their expertise available to facilitate complex operations necessary for illicit activities (Catino 2018). Analyses of the roles of 60 outsiders reveal their roles in solving organizational problems that are typical of both legal and criminal enterprises.[63] As knowledge brokers, they reduce information asymmetry by putting the mafia in touch with entrepreneurs, public officials, and others (such as those who grant preferential access to public tenders) who are seen as "approachable"— in other words, corruptible. They identify potential clients, business partners, front people for phantom companies, individuals seeking credit, or law enforcement personnel who can provide warnings about investigations. They can guarantee communication between the members of the mafia organization itself (e.g., when some are in prison). As knowledge providers, white-collar workers make their highly specialized skills available to serve a mafia's economic and entrepreneurial interests in a continuous process of creating criminal opportunities. This allows the mafia to recycle, manage, and reinvest illicit capital in the financial, banking, corporate, and real estate sectors—fundamental activities for the criminal enterprise, but ones that would be impossible to carry out without active collaboration of white-collar workers.

These relationships between mafias and outsiders demonstrate an evolution of relationships and blur lines between views of entrepreneurs as being either victims or colluders. Many instead are vital business partners of the mafia organization.[64] Increasingly frequently, the professionals and entrepreneurs seek out a relationship with the mafia. Exchanges can

[62] Its role has been analyzed in the *Fata Morgana*, *Reghion*, and *Mammasantissima* investigations (three investigations of the Tribunale di Reggio Calabria in 2016)

[63] The analysis is based on 40 investigations into mafia groups carried out from 2008 to 2017 in northern Italy (Lombardy mainly, Piedmont, Emilia Romagna, Veneto, Liguria) and is accompanied by semistructured interviews with privileged witnesses, such as magistrates and experts from LEAs involved in the investigation (Catino 2018).

[64] The *entrepreneur as victim* gives in to duress, suffering unjust damage due to intimidation; the *entrepreneur as colluder* establishes a symbiotic relationship with the organization and gains advantages (Corte Suprema di Cassazione Penale 2015; Turone 2015). For a detailed description of such figures, see Sciarrone (2009).

continue over time and be mutually beneficial. The relationship is aimed at developing business that is redefined over time based on changing circumstances. Professionals from the legal world provide ideational, creative, and entrepreneurial contributions.

Several judicial investigations examined in recent studies show that professionals, attracted by earnings and economic opportunities, seek out mafia relationships in legal markets to obtain their "protection" and extralegal services (Moro and Catino 2016; Catino 2018). Some emblematic examples emerge from "Operation Aemilia," the largest anti-mafia operation in Emilia Romagna (Tribunale di Bologna 2015). The investigation showed that the 'Ndrangheta did not have to threaten entrepreneurs in order to enter markets, but responded to preexisting needs for false invoicing and illicit earnings. They proved to be capable and reliable service providers.

In other words, politicians, entrepreneurs, and white-collar workers have realized that mafia collaborations can be useful. Given this, no threats are needed. Violence emerges later, though not always, when things go wrong. One example is banking and financial consultant Roberta Tattini, who provided professional advice to the 'Ndrangheta group headed by Nicolino Grandi Aracri, introducing clan members to other financial operators and identifying new business opportunities. Aware of the identity of her client, even boasting about his criminal qualifications in a phone call to her father, Tattini believed that the collaboration, and the more than 100 companies in the boss's hands, would increase her own economic and professional opportunities.

Another example emerges from "Operation Giotto" (Tribunale di Milano 2016), involving criminal associations aimed at tax evasion and other tax offenses for the benefit of the Cosa Nostra's Laudani clan. Ghost companies produced false invoices and provided compliant front men. Cash was obtained to be used to bribe figures from public administrations and private companies, thus obtaining lucrative contracts for the benefit of the companies the clan controlled. The system could not have worked without the assistance of knowledge brokers and knowledge providers. Brokers bridged the information asymmetry between the mafia clan in Sicily and the individuals to be bribed in Lombardy and Piedmont. An ex-trade unionist put his network of relationships and knowledge at the mafia clan's disposal. Accountants invented fictitious companies that handled legal and tax matters, something the mafia could not do due to their lack of specialized knowledge.

Cases such as these show how outsiders can shape and adapt mafia activity, rather than the other way around. In order to understand how mafias operate in nontraditional areas, and other areas as well, it is essential to understand the behavior of complicit outsiders. Knowledge providers and brokers enable the mafia organization to do things it otherwise could not, providing capacities more significant in some cases than those of mafia members. As Europol recommends, "Straw men and professionals aiding and abetting must be considered as affiliates to the Clan or Family they knowingly help" (2013, p. 18). They augment the mafia organization's capabilities and ensure that processes that would otherwise occur slowly and with difficulty are carried out relatively quickly and easily. Collaborators of this kind should be a focus of future research and debate since, without them, the presumed omnipotence of mafia organizations would come into question.

REFERENCES

Albini, Joseph L. 1971. *The American Mafia: Genesis of a Legend*. New York: Appleton-Century-Crofts.
Allum, Felia. 2016. *The Invisible Camorra: Neapolitan Crime Families across Europe*. Ithaca, NY: Cornell University Press.
Alongi, Giuseppe. 1890. *La Camorra, Studio di Sociologia Criminale*. Turin: Edizioni Bocca.
Anderson, Annelise G. 1979. *The Business of Organized Crime: A Cosa Nostra Family*. Stanford, CA: Hoover Institution.
———. 1995. "Organized Crime, Mafia and Governments." In *The Economics of Organized Crime*, edited by Gianluca Fiorentini and Sam Peltzman. Cambridge: Cambridge University Press.
Arlacchi, Pino. 1988. *Mafia Business: The Mafia Ethic and the Spirit of Capitalism*. Oxford: Oxford University Press.
———. 1993. *Men of Dishonor: Inside the Sicilian Mafia; An Account of Antonino Calderone*. New York: William Morrow.
———. 1994. *Addio Cosa Nostra. La Vita di Tommaso Buscetta*. Milan: Rizzoli.
Asmundo, Adam, and Maurizio Lisciandra. 2008. "The Cost of Protection Racket in Sicily." *Global Crime* 9(3):221–40.
Baarda, Charlotte. 2015. "Human Trafficking for Sexual Exploitation from Nigeria into Western Europe: The Role of Voodoo Rituals in the Functioning of a Criminal Network." *European Journal of Criminology* 13(2):257–73.
Barbagallo, Francesco. 2010. *Storia della Camorra*. Bari: Laterza.

Blok, Anton. 1974. *The Mafia of a Sicilian Village, 1860–1960*. New York: Polity.

Bonanno, Joseph. 1983. *A Man of Honor: The Autobiography of Joseph Bonanno*. New York: Simon & Schuster.

Boulding, Kenneth E. 1964. "A Pure Theory of Conflict Applied to Organizations." In *The Frontiers of Management Psychology*, edited by George Fisk. New York: Harper & Row.

Calderoni, Francesco. 2014*a*. "Measuring the Presence of the Mafias in Italy." In *Organized Crime, Corruption, and Crime Prevention*, edited by Stefano Caneppele and Francesco Calderoni. New York: Springer.

———. 2014*b*. "Mythical Numbers and the Proceeds of Organised Crime: Estimating Mafia Proceeds in Italy." *Global Crime* 15(1–2):138–63.

Calderoni, Francesco, Giulia Berlusconi, Lorella Garofalo, Luca Giommoni, and Federica Sarno. 2016. "The Italian Mafias in the World: A Systematic Assessment of the Mobility of Criminal Groups." *European Journal of Criminology* 13(4):413–33.

Campana, Paolo. 2011. "Eavesdropping on the Mob: The Functional Diversification of Mafia Activities across Territories." *European Journal of Criminology* 8:213–28.

———. 2013. "Understanding Then Responding to Italian Organized Crime Operations across Territories." *Policing* 7(3):316–25.

———. 2016. "The Structure of Human Trafficking: Lifting the Bonnet on a Nigerian Trafficking Network." *British Journal of Criminology* 56:68–86.

Caneppele, Stefano. 2014. *Le Mafie Dentro gli Appalti. Casi Studio e Modelli Preventivi*. Milan: Franco Angeli.

Caneppele, Stefano, and Sara Martocchia. 2014. "Italian Mafias, Public Procurement, and Public Works in Southern Italy." In *Organized Crime, Corruption, and Crime Prevention: Essays in Honor of Ernesto U. Savona*, edited by Stefano Caneppele and Francesco Calderoni. Cham, Germany: Springer.

Catino, Maurizio. 2014. "How Do Mafias Organize? Conflict and Violence in Three Mafia Organizations." *European Journal of Sociology* 55(2):177–220.

———. 2018. "Colletti bianchi e mafie. Le relazioni pericolose nell'economia del Nord Italia." *Stato e Mercato* 1:149–88.

———. 2019. *Mafia Organizations: The Visible Hand of Criminal Enterprise*. Cambridge: Cambridge University Press.

Catino, Maurizio, and Francesco N. Moro. 2018. "High-Profile Mafia Murders: Understanding Targeted Assassinations Carried Out by Organized Crime in Italy." In *Mafia Violence: Political, Symbolic, and Economic Forms of Violence in Camorra Clans*, edited by Monica Massari and Vittorio Martone. London: Routledge.

CENSIS. 2009. *Il Condizionamento delle Mafie sull'Economia, sulla Società e sulle Istituzioni del Mezzogiorno*. Rome: Centro Studi Investimenti Sociali.

Ciconte, Enzo. 1996. *Processo alla 'Ndrangheta*. Bari: Laterza.

Ciconte, Enzo, Vincenzo Macrì, and Francesco Forgione. 2010. *Osso, Mastrosso, Carcagnosso*. Soveria Mannelli, Italy: Rubbettino.

CNEL. 2010. *L'Infiltrazione della Criminalità Organizzata nell'Economia di Alcune Regioni del Nord Italia*. Rome: Osservatorio Socio-Economico sulla Criminalità.

Cohen, Wesley M., and Daniel Levinthal. 1990. "Absorptive Capacity: A New Perspective on Learning and Innovation." *Administrative Science Quarterly* 35(1):128–52.

Coleman, James S. 1988. "Social Capital in the Creation of Human Capital." *American Journal of Sociology* 94:95–120.

———. 1990. *Foundations of Social Theory*. Cambridge, MA: Belknap/Harvard University Press.

CROSS. 2014. *Secondo Rapporto Trimestrale sulle Aree Settentrionali per la Presidenza della Commissione Parlamentare di Inchiesta sul Fenomeno Mafioso*. Rome: Osservatorio sulla Criminalità Organizzata.

Dalla Chiesa, Nando. 2014. *La Scelta Libera. Giovani del Movimento Antimafia*. Torino: EGA-Edizioni Gruppo Abele.

———. 2016. *Passaggio a Nord. La Colonizzazione Mafiosa*. Milan: Melampo Editore.

De Blasio, Abele. 1897. *Usi e Costumi dei Camorristi. Storie di Ieri e di Oggi*. Naples: Pierro.

Della Porta, Donatella, and Alberto Vannucci. 2012. *The Hidden Order of Corruption: An Institutional Approach*. Farnham: Ashgate.

Di Cagno, Giovanni, and Gioacchino Natoli. 2004. *Cosa Nostra Ieri, Oggi, Domani*. Bari: Edizioni Dedalo.

Dickie, John. 2012 *Mafia Brotherhoods*. London: Sceptre.

Di Fiore, Gigi. 2016. *La Camorra e le Sue Storie: La Criminalità Organizzata a Napoli dalle Origini alle Paranze dei Bimbi*. Novara: UTET.

Di Matteo, Nino, and Salvo Palazzolo. 2015. *Collusi. Perché Politici, Uomini delle Istituzioni e Manager Continuano a Trattare con la Mafia*. Milan: BUR.

Dino, Alessandra. 2006. *Pentiti*. Rome: Donzelli.

———. 2008. *La Mafia Devota*. Rome-Bari: Laterza.

Dugato, Marco, Serena Favarin, and Luca Giommoni. 2015. "The Risks and Rewards of Organized Crime Investments in Real Estate." *British Journal of Criminology* 55(5):944–65.

EMCDDA. 2014. *European Drug Report 2014: Trends and Developments*. Lisbon: European Monitoring Centre for Drugs and Drug Addiction.

Eurispes. 2008. *'Ndrangheta Holding: Dossier 2008*. Rome: Istituto di Studi Politici, Economici e Sociali.

Gambetta, Diego. 1993. *The Sicilian Mafia: The Business of Private Protection*. Cambridge, MA: Harvard University Press.

Gambetta, Diego, and Peter Reuter. 1995. "Conspiracy among the Many: The Mafia in Legitimate Industries." In *The Economics of the Organized Crime*, edited by Giovanni Fiorentini and Sam Peltzman. Cambridge: Cambridge University Press.

Gratteri, Nicola, and Antonio Nicaso. 2018. *Storia Segreta della 'Ndrangheta*. Milan: Mondadori.

Hannan, Michael T., and John Freeman. 1977. "The Population Ecology of Organizations." *American Journal of Sociology* 82(5):929–64.

———. 1989. *Organizational Ecology*. Cambridge, MA: Harvard University Press.

Hess, Henner. 1973. *Mafia and Mafioso: The Structure of Power*. Lexington, MA: Lexington Books.

———. 1998. *Mafia and Mafiosi: Origin, Power and Myth*. London: Hurst.

Hobsbawm, Eric J. 1959. *Primitive Rebels: Studies in Archaic Forms of Social Movements in the 19th and 20th Century*. New York: Norton.

Ianni, Francis A. J. 1972. *A Family Business: Kinship and Social Control in Organized Crime*. Ithaca, NY: Russell Sage Foundation.

Ingrascì, Ombretta. 2015. "La Mafia Russa in Italia. Lavori in corso." *Rivista di Studi e Ricerche sulla criminalità organizzata* 1(1):37–55.

Kleemans, Edward R. 2007. "Organized Crime, Transit Crime, and Racketeering." In *Crime and Justice in the Netherlands*, edited by Michael Tonry and Catrien Bijleveld. Chicago: University of Chicago Press.

La Spina, Antonio. 2014. "The Fight against the Italian Mafia." In *The Oxford Handbook of Organized Crime*, edited by Letizia Paoli. Oxford: Oxford University Press.

Legambiente. 2012. *Rifiuti Spa. Dieci Anni d'inchieste sui Traffici Illegali di Rifiuti. I Risultati Raggiunti e le Proposte per un Nuovo Sistema di Tutela Penale dell'ambiente*. Rome: Legambiente.

Lestingi, Francesco. 1880. "La Mafia in Sicilia." *Archivio di Psichiatria e Antropologia Criminale* 1:291–94.

Lin, Nan. 2001. *Social Capital: A Theory of Social Structure and Action*. Cambridge: Cambridge University Press.

Lombardo, Robert M. 2013. *Organized Crime in Chicago: Beyond the Mafia*. Champaign: University of Illinois Press.

Lupo, Salvatore. 2011*a*. *History of Mafia*. New York: Columbia University Press.

———. 2011*b*. *Il Tenebroso Sodalizio. Il Primo Rapporto di Polizia sulla Mafia Siciliana*. Rome: XL Edizioni.

———. 2015. *The Two Mafias: A Transatlantic History, 1888–2008*. New York: Palgrave Macmillan.

Mancuso, Marina. 2014. "Not All Madams Have a Central Role: Analysis of a Nigerian Sex Trafficking Network." *Trends in Organized Crime* 17(1):66–88.

Marmo, Marcella. 2011. *Il coltello e il Mercato. La Camorra Prima e Dopo l'Unità d'Italia*. Naples: L'ancora del Mediterraneo.

Massari, Massari. 2001. *La criminalità mafiosa nell'Italia centro-settentrionale*. In *Mafie nostre, mafie loro*, edited by Stefano Becucci and Monica Massari. Turin: Comunità.

———. 2014. "The Sacra Corona Unita: Origins, Characteristics, and Strategies." In *The 'Ndrangheta and Sacra Corona Unita: The History, Organization and Operation of Two Unknown Mafia Groups*, edited by Nicoletta Serena. Cham, Germany: Springer.

Mattioni, Alice. 2013. "I Movimenti Antimafia in Italia." In *Atlante delle Mafie (Volume II)*, edited by Enzo Ciconte, Francesco Forgione, and Isaia Sales. Soveria Mannelli, Italy: Rubbettino Editore.

Mirenda, Litterio, Sauro Mocetti, and Lucia Rizzica. 2017. *The Real Effects of 'Ndrangheta: Firm Level Evidence*. Rome: Banca d'Italia.

Mizruchi, Mark S., and Mina Yoo. 2005. "Interorganizational Power and Dependence." In *Companion to Organizations*, edited by Joel A. C. Baum. Oxford: Blackwell.

Monnier, Marco. 1862. *La Camorra. Notizie Storiche Raccolte e Documentate*. Florence: Barbera.

Moro, Francesco N., and Maurizio Catino. 2016. "La Protezione Mafiosa nei Mercati Legali. Un Framework Analitico ed Evidenze Empiriche in Lombardia." *Stato & Mercato* 3:311–52.

Moro, Francesco N., and Salvatore Sberna. 2018. "Transferring Violence? Mafia Killings in Non-Traditional Areas: Evidence from Italy." *Journal of Conflict Resolution* 62(7):1579–601.

Moro, Francesco N., and Matteo Villa. 2017. "The New Geography of Mafia Activity: The Case of a Northern Italian Region." *European Sociological Review* 33:46–58.

Natoli, Gioacchino. 2006. "Italia e Usa: Esperienze a Confronto." In *Pentiti*, edited by Alessandra Dino. Rome: Donzelli.

Natoli, Luigi. 1971. *I Beati Paoli*. Palermo: Flaccovio Editore.

Nelson, Richard R., and Sidney G. Winter. 1982. *An Evolutionary Theory of Economic Change*. Cambridge, MA: Harvard University Press.

Ocasio, William. 2005. "Organizational Power and Dependence." In *Companion to Organizations*, edited by Joel A. C. Baum. Oxford: Blackwell.

OSPA, and Corrado Stajano. 2010. *Mafia. L'Atto d'Accusa dei Giudici di Palermo*. Rome: Editori Riuniti (contains sections from OSPA 1985, *Ordinanza Sentenza della Corte di Assise di Palermo contro Abbate Giovanni + 706*, Palermo, 08.11.1985, 40 vols.).

Paliotti, Vittorio. 2007. *Storia della Camorra*. Rome: Newton Compton.

Paoli, Letizia. 2003. *Mafia Brotherhoods: Organized Crime, Italian Style*. Oxford: Oxford University Press.

———. 2004. "The Illegal Drugs Market." *Journal of Modern Italian Studies* 9(2):186–207.

———. 2014. "The Italian Mafia." In *The Oxford Handbook of Organized Crime*, edited by Letizia Paoli. Oxford: Oxford University Press.

Paoli, Letizia, Victoria A. Greenfield, and Andries Zoutendijk. 2013. "The Harm of Cocaine Trafficking: Applying a New Framework for Assessment." *Journal of Drug Issues* 43(4):407–36.

Pignatone, Giuseppe, and Michele Prestipino. 2019. *Modelli Criminali. Mafie di Ieri e di Oggi*. Bari-Roma: Laterza.

Pinotti, Paolo. 2015. "The Economic Costs of Organised Crime: Evidence from Southern Italy." *Economic Journal* 125(586):203–32.

Pitrè, Giuseppe. 1889. *Usi, Costumi, Credenze e Pregiudizi del Popolo Siciliano*. Palermo: Libreria Pedone Lauriel.

Ramella, Francesco, and Carlo Trigilia. 1997. "Associazionismo e Mobilitazione Contro la Criminalità Organizzata nel Mezzogiorno." In *Mafia e Società Italiana. Rapporto '97*, edited by Luciano Violante. Rome-Bari: Laterza.

Reuter, Peter. 1984. "The (Continued) Vitality of Mythical Numbers." *Public Interest* 75:135–47.

Riccardi, Michele. 2014. "When Criminals Invest in Businesses: Are We Looking in the Right Direction? An Exploratory Analysis of Companies Controlled by Mafias." In *Organized Crime, Corruption, and Crime Prevention: Essays in Honor of Ernesto U. Savona*, edited by Stefano Caneppele and Francesco Calderoni. Cham, Germany: Springer.

Sales, Isaia. 1988. *La Camorra, le Camorre*. Rome: Editori Riuniti.

———. 2016. *I Preti e i Mafiosi*. Soveria Mannelli, Italy: Rubbettino.

Santino, Umberto. 2010. *Storia del Movimento Antimafia*. Rome: Editori Riuniti.

Savona, Ernesto U. 2010. "Infiltration of the Public Construction Industry by Italian Organised Crime." In *Situational Prevention of Organized Crimes*, edited by Karen Bullock, Ronald V. Clarke, and Nick Tilley. Cullompton, Devon: Willan.

Savona, Ernesto U., and Giulia Berlusconi. 2015. *Organized Crime Infiltration of Legitimate Businesses in Europe: A Pilot Project in Five European Countries*. Final Report of Project ARIEL—Assessing the Risk of the Infiltration of Organized Crime in EU MSs Legitimate Economies. Trento: Transcrime/Università degli Studi di Trento.

Savona, Ernesto U., Francesco Calderoni, Gian Maria Campedelli, Tommaso Comunale, Marco Ferrarini, and Cecilia Meneghini. 2018. *Recruitment into Mafias: Criminal Careers of Mafia Members and Mafia Bosses*. Intermediate Report of Project PROTON—Modelling the Processes Leading to Organised Crime and Terrorist Networks. Milan: Transcrime/Università Cattolica del Sacro Cuore.

Savona, Ernesto U., and Michele Riccardi. 2015. *From Illegal Markets to Legitimate Businesses: The Portfolio of Organised Crime in Europe*. Final Report of Project OCP—Organised Crime Portfolio. Trento: Transcrime/Università degli Studi di Trento.

Schneider, Jane C., and Peter T. Schneider. 1976. *Culture and Political Economy in Western Sicily*. New York: Academy Press.

Sciarrone, Rocco. 2009. *Mafie Vecchie, Mafie Nuove. Radicamento ed Espansione*. Rome: Donzelli.

———. 2014. *Mafie del Nord. Strategie Criminali e Contesti Locali*. Rome: Donzelli.

Sergi, Anna. 2016. "A Qualitative Reading of the Ecological (Dis)Organization of Criminal Organization: The Case of the Famiglia Basilischi in Italy." *Trends in Organized Crime* 19(2):149–74.

———. 2018. "Polycephalous 'Ndrangheta: Crimes, Behaviours, and Organisation of the Calabrian Mafia in Australia." *Australian and New Zealand Journal of Criminology*, https://doi.org/10.1177percent2F0004865818782573.

Sergi, Anna, and Anita Lavorgna. 2016. *'Ndrangheta*. London: Palgrave Macmillan.

Sergi, Pantaleone. 2003. *Gli Anni dei Basilischi. Mafia, Istituzioni e Società in Basilicata*. Milan: Franco Angeli.

Sparagna, Roberto M. 2015. "Metodo Mafioso e c.d. Mafia Silente nei Più Recenti Approdi Giurisprudenziali." *Diritto Penale Contemporaneo*, https://www.penalecontemporaneo.it.

Teece, David, Gary Pisano, and Amy Shuen. 1997. "Dynamic Capabilities and Strategic Management." *Strategic Management Journal* 18(7):509–33.

Thompson, James D. 1967. *Organizations in Action*. New York: McGraw-Hill.
Transcrime. 2013. *Progetto PON Sicurezza 2007–2013. Gli Investimenti delle Mafie*. Rapporto Linea 1. Rome: Ministero dell'Interno.
Truzzolillo, Fabio. 2013. "Criminale e Gran Criminale. La struttura Unitaria e Verticistica della 'Ndrangheta delle Origini." *Meridiana* 77(2):203–32.
Turone, Giuliano. 2015. *Il delitto di Associazione Mafiosa*. Milan: Giuffrè.
Vannucci, Alberto. 2012. *Atlante della Corruzione*. Torino: Gruppo Abele.
Varese, Federico. 2006. "How Mafias Migrate: The Case of the 'Ndrangheta in Northern Italy." *Law and Society Review* 40(2):411–44.
———. 2011. *Mafias on the Move: How Organized Crime Conquers New Territories*. Princeton, NJ: Princeton University Press.
———. 2012 "The Structure and the Content of Criminal Connections: The Russian Mafia in Italy." *European Sociological Review* 29(5):899–909.
———. 2017*a*. *Mafia Life: Love, Death and Money at the Heart of Organized Crime*. London: Profile.
———. 2017*b*. "What Is Organised Crime?" In *Redefining Organised Crime*, edited by Stefania Carnevale, Serena Forlati, and Orsetta Giolo. Portland, OR: Hart.
———. 2020. "How Mafias Migrate: Transplantation, Functional Diversification and Separation." In *Organizing Crime: Mafias, Markets, and Networks*, edited by Michael Tonry and Peter Reuter. Chicago: University of Chicago Press.
Visconti, Costantino. 2015. "I giudici di Legittimità Ancora alle Prese con la 'Mafia Silente' al Nord: Dicono di Pensarla allo Stesso Modo, ma Non è Così." *Diritto Penale Contemporaneo*, https://www.penalecontemporaneo.it.
Von Lampe, Klaus. 2012. "Transnational Organized Crime Challenges for Future Research." *Crime, Law, and Social Change* 58(2):179–94.
Weber, Max. 1978. *Economy and Society*. Berkeley: University of California Press. (Originally published 1922.)
Zuckerman, Ezra W. 2010. "Speaking with One Voice: A 'Stanford School' Approach to Organizational Hierarchy." In *Stanford's Organization Theory Renaissance, 1970–2000*, edited by C. Bird Schoonhoven and F. Dobbin. Bingley, UK: Emerald Group.

SOURCES: JUDICIAL, INVESTIGATIVE, POLITICAL

Corte d'Appello di Catanzaro. 2018. *Cerimonia di inaugurazione dell'anno giudiziario*, Estratto della Relazione sull'amministrazione della giustizia del Presidente della Corte d'Appello, Domenico Introcaso.
Corte Suprema di Cassazione Penale. 2015. Sentence no. 24771.
CPA. 1992. *Audizione del Collaboratore di giustizia Leonardo Messina*. Rome: Commissione Parlamentare Antimafia.

————. 1994. *Relazione sulle Risultanze dell'attività del Gruppo di Lavoro Incaricato di Svolgere Accertamenti su Insediamenti e Infiltrazioni di Soggetti ed Organizzazioni di Tipo Mafioso in Aree Non Tradizionali*. Rome: Commissione Parlamentare Antimafia.

————. 1998. *Relazione sui Sequestri di Persona a Scopo di Estorsione*. Rome: Commissione Parlamentare Antimafia.

————. 2000. *Report sul Crimine Organizzato in Campania*. Rome: Commissione Parlamentare Antimafia.

————. 2008. *Relazione Annuale sulla 'Ndrangheta*. Rome: Commissione Parlamentare Antimafia.

————. 2010. *Audizione del Procuratore Distrettuale Antimafia di Reggio Calabria Dottor Giuseppe Pignatone*. Rome: Commissione Parlamentare Antimafia.

————. 2017. *Relazione sulle Infiltrazioni di Cosa Nostra e della 'Ndrangheta nella Massoneria in Sicilia e in Calabria*. Rome: Commissione Parlamentare Antimafia.

————. 2018. *Relazione Conclusiva*. Rome: Commissione Parlamentare Antimafia.

DDA Palermo. 2008. *Direzione Distrettuale Antimafia* (Anti-mafia District Directorate), *Squadra Mobile* (Flying squad) in 2006, *Operazione Gotha*, April 21.

DIA. 2010. *Relazione del Ministro dell'Interno al Parlamento. Attività Svolta e Risultati Conseguiti (Luglio-Dicembre)*. Rome: Direzione Investigativa Antimafia.

————. 2017. *Relazione del Ministro dell'Interno al Parlamento. Attività Svolta e Risultati Conseguiti (Luglio-Dicembre)*. Rome: Direzione Investigativa Antimafia.

DNA. 2010. *Relazione Annuale sulle Attività Svolte dal Procuratore Nazionale e dalla Direzione Nazionale Antimafia e Antiterrorismo Nonché sulle Dinamiche e Strategie della Criminalità Organizzata di Tipo Mafioso nel Periodo 1 Luglio 2008-30 Giugno 2009*. Rome: Direzione Nazionale Antimafia.

————. 2017. *Relazione Annuale sulle Attività Svolte dal Procuratore Nazionale e dalla Direzione Nazionale Antimafia e Antiterrorismo Nonché sulle Dinamiche e Strategie della Criminalità Organizzata di Tipo Mafioso nel Periodo 1 Luglio 2015-30 Giugno 2016*. Rome: Direzione Nazionale Antimafia.

Europol. 2013. *Threat Assessment: Italian Organised Crime*. The Hague: European Police Office.

Ministero dell'Interno. 2017. *Relazione sui Programmi di Protezione, sulla Loro Efficacia e sulle Modalità Generali di Applicazione per Coloro che Collaborano con la Giustizia (secondo semestre 2015 e primo semestre 2016)*. Rome: Ministero dell'Interno.

Polizia e Carabinieri di Palermo. 1982. *Rapporto Greco Michele+161, n.2832/2*.

Procura della Repubblica di Palermo. 1989. *Procedimento Penale Contro Greco Michele ed altri, n.3162/89*.

Tribunale di Bologna. 2015. *Ordinanza di Applicazione di Misure Cautelari Coercitive, Aiello+202—Operazione Aemilia*.

Tribunale di Milano. 2010. *Ordinanza di Applicazione di Misura Coercitiva, Agostino Fabio+159—Operazione Infinito*.

————. 2014. *Ordinanza di Applicazione di Misura Coercitiva con Mandato di Cattura—Operazione Insubria*.

————. 2016. *Ordinanza Applicativa di Misura Cautelare, Giardino Massimiliano+10—Operazione Giotto*.

Tribunale di Napoli. 2008. *Ordinanza di Applicazione della Misura Cautelare Coercitiva Personale nei Confronti di Ammutinato Salvatore+132.*

————. 2011. *Ordinanza di Applicazione della Misura Cautelare Coercitiva Personale nei Confronti di Buanno Fabio e altri.*

Tribunale di Palermo. 2005. *Grande Mandamento.* Fermo di indiziati di reato, RG. PM. DDA 3779/03.

————. 2008. *Gotha.* Sentenza di rito abbreviato, N. 1579/07.

————. 2018. Corte d'appello, *Sentenza di primo grado*, No. 2/2018 Reg. Sent., 20 April (Processo Trattativa).

Tribunale di Palermo (DDA). 2008. *Old Bridge.* N. 11059/06 R. mod. 21 D.D.A.

————. 2008. *Perseo.* Fermo di indiziati di delitto art. 384 segg.

Tribunale di Reggio Calabria. 2001. *Sentenza della Corte di Assise, Seconda Sezione Penale—Operazione Olimpia.*

————. 2010. *Decreto di Fermo di Indiziato di Delitto, artt. 384 e ss. c.p.p.—Operazione Crimine.*

————. 2014. *Ordinanza di Applicazione di Misure Coercitive di Natura Cautelare, Amabile Michele+22—Operazione New Bridge.*

————. 2015a. *Fermo di Indiziato di Delitto—Operazione Columbus I.*

————. 2015b. *Fermo di Indiziato di Delitto—Operazione Columbus II.*

Tribunale di Roma. 1985. *Sentenza di Primo Grado Contro Matarazzo Giovanna+82, Settima Sezione Penale.*

Tribunale di Santa Maria Capua Vetere. 2013. *Processo a Carico di Antonucci Esterino+altri, Prima Sezione Penale.*

Tribunale di Torino. 2011. *Operatione Minotauro*, No. 6191/2007 R.G.N.R. DDA + 4775/09 R.G. GIP, p. 1271.

————. 2014. *Operazione San Michele*, Ordinanza di applicazione di misura cautelare di Aracri Francesco + 25, Giudice per le indagini preliminari Elisabetta Chinaglia, 5 aprile.

Letizia Paoli

What Makes Mafias Different?

ABSTRACT

Organized crime, a fuzzy concept, has been defined in many different, sometimes contradictory ways. Five sets of mafia organizations have for decades been considered the core of organized crime: the American Cosa Nostra, the Italian Cosa Nostra and 'Ndrangheta, Chinese triads, and Japanese yakuza. These organizations—mafias for short—share seven typifying characteristics: longevity and thus premodern roots and, with rare exceptions, male-only membership; large size; a formalized and complex internal structure; an elaborate cultural apparatus meant to generate lifelong commitment, new identity, and fictive kinship ties; multifunctionality; the goal of political dominion and capacity to provide governance services; and long-standing popular legitimacy and power-sharing with local state authorities. The first and the last characteristics point to reasons for the mafias' consolidation and persistence: except for the American Cosa Nostra, all emerged in contexts of state weakness or absence and benefited from willingness of state representatives to acknowledge their power. Reduced willingness of state authorities and communities to accept mafias' power, coupled with premodern features of their structure and culture, explain a further common trait: with the partial exception of the 'Ndrangheta, all have experienced considerable decline in recent decades.

At least since Joe Valachi's televised hearings before the Permanent Subcommittee on Investigations of the US Senate in 1963, the Italian American Cosa Nostra has been prominent in public imagination, seen as the

Electronically published June 5, 2020
   Letizia Paoli is professor of criminology at the KU Leuven Faculty of Law, Belgium. She is grateful to Bryan Peters for excellent research assistance.

embodiment of organized crime. This view was popularized by the release of the first *Godfather* film in 1972 and has been reinforced by the lasting success of the *Godfather* trilogy and production of more than 450 films featuring Italian American mafiosi since 1972 (Santopietro 2012; Italic Institute of America 2015).[1] Southern Italian mafia organizations, particularly the Sicilian Cosa Nostra, took on this mythic status.

The Chinese triads and Japanese yakuza are often put on a par with the Italian and American mafias (e.g., von Lampe 2008). They share many characteristics, justifying placing them all in a common category, even if the triads and yakuza are older and larger. Triads and yakuza consist of consortia, or associations, of basic units, or groups, rather than a single consortium like the two Cosa Nostras and the Italian 'Ndrangheta. Much like the Italian mafias, triads and yakuza have inspired hundreds of movies, also catching the public imagination in their countries (e.g., Schilling 2003).

The American and Sicilian Cosa Nostra, the Calabrian 'Ndrangheta, the Chinese triads, and the Japanese yakuza have since the 1980s been regarded as iconic criminal organizations, as exemplary of organized crime, no matter how organized crime is defined. I collectively call them mafia organizations or, for short, mafias, and in this essay summarize what is known about them. With an approach strongly influenced by the sociology of Max Weber (e.g., [1921] 1978), I provide a comparative analysis of these organizations in order to identify their common, typifying characteristics (and minor differences), and the reasons for their consolidation and recent decline.

Seven shared traits characterize the five mafias. Four concern the organizations; three relate to their interactions with their environments. First, mafias are long-standing. Second, they are large consortia. Third, all have ruling bodies and, fourth, an elaborate cultural apparatus. Because of their premodern origins and criminalization they have, fifth, not taken part in the functional differentiation typical of modernity. They are inherently multifunctional and not exclusively interested in profit maximization. Sixth, they have claimed and long exercised political

---

[1] As late as 2016, US President Barack Obama described the first two *Godfather* films as his favorite movies (Shamsian 2016). Several quotes from the *Godfather*—including "I'll make him an offer he can't refuse," "keep your friends close, but your enemies closer," and "going to the mattresses"—have entered into American parlance.

dominion in their home territories, providing governance services and competing with local governments. Seventh, they long enjoyed substantial popular legitimacy and often entered into effective, sometimes official, power-sharing arrangements with local governments.

This is an alternative, novel way to deal with the apparently intractable ambiguity of the term "organized crime." The seven typifying characteristics can be used as benchmarks to assess other organized crime actors. Peter Reuter and I have done this in another essay (Reuter and Paoli 2020), in which we analyze contemporary criminal organizations in Latin America and compare them with the five mafias.

This characterization of the five mafias combines the main insights of evolving academic debates since the 1960s. Studies in Sicily in the 1960s identified mafiosi's functions in their local societies and the cultural codes they relied on to justify their power (Hess 1973; Blok 1975; Schneider and Schneider 1976). These studies, however, usually denied the existence of mafia organizations, as did some scholars in the US until the 1970s (e.g., Albini 1971). After testimonies of mafia turncoats and criminal investigations irrefutably proved the existence of the US and Sicilian Cosa Nostras and the Calabrian 'Ndrangheta, researchers in the United States, Italy, and elsewhere focused on mafias' criminal activities, conceptualizing them as profit-maximizing criminal enterprises (e.g., Arlacchi 1988). Gambetta's seminal 1992 book shifted the focus to the Sicilian mafia's provision of governance services. This perspective was applied to other mafias and led to recognition of mafias' political power (Varese 2001; Hill 2003). Historical research in Italy and elsewhere documented the many functions performed by mafias and their members and their adaptability to changing political regimes (Murray 1994; Ownby 1996; Lupo 2009). More sociological studies analyzed and emphasized mafias' cultural apparatus and organizational structures, their accomplishment of multiple functions, and their internal and external legitimation (Paoli 2003; Santoro 2007).

This essay is organized as follows. Section I reviews the main concepts used in this field and explains how I use them here. Section II briefly considers other criminal organizations in addition to the mafias and fleshes out the mafias' seven typifying characteristics. Sections III to X discuss each trait in more detail. A table at the end of each of those seven sections summarizes the key data for each characteristic and organization. Section XI considers mafias' common decline. The final section recapitulates the main findings and discusses policy implications.

I. Key Concepts

The concept of organized crime has had a winding history, with many partly contradictory meanings attached to it since the expression began to be used in the United States at the turn of the twentieth century (see, e.g., Varese 2010; for a list of definitions, see von Lampe 2019). Mafia is a word of uncertain origin that was first used in Italy after the country's unification in 1861 (Gambetta 1992) and that has been given very different meanings. In this section, I briefly summarize the academic and policy debate on each term, explain the approach adopted here, and provide my definition of criminal organization.

A. Organized Crime and Criminal Organization

Understanding of organized crime has shifted back and forth since the 1920s between two competing notions: a set of large, long-lasting, well-structured criminal organizations whose members systematically engage in crime, taking advantage of that structure; and a set of criminal activities requiring coordination, and particularly the provision of illegal goods and services, mostly carried out for monetary gain (Paoli and van der Beken 2014). This dichotomy was singled out by Smith (1991) as "who" (criminal actors) and "what" (criminal activities). More recently, Hagan (2006, p. 134) proposed a distinction between "Organized Crime" (capitalized) to refer to criminal organizations and "organized crime" to refer to criminal activities that require a degree of organization (Papachristos and Zhao 2015; von Lampe 2016).

The Italian American Cosa Nostra was long considered the archetype of the "who" notion of organized crime. For Peter Reuter, for example, organized crime consists of "organizations that have durability, hierarchy, and involvement in a multiplicity of criminal activities. . . . The Mafia provides the most enduring and significant form of organized crime" (1983, p. 175; Jacobs 2020).

Largely based on findings of US congressional committees (US Senate 1951, 1957, 1963, 1988) and other public bodies (e.g., Task Force on Organized Crime 1967), the mafia-centered conception was from the late 1960s onward rejected by many, if not most, North American academics (e.g., Hawkins 1969). To avoid the ethnically loaded term "organized crime," some proposed the term "illegal enterprise" (e.g., Smith 1975; Haller 1990). The terms *illegal enterprise* and *organized crime* ended up being used interchangeably, creating confusion in both academic and policy debates (Yeager 2012).

For some scholars, the identification of organized crime with "what," the provision of illegal goods and services, is complete. Van Duyne, for example, asks: "What is organized crime without organizing some kind of criminal trade; without selling and buying of forbidden goods and services in an organizational context? The answer is simply nothing" (1997, p. 203). Other scholars (e.g., Edwards and Levi 2008) and most official reports on organized crime (e.g., by the German Bundeskriminalamt or Federal Police Office, BKA 2018) include both some forms of "illegal transfers" and predatory crimes, such as robberies, extortions, embezzlement, and frauds, sometimes depending on the size and durability of the group involved. Unlike the provision of illegal goods and services, these transfers do not create value; they shift it from one person to another.

This loose understanding of organized crime in terms of profit-making criminal activity has allowed organized crime to become a useful policy term even in European countries that have no significant mafia problems. It inspires the statutory and bureaucratic definitions of organized crime used by law enforcement agencies in most European countries except Italy. The definition adopted by the UK Serious and Organized Crime Agency in 2012, for example, is broad and loose, has a clear focus on profit-making crimes, and contains no organizational requirements: "Organised crime is defined as those involved, normally working with others, in continuing serious criminal activities for substantial profit, whether based in the UK or elsewhere" (SOCA 2012).[2]

Reconciliation of the "who" and the "what" conceptions of organized crime has been achieved by watering down the notion of "who." The term now encompasses, in addition to genuine criminal organizations, a variety of other actors, more or less loosely organized, and in some cases even individuals. This approach is visible in the most recent, high-level US policy documents on the topic, the *Law Enforcement Strategy to Combat International Organized Crime* (US Department of Justice 2008) and the *Strategy to Combat Transnational Organized Crime* (White House 2011). Organized crime is initially described in both as a set of criminal organizations primarily interested in committing crimes for gain: "Organized crime refers to those self-perpetuating associations of individuals

---

[2] The UK government has shifted to an even broader conceptualization of serious and organized crime: "individuals planning, coordinating and committing serious offenses, whether individually, in groups and/or as part of transnational networks" (Home Office 2018, p. 11).

who operate internationally for the purpose of obtaining power, influence, monetary and/or commercial gains, wholly or in part by illegal means, while protecting their activities through a pattern of corruption and/or violence" (US Department of Justice 2008, p. 2; see also White House 2011). However, in line with most academic research and international policy developments, US policy makers also endorse a looser understanding: "There is no single structure under which transnational criminals operates; they vary from hierarchies to clans, networks, cells, and may evolve to other structures" (US Department of Justice 2008, p. 2). Moreover, as in other policy contexts, the initial focus on criminal groups gives way to a listing of illegal market activities, under the assumption that transnational organized crime is responsible for them (White House 2011).

The watering down of the "who" has been reinforced by adoption of the offense of "criminal organization" as an anchor for the definition of organized crime within the European Union (e.g., Europol 2013a). In EU criminal law and, thus, in the criminal laws of all EU member states, a criminal organization is committed whenever more than two people cooperate over time in commission of serious criminal offenses (Council of the European Union 2008). This definition might serve useful purposes within criminal law. Its breadth, though, has been said to hamper development of EU criminal justice policy (e.g., Calderoni 2010) and makes it unsuitable for use as an analytic device.

The 2000 UN Convention against Transnational Organized Crime, the most important international instrument, has also adopted "a minimum common denominator" definition of organized crime, with no strict criteria concerning numbers of members or group structure (Paoli 2002a, p. 208). Article 2, paragraph (a) provides: "'Organized criminal group' shall mean a structured group of three or more persons, existing for a period of time and acting in concert with the aim of committing one or more serious crimes or offenses established in accordance with this Convention, in order to obtain, directly or indirectly a financial or other material benefit" (UNGA 2000, p. 25). Thus, investigative methods and other statutory measures included in the convention and adopted by the parties can be applied to cliques, gangs, and networks that are far removed from the images of mafia that dominate media and political discourse (Levi 2012, p. 597).

Given the fuzziness of the concept and the increasing focus on profit-making, several scholars (e.g., Naylor 2003; Edwards and Levi 2008) have suggested getting rid of the term "organized crime" altogether and focusing on the organization of crime for gain.

In this essay, I adopt the first part of that advice but not the second and focus on the criminal organizations that have traditionally been at the core of organized crime. My definition of "organization" is more restrictive than the legal ones and draws from the classical definition of organization given by Max Weber ([1921] 1978, p. 48): "a social relationship which is either closed or limits the admission of outsiders [and whose] regulations are enforced by specific individuals: a chief and, possibly, an administrative staff, which normally also has representative powers." Similar definitions are standard in organization studies (see, e.g., Tolbert and Hall 2009). Criminal organizations are seen as social entities that are relatively large, long-lasting, distinguish members from nonmembers, have an internal structure, with their own ruling bodies and subculture, and are either criminal per se or directly, or indirectly through their members, routinely engage in profit-making and other criminal activities. I focus exclusively on what Jacobs (2020) calls "organized crime organizations," that is, criminal organizations that emphasize the achievement of members' financial and material benefits over other aims.[3]

The five sets of entities I focus on, with the partial exception of the yakuza, are undoubtedly criminal organizations by contemporary standards. Nonetheless, I seldom use the adjective "criminal" in this essay while discussing their histories because four of the five (the American Cosa Nostra is the exception) were neither substantively nor formally criminalized for a considerable portion of their existence. Referring to them as criminal organizations would obscure that reality.

B. Mafia

The term "mafia" also has ambiguities. It was long used to signify a cultural attitude and form of power that spread in parts of Sicily and Calabria in the second half of the nineteenth century during the transition from feudalism to modernity. This "culturalist" view denied the existence of mafia organizations (Hess 1973; Blok 1975). Beginning in the mid-1980s, when judicial investigations began to provide clear, solid proof of their existence, "mafia" was conceptualized as an illicit enterprise,

---

[3] "Organized crime organization" is a more precise term than "criminal organization," but I seldom use it. It rings awkwardly to the ear and has seldom been used other than by Jacobs.

and its economic activities became the focus of academic analyses (e.g., Arlacchi 1988; Santino and La Fiura 1990; Catanzaro 1992).

With the publication of Diego Gambetta's *The Sicilian Mafia* in 1992, another functionalist interpretation of "mafia" became dominant. In his view, the Sicilian mafia is "a specific economic enterprise, an industry which produces, promotes, and sells private protection" (1992, p. 1). This conceptualization emphasizes an important function historically performed by Sicilian mafia groups but neglects many other activities in which they and their members historically engaged (e.g., Nelken 1995). This conceptualization has been applied to other criminal organizations and groups in Italy and elsewhere (Varese 2001; Hill 2003), but it obscures the inherently political nature of mafia organizations (Santoro 2007). It also almost paradoxically implies that a group can or cannot be labeled as mafia depending on the geographical (e.g., Campana 2011) or historical context (e.g., Hill 2003) in which it operates and thus whether it is able to sell protection services.

For these reasons, I eschew a strict functionalist interpretation of mafia. I start from historical entities that over time have been considered exemplary of organized crime. I characterize them as a specific set of organizations—that is, mafia organizations—and rely on a conceptual framework inspired by Weber's work to identify their typifying characteristics. For the sake of simplicity, if not historical precision, I call them all "mafias." This term is used by several scholars (e.g., Varese 2011) and has become a policy category not only in Italy[4] but elsewhere, including China.[5]

II. Mafias versus Other Criminal Organizations

Mafias are, of course, not the only criminal organizations, even if we exclude those that systematically use terrorist methods and usually aim at political change.[6] In this section I briefly discuss the other main "organized crime organizations," justify my choice to focus only on the five mafias, and identify their typifying characteristics.

---

[4] The offense of *associazione a delinquere di tipo mafioso* (mafia-type criminal organization) was added in 1982 to the Italian penal code (Article 416bis), bringing the sociological concept of mafia into the criminal code (Turone 2008; Calderoni 2010).

[5] Since 2002 the Chinese government has designated the best organized, most stable, and most dangerous criminal groups as "mafia-like gangs" (Chin 2014, pp. 221–22).

[6] See Schmid (2004) for an excellent summary of the debate on the definition of terrorism.

A. Focusing on Five Mafias

The main other criminal organizations are the post-Soviet *vory-v-zakone* (i.e., thieves-with-a-code-of-honor; Varese 2001, pp. 125–44), drug trafficking organizations or "cartels" in Colombia and Mexico (Thoumi 2014; Atuesta and Pérez-Dávila 2018), and (prison) gangs and other criminal organizations in several South and Central American countries. The last group includes the US–Central American Mara Salvatrucha or MS-13 and Barrio 18 (Cruz 2010), and the Brazilian Primeiro Comando da Capital (First Command of the Capital, also known as PCC, its Portuguese acronym) and Comando Vermelho (Portuguese for Red Command; Lessing 2018). Some of these organizations—particularly the Colombian and Central American ones—have attracted much public and media attention in recent times[7] and are responsible for much more violence than the mafias are.[8] Reuter and Paoli (2020) analyze some of these criminal organizations.

Reuter and Paoli also discuss "candidate" criminal organizations, including the Neapolitan camorra, motorcycle gangs (von Lampe and Blokland 2020), and several terrorist, paramilitary, and military organizations that have progressively focused on profit-making rather than their original political aims.

The Neapolitan camorra is often considered to be a criminal organization and a mafia (Saviano 2008; Allum 2016; Catino 2019, 2020). I exclude it because judicial investigations and academic studies have shown that the many criminal groups operating in and around Naples do not constitute a unitary criminal organization (e.g., Sales 1993). This is acknowledged even by scholars who consider the camorra to be a mafia organization. Catino, for example, writes: "The Camorra today is a population of criminal organizations (clans) in competition/conflict. .... In contrast with the Sicilian Cosa Nostra and the 'Ndrangheta, the Camorra is not a unified organization and no single higher-level body of coordination exists (such as the family or group of families) able to coordinate the entire criminal system" (2019, p. 156).

[7] More than 15 movies have been dedicated to Pablo Escobar, the former leader of the Medellin cartel (IMDb 2020).

[8] Central American countries—in particular, El Salvador, Honduras, Guatemala, and Mexico—have among the highest homicide rates in the world. Violence there is due to a multiplicity of factors but is strongly influenced by the presence of organized crime groups and gangs (UNODC 2019).

A criminal organization called camorra was active in the prisons and city of Naples during the nineteenth century (Behan 1996); some contemporary camorra groups draw inspirations from its rituals and symbols. Unlike the Cosa Nostra and 'Ndrangheta, though, no continuity can be established between the nineteenth-century camorra and the contemporary crime groups. As Sales (2001, p. 468) put it, "If camorra means a criminal organization that ruled over Naples' popular and plebeian strata, we can safely say that it started and ended in the nineteenth century." Monzini (1999) takes a similar position.

At least three considerations support a focus on the mafias. First, since the publication of Peter Reuter's *Disorganized Crime: The Economics of the Visible Hand* (1983), a consensus has emerged among scholars that criminal organizations are the exception not the rule in the vast panorama of organized crime. Most exchanges in illegal or criminal markets of developed countries are carried out by criminal enterprises, which are frequently referred to as organized crime but are much smaller and more ephemeral than mafia or other criminal organizations. This realization underlies the "illegal enterprise paradigm" that has become mainstream and is shared by many law enforcement and policy agencies (e.g., Europol 2013*a*).[9] Given the rarity of criminal organizations, it is analytically interesting and policy relevant to understand when, why, and under what conditions they, and especially mafias, have emerged.

Second, the mafias of Italian origin, the Chinese triads, and Japanese yakuza constitute an archetype or model of organized crime in the public imagination, and in a considerable part of the policy and academic debates. Their common characteristics can be used as a standard against which to assess other criminal organizations. The identification of a benchmark based on comparative analysis of the iconic mafia organizations may bring clarity to confused and confusing debates about definitions of organized crime and provide a basis for classification of organized crime actors.

Third, despite an abundant literature on mafias, especially those of Italian origin, there have been few attempts to compare them systematically (Paoli 2002*b*; Catino 2019, 2020).

---

[9] Unlike scholars, some law enforcement and policy agencies often argue that networks of criminal enterprises have replaced more hierarchical forms of organizations (e.g., Europol 2003). That thesis, though, seems to reflect a shift in the agencies' interpretative frames rather than the evolution of organized crime actors.

B. Seven Typifying Characteristics

I have identified seven typifying characteristics of the five mafias: longevity; size; formalized, complex structure; cultural apparatus; multifunctionality; political dominion and governance; and popular legitimacy and state toleration.

1. *Longevity.* They have all existed for at least a century. The American Cosa Nostra is the youngest. No other organized crime organization, other than the five mafias I discuss, is as old even as the American Cosa Nostra except for the *vory-v-zakone*, whose association consolidated in Soviet prisons and labor camps in the late 1920s, had its heyday after the implosion of the Soviet Union in 1991, and has since been much weakened (Varese 2001; Volkov 2014). It is the closest to the mafias, with which it shares several traits besides longevity. A few contemporary criminal organizations, such as the Mexican Sinaloa cartel, have been in operation for several decades, but none existed before World War II (Astorga 1999). Most criminal enterprises supplying prohibited goods and services are more ephemeral, existing for a few years at most. Conversely, many gangs and bandit groups that were active until the early nineteenth century in western Europe—and are especially well documented in the Benelux countries—have been disbanded. Some of these groups were fairly formalized and had organizational and functional similarities with mafia organizations, but they were swept away once governments were able to monopolize the use of violence, regulate markets, and provide effective protection and mediation services to their citizens and enterprises (Egmond 2004; Fijnaut 2014).

The five mafias' longevity implies that they originated in premodern times when state authorities had not yet monopolized the use of violence or were, as in the first Chinese settlements in Southeast Asia, utterly absent (Ownby and Heidhues 1993). Mafias' premodern roots influence their structure and culture. They also probably explain why mafias, with very rare exceptions in the 'Ndrangheta and triads, recruit only males into their ranks (Ciconte 1992, pp. 80–85; Chu 2005, p. 6)

2. *Size.* There is considerable variability in size among the five mafia organizations, but all have had at least a few thousand members for at least several decades. The Chinese triads and Japanese yakuza at their peaks had more than 230,000 and 180,000 members, respectively. Although not all triad members are criminally active, these figures refer only to members who had been ritually affiliated. Many more people cooperate with them in looser partnerships to arrange trades and commit

crimes. Most other, nonmafia, criminal organizations do not use initiation ceremonies or other means to separate members from nonmembers, making it difficult to assess their membership. Even with these caveats in mind, few criminal organizations have for more than a decade maintained a large membership comparable to those of the mafias.

The only exceptions are represented by some candidate "criminal" organizations. Among them are armies gone awry, such as the Chinese Kuomintang in post–World War II Burma (McCoy 1991), and militias and terrorist organizations, such as the Revolutionary Armed Forces of Colombia–People's Army (known as FARC), which had a military structure and operated in the context of virtual state absence (Brittain 2010; Norman 2018). Both the Kuomintang and the FARC deserve to be considered examples of organized crime, because over time they derived a growing and eventually preponderant share of their resources from organization and protection of drug production and trafficking (opium for the Kuomintang; coca for the FARC).

Outlaw motorcycle gangs also constitute, in my view, candidate criminal organizations. With formalized structures and well-defined recruitment procedures, they are organizations pursuant to my Weberian definition. However, I regard them as candidate rather than full-fledged criminal organizations because in most countries they are considered legitimate albeit problematic organizations. As von Lampe and Blokland (2020) report, most motorcycle gangs are registered legal entities, and some have copyrighted their colors and patches to prevent unauthorized use. The Hells Angels have gone to court to challenge unauthorized use of their name and logo. Despite the frequent use of the epithet "outlaw," these organizations are not fully criminalized, even if several US public bodies characterize them as organized crime syndicates (e.g., President's Commission 1986*b*). The US Department of Justice (2014) lists them as "organizations whose members use their motorcycle clubs as conduits for criminal enterprises." Dutch courts were the first to issue nationwide bans on some whole organizations or "clubs," including the Bandidos in 2017 and the Hell's Angels in 2019 (*Agence France-Press* 2019), and not only on local branches, known as chapters.

Observers disagree on whether motorcycle gangs should be classified as criminal organizations. For Barker (2014, pp. 13–14), for example, this is an empirical question, which has to be answered separately for each club or chapter depending on their members' and leaders' involvement in criminal activities. The largest motorcycle gangs are larger than the smaller mafias. Hells Angels in the early 1980s had an estimated 4,500 members, and non-US clubs, such as Australia's Rebels MC and The Netherlands' Satudarah MC, have become bigger than US clubs in recent decades (von Lampe and Blokland 2020).

3. *Formalized, Complex Structure.* The five mafias have formalized and complex internal structures, creating a clear-cut separation between members and nonmembers and having ruling bodies within each group and often also within the consortia. Only the candidate criminal organizations just discussed rival the mafias in formalization and complexity of their internal structures.

Mafia organizations constitute segmentary societies—consortia composed of several units that recognize each other as part of the same consortium. This organizational model used to be widespread in simple societies (Smith 1974). It is similar to that of the *vory-v-zakone* and the motorcycle gangs, which are also consortia of fairly autonomous units. Terrorist organizations and militias, such as the FARC, by contrast, tend to have more bureaucratic, centralized structures (Brittain 2010).

4. *Cultural Apparatus.* Mafia organizations possess a complex set of cultural codes, rituals, norms, and sanctions through which they create a collective identity, justify their existence, and aim to generate a lifelong commitment, a new identity, and fictive kinship ties among their members. There are few parallels among other criminal organizations; *vory-v-zakone* and the motorcycle gangs come closest.

To secure members' lifelong allegiance, mafia organizations impose status and fraternization contracts upon their members through elaborate initiation ceremonies (Weber [1921] 1978, pp. 671–73). Such contracts were widespread in premodern societies and are quite different from the employment contracts that are standard in contemporary bureaucracies. Being long-term and nonspecific, status and fraternization contracts guarantee the group bosses extraordinary flexibility, as members in principle cannot disobey orders. However, such contracts can credibly be imposed only on individuals who have been socialized into a subculture, thus restricting the pool of potential recruits. The subcultures underpinning the status and fraternization contracts have come under increasing strain due to the modernization of host societies and progressive delegitimization of mafia organizations.

5. *Multifunctionality.* Throughout their existences, mafia organizations have carried out a variety of functions, aiming at both money and power, engaging in numerous illegal and legal activities, and allowing

members considerable autonomy in their money-making activities. Mafias' multifunctionality is a heritage of their premodern roots: until the consolidation of modern states, there were no clear-cut boundaries between force-using and profit-seeking enterprises; mafias have not experienced functional differentiation because of their progressive criminalization. Although members are heavily involved in illegal businesses today, it is reductive to conceive mafias merely as profit-seeking criminal enterprises. All mafias arose before the consolidation of contemporary illegal markets, and, possibly excepting the American Cosa Nostra, profit maximization is not even today their exclusive, or even their main, aim.

All criminal organizations show some degree of multifunctionality. Even when they are primarily interested in making money through an economic activity, such as drug trafficking, as in the case of the Colombian and Mexican drug cartels, they end up exercising at least proto-political functions (e.g., Weber [1921] 1978, pp. 53–56) to secure the loyalty of their members, the cooperation and subordination of their collaborators, and the passivity and silence of the wider communities. Multifunctionality is reduced to a bare minimum in criminal enterprises that are continuously set up, and disbanded, to trade in prohibited products in western countries. Some are able to traffic in multiple products at the same time, but all try to minimize the use of violence to solve conflicts and secure their property rights, because violence attracts undesired law enforcement attention (Pearson and Hobbs 2001).

6. *Political Dominion and Governance.* Mafia organizations distinguish themselves from criminal enterprises and from many other criminal organizations through their claim to exercise political dominion in their home areas (Weber [1921] 1978, p. 54), not only among organization members and collaborators, and their long-standing ability to deliver governance services. They are thus inherently political organizations and can be conceived of as small proto-states that throughout their history have struggled with varying degrees of success to force their bodies of rules onto the entire population of their territory and to endow them with legitimacy. They have never succeeded in neutralizing all rival power centers (Tilly 1985, 1988).

7. *Popular Legitimacy and Power-Sharing Agreements.* Mafias have long enjoyed a considerable degree of popular legitimacy and have entered into effective, sometimes even official, power-sharing arrangements with local state institutions. No other organized crime actors have enjoyed such

long-standing legitimacy both in the communities within which they operate and with local state authorities.

These seven common characteristics distinguish mafias from other organized crime organizations, even if some possess some of these characteristics to some degree or even fully. The first four are internal characteristics. The other three are external and concern the organizations' actions in, and interactions with, their environment. Some other criminal organizations show similarities with the mafias in their size, internal structure, or culture. Others have developed similar patterns of interaction with their environments.

Mafias can be conceptualized in terms of their typifying characteristics. They are organizations consisting of long-standing and large consortia of fairly autonomous but homologous units, which are distinct from the blood families of their members, have their own ruling bodies, recognize each other as part of the same consortium, and have sometimes developed higher level coordinating bodies. They rely on an elaborate cultural apparatus to secure lifelong allegiance and subordination from their members and create fictive brotherhoods ties among them. Throughout their histories they have performed multiple functions to enhance their members and particularly their bosses' interests. They have claimed rights to exercise political dominion in their areas of settlement, long providing effective governance services and, despite their progressive, formal, and substantive criminalization, their power has long been recognized by local communities and representatives of state authorities.

There is an eighth common trait, which is, however, accidental and not typifying. With the partial exception of the 'Ndrangheta, all have experienced a considerable decline in recent decades. This has affected many, if not most, of their typifying characteristics.

III. Longevity

With the exception of the American Cosa Nostra, which grew out of its Sicilian counterpart early in the twentieth century, all five mafias have existed for more than 150 years and have their roots in premodern times. All existed before local governments established control over a given territory and managed to monopolize the use of violence (table 1).

TABLE 1

Mafias' Longevity

Sicilian Cosa Nostra	Calabrian 'Ndrangheta	American Cosa Nostra	Japanese Yakuza	Chinese Triads
Continuous existence since 1860s	Continuous existence since 1860s	Founded in 1920s, offspring of Sicilian Cosa Nostra	Predecessor groups (*bakuto*/gamblers and *tekiya*/peddlers) active since 1700s	Predecessor organization (Tiandihui) founded around 1760, similar groups even earlier

SOURCE.—Author's elaboration drawing on sources cited in text.

A. Sicilian and Calabrian Mafias

The Sicilian and Calabrian mafias date back to middle of the nineteenth century (Pezzino 1990; Ciconte 1992; Lupo 1993). The earliest reference to antecedents in Sicily was in 1838 in a report by the Procuratore Generale del Re, Pietro Calà Ulloa ([1838] 1961, pp. 233–35):

> In many villages, there are unions or fraternities—kinds of sects—
> which are called *partiti*, with no political color or goal, with no
> meeting places, and with no other bond but that of dependency on
> a chief, who is a landowner in some cases, and in others a priest. A
> common fund serves their needs, sometimes to exonerate an official,
> sometimes to defend him, sometimes to protect a defendant,
> sometimes to charge an innocent. These form many small
> governments inside the government.

Many other sources, especially after Italian unification in 1861, document the presence of mafia associations in Sicilian towns (Paoli 2003, pp. 33–36). Although the Calabrian mafia has historically received much less attention than its Sicilian counterpart, several documents—primarily judicial statements and police reports from the early twentieth century but also poems and novels—show the existence in Calabria of well-structured mafia associations since the late nineteenth century (Ciconte 1992; Gratteri and Nicaso 2010).

In both western Sicily and southern Calabria, the predecessors of contemporary mafias developed and consolidated in a power vacuum left first by the Bourbon monarchy, which dominated southern Italy until 1860, and then by the Italian state. The Bourbons were unable to control the disintegration of the feudal political and economic systems in the Kingdom of the Two Sicilies. On paper, the Bourbons, fully restored to power after the 1815 Vienna Congress, officially completed the transition from feudal institutions to those typical of an administrative monarchy by the end of the 1820s. In reality, the changes were much more ambiguous. New state structures proved to have only a weak territorial grip and to be largely ineffective in exercising social regulation; the sale of former feudal property began only after 1860 (Pezzino 1992; Lupo 2009).

For many years after unification in 1861, the new Italian government fared even worse. It alienated southern sympathies and was unable to penetrate large parts of the south or to guarantee public safety. As Leopoldo Franchetti put it in 1876, late-nineteenth-century western Sicily "was a society whose orders were all founded on the assumption that no public authority exists" (1993, p. 14). Franchetti notes that "the abolition of feudalism, far from decreasing private violence, ended up making it more widespread and 'democratic.'" This analysis also applies to large parts of Calabria. Diverse figures in both regions, ranging from landowners struggling to maintain their quasi-feudal privileges to members of both the urban bourgeoisie and the lower classes seeking social ascent, resorted to violence to protect their interests. Their advocates set up associations and gangs of various types, using violence to promote common and individual interests. Some of them, and particularly those that succeeded in consolidating, are direct ancestors of Cosa Nostra and the 'Ndrangheta.

B. Chinese Triads

The Chinese triads evolved from a variety of organizational forms—variously known as brotherhood, *hui*, secret society, and *kongsi*—developed by non-elite Chinese in South China and Southeast Asia beginning in the seventeenth century. The Tiandihui, from which the name triad derives, is only the most famous of many associations clustered around the notion of fictive kinship. Tiandihui's founding around 1760 makes the contemporary triads the oldest existing organized crime group; however, not all contemporary triads are directly descended from the Tiandihui (Murray 1994).

Tiandihui and many other brotherhoods flourished in contexts in which "the Confucian state and Confucian local elite were either weak or absent" (Ownby 1993, p. 16). In Taiwan and Southeast Asia, then a frontier for thousands of mainland Chinese, the brotherhoods provided mutual aid and protection to young single men who had lost the protection of their lineage, their village, and the Chinese state. In mainland South China, political and economic change produced significant numbers of marginal young men who also found organization on the basis of fictive kinship useful. Unrest caused by protracted and disruptive transition in the late seventeenth century from the ethnic Chinese Ming to the Manchu Qing dynasty was followed in the eighteenth century by rapid population growth in a violent region already pressed for arable land (Ownby 1993, 1996).

In some cases, the brotherhoods were in that period little more than ad hoc survival strategies—some protective, some predatory, some both (Perry 1980, pp. 1–9). In other instances, most prominently in the case of the Tiandihui, the associations facilitated cooperation and organization on a remarkable scale, providing an organizational model for the existing triads. This model was replicated many times within Chinese communities. Both social groups and individuals were for many decades forced to transform themselves in, or join, a triad in order to obtain protection from established triads (Chu 2000, p. 18).

C. Japanese Yakuza

The ancestors of the modern yakuza associations, itinerant bands of Japanese roadside gamblers (known as *bakuto*) and peddlers (*tekiya*), have been active since the early eighteenth century (Kaplan and Dubro 1987). These associations provided structure, protection, and mutual aid to nonelite, disenfranchised young men struggling to survive and to ascend socially while the traditional social order was crumbling at the dawn of the early modern era.

The tekiya were organized according to feudal status, with ranks still adopted by the contemporary yakuza. The associations established control over portable booths at market fairs in temples and shrines. Tekiya bosses controlled not only their younger members but also the allocation of stalls and even the availability of certain goods. They collected rent and protection money and pocketed the difference from the rental payments required by the shrine or temple. They also restricted widespread fraudulent practices and negotiated with each other and feudal lords to prevent or at least limit turf wars.

Bakuto were especially active along Japan's trade routes, such as the Tokaido highway that connected Kyoto, the old capital, with Tokyo and along which nobles and their servants and couriers frequently traveled. Bakuto offered card games and entertainment: the name "yakuza" comes from this tradition and refers to the worst outcome in a card game. Like the tekiya, the bakuto formed associations based on the principle of fictive kinship and a set of strict rules and sanctions, including the practice of cutting the top joints of the little fingers for serious violations. This became a mark of recognition for the whole yakuza (Iwai 1986).

D. American Cosa Nostra

Only the American mafia or Cosa Nostra is comparatively younger. It consolidated as a distinct organization in the 1920s in the favorable breeding ground of Prohibition and political urban machines (Nelli 1976; Jacobs 2020). However, precursors can be traced to the late 1800s (Albanese 2014, pp. 1–2). More importantly, the American Cosa Nostra is an offshoot of the Sicilian Cosa Nostra and thus also has premodern roots.

E. Male-Only Membership

Probably because of their premodern roots, all five mafias, with very few exceptions, admit only males into their ranks (Ciconte 1992, pp. 80–85; Chu 2005, p. 60). Women have nonetheless played important roles in the southern Italian and American mafias by socializing offspring into the mafia subculture and, through marriage, creating ritual kinship ties between biological families within mafia groups (Selmini 2020). With the intensification of law enforcement pressures since the early 1990s, women in southern Italy have become more involved in criminal money-making activities and maintaining business continuity when their husbands, brothers, and sons are imprisoned (Fiandaca 2007; Scaglione 2016, p. 64).

IV. Size

All five mafias have at least a few thousand members and are much larger than other criminal enterprises operating in illegal markets of developed countries. The difference in size among the five mafias, however, is considerable (table 2). The American Cosa Nostra never had more than 3,000 ritually affiliated (or "made") members (President's Commission on Organized Crime 1986a). Chinese triads in the 1950s counted more than 300,000 in Hong Kong alone (Morgan 1960). Many Chinese people, though, joined triads to receive protection and were not criminally active. Although no exact figure can be established, the proportion of Italian American mafia members who did not actively engage in criminal activities was probably much lower.

TABLE 2
Mafias' Size and Geographic Spread

	Sicilian Cosa Nostra	Calabrian 'Ndrangheta	American Cosa Nostra	Japanese Yakuza	Chinese Triads
Peak membership	3,000 (early 1990s)	10,000 (early 1990s)	3,000 (1970s)	184,000 (1963)	300,000 in Hong Kong (1950s); many not criminally active
Most recent membership	2,000 or less (2000s); now unclear	Latest: 10,000 (2009)	Less than 1,000 (2014)	34,500, including associates 18,600 full members (2016)	160,000 (early 1990s; now unclear)
Number of consortia	1 consortium, 90–100 units at peak	1 consortium, composed of about 150 units	1 consortium, 24 units at peak; since 1990s fewer	24 consortia; unclear number of units	14 consortia in Hong Kong (50 in 1990s); number unclear in Taiwan
Size of units	As little as 5–10; at peak, 50	20–300	At peak 200 and 800 associates; now as few as 5–10	Largest is Yamaguchi-gumi, 4,700 members	Hong Kong, Sun Yee On: 25,000 members; Taiwan, Bamboo Union: 10,000 members; most units smaller
Geographic spread	Western Sicily, limited presence in eastern, southern parts; no families outside Sicily; single members / subunits in Europe and Latin America	Southern Calabria; units in northern Calabria, northern Italy, Canada, Australia; single members / subunits in Europe and Latin America	Major cities of Northeast and Midwest; limited presence in West and South; hardly any foreign activity	Throughout Japan; minimal foreign presence and activity	Originally China and Chinese diaspora; since 1949 mostly Hong Kong, Taiwan; cities in Southeast Asia, USA; since 1990s limited presence in China

SOURCE.—Author's elaboration drawing on sources cited in text.

While not all made members are criminally active, made members often cooperate with nonmembers in their profit-making criminal activities. The number of these associates varies depending on the organization and the period and often cannot be estimated with precision. A further, even less clear-cut, circle is composed of relatives, friends, and acquaintances of the made members (Bouchard 2020). As a rule, these supporters do not directly engage in criminal activities with made members but protect the group from external attention and law enforcement investigations and enhance the group's social capital and power, especially at times of elections.

The core memberships of four of the five mafias, the 'Ndrangheta being the exception, have shrunken considerably in recent decades. Only two—the Calabrian 'Ndrangheta and the Chinese triads—ever developed a strong international network.

A. Consortia

According to very precise statistics of the Japanese police, yakuza groups had 184,000 members in 5,216 gangs at their peak in 1963. Since then, there has been a steady decline. Membership stood at approximately 34,500 at the end of 2017 (NPA 2018). Journalistic sources, referring to official data, report that the decline in real members, not counting associates, has been steeper, dropping to 18,100 at the end of 2016 (e.g., Noboru 2018).

By early 2018, the Japanese police identified 24 *boryokudan* groups, which are more properly understood as associations or "syndicates" of groups (Hill 2004). The Yamaguchi-gumi, the largest, founded in 1915, is based in the Osaka-Kobe region and had 4,700 members in early 2018. Membership of the next three largest groups ranged between 2,000 and 2,900. Two, the Inagawa-kai and Sumiyoshi-kai, are based in Tokyo. The third is a splinter of the Yamaguchi-gumi; it separated in 2015. The primacy of the Yamaguchi-gumi is more marked than police data suggest, because many bosses of other syndicates, including the Inagawa-kai, have alliances or brotherhood links with senior Yamaguchi-gumi members (Hill 2014, p. 236). All other boryokudan are much smaller. None had more than 560 members, and six had less than a hundred (NPA 2018, pp. 28–29). Many of the smaller syndicates have lost members. The biggest have become relatively more powerful in recent decades.

Membership estimates of the Chinese triads are far less precise because triads are more loosely organized, spread across several countries, and generally subject to more stringent state pressures than the yakuza. An estimated 300,000 triad members lived in Hong Kong during the 1950s; the local triads were joined by mainland triads, such as the 14K, which relocated after the Chinese Communist Party took power in 1949 (Morgan 1960). Membership in Hong Kong had fallen to roughly 160,000 by the early 1990s, when about 50 triads were active (Chin 2014, p. 220). Overall membership and the number of the triads have further decreased since Communist China took over Hong Kong in 1997. While I was not able to find recent official or scholarly estimates of overall contemporary membership, only 14 of the 50 Hong Kong triads appear to remain active (Chin 2014, p. 220).

Organizations similar to Hong Kong's triads can also be found in Taiwan. They were largely founded by mainland Chinese who followed Chiang Kai-shek to Taiwan in 1949 (Kaplan 1992). The Bamboo United, the Four Seas, and the Celestial Alliance are reputed to be among the most powerful (Chin 2003). Much like the yakuza, triads consist of multiple consortia that operate independently, each consisting of largely autonomous units. The largest triad in Hong Kong is Sun Yee On, which according to media figures has an estimated 25,000 members. The second and third largest are the Wo Group and 14K triads, which are also loose consortia; each has roughly 20,000 members. The largest Taiwanese triad, the Bamboo Union Gang, reportedly had more than 10,000 members at the beginning of the current century (Huang 2007, p. 129). Only a fraction of triad members were and probably still are criminally active. Fijnaut (2014, p. 58) estimates about 30 percent in early twentieth-century Hong Kong, adding that the remaining members joined only to receive protection and to receive help in finding jobs.

Italian and Italian American mafia organizations have always been much smaller. The largest at least since World War II has been the Calabrian 'Ndrangheta. Since the early 1990s, its membership has repeatedly been estimated at about 10,000 made members (e.g., Commissione Antimafia XVI 2010, p. 5; DNA 2017).

The Sicilian and American Cosa Nostras are even smaller. The formal Sicilian membership was estimated at 3,000 members in the mid-1990s and has probably declined to 2,000 or fewer (e.g., Ministero dell'Interno 2012b, 2019). Cosa Nostra has traditionally been much more selective in its recruitment policies than the 'Ndrangheta. It has also been more seriously hit by law enforcement action, and its popular legitimacy has been more seriously challenged (Ministero dell'Interno 2018, 2019).

The American Cosa Nostra had about 3,000 made members at its peak in the 1970s, according to statements by the then director of the FBI to the 1986 President's Commission on Organized Crime (1986*b*, p. 35; Reuter 1995, p. 91). The 1986 estimate was 1,700 made members. More recent estimates place the number at fewer than 1,000 (e.g., Jacobs and Gouldin 1999, p. 176; Albanese 2014, p. 152).

B. Units

Individual Italian and American mafia groups are sometimes larger than most other criminal enterprises active in the illegal markets of developed countries but much smaller than Asian mafia organizations. The largest units among mafias of Italian origin are within the 'Ndrangheta. Units of 250–300 members are not uncommon (Commissione Antimafia XVI 2010, p. 5). Credible estimates of associate numbers are unavailable; they likely vary for each group, depending on its location and the criminal activities it specializes in. There is no doubt, though, that each unit— called *locale* in the 'Ndrangheta slang—is embedded in a much wider circle of relatives, friends, and acquaintances. In 2010, Giuseppe Pignatone, then chief prosecutor of Reggio Calabria, estimated this broader circle at 1,500–2,000 people for a locale of 250 made members (Commissione Antimafia XVI 2010, p. 5).

The most powerful American Cosa Nostra groups, such as the New York Genovese and Gambino families, in their heydays had more than 200 members (US Senate 1988, pp. 776–800). Raab (1998*a*, 1998*b*) estimated that there were four or five associates for each sworn member. In this century, the average numbers of both members and associates have probably declined. Cosa Nostra families in Cleveland, Los Angeles, and Tampa have been dismantled; memberships presumably shrank prior to their ends (Albanese 2014, p. 152).

With few exceptions, Sicilian mafia units have been much smaller. A detailed analysis of the 56 mafia families in the city and province of Palermo, Sicily's capital, carried out jointly in the early 1990s by all Italian police forces, concluded that the average number was about 25. This figure included sworn members and associates (Gruppo Interforze 1993*a*, 1993*b*). If the latter are excluded, many mafia families had fewer than 10 "made" members (Paoli 2003, pp. 28–29). Intensification of law enforcement pressure since the early 1990s, difficulties in recruiting new members (DNA 2017, p. 44), and resulting declines in membership make it unlikely that Sicilian mafia families have become larger.

C. Geographic Spread

There are also considerable differences in geographic spread. With few exceptions, of which creation of the American Cosa Nostra is the most notable, the Sicilian Cosa Nostra has never had expansionary ambitions or established whole units outside Sicily. Cosa Nostra has never even established families in, let alone controlled, the whole island. Its stronghold has always been the western part, especially the provinces of Palermo, Trapani, and Agrigento. In other Sicilian provinces, Cosa Nostra has had only limited presence or been largely absent (Ministero dell'Interno 2012*b*, 2019). For example, it traditionally had only one family in the province of Catania, Sicily's second largest city (Arlacchi 1993). There has never been a Cosa Nostra family in the southern provinces of Ragusa. Outside Sicily, Cosa Nostra has since World War II had only individual made members or subunits, such as a mafia family from central Enna province, in the suburbs of Milan, which was identified in 2016 (Ministero dell'Interno 2019, p. 62).

The Calabrian 'Ndrangheta has a much broader spread. Although most units are rooted in the southern part of Calabria, the 'ndranghetisti has over decades created and recognized units in northern Italy. According to the Commissione Antimafia of the Italian Parliament (2010, p. 5), 500 'ndranghetisti were active there in 2010, divided into about 25 locali (Sciarrone 2009, 2014; Varese 2011; DNA 2017, pp. 19–30). Members also operate in several European countries, primarily Belgium, the Netherlands, Germany, and Spain. Some are descendants of earlier generations of migrants; others have moved in order to hide from Italian law enforcement authorities or oversee wholesale drug shipments from locations closer to points of entry into Europe (KLPD 2011; Europol 2013*b*; Calderoni et al. 2016). Cocaine now primarily enters through the ports of Rotterdam and Antwerp. Spain was earlier also an important transit country and remains the main entry point for Moroccan hashish (EMCDDA and Europol 2019). Several 'ndranghetisti are active in Latin American countries, from which they arrange large-scale cocaine shipments (Gratteri and Nicaso 2018).

Locali have also been established in other countries including Switzerland, Germany, Canada, and Australia (Sergi and Lavorgna 2016; DNA 2017, pp. 19–30). The Canadian and Australian branches can be traced to large migration flows in the early twentieth century, but unlike the American Cosa Nostra, they have not become independent organizations and have remained subordinate to the Calabrian organization (DDA Reggio Calabria 2010).

The American Cosa Nostra's 24 families were primarily located in major metropolitan areas in the Northeast and Midwest, although families were formerly reported in the West and South, and some Cosa Nostra members were heavily involved in development of the casino industry in Las Vegas (Albanese 2014, p. 11; Jacobs 2020). The five most prominent families have always been based in New York. The American Cosa Nostra has never branched out internationally.

The Japanese yakuza never expanded abroad, but its groups are spread throughout Japan. Only since asset forfeiture for organized crime money was authorized in 1999 have yakuza begun investing money abroad. Yakuza are reported to operate in Korea, China, Macau, Hong Kong, and Singapore (Calderón 2012, pp. 158–59).

The Chinese triads have by far the largest international spread. Reflecting migration from mainland China since the sixteenth century, brotherhood associations similar to the triads were established in Malaysia, Borneo, and Singapore. Since the early twentieth century, triads have flourished in Hong Kong, which became their main seat after the Communist Party took power in 1949. Sustained migration flows have continued in more recent times, and triad representatives are today active in numerous countries ranging from Burma to the United States. They have also reentered mainland China. However, they do not occupy a controlling position even in relation to Chinese organized crime (Xia 2006; Chin 2014; Wang 2017).

Mafia organizations are on average much larger than criminal enterprises, but they tend to be rooted and to remain in particular regional or national settings. Even the triads' international spread appears to result more from Chinese migration flows and dramatic upheavals in China and neighboring countries than from expansionary strategies. This is consistent with Varese's (2020) theory that international movements of mafias are rare and highly contingent.

V. Formalized, Complex Structure

All five mafias have formalized, complex internal structures that include ruling bodies in each unit and usually higher level coordinating bodies (table 3). The existence of these ruling bodies sets mafias apart from

TABLE 3
Mafias' Internal Structure

	Sicilian Cosa Nostra	Calabrian 'Ndrangheta	American Cosa Nostra	Japanese Yakuza	Chinese Triads
Segmentary structure	Yes	Yes	Yes	Yes	Yes
Higher coordination body	Higher coordination bodies since 1950s, primarily for regulation of violence; not clear if active	Higher coordination bodies since 1990s, primarily for regulation of violence	Higher coordination bodies since 1930s, primarily for regulation of violence; unclear if active	Centralization since 1960s, three large consortia; partial coordination mechanisms	No coordination or centralization, but selection
Command positions within consortia	NA	NA	NA	Yamaguchi-gumi has bureaucratic headquarters; others lighter structures	Past bureaucratic headquarters dismantled; some triads run by coordinating bodies
Ranks and command positions within unit	Command positions; no ranks in units	Ranks and command positions, each unit	De facto ranks and command positions, each unit	Ranks and command positions, each unit	Ranks and command positions, each unit; sharply simplified

SOURCE.—Author's elaboration drawing on sources cited in text.

the blood families of their leaders and, in a Weberian perspective (Weber [1921] 1978, p. 48), makes them true organizations.

The coordinating bodies are often not fully institutionalized, and in most, mafias have limited authority. Mafias were originally segmentary societies without central political organs and with societal boundaries that coincided with the maximum range of structurally similar units (Smith 1974, p. 98). This organizational model has often been found by anthropologists in simple "primitive societies." It is close to what Catino (2020) calls "clan-based." In other words, mafias are characterized by Durkheim's ([1893] 1964) "mechanical solidarity"; solidarity derives from replication of corporate and cultural forms. Southern Italian mafia defectors have emphasized the idea that each Cosa Nostra family belongs to a larger whole (e.g., Tribunale di Palermo 1989, p. 63).

While the higher level coordinating bodies have limited powers, individual units of all the mafias have well-defined ruling bodies, which are mostly reinforced by internal systems of stratification.

A. Coordination

Higher level coordinating bodies were established in mafias of Italian origin beginning in the 1930s—first in the American Cosa Nostra, then in the 1950s in the Sicilian Cosa Nostra, and during the 1990s in the 'Ndrangheta (Maas 1969, pp. 33–34; Tribunale di Palermo 1985; US Senate 1988; DDA Reggio Calabria 1995). Composed of the most important family chiefs, they are known as "commissions" in the Cosa Nostras and *crimine* in the 'Ndrangheta. These bodies are not comparable to boards of directors of companies; they have rarely had responsibility for planning or coordination of profit-making activities. They were set up primarily to mediate conflicts and regulate use of violence against members of other mafia units and high-level government officials (Catino 2019, pp. 146–56).

Only the 'Ndrangheta's commission remains operative (DDA Reggio Calabria 2010). The two commissions of the Sicilian Cosa Nostra—one coordinating the families of the Palermo province and the other of the whole region—were disbanded in the 1990s. It became too dangerous to assemble the most important members of mafia groups in one place at one time; most commission members were imprisoned. When an attempt was made in 2018 to reestablish a commission in the Palermo province, the new leaders were immediately arrested (Ministero dell'Interno 2018). The existence of a commission comprising four of the five New York City families was proved in the so-called commission case (*United*

States v. Salerno) in 1986, but it is unclear whether it still functions (Albanese 2014; Jacobs 2020). If so, it has limited powers over the families. This suggests that the American Cosa Nostra—like its Sicilian counterpart—has resumed its original segmentary structure.

In Japan, three consortia or "syndicates" (Hill 2003)—the Yamaguchi-gumi, Sumiyoshi-kai, and Inagawa-kai—incorporate more than a third of the yakuza known to the police (NPA 2018). Not least because of tolerance shown by Japanese authorities, the Yamaguchi-gumi is coordinated by a visible headquarters composed of a large number of executive roles and subcommittees that create "a quasi-feudal organizational structure" (Hill 2014, p. 236). In 2007, for example, the headquarters consisted of 93 members. One was the *kumi-chō* (supreme leader), 25 constituted the senior executive cadre, and the remaining 67 were *chokkei kumi-chō* (leaders of powerful groups). The last group comprised bosses of lower level groups, resulting in a pyramidal structure (Hill 2003, p. 69). Decisions of the executive cadre and other relevant information were announced at monthly meetings attended by all members of the headquarters. Control was also exercised through regional blocks consisting of different units within the same geographical area. These were overseen by a designated senior member whose job was to ensure that instructions from the headquarters were relayed to the individual units and that conflicts were resolved amicably.

In other Japanese consortia, such as the Sumiyoshi-kai, though, the central power was traditionally much less controlling: a president was selected by the leaders of the largest and most powerful units; the president's primary task was to adjudicate disputes (Hill 2003). Hill (2014) later observed that Sumiyoshi-kai reorganized to achieve more central control.

No overarching coordinating body has emerged within the yakuza that claims to represent or loosely coordinate all of the syndicates along the lines of the Cosa Nostra and 'Ndrangheta commissions. However, loose associations have attempted to do so on a regional scale, bringing together several consortia. In the Tokyo area, for example, the leaders of the major bakuto consortia, including Sumiyoshi-kai and Inagawa-kai, meet regularly on the twentieth of the month to minimize conflicts and avoid antagonizing government representatives. The leaders also hold regular meetings with representatives of a similar association comprising the Tokyo-based tekiya groups (Hill 2003, pp. 70–71).

Some powerful triads, such as Sun Yee On and Wo Group in Hong Kong and the Bamboo Union Gang in Taiwan, have also at times established higher level coordinating bodies. At least until 1942 they were run by well-structured, visible headquarters similar to the yakuza syndicates. Under the leadership of Shan Chu (the Mountain Master), the triad headquarters consisted of several senior officials and was organized into five departments: general affairs section, recruiting section, organization section, liaison section, and education and welfare section (Morgan 1960). Even then, however, the headquarters' powers were limited and its main functions were to resolve disputes, thus avoiding warfare, and to organize initiations of new members.

Because of increased law enforcement pressures, not even the four largest triad societies active in Hong Kong at the turn of the current century retained formalized and stratified higher level coordinating bodies (Chu 2000, pp. 22–26). In our time, though, a well-organized triad consortium is run by a central committee composed of the most influential and senior officials. The chairman and treasurer are often elected at annual or biannual meetings. The central committee leadership decides promotions, supervises internal discipline, mediates internal and external conflicts, and occasionally runs promotional activities, such as martial arts demonstrations during Chinese festivals. Leaders do not, however, meddle in subordinate units' or members' entrepreneurial activities or regularly share in their gains aside from gifts presented during special festivities. Apparently, though, not all contemporary triads are organized in this way. According to testimonies cited by Chu (2000, p. 29), by the mid-1980s the 14K had no centralized structure and its units operated independently, though they shared the same name and structure and occasionally cooperated.

Yakuza consortia thus have traditionally had much more centralized leadership than the other four mafias. The power of the yakuza headquarters should not, however, be exaggerated. In all five mafias, the individual units have a high degree of autonomy especially in planning and executing profit-making activities. Higher level coordinating bodies or headquarters exert only weak control over individual units or members (Hill 2003, p. 70). That is why it is a mistake to conceive of these organizations as hierarchical, rationally managed, modern bureaucracies as Cressey (1969) did.

B. Ranks and Leaders

The individual units of all the mafia organizations have well-defined ruling bodies—the distinguishing trait of an organization according to Weber ([1921] 1978, p. 48).

The Sicilian and Italian American mafia groups have (or had) basically the same command positions, called by the same or similar names (Cressey 1969; Anderson 1979). Heading each Cosa Nostra family is a representative (*rappresentante*) or family head (*capofamiglia*) who constitutes the highest group authority. The family chief is elected every year, but elections are often a formality, and the most powerful member is easily reelected. The chief has an underboss (*sottocapo*) whom he can choose himself and one or more counselors (*consiglieri*) who are elected by the members. They assist him in the most important decisions and, at the same time, monitor his management of the family. In larger families, the chiefs select one or more unit heads (*capidecina*; *capiregime* in the American mafia) who coordinate units of about 10 people (Anderson 1979; Tribunale di Palermo 1985; Catino 2019, 2020).

The selection procedures and the competencies of the Cosa Nostra ruling bodies derive, in theory, from a principle of direct democracy, the embodiment on a structural level of feelings of equality, solidarity, and fraternity created by fictive kinship bonds and reflected in the lack of formal ranks. However, in many Cosa Nostra families, power within single families has been repeatedly, sometimes for decades, held by shrewd leaders with special military or political skills or by representatives of powerful blood families.

The sizes of some American mafia families favored internal stratification and segmentation. In the late 1980s, for example, the "soldiers" of the Genovese family were divided into 14 regimes, each headed by a chief, with support from the underboss and counselors. Only for the most serious questions could a unit leader talk directly to the family chief. As a result, many rank-and-file members never met their chiefs—an unlikely scenario in Sicily (Maas 1969).

Greater stratification and segmentation characterize the other three mafia organizations. Within each 'Ndrangheta unit, for example, there is both an internal ranking system and a subdivision between a higher and a lower section; only the older, higher ranking members have access to the higher section (DDA Reggio Calabria 1995; Catino 2019). Elections are regularly held to select members of the appropriate ranks to the command positions of each section. As in the Cosa Nostras, elections often confirm preexisting power relations among members and their informal factions.

The Hong Kong triads have simplified their complicated traditional ranking systems, reducing them to three: 426 Red Pole, the rank that now allows a member to run for all ruling positions; 49, the ordinary members; and Blue Lanterns, the new recruits. Despite this simplification, each unit remains "hierarchical" (Chu 2000, p. 29). It is headed by an area boss, who commands 15–20 members and often also commands subordinate juvenile gang members (Chu 2000, pp. 27–28).

There are three overlapping hierarchies within each yakuza family: a formal administrative hierarchy, a hierarchy based on fictive kinship ties, and a hierarchy within the internal groups (Stark 1981, pp. 61–88; Hill 2003, pp. 65–68). The first hierarchy defines members' ranks, command positions, and associated tasks, duties, and privileges. Its five ranks include the family head or boss, senior executives, executives, soldiers, and trainees. The family head is the manager, often aided by one or more advisors. The soldiers are responsible for guard duties, driving, running the office, and supervising apprentices, who are given the most menial tasks (Iwai 1986).

In addition to this formal hierarchy, social bonds are based on the fictive kinship relationships of father-son and brother-brother; these relationships might evolve depending on the success of the younger members. If an executive has more than one "son," he might also form his own internal group, which might develop its own internal hierarchy. Usually composed of fewer than 10 members, such groups tend to manage most day-to-day business.

In the other mafia organizations, despite their complex formal structures, most business activities, except for extortion and the most glaring violent crimes, are conducted not by the families as such but by what anthropologists call "action sets," temporary coalitions that pursue specific goals and disband once their goals are achieved (Blok 1975; Schneider and Schneider 1976). Sometimes a family (especially in organizations such as the Sicilian Cosa Nostra with small families) or one of its subunits runs a legal or illegal business directly. More often, however, members set up short-term illegal enterprises or legal firms with other members, associates, or even nonmembers; these entities remain sharply distinct from the mafia organizations to which the members belong (Jacobs and Gouldin 1999, p. 138; Paoli 2003, pp. 144–48). Yakuza are expected to share some of their profits with their "fathers"—until the 1970s, a percentage, which then became a fixed amount—to prevent cheating (McKenna 1996; Hill 2003, pp. 66–67). Similarly, triad bosses receive payments from members in the form of envelopes stuffed with cash on significant days such as the Chinese New Year (Van Oudenaren 2014). In the Cosa

Nostras and 'Ndrangheta, this practice is less formal, but lower level members running a profitable enterprise are wise (and safer) to share their revenues with the bosses.

VI. Cultural Apparatus

All five mafia organizations have developed a complex cultural apparatus that has few parallels among other criminal enterprises. Only the post-Soviet *vory-v-zakone* and outlaw motorcycle groups employ comparable cultural codes, rituals, norms, and sanctions. The cultural apparatus is meant to create the organization's collective identity, justify its existence, and generate lifelong commitments, new identities, and fictive kinship ties among members (table 4).

A. Status and Fraternization Contracts

Ritual kinship, seemingly odd in contemporary societies, has been a persistently used form of social organization since at least the Middle Ages (Ownby 1996). Clawson (1989, p. 15) points out that "in societies where kinship remained the primary basis of solidarity relations, fraternal association was effective because it used quasi-kin relations to extend bonds of loyalty and obligation beyond the family, to incorporate people into kin networks, or to create new relations having some of the force of kinship." Guilds, journeymen's societies, religious confraternities, village youth brotherhoods, and whole cities were founded on a metaphor of brotherhood; other fictive kin relations, such as godparenthood, played a central role in late medieval and early modern Europe.

Fictive kinship is not peculiar to the Western world. The "father-son" relationship at the core of the yakuza groups has been a pillar of Japanese society since at least the eighteenth century and declined only with Japanese modernization in the last 50 years (Ishino 1953). Hill (2003, p. 68) reports that such relationships existed within the Japanese police. Scholars of Chinese history have stressed a continuum linking secret societies to brotherhoods and widespread use of blood oaths in Chinese society since the seventeenth century (Ownby 1993).

Mafias do not bind their members with a conventional contract as a modern firm or government bureaucracy would do; they are founded on what Max Weber ([1921] 1978, pp. 671–73) called "status and fraternization contracts." Status contracts require lifelong commitment and assumption of a new identity. The first requirement was understood by

TABLE 4

Mafias' Elaborate Cultural Apparatus

	Sicilian Cosa Nostra	Calabrian 'Ndrangheta	American Cosa Nostra	Japanese Yakuza	Chinese Triads
Status and fraternization contracts	Yes	Yes	Yes	Yes	Yes
Initiation rituals	Yes	Yes	Yes	Yes	Yes
Founding myths	Yes	Yes	Yes	Yes	Yes
Membership symbols	No visible membership symbols	Elaborate membership symbols	No visible membership symbols	Elaborate membership symbols	Elaborate membership symbols
Dispute resolution mechanisms	Yes	Yes	Yes	Yes	Yes
Legal code	Nonwritten legal code	Partially written legal code	Nonwritten legal code	Written legal codes	Legal codes, in the past written

SOURCE.—Author's elaboration drawing on sources cited in text.

Judge Giovanni Falcone, who observed that admission to Cosa Nostra "commits a man for all his life. Becoming a member of the mafia is equivalent to being converted to a religion. You never stop being a priest, nor being a mafioso" (Falcone and Padovani 1993, p. 97). In the triads there is the saying "once a triad, always a triad" (Chu 2000, p. 34). An oath new members must swear is: "If I should change my mind and deny my membership to the Hung family [triad], I will be killed by a myriad of swords" (Morgan 1960, pp. 157–60). To ensure that the lifelong commitment is real, mafias test and train prospective members for a long time, sometimes several years (Commissione Antimafia XI 1992, pp. 514–15; DDA Reggio Calabria 1995, pp. 363–64; Hill 2014).

In the yakuza and, to a smaller extent, the 'Ndrangheta and the Chinese triads, the lifelong commitment is expressed with tattoos (Ciconte 1992, pp. 40–42). Yakuza, in particular, often have their whole torso and thighs tattooed through a slow, painful, and expensive process (Seymour 1996, pp. 25–26). Finger amputation is generally performed as a punishment, apology, or demonstration of commitment, but absence of one or more fingertips is a recognizable and permanent yakuza trademark. Police data from the mid-1990s indicated that one-third of all yakuza lacked at least one fingertip (Hill 2014, p. 237).

In the Cosa Nostras and the 'Ndrangheta[10] the assumption of a new identity is centered on the role of "man of honor." The code of honor, traditionally widespread in many premodern Mediterranean societies, requires a man to defend his person and property, including his women, by himself, without the help of law enforcement authorities. Prospective members of the three mafia organizations are sometimes required to prove their honor by committing violent crimes, in the past preferably a murder (Stajano 1992, pp. 71–72; Catino 2015, p. 544). In the Italian and American mafia worlds, the code of honor also implies respect of organization rules and subordination to the mafia family. A related code, omertà, emphasizes the duty to keep the internal affairs of the mafia organization, and in Sicily and the United States its existence, secret (Finckenauer 2001, pp. 1–2; Paoli 2003, pp. 72–75, 108–12).

The first two of three "Commandments of tekiya" adopted by tekiya groups in Japan since the eighteenth century echo these expectations:

---

[10] 'Ndrangheta in Calabrian dialect means "society of the men of honor" (Gratteri and Nicaso 2010).

"Do not touch the wife of another member." This rule is a corollary of the code of honor and was particularly important among tekiya, because, as peddlers, they left their wives alone for months. Similarly, "do not reveal the secrets of the organization to the police" is akin to omertà (Kaplan and Dubro 1987, p. 26).

The third commandment—"keep strict loyalty to the father-son relationship"—indicates that the contract used by mafia organizations, like most status contracts, is also a contract of fraternization. New members are bound to become brothers (or sons) of older members and to share a regime of "generalized reciprocity," which presupposes an altruistic attitude and behavior without expecting any short-term reward (Sahlins 1972, pp. 193–200). Mafia members are obligated to help each other materially and financially when requested or in case of need and unfailingly to honor principles of sincerity and correctness in their interactions; the expectation of reciprocity is left undefined.

In all mafias, the kin-like relationship is established through ritual. Entrance involves a ceremony of affiliation, a true "rite of passage." The ritual marks assumption of the new status of member of a brotherhood. The main steps of the Cosa Nostra ceremonies of initiation are well known: candidates are presented to the family by the "men of honor" responsible for their training and for assessing their criminal reliability. After the family head explains the main rules, each recruit is asked to choose a godfather among those present who then makes a small cut on the index of his right hand so that blood drops on the image of a saint. Finally, the new member swears an oath of faithfulness with this picture burning in his hands (e.g., Falcone and Padovani 1993, pp. 85–97; Jacobs and Gouldin 1999, p. 138).

The initiation rituals traditionally staged by the triads were much more complex and could last as long as 3 days and involve up to 18 steps. The new members completed a mystical journey, recreating the passion of the five founder-members of the fraternity, swore 36 oaths, drank their own blood and a mixture of wine and the blood of all the recruits (pre-HIV), and were taught recognition signs (Morgan 1960). However, simplified ceremonies have become the rule since the 1990s; they contain the basic elements of the traditional ceremonies but seldom last more than an hour (Chu 2000, pp. 32–34). In the yakuza, fictive kinship ties are established through the exchange of sake in the *sakazuki* ceremony, with the share of sake in the participants' cups symbolizing the latter's kinship hierarchy (Hill 2003, p. 67).

Elements of high symbolic salience are employed by all mafia organizations. All, for example, make extensive reference to the iconography and terminology of the dominant local religion. Taoist or Buddhist religious symbols are used in the ceremonies of the Chinese triads and similar groups (Chesneaux 1971; Ownby 1996). In the 'Ndrangheta, the ceremony is called baptism (Ciconte 1992, pp. 32–35). In both southern Italian mafias, the ceremony includes burning the image of a saint in the new member's hands.

Four of the five mafias use blood in their rituals. The symbolism is evident: religious references give a sacral valence and reinforce the ritual's authority. Blood has multiple meanings. It refers to a process of rebirth to which the candidate is called, implies "natural" kinship with all members, and points to the ultimate punishment in case of betrayal. "One goes in and comes out of the Cosa Nostra with blood," the Catanese informant Antonino Calderone was told at the moment of his affiliation. "You will see for yourselves, in a little while, how one enters with blood. And if you leave, you'll leave with blood because you'll be killed" (Arlacchi 1993, p. 68; see also Chu 2000, p. 33).

The kinlike relations are reinforced with symbols and codes drawn from the kinship language. While the basic units of the Sicilian and American Cosa Nostra and the yakuza are called families, such groups are clearly different from members' biological families—no women are allowed—but use of the term evokes and prescribes the cohesion and solidarity of blood ties.

B. Norms, Myths, and Symbols

All mafias have developed normative codes that do not recognize and even oppose state laws. These make them a separate "law community," establishing and enforcing its own "special law" (Weber [1921] 1978, pp. 694–96). A former member of a Sicilian mafia family was, for instance, often told that "Cosa Nostra [does] ... not recognize the authority of state, to which it was and it will always be opposed. ... Our homeland is the family, and it must be defended to the last" (Bettini 1994, pp. 86–88; see Catino 2015).

Like all fully fledged legal orders, mafias' normative codes include "primary" and "secondary" rules, a distinction proposed in the 1960s by H. L. A. Hart (1994). Primary rules establish obligations and require members to do or abstain from particular actions. Some mafias had written codes of such norms (e.g., Morgan 1960; Catino 2015); all have rules that overlap with custom and are thus easier to change. In the Cosa Nostras and the 'Ndrangheta, for example, the prohibition of extramarital affairs progressively fell into disuse along with general changes in cultural norms in their societies (Colaprico and Fazzo 1995, pp. 86–96). Traditional prohibitions of drug trafficking by four of the five mafias (excluding the triads) have likewise been relaxed following repeated violations by members (Hill 2003, pp. 49, 70; Paoli 2003, p. 131).

Mafias also traditionally have secondary rules that prescribe how primary rules can be ascertained, introduced, eliminated, and varied, and their violation conclusively determined. For Hart (1994, p. 94), this marks the passage "from the pre-legal into the legal world." All mafias have developed "rules of adjudication" that empower their ruling bodies (chiefs of single units and higher level coordinating bodies) to make authoritative decisions whether rules have been broken, to resolve disputes, and to impose sanctions. The Yamaguchi-gumi—with its monthly headquarters meetings and formalized procedures for communication of decisions—has clear "rules of change," which specify how new rules can be enacted and old rules eliminated. Written codes, when they were developed, were augmented by "rules of recognition," allowing conclusive identification of primary rules of obligation.[11]

Mafias further support their "imagined communities" (Anderson 1983) through a complex cultural apparatus. They all have founding myths, which portray their founders as Robin Hoods who steal from the rich and care for the poor (Chu 2000, p. 11; Hill 2003, p. 38). The 'Ndrangheta and the Asian mafias, all widely accepted in their communities until well into the second half of the twentieth century, had sophisticated signs of recognition, including passwords, phrases, poems, hand signs, gestures, and seals. Such signs are used much less since the 1990s in all three mafias because they have gone out of fashion and can be easily exploited by police (Chu 2000, pp. 35–37; Gambetta 2011; Hill 2014).

C. Advantages of Fictive Kinship

Fictive kinship ties give mafias flexibility that has no parallel in contemporary business firms in which employment contracts are purposive.

---

[11] See Paoli (2003) for detailed analysis of the normative codes of Cosa Nostra and 'Ndrangheta. For the definition of the three types of secondary rules, see Hart (1994, pp. 91–99).

Mafia units can be exploited in pursuit of any short-term gains sought by their leaders. Subordinates in a regime of generalized reciprocity have no choice whether to execute superiors' orders. Unlike in ordinary commercial contracts, the commitment to a mafia organization is long-term, nonspecific, and so comprehensive that members are expected if ordered to deny family and friendship bonds and to sacrifice their lives. Even today, reliance on status contracts strengthens mafias' multipurpose nature.

In exchange, individual members benefit from the group's collective actions and reputation. The reputation is primarily exploited by members in conduct of licit and illicit businesses. When management of criminal activities (particularly extortion and sometimes drug trafficking) is centralized, proceeds are divided among members. This was fully institutionalized in most Calabrian and some Sicilian mafia groups between the 1970s and 1990s; group chiefs paid regular salaries to all members each month. Many units have a common account to be used to cope with members' exceptional financial needs, pay their legal expenses, support families of the imprisoned or dead members, and occasionally subsidize monthly salaries.

Thus, as in other premodern ritualized relationships (Eisenstadt and Roniger 1984), mafias appear to be characterized by "a peculiar and distinct type of combination of instrumental and solidary relationship, in which the solidarity provides the basic framework, yet within this framework various instrumental considerations, albeit very diffusely defined, are of paramount importance" (Eisenstadt 1956, p. 91). In other words, mafia organizations represent a combination of specific exchange with what is termed "generalized exchange" in anthropological literature. This last expression, coined by Marcel Mauss (1990) and elaborated by Claude Levi-Strauss (1969), distinguishes the nonutilitarian and unconditional relationships necessary to establish conditions of basic trust and solidarity in society and to uphold what Durkheim called the "pre-contractual elements of social life" (Eisenstadt and Roniger 1984). Mafia membership is typified by a crisscrossing of instrumentality and solidarity, of personal selfishness and unconditional involvement. Failure to take account of both sides of this relationship misunderstands its deeper meaning and strength.

Some heavy constraints, though, are also associated with status and fraternization contracts. They are important contributors to mafia organizations' contemporary decline.

VII. Multifunctionality

Throughout their existence, all five mafias have performed a variety of functions, most of which are not related to provision of illegal goods and services (see table 5). If there is a preeminent function, it is provision of mutual aid. The *Procuratore del Re* Lestingi observed in 1884 that the "essential character of the mafia" lies in "its aid without limits and without measure, and even in crimes" (1884, p. 453). Likewise, the Tiandihui's "main purpose was to form pseudo-familial networks among unacquainted people through the rituals of sworn brotherhoods for mutual protection," and "it aimed to offer a worldwide 'life insurance scheme' for its members" (Chu 2000, p. 12; see also Ownby 1996).

Enhancement of members' interests through mutual aid seems always to have been the main "official goal" of mafia organizations. This general aim has been interpreted and applied in many different ways over time. It has been translated into a plurality of "operative goals" across the whole spectrum of legality (Perrow 1961).

A. The Case of the Early Triads

This intermingling of goals and activities is well illustrated by the history of the triads from the eighteenth to the early twentieth century. In Taiwan and southern Fujian province, for example, the Tiandihui operated largely as a rebellious organization in the late eighteenth and early nineteenth centuries, as demonstrated by its key role in Lin Shaungwen's rebellion in Taiwan of 1787–88. In Guangdong province, the Tiandihuit became chiefly a vehicle for robbery, while in western Fujian–eastern Jiainxi region, it intermingled with local cults and appears to have functioned as a form of popular religion (Ownby 1996, p. 26).

In the second half of the nineteenth and the early twentieth centuries, triad societies and their members participated in rebellions against the Qing government such as the Taiping Rebellion of 1850–64 in Guangdong. Sun Yat-Sen's overthrow of the Qing dynasty in 1912 was also heavily supported by overseas triads; Sun Yat-Sen was a member of Kwok On Wui Triad of Honolulu (Chu 2000, p. 15). Contrary to the "primitive revolutionaries" thesis advanced by Jean Chesneaux (1971) and others in the 1960s and 1970s, however, triads cannot be reduced to their engagement with political change (Ownby 1993 and 1996).

A considerable share of triad members and entire triad units engaged throughout their history in profit-making activities. Some were completely legitimate. Triads and other secret societies, for example, played

TABLE 5

Mafias' Multifunctionality

	Sicilian Cosa Nostra	Calabrian 'Ndrangheta	American Cosa Nostra	Japanese Yakuza	Chinese Triads
Commitment to mutual aid	Yes	Yes	Yes	Yes	Yes
Illegal market activities	Heroin smuggling in 1980s; local drug trafficking since then	Drug trafficking since 1980s; since 1990s, large-scale cocaine smuggling	Gambling, loansharking, property crime, heroin trafficking in Northeast	Gambling, prostitution, amphetamine trafficking	Drug trafficking, smuggling of goods and people, counterfeiting, and fraud
Presence in legal economy	Throughout: extortion, involvement in different legal activities; since 1970s: manipulation of public tenders	Throughout: extortion, involvement in different legal activities; since 1970s: manipulation of public tenders	Limited and declining extortion, involvement in different legal activities including casinos and local markets in New York	Throughout: extortion, involvement in different legal activities; since 1980s: real estate and stock markets	Throughout: extortion, involvement in different legal activities; since 1950s: real estate

SOURCE.—Author's elaboration drawing on sources cited in text.

a crucial role in organization of workers in tin mines in the interior of Malaysia. An offshoot of the Tiandihui played a similar role in plantation agriculture in what is now Singapore. Similar brotherhoods known as *kongsis* functioned as mining corporations in western Borneo and Bangka, operating in surprisingly egalitarian ways (Heidhues 1993; Trocki 1993). From the beginning, however, triads and their members also engaged in criminal activities, including salt and opium smuggling, robbery, violence, extortion, and piracy (Sinn 1989, p. 13; Wang 2017, pp. 22–31).

Triads and their members were quick to exploit opportunities at the edge of legality. Soon after the British established a colony on Hong Kong Island in 1842, opportunities arose for triad members who had migrated to Hong Kong from mainland China. Hong Kong became the gateway for two international trades: trafficking of opium from India via Hong Kong to China and trade in Chinese labor to Southeast Asian countries, Australia, and America. The opium trade was legal in Hong Kong and actively promoted by British authorities, but it was illegal in China from the Qing dynasty's first opium suppression edict in 1729 until the end of the Second Opium War in 1858 (Zhou 1999, pp. 12–18). The trade in Chinese "coolies" was also legal in early Hong Kong: triad members often owned or otherwise controlled boardinghouses where coolies stayed prior to shipment overseas. However, boardinghouse owners also extensively engaged in extortions that would be criminal today.

In those same years, though, triad membership provided protection to laborers and peddlers who moved from South China to Hong Kong. Triads arose among natives of specific regions. The Fuk Yee Hing, for example, long exclusively attracted and protected Chiu Chow and Hoklo people from northern Guangdong province. Migrants were often robbed by bandits; many joined triads before arriving in Hong Kong. Once there, the society dealt with employment, welfare, and funeral problems. Of 10,000 estimated members before 1941, less than a third were believed to use triad bonds for other purposes (Chu 2000, p. 17). Other triad societies, like the tekiya in Japan, emerged to protect peddlers. The Hung Shing Wui from Canton united members of the hawking community and monopolized the hawking trade in Hong Kong. In the late nineteenth century other triads were established in Hong Kong to organize and protect specific trades. In 1909 these triads formed the Wo group, which remains one of the main triad consortia (Chu 2000, pp. 17–18).

With time, almost paradoxically, new triads were established to protect their members from victimization by established triads. The Tung

Lok Tong Triad, for example was founded in 1910 by coolies of the government hospital in the Western District of Hong Kong to protect them from extortion by members of the Wo group (Morgan 1960, p. 67). As recently as the 1970s, some trade unions, such as the Kwon Hung Painters' Guild, transformed themselves into fully fledged triads in order to protect their members (Chu 2000, p. 20).

The flexibility and ability of mafia organizations to adapt to changing conditions can be understood when they are seen as functionally diffused organizations. They have been used by their members to achieve a multiplicity of goals and to perform diverse functions. The members of the first secret societies "originally organized for one purpose sometimes found themselves mobilized for different ends, and simultaneously involved in activities where the distinctions between 'legal' and 'illegal,' 'protection' and 'predation,' or 'orthodox' and 'heterodox' blurred" (Murray 1994, p. 2). No single encompassing function or goal, such as the provision of protection (e.g., Gambetta 1992), characterizes mafia organizations throughout their histories.

A functionalist approach is particularly unsuitable for understanding mafia organizations. Given their histories and the criminalization processes they have experienced, they could hardly take part in the process of functional differentiation that has characterized most societies since the early twentieth century. Mafia organizations have always remained functionally diffuse.

B. Profit Maximizers?

Making money was traditionally neither the exclusive nor the main goal for many, if not most, mafia members. Until the 1960s, for example, few members of the Sicilian and Calabrian mafias were substantially wealthy. Most earned their livings by their own legal means and professions, which they had usually started before entering the mafia group (Tribunale di Palermo 1984; Tribunale di Marsiglia 1987). Of 218 mafiosi identified by Questore Sangiorgi at the beginning of the twentieth century, the largest group (45) included employees running and safeguarding agricultural companies, 27 were farmers and farm laborers, 26 were small- to medium-scale landowners, 25 were brokers and merchants, and a smaller number were retailers (Hess 1973, p. 54; Lupo 1993, pp. 83–85). Mafiosi in Sicily and Calabria continued to adhere to value systems of their premodern rural settings and long valued acquisition of respect more than accumulation of wealth.

Only since the 1960s have the Italian mafias undergone an "entrepreneurial transformation" (Arlacchi 1988). Since then, members have invested increasing energies in wealth maximization, adapting to modernization processes in which wealth became the main marker of social position (Arlacchi 1988, pp. 57–61). The entrepreneurial transformation of the American mafia began much earlier, prompted by Prohibition from 1920 to 1933, which created undreamed-of moneymaking opportunities. The bootlegging organization set up by John Torrio and Al Capone in Chicago, for example, grossed at least $60 million annually from beer and other alcohol and maybe as much as $240 million (Nelli 1976, p. 150).

Almost 50 years later, drug trafficking provided the Sicilian mafias with a comparable moneymaking opportunity. Production and export of heroin to the United States proved particularly profitable from the late 1970s to the mid-1980s. Traffickers relied on a network of recently immigrated Sicilian men of honor and members of New York's Bonanno mafia family. Many used pizzerias as fronts. Ensuing prosecutions became known as the Pizza Connection case. This is the largest cooperative scheme ever documented between Sicilian and American Cosa Nostra members (Jacobs, Panarella, and Worthington 1994, pp. 129–66).

C. Illegal Profit-Making Activities

American Cosa Nostra families have never controlled the US drug market or been a major player except concerning heroin in the Northeast. For many decades after Prohibition, gambling provided Italian American mafias with their largest revenues (Nelli 1976, pp. 222–33; Anderson 1979, pp. 50–63; Jacobs 2020). Since the 1980s, legal gambling has been increasingly available, which made illegal gambling much less profitable. American mafiosi have engaged in more traditional criminal activities including loansharking, property crimes such as cargo theft and hijacking, theft of equipment and materials from construction sites, and, since the 1980s, a variety of frauds (Jacobs and Gouldin 1999, pp. 139–55; Finckenauer 2001, pp. 2–3).

Except briefly during the 1980s, Sicilian Cosa Nostra families have not had significant stakes in international drug trafficking (Paoli 2003, pp. 215–16; Europol 2013*b*). Some 'Ndrangheta units have maintained a sustained presence in transcontinental cocaine smuggling and wholesale drug trafficking in western Europe. However, the 'Ndrangheta does not have the "de facto monopoly on the import of Colombian cocaine into Europe" claimed by the Italian Parliamentary Antimafia Commission

(Commissione Antimafia XV 2008, p. 19) and some other Italian observers (e.g., Forgione 2009).

Families and members of the two Cosa Nostras and the 'Ndrangheta have since the 1950s been involved in, sometimes locally controlled, several legitimate markets. Their involvement in the legitimate economy has often involved extortionate practices.

Despite exaggerated "mythical numbers" (Reuter 1984) about mafia profits and activities regularly published in Italy (e.g., Eurispes 2008; SOS Impresa 2012), no one has sufficient data even roughly to estimate mafias' revenues from criminal activities except concerning the yakuza. In 1989, the Japanese police estimated total yakuza income of 1.3 trillion yen ($11.8 billion; Hill 2014, p. 239). Even for the yakuza, though, the estimates are questionable. According to Hill (2003, p. 93), revenues from links with big business were excluded because the subject was too politically sensitive. This and later efforts, however, show the breadth of yakuza activities, which range from unambiguously illegal activities to venture capitalism and securities trading. McNeil and Adelstein (2008) reported that the yakuza had penetrated hundreds of Japan's listed companies and were capable of manipulating the stock prices of many.[12]

Gambling, the traditional bakuto business, is now of marginal economic significance. One analysis of the underground economy estimates that gambling and bookmaking accounted for 7 percent of illegal yakuza income in 2000, down from 21 percent in 1989 (Hill 2014, p. 239). Many yakuza syndicates officially shun drugs, but arrest statistics and police estimates indicate routine engagement in the amphetamine trade. Tamura in the late 1980s showed that yakuza dominated the wholesale trade but that yakuza and nonyakuza dealers were equally involved at street level (Hill 2014, p. 240). Yakuza groups and their members also import foreign sex workers (sometimes tricking them into indentured servitude) and help control them afterward (Hill 2003).

Yakuza have achieved a foothold in the hospitality sector, and many others, through their protection services, provide a mechanism for resolving disputes in a country with inefficient civil courts. In other ways they use their reputations inventively. For example, they might purchase an apartment in a building, then make their presence known in order to induce the owner to buy them out at a premium price. Yakuza groups

---

[12] For an overview of yakuza involvement in financial crime, see Kawasaki (2010).

and skilled members, such as the Inagawa-kai boss Ishii Susumu in the 1980s, have become heavily involved in the financial sector through extortion and collusion with prominent firms (Hill 2003, pp. 182–83).

In recent decades, triads and their members have also engaged in a broad range of criminal activities including drug trafficking, smuggling of other goods and people, counterfeiting, swindles, the sex trade, and money laundering. Triad members often cooperate with legitimate businessmen in legal activities, such as selling new apartments (Chu 2000; Van Oudenaren 2014).

Despite mafias' broad range of profit-making activities, law enforcement sources show that their revenues and market shares have in many cases shrunken considerably (Zhang and Chin 2003; Noboru 2018; Ministero dell'Interno 2019; Jacobs 2020). Causes include increased law enforcement pressure, more effective criminal justice and administrative controls, increased competition from other criminal organizations, poor strategic choices, and organizational weaknesses.

VIII. Political Dominion and Governance

Mafias' goal to exercise political dominion and their ability to provide governance through the use or threat of violence distinguish them from other criminal enterprises (table 6; Schelling 1971). Gambetta described the Sicilian mafia as "a specific economic enterprise, an industry that produces, promotes, and sells private protection" (1992, p. 1). Provision of protection is one of the most important functions historically played by other mafias. Gambetta (1992, p. 6) was unpersuaded by Charles Tilly's functional analogy to the state. Tilly observed that "Sicily's problem is not a shortage but a surfeit of government" (1988, p. xxiii; see also Tilly 1985). In Tilly's view, mafia groups constituted many small proto-states, none of which had succeeded in legitimizing its monopoly of physical force.

A. Violence

Violence, although not often employed against outsiders, is the backbone of mafias' political power and their capacity to sell or impose protection. Violence is used primarily to secure obedience from members and to punish those who betrayed or did not respect their authority. It is also routinely employed to threaten, render inoffensive, or even physically eliminate whoever endangers the power positions and the business activities

TABLE 6

Mafias' Goal of Political Dominion and Governance Services

	Sicilian Cosa Nostra	Calabrian 'Ndrangheta	American Cosa Nostra	Japanese Yakuza	Chinese Triads
Political dominion	De facto local political dominion until 1960s; less success since then	De facto local political dominion but with declining success	No ambition to exercise political dominion; control of trade unions in 1960–80s	De facto local political dominion	Political dominion until 1949 (China) and 1980s (HK); since then decline and disruption
Protection services	Protection/extortion, legal and illegal markets	Protection/extortion, legal and illegal markets	Protection/extortion, legal and illegal markets	Protection/extortion, legal and illegal markets	Protection/extortion, legal and illegal markets
Control of criminal world	No control of criminal world even within strongholds	Control of criminal world within strongholds	No control of criminal world even within strongholds	Seeming control of criminal world	No control of criminal world even in Hong Kong at least since 1990s
Timing and extent of violence	Local peaks of violence in 1980–90s, including "excellent murders"; strong decline since then	Local peaks of violence in 1980–90s; strong decline since then, only inward-oriented	Very limited use of violence, only inward-oriented	Very limited use of violence, only inward-oriented	Very limited use of violence, only inward-oriented

SOURCE.—Author's elaboration drawing on sources cited in text.

of the organizations, their units, or their members. Through effective threats and selective use of violence, mafias have long tried—with substantial success—to impose their will on their home territories. In Weberian terms, they began as "voluntary associations," claiming authority only over voluntary members, but often acted as "compulsory organizations" whose legal order is imposed on outsiders ([1921] 1978, p. 52).

Mafias can be regarded as political organizations that guarantee the continuation and validity of their own legal order within a territory by means of threats and use of force (Weber [1921] 1978, p. 54). Each Cosa Nostra and 'Ndrangheta unit claims sovereignty over a well-defined territory, which usually corresponds to a village or a city district. The Sicilian mafia defector Leonardo Messina explained to the Parliamentary Antimafia Commission: "You must keep in mind that the families have their own businesses and that these concern everything related to the territory of the families themselves. For example, if in the community of Rome there were a family, everything that belongs to the community would interest it, whether politics, public works, extortions, drug trafficking, et cetera. In practice, the family is sovereign, it controls everything that happens on that territory" (Commissione Antimafia XI 1992, p. 516).

Although many mafia rules are no longer systematically enforced, Sicilian and Calabrian mafia groups exercise a form of sovereignty through a generalized system of extortion. They tax many, if not most, productive activities carried out within their territories. They do not hesitate to intervene when asked to mediate conflicts, guarantee property rights, and enforce rules consistent with their own legal order, such as those concerning female honor (Paoli 2003, pp. 154–72). Contemporary men of honor take these duties seriously. Giovanni Brusca, a high-level Cosa Nostra member who became a mafia witness, recounts that he "helped lots of people recover their cars." If the stolen vehicle had already been taken apart, his men would steal another of the same model and color in order to satisfy the request for help (Lodato 1999, p. 73).

Southern Italian mafia families prefer to achieve their aims by colluding with politicians, but some, particularly in the Cosa Nostra, have killed state officials or representatives who posed threats or failed to honor corrupt agreements. Between the late 1970s and the early 1990s, Cosa Nostra assassinated dozens of policemen, prosecutors, judges, and politicians. The 'Ndrangheta coalesced with right-wing political groups in protests in Reggio Calabria in 1970 (Ciconte 1992). In December

1984, Cosa Nostra bombed an express train from Naples to Milan, killing 16 and wounding 266, in order to deflect law enforcement and public attention from antimafia investigations by Judge Giovanni Falcone (Höbel and Iannicelli 2006).

Cosa Nostra's challenge to state power climaxed in 1992–93. Palermitan judges Giovanni Falcone and Paolo Borsellino were murdered in two spectacular bomb explosions in 1992. In 1993, to demonstrate its national power, Cosa Nostra organized bombings in Rome, Florence, and Milan (Stille 1995). Since then southern Italian mafia groups have realized that extreme violence against outsiders is not in their own best interests and have generally abstained from it.

Faced with much stronger and less accommodating state authorities, American Cosa Nostra families never dared kill state representatives (Jacobs 2020). Except for waves of blackmail allegedly orchestrated by the Mano Nera among Italian migrants early in the twentieth century, American mafia families have never managed to impose systematic extortion systems even within Italian communities (e.g., Nelli 1976, pp. 69–100; Jacobs 2020).

American Cosa Nostra families nonetheless exercised considerable power through labor racketeering. This activity, virtually unknown in Italy, is the closest substitute to the political power exerted by Italian mafiosi in their local areas. A former member of New York's most powerful mafia family recalls, "We got our money from gambling but our real power, our real strength came from the unions. . . . In some cases we got money from our dealing with the unions, in some cases we got favors such as jobs for friends and relatives, but more importantly, in all cases we got power over every businessman in New York" (US Senate 1988, p. 225).

Union power was frequently turned into profit, as Cosa Nostra members embezzled and defrauded the unions and their pension and welfare funds, sold labor peace, took payoffs in exchange for sweetheart contracts, and used their leverage on unions to obtain ownership interests in businesses and operate business cartels. Cosa Nostra's influence in the Laborer's International Union of North America, for example, guaranteed a powerful presence in the construction industry, especially in New York and Chicago (President's Commission on Organized Crime 1986b; Reuter 1987; Goldstock et al. 1990).

Especially in historic Chinese communities in frontier regions of Southeast Asia, the political power of Tiandihui and other brotherhoods was less restrained than that of their Italian counterparts. According to Trocki (1993, p. 93): "There was no "secret society" in the Lanfang, Thaikong, or the other Borneo *kongsis*, secrecy being unnecessary in a community made up entirely of Chinese members and dominated by the Tiandihui. Whether or not there was a secret ritual, there was certainly ritual sanctifying the oaths of brotherhoods that bound the entire *kongsi* together. Secrecy became necessary only when the Chinese lived near or under the control of an actual state authority."

Ngee Heng, "the original Chinese institution in Singapore," organized the local pepper and medicinal herb economy and maintained order among Chinese migrants. Singapore became a British colony in 1819, but Ngee Heng "exercise[d] nearly supreme power" in the countryside until at least the mid-nineteenth century. Its economic power and political authority transcended colonial boundaries and extended to neighboring regions controlled by the Dutch and Malay (Trocki 1993).

Even when triad societies became formally illegal, at different times in different places, they performed political and economic functions in Chinese diaspora communities and in mainland China until the 1949 Communist takeover. The Green Gang, a Tiandihui offshoot, until the 1930s exercised political and unprecedented economic power in Shanghai, which had become China's main commercial and industrial center in the late nineteenth century. The two foreign jurisdictions within Shanghai, the International Settlement and the French Concession, adopted the strategy of "using a thief to catch a thief ... police officers recruited the most powerful and successful gangsters into their detective squads" (Martin 1996, p. 33). Huang Jinrong, a Green Gang boss, made a career in the 1920s in the French Concession police force and enabled it to reduce local crime rates considerably. Other gang bosses diverted police action from themselves and their gangs and dominated the criminal underworld and its two most profitable illegal activities, gambling and opium sales (Martin 1996).

The triads' power in mainland China was ended by the Japanese invasion of 1937 and the Communist takeover of 1949, but their political and economic power in Hong Kong persisted longer. Up to the 1970s they provided extensive governance services to Chinese migrants from the mainland. Triads provided a modicum of order in Kowloon District and other socially disorganized areas of the city (Huang 2007).

Since the 1970s, though, the triads' power in Hong Kong has substantially declined (Chin 1996; Chu 2000), though triad members use the remnants of their political power when they can. Low-level affiliates were paid to attack prodemocracy protestors in October 2014 (Varese and Wong 2018). Triad members attacked antigovernment protesters again in July 2019, allegedly in collusion with the police (Ramzy 2019).

Yakuza groups have not always had strong connections to specific territories (Stark 1981; Kaplan and Dubro 1987; Hill 2003, 2014), Nonetheless, early yakuza groups protected their members and as early as the mid-eighteenth century guaranteed safety and order in open-air markets and along the highways, often at the request of local religious authorities (Hill 2003, p. 37). Yakuza have remained in the business of protection in many legal and illegal markets.

Clear separation of government and business is a modern development. Before the modern period, it was otherwise (Schumpeter 1981, pp. 169, 201). Separation of force-using enterprises from profit-seeking enterprises occurred at different times in different places. In the case of mafias, that differentiation has only minimally occurred. The mafias emerged in contexts in which the separation had not yet occurred and, because of their criminalization, have not taken part in the later process of differentiation.

B. Protection Rackets and Legal Markets

Units or members of mafias have repeatedly been able to gain shares, and sometimes control, of legal markets by use of extortion. Only in its simplest form does extortion involve transfer of money. Often it involves payments in kind, such as purchase of unnecessary protection services or of goods at higher prices or forced participation in a company or public contract.

Beginning in the 1950s, mafia members—first in Sicily and then in Calabria—established building companies to gain subcontracts for clearance of major public works sites; their ambitions grew in subsequent decades. In the 1980s building companies close to mafia families secured large shares of public work contracts by entering into corrupt agreements with governmental and building company personnel (e.g., Paoli 2003, pp. 147–48).

Thanks to better government controls, Italian mafia groups' grip on large building projects seems to have declined (La Spina 2014). Both criminal justice system investigations (e.g., Tribunale di Milano 2010) and scholarly studies of 'Ndrangheta settlements in northern Italy (Sciarrone 2009, 2014; Varese 2011) show that mafia families can no longer manipulate assignment processes for large public tenders, as they did especially in Sicily in the 1980s (Tribunale di Palermo 1991). Instead, they influence assignment of relatively small projects, or their firms perform relatively minor tasks in large infrastructure projects.

However, the families' reach has diversified and includes public services ranging from garbage collection and disposal to health sector procurement (DDA Calabria 2010). The combination of violence and profits from drug trafficking has enabled some mafia groups to control local market sectors. In the 1970s and 1980s, mafia groups in parts of Sicily controlled the local supply of cement. In the 1990s, 'Ndrangheta groups monopolized the meat sector in Reggio Calabria (Tribunale di Reggio Calabria 1994, pp. 124–26; DDA Reggio Calabria 2010, pp. 2083–580). Mafia groups are entering new sectors such as alternative energy. In 2013 a high-profile wind energy entrepreneur was identified as a straw man for an important Cosa Nostra boss; his companies and properties, allegedly worth over €1.3 billion, were seized (Palazzolo 2013).

Italian mafias have not been able to monopolize any sector of the legal or illegal economies outside of southern Italy or even in any region of southern Italy (Europol 2013*b*; Paoli 2014). Cosa Nostra's power is not unchallenged even within its strongholds. Because of the rigidity of their recruitment policies, Cosa Nostra families often find themselves at a disadvantage with local competitors and are unable to control the entire underworld (Lodato 1999, p. 67). Even in Palermo, Cosa Nostra has tolerated the consolidation of several Nigerian crime groups that run retail drug sales and exploit prostitution in several neighborhoods (Patanè 2019).

Many contemporary yakuza activities can best be analyzed as forms of protection. Yakuza groups impose protection on street vendors and the whole hospitality sector, which includes restaurants, nightclubs, hostess bars, snack joints, and sexual service establishments. In the 1980s and 1990s, two-thirds of bars, clubs, and restaurants were paying for protection in monthly amounts varying between a few hundred dollars and $10,000 (Hill 2003, pp. 94–96). Yakuza groups and members also engage in labor brokering, particularly in the construction industry. Like Italian mafia families, they extort protection fees from construction companies, own their own companies, and participate in rigging bids. Given the long-standing inefficiency of Japanese civil courts (Milhaupt and West 2000), yakuza offer different forms of extralegal fixing, including debt collection and bankruptcy management. Sometimes they engineer civil disputes as pretexts for compensation; the practice is widespread but difficult to prosecute because victims, recognizing yakuza insignia, often pay without threats being made.

The triads have throughout their history provided effective protection services in both illegal and legal markets. The Sanxin gonksi, founded in 1918 by three Shanghai tycoons, controlled opium sales in the French Concession and the International Settlement and dominated the trade in other parts of the city and South China. Functioning like an insurance company, the Sanxin Company provided effective protection to opium traders in exchange for a 10 percent protection fee. It earned about Ch $56 million per year, "equating to 14–20 percent of the total state revenue" (Wang 2017, p. 419). The owners also acquired important stakes and influence in banking, shipping, and food supply (Martin 1996).

C. The Violence Paradox

The paradox is that mafias have exercised political dominion and imposed protection rackets effectively, while using violence sparingly. All have further restricted their use of violence in recent years.

The yakuza, in a country with exceptionally low homicide rates, has repeatedly been accused of staging mafia wars. The total number of homicides that can be attributed to it, however, is tiny. The most serious intergang war lasted over 5 years (1985–89) and involved 25 deaths and 70 injuries. Hill (2004, p. 109) notes that "between 1992 and 2001 the average number of fatalities and injuries due to yakuza inter-gang conflict were 3.1 and 11.5." Rankin (2012a) reported a sharp decline in yakuza-related shooting incidents from 2000 to 2011; even in 2000 the number was less than 200. Even the split within the Yamaguchi-gumi since August 2015 has not caused a gang war. Only about a hundred violent incidents had been reported by the Japanese police as of October 2017. Most were minor. There was one murder (Nippon.com 2017). The modern Hong Kong triads likewise, reflecting the society in which they operate, make little use of violence and possess few firearms (Chu 2000).

Use of violence by the American Cosa Nostra is rarely necessary, especially against people who are not professional criminals. Several mafia bosses, though, were killed in the 1990s in interfamily conflicts (Jacobs 2020). The Sicilian Cosa Nostra and the 'Ndrangheta probably used violence most unrestrainedly until the early 1990s, but that too has drastically declined. Sicily recorded no mafia murders in 2016, down from 253 in 1991. Calabria had three mafia murders in 2015, down from 165 in 1991 (ISTAT, various years). These spectacular reductions are related to mafias' declining popular legitimacy and decreased tolerance by state institutions.

IX. Popular Legitimacy and Power-Sharing Agreements
With the partial exception of the America Cosa Nostra, all mafia organizations long enjoyed considerable degrees of popular legitimacy. Their political power was acknowledged by state representatives and even state authorities (table 7). Mafias' protection and mediation services effectively met needs in the population, at least partly substituting for an absent or weakened state. Those services and the resonance of their subcultures with the values and norms of the larger societies in which they operated helped them consolidate their popular legitimacy for many decades, including today in parts of southern Italy and Japan.

Beginning at different times mostly during the twentieth century, mafias have begun losing—or largely lost—their popular legitimacy. This process was fostered and reinforced by more punitive antimafia laws and intensified law enforcement. Profit-making and governance activities have been curbed, and corrupt exchanges with politicians and government officials have become riskier, more fragile, more secretive, and rarer.

A. The Triads
The local power of the Tiandihui and similar brotherhoods was long accepted by British and other European colonial powers. The British in Malaya employed secret society headmen in a form of "indirect rule" until the 1890s, "as if they were chiefs in a tribal society" (Ownby 1993, p. 12). Once outlawed, the brotherhoods began to decline and to lose popular legitimacy and market control (Ownby 1993, pp. 19–20). The process was accelerated by establishment of opium monopolies, a general decline in opium consumption (Dikötter, Laamann, and Zhou 2004), and decolonization.

The Qing government in mainland China was much less tolerant of triads and other secret societies than were colonial authorities in Southeast Asia. It legislated against the Tiandihui as early as 1792 (Chu 2000, p. 135), but was largely unable to enforce the prohibition in the more anarchic southern part of the country (Murray 1994, pp. 28–37). In Shanghai the colonial authorities cooperated closely and openly with the heads of the Green Gang (Martin 1996).

A similar pattern of formal proscription coupled with de facto acquiescence and open cooperation occurred in Hong Kong. The colonial government criminalized triad societies in 1845, 3 years after the British took possession (Chu 2000, p. 135). However, the colonial government

TABLE 7

Mafias' Popular Legitimacy and Power-Sharing Agreements with State Authorities

Sicilian Cosa Nostra	Calabrian 'Ndrangheta	American Cosa Nostra	Japanese Yakuza	Chinese Triads
Popular legitimacy in the past; decline since 1960s	Popular legitimacy in the past; decline since 1960s	Limited and declining popular legitimacy since 1940s	Popular legitimacy in past; decline since 2000s	Popular legitimacy in Chinese communities in the past; decline since 1990s
De facto power-sharing with local state representatives in strongholds; decline in extent and legitimacy since 1980s	De facto power-sharing with local state representatives in strongholds; decline in extent and legitimacy since 1990s	De facto power-sharing with local state representatives in big cities until 1940s; between 1950 and 1980s, control of labor unions	Quasi-public power-sharing agreements with local governments and full legality until 2001; since then regulated	Power-sharing with local governments; de facto or full legality until early 20th century in European colonies, 1949 in China, and 1970s in Hong Kong

SOURCE.—Author's elaboration drawing on sources cited in text.

attitude toward the triads was as ambiguous and tolerant as those of European colonial authorities elsewhere, and lasted much longer. Until the 1960s and early 1970s, there was extensive corruption among the Hong Kong police. One third of Chinese police officers in Hong Kong in the early 1970s were estimated to be triad members (Booth 1990); the favors they granted the triads were often authorized by their British supervisors. Chu (2000) argues that the triads were "licensed" by corrupt police officers and that this allowed them to control some legal markets and divide and maintain their territories. This is consistent with the model developed by Schelling (1967) in which criminal organizations collect rents generated by monopoly control by corrupt police.

Since the mid-1970s, corruption in Hong Kong has declined dramatically. The Independent Commission against Corruption, established in 1974, effectively curbed public corruption, making Hong Kong one of the least corrupt places in the world; this has continued under Chinese sovereignty since 1997 (TI 2019). Triads have maintained their political power longer in Taiwan. In the 1980s, they were able to manipulate the outcomes of local elections; current and past members have been elected to national and local public office (Zhang and Chin 2003). Baum (1996) questioned whether Taiwan was ruled by gangsters.

B. The Italian Mafias

Italian mafia organizations have continuously been embedded in backward, often rural societies at the periphery of the world system. They long performed quasi-state functions, providing protection and mediation services and having greater legitimacy than state authorities. It was common, especially in inland Sicily, to go to mafia chiefs to recover stolen property, especially cattle, which were the most precious property (e.g., Alongi 1977, pp. 82–96). Mafia mediation was usually more effective than any police intervention, something recognized even by the "Iron Prefect," Cesare Mori (1993, pp. 72–73), who conducted ruthless antimafia campaigns during the first 10 years of the fascist regime. The mafia groups enforced norms inspired by the code of honor that were widespread in society at large but not recognized by the state. They intervened in order to restore the honor of a woman who had been seduced or to preserve her virginity (Hess 1973, pp. 137–38; see also Ciconte 1992, pp. 220–22). Mafia groups' legitimacy, especially in Calabria, meant that they had no need to hide themselves long after the end of World War II (Alvaro 1955; Ciconte 2011; Dimico, Isopi, and Olsson 2017, pp. 1096–97).

After initial unsuccessful attempts until 1876 to crack down on mafia groups, Italian ruling classes came to terms with mafia representatives. This was reinforced by progressive extension of the suffrage, which made southern votes crucial to defend the northern bourgeoisie's power, which was threatened by workers' and peasants' protests and by the rise of the Socialist and Popular parties. Mafia representatives were openly supported by most local state representatives, including even the prefects, the direct representatives of the central government (Salvemini 1962).

Inclusion within political networks was facilitated by most mafia chiefs, especially in Sicily. They only rarely openly opposed state institutions or publicly promoted noncompliance with state laws. Government agencies condemned mafia violence and occasionally responded fiercely to its most violent manifestations. As a rule, however, they came to terms with mafia power and effectively delegated the maintenance of public order in areas of western Sicily and southern Calabria to it. The state's authority was weak, and the personal safety of state officials was in danger. At least through the mid-twentieth century, many mafia chiefs were protected by state acquiescence (Commissione Antimafia XI 1993, p. 54). Even the Military Allied Government that occupied southern Italy in 1943 appointed numerous mafia chiefs as mayors in western Sicily and the province of Reggio Calabria (Renda 1987, pp. 15–97).

After World War II, many mafia bosses, particularly in Sicily, were considered by politicians in the dominant Christian Democracy party to be respectable and suitable partners; they were valued for their ability to deliver votes. Giulio Andreotti symbolizes these "evil pacts." He was one of the most important Italian politicians in the postwar period, served in parliament from 1948 until 2013, was prime minister seven times, and was a government minister countless times. In 2004 Italy's Supreme Court concluded that he collaborated with Cosa Nostra until 1980; he could not be convicted because the statute of limitations had expired (Lupo 1996; Santino 1997; Corte Suprema di Cassazione 2004).

In our time, mafia bosses have little difficulty finding hidden allies among local politicians who want their electoral support. This is evidenced by government efforts to control mafia corruption. Between 1991 and June 2019, more than 249 municipal councils were dismissed because of mafia connections, more than 60 of them two or three times (Avviso Pubblico 2019). The council of Reggio Calabria, Calabria's most populous was dismissed in 2012. The 'Ndrangheta's political influence in southern Calabria is particularly strong. Mafia members, their relatives, and associates make up 10–20 percent of the local population in the province of Reggio Calabria. They control up to 40 percent of the votes in many small and medium-sized municipalities (Arlacchi 1988, pp. 137–40; Commissione Antimafia XVI 2010).

Mafia groups' political power is not only local. Numerous investigations in Calabria and Sicily demonstrate that regional and national politicians continue to accept mafia electoral support in exchange for favors. Totò Cuffaro, a former regional president, was sentenced in 2011 to 7 years imprisonment for abetting Cosa Nostra (Corte Suprema di Cassazione 2011; Bianconi 2015). Marcello Dell'Utri and Amedeo Matacena, former members of the European and Italian parliaments for Silvio Berlusconi's party Forza Italia, were convicted respectively of abetting Cosa Nostra and 'Ndrangheta (*Huffington Post* 2014; Candito 2017).

Politicians could not, however, protect Cosa Nostra when it openly challenged state power in the early 1990s by killing Judges Falcone and Borsellino and bombing Rome, Florence, and Milan (Stille 1995). Those events were a turning point. They triggered unprecedented intensification of law enforcement action, as Bernardo Provenzano, then leader of Cosa Nostra, acknowledged in a wiretapped conversation (Ministero dell'Interno 2001, p. 10). Almost all Sicilian mafia bosses were arrested, as were many, if not most, of their associates. Between 1992 and June 2018, the Direzione Investigativa Antimafia (DIA; Ministero dell'Interno 2019) issued several thousand arrest warrants for the offense of membership in a mafia organization. The DIA figures imply that the likelihood of being arrested has become very high, especially since three other police agencies also engage in antimafia activities. Most arrested mafia members were convicted and given long prison sentences. As of June 2013, 6,758 people were in prison for involvement in mafia-type organizations (Ministero della Giustizia 2013; 416*bis*). Of these, 645 of them were subject in December 2009 to a special high-security incarceration regime for mafia members (Ministero della Giustizia 2011). The financial drain has also been unprecedented. DIA (2013) alone seized assets worth €11 billion from mafia groups between 1992 and 2011 and confiscated €1.8 billion. Prosecutors charged both mafia members and their political protectors.

A broad long-term process of mafia delegitimization began after World War II. Initiated by small, primarily Sicilian, elites, it gained popular support after the murder in Palermo in 1982 of General Dalla Chiesa. New generations of criminal justice officials who were trained during and after the 1968 Cultural Revolution have played crucial roles (Ginsborg 1998). They rejected traditional acquiescence to local politicians and mafia leaders' power-sharing and took the lead in antimafia investigations and trials. Members included Giovanni Falcone, Paolo Borsellino, and other investigative judges who wrote the indictment for the first *maxiprocesso* in 1984–85. This case proved for the first time the existence of the Sicilian Cosa Nostra and led to the conviction of over 400 of its members (Tribunale di Palermo 1987).

The antimafia movement has surged since the early 1990s, mobilizing large numbers of people in Sicily and, to a lesser extent, in other southern regions. Important new participants included the Italian and Sicilian Employers' Associations and the Catholic Church, which had previously remained silent. Numerous antimafia and antiracketeering associations were established (Santino 2000; Libera 2020). Traditional mafia values of honor and omertà no longer attract public supporters. Even children of mafia bosses publicly oppose the mafia (Arlacchi 2010, p. 268).

C. The American Cosa Nostra

American Cosa Nostra's political power was never as widespread, effective, or legitimate as the Sicilian mafia's. Traditional mafia subculture found much less resonance in America than in southern Italy. American mafiosi were too few and too scattered to achieve political dominion. Except for New York, few cities contained sufficiently high concentrations of Italian immigrants over whom mafia families could exert political dominion. Consolidation of power was made especially difficult by high population turnover; newcomers from overseas successively replaced earlier arrivals who moved away. Migrants came from all parts of Italy, and many were unwilling to recognize mafia claims; most had not encountered mafias at home. Mafiosi were occasionally asked to resolve disputes and mediate conflicts but never gained the prestige and influence of mafiosi in Italy (Nelli 1976, pp. 37, 137).

Tolerance of and collusion with mafias by American public authorities have been more limited than in Italy. Cosa Nostra leaders in New York, Boston, and Chicago exerted considerable influence on politicians, politics, and the police from the 1920s through World War II (Nelli 1976, pp. 190–93; Jacobs and Gouldin 1999, p. 156). However, their influence declined rapidly as urban machines disappeared and federal law enforcement agencies attacked corrupt relationships between mafiosi and local police (Reuter 1995). American Cosa Nostra members since the 1970s have been unable to rely on strong connections with high-ranking politicians and government officials. Since the 1980s they have been hard hit by relentless criminal investigations and administrative reforms (Jacobs

1999). Almost all leading Cosa Nostra figures of the 1980s and 1990s are in prison serving lengthy sentences or life without parole. Prospective bosses have little likelihood of reviving illicit enterprises. Cosa Nostra progressively lost the allure that it had had among Italian Americans (Finckenauer 2001, p. 1).

D. The Yakuza

Yakuza groups have long enjoyed considerable popular legitimacy. Milhaupt and West (2000), for example, showed that lack of efficient legal mechanisms for conflict resolution created a demand for a "dark side of private ordering, " a necessary evil, that yakuza provided. Through the early 1990s, yakuza's services were highly valued in business sectors most affected by Japan's economic bubble. High-ranking yakuza supplied money to financial companies at short notice when it was really needed, and in the real estate industry acquired land within tight time limits and provided workers for dangerous jobs (Hirotoshi 2017).

The yakuza has not been fully criminalized. Yakuza groups were fully legal until 1991; they had phone listings and official offices, whose entrances bore the group name and emblem (Kaplan and Dubro 1987; Seymour 1996). Yakuza groups continue today to be regulated rather than fully criminalized. This does not mean, though, that there have been no ups and downs in relations with state authorities.

Japan's first modern government, the Meiji that defeated the feudal regime, initially prohibited gambling and fought the bakuto groups, even though some had supported the Meiji overthrow of the Tokugawa shogunate. Government hostility, however, did not last long, and controls on gambling were soon relaxed. Faced with an increasingly confrontational labor movement, both governments and industrialists sought help from bakuto and tekiya groups in breaking strikes and assuring labor acquiescence. As a result, yakuza developed links with right-wing groups, nationalistic politicians, and military officials. However, those contacts did not protect many yakuza from law enforcement targeting during World War II when full mobilization of the economy made yakuza's labor market controls unnecessary.

Yakuza came back immediately after World War II. Resources were scarce, and state capacities had collapsed. Only tekiya and to a lesser extent bakuto groups had the skills and contacts to create and control black markets that supplied food to millions of Japanese. Weakened by American occupying forces, the Japanese police lacked means to challenge yakuza's power; a 1946 ordinance granted yakuza jurisdiction over the

Tokyo markets (Hill 2004, p. 44). Elsewhere, too, yakuza were given free rein. In Nagahama, the local yakuza boss sat in the city council and served as head of the city's police commission. Police forces in many other towns depended on donations, including from yakuza, to operate (Hill 2004, p. 54).

Once fear of communism cooled American resolve to purge right-wing extremists from Japan's government and business elites, yakuza leaders "became an integral part of a conservative nexus that was a rein-carnation of the prewar nationalist version [of violent political support groups]" (Siniawer 2008, p. 150). Conservative politicians, right-wing extremists, and yakuza formed anticommunist organizations similar to those in prewar times. In 1952, senior conservative politicians enlisted yakuza to protect the Diet building against left-wing protestors trying to prevent passage of the Subversive Activities Bill. In 1959 and 1960 yakuza helped curb left-wing demonstrations intended to block passage of a revised security treaty with the United States. When, after the treaty was ratified, rioting threatened to disrupt a planned visit by US President Dwight Eisenhower, Tokyo yakuza and right-wing groups were re-cruited to protect him (Kaplan and Dubro 1987, pp. 104–7; Siniawer 2008, pp. 166–68).

Yakuza's links with high-level politicians in the 1950s and 1960s were open and intense. The relationship was promoted by Yoshio Kodama, said to have been "perhaps the most powerful single individual within the LDP" (Kaplan and Dubro 1987, p. 84), The LDP or Liberal Dem-ocratic Party uninterruptedly ruled Japan in the second half of the twen-tieth century. Politicians profited from yakuza support in many ways: raising funds, organizing voters, and discrediting opponents. They re-paid such favors through high-level protection and contacts. In 1971 former Prime Minister Kishi and former Education Minister Kakamura guaranteed bail for a Yamaguchi-gumi boss arrested for murder (Kaplan and Dubro 1987, p. 145).

Since the 1970s, and especially since the Lockheed bribery scandal in 1976 that led to Kodama's fall, politicians' contacts with yakuza have be-come more secretive. They still occur, though, and numerous national politicians including cabinet ministers have been caught in recent de-cades in transactions with prominent yakuza (Hill 2004). In 1987, for ex-ample, Takeshita Noboru and Kanemaru Shin, two of the most impor-tant politicians in Japan, sought help from Ishii of the Inagawa-kai in silencing a right-wing organization that was undermining Takeshita's campaign to become prime minister. Such corrupt exchanges, once generally known, have become scandals and led to the downfall of the politicians involved, but high-level contacts persist. As of 2008, at least six LDP cabinet ministers had yakuza links (Hill 2014).

Japan's mafia organizations did not place all bets on a single political party. Before the 2009 election, the Yamaguchi-gumi headquarters instructed its branches to support the Democratic Party of Japan. This effectively defeated LDP and ended its postwar dominance. Yamaguchi-gumi's decision was apparently not only based on opportunism; its leadership was allegedly frustrated by increasingly harsh law enforcement operations (Adelstein 2010).

Yakuza's relations with the police followed a similar path. In the immediate postwar years the police relied on yakuza to maintain order and for its own protection (Hill 2014, pp. 58–59). Relations, however, became progressively less cooperative, less visible, and more differentiated over time. Wider societal changes affected yakuza's legitimacy. Japan's police were empowered by recentralization and by establishment of the National Police Agency (NPA). According to Hill (2014), the NPA through its investigations and legislative changes it has promoted has limited yakuza's power. The police in the early 1990s launched the "summit strategy": it involved arrests of hundreds of high-ranking yakuza, taking control of their illegal income sources, and temporary disbanding of several yakuza consortia.

The NPA was the driving force behind adoption in 1991 of the Act on Prevention of Unjust Acts by Organized Crime Group Members, or antiboryokudan law. It enabled the Public Safety Commission to designate certain groups as boryokudan, imposed administrative controls over semi-illegal "violent demands" by members of these groups, limited use of gang offices during intergroup conflicts, and established a regional center to assist boryokudan victims and promote the groups' eradication. These provisions look mild by Western standards. Complaints have been made by Japanese scholars and police officers, partly because the most stringent proposed provisions were not enacted. There is no doubt that adoption of the Act on Prevention of Unjust Acts by Organized Crime Group Members was a watershed event (Hill 2004, pp. 245–47).

Relationships between yakuza and police at local levels are not, however, always hostile. Many local police prefer to maintain amicable relationships in order to obtain information about street and violent crimes and about expelled members (who may become rogue lone wolf criminals), and are willing to tolerate yakuza's activities so long as they are victimless and consensual. There have also been cases of outright corruption. In 1986, 124 police officers in Osaka were dismissed or disciplined for accepting bribes to warn yakuza bosses of impending raids of gaming machine operations (Kaplan and Dubro 1987, pp. 157–59). Corrupt exchanges have persisted into the twenty-first century (Rankin 2012*b*), promoted by a deep-rooted culture of gift-giving and reciprocity, often manifested in the giving of envelopes filled with cash. Nonetheless, it is fair to say that relations between yakuza and police are less symbiotic and legitimate than in the 1950s and 1960s.

"Yakuza exclusion ordinances" enacted in many prefectures since 2010 are a sign of changing attitudes. Those ordinances prohibit citizens and companies from doing business with yakuza and thereby cut them off from legitimate sources of income. Local ordinances, in force throughout Japan, have much the same effect (Noboru 2018). Law enforcement agencies are also getting tougher. In 2017, the Japanese police arrested 17,737 boryokudan members, more than half the total number (NPA 2018, p. 30).

These initiatives reflect increasingly critical societal attitudes. Many Japanese accept yakuza's chivalry myth and its mutual aid ideology, which are incessantly glamorized by the Japanese entertainment industry. They also appreciate yakuza's positive sides. For example, yakuza groups won much praise for quick and extensive help after the 2011 tsunami and Fukushima nuclear disaster. Rankin (2012*b*) observes, "It appears that awareness of the fundamental criminality of the yakuza does not preclude a degree of respect for their achievements."

However, attitudes are changing. Every year hundreds of lawyers, demanding an official ban, hold an antiyakuza protest march in front of Yamaguchi-gumi headquarters (McNeil and Adelstein 2008; Adelstein 2017). When Yamaguchi-gumi in 2018 held its annual Halloween event for Kobe's children, more than 100 protesters gathered outside, stressing that the treats came from criminal proceeds and calling for deportation of violent gangs (Shim 2018). Local residents in other cities have also organized "boryokudan office removal campaigns," which have been supported by the Japanese police (NPA 2018, p. 30).

Increasing restrictions on profit-making legal activities, and much diminished opportunities in real estate and finance since Japan's economic bubble burst, have forced rank-and-file members to rely on predatory activities, frauds, and amphetamine trafficking to support themselves and pay yakuza membership fees. Until recently yakuza caused little visible harm to ordinary citizens; this shift has tarnished their popular image.

Delegitimization has been acknowledged by Yoshinori Oda, a high-ranking, defecting member of the Yamaguchi-gumi: "After Japan's economic bubble, we became a bunch of money worshipping thugs, no better than common mafia across the world. Yakuza are engaging in 'wire-me-the-money' fraud (which preys on the elderly) and I'd like to make them stop. It's these things that have made the public dub us 'antisocial forces'" (Adelstein 2017). It remains to be seen whether Oda's plan, announced at a press conference, to establish a "humanitarian organization," return to yakuza's old principles, limit criminal activity to traditional protection services, and operate "peace patrols" to prevent street crime will stop yakuza's delegitimization.

X. The Decline

All five mafias have lost legitimacy and government tolerance. The process started at different times in different places and varies in details but has affected mafias' other typifying characteristics (except longevity).

Membership in most, if not all, has shrunk considerably. Sicilian Cosa Nostra's membership declined by a third between the early 1990s and 2017 (Ministero dell'Interno 2019). The American Cosa Nostra has retained a third of the 3,000 members it had in the 1970s (Albanese 2014, p. 152). Yakuza's membership in 2017 was 18 percent of members and associates at its peak in 1963 (NPA 2018). Declines in both full members and associates accelerated after 2005, with a 10 percent drop in full members between 2016 and 2017 (Nippon.com 2017; Noboru 2018).

The American Cosa Nostra, the triads, and yakuza, and probably the Sicilian Cosa Nostra, have shut down units and, in the case of the triads, whole consortia. In 1999, a high-ranking Hong Kong police officer reported that only five triads remained active (Sun Yee On, Wo Shing Wo, 14K, Wo On Lok, and Wo Hop To; Zhang and Chin 2003, p. 484). The recent split within the Yamaguchi-gumi is a sign of weakness, not strength.

In some organizations, organizational complexity has been reduced. The two Cosa Nostras have reverted to their original segmentary structures, probably not convening regular meetings of their interfamily coordinating bodies, the "commissions," for many years (Ministero dell'Interno 2019; Jacobs 2020). The structures of most triads and, within each consortium, the single units, have been simplified (Chu 2000, pp. 22–26). Zhang and Chin (2003, p. 484) quote a police officer who observed, "While the traditional structure of a triad society can be well organized, nowadays triads are only a collection of loose-knit groups or gangs."

Mafias' elaborate cultural apparatus has also come under pressure. Many rituals, symbols, and norms are increasingly seen as cumbersome, as outmoded legacies of a remote past. Within the Hong Kong triads, initiation ceremonies have been much simplified (Chu 2000, pp. 32–34). An increasing number of recruits experience a shortened procedure known as "hanging the blue lantern." This is verbal recognition of a new triad member without oath or ritual, and usually takes less than 5 minutes. People recruited in this way in the past were not considered to be full members but only probationers with full initiation to come later. In this century some triads seem to have abandoned initiation ceremonies entirely from fear of undercover police agents (Lo and Kwok 2012; Lilias 2014).

Mafias' cultural apparatus is losing its grip on current members and its appeal to prospective ones. In the Italian and American mafias the code of honor with its restrictive sexual norms looks increasing backward and awkward (Colaprico and Fazzo 1995). Reflecting modernization in the broader society, mafiosi since the 1970s in Sicily and Calabria—and earlier in the United States—have identified honor with wealth, devoting increasing time and energy to maximizing profits (Arlacchi 1988). Successful entrepreneurial transformations have weakened in-group morality and increased the gap between mafia ideology and tradition and what mafiosi do in everyday life (Paoli 2003).

Similar developments have affected the cultural apparatuses of Hong Kong triads and yakuza (Chin 2014; Adelstein 2017). Most mafia members realize that their organizations' values and ideology are routinely ignored, especially by higher-ranking members. Lower-level members feel entitled to do the same when compliance entails heavy personal sacrifices—as it often does, given increased law enforcement pressures.

New members who have grown up in societies that regard economic success as the basis of social reputation subscribe only superficially to mafia traditions and prescriptions. Adhesion to a mafia group has become primarily instrumental, based on utilitarian assessments of costs and rewards (Chu 2000, p. 34).

As a result, starting in the 1980s an unprecedented number of Hong Kong triad members began switching societies (Chu 2000, p. 34). A similar pattern has more recently developed in the yakuza, where punishments of breakaway members and groups are no longer applied: "Before, it was the end for gangsters who received these punishments," notes Sakurai Kenji, a former Yamaguchi-gumi boss. "But now they've lost their power. It doesn't matter if you've been given *hamon* or *zetsuen* [the two main punishments against defectors]. You can still be welcomed at an opposing group. If members aren't scared of getting these punishments, they can do what they like. The rules have changed, and it's making people nervous" (Nippon.com 2017). More than 4,000 members formally left the yakuza between 2011, when the exclusion ordinances were passed, and 2017, according to police data (Hoshino and Kamada 2018; Noboru 2018). Unprecedented numbers of American and southern Italian mafiosi, including high-ranking members, motivated by availability of witness protection programs, have cooperated with criminal justice agencies, providing precious evidence against former associates and bosses but also against their political protectors (Lupo 2009; Ministero dell'Interno 2012*a*; Jacobs 2020).

The Sicilian Cosa Nostra has tried to stop the flood of defectors by reasserting old principles. Cosa Nostra's leadership has reportedly restricted the number of new initiations and, following 'Ndrangheta's example, increasingly relies on natural rather than fictive family ties (Balsamo 2006, p. 377; Scaglione 2016, p. 64). Given the parallel trends affecting all mafias and the underlying socioeconomic and political changes, long-term processes of delegitimization and loss of members' unconditional allegiance are unlikely to reverse.

Mafias' traditional ideologies are increasingly unappealing to prospective members. Particularly in the United States, mafia groups have been increasingly unable to attract young, able, intelligent, ambitious Italian Americans. Many high-ranking mafiosi have discouraged their own sons (Reuter 1995; Arlacchi 2010). The strict recruitment criteria and procedures of Italian and American mafias hinder internalization of the competencies needed to compete successfully in international illegal markets and infiltrate legitimate industries. And, because they often require prospective members to prove their honor by committing violent crimes, mafias often end up selecting tough, poorly educated felons.

Hong Kong triads since the late 1990s have relaxed recruitment criteria and admitted even some Hong Kong–born Indians and Pakistanis (Chin 2014). Nonetheless, triads' formalized selection procedures hamper development of connections and competencies necessary to organize transcontinental illegal ventures (Zhang and Chin (2003).

Only 'Ndrangheta seem at least partly to have overcome some of these constraints. Defectors are much less common because of its reliance on natural, rather than fictive, blood ties among members. Scions of several powerful 'Ndrangheta families have obtained university degrees, thus acquiring specialized expertise (DDA Reggio Calabria 2010). Last but not least, 'Ndrangheta has also benefited from the backwardness of its home territories, which remain more tolerant of mafia groups' political and economic power than are people in other mafias' areas.

'Ndrangheta has also been more successful than other mafias in its illegal profit-making activities. Extensive branches in northern Italy, western Europe, Canada, and Australia, and perhaps their leaders' entrepreneurial acumen have enabled some 'Ndrangheta groups to continue to play significant roles in the world cocaine market.

The scales of the other mafias' traditional illegal activities are much reduced, and they have not established successful roles in new markets. Declines are sometimes products of policy changes, such as legalization of gambling in the United States (Coryn, Fijnaut, and Littler 2008). Other causes include enhanced law enforcement pressures, peripheral positions, and lack of production and transshipment contacts, as in the case of heroin trafficking for the Sicilian and American Cosa Nostra (Paoli 2003).

Zhang and Chin (2003, 2006, 2008; Chin and Zhang 2015) have persuasively demonstrated that contemporary triads do not control or even occupy important positions in drug or human smuggling, two of the most profitable organized crime activities in Asia. Likewise, though triads from Hong Kong and Taiwan reentered mainland China in the early 1980s, they have remained subordinate to local organized crime groups (Xia 2006). Zhang and Chin (2003) argue that a "structural deficiency" explains why triads have not seized new opportunities in transnational crime. Because they and their traditional activities such as gambling, prostitution, and loansharking are geographically constrained, they are not well suited to fluid transnational market conditions. Southern Italian mafia groups have been unable to, or are uninterested in, playing roles in human smuggling, an activity that has boomed. Their home regions have become entry points for hundreds of thousands of African and Middle Eastern migrants (Campana 2020).

Mafia organizations draw the bulk of their revenues from legitimate sectors such as real estate and government contracts, even though their involvement, frequently involving corruption, extortion, and manipulation of public tenders, is illegal or of dubious legality (Paoli 2003; Zhang and Chin 2003; Sciarrone 2014). Even those activities have been seriously disrupted by more effective regulation and intensified controls. Successful civil RICO cases in the United States have since the 1980s prompted thorough reform of most unions and businesses that were once controlled by Cosa Nostra. This litigation, together with the declining strength of unions generally, much reduced Cosa Nostra's influence on the American economy (Jacobs 2020).

Higher level yakuza can make easy money in the financial and real estate sectors, but lower level yakuza are increasingly barred by the exclusion ordinances from offering protection services in the legitimate economy. They lament the difficulties of making a living and supporting a family, problems that have contributed to the recent wave of defections (Noboru 2018). In all contexts, mafia organizations are less able than previously to exercise political dominion, because the local populations are less willing to accept their power and state representatives no longer are willing to share theirs.

XI. Looking Forward

Five organized criminal organizations, mafias, exemplify organized crime: the America and Sicilian Cosa Nostras, the Calabrian 'Ndrangheta, the Chinese triads, and the Japanese yakuza. They are true organizations in sociological and legal senses. They are anomalies in contemporary organized crime.

All five emerged in times and places in which modern state institutions had not consolidated, were weak, or—as in the case of colonial powers in Asia—preferred to exercise their powers indirectly. A paradox emerges. Except for the American Cosa Nostra, mafias, the most iconic criminal organizations, were not substantively or even formally criminalized for a considerable portion of their existence. They were considered legitimate by local populations and representatives of local and sometimes national state authorities. In some cases—especially in Japan—they have been formally legal.

Declines experienced by all mafias, with the partial exception of the 'Ndrangheta, reflect reduced tolerance from state authorities. This has been promoted by, and reinforces, mafia organizations' progressive loss of popular legitimacy. Even this eighth, accidental, shared mafia characteristic points to the importance of the state's role in enabling consolidation, survival, or decline of mafias.[13]

This comparative analysis shows that law enforcement investigations have been fundamentally important in weakening mafias' power and their reputations for impunity (Catino 2020; Jacobs 2020). In most countries, including Italy and the United States, criminal justice policy initiatives have successfully complemented administrative and civil law measures. Examples include the cleaning up of the Fulton fish market in New York City, long infested by Cosa Nostra; the dismissal in Italy of hundreds of city councils that had been infiltrated by mafia groups; and the curbing of police and political corruption in Hong Kong, which has transformed an administration known for its triad connections into one of the least corrupt in the world. The effectiveness of these non-criminal-justice interventions is most evident in Japan, a country that continues to use the criminal law sparingly in controlling its local mafia. The yakuza exclusion ordinances issued by many prefectures have considerably reduced yakuza's revenues and power and accelerated its delegitimization.

State actions against the mafias have been intertwined with, and supported by, civil society initiatives. Enlightened small groups within the criminal justice apparatus and the civil society initially took the lead, and antimafia movements have steadily gained popular support (Schneider and Schneider 2003; Rakopoulos 2014; Shim 2018). Long-standing support for mafia groups in the general population and among state representatives has declined and weakened, thus undermining mafias' power.

This is not a time, however, for excessive optimism. Mafias have over the decades demonstrated extraordinary flexibility and resilience in the face of changing political and socioeconomic conditions. All five, though diminished, survive. They can rely on formalized structures with well-delineated command positions and elaborate cultural apparatuses. Some of their cultural codes and rites look increasingly out of step with contemporary cultural norms, but their insistence on family ties, whether blood or fictive, resonates with some parts of local populations. The widespread acceptance and tolerance of patronage relationships in Italy

---

[13] The key role of the state in consolidation and survival of mafia-type organizations emerges from broader comparative and historical analyses. Many gangs and criminal associations were active until the early nineteenth century in northern Europe but were swept away by the rise of modern state institutions (Fijnaut 2014).

and Japan encourage corrupt agreements between mafiosi and politicians. In places such as southern Italy that are characterized by chronic high levels of unemployment, mafia careers may continue to attract youngsters with inadequate educations and few hopes of finding appealing conventional jobs. The Cosa Nostra endures even in the United States despite nearly five decades of relentless law enforcement actions. Mafias will not easily be swept away.

REFERENCES

Adelstein, Jake. 2010. "The Last Yakuza." *World Policy*, August 3. https://worldpolicy.org/2010/08/03/the-last-yakuza/.

———. 2017. "Yakuza Revolution: From Bruisers to Boy Scouts?" *The Daily Beast*, March 3. https://www.thedailybeast.com/the-yakuza-is-rebranding-as-a-humanitarian-organization.

Agence France Press. 2019. "Hells Angels Banned by Dutch Court in Biker Gang Crackdown." *Guardian* (May 29). https://www.theguardian.com/world/2019/may/29/hells-angels-banned-by-dutch-court-in-strike-against-biker-gangs.

Albanese, Jay S. 2014. "The Italian-American Mafia." In *The Oxford Handbook of Organized Crime*, edited by Letizia Paoli. Oxford: Oxford University Press.

Albini, Joseph L. 1971. *The American Mafia: Genesis of a Legend*. New York: Appleton Century Crofts.

Allum, Felia. 2016. *The Invisible Camorra: Neapolitan Crime Families across Europe*. Ithaca, NY: Cornell University Press.

Alongi, Giuseppe. 1977. *La maffia*. Palermo: Sellerio. (Originally published 1886. Rome: Bocca.)

Alvaro, Corrado. 1955. "La fibbia." *Corriere della Sera*, September 17.

Anderson, Annelise G. 1979. *The Business of Organized Crime: A Cosa Nostra Family*. Stanford, CA: Hoover Institution.

Anderson, Benedict. 1983. *Imagined Communities: Reflections on the Origin and Spread of Nationalism*. London: Verso.

Arlacchi, Pino. 1988. *Mafia Business. The Mafia Ethic and the Spirit of Capitalism*. Oxford: Oxford University Press.

———. 1993. *Men of Dishonor: Inside the Sicilian Mafia; An Account of Antonino Calderone*. New York: William Morrow.

———. 2010. "Postfazione: L'Occasione Perduta." In *Gli Uomini del Disonore: La mafia siciliana nella vita del grande pentito Antonino Calderone*. Milan: Il Saggiatore.

Astorga, Luis 1999. "Drug Trafficking in Mexico: A First General Assessment. Management of Social Transformations." MOST Discussion Paper no 36. Paris: UNESCO.

Atuesta, Laura, and Yocelyn S. Pérez-Dávila. 2018. "Fragmentation and Cooperation: The Evolution of Organized Crime in Mexico." *Trends in Organized Crime* 21(3):235–61.

Avviso Pubblico. 2019. *Amministrazioni Sciolte per Mafia: Dati Riassuntivi*. https:// www.avvisopubblico.it/home/home/cosa-facciamo/informare/documenti-tema tici/comuni-sciolti-per-mafia/amministrazioni-sciolte-mafia-dati-riassuntivi/.

Balsamo, Antonio. 2006. "Organised Crime Today: The Evolution of the Sicilian Mafia." *Journal of Money Laundering Control* 9(4):373–78.

Barker, Thomas. 2014. *Outlaw Motorcycle Gangs as Organized Crime Groups*. Cham: Springer Briefs in Criminology.

Baum, Julian. 1996. "Hard Guys Get Hit: Public Outrage Spurs Crackdown on Gangs." *Far Eastern Economic Review*, February 19, pp. 18–20.

Behan, Tom. 1996. *The Camorra*. London: Routledge.

Bettini, Marco. 1994. *Pentito. Storia di Mafia*. Turin: Bollati Boringhieri.

Bianconi, Giovanni. 2015. "Totò Cuffaro esce da Carcere di Rebibbia: «Bello respirare la libertà»." *Il Corriere della Sera*, December 15. https://www.corriere .it/cronache/15_dicembre_13/toto-cuffaro-esce-carcere-rebibbia-bello-respi rare-liberta-2e092f70-a17d-11e5-80b6-fe40410507f1.shtml?refresh_ce-cp.

BKA (Bundeskriminalamt). 2018. *Lagebild Organisierte Kriminalität Bundesrepublik Deutschland*. Wiesbaden: BKA.

Blok, Anton. 1975. *The Mafia of a Sicilian Village, 1860–1960: A Study of Violent Peasant Entrepreneurs*. New York: Harper Torchbooks.

Booth, Martin. 1990. *The Triads: The Chinese Criminal Society*. London: Grafton.

Bouchard, Martin. 2020. "Collaboration and Boundaries in Organized Crime: A Network Perspective." In *Organizing Crime: Mafias, Markets, and Networks*, edited by Michael Tonry and Peter Reuter. Chicago: Chicago University Press.

Brittain, James J. 2010. *Revolutionary Social Change in Colombia: The Origin and Direction of the FARC-EP*. London: Pluto.

Calà Ulloa, Pietro. 1961. "Considerazioni sull Stato Economico e Politico della Sicilia, Riservatissima al Ministro della Giustizia Parisio in Napoli." In *Il riformismo Borbonico nella Sicilia del Sette e dell'Ottocento. Saggi storici*, edited by Ernesto Pontieri. Naples: Edizioni Scientifiche Italiane. (Originally published 1838.)

Calderón, Ania. 2012. "Global Vice: The Expanding Territory of the Yakuza." *Journal of International Affairs* Fall/Winter:155–61.

Calderoni, Francesco. 2010. *Organized Crime Legislation in the European Union: Harmonization and Approximation of Criminal Law, National Legislations and the EU Framework Decision on the Fight against Organized Crime*. Heidelberg: Springer.

Calderoni, Francesco, Giulia Berlusconi, Lorella Garofalo, Luca Giommoni, and Frederia Sarno. 2016. "The Italian Mafias in the World: A Systematic Assessment of the Mobility of Criminal Groups." *European Journal of Criminology* 13(4):413–33.

Campana, Paolo. 2011. "Eavesdropping on the Mob: The Functional Diversification of Mafia Activities across Territories." *European Journal of Criminology* 8:213–28.

Candito, Alessia. 2017. "Mafia, Sequestrati 10 Milioni all'ex Deputato di Fi Amedeo Matacena. C'è Anche una Nave." *La Repubblica*, December 21. https://www.repubblica.it/cronaca/2017/12/21/news/mafia_sequestrati_10_mi lioni_all_ex_deputato_di_fi_amedeo_matacena_c_e_anche_una_nave-184759236/.

Catanzaro, Raimondo. 1992. *Men of Respect: A Social History of the Sicilian Mafia*. New York: Free Press.

Catino, Maurizio. 2015. "Mafia Rules. The Role of Criminal Codes in Mafia Organizations." *Scandinavian Journal of Management* 31(4):536–48.

———. 2019. *Mafia Organizations: The Visible Hand of Criminal Enterprise*. Cambridge: Cambridge University Press.

———. 2020. "Italian Organized Crime since 1950." In *Organizing Crime: Mafias, Markets, and Networks*, edited by Michael Tonry and Peter Reuter. Chicago: Chicago University Press.

Chesneaux, Jean. 1971. *Secret Societies in China in the Nineteenth and Twentieth Century*. London: Heinemann.

Chin, Ko-Lin. 1996. *Chinatown Gangs*. New York: Oxford University Press.

———. 2003. *Heijin: Organized Crime, Business, and Politics in Taiwan*. Armonk, NY: M. E. Sharpe.

———. 2014. "Chinese Organized Crime." In *The Oxford Handbook of Organized Crime*, edited by Letizia Paoli. Oxford: Oxford University Press.

Chin, Ko-Lin, and Sheldon X. Zhang. 2015. *The Chinese Heroin Trade: Cross-Border Drug Trafficking in Southeast Asia and Beyond*. New York: New York University Press.

Chu, Yiu-kong. 2000. *The Triads as Business*. London: Routledge.

———. 2005. "Hong Kong Triads after 1997." *Trends in Organized Crime* 8(3):5–12.

Ciconte, Enzo. 1992. *'Ndrangheta dall'Unità ad Oggi*. Bari: Laterza.

———. 2011. *'Ndrangheta*. Soveria Mannelli: Rubbettino Editore.

Clawson, Mary Ann. 1989. *Constructing Brotherhood. Class, Gender, and Fraternalism*. Princeton, NJ: Princeton University Press.

Colaprico, Piero, and Luca Fazzo. 1995. *Manager calibro 9. Vent'anni di malavita a Milano nel racconto del pentito Saverio Morabito*. Milan: Garzanti.

Commissione Antimafia XI. 1993. *Relazione sui rapporti tra mafia e politica con note integrative*. Doc. XXIII, no. 2, XI Legislature. Rome: Camera dei Deputati.

Commissione Antimafia XI, Commissione Parlamentare d'inchiesta sul fenomeno della mafia e sulle altre associazioni similari. 1992. *Audizione del collaboratore di giustizia Leonardo Messina*. XI Legislature. Rome: Camera dei Deputati.

Commissione Antimafia XV. 2008. *Commissione parlamentare d'inchiesta sul fenomeno della criminalità organizzata mafiosa o similare. Relazione annuale sulla 'Ndrangheta*. Doc. XXIII, no. 3, XV Legislature. Rome: Camera dei Deputati.

Commissione Antimafia XVI. 2010. *Commissione parlamentare d'inchiesta sul fenomeno della mafia e sulle altre associazioni criminali, anche straniere. Audizione del Procura tore Distrettuale Antimafia di Reggio Calabria, dottor Giuseppe Pignatone*. XVI Legislature. Rome: Camera dei Deputati.

Corte Suprema di Cassazione. 2004. Sentenza n. 9691/2004.

———. 2011. Sentenza 19 aprile 2011 n. 15583.

Coryn, Tom, Cyrille Fijnaut, and Alan Littler. 2008. *Economic Aspects of Gambling Regulation: EU and US Perspectives*. Leiden: Martinus Nijhoff.

Council of the European Union. 2008. "Council Framework Decision 2008/841/JHA of 24 October 2008 on the Fight against Organised Crime." *Official Journal of the European Union* L300:42–45.

Cressey, Donald R. 1969. *Theft of a Nation: The Structure and Operations of Organized Crime in America*. New York: Harper & Collins.

Cruz, J. Miguel. 2010. "Central American Maras: From Youth Street Gangs to Transnational Protection Rackets." *Global Crime* 11(4):379–98.

DDA (Direzione Distrettuale Antimafia) Reggio Calabria, Procura della Repubblica di Reggio Calabria. 1995. "Richiesta di ordini di custodia cautelare in carcere e di contestuale rinvio a giudizio nel procedimento contro Condello Pasquale + 477." July.

———. 2010. Decreto di fermo di indiziato di delitto—artt. 384 e segg. c.p.p.—nei confronti di A. A.M. + 156.

DIA (Direzione Investigativa Antimafia). 2013. *Valori dei sequestri e delle confische dal 1992—2011 and dati complessivi ordinanze di custodia cautelare*. http://www.interno.gov.it/dip_ps/dia/page/rilevazioni_statistiche.html.

Dikötter, Frank, Lars Laamann, and Zhou Xun. 2004. *Narcotic Culture: A History of Drugs in China*. Chicago: University of Chicago Press.

Dimico, Arcangelo, Alessia Isopi, and Ola Olsson. 2017. "Origins of the Sicilian Mafia: The Market for Lemons." *Journal of Economic History* 77(4):1083–115.

DNA (Direzione Nazionale Antimafia e Antiterrorismo). 2017. *Relazione annuale sulle attività svolte dal Procuratore nazionale e dalla Direzione nazionale antimafia e antiterrorismo nonché sulle dinamiche e strategie della criminalità organizzata di tipo mafioso nel periodo 1° luglio 2015–30 giugno 2016*. Prot. 12720/2017/PNA, April 12.

Durkheim, E. 1964. *The Division of Labor in Society*. New York: Free Press. (Originally published 1893. Paris: Félix Alcan.)

Edwards, Adam, and Michael Levi. 2008. "Researching the Organization of Serious Crimes." *Criminology and Criminal Justice* 8:363–88.

Egmond, Florike. 2004. "Multiple Underworlds in the Dutch Republic of the Seventeenth and Eighteenth Centuries." In *Organized Crime in Europe: Concepts, Patterns, and Control Policies in the European Union and Beyond*, edited by Cyrille Fijnaut and Letizia Paoli. Dordrecht: Springer.

Eisenstadt, Shmuel N. 1956. "Ritualized Personal Relations. Blood Brotherhood, Compadre, etc.: Some Comparative Hypotheses and Suggestions." *Man* 56:90–95.

Eisenstadt, Shmuel N., and Luis Roniger. 1984. *Patrons, Clients and Friends: Interpersonal Relations and the Structure of Trust in Society*. Cambridge: Cambridge University Press.

EMCDDA (European Monitoring Centre on Drugs and Drug Addiction) and Europol. 2019. *EU Drug Markets Report 2019*. Luxembourg: Publications Office of the European Union.

Eurispes. 2008. *'Ndrangheta Holding—Dossier 2008*. Rome: Eurispes.

Europol. 2003. *2003 European Union Organised Crime Report*. Luxembourg: Office for the Official Publications of the European Communities.

———. 2013a. *SOCTA 2013: EU Serious and Organised Crime Threat Assessments*. Gravenzande: Deventer.

———. 2013b. *Threat Assessment: Italian Organized Crime*. The Hague: Europol.

Falcone, Giovanni, and Marcelle Padovani. 1993. *Men of Honor: The Truth about the Mafia*. London: Warner. (Originally published 1991. Milan: Rizzoli.)

Fiandaca, Giovanni, ed. 2007. *Women and the Mafia*. New York: Springer.

Fijnaut, Cyrille. 2014. "Searching for Organized Crime in History." In *The Oxford Handbook of Organized Crime*, edited by Letizia Paoli. Oxford: Oxford University Press.

Finckenauer, James O. 2001. *La Cosa Nostra in the United States*. Washington, DC: National Institute of Justice, International Center.

Forgione, Francesco. 2009. *Mafia Export: Come 'Ndrangheta, Cosa Nostra e Camorra Hanno Colonizzato il Mondo*. Baldini: Castoldi Dalai.

Franchetti, Leopoldo. 1993. *Condizioni Politiche ed Amministrative della Sicilia*. Rome: Donzelli. (Originally published 1876.)

Gambetta, Diego. 1992. *The Sicilian Mafia: The Business of Private Protection*. Cambridge, MA: Harvard University Press.

———. 2011. *Codes of the Underworld: How Criminals Communicate*. Princeton, NJ: Princeton University Press.

Ginsborg, Paul. 1998. *L'Italia del Tempo Presente. Famiglia, Societa Civile, Stato, 1980–1996*. Turin: Einaudi.

Goldstock, Ronald, Martin Marcus, Thomas D. Tacher II, and James J. Jacobs. 1990. *Corruption and Racketeering in the New York City Construction Industry: The Final Report of the New York State Organized Crime Task Force*. New York: New York University Press.

Gratteri, Nicola, and Antonio Nicaso. 2010. *Fratelli di sangue: Storie, boss e affari della 'Ndrangheta, la mafia più potente del mondo*. Milan: Oscar Mondadori.

———. 2018. *Storia segreta della 'ndrangheta: Una lunga e oscura vicenda di sangue e potere (1860–2018)*. Milan: Mondadori.

Gruppo Interforze. 1993a. "Bozza relativa alle famiglie mafiose della provincia di Palermo redatta dal gruppo interforze di quella città e consegnata in via informale." Unpublished report. Rome: Ministero dell'Interno.

———. 1993b. "Bozza relativa alle famiglie mafiose della città di Palermo redatta dal gruppo interforze di quella città e consegnata in via informale." Unpublished report. Rome: Ministero dell'Interno.

Hagan, Frank E. 2006. "'Organized Crime' and 'Organized Crime': Indeterminate Problems of Definitions." *Trends in Organized Crime* 9(4):127–37.

Haller, Mark. 1990. "Illegal Enterprise: A Theoretical and Historical Interpretation." *Criminology* 28(2):207–35.

Hart, Herbert, L. A. 1994. *The Concept of Law*, 2nd ed. Oxford: Clarendon.

Hawkins, Gordon. 1969. "God and the Mafia." *Public Interest* 14 (Winter):24–51.

Heidhues, Mary F. Somers. 1993. "Chinese in West Borneo and Bangka: Kongis and Hui." In *"Secret Societies" Reconsidered: Perspectives on the Social History of Modern South China and Southeast Asia*, edited by David Ownby and Mary F. Somers Heidhues. Amonk, NY: M. E. Sharpe.

Hess, Henner. 1973. *Mafia and Mafiosi: The Structure of Power*. Westmead: Saxon House. (Originally published 1970. Tübingen: Mohr.)

Hill, Peter B. 2003. *The Japanese Mafia: Yakuza, Law, and the State*. Oxford: Oxford University Press.

———. 2004. "The Changing Face of the Yakuza." *Global Crime* 6(1):97–116.

————. 2014. "The Japanese Yakuza." In *The Oxford Handbook of Organized Crime*, edited by Letizia Paoli. Oxford: Oxford University Press.

Hirotoshi, Itō. 2017. "Hard-Up Yakuza Struggle to Earn a Living." Nippon.com, November 8. https://www.nippon.com/en/features/c04202/hard-up-yakuza -struggle-to-earn-a-living.html?pnum = 1.

Höbel, Alexander, and Gianpaolo Iannicelli. 2006. *La strage del treno 904. Un contributo delle scienze sociali*. Santa Maria Capua Vetere: Ipermedium.

Home Office. 2018. *Serious and Organised Crime Strategy*. Presented to Parliament by the Secretary of State for the Home Department by Command of Her Majesty. London: Home Office.

Hoshino, Tetsuya, and Takuna Kamada. 2018. *Third-Party Policing on Organized Crime: Evidence from the Yakuza*. University Park: Pennsylvania State University.

Huang, Hua-Lun. 2007. *From the Asian Boys to the Zhu Lian Bang (The Bamboo Union Gang): A Typological Analysis of Delinquent Asian Gangs*. Lafayette: Springer.

Huffington Post. 2014. "Sentenza Marcello Dell'Utri, la Cassazione Conferma la Condanna a 7 Anni," September 5. https://www.huffingtonpost.it/2014/05 /09/sentenza-marcello-dellutri-condanna_n_5295649.html.

IMDb (Internet Movie Database). 2020. "Most Popular Pablo Escobar Movies and TV Shows." https://www.imdb.com/search/keyword/?keywords = pablo -escobar.

Ishino, Iwao. 1953. "The Oyabun-Kobun: A Japanese Ritual Kinship Institution." *American Anthropologist* 55:695–707.

ISTAT (Istituto Nazionale di Statistica). Annual. *Statistiche giudiziarie penali*. Rome: Istat.

Italic Institute of America. 2015. "Film Study 2015 (1919–2014)." http://www .italic.org/imageb1.htm.

Iwai, Hiroaki. 1986. "Organized Crime in Japan." In *Organized Crime: A Global Perspective*, edited by Robert J. Kelly. Totowa, NJ: Rowman & Littlefield.

Jacobs, James. B. 1999. *Gotham Unbound: How New York City Was Liberated from the Clutches of Cosa Nostra*. New York: New York University Press.

————. 2020. "The Rise and Fall of Organized Crime in the United States." In *Organizing Crime: Mafias, Markets, and Networks*, edited by Michael Tonry and Peter Reuter. Chicago: Chicago University Press.

Jacobs, James B., and Lauryn P. Gouldin. 1999. "Cosa Nostra: The Final Chapter?" In *Crime and Justice: A Review of Research*, vol. 25, edited by Michael Tonry. Chicago: University of Chicago Press.

Jacobs, James B., with the assistance of Chistopher Panarella, and Jay Worthington. 1994. *Busting the Mob*. New York: New York University Press.

Kaplan, David. 1992. *Fires of the Dragon: Politics, Murder and the Kuomintang*. New York: Atheneum.

Kaplan, David E., and Alec Dubro. 1987. *Yakuza: The Explosive Account of Japan's Criminal Underworld*. London: Futura.

Kawasaki, Tomomi. 2010. "Big Investment Fraud and 'Yakuza Money' Crime: Two Perspectives of Financial Crime in Japan." *Asian Criminology* 5:89–98.

KLPD (Korps landelijke politiediensten). 2011. "The 'Ndrangheta in the Netherlands: The Nature, Criminal Activities, and Modi Operandi on Dutch Territory." Amsterdam: Korps landelijke politiediensten (National Police Corps).

La Spina, Antonio. 2014. "The Fight against the Italian Mafia." In *The Oxford Handbook of Organized Crime*, edited by Letizia Paoli. Oxford: Oxford University Press.

Lessing, Benjamin. 2018. *Making Peace in Drug Wars: Crackdowns and Cartels in Latin America*. Cambridge: Cambridge University Press.

Lestingi, Ferdinando. 1884. "L'Associazione della Fratellanza nella Provincia di Girgenti." *Archivio di Psichiatria, Antropologia Criminale e Scienze Penali* 5:452–63.

Levi, Michael. 2012. "The Organization of Serious Crime for Gain." In *The Oxford Handbook of Criminology*, edited by Mike Maguire, Rodney Morgan, and Robert Reiner. Oxford: Oxford University Press.

Lévi-Strauss, Claude. 1969. *The Elementary Structures of Kinship*. Boston: Beacon. (Originally published 1949.)

Libera. 2020. La storia dell'Associazione. https://www.libera.it/schede-7-la_storia _dell_associazione.

Lilias, Per. 2014. "What Has Happened to Hong Kong's Triads?" *Time*, February 28. https://time.com/10445/hong-kong-triads-have-lower-profile/.

Lo, T. Wing, and Sharon Ingrid Kwok. 2012. "Traditional Organized Crime in the Modern World: How Triad Societies Respond to Socioeconomic Change." In *Traditional Organized Crime in the Modern World: Responses to Socioeconomic Change*, edited by Dina Siegel and Henk van de Bunt. Boston: Springer.

Lodato, Saverio. 1999. *Ho Ucciso Giovanni Falcone. La Confessione di Giovanni Brusca*. Milan: Mondadori.

Lupo, Salvatore. 1993. *Storia della mafia dalle origini ai giorni nostri*. Rome: Donzelli.

———. 1996. *Andreotti, la Mafia, la Storia d'Italia*. Rome: Donzelli.

———. 2009. *History of the Mafia*. New York: Columbia University Press. (Originally published 1996. Rome: Donzelli.)

Maas, Peter. 1969. *The Valachi Papers*. New York: Bantam.

Martin, Brian G. 1996. *The Shanghai Green Gang: Politics and Organized Crime, 1919–1937*. Berkeley: University of California Press.

Mauss, Marcel. 1990. *The Gift: The Form and Reason for Exchange in Archaic Societies*. London: Routledge. (Originally published 1923–1924, *L'Année Sociologique*, 2nd series.)

McCoy, Alfred W. 1991. *The Politics of Heroin: CIA Complicity in the Global Drug Trade*. Brooklyn, NY: Lawrence Hill.

McKenna, James J. 1996. "Organized Crime in Hong Kong." *Journal of Contemporary Criminal Justice* 12(4):316–28.

McNeill, David, and Jake Adelstein. 2008. "Yakuza Wars." *Asia-Pacific Journal* 6(9):1–9.

Milhaupt, Curtis, and Mark D. West. 2000. "The Dark Side of Private Ordering: An Institutional and Empirical Analysis of Organized Crime." *University of Chicago Law Review* 67(1):41–98.

Ministero della Giustizia. 2011. *Anno Giudiziario 2010: Relazione del Ministero–Dipartimento dell'Amministrazione Penitenziaria*. Rome: Ministero della Giustizia.
———. 2013. *Detenuti Presenti per Tipologia di Reato. Situazione al 30 giugno 2013*. http://www.giustizia.it/giustizia/it/mg_1_14_1.wp?facetNode_1 = 0_2andprevi siousPage = mg_1_14andcontentId = SST935038.
Ministero dell'Interno. 2001. *Relazione semestrale sull'attività svolta e i risultati conseguiti dalla Direzione Investigativa Antimafia nel secondo semestre del 2000*. Rome: Ministero dell'Interno.
———. 2012*a*. *Relazione al Parlamento Sulle Speciali Misure di Protezione, sulla loro Efficacia e sulle Modalità Generali di Applicazione—1 luglio–31 dicembre 2011*. Rome: Ministero dell'Interno.
———. 2012*b*. *Relazione Semestrale sull'Attività Svolta e i Risultati Conseguiti dalla Direzione Investigativa Antimafia—gennaio-giugno 2012*. Rome: Ministero dell'Interno.
———. 2018. *Relazione Semestrale sull'Attività Svolta e i Risultati Conseguiti dalla Direzione Investigativa Antimafia—gennaio-giugno 2018*. Rome: Ministero dell'Interno.
———. 2019. *Relazione Semestrale sull'Attività Svolta e i Risultati Conseguiti dalla Direzione Investigativa Antimafia—luglio–dicembre 2018*. Rome: Ministero dell'Interno.
Monzini, Paola. 1999. *Gruppi criminali a Napoli e Marsiglia: la delinquenza organizzata nella storia di due città: 1820–1990*. Catanzaro: Meridiana Libri.
Morgan, W. P. 1960. *Triad Societies in Hong Kong*. Hong Kong: Government Press.
Mori, Cesare. 1993. *Con la Mafia ai Ferri Corti*. Naples: Flavio Pagano. (Originally published 1932. Milan: Mondadori.)
Murray, Dan H., with the assistance of Qin Baoqi. 1994. *The Origins of the Tiandihui: The Chinese Triads in Legend and History*. Stanford, CA: Stanford University Press.
Naylor, R. Thomas. 2003. "Towards a General Theory of Profit-Driven Crimes." *British Journal of Criminology* 43:81–101.
Nelken, David. 1995. "Review of *The Sicilian Mafia: The Business of Private Protection*, by Diego Gambetta." *British Journal of Criminology* 35(2):287–89.
Nelli, Humbert. S. 1976. *The Business of Crime: Italians and Syndicate Crime in the United States*. New York: Oxford University Press.
Nippon.com. 2017. "Fragmented Yamaguchi-gumi: A Sign of Changing Yakuza Times," October 4. https://www.nippon.com/en/features/c04201/fragmented-yamaguchi-gumi-a-sign-of-changing-yakuza-times.html.
Noboru, H. 2018. "No Way Out: The Dilemma of Japan's Ex-yakuza." Nippon.com, January 5. https://www.nippon.com/en/currents/d00372/no-way-out-the-dilemma-of-japanpercentE2 percent80percent99s-ex-yakuza.html.
Norman, Susan V. 2018. "Narcotization as Security Dilemma: The FARC and Drug Trade in Colombia" *Studies in Conflict and Terrorism* 41(8):638–59.
NPA (National Police Agency). 2018. *Police of Japan 2018*. Tokyo: National Police Agency. https://www.npa.go.jp/english/Police_of_Japan/POJcontents.html.
Ownby, David, 1993. "Secret Societies Reconsidered." In *"Secret Societies" Reconsidered: Perspectives on the Social History of Modern South China and*

Southeast Asia, edited by David Ownby and Mary F. Somers Heidhues. Armonk, NY: M. E. Sharpe.

———. 1996. *Brotherhoods and Secret Societies in Early and Mid-Qing China: The Formation of a Tradition*. Stanford, CA: Stanford University Press.

Ownby, David, and Mary F. Somers Heidhues, eds. 1993. *"Secret Societies" Reconsidered: Perspectives on the Social History of Modern South China and Southeast Asia*. Armonk, NY: M. E. Sharpe.

Palazzolo, Salvo. 2013. "Confisca Miliardaria al re dell'Eolico." *La Repubblica*, April 4. http://ricerca.repubblica.it/repubblica/archivio/repubblica/2013/04 /04/confiscamiliardaria-al-re-delleolico.html?ref=search.

Paoli, Letizia. 2002*a*. "The Implementation of the UN Convention against Transnational Organized Crime: Concepts and Actors." In *The Containment of Transnational Organized Crime: Comments on the UN Convention of December 2000*, edited by Hans-Jörg Albrecht and Cyrille Fijnaut. Freiburg: Edition Iuscrim.

———. 2002*b*. "The Paradoxes of Organized Crime." *Crime, Law and Social Change* 37(1):51–97.

———. 2003. *Mafia Brotherhoods: Organized Crime, Italian Style*. New York: Oxford University Press.

———. 2014. "The Italian Mafia." In *The Oxford Handbook of Organized Crime*, edited by Letizia Paoli. Oxford: Oxford University Press.

Paoli, Letizia, and Tom Vander Beken. 2014. "Organized Crime: A Contested Concept." In *The Oxford Handbook of Organized Crime*, edited by Letizia Paoli. Oxford: Oxford University Press.

Papachristos, Andrew V., and Sandy Y. Zhao. 2015. "Crime: Organized." In *International Encyclopedia of the Social and Behavioral Sciences*, edited by Neil J. Smelser and Paul B. Baltes. Amsterdam: Elsevier.

Patanè, Francesco. 2019. "Palermo: terzo blitz contro la mafia nigeriana, smantellata base operativa a Ballarò." *La Repubblica*, July 11. https://palermo .repubblica.it/cronaca/2019/07/11/news/palermo_terzo_blitz_contro_la_mafia _nigeriana_smantellata_base_operativa_a_ballaro_-230930235/.

Pearson, Geoffrey, and Dick Hobbs. 2001. *Middle Market Drug Distribution*. London: Home Office Research, Development and Statistics Directorate.

Perrow, Charles. 1961. "The Analysis of Goals in Complex Organizations." *American Sociological Review* 26:854–66.

Perry, Elizabeth J. 1980. *Rebels and Revolutionaries in North China, 1845–1945*. Stanford, CA: Stanford University Press.

Pezzino, Paolo. 1990. *Una Certa Reciprocità di Favori. Mafia e Modernizzazione Violenta nella Sicilia Postunitaria*. Milan: Angeli.

———. 1992. *Il Paradiso Abitato dai Diavoli. Società, élites, Istituzioni nel Mezzogiorno Contemporaneo*. Milan: Angeli.

President's Commission on Organized Crime. 1986*a*. *The Edge: Organized Crime, Business, and Labor Unions*. Washington, DC: US Government Printing Office.

———. 1986*b*. *The Impact: Organized Crime Today*. Report to the President and the Attorney General. Washington, DC: US Government Printing Office.

Raab, Selwyn. 1998*a*. "A Who's Who, and Who's Where, of Mafia Families." *New York Times*, April 27, sec. B:4.

———. 1998*b*. "Mob's 'Commission' No Longer Meeting, as Families Weaken." *New York Times*, April 27, sec. B:1.

Rakopoulos, Theodoros. 2014. "Cooperative Modulations: The Antimafia Movement and Struggles over Land and Cooperativism in Eight Sicilian Municipalities." *Journal of Modern Italian Studies* 19(1):15–33.

Ramzy, Austin. 2019. "What Are the Triads, and What Is Their History of Violence?" *New York Times*, July 24. https://www.nytimes.com/2019/07/24/world/asia/hong-kong-triads-protests.html.

Rankin, Andrew. 2012*a*. "21st-Century Yakuza: Recent Trends in Organized Crime in Japan—Part 1." *Asia-Pacific Journal* 10(7–2):1–27.

Rankin, Andrew. 2012*b*. "21st-Century Yakuza: Recent Trends in Organized Crime in Japan—Part 2." *Asia-Pacific Journal* 10(7–1):1–21.

Renda, Francesco. 1987. *Storia della Sicilia dal 1860 al 1970*, Vol. 3. Palermo: Sellerio.

Reuter, Peter. 1983. *Disorganized Crime: The Economics of the Visible Hand*. Cambridge, MA: MIT Press.

Reuter, Peter. 1984. "The (Continued) Vitality of Mythical Numbers." *Public Interest* 75(Spring):135–47.

———. 1987. *Racketeering in Legitimate Industries: A Study in the Economics of Intimidation*. Prepared for the National Institute of Justice, US Department of Justice. Santa Monica, CA: Rand.

———. 1995. "The Decline of the American Mafia." *Public Interest* 120:89–99.

Reuter, Peter, and Letizia Paoli 2020. "How Similar Are Modern Criminal Organizations to Traditional Mafias?" In *Organizing Crime: Mafias, Markets, and Networks*, edited by Michael Tonry and Peter Reuter. Chicago: Chicago University Press.

Sahlins, Marshall. 1972. *Stone Age Economics*. Chicago: Aldine Atherton.

Sales, Isaia. 1993. *La camorra. Le camorre*. Rome: Editori Riuniti.

———. 2001. "Camorra." In *Appendice 2000*. Rome: Treccani.

Salvemini Gaetano, G. 1962. *Il Ministro della Mala Vita e Altri Scritti sull'Italia Giolittiana*. Milan: Feltrinelli.

Santino, Umberto. 1997. *L'Alleanza e il Compromesso. Mafia e Politica dai Tempi di Lima e Andreotti ai Giorni Nostri*. Soveria Mannelli: Rubbettino.

———. 2000. *Storia del Movimento Antimafia. Dalla Lotta di Classe all'Impegno Civile*. Rome: Editori Riuniti.

Santino, Umberto, and Giovanni La Fiura. 1990. *L'impresa mafiosa. Dall'Italia agli Stati Uniti*. Milan: Angeli.

Santopietro, Tom. 2012. *The Godfather Effect: Changing Hollywood, America, and Me*. New York: Thomas Dunne.

Santoro, Marco. 2007. *La voce del padrino: Mafia, cultura, politica*. Verona: Ombre corte.

Saviano, Roberto. 2008. *Gomorrah: Italy's Other mafia*. New York: Macmillan.

Scaglione, Attilio. 2016. "Cosa Nostra and Camorra: Illegal Activities and Organisational Structures." *Global Crime* 17(1):60–78.

Schelling, Thomas C. 1967. "Economics and the Criminal Enterprise." *Public Interest* 7:61–78.

———. 1971. "What Is the Business of Organized Crime?" *American Scholar* 40(4):643–52.

Schilling, Mark. 2003. *The Yakuza Movie Book: A Guide to Japanese Gangster Films*. Berkeley, CA: Stone Bridge.

Schmid, Alex. 2004. "Terrorism: The Definitional Problem." *Case Western Reserve Journal of International Law* 36:371–415.

Schneider, Jane, and Peter Schneider. 1976. *Culture and Political Economy in Western Sicily*. New York: Academic Press.

———. 2003. *Reversible Destiny: Mafia, Antimafia, and the Struggle for Palermo*. Berkeley: University of California Press.

Schumpeter, Joseph A. 1981. *Capitalism, Socialism, and Democracy*. London: Allen & Unwin.

Sciarrone, Rocco. 2009. *Mafie Vecchie, Mafie Nuove: Radicamento ed Espansione*. Rome: Donzelli.

———. 2014. *Mafie del Nord: Strategie Criminali e Contesti Locali*. Rome: Donzelli.

Selmini, Rossella. 2020. "Women in Organized Crime." In *Organizing Crime: Mafias, Markets, and Networks*, edited by Michael Tonry and Peter Reuter. Chicago: Chicago University Press.

Sergi, Anna, and Anita Lavorgna. 2016. *'Ndrangheta: The Glocal Dimensions of the Most Powerful Italian Mafia*. Cham: Palgrave Macmillan.

Seymour, Christopher. 1996. *Yakuza Diary: Doing Time in the Japanese Underworld*. New York: Atlantic.

Shamsian, Jacob. 2016. "Here Are All of Barack Obama's Favorite Things." *Insider*, July 28. https://www.insider.com/president-barack-obama-favorite-movies-books-tv-shows-music-2016-7.

Shim, Elizabeth. 2018. "Japan Crime Ring Distributes Treats to Children at Halloween Event." *UPI*, October 31. https://www.upi.com/Top_News/World-News/2018/10/31/Japan-crime-ring-distributes-treats-to-children-at-Halloween-event/9021541001540/.

Siniawer, Eiko M. 2008. *Ruffians, Yakuza, Nationalists: The Violent Politics of Modern Japan; 1860–1960*. Ithaca, NY: Cornell University Press.

Sinn, Elizabeth. 1989. *Power and Charity: The Early History of the Tung Wah Hospital, Hong Kong*. Hong Kong: Oxford University Press.

Smith, Dwight, Jr. 1975. *The Mafia Mystique*. New York: Basic.

———. 1991. "Wickersham to Sutherland to Katzenbach: Evolving an 'Official' Definition for Organized Crime." *Crime, Law, and Social Change* 16(2):138–42.

Smith, Michael G. 1974. *Corporations and Society*. London: Duckworth.

SOCA (Serious and Organised Crime Agency). 2012. *Organised Crime Groups*. http://www.soca.gov.uk/threats/organised-crime-groups.

SOS Impresa. 2012. *Le mani della criminalità sulle imprese—XIII Rapporto di SOS Impresa*. Reggio Emilia: Aliberti Editore.

Stajano, Corrado, ed. 1992. *Mafia: L'atto d'accusa dei giudici di Palermo*. Rome: Editori Riuniti. (Contains sections from Tribunale di Palermo. Ufficio Istruzione

Processi Penali. 1985–1992. *Ordinanza-sentenza di rinvio a giudizio nei confronti di Abbate Giovanni + 706*. Palermo, November 8, 40 vols.).

Stark, David. H. 1981. "The Yakuza: Japanese Crime Incorporated." PhD dissertation, Department of Political Science, University of Michigan, Ann Arbor.

Stille, Alexander. 1995. *Excellent Cadavers: The Mafia and the Death of the First Italian Republic*. London: Jonathan Cape.

Task Force on Organized Crime, President's Commission on Law Enforcement and Administration of Justice. 1967. *Task Force Report: Organized Crime*. Washington, DC: US Government Printing Office.

Thoumi, Francisco E. 2014. "Organized Crime in Colombia: The Actors Running the Illegal Drug Industry." In *The Oxford Handbook of Organized Crime*, edited by Letizia Paoli. Oxford: Oxford University Press.

TI (Transparency International). 2019. *Corruption Perceptions Index 2018*. https://www.transparency.org/cpi2018.

Tilly, Charles. 1985. "War Making and State Making as Organized Crime." In *Bringing the State Back In*, edited by Peter Evans, Dietrich Rueschemeyer, and Theda Skocpol. Cambridge: Cambridge University Press.

———. 1988. "Foreword." In *The Mafia of a Sicilian Village, 1860–1960: A Study of Violent Peasant Entrepreneurs*, edited by Anton Blok. New York: Polity.

Tolbert, Pamela S., and Richard H. Hall. 2009. *Organizations: Structures, Processes and Outcomes*, 10th ed. Abingdon: Routledge.

Tribunale di Marsiglia, Ufficio Istruzione Processi Penali. 1987. *Verbali di interrogatorio reso dal collaboratore di giustizia, Antonino Calderone*.

Tribunale di Milano, Ufficio del giudice per le indagini preliminari. 2010. *Ordinanza di applicazione di misura coercitiva nei confronti di Agostino Fabio + altri/ n. 8265/06*.

Tribunale di Palermo, Corte di Assise. 1987. *Sentenza nei confronti di Abbate Giuseppe + altri*. December 16.

Tribunale di Palermo, Ufficio del Giudice per le Indagini Preliminari. 1991. *Ordinanza di custodia cautelare in carcere nei confronti di Morici Serafino + 4*. July 9.

Tribunale di Palermo, Ufficio Istruzione Processi Penali. 1984. *Verbali di interrogatorio reso dal collaboratore di giustizia, Tommaso Buscetta*.

———. 1985. *Ordinanza-sentenza di rinvio a giudizio nei confronti di Abbate Giovanni + 706*. November 8.

———. 1989. *Verbali di interrogatorio reso dal collaboratore di giustizia, Francesco Marino Mannoia*.

Tribunale di Reggio Calabria, Ufficio del Giudice per le Indagini Preliminari. 1994. *Ordinanza di custodia cautelare in carcere nei confronti di Labate Pietro + 17*. January 7.

Trocki, Carl. A. 1993. "The Rise and Fall of the Ngee Heng Kongsi in Singapore." In *"Secret Societies" Reconsidered: Perspectives on the Social History of Modern South China and Southeast Asia*, edited by David Ownby and Mary F. Somers Heidhues. Amonk, NY: M. E. Sharpe.

Turone, Giuliano. 2008. *Il delitto di associazione mafiosa*. Milan: Giuffrè.

UNGA (United Nations General Assembly). 2000. *Crime Prevention and Criminal Justice: Report of the Ad Hoc Committee on the Elaboration of a Convention against Transnational Organized Crime on the Work of Its First to Eleventh Sessions*. A/SS/383, November 2.

UNODC (United Nations Office on Drugs and Crime). 2019. *Global Study on Homicide 2019*. Vienna: UNODC.

US Department of Justice. 2008. *Overview of the Law Enforcement Strategy to Combat International Organized Crime*. Washington, DC: United States Government Printing Office. http://www.justice.gov/ag/speeches/2008/ioc-strategy-public-overview.pdf.

———. 2014. *Motorcycle Gangs*. http://www.justice.gov/criminal/ocgs/gangs/motorcycle.html.

US Senate. 1951. *Third Interim Report of the Special Committee to Investigate Organized Crime in Interstate Commerce (Kefauver Committee)*. 81st Cong., 2d sess. Washington, DC: US Government Printing Office.

US Senate, Committee on Government Operations. 1963. *Hearings of Joseph Valachi before the Permanent Subcommittee on Investigations of the Committee on Government Operations*. Washington, DC: US Government Printing Office.

US Senate, Judiciary Committee. 1957. *Investigations on Improper Activities in the Labor or Management Field*. Hearings. Washington, DC: US Government Printing Office.

US Senate, Permanent Subcommittee on Investigations of the Committee on Governmental Affairs. 1988. *Organized Crime: Twenty-Five Years after Valachi*. Hearings. 100th Cong., 2d sess. Washington, DC: US Government Printing Office.

Van Duyne, Peter C. 1997. "Organized Crime, Corruption and Power." *Crime, Law, and Social Change* 26:201–38.

Van Oudenaren, John S. 2014. "Enduring Menace: The Triad Societies of Southeast China." *Asian Affairs: An American Review* 41(3):127–53.

Varese, Federico. 2001. *The Russian Mafia: Private Protection in a New Market Economy*. Oxford: Oxford University Press.

———. 2010. "What Is Organized Crime?" In *Organized Crime*, edited by Federico Varese. London: Routledge.

———. 2011. *Mafias on the Move: How Organized Crime Conquers New Territories*. Princeton, NJ: Princeton University Press.

———. 2020. "How Mafias Migrate: Transplantation, Functional Diversification, and Separation." In *Organizing Crime: Mafias, Markets, and Networks*, edited by Michael Tonry and Peter Reuter. Chicago: Chicago University Press.

Varese, Federico, and Rebecca W. Y. Wong. 2018. "Resurgent Triads? Democratic Mobilization and Organized Crime in Hong Kong." *Australian and New Zealand Journal of Criminology* 51(1):23–39.

Volkov, Vadim. 2014. "The Russian Mafia: The Rise and Extinction." In *Oxford Handbook of Organized Crime*, edited by Letizia Paoli. New York: Oxford University Press.

Von Lampe, Klaus. 2008. "Organised Crime in Europe: Conceptions and Realities." *Policing* 2(1):7–17.

———. 2016. *Organized Crime: Analyzing Illegal Activities, Criminal Structures, and Extralegal Governance*. Thousand Oaks, CA: Sage.

———. 2019. *Definitions of Organized Crime*. http://www.organized-crime.de /organizedcrimedefinitions.htm.

Von Lampe, Klaus, and Arjan Blokland. 2020. "Outlaw Biker Clubs and Organized Crime." In *Organizing Crime: Mafias, Markets, and Networks*, edited by Michael Tonry and Peter Reuter. Chicago: Chicago University Press.

Wang, Peng. 2017. *The Chinese Mafia: Organized Crime, Corruption, and Extralegal Protection*. Oxford: Oxford University Press.

Weber, Max. 1978. *Economy and Society: An Outline of Interpretive Sociology*, edited by Guenther Roth and Claus Wittich. Berkeley: University of California Press. (Originally published 1921. Tübingen: J. C. B. Mohr.)

White House. 2011. *Strategy to Address Transnational Organized Crime: Addressing Converging Threats to National Security*. Washington, DC: White House.

Xia, Ming. 2006. "Assessing and Explaining the Resurgence of China's Criminal Underworld." *Global Crime* 7(2):151–75.

Yeager, Matthew G. 2012. "Fifty Years of Research on Illegal Enterprise: An Interview with Mark Haller." *Trends in Organized Crime* 15:1–12.

Zhang, Sheldon X., and Ko-Lin Chin. 2003. "The Declining Significance of Triad Societies in Transnational Illegal Activities." *British Journal of Criminology* 43(3):463–82.

———. 2006. "Snakeheads, Mules, and Protective Umbrellas: A Review of Current Research on Chinese Organized Crime." *Crime, Law, and Social Change* 50:177–95.

———. 2008. "Enter the Dragon: Inside Chinese Human Smuggling Organizations." *Criminology* 40(4):737–68.

Zhou, Yongming. 1999. *Anti-drug Crusades in Twentieth-Century China: Nationalism, Identity, and State Building*. Lanham, MD: Rowman & Littlefield.

Peter Reuter and Letizia Paoli

How Similar Are Modern Criminal Syndicates to Traditional Mafias?

ABSTRACT

Five organizations exemplify organized crime organizations, or "mafias": the American and Sicilian Cosa Nostras, the Calabrian 'Ndrangheta, Chinese triads, and Japanese yakuza. Newer syndicates have emerged that are often called organized crime organizations but most importantly differ from the cxemplars. Drug trafficking syndicates in Colombia and Mexico are large, wealthy, and extraordinarily violent but have proven fragile in the face of aggressive law enforcement, do not have fully formalized internal structures or elaborate cultures, and only occasionally attempt to exercise political power or provide dispute settlement services in the criminal world. The Primeiro Comando da Capital in Sao Paulo, originally a prisoner self-protection group, comes closer. It has a formalized internal structure and an elaborate culture that permit it partly to control drug markets and provide an alternative justice system in parts of Brazil. Rio de Janeiro's Commando Vermelho, also originally prison-based and now extensively involved in drug trafficking, has some mafia-like characteristics. Other criminal syndicates are better thought of as "candidate criminal organizations" because they are not fully consolidated (e.g., the Neapolitan camorra), are not fully criminalized (e.g., Hells Angels), or aim mainly at political subversion and have only subsidiary involvement in profit-making crimes (e.g., the Colombian FARC).

Electronically published June 1, 2020

Peter Reuter is professor of public policy and of criminology at the University of Maryland. Letizia Paoli is professor of criminology in the Faculty of Law at the KU Leuven. They are grateful to Bryan Peters for extremely helpful research assistance.

223

The label "organized crime" is freely conferred in modern times on a heterogeneous set of entities. Official definitions allow the term to be applied to very modest illegal enterprises; three men and a dog regularly selling cannabis may be called organized crime. For example, the definition adopted by the United Kingdom's Serious and Organized Crime Agency in 2012 is broad and loose, has a clear focus on profit-making crimes, and sets no organizational requirements: "Organised crime is defined as those involved, normally working with others, in continuing serious criminal activities for substantial profit, whether based in the UK or elsewhere" (SOCA 2012; see also BKA 2018).[1]

The legal offense of criminal organization, increasingly treated as a synonym for organized crime (e.g., Europol 2013), is also broad and loose. In European Union criminal law and, thus, in the criminal laws of all EU member states, criminal organization requires no more than two people to cooperate for a certain period of time in the commission of serious criminal offenses (Council of the European Union 2008; Calderoni 2010). In such official definitions, and in some proposed by scholars (e.g., Felson 2009, pp. 159–60), organized crime seems to mean little more than co-offending by more than two perpetrators. Known as the illegal enterprise paradigm, this understanding equates organized crime with profit-making criminal activities, in particular the provision of illegal goods and services (e.g., van Duyne 1997; Edwards and Levi 2008).

Despite these loose definitions, in public imagery and political rhetoric, organized crime is still identified with large-scale, long-lasting, well-structured, and presumably powerful criminal organizations. Since about 1960, the American mafia or Cosa Nostra has served as the embodiment of this second understanding of organized crime. Since the 1980s, Cosa Nostra's Sicilian counterpart and a few other organizations have taken on similar mythical status. The alleged growing presence and reach of criminal organizations have been repeatedly used to justify expanded state powers. For example, the European Union's first policy intervention concerning organized crime opened with the claim: "Organized crime is increasingly becoming a threat to society as we know it and want to

---

[1] The UK government (see p. 11 at https://assets.publishing.service.gov.uk/government/uploads/system/uploads/attachment_data/file/752850/SOC-2018-web.pdf) has shifted to the even broader category of serious and organized crime, defined as "individuals planning, coordinating and committing serious offences, whether individually, in groups and/or as part of transnational networks."

preserve it. Criminal behavior no longer is the domain of individuals only, but also of organizations that pervade the various structures of civil society, and indeed society as a whole" (European Commission 1997, p. 1).

Given this dual understanding of organized crime in terms of both criminal activities and criminal organizations, the term has lost coherence as the basis for justifying expanded powers of the state or for research. We do not in this essay propose a new and competing definition of organized crime but attempt to learn from organizations to which application of the label is uncontroversial. Five sets of criminal organizations are considered exemplars of organized crime, namely the American Cosa Nostra, Sicilian Cosa Nostra, Calabrian 'Ndrangheta, Chinese triads, and Japanese yakuza. These are regularly called "mafias" or "mafia organizations" (see, e.g., Catino 2019, 2020; Paoli 2020; Varese 2020). Catino (2019) also includes the Neapolitan camorra and the Russian mafia. We explain below why we disagree, but note that some parts of the so-called Russian mafia, specifically the fraternal association *vory-v-zakone* (thieves with a code of honor), and some groups of the camorra, come close.

In this essay we examine some of the most prominent of the newer entities that are consistently called organized crime. To what extent are they criminal organizations in a sociological and not just legal sense? Do they share the distinctive characteristics of the "iconic five" mafia organizations?

The definition of criminal organization used here is much more restrictive than the legal offense of criminal organization or conventional understandings of the term "organized crime." We apply the classical definition of organization given by Max Weber ([1922] 1978, p. 48): "a social relationship which is either closed or limits the admission of outsiders [and whose] regulations are enforced by specific individuals: a chief and, possibly, an administrative staff, which normally also has representative powers." Definitions that draw on Weber are widely used in organization studies (e.g., Tolbert and Hall 2009). Criminal organizations, as we use the term, are social entities that are relatively large, have clear barriers to entry, an internal structure, and their own rules. They are either entirely criminal in purpose or routinely engage in criminal activities, whether for profit or for other purposes, directly or indirectly (i.e., through their members). Like other organized crime scholars, we do not include terrorist organizations in this category, unless their involvement in profit-making criminal activities comes to rival their original political cause, as for example in case of the FARC (Fuerzas Armadas Revolucionarias de Colombia [Revolutionary Armed Forces of Colombia]) in Colombia. In this respect, the term "organized crime organization," which Jacobs (2020) has recently proposed, would be more precise than the generic expression "criminal organization." However, the term "organized crime organization" rings awkwardly to the ear and would add yet another label to an already bulging armory.

Drawing on the extensive literature on the five mafias, we believe that the following seven characteristics typify them:

Longevity. The five mafias have all existed for at least a century. That longevity has been a source of power, since it creates an expectation of survival and enhances reputation and thus the capacity to intimidate by threat alone. Mafias' extraordinary longevity implies that they developed in premodern contexts in which state authorities had not yet monopolized the use of violence or were, as in the first Chinese settlements in Southeast Asia (e.g., Ownby and Somers Heidhues 1993), utterly absent. The American mafia is an apparent exception to the claim of premodernity but was explicitly modeled on the Sicilian Cosa Nostra. Mafias' premodern roots also influence their structure and culture.

Large size. All five mafias have in their histories had at least a few thousand members for several decades. The Chinese triads and Japanese yakuza had more than 230,000 and 180,000 members, respectively, at their peaks (Morgan 1960; NPA 2018). Although not all triad members were criminally active, these figures refer only to members who have been ritually affiliated. As is typical of true organizations, mafias clearly distinguish members from nonmembers.

Formalized and complex structure. As is required for a true organization, each of the five mafias has an internal set of rules and hierarchies; these are highly formalized and complex. They also have ruling bodies within each group and often also across groups that make up the consortia. Mafia organizations are segmentary societies—that is, consortia composed of several units that recognize each other as part of the same consortium. All five have mechanisms for dispute settlement, though their strength varies substantially.

Elaborate cultural apparatus. This constitutes an effort to generate an enduring commitment to the organization and a sense of family and identity. Mafia organizations often have initiation rituals, written sets of norms and penalties, and procedures to deal with violations. This enables them to create a collective identity, justify their existence and generate lifelong commitments, new identities, and fictive kinship ties among their members.

The contracts binding members to mafias are very different from the narrowly drawn employment contracts that are standard in contemporary bureaucracies and corporations, as well as in many illegal enterprises. The long-term and broad mafia contracts, and the fictive families they create, give mafia bosses extraordinary flexibility; in principle no order can be disobeyed by the members. However, in order to be effective, these contracts can be imposed only on candidates who are already socialized into certain values and norms, thus limiting the pools of eligible members.

Multifunctionality. All five mafias have engaged in a wide variety of activities, both legal and illegal. Some aim principally at increasing the organization's power within the community or even further afield; others are purely profit-making. There is rarely an effort to control the money-making activities members participate in. Profit-making activities, propelled by the late twentieth-century emergence of mass drug markets, have become more important, but historically the development and wielding of power were the mafias' distinctive feature. With the possible exception of the American Cosa Nostra, profit maximization even today is not their exclusive, or even their main, aim.

Goal of political dominion and long-standing ability to provide governance services. Mafia organizations are different from illegal enterprises and from other criminal organizations because they claim to exercise a local political dominion that extends beyond their members and collaborators. They also deliver certain governance services, particularly related to settlement of disputes and provision of personal security. They are thus inherently political organizations that have tried over time, with varying degrees of success, to enforce their rules on certain communities. They have attempted to endow themselves with legitimacy but have never succeeded in neutralizing all rival centers of power (Tilly 1985, 1988).

Popular legitimacy and power sharing. With their claim to exercise a political dominion, mafias have long enjoyed a considerable degree of popular legitimacy and have entered into de facto, or sometimes even official, power-sharing arrangements with local state institutions. No other organized crime actors have enjoyed such long-standing legitimacy from both the communities within which they operate and local state authorities.

Using Weber's definition of organization and this list of mafias' typifying characteristics as benchmarks, we focus first on the criminal syndicates of three Latin American countries, Colombia, Mexico, and Brazil. These are described in some detail since this requires integrating a scattered literature. Our comparative analysis shows that few of these criminal syndicates can be formally defined as organizations. In particular, all the prominent drug trafficking syndicates in Colombia and almost all in Mexico fail the most basic test of an organization. They have neither strict criteria to distinguish members from nonmembers nor a formalized internal structure with clear command positions. Moreover and perhaps surprisingly, neither the earlier nor the newer drug trafficking syndicates in Colombia and Mexico rely on a premodern, elaborate cultural apparatus such as those of traditional mafias to secure their members' allegiance. They usually show much less ambition than traditional mafias to exercise political power or provide dispute settlement services to other criminals or the broader population. The Sao Paulo Primeiro Comando da Capital (PCC) is by far the most developed in its internal structure, culture, and governance functions. The PCC is clearly a criminal organization in the Weberian sense and, though only 25 years old, appears well launched to become a powerful and enduring mafia if it can survive the departure of its charismatic leader. The Commando Vermelho (Red Command in Portuguese, also known as CV) in Rio de Janeiro may have many mafia characteristics; the evidence is less clear.

We then consider more heterogeneous sets of entities more briefly. One set comprises "not fully consolidated criminal organizations" such as the Neapolitan camorra, groups that emerged in Eastern Europe after the end of communism (Russia and Albania), and some emergent groups in Western Europe. We treat the camorra in detail because in the distant past it almost certainly was a mafia organization. Another set comprises offshoots of voluntary or sports associations, including the motorcycle gangs. These are true organizations, but we refer to them as candidate criminal organizations because they are not fully criminalized. The final set includes terrorist, paramilitary, and military groups that draw a growing share of their revenues from profit-making criminal activities, thus shifting away from their original subversive or military objectives.

The literature on the relatively new Latin American syndicates is not nearly as rich as that on the older five mafias. For example, there are no studies of the internal dynamics of Mexican drug-trafficking syndicates based on long-term undercover investigations (as with Donny Brasco for the American mafia; Pistone 1988) or extended statements by high-level informants (such as the *pentiti* for the Sicilian Cosa Nostra; e.g., Commissione Parlamentare Antimafia 1992).[2] The Brazilian literature is better but still weaker than for the historical syndicates. Lessing (2018) provides an outstanding analytic account of the dynamics of drug wars in Brazil, Colombia, and Mexico but with primary emphasis on the relationships between the syndicates and government policy. Our analysis of these syndicates is correspondingly limited. Time and space limitations prevent consideration of comparably powerful groups in three smaller and poorer Latin American countries, El Salvador, Guatemala, and Honduras, which constitute the Northern Triangle of Central America (Miguel Cruz 2010; Seelke 2016).

Why is it useful to establish whether some of the most prominent contemporary criminal syndicates are organizations and which traits they share with mafias? First, we see this essay as the beginning of an effort to develop a categorization of contemporary organized crime actors. Despite the subject's media salience, the burgeoning literature on organized crime, and numerous policy initiatives targeting organized crime, systematic comparisons of criminal entities are rare (i.e., Krauthausen 1997; Paoli 2002; Catino 2019). Comparative analysis has been hampered not only by the lack of data but also by confusion and ambiguities surrounding the concepts of organized crime and criminal organization. As a result, the varieties of organized crime actors have not been categorized. The comparative analysis of organized crime actors also provides a novel approach for bringing some clarity to the confused and confusing debate about the nature of organized crime. Previous efforts have looked for a consensus definition of organized crime but have mostly ended in identifying only basic, generic features and have not generated much progress.[3] Given the fuzziness of the concept and the increasing focus

---

[2] A rare exception is Human Rights Clinic (2017), analyzing testimony in a number of US federal trials of the Zetas, a Mexican criminal syndicate. It is telling that this represents detail not generated within Mexico itself.

[3] Varese (2010), for example, analyzed a database of 115 definitions of organized crime primarily from criminologists, criminal justice agencies, and statutes, which had been created by Klaus von Lampe; see von Lampe (2019) for the most recent version of the database. Varese presented statistical descriptions of the occurrence of specific features of the definitions over time (1915–2009) and across 23 countries (but mostly from the United States). He distinguished between organizations and activities in his review of definitions. For organizations, concepts such as specialization, hierarchy, and networks are most frequently mentioned. For activities, the list of relevant dimensions is slight: just monopoly and provision of illegal goods and services.

on prohibited profit-making activities, it is no surprise that several scholars (e.g., Naylor 2003; Edwards and Levi 2008) have suggested getting rid of the term "organized crime" altogether and focusing instead on the organization of crime for gain.

Since the 1980s, scholars (e.g., Bouchard and Morselli 2014) and a growing number of policy and law enforcement agencies worldwide (e.g., Europol 2003; White House 2011) have observed that true criminal organizations are the exception rather than the rule in the vast panorama of organized crime. Most exchanges in the illegal or criminal markets of developed countries are carried out by criminal enterprises, which are also frequently referred to as organized crime but are smaller and more ephemeral than mafias or other criminal organizations.

Second, we believe that research would profit from a focus on the distinctive features of mafias. This is not only because the five mafias—most prominently the American and Sicilian Cosa Nostras—have since the 1960s been considered exemplars. The ambition to exercise political dominion and provide competing dispute resolution and other governance services presents a distinctive threat of mafias to the legitimacy of the state. The five mafias all developed as responses to the failure of government to provide security of property and sometimes persons; profit-making criminal activities were not necessarily the first activities they undertook. If more modern criminal syndicates are able to imitate the mafias and present themselves as credible alternatives to the governments of failing states, that failure will be more difficult to reverse.

Multiple dimensions of research are affected by whether mafias and other criminal organizations are present. For example, there is a growing interest in the criminal careers of those involved in organized crime (Kleemans and van Kopen 2020). Mafias, with their emphasis on lifelong commitment and demanding initiation rituals, create distinct pathways; sheer economic ability counts for less in advancing in the organization. Military or political skills might also be essential to make a career in other criminal syndicates that share mafias' governance ambitions or are involved in open conflicts with state authorities or competing syndicates. Network analysis, used to understand the relationships among offenders in organizations or markets (Bouchard 2020), will require a different interpretation if mafias or other real organizations are present, whether or not these organizations are fully criminalized or are military bureaucracies or militias once fully dedicated to a revolutionary cause.

The essay is organized as follows. Sections I through III present relatively detailed descriptions of the Colombian, Mexican, and Brazilian drug-trafficking syndicates. Section IV presents a comparative analysis of the Latin American cases. Section V provides a much briefer discussion of a variety of entities that have been, we think, mischaracterized as organized crime and why they differ from mafias. Section VI concludes.

I. Colombian Drug "Cartels"[4]

The growth of the United States cocaine market in the 1980s provided the basis for a large refining and export industry in Colombia. That generated the most visible and politically active criminal syndicates of modern times. The cocaine "cartels," the standard but inaccurate name given to these trafficking syndicates, challenged the Colombian national government in the late 1980s. In 1989 they assassinated the leading presidential candidate (Luis Carlos Galan) and shot down a civilian jet plane with 139 passengers that they believed carried another political leader threatening their activities. This violence led to a military crackdown; the US government provided substantial resources and expertise to that effort. The result by 1995 was the removal by death or incarceration of the leadership of these syndicates. The cocaine trade continued unabated but in a very different form, with a relatively large number of small enterprises. It is useful then to divide the analysis between the pre- and postcrackdown periods.

A. The Cocaine Cartels in the 1980s

Two syndicates dominated the Colombian cocaine industry in the 1980s, one associated with Medellin, the other with Cali, Colombia's second and third largest cities. Each was identified with a few prominent leaders. Each one adopted its own distinct strategy in dealing with the government. They are called cartels, which suggests a capacity to fix prices and control markets; there is no evidence that they had such power and they are best thought of as syndicates, with many individual groups as members coordinating some of their activities, such as contributing cocaine for large shipments to the United States.

[4] A comprehensive English-language history of Colombian drug trafficking organizations is apparently not available. Useful sources include Thoumi (2014), Ramirez (2017), and Norman (2018).

The cartels were involved in politics, but for narrow self-protective purposes. A critical issue for the leaders was whether Colombia would sign an extradition treaty with the United States (Restrepo and Guizado 2003, pp. 261–63). They were confident they could evade much restriction if sentenced in Colombia but correctly feared confinement in the United States. Many political assassinations in this period were aimed to deter the government from signing an extradition treaty, with varying success over time (Lessing 2018).

No criminal figure so captured the popular imagination in the late twentieth century as Pablo Escobar, the most prominent of the Medellin traffickers.[5] Escobar created a complex myth, involving both extreme violence and social activism (Restrepo and Guizado 2003; Arias 2010). The violence was brazen; Escobar was willing to announce the amount he would pay for the killing of a police officer in Medellin (Lessing 2018). After some years of cooperation, he also became aggressive in his treatment of other traffickers, killing many in disputes about transactions or territory. At the same time Escobar ostentatiously donated money for low-income housing in his home city and succeeded in getting elected as an alternate member of Congress (Restrepo and Guizado 2003; Bowden 2007).[6] In a country long dominated by an oligarchy that provided little social mobility, a rich drug dealer apparently with a social conscience had a certain appeal (Thoumi 2002, 2012). Carlos Lehder, another prominent member of the Medellin cartel also had political ambitions, albeit of a generally fascist tendency (Lee, 1991 p. 9). However, there was no effort to create a legend of social justice in the trafficking enterprises themselves; the philanthropy was personal, associated with the leader rather than the syndicate—similar to the Gates Foundation rather than the Microsoft Foundation.

The Drug Enforcement Administration (DEA) estimated at the end of 1980s that about 24,000 people were part of the Medellin and Cali cartels (Krauthausen 1997, p. 162). It is unclear, though, how many of these people really were members of the two syndicates. The major exporters, as well as the traffickers that controlled specific export routes, sometimes internalized the services, paying regular salaries to their

---

[5] A good discussion of Escobar's grip on the twenty-first-century Colombian imagination is provided in a 2018 *New Yorker* article (Anderson 2018).

[6] Escobar was forced to resign 2 years after his election, when the source of his wealth was revealed.

employees. At other times they bought the same services on the market. Low-level participants in the drug industry primarily worked under conventional job contracts similar to those of employees of legal businesses owned by the *narcos*. Big shipments often consisted of product from several drug-trafficking groups; they shared the risks, with some *narcos* "controlling" a specific route. In this sense they played the role of historical figures such as caravan leaders in the desert (Krauthausen 1997, pp. 162–76) or ship owners sailing from Genoa or another Italian sea republic in the late Middle Ages.

The core of the drug-trafficking groups composing the cartels often included brothers, such as the brothers Rodríguez Orejuela, who founded the Cali cartel, or several relatives as in the case of Pablo Escobar. According to Krauthausen (1997, p. 187), Escobar's group even at its peak consisted of only a modest number of people, probably not many more than 50. Escobar surrounded himself with a few trusted relatives, accountants, and other low-level employees, who were principally responsible for organizing his hiding places. This suggests that even at its core the Medellin cartel did not rely on lifelong status and fraternization contracts, as mafias do. Krauthausen further notes that the cartels, much like legitimate businesses, screened their employees and partners, avoiding people with addiction or other psychological problems.

The Colombian syndicates also insisted that employees and partners respect the code of silence but again, unlike the mafias, did not seek to inculcate these values in members through initiation rituals, ad hoc norms, and symbols. Instead they attempted to secure allegiance through compensation and threats. The best documented study of traffickers (Kenney 2007) points to recruitment that was much closer to corporate hiring than to initiation into a mafia family and relied more on threats and deterrence than the internalization of a specific subculture. "Recruits may be asked to provide contact information for their immediate family members as a hedge against cooperating with the police. For similar reasons, some enterprises require potential employees to fill out an application that details previous work experience and supplies personal information to their employer" (Kenney 2007, p. 250). Nor were individuals permanently identified with a specific enterprise. "Traffickers that avoid apprehension readily migrate to other nodes or networks when their former colleagues are jailed. 'This happens a lot, depending on your role,' explains Nestor. 'Say one guy gets popped, you go work for another group or another guy'" (Kenney 2007, p. 256). Kenney notes that friendship and family relations play a role in recruitment, but that is true of conventional enterprise hiring as well.

While the units at the core of the cartels were never very large, there is evidence that some distribution cells organized by the cartels in the United States were more substantial. Fuentes (1999) describes organizations primarily in the New York metropolitan area with hundreds of employees. He invokes Weberian concepts of organization to describe the individual components ("cells"), though he also emphasizes the turnover in the workforce.

The Colombian cartels, like other criminal syndicates, had to protect themselves from the challenges of competitors and other underworld figures without resorting to police and courts. In particular their leaders had to demonstrate command of violence to maintain their credibility and market shares. However, the exercise of violence was not equally distributed across the component parts of the cartel; some suborganizations were more willing and able to command violence than others. Even within the Medellin cartel itself, the Escobar and Gonzalo Rodríguez Gacha groups had far fewer qualms than other drug-trafficking groups about employing violence to punish people who committed infractions and kill uncooperative representatives of the state authorities. This is why Krauthausen (1997, p. 185) concludes that Escobar's and Rodríguez Gacha's "goals and action were distinctively military and political," even if they also earned huge sums with drug trafficking. In particular, Escobar emerged as the guarantor of most trafficking deals and even set up *oficinas* (in effect, bureaus) that could help other traffickers reclaim cocaine or money if their business partners tried to cheat them (McDermott 2015). Because of such service, Escobar was often invited by other trafficking groups to take a share of shipments (Hylton 2008).

Because of its pronounced military functions, Rodríguez Gacha's group had the appearance of a paramilitary formation, with a formalized hierarchy and a clear division of labor. Despite its even more pronounced function of protection, Escobar's group was less formalized. Rather than developing an in-house capability, Escobar outsourced the use of violence and relied on the leaders of Medellin street gangs; he bought violent services on the market, mostly from young members of city gangs or other thugs (Lamb 2010). These worked for Escobar as long as he could pay them. "Recuerde: Los extrabitables sí pagamos" ("Remember that we the Extrabitables really pay") stated a flier distributed by Escobar in Medellin. And thanks to a large pool of mercenary hit men, Escobar exercised firm control of the drug industry of the whole department of Antiochia right up to his arrest.

There are references to very large numbers of traffickers, both large and small, suggesting that the individual units were moderate in size. For example, Bunker and Sullivan (1998) mention "223 top traffickers" who formed the MAS,[7] an alliance that challenged left-wing guerillas who had kidnapped the sister of a leading Cali trafficker. Lee (1991) says that one official report estimated that there were 200 individual trafficking groups in the Medellin cartel.

For the dozen or so years that the Medellin cartel operated, there were numerous instances of battles among the leaders, at the same time that the same men were involved in collaborative trafficking efforts. A massive cocaine refining facility found in the jungle in 1984 (Tranquilandia) was apparently the result of collaboration among 14 different trafficking groups (Lee 1991). However, numerous accounts refer to Escobar's killing of others in the cartel (e.g., Duncan 2014; Lessing 2018). In the end, other traffickers assisted the state in tracking down Escobar; indeed, they formed a team specifically for that purpose (Bowden 2007). There seemed to be no dispute resolution mechanism, though the cartel had a board of directors for operational purposes. That board met only occasionally and apparently focused on coordinating shipments (Kenney 2007).

The Medellin and Cali cartels were substantial enough entities that they met on a number of occasions with senior members of the national government to discuss potential deals under which the traffickers would be able to retain some of their wealth in return for abandoning the drug trade (Clawson and Lee 1996). It is claimed that in these meetings the traffickers offered to pay off the Colombian national debt in return for a peace agreement; the government reportedly declined the offer (Lessing 2018).[8]

The two cartels adopted different protective strategies (Thoumi 2014). Where Medellin consistently challenged the state with assassinations, Cali relied on corruption. Many members of the Colombian congress

---

[7] Muerte a Secuestradores (Death to Kidnappers).

[8] We are skeptical about this claim. No reference we have found provides any direct documentation of these meetings or of the content of the discussions. In heavily sourced studies such as Lessing's (2018), this is a notable absence.

were known to have taken bribes from Cali traffickers.[9] The government responded to the 1989 Medellin assassination of Galan and the shooting down of a civilian airline with a campaign involving use of the military as well as police forces. Escobar was initially locked up in a luxurious prison following negotiations; he escaped and was killed in a shoot-out in 1993. The Cali group was eliminated by 1995 via a different mechanism. After it became known that the Cali cartel had funded the successful campaign of President Ernesto Samper, his administration had no option but to crack down on the major traffickers, in particular the Rodriguez-Orejuela brothers (Felbab-Brown 2009; Snyder and Durán Martínez 2009, p. 84).

Also important for their development as criminal syndicates were differences in how they invested in the legal economy (Thoumi 2014). The Medellin cartel purchased large tracts of farmland for cattle grazing. They created heavily armed gangs to purchase land at low prices from local farmers and to protect against guerillas. The gangs also challenged the national authorities in the rural areas. The Cali traffickers instead invested in urban properties and sought political protection for those properties rather than challenge the government directly. That made Medellin a more tempting target for a government crackdown, even before it directly attacked the national government.

The two cartels undertook other criminal activities; having assembled such massive firepower, it would be surprising if they had not. For example, Garzon (2010) reports that they were involved in general extortion. However, the very paucity of description of other activities suggests that they were not important sources of revenue. Moreover, no source suggests that the cartels or their representatives were interested in providing effective governance services to either the rest of the non-drug-related underworld or the general population. The two cartels were active in the United States but only in marketing cocaine; they never established a broader criminal presence in American cities (Florez and Boyce 1990, pp. 83–84).

---

[9] Twelve Colombian legislators were imprisoned for accepting bribes from the Cali Cartel during the 1994 "Proceso 8.000" election scandal. Insiders, including President Samper's campaign treasurer, Santiago Medina, estimated that at least 70 percent of congressmen accepted cartel funds (Lee and Thoumi 1999, p. 71). At one point, 170 of 230 legislators were under investigation for cartel-related political corruption (Carrigan 1996, p. 6).

The cores of the Cali and Medellin cartels might have constituted small true organizations with well-defined memberships, but they were still much different from the mafias. The dispute resolution mechanism was weak and abjectly failed in the latter stages of Escobar's career. The political claims were associated with individuals and not the syndicates. In addition to the differences in internal structure, culture, degree of multi-functionality, and claims to exercise a political dominion, the two cartels failed the longevity test; they lasted less than 20 years and did not survive beyond the first generation of leaders. The Medellin cartel challenged the national government frontally, as did the Sicilian Cosa Nostra in the 1990s. While the Sicilian Cosa Nostra was diminished as a result, the Medellin cartel as such was eliminated. The Cali cartel, though it avoided confrontation, was also eliminated by the government once the Samper administration (1994–98) was forced by US pressure to crack down.

B. Post-Cartel

The elimination of the cartels' leadership in the early 1990s created only a temporary interruption to the flow of cocaine to the United States but had a lasting effect on the organization of the drug trade (Lee 2002, pp. 538–39). Certainly there were no successors to Escobar and the Rodriguez-Orejuela brothers, larger-than-life figures who presented challenges to the Colombian establishment. However, it is not clear that much changed operationally. The smaller syndicates remained capable of cooperating and bringing large quantities of cocaine together to ship to the United States, as is indicated by very large individual seizures (multiple tons) that have consistently occurred since the end of the two cartels.[10]

The drug trade has been through perhaps three successive transformations, more than we can elaborate on in this subsection. Drawing on an unpublished 2012 study by Peter Reuter and Daniel Rico, we describe the major drug-dealing syndicate in the second phase of the cocaine trade, between about 2002 and 2012.

---

[10] Attesting to the cartel's capabilities, 92 percent of cocaine samples seized in 2016 in the continental United States were of Colombian origin (DEA 2017, p. 2). On February 28, 2019, officials at the Port of Newark seized 3,200 pounds of cocaine, worth an estimated $77 million, on board a container ship that had recently arrived from Colombia (Watkins 2019). In a similar incident on June 2, 2016, Miami-based Customs and Border Protection agents seized approximately 2,000 pounds, with a reported street value of $27 million, from a general cargo vessel recently arrived from Haiti (*Maritime Executive* 2016).

Following the dismantling of the Cali and Medellin cartels in the early 1990s, there was a period in which cocaine trafficking was conducted by small, essentially anonymous, criminal gangs. Starting around 1998, right-wing paramilitary groups emerged under the loose heading of the AUC (United Self-Defense Forces of Colombia) that eventually depended on drug revenues for most of their income.[11] After 2002, when the government began negotiations to reintegrate the paramilitary groups back into society, a set of purely criminal groups emerged, loosely labeled BACRIM ("bandas criminales"; McGovern 2016; Nussio 2018).

The biggest of these gangs, Los Rastrojos, was formed in 2002 as the armed wing for one of the leaders (Varela) contending for control of the Cartelo de Norte Valle (NDVC). Internal fighting led to Varela's murder in 2008, but his armed wing remained a powerful player in the drugs, extortion, and kidnapping businesses (*InSight Crime* 2017). After 2008 it was led by two brothers, Javier Antono Calle Serna and Luis Enrique Calle Serna.

As the name of its predecessor syndicate (Norte de Valle) suggests, Los Rastrojos was for some years regionally focused, operating in the Pacific coast region of Colombia. After 2008 it expanded into other regions previously dominated by one of its rivals, Los Urabenos, particularly in the Caribbean coast (the department of Antioquia).

Given their paramilitary origin, Los Rastrojos most probably had some formalized internal structure with (pseudo-)military command positions. There were both regional- and municipal-level management structures. As in the case of the Medellin cartel, it is difficult to estimate its membership not least because the syndicate was not highly centralized and considerable autonomy was given to the individual units. Los Rastrojos was estimated to have more members than any of the other BACRIM groups and possibly as much as 50 percent of the BACRIM total, with influence in 100 municipalities. As a Colombian national security officer noted in an interview, "It is not an easy task to define who is a member of Los Rastrojos: the individual that provides the cars and transportation for the commanders is a supplier but is not a member of the structure. We also found that smaller organizations use the name to commit extortions, but when we conducted investigations we found

---

[11] The International Crisis Group (ICG 2007, p. 4) reports that Castano, the AUC leader, admitted that in 2000, 70 percent of the paramilitary income came from drugs.

that they have no relationship with the structure, they are only using the 'bad will' reputation for extortive purposes. The name had become a 'trademark,' sometimes paid for and sometimes not" (Reuter and Rico 2012, pp. 6–7).[12]

For about a decade, the syndicate exported large quantities of cocaine. In December 2010, Colombian police seized 6 tons of cocaine in the port of Buenaventura that was purportedly the property of Los Rastrojos, which was also connected to a seizure of $27 million in US currency on a ship coming from Mexico, believed to be payment by Mexico's Sinaloa cartel (*InSight Crime* 2011). In contrast to their predecessor syndicates, they retailed drugs in Colombia itself. A distinctive feature of this syndicate was its active involvement in all stages of production and export to Mexico (transiting to the United States) in close cooperation with the Sinaloa cartel, which was a business partner, not just a buyer. However it stuck to its core competence, the management of criminal activity, rather than direct participation in the drug trade, in particular the upstream activities of growing and processing.

Los Rastrojos was involved in a wide variety of other criminal activities. For example, there were reports after 2010 that both the principal left-wing guerilla group FARC and BACRIM (including Los Rastrojos) extorted the rapidly expanding illegal gold mining industry, which is largely populated by micro-enterprises (Romero 2011). However, there is a dearth of specifics on other profit-making activities. They extorted both legitimate and criminal entrepreneurs in the areas they controlled. They were also participants in siphoning oil from Colombian pipelines, as well as smugglers of contraband gasoline from Ecuador. In Medellin, the regional leader of Los Rastrojos has been a principal in the pirate CD market (Reuter and Rico 2012).

The syndicate, like all its competitors and predecessors, had a fearsome reputation for use of violence for instrumental purposes. Government officials believe that the national leadership of Los Rastrojos in its later years attempted to restrain the regional units from undertaking high-profile violent activities, in particular massacres, a common occurrence in the past. The reasoning was that these attract unnecessary government attention. To reinforce this message, financial fines were levied

[12] From the same interview: "It sounds simple but to estimate the real size of the organization and the areas of influence is a very complex task" (Reuter and Rico 2012, p. 7).

on regions in which such events occurred, which caused a reduction in the share of cocaine revenues returned to the regional leadership. However, like the Medellin and Cali cartels, Los Rastrojos made no effort to offer governance services to the broader population (interviews with officials in Reuter and Rico 2012).

C. Relations with Political Actors

Despite its right-wing paramilitary origins, Los Rastrojos built working relationships with both FARC and ELN (National Liberation Army), the two main left-wing guerillas active in Colombia. These alliance decisions were made at the regional, rather than national, level. Thus some units still fought FARC, as indicated by a February 2011 report of a clash between the two entities in which 15 people were killed.[13]

The FARC sold Los Ratrojos the coca base; it also provided protection for the processing labs. In exchange Los Rastrojos provided other raw materials for the production process, especially gasoline, which was a critical resource for the FARC; Los Rastrojos owned gasoline stations and trucks for gasoline transportation (interview with Navy official; Reuter and Rico 2012, p. 12).

The gang was well armed but reluctant to attack the government. "Los Rastrojos had a big arsenal of rifles and munitions that they have decided not to use against the army or the police, for strategic reasons. They know fighting is a costly activity, and let the FARC attack our forces" (interview with Army intelligence analyst; Reuter and Rico 2012, p. 12).

Los Rastrojos was deeply involved in corruption, aimed primarily at local rather than national government officials. The purpose seemed to be less concerned with protection of drug-trafficking activities, at least directly, than with obtaining access to government contracts and facilities for money laundering. It did not neglect national influence; for example,

---

[13] See http://colombiareports.com/colombia-news/news/14291-15-dead-in-farc-los -rastrojos-clash.html. An Army intelligence officer speculated as to why the relationship was cooperative in only some areas: "In Cauca the FARC is strong enough to conduct the narcotics business without Los Rastrojos, so they don't want them around; the FARC decided to cooperate with other BACRIM that are enemies of Los Rastrojos." The decisions about alliance under this interpretation lie with the FARC. However, even this observer offered a counterexample in which it appeared to be Los Rastrojos that initiated the relationship: "Two years ago the Urabeños worked with the FARC in the northwest of the country, smuggling cocaine to Central America, but Los Rastrojos offer a better deal for the 58th front of the FARC and now both groups are fighting against the Urabeños" (Reuter and Rico 2012, pp. 11–12).

in the 2010 national elections, it was accused of intimidating some voters and paying others in the department of Narino (Borkan 2010).

InSight Crime, the most authoritative independent source of information about Latin American organized crime, more or less declared Los Rastrojos to have been eliminated as an important player by 2012: "The group imploded in 2012 with the fall of three of its main leaders" (*InSight Crime* 2017). However, in 2019 *InSight Crime* reported major incidents, such as a massacre of 12 Los Rastrojos members in a factional fight on the Venezuelan border, where the syndicate has been involved in the theft of fuel (Venezuela Investigative Unit 2019). It seems to have survived despite the frequent turnover in leadership but to have been weakened, particularly in its core drug-selling activities.

It is easy to dismiss the candidacy of the post-cartel criminal groups as mafias. In the case of the Rastrojos (and a few other federations of the same generation such as Los Urbaneos), it can be safely argued that they were organizations at least in their core groups, not least because of their military setup. They were successful criminal enterprises with unstable leadership. However, they made no effort to create fictive families or other social bonds, had a minimal dispute resolution mechanism, no apparent succession rules, and no claim to broad governance or popular legitimacy. They undertook a range of criminal activities and had a substantial geographic spread within Colombia but not elsewhere.

II. Mexican Drug-Trafficking Syndicates

For more than three decades, Mexican drug-trafficking syndicates (usually referred to as DTOs, the acronym of "drug-trafficking organizations") have occupied a prominent place in the American vision of the drug supply problem. Essentially all illegal drugs imported into the United States are either produced in Mexico (heroin, marijuana, and methamphetamine) or pass through (cocaine) on their way to US markets (US Department of State 2019, p. 212).[14] This has led to a view that the Mexican DTOs are uniquely rich, with estimates of annual revenues regularly in the tens of billions of dollars (e.g., National Drug Intelligence

---

[14] Synthetic opioids, in particular fentanyl, are now the principal source of fatal overdoses in the United States, even though the quantity consumed is tiny. These new drugs are produced mostly in China, but a substantial share is imported via Mexico (Pardo et al. 2019).

Center 2008), though a more realistic estimate puts it in the low billions (Kilmer et al. 2010). Since 2006 the extraordinary number and gruesomeness of homicides involving Mexican DTOs have riveted attention. For example, in 2008 La Familia Michoacana threw five decapitated heads onto the dance floor of a disco club to demonstrate its power; it also threw a bomb into a crowd celebrating Independence Day for the same purpose (Felbab-Brown 2011). A good quality literature on the effect of government actions against DTOs has emerged; for example, there are sophisticated analyses of the consequences of incarcerating a DTO leader on violence in his territory, showing that it led to greater violence both in that territory and in those neighboring (Calderón et al. 2015; Osorio 2015; Duran-Martinez 2017). However, less attention has been paid to many of the dimensions of our concern, such as recruitment, organizational structure, nondrug activities, and governance.

A further complication is that Mexico now has many large-scale criminal syndicates that have a variety of origins, structures, and behaviors. For example, the Zetas is a relatively recent syndicate formed out of defectors from elite[15] military units in the late 1990s and initially affiliated with the Gulf cartel.[16] The Zetas' power rested primarily on its willingness to use extreme and spectacular violence in almost any situation, including assassinations of politicians, grenade attacks, car bombs, and display of bodies or body parts of murdered victims (Correa-Cabrera 2017; Felbab-Brown 2019, p. 2). Although the Zetas also bribed local and state politicians and government officials, it did not seek high-level government protection or power-sharing agreements. It was also not interested in gaining popular legitimacy through the delivery of dispute settlements or other governance services. It instead used its military power to achieve political dominion by fear, to extort both legal and illegal activities such as the smuggling of migrants in its areas of settlement, and to become involved in a variety of illegal profit-making activities,

[15] The adjective "elite" is almost universally applied to the Zetas' origins; this seems to refer to the training that its original members received in the Mexican and Guatemalan Armies from Israeli and US Special Forces (Grayson and Loga 2012, p. 46, Correa-Cabrera 2017, pp. 21–22, 57–58).

[16] The Zetas was originally a component of the Gulf cartel; its members separated into a competitive group in 2003, following the arrest of the Gulf cartel leader, Osiel Cardenas Guillen (Atuesta and Perez-Davila 2018).

including kidnappings, prostitution, pirating DVDs, and sale of black-market oil in addition to drug trafficking (Correa-Cabrera 2017).

The Sinaloa cartel can trace its origins back to pre–WWII drug trafficking and has at least until recently largely remained focused on drug trafficking. Rather than openly challenging government authority, the Sinaloa cartel was through the second half of the twentieth century closely tied to the political structure and has shown a capacity to negotiate the resolution of community conflicts, at least on occasion, thus gaining some partial local legitimacy (Astorga 2012). Thus any effort to summarize the whole set of DTOs in a single characterization risks distortion.

Our focus is on the current configuration of DTOs. An assessment of their capabilities is likely to be different from the situation in the late twentieth century. To that extent, Mexico resembles Colombia. Relationships with the state have changed dramatically over the last 20 years. When the PRI (Institutional Revolutionary Party) dominated politics at all levels (federal, state, municipal), the party maintained a close corrupt relationship with approximately five drug-trafficking syndicates that kept violence at a modest level (Snyder and Duran-Martinez 2009; Lessing 2018). The corruption involved both law enforcement and political authority (Astorga 1999). One former governor wrote of adherence by the drug-trafficking syndicates to 10 principles in return for protection:

(1) there should be no bodies on the streets; (2) criminals were not allowed to sell drugs in schools; (3) there should be no media scandals; (4) traffickers should allow periodic drug seizures and arrests of low members; (5) traffickers must generate economic revenues for their communities; (6) there should be no proliferation of gangs; (7) criminals should not pact directly with the police or the judiciary; (8) mistakes are to be punished with imprisonment by the authorities, not with execution by rivals; (9) criminals must respect territorial boundaries; and (10) profits from illicit markets should be reinvested in Mexico. (Monreal Ávila 2008)[17]

The gradual erosion of PRI's political dominance, starting with the loss of some state governorships in the 1990s and then the 2000 election of Vicente Fox, the first non-PRI president in 71 years, led to a more

---

[17] This summary has a beguiling crispness and comprehensiveness. It should probably not be taken too literally but rather as a rough guide to the nature of the agreement.

complex relationship between government and DTOs. Drug-trafficking-related violence rose sharply during Fox's administration, though the national homicide rate fell from 13 per 100,000 in 2000 to 8 in 2007 (Heinle, Ferreira, and Shirk 2014). According to Correa-Cabrera (2017), the increase in drug-related violence was not only due to the decline of one-party rule. It was also promoted by the Zetas, its extensive and brutal use of violence, and its attempt to impose its power in the northeastern Mexican state of Tamaulipas and other parts of Mexico: "a new militarized criminal organization brought with it the militarization of other criminal groups and the militarization of the security strategy in Mexico" (Correa-Cabrera 2017, p. 39). Existing drug-trafficking syndicates felt obliged to set up enforcer wings. The Sinaloa cartel, for example, established Los Negros, an enforcer group similar to Los Zetas, while the Empresa in Michoacán founded La Familia Michoacana, after breaking up a previous alliance with the Zetas and the Gulf cartel.

Drug-related homicides included intersyndicate killings, assassination of police and local political figures, and occasional killings of innocent parties apparently aimed to amplify the violent reputations of the newer syndicates and the armed wings of the older ones (e.g., Lacey 2008; Reuter 2009). Many of the victims' bodies were accompanied by notes declaring which group had committed the murder and what message the killing was supposed to send (Atuesta 2017). Syndicates also started using traditional media and social media to justify their brutal deeds, distributing shocking narco-videos of assassinations and publishing communiques in important newspapers, thus spreading the impression of an unmanageable country (Correa-Cabrera 2017, pp. 30–31). The homicide rate dramatically accelerated with the decision by President Calderon in late 2006, following his very narrow victory over the left-wing PRD's (Democratic Revolutionary Party) Andres Manuel Lopez Obrador, to bring in the military to crack down on the criminal syndicates. From 2007 through to this writing in 2019, the national homicide rate has been extremely high by historical and global standards, at approximately 25 per 100,000 in 2018 (INEGI 2019). Moreover, in 2020 the government estimated that 60,000 individuals had "disappeared" between 2007 and 2019, presumably homicide victims but with bodies that had been buried in mass graves so they did not show up in the official statistics; many are thought to be killings related to the drug trade (Sheridan 2020).

Mexican criminal syndicates are very large, but systematic membership or employment estimates do not exist in the published literature. Astorga (2012), in the course of debunking estimates of various dimensions of the Mexican drug trade (e.g., revenue, cultivation area), offered no estimates of the syndicates' membership. Bunker (2010) reports a total of about 100,000 in just the largest two DTOs (Sinaloa and Gulf cartels), without providing a specific source for the number or specifying the inclusion criteria. A review of many sources has turned up no estimates, but the impression is of individual syndicates that have thousands, if not tens of thousands, of members or regular associates.[18] As in the case of the Colombian cartels, membership has to be understood in a loose way; the estimates refer to the people who variously participated in drug trafficking or other criminal activities. No data suggest that, as in the mafias, there is a clear-cut distinction between members and nonmembers.

Some syndicates have become institutionalized, in the sense of surviving the departures (typically through killings) of their founders. For example, the Gulf cartel lost its long-term leader Osiel Cardenas Guillen in 2003 but continued to function as a major syndicate, though losing its armed wing that became Los Zetas. However, many of the more recent syndicates have proven fairly ephemeral. For example, Los Caballeros Templarios emerged as a breakaway from La Familia in 2011 but did not survive the capture of its leader in 2015 (Atuesta and Perez-Davila 2018, p. 245). Even the Zetas has not been able to consolidate. Although it was reported to be "the criminal group with highest presence in the nation, even above the Sinaloa cartel" in 2012 (quoted in Correa-Cabrera 2017, p. 49), by 2014 it had started to disintegrate. It was targeted by Mexican, US, and Guatemalan law enforcement agencies and by rival syndicates. As Daniel Haering observes, "the old networks were disrupted by the Zetas, and now the Zetas have disintegrated into Zetillas. They are splinter groups (*grupúsculos*), not big operators" (International Crisis Group 2014, p. 12).

---

[18] Estimates place the number of persons employed by Mexican cartels at approximately 450,000 (Chew Sánchez 2014, p. 26). Although there is some consensus that Cartel de Jalisco Nueva Generación (CJNG) is currently one of the largest and most powerful (Jones 2018, p. 20; Congressional Research Service 2019, p. 18), size estimates for individual cartels are few and far between. Chalk (2011, p. 26) noted that the La Familia cartel had 4,000 members in 2010. None of these figures is well documented.

Recruitment seems often to be open rather than based on kinship. For example, it was claimed in 2012 that the cartels used social media for recruitment (Looft 2012). The Zetas recruited its core members from specific Mexican and Guatemalan army units, using military training and discipline to secure members' allegiance and create a sense of belonging. From 2003 onward, once it expanded beyond its original basis in Tamaulipas, the Zetas also allowed local criminal groups and thugs to use its brand (Correa-Cabrera 2017).

The Sinaloa cartel, one of the most durable and significant syndicates, appears to be different. "The Sinaloa cartel's central bond is blood. Many of its members are related by birth or by marriage" (*InSight Crime* 2019). Some of both the older and newer syndicates have spawned their own popular music, ballads that are regularly performed on local radio stations (Guevara 2013, pp. 141, 147; Campbell 2014, p. 72).

There are no reports of any rituals associated with membership or the creation of fictive family ties. La Familia Michoacana and its splinter group Los Caballeros Templarios (or the Knights Templar) may be exceptions. They have used evangelism, an eccentric Christian credo, and regional identities to enhance their legitimacy among their members and the local population and justify their extreme use of violence (Grayson 2010; Felbab-Brown 2019).

Some features we infer from absence of any mention in the extensive literature that has developed. No study except Felbab-Brown (2019)[19] refers to governance functions provided by the syndicates either across product or service markets or across syndicates in drug trafficking. The extraordinary level of violent conflict between various groups provides evidence that no mechanisms have developed to replace the PRI in its role of ensuring peace in the drug trade.

Correa-Cabrera (2017) and Atuesta and Perez-Davila (2018) suggest that the violence is not merely a direct response to the government crackdown but also results from the fragmentation of existing syndicates generated by the spread of Zetas' militarized tactics and the fractionation of political authority with the breakdown of the PRI monopoly.

---

[19] "In contrast to the criminal groups choosing to rule through sheer might alone, others, such as La Familia Michoacana, Los Templarios, and the Sinaloa cartel, have been providing a variety of governance functions beyond the distribution of handouts, such as the adjudication of disputes and enforcing judgments, thereby acquiring authority and political capital" (Felbab-Brown 2019, p. 13). We have been unable to find any confirming evidence for this statement by a well-regarded scholar.

This fragmentation is illustrated by the 5-year time line for the 2006 Sinaloa cartel in Atuesta and Perez-Davila (2018). Over those years it fractured into as many as 10 coexisting criminal groups. Atuesta and Perez-Davila (2018) concluded that the five DTOs that existed in 2006 had become 80 distinct syndicates/formations by 2011. Beittel (2019) offers different figures but makes the same point. Golz and D'Amico (2018) argue that the pressure against leading traffickers benefited smaller DTOs.

Atuesta and Perez-Davila (2018) identify six shifting alliances among various syndicates, combining temporarily to resist attacks by a common enemy. For example:

i.   The Gulf cartel and Los Zetas to confront the Sinaloa cartel;
ii. The Gulf cartel and La Familia Michoacana to confront Los Zetas, which wanted to enter Michoacan;
iii. La Resistencia, Los Zetas, and the Cartel del Pacifico Sur to confront La Barbie.

The alliances are quite short-lived, dissolving when the threat goes away and easily generating conflict among DTOs that were just recently allies.

There are passing references to other income-generating activities of the DTOs in recent years (e.g., Felbab-Brown 2019[20]). According to Correa-Cabrera (2017), the Zetas was the first to use its military power to impose its presence in non-drug-related criminal activities, and the same strategy was copied by other syndicates. Kidnapping and extortion of legitimate businesses in major cities are important potential revenue sources, though no systematic revenue estimate is available. Theft of oil from the poorly maintained distribution system of the national oil company, PemEx, may provide substantial revenues (Beittel 2019). None of the other sources that are regularly mentioned (e.g., services for human smuggling or extortion of farmers in rural areas where poppy and marijuana growing is concentrated) have much plausibility as providing revenues comparable to those obtained from drug smuggling (Kilmer et al. 2010).

---

[20] "Criminal groups have also become directly involved in fuel theft and its illegal distribution, kidnapping, and many other prohibited activities, such as illegal logging" (Felbab-Brown 2019, p. 12).

In sum, the current Mexican criminal syndicates, even the largest and most enduring ones, have few of the characteristics associated with mafias. They are large, and some have broad geographic spread within Mexico and operate (in terms of supply chains and sales) in other countries. Their longevity is in question, though a small number have lasted already a half-century with successful leadership succession. They may also have a formal management structure, but related only to drug trafficking rather than to broader purposes. There is no clear-cut distinction between members and nonmembers. Recruitment is for employment in an illegal business, not joining a fraternal type of organization. There are no rituals or, with the partial exception of the Familia Michoacana and Knights Templar, an elaborate cultural apparatus. The primary aim of most syndicates continues to be making money from drug production and trafficking. However, following the Zetas' example, more and more groups have used their military power to diversify their criminal activities and increase their multifunctionality. With the spread of military tactics and the increasing use of violence, many current formations have begun behaving more like "power syndicates" rather than mere "enterprise syndicates," to refer to Alan Block's (1983) famous dichotomy. The Zetas and its rivals have also claimed control over specific territories. However, with few exceptions (La Familia Michoacana, the Knights Templar, the Jalisco Gang, and New Generation in its earliest days), they have made no serious effort to provide governance services and thus secure popular legitimacy, beyond terrorizing the local population. Although all syndicates bribe or intimidate local and state government officials and politicians, they no longer seem able to establish stable power-sharing agreements with governments even at the local level.

The drug-trafficking syndicates of the PRI era have a greater claim to mafia status in relation to their stability, legitimacy, and power-sharing agreement. However, even before 2000 there were important differences. In their heydays, the Sinaloa and Gulf cartels were loose alliances of fairly autonomous groups mostly formed around a successful drug producer or smuggler and run by a dominant blood family. There was never a formalized internal structure with clear-cut command positions and procedures to assign them. The cultural apparatus was also much less strong. None of the sources consulted ever mentions initiation rituals, founding myths, organizational symbols, or codes of written rules. Although some syndicate members engaged in other criminal activities, drug production and smuggling were the dominant activities. And although they occasionally provided governance services (and jobs) in their areas of settlement, thus gaining some popular legitimacy, they never tried to exercise political dominion or impose generalized extortion regimes to gain control of legitimate economic sectors. Notwithstanding their considerable revenues and the local influence of their leaders, the traditional syndicates were more instruments of the government than independent entities with the capacity to influence or even control government. A collapse of monopoly party control of government at all levels led to their decline.[21]

III. Brazilian Criminal Syndicates

There are two major criminal syndicates in Brazil, associated with the two largest cities, Rio de Janeiro and Sao Paulo. Both have emerged fairly recently. They have distinct histories and structures. They present more complex interpretive issues for our framework than do the DTOs in Colombia and Mexico, but both can be considered organizations in the Weberian sense and are closer to the mafia model than the Colombian and Mexican syndicates.

A. Rio de Janeiro

Since the mid-1980s, the Comando Vermelho (Portuguese for Red Command, also known as CV) has been the dominant criminal organization in Rio, run from prison but rooted in the favelas of the city (Lessing 2018). The CV command is collective and has changed over time. There appear to be no rituals of initiation or claims of fictive brotherhood. The CV originated as a prison gang aimed at protecting prisoners from a brutal prison management system; the founders included both ordinary convicts and left-wing political prisoners with whom the former were incarcerated during the military dictatorship of 1964–85 (Garzon 2010; Ramos da Cruz and Ucko 2018). Penglase (2008) describes how the early leadership emphasized the diffusion of norms to improve communal prison life, quoting a participant: "The repercussion in the entire system was enormous. Very quickly the rules of the Fundo [the code of conduct] were adopted in all prisons: death to anyone who assaults or rapes fellow

---

[21] This is consistent with the well-known model of organized crime offered by Tom Schelling (1971), in which the mafia is hired by a monopolist police department as an efficient means for collecting the rents extracted by a corrupt agency.

prisoners; conflicts brought from the street must be left outside of prison; violence only to attempt to escape; constant struggle against repression and abuse" (p. 126).

Having developed a capacity for contingent violence, the CV lost its political ideology and branched out into drug selling (Lessing 2018). The CV does not control the drug trade at the local level, but its members and agents contest specific territories against affiliates of two smaller prison gangs (Hirata and Grillo 2019). "The CV is most accurately described as a loose association of drug traffickers who come together for reciprocal assistance yet who act with great degrees of autonomy" (Penglase 2008, p. 123). "The so-called 'commands' of the drug trade in Rio are basically networks formed by tacit and precarious accords between 'owners' of the various sales zones (some of whom also serve as distributers for smaller zones), most of whom are serving jail terms in maximum security prisons" (Misse 2007, p. 149).

The CV is involved in other criminal activities beyond drug trafficking. Though the list provided by Misse (2007) does not suggest that these are major sources of income, other studies indicate that some kinds of theft and extortion are significant in terms of revenue (Penglase 2008, pp. 128–30; Garzon 2010, pp. 63–67; Ramos da Cruz and Ucko 2018, pp. 47–48).

Since the 1980s CV has battled the government openly, and the resulting violence is extraordinary, generating annual homicide rates of more than 50 per 100,000 in the city (Zdun 2011; Murray, Cerqueiro, and Kahn 2013). The police in Rio regularly kill more than 1,000 persons annually, roughly 10 percent of all homicides; most of these deaths are suspected to be executions of drug dealers (Lessing 2018). Police violence is accompanied by extreme police corruption. The relationship between the CV and police is complicated; in some areas they compete in offering extortionate protection, in others they are collaborators (Araujo 2019).

CV's drug gangs constitute a broad presence in the favelas of Rio (Garzon 2010; Hirata and Grillo 2019). They act as enforcers of norms, for example brutally punishing rapists; the extent and form of such enforcement vary according to the whims of the locally dominant trafficker (Arias and Rodrigues 2006). The traffickers are also brought in to resolve local disputes, again with considerable local variation in the formality and fairness of the process: "The politics of trafficker dispute resolution focus intensely on maintaining support among the critical segment of the population closest to drug dealers" (Arias and Rodrigues 2006, p. 74). Wolff

(2015) provides a similar analysis, comparing the emergence of drug gangs as the resolvers of disputes in Rio with the failure of their counterparts in Recife to achieve the same status. There is no suggestion in the literature that the CV as a federation of traffickers has rules about these matters. Rather, individual gang leaders sometimes seek to develop community support and prevent informing to the police by providing a rough justice. As Penglase (2008, p. 123) notes, "It is difficult to generalize about a group as amorphous as the CV. Because favela-level drug bosses have a wide degree of local autonomy, there is considerable variation in practices among those who consider themselves to be part of the CV."

B. Sao Paulo

Sao Paulo has been dominated for 25 years by a syndicate controlled from prison (Millard and Hundleby 2015).[22] This group was formed by eight prisoners in 1993 under the name of Primeiro Comando da Capital (PCC), following a deadly riot that resulted in the death of 111 prisoners in one prison. The PCC, like the CV, started as an effort by prisoners to prevent violence within the prison, both by guards and by inmates. It developed a lengthy set of principles, excerpts of which are included in Garzon (2010, p. 74). Typical of the high moral tone is: "The Party does not allow lies, betrayal, envy, greed, slander, selfishness, or personal interest. It requires truth, loyalty, manliness, solidarity, and common interest for the good of all, because we are one for all and all for one." Just one study refers to initiation rites, taking the form of baptisms (Dias and Salla 2013).

Though there has been turnover in leadership, the leaders have all been in long-term imprisonment. A coup in 2002 replaced the eight-person command with a single individual (pseudonym Marcola) who established a very different system of control, relying largely on explicit rules, procedural fairness, and detailed record keeping. This is so distinctive that we provide a relatively lengthy summary of its operation and consequences (Lessing and Willis 2019; Perla Diógenes de Aquino 2019).

The vast majority of PCC members at any one time are incarcerated. Size estimates are highly variable ranging from 6,000 incarcerated and 5,200 outside prison in Sao Paulo (Millard and Hundleby 2015) to 29,000 altogether (Lessing and Willis 2019). All authorities and observers agree that the PCC operates in many Brazilian states and a growing

---

[22] An excellent concise history of the PCC is provided by Coutinho (2019).

number of other Latin American countries. For example, in June 2019 *InSight Crime* reported that the PCC was responsible for a massacre of 10 prisoners in Paraguay (Marcela Zuñiga 2019). In June 2018 it reported that the PCC was very active in Bolivia and Venezuela (Albaladejo 2018).

PCC has a multilevel hierarchical structure, even including some specialized bureaus providing functions such as legal and financial services outside of prison. It also has a highly formalized system of tribunals to judge specific offenses by members, for example of stealing organizational funds (Willis 2017). The PCC keeps tribunal records of the nature of the offense and the sentence delivered; only a few offenders are executed. There is a graded set of punishments for the most common of offenses, which is nonpayment of drug debts; a first offense leads to a 15-day suspension and no access to drugs for selling during that period. The third offense leads to expulsion from the organization. The system deals also with other crimes, even those that are in no way connected to the PCC, manifesting the organization's founding as a resistance to state violence in the prisons. Lessing and Willis (2019) obtained hundreds of seized PCC documents covering a 13-month period in 2011–12. These included "everything from membership rolls, excel spreadsheets of marijuana, crack and cocaine sale by area code by week, the organization's 'gun library' and an outline of a new fund to help members get 'back on their feet' following release from prison with a $2500 equivalent loan and access to a gun." Lessing and Willis (2019) find "vast, consignment-based trafficking operations whose profits fund collective benefits for members' families; elaborate bureaucratic procedures and recordkeeping; and overwhelmingly nonviolent punishments for debt-nonpayment and misconduct" (p. 584). These are the kinds of records one would expect to find in a legal bureaucracy or corporation.

Biondi (2016) notes a remarkable decline in Sao Paulo homicides that have accompanied this shift to a formal system of "justice by criminals," in stark contrast to the arbitrariness of the state-operated criminal justice system. Whereas in 1999 the Sao Paulo state prison system with 52,000 inmates had 117 killings (a rate of more than 200 per 100,000), in 2007 a prison system with over 150,000 inmates had only 11 killings (about 7 per 100,000). In the state of Sao Paulo, the overall homicide rate fell from a peak of 44 in 1999 to about 10 in 2014 (Lessing and Willis 2019). The PCC, in contrast to Rio's CV, has generally avoided confrontation with the state. Nonetheless, the PCC under Marcola's leadership has not hesitated to use violence strategically. Most notoriously, in May 2006, it initiated a series of attacks against the government that led to 560 deaths, including 59 public agents, mostly police. That led to negotiations with the government that produced agreements about the conditions of incarceration of the leadership (Coutinho 2019).

Available PCC income estimates suggest that it is modest. The organization is funded by fixed monthly payments, with higher rates for outside members ($130) compared with the incarcerated ($13) (Garzon 2010). In 2005 an official inquiry using seized PCC financial records estimated annual dues income of only about $5 million (Garzon 2010, p. 76). Millard and Hundleby (2015) estimate a total of $50 million per annum, with another $100 million being earned by its members but not flowing to the organization. Perhaps the incarceration of most members explains that relatively low figure. If all the money is earned by the outside members, Millard and Hundley's membership estimate suggests an average of about $30,000 per annum. In a state with average annual earnings of $8,000 in 2012 (probably the year to which the drug revenue data refer), that may be enough to attract a lot of young men. Lessing and Willis analyze the seized records for one large area of the Sao Paulo state market, with a population of 14 million (2019, p. 597). They identify 500 PCC customers (presumably low-level wholesalers) handling a total of 650 kilograms of crack and cocaine in 19 weeks (roughly 1,800 kilograms per annum). The implied annual cocaine revenue is only about $10 million. Lessing (personal communication, May 1, 2019) reports that PCC is not the dominant cocaine supplier to the regional market. It is hard to reconcile all these estimates, but they are consistent in suggesting that the PCC is not, by the standards of drug-trafficking syndicates in other countries, a rich organization.

Millard and Hundleby (2015) report a large variety of violent income-generating offenses conducted under PCC auspices: kidnap and ransom, vehicle and cargo robberies, and residential condominium assaults are typical of the list. Aquino (2019) emphasizes the importance of the PCC's early role in organizing and carrying out very high-value armed robberies; not only did that provide substantial income but conferred considerable prestige on the organization.[23] Coutinho (2019) makes similar

---

[23] In 2018 Sao Paulo officials seized a large set of PCC records. They concluded that "in its home state of São Paulo, authorities estimate the PCC has nearly doubled its ranks from 6,000 in 2012 to almost 11,000 today. Elsewhere in Brazil, the number of PCC members is estimated to have grown from just over 3,000 in 2014 to more than 20,000 today." They

points, estimating that the PCC may be responsible for about half of the 3,000 ATM robberies that occur each year in Brazil. Lessing (personal communication, May 1, 2019) suggests that nondrug activities are undertaken by members, whose prestige in the criminal world is enhanced by membership in the PCC but that their activities do not require permission from the PCC leadership.

IV. Comparative Analysis

All three Latin American countries discussed here host very prominent criminal syndicates. In each country the numbers of members and affiliates is large by historical standards, almost comparable to the triads and the yakuza at their peak. For Colombia and Mexico, official estimates of revenues may be exaggerated, but the true figures are undoubtedly very large, in the billions of dollars. For Brazil the revenues might be smaller, but the geographic and criminal breadth of the CV and the PCC is substantial.

Latin American criminal syndicates are distinct in many other ways from mafia organizations. Almost none of them have a very long history, and, with exceptions of a few in Mexico, they have not survived through several generations of leadership. Except for the PCC, their internal structures are much less formalized, so much so that it is difficult even roughly to estimate their memberships. Moreover, the old, large, apparently dominant syndicates in Colombia and Mexico have become increasingly fragmented as a result of government action and, in Mexico, intergang conflicts. Even if some Latin American criminal syndicates and groups promote self-legitimizing songs and, in Rio de Janeiro, even parties to promote their image and find new recruits, their cultural apparatus seems to be much less developed than that of mafia organizations. Unlike the latter, moreover, they are not based on premodern lifelong status or fraternization contracts but attract their personnel on the basis of utilitarian exchanges and maintain their loyalty primarily through deterrence. They show limited multifunctionality, and most are principally identified with just one criminal activity, drug trafficking. Only the PCC in Sao Paulo also aims systematically to provide some general governance

---

also estimated organizational income at $100–$200 million. None of these figures have a strong enough provenance to be given much weight (Albaladejo 2018).

services beyond attempting to solve conflicts among their own members, while some CV gang leaders also do that more sporadically. Consequently even their popular legitimacy is generally contested or at least fleeting, even if some syndicates or, more frequently, their leaders in specific periods spent considerable sums of money on benevolent projects.

In Mexico, the traditional syndicates had long-standing agreements with the once-dominant political party, PRI, which occupied the entire state structure for over 70 years. In all other contexts, though, power-sharing agreements between the criminal syndicates and state representatives have been based on bribes rather than a shared Weltanschauung. The agreements have largely focused on guaranteeing impunity—or at least mild treatment—for the syndicate leaders. In contrast to the five mafia organizations, some Mexican syndicates since the end of the PRI monopoly have employed violence unrestrictedly, causing thousands of innocent deaths in their operating areas.

Brazil is the most interesting case. The recent literature on Brazilian organized crime, even just that available in English, is relatively rich.[24] The sketch provided above is very summary. It suggests that the PCC in Sao Paulo not only meets our definition of criminal organizations but is more ambitious in its purpose and aims than its Colombian and Mexican counterparts, or even Rio's CV. The PCC, much like the iconic mafias, is truly a multifunctional organization, aiming to provide governance in addition to making money from crime. It offers in some ways a new form. None of the historical models have been continuously controlled from prison, even though leaders often spent time in prison and could maintain control while doing so.[25] While some of the five mafias have had their roots in providing an alternative to a weak state, providing an alternative justice (as in the famous opening scene of *The Godfather*), the PCC's strong normative base, with its effort to challenge the state by offering a highly bureaucratized and apparently fair system of justice both to its members and to at least some other citizens, is extreme. It differs from the Colombian and Mexican cases in that drug trafficking, though perhaps the largest source of revenues, is not its motivating activity.

[24] For example, the second issue of the new *Journal of Illicit Economies and Development* is devoted entirely to Brazilian illegal markets and their consequences.

[25] Jacobs (2020) reports that in the American mafia there was no rule that a capo had to give up control when incarcerated.

A critical issue is how much the PCC depends on the charismatic authority of one man, Marcola. Surviving for 15 years in prison as head of a criminal organization is itself an impressive achievement. Whether the organization can continue after his departure, voluntary or not, is a fair question.

Table 1 summarizes our view of the extent to which the Colombian and Mexican drug-trafficking syndicates and Brazilian criminal organizations exhibit the characteristics of the five mafias. The task is complicated by the occasional exceptions. For example, Correa-Cabrera (2017) and Felbab-Brown (2019) observe that the short-lived La Familia Michoacana, notwithstanding its gruesome behavior, tried to inculcate a religious quality to membership; that is unique or at least very rare. Some cells have question marks, representing gaps in the literature. Others have quite tentative judgments, reflecting the same limited insights from research and journalistic sources.

V. Candidate Criminal Organizations

Next to the mafia organizations and the Latin American syndicates, we identify several candidate criminal organizations and classify them into three main categories:

- Not fully consolidated criminal organizations,
- Offshoots of voluntary associations, and
- Terrorist, paramilitary, and military organizations gone awry.

For each category we explain why we do not regard them as yet to be a fully criminal organization. The aim is to demonstrate the range of large-scale criminal entities and of countries in which they appear.

A. Not Fully Consolidated Criminal Organizations

Using the sociological, Weberian definition of organization, the Neapolitan camorra and other Italian short-lived criminal associations and post-Soviet Russian and Albanian organized crime groups are prominent examples of the first category of candidate criminal organizations. Some instances of illegal governance and entrepreneurship in western Europe also fall short of meeting the basic characteristics of an organization. Though sometimes called organized crime, they are even more distant than the first examples from mafia organizations.

1. *The Camorra.* According to many commentators and government agencies (e.g., Saviano 2008; US Department of Treasury 2012), the camorra constitutes a criminal organization and Italy's third mafia organization after the Sicilian Cosa Nostra and Calabrian 'Ndrangheta. We consider it only a candidate criminal organization, because the camorra is not even a confederation of crime groups.

Catino (2019) provides a history of the Neapolitan camorra, emphasizing its emergence in the nineteenth century as a set of geographically defined criminal groups with a powerful higher level body to coordinate activities. However, he emphasizes what has changed. "This model vanished in the early decades of the twentieth century and no trace remains nowadays of this original organizational structure.... Rather than speak of a single mafia organization we should speak of 'Camorre' in the plural. . . . Unlike other mafias, where it is possible to locate one prevailing organizational model, the Camorra has four quite different competing models" (pp. 169–70). Catino (2019) goes on to note that "the most significant phenomenon in the evolution of the Camorra is the multiplication of clans and families. While in 1861 there were 16 clans and families, today there are around 128" (p. 172).

Catino (2020) continues to refer to the camorra as a mafia but emphasizes the many differences between it and the other Italian mafias. For example, he notes the lack of a coherent strategy and the much higher level of homicides, representing the camorra groups' inability to resolve disputes. Between 1983 and 2018 these groups were responsible for almost as many homicides as the Sicilian Cosa Nostra and the Calabrian 'Ndrangheta combined. This is also why Campania, the region hosting camorra, has historically had a much higher homicide rate than either Sicily and Calabria, even though that rate has declined significantly since the early 1990s (Massari and Martone 2018).

The camorra thus offer the instance of a one-time mafia that broke up into a set of competing criminal groups. Contemporary camorra groups are not only competing, but also varied. In its most recent report, the Italian Ministry of the Interior speaks of a "camorra system . . . characterized by the coexistence of clans with diversified setups and operative strategies." The Ministry further notes that "these characteristics make it difficult to give an unequivocal definition" and "very different criminal realities continue to cohabit in the same territories" (Ministero dell'Interno 2020, p. 138). While a few of the current camorra groups form syndicates, if not fully fledged organizations according to our Weberian definition, others are much more disorganized and ephemeral.

TABLE 1
Latin American Syndicates: To What Extent Are They Mafias?

	Colombia pre-1993	Colombia post-1993	Mexico pre-2000	Mexico post-2000	Rio de Janeiro CV	Sao Paulo PCC
Longevity (leadership succession)	Lasted <20 years; failed to survive leadership loss	Frequent turnover of syndicate names and leaders	A few going back at least to the 1950s, with multiple generations of leaders	Few older syndicates still existing but also numerous new, mostly short-lived syndicates	>35 years; multiple generations of leaders	>25 years; dominant single leader for 20 years
Size:						
Clear-cut distinction members/nonmembers (associates)	No	No	No	No	Yes	Yes
Number of members (associates)	Many tens of thousands	Many tens of thousands	>100,000 in total (including occasional service providers)	>100,000 in total (including occasional service providers)	~20,000 (probably members only)	>10,000 members
Internal structure:						
Type of syndicate	Consisted of not formalized, largely autonomous units, mostly run by blood family	Some followed on smaller scale pre-1993 model; others originated from right-wing paramilitary groups	Consisted of not formalized, largely autonomous units, mostly run by blood family	For older syndicates as pre-2000; Zetas founded by defectors of military units and special forces, as armed wing of other syndicate, later independent; later groups either followed Zetas model or attempted to create ritual family ties	Rose as unitary single prison gang, but outside prison units operate with large degree of autonomy	Rose as unitary single prison gang; autonomy of units outside prisons unclear
Higher-level coordinating bodies?	Prominent leader(s) in each syndicate, but	Prominent leader(s) in each syndicate, but	Prominent leader(s) in each syndicate, but		Elite of older members in prison; unclear if fit	

[coordinating bodies]	no formalized higher level coordinating bodies	but no formalized higher level co-ordinating bodies	no formalized higher level coordinating bodies	As of pre-2000 but more frequent shifts of alliances and splits	constitutes a formal coordinating body	Yes, eight-person command, substituted in 2002 by supreme leader
Ranks and command positions	No ranks, only basic command apparatus with few formalized positions or procedures to assign them	No known ranks, but (pseudo-) military command positions in some, e.g., Los Rastrojos	No ranks, only basic command apparatus with few formalized positions or procedures to assign them	No known ranks, but (pseudo-) military command positions in some, e.g., Los Zetas	No ranks, perhaps clear-cut command positions in prison but not outside	No ranks, but multi-level hierarchy of command positions
Cultural apparatus:						
Status and fraternization contract	No; some low-level positions assigned through regular employment contracts	No, paramilitary discipline functions as partial substitute; some low-level positions assigned through regular employment contracts	No; some low-level positions assigned through regular employment contracts	No; military discipline functions as partial substitute in Zetas; some low-level positions assigned through regular employment contracts	Probably yes	Yes
Initiation rituals	No	No	No	No; military training functions as partial substitute in Zetas	Unclear, but probably yes	Yes
Founding myths, ideology, and membership symbols	No	No	No	No, with exception of La Familia Michoacana; military training and discipline function as partial substitute in Zetas	Unclear, but probably yes	Yes
Dispute resolution mechanisms	In most no, but *oficinas* in Medellín cartel	No	No	No	Unclear, but probably yes	Yes
Legal code						

TABLE 1 (*Continued*)

	Colombia pre-1993	Colombia post-1993	Mexico pre-2000	Mexico post-2000	Rio de Janeiro CV	Sao Paulo PCC
	No written rules; loyalty achieved through family ties, monetary rewards, and violence	No written rules; loyalty achieved through family ties, monetary rewards, military discipline, and violence, especially employee hostage identification	No written rules; loyalty achieved through family ties, monetary rewards, and violence	No written rules, except in La Familia Michoacana; loyalty achieved through family ties, military discipline, monetary rewards, and violence	Rules of behavior in prison; at least a commercial code for outside activities	Yes, highly structured rules and sanctions
Multifunctionality:						
Illegal activities	Specialized in cocaine production and trafficking; used coercion to protect/enhance land ownership	Specialized in cocaine production and trafficking; extortion of both criminal and legal markets	Specialized in heroin production and drug trafficking; occasional engagement in other criminal activities	Most specialized in heroin production and drug trafficking but growing involvement, especially of newer syndicates, in other criminal activities	Active in many criminal markets and crimes	Active in many criminal markets and crimes
Presence in legal economy	Presence primarily meant to facilitate drug trafficking and launder proceeds; no or very limited extortion; no known ambition to control legal economic sectors	Presence primarily meant to facilitate drug trafficking and launder proceeds; no or very limited extortion; no known ambition to control legal economic sectors	Presence primarily meant to facilitate drug trafficking and launder proceeds; no known ambition to control legal economic sectors	In most cartels same as in pre-2000 period; newer ones, especially Zetas, attempt to impose extensive extortion regimes and aim to control legal economic sectors	Extent and purpose of presence in legal economy is unclear; no known ambition to control legal economic sectors	Extent and purpose of presence in legal economy is unclear; no known ambition to control legal economic sectors

Governance services:

Goal of political dominion	No goal of political dominion	No goal of political dominion	No goal of political dominion, but occasional, limited governance services in areas of settlement	No governance services; dominion imposed by fear	Political dominion in prison but no generalized claim to exercise it outside; resolve disputes in community	Political dominion in prison but no generalized claim to exercise it outside; resolve disputes in community
Protection services	No or very limited extortion	No or very limited extortion	No or very limited extortion	Mostly not, but some newer ones, especially Zetas, extort both legal and illegal businesses	Extortion of legal and informal businesses but extent unclear	No information
Control of criminal world?	No claim to exert control	Unknown	No claim to exert control	For most syndicates, no claim to exert control, but some newer ones, especially Zetas, exert such claim in areas of settlement	Claim to control local prisons and Rio favelas but extent of effective control unclear	Extensive control of local prisons and criminal world
Extent of violence	Unrestrained use of violence, especially by Medellin cartel	Substantial	Limited use of open violence	Unrestrained and strategic use of violence, especially by newer syndicates, e.g., Zetas	Unrestrained use of violence	Limited use of open violence; effective control of violence in prisons
Popular legitimacy and power-sharing agreements	Legitimacy pursued by a few leaders as entrepreneurs/benefactors, not the syndicates; no power-sharing agreements but extensive corruption and intimidation of government officials and politicians	No legitimacy claim or power-sharing agreements; extensive corruption and intimidation of government officials and politicians	Limited popular legitimacy; subservient to PRI until 1990s, systematic sharing of drug revenues with local and federal government officials and politicians	Very limited popular legitimacy despite popular songs romanticizing syndicates; no power-sharing agreements but extensive corruption and intimidation of government officials and politicians	Considerable legitimacy in prisons and favelas, primarily through providing an alternative to police; de facto power-sharing or rivalry with local corrupt police, but no backing by central government	High level of legitimacy in prisons; quasi-official power-sharing in prisons and, to a lesser extent, outside

SOURCE.—Authors' original.

Most current camorra groups consist in their core of one or more blood families, which can rely on a circle of associates for their criminal activities. This circle can expand or contract depending on current needs. Associates are recruited in the extensive local underworld, the numerous participants in the local underground economy, and from legitimate companies, liberal professions, and even the political class. Unlike the mafias, these family-based camorra groups do not routinely conduct ceremonies of initiation so that it is difficult to distinguish the members from the nonmembers.[26]

The ruling bodies of both the single camorra groups and their alliances are rudimentary compared with those of Cosa Nostra and the 'Ndrangheta. They neither are fully institutionalized nor are ruling body members selected through formal procedures. Within the alliances, there is no higher level body coordinating the groups' activities and mediating intergroup conflicts. Within each family-based camorra group, the leader is the most skillful or violent member of the core blood family. He rules together with his brothers, close relatives, and sometimes a limited number of associates. Within the alliances, decisions on key matters are taken through negotiations among the leaders of the dominant camorra groups. Occasionally a particularly skillful *camorrista* may obtain the position of first among equals, as Francesco Schiavone (aka Sandokan) did in the 1990s in the Casalesi cartel.

The cultural apparatus is also reduced to a minimum. As a rule, family-based camorra groups use no symbols or rituals to secure allegiance. For that purpose, they rely on financial and other material benefits and on threats. In both their internal structure and culture, family-based camorra groups are more similar to Colombian and Mexican drug trafficking syndicates than to the mafias of neighboring Sicily and Calabria.

Camorra groups frequently form alliances, further complicating the investigator's task of establishing who belongs to which group. While many alliances are short-lived, some have lasted for several decades. One long-term alliance is the so-called Casalesi cartel, which is based in the Caserta province north of Naples. Since the 1990s, it has had three family-based crime groups at its core: the Schiavone, Zagaria, and Bidognetti groups. The Casalesi have been one of the most, if not

---

[26] A few *camorristi*, such as Antonio Bardellino and Michele Zagaria, were ritually admitted to the Sicilian Cosa Nostra during the 1970s (Tribunale di Palermo 1985). However, the link with Cosa Nostra broke down soon afterward, and no Cosa Nostra rituals were imported into the camorra.

the most, powerful camorra syndicates. Through their networks of associates, including less powerful crime groups, the Casalesi could mobilize up to 9,000 associates at the peak of their power in the 1990s (CSM 2020). The units constituting the cartel have always maintained a considerable degree of autonomy, but both the core and the satellite crime groups and even their looser associates have profited from the reputation and power of the Casalesi cartel. Similarly, the so-called Alleanza di Secondigliano was founded by four family-based camorra groups of Naples and its outskirts—Contini, Bosti, Licciardi, Mallardo—and has been operating since the 1980s (Ministero dell'Interno 2020, pp. 146–47). Three of the founders, each representing a constituent camorra group, had married three sisters, thus becoming relatives. The core groups, and others that have at times joined the alliance, have maintained an even higher degree of entrepreneurial autonomy than the groups of the Casalesi cartel.

The Casalesi and the other "established" camorra groups are similar to mafia organizations in Sicily and Calabria in aiming to exercise political dominion in their areas of settlement. Some constituent families of the Casalesi cartel, for example, provided protection services in rural areas, much as the Sicilian and Calabria Mafiosi did, from about the 1950s to the 1980s (Sales 1993), and they have not given up this activity in recent times. Another element of similarity with the Sicilian and Calabria mafia organizations is the ability of many camorra groups to infiltrate local government, which has helped them manipulate public tenders and gain many public contracts. In the Caserta province, for example, the Casalesi cartel's influence on local government is pervasive: even the Italian Ministry of the Interior observes, "the public administration of the territory has aimed to meet camorra's interests at the same time as the local corrupt policy-makers, thanks to their links with criminality, have consolidated their decision-making power and satisfied their personal ambitions" (Ministero dell'Interno 2012, p. 166).

The Casalesi cartel distinguishes itself from all Cosa Nostra and many 'Ndrangheta groups in the entrepreneurial acumen shown by its leaders since the 1970s. Thanks to that acumen, the cartel's power of intimidation and the readiness of many Campanian entrepreneurs to become associates, the Casalesi have been able to acquire, or at least influence, many businesses in the Caserta province, gain control of several local economic sectors, and expand their business activities outside the province (Corte di Assise Santa Maria Capua Vetere 2006; Saviano 2008).

Other camorra groups are less durable formations that developed around a charismatic chief. These gangs might expand very rapidly for a while and make money through a variety of illegal activities. However, they usually have a more limited number of associates in the legal economy and public administration than the more established family-based groups and are less able to exercise political dominion in their specific areas. The Nuova Camorra Organizzata (or NCO) constitutes the most prominent example of this second type of camorra group. The NCO was founded by Raffaele Cutolo while he was in prison in the early 1970s and lasted until the late 1980s. Much like the leaders of the Brazilian and Central American prisons gangs, Cutolo remained imprisoned throughout the NCO's existence. To attract new affiliates and secure new allegiances, Cutolo resorted to the rituals, ranks, slang, codes, and rules of the nineteenth-century camorra. Presenting itself as a brotherhood, the NCO also paid salaries to the poorest of its imprisoned members. It set up a court to settle internal conflicts. Thanks to its elaborate cultural apparatus and solidarity vis-à-vis poorer members, Cutolo was able to enlarge the NCO's ranks very rapidly. At its peak in the early 1980s, the NCO had about 7,000 members (Sciarrone 1998, pp. 65–68). Cutolo also gained the unconditional loyalty and allegiance of most NCO members. "The correspondence in prisons among its affiliates," the Parliamentary Antimafia Commission noted in 1993, "is very intense and full of expressions of gratitude to the chief who sometimes presented himself as a guru and in other cases as a modern criminal boss" (Commissione Parlamentare Antimafia 1993, pp. 43–44).

The NCO's revenues were generated through a variety of criminal activities, including drug trafficking and dealing, cigarette smuggling, illegal gambling, and extortion of legitimate businesses. The NCO (and other camorra groups) also profited from the acquisition of many emergency public contracts issued after the 1980 earthquake in Campania (Commissione Parlamentare Antimafia 1993). In the late 1970s, Cutolo felt strong enough to attempt to impose a tax on each box of smuggled cigarettes that landed in Naples and to seek control over the central neighborhoods of Naples (Corte Suprema di Cassazione 1987). These attempts, though, prompted rival clans to form a coalition, the Nuova Famiglia, which initially copied the NCO's rituals to secure their members' allegiance. Weakened by very violent fights with this coalition and subsequent criminal investigations, the NCO disintegrated in the second half of the 1980s. The Nuova Famiglia disbanded soon afterward when a conflict arose among the crime groups composing it, which soon reverted to their usual "patriarchal" style of domination (Monzini 1999).

Next to family-based syndicates and the gangs led by a charismatic leader, there are also loose gangs of juvenile and adult offenders, primarily drawn from the city working class. Even the police acknowledge that these gangs are primarily co-offending groups of criminals rather than organized crime (Ministero dell'Interno 2020, pp. 138–41). The composition of many gangs and the alliances among them are so unstable that law enforcement agencies often have difficulties in finding evidence of the offense of mafia-type criminal organization (Ministero dell'Interno 2012, pp. 130–37).

Organizational differences are matched by entrepreneurial diversity. Some groups, especially in the city of Naples, draw most of their revenues from the control of local drug distribution DNA (2017, pp. 66–75). Others are specialized in international drug trafficking. Giuseppe Polverino from the Marano group from the town of the same name at the outskirts of Naples was long known as "Mr. Hashish." According to Italian law enforcement agencies he was the main smuggler of Moroccan hashish into Europe at least until his arrest in Spain in 2012 (Allum 2016, pp. 157–58). Thanks to high-level drug trafficking and the clever reinvestment of drug-trafficking proceeds in several economic sectors, Polverino and his associates accumulated considerable wealth. Assets worth over 1 billion euros were seized from them on a single occasion in 2011 (Europol 2013, pp. 12–13).[27] Other camorra groups have become very skilled in the distribution of a wide range of counterfeited products. They both manufacture these products in the Naples and Caserta provinces and import them from China. Camorra groups are also proficient in counterfeiting currencies, which they then sell to crime groups all over Europe (Europol 2013, p. 17).

Some of these groups have been much weakened or even dissolved as a result of enhanced law enforcement pressure in the first two decades of the twenty-first century (DNA 2017, p. 67). The law enforcement successes have been facilitated by the decision of many camorra representatives, including the bosses of several groups, to become state witnesses,

---

[27] Seizure figures can exaggerate the value of the assets lost by the criminals. For example, properties are often subject to mortgages; the owner will lose only his investment, not the full value of the property.

following arrest. As of June 30, 2016, there were 561 former criminals from Campania in the state witness protection program; the numbers in Sicily and Calabria were 305 and 164, respectively (Ministero dell'Interno 2017, p. 12). This testifies to the weakness of associational bonds and the prevalence of a more utilitarian logic within camorra groups compared with those of the Sicilian Cosa Nostra and the Calabrian 'Ndrangheta. In 2018 and 2019, for example, the sons of the leaders of both the Bidognetti and Schiavone families started cooperating with criminal justice authorities, thus weakening the Casalesi cartel.

In sum, despite the fact that some camorra groups score high on the more external typifying characteristics of mafia organizations (e.g., multifunctionality, claim to exercise political power), we classify the camorra as a candidate criminal organization, because no single such organization exists. Some cartels coordinating camorra groups are clearly syndicates and have many similarities with the Colombian and Mexican drug-trafficking syndicates. We stop short of calling them organizations because they fail to meet the basic defining criterion of organization, namely clear boundaries, and do not have institutionalized command positions. Conversely, the NCO met the requirements of our sociological definition of organization, but lasted less than two decades.

2. *Russian and Albanian Organized Crime.* Russia's *vory-v-zakone*, "thieves-in-law" or "thieves professing the code," constitute the criminal organization that most closely resembles the five iconic mafias, even if some significant differences remain in the internal structure, breeding ground, and evolution. Catino (2019) includes them as a mafia. The *vory*'s society is at least as old as the youngest mafia, the American Cosa Nostra. It most probably emerged in the late 1920 and early 1930s in the Soviet prisons and labor camps, although some sources (e.g., Rossi 1989; Shinar 2016) maintain that the society existed in prerevolutionary times (Varese 2001, pp. 146, 160–61; Cheloukhine 2008). Like the mafias, it only admitted men. Unlike the mafias, the *vory*'s society included only a selected elite group of professional criminals and not their criminal manpower or even the *avtoritety*, the heads of many crime groups (Varese 2001, pp. 125–41). There were, in other words, no groups belonging to the *vory*'s society, only individuals. Six hundred *vory* were known to police sources just before the dissolution of the Soviet Union in December 1991 (Handelman 1995, p. 28). Given the organization's selectivity, there was no elaborate ranking system or command structure within it. *Vory* were classified only as junior or senior. Within the senior category, some

had more prestige than others and sometimes took strategic decisions for the whole society; however, they did not form a well-defined ruling body (Handelman 1995, p. 39).

Like the mafias, the *vory*'s society had an elaborate cultural apparatus, including rituals, a jargon, tattoos, and even a parallel normative code in open opposition to state laws. Much like the mafias, it also imposed a status and fraternization contract on its members, expecting a lifelong commitment and brotherly solidarity, which was symbolized by the *obshchak*, the communal fund. Their ideology was even stricter than that of the mafias. *Vory* were expected to live exclusively on thefts and black-market dealing when not in prison and were prohibited from having any contact with state representatives (Handelman 1995, pp. 28–45; Varese 2001, pp. 145–59).

The *vory* long constituted a parallel authority in the Gulag archipelago despite the Soviet state's efforts to weaken them in the late 1940s and early 1950s. Given their bases in prisons and the lack of direct manpower, the *vory* never, unlike the mafias, tried to rule the broader society beyond the criminal underworld. And even within the underworld, their power was largely due to their reputation and capability to solve conflicts, rather than their direct command of violence. As an informer told Varese (2001, pp. 140–41), "it is not the case that each group pays into the *obshchak* once a month, as a company does with his employees. The groups pay when they feel like it, as a sort of charity to support the criminal population in prison, or as a sign of respect for the *vory*. The treasurer of the *obshchak* asks for money when he needs it. Alternatively, groups pay into the *obshchak* when the *vor* does something in particular. Also the *vor* of our city is very respected in Moscow and can get help from all over Russia."

The *vory* had their heydays after the implosion of the Soviet Union in 1991. They obtained or extorted contributions for their *obshchak* from many criminals and used their parallel justice tradition and skills to settle disputes both among criminals and among businesses that state courts were unable to deal with (Varese 2001, pp. 123–41).

But even in the 1990s, *vory* were just one branch of post-Soviet Russian organized crime. Many, less formalized formations arose from sports societies and martial arts clubs and the military, especially the Cossacks, Afghan war participants, and later mercenaries who fought in conflicts in Abkhasia and Transdniestria (Volkov 2014). Other crime groups, such as the Chechens, were ethnically based, with no clear-cut boundaries or institutionalized command positions (Varese 2001, pp. 177–79). Galeotti

(2012, p. 2) notes that "unlike other international criminal organizations (yakuza, Chinese triads, or Cosa Nostra), Russian criminal groups do not have a rigid control structure. They act opportunistically." A Russian police officer specializing in the control of organized crime similarly reported at the beginning of the 1990s that "representatives of the new type of criminal world pay no attention to the *vory*. In prison, of course, everyone has to bow to the traditions. But outside, if a criminal has money and his own fighters, he can act independently" (Handelman 1995, p. 42).

In the early 1990s, many of these different crime groups were not only active in the liberalized post-Soviet illegal markets, but also extorted legitimate businesses and occasionally offered effective protection, exploiting the power void left by the implosion of the Soviet state. Although some of these groups consisted of dozens, if not hundreds, of members and had a hierarchical structure, most have disbanded since the turn of the century and lost their governance functions (Sokolov 2004). Volkov (2014, pp. 170–75) has no qualms speaking of "extinction of the Russian mafia" and identifies three structural causes for such process: the consolidation of a private security industry, which provides protection services more reliably than criminal groups did; the strengthening of the state and of its law enforcement under Putin's leadership; and that many leaders of the most successful criminal groups preferred to become associates or investors in legitimate businesses. Many *vory* lacked necessary skills; the *vory* and many lower level, less skilled, more violent associates have been progressively marginalized, arrested, or killed. As of 2008, according to the then Russia's Minister of the Interior, Rashid Nurgaliev, fewer than 100 *vory* remained active on Russian territory (Schwirtz 2008).

Albanian organized crime has been prominent in Europe since the 1990s, using violence to further its drug dealing and other illegal market ventures, such as sex trafficking and loan sharking (Xhudo 1996; Zhilla and Lamarri 2015). Jana Arsovska (2015, 2016) has authoritatively shown that much like the camorra, Albanian organized crime consists of a variety of criminal groups largely reliant on family or friendship ties. It has no formalized internal structure, elaborate subcultural apparatus, or political power.

3. *Illegal Governance and Entrepreneurship in Western Europe.* Even in western Europe, with its high degree of government legitimacy and power, some groups occasionally provide temporary governance services in illegal markets. Such figures have been identified in a few English

cities and towns by Campana and Varese (2018). However, lacking a formalized structure, including institutionalized command positions and a well-defined cultural apparatus, the groups surrounding these figures do not possess any of the seven typifying characteristics of mafia organizations. Even their provision of governance has never become fully institutionalized before the group was broken up by the police.

A few blood families in the southern part of the Netherlands have shown a surprising degree of intergenerational involvement in various criminal activities, including thefts, other property crimes, and smuggling of a variety of illegal goods across borders (Moors and Spapens 2017). Since the 1960s, the southern province of North Brabant has played a key role in the production of ecstasy and amphetamines for the whole world market. With extensive cannabis plantations, it also feeds the illegal and semi-illegal markets for cannabis in Netherlands and many surrounding countries (Colman et al. 2018; Tops et al. 2018).

Despite their entrepreneurial success and occasional attempts to infiltrate legitimate economic activities and public life, southern Dutch crime groups remain only candidate criminal organizations. They are generally small and mostly ephemeral; they do not possess a formalized criminal structure or elaborate cultural apparatus. Moreover, their sole aim is making money from crime, and they have no interest in imposing governance services on the broader population or becoming an alternative to the state (van de Bunt and Kleemans 2007; Spapens 2016).

B. Offshoots of Voluntary or Sport Associations

A second category of candidate criminal organizations consists of offshoots of voluntary organizations. Several crime groups in Russia—and in other eastern European countries (e.g., Kaplan 1998)—emerged from sports societies and martial arts clubs. As Volkov (2014) notes, in the chaotic post-Soviet period, members of these clubs—and especially boxers, wrestlers, karate masters, and the like—possessed qualities that made them fit for violent entrepreneurship, including the ability to use violence, discipline, and countrywide networks. However, much as the Uralmash, one of these criminal groups, has transformed into an influential regional business group, most Russian criminal groups based on sport associations have either much reduced their criminal activities or have disbanded due to the increasing pressure of Russian state authorities.

In Western countries, the most prominent example of this category is represented by outlaw motorcycle gangs such as the Hells Angels and

Bandidos and Europe-based gangs such as Satudarah (see von Lampe and Blokland 2020). These gangs meet most of the requirements of large-scale criminal organizations. The most established go back to the 1930s and have thousands of members spread across many countries. They are also divided into chapters, each with well-defined command structures and detailed appointment procedures. Though they do not have outright ceremonies of initiation, they clearly separate members from nonmembers, much as mafias do. Much like mafias, they expect a long-term commitment from their members and expect quasi-brotherhood ties and mutual aid among the latter. Like the mafias, outlaw motorcycle gangs were not founded to conduct criminal activities or just to make money. They also show considerable multifunctionality, including their members' engagement in a plurality of criminal activities. Last but not least, some of their leaders claim to, and sometimes effectively, govern part of the underworld, especially the sex industry.

Nonetheless, they remain candidate criminal organizations because these gangs are still considered legitimate, if problematic, organizations in most countries despite the frequent epithet "outlaw." As von Lampe and Blokland (2020) report, most outlaw motorcycle gangs are registered legal entities and some even have copyrighted their colors and patches to prevent unauthorized use.

This means that, despite frequent use of the epithet "outlaw," these organizations are not fully criminalized, even if they have been listed as organized crime syndicates by several US public bodies (e.g., President's Commission on Organized Crime 1986). The US Department of Justice (2014) characterizes them as "organizations whose members use their motorcycle clubs as conduits for criminal enterprises." Dutch courts were the first to issue nationwide bans on some whole organizations or "clubs," including the Bandidos in 2017 and the Hells Angels in 2019 (Agence France-Press 2019), and not just some of local branches, known as chapters. Even leaving official categorizations aside, observers disagree on whether motorcycle gangs should be classified as criminal organizations. According to Barker (2014, pp. 13–14), for example, this is an empirical question, which has been answered separately for each club or even chapter depending on their members' and leaders' involvement in criminal activities. The relationship of the gang to member criminality varies a great deal. In some chapters the criminal activities involve the chapter itself; in others there are individual offenders who find the chapter a useful setting in which to operate.

C. Terrorist, Paramilitary, and Military Organizations

The last category of candidate criminal organizations consists of terrorist organizations and militias. In a few extreme cases, it even includes offshoots of military organizations gone awry, when they start drawing a large share of their resources from the organization and protection of organized crime activities, typically drug production and trafficking. Following Schmid (2004) and others, we note the inherently controversial nature of the label "terrorism" and the fluidity of the distinction between terrorist organizations and militias.

Whereas many terrorist groups are short-lived and ephemeral (LaFree, Dugan, and Miller 2015), some of the largest and longest-lasting terrorist groups and militias, such as the Irish Republican Army (e.g., Dingley 2012) and the Colombian FARC, have long been considered criminal organizations by governments. It is beyond the scope of this essay to establish to what extent each of the many prominent terrorist groups is comparable with mafia organizations. In the following subsections we briefly discuss just the FARC and Colombian paramilitaries and two Burmese[28] examples: United Wa State Army and Party, and the Kuomintang, the latter being an extreme case of a military organization that has transformed itself into an organized crime entity.

1. *The FARC and the Paramilitaries in Columbia.* Founded in the 1960s, the FARC lasted until at least 2017, when it formally agreed to terms effectively of surrender to the Colombian government.[29] With an army of 20,000 "soldiers" at its peak in the early 2000s (Otis 2014), it certainly was large. At least until 2009, it also had a formalized, hierarchical internal structure and an elaborate subculture, which were more bureaucratic and thus more "modern" than those of mafia organizations. Like mafias, the FARC long showed considerable multifunctionality and de facto operated for a long time as a quasi-state authority in about a third of Colombia's territory, enjoying a certain degree of legitimacy (Eccarius-Kelly 2012).

Moreover, despite its original Marxist program of agrarianism and anti-imperialism, the FARC entered the drug business during the 1980s, thus adding a standard organized crime component to its original insurgent

---

[28] We refer to them as "Burmese" simply because the events narrated here occurred mainly during the time before the country was renamed Myanmar.

[29] In 2019 a major faction of the FARC announced that the government had failed to provide the basic protections set out in the peace agreement and that its members would return to conflict (Acosta and Cobb 2019).

aims and practices. Until the 2017 peace agreement, the FARC not only extracted protection money from the peasants growing coca and poppies and from the traffickers trading in semimanufactured or finished products, but it had also become a key player in the refining and sale of coca paste, earning at least US$1 billion per year (Otis 2014).

In 1997 most right-wing paramilitary groups coalesced into the United Self-Defense Forces of Colombia (known as AUC, the acronym from the Spanish initials), which profited extensively from the cocaine industry through both extortion of producers and traffickers and direct participation in the trade (Vargas 2005, pp. 212–14). However, like many other insurgent groups, the AUC is too ephemeral to seriously merit the term "organization," being almost completely demobilized in 2005 and 2006.

2. *The United Wa State Army and Party.* The United Wa State Army and Party are certainly organizations, again more bureaucratic and modern than mafia organizations. However, they are not clearly "criminal." Respectively known as UWSA and UWSP,[30] they have undergone a spectacular transformation from an insurgent Marxist group to a major opium- and heroin-producing organization and, more recently, to an almost fully fledged, though not internationally recognized, state authority that has banned opium production since 2005.

The UWSA was the largest splinter group from the Communist Party of Burma (CPB), consisting of 8,000–10,000 men at the time of the split in 1989 (Milsom 2005).[25] It incorporated a smaller group dominated by three ethnic Chinese brothers, the Wei, with decades-long experience in the opiate trade.

Within a few months of the creation of the UWSA, cease-fire agreements were struck between Burma's military government and the main former CPB forces. In exchange for promises not to attack government forces and to sever ties with other rebel groups, the CPB mutineers were granted permission to engage in any business, including, almost inevitably, opiate production and trafficking (Davis and Hawke 1998; Altsean-Burma 2004, pp. 50–51). A nonmedical opiate industry was de facto legalized.

Initially, Burma's opium production boomed under the ex-CPB quasi-state authorities. Between 1988 and 1993, the opium harvest grew by

---

[30] For reasons of simplicity we refer to both of them by using the more common acronym of UWSA.

60 percent, and a string of new, large heroin refineries were set up near the main growing areas (Lintner 2002, pp. 263, 272–74). At least until the beginning of the twenty-first century, the refineries were run both by the militia commanders and by independent traffickers who were obliged to pay a "protection" tax to the militias.

Though the UWSA was designated as a "drug kingpin" in 2003 by the United States, the Burmese government long gave the leaders of the UWSA legitimacy as "leaders of the national races" (Ball 1999, p. 4). It allowed them to invest illicit proceeds in the legitimate economy. More recently, though, the relationship has become tenser, and three rounds of inconclusive peace talks were held between 2016 and 2018 (Lintner 2019).

Unexpectedly in 2005 the UWSA banned opium production in the areas under its control, following earlier bans of two other splinter groups. It forcibly moved many opium-farming villages from their hill locations to riverine plains to induce them to grow other crops (Paoli, Greenfield, and Reuter 2009, pp. 139–42). As a result, Burma's potential opium production fell from 1,760 tons in 1996 to 310 tons in 2005. Although Myanmar's production has fluctuated since 2006 with a total of 550 tons in 2017, "there are hardly any poppy fields" left in the Wa region (UNODC 2017, p. 8).

3. *The Kuomintang.* The de facto stateless northeastern Burmese Shan State also provides an extreme example of a regular military organization that turned criminal. This is the Nationalist Chinese Kuomintang (KMT), which operated for several decades in northeastern Burma after being expelled from China by Mao Zedong's communist troops in 1949. The newly independent Burma, weakened by the assassination of its designated leader and his closest associates in 1947 by ethnic rivalries, and by army mutinies, had no means to oust this leftover army. The KMT received plenty of weapons, supplies, and technical support from the Nationalist Chinese headquarters in Taiwan and its covert allies, most notably the United States and Thailand. From late 1952 onward, the KMT became the only effective government authority in the territories between the Salween River and the Chinese border (Kokang, Wa, and Kengtung states), extracting taxes and customs duties (McCoy 1991, pp. 162–78; Lintner 2002, pp. 236–38).

Unsurprisingly, because the territories conquered by the KMT were Burma's major opium-producing regions, a significant part of KMT revenues came from the taxation of opium producers and traffickers; the KMT required that every hill-village farmer pay a heavy annual opium tax. The KMT centralized the wholesale transportation of opium into

Thailand, where it long enjoyed the full protection of Thai authorities (Lintner 2002, pp. 242–44). This may explain why there was a rapid increase in local opium production (McCoy 1991, p. 173). In 1962, the KMT's two main Burmese armies moved their headquarters into Thailand, and, once Taiwan cut back financial support, they increasingly relied on the opium traffic to finance their military operations. They remained major actors in the opium trade, and later heroin production, of the Golden Triangle until the 1980s. Only in 1984 after a new democratic government was installed did the Thai government crack down on the remnants of the KMT (McCoy 1991, pp. 354–55, 432–33).

As these last examples (FARC, UWSA, KMT) show, in conditions of total breakdown or absence of state authority, it becomes difficult to draw clear-cut boundaries among organized crime groups, criminal profit-driven organizations, terrorist organizations, militias, and even states. No doubt, in their heydays, the FARC and Kuomintang exercised, and the UWSA still exercises, governance functions to an even larger extent than any mafia has ever done (with the exception of the triads in Southeast Asia until the nineteenth century). As Tilly (1988, p. xx) noted long ago, "One might imagine a continuum running from anarchy to banditry to mafia to routine government. The defining feature of that continuum is the extent to which control over the use of force is concentrated in a single organization." As in the case of mafia organizations and most collective entities active in (de facto) stateless contexts, for militias, too, it is hardly possible to distinguish economic from political functions. Neither militias (including military organizations gone awry) nor mafia organizations can be classified as exclusively governmental or business enterprises. Profit- and power-oriented activities are present and closely intertwined in these clusters of actors. Moreover, it is even awkward to apply the adjective "criminal" to many militias or mafia organizations because the closest state authorities have sometimes not even formally criminalized or attempted to suppress them. They have themselves exercised power and even held a considerable degree of popular legitimacy. Crime is a term that modern state authorities use to express censure and disapproval, and in the case of both sets of organizations the state was instead conniving, tolerant, or just not there.

VI. Concluding Comments

We began by identifying seven common characteristics of organized crime organization that we and almost all observers and scholars call the five "iconic" mafias. Though each of the five has a distinctive history and setting, there are enough commonalities that bundling them in one category is reasonable.

We mostly discussed whether other modern criminal syndicates share many of the same characteristics. The powerful syndicates that have in the latter part of the twentieth century emerged in Colombia, Mexico, and Brazil are often considered exemplary of organized crime. These syndicates, however, do not possess many of the typifying characteristics of the iconic five, and in some cases it is unclear whether they should even be considered organizations in the sociological sense; they do not have a clear boundary between members and others. The prison-based PCC in Sao Paulo seems to come closest, with longevity as yet the one missing element, which, by definition, can be achieved over time. It is surprising how few of the obvious candidate entities, particularly the Colombian and Mexican DTOs, have many of the typifying characteristics of the iconic five. However, we make no claim that we have conducted an exhaustive study of potential criminal syndicates. For example, the prison-based gangs in El Salvador and Guatemala, such as the MS-13 (Mara Salvatrucha 13) or 18th Street gang, facing extremely weak and brutal governments, have many similarities with the PCC and, like the latter, may share some characteristics of the five iconic mafias, even if they are relatively young.

Mafias are not necessarily the most damaging form of organized crime. If a country had to choose between the recklessly homicidal Mexican drug-trafficking syndicates and the more subtle Sicilian Cosa Nostra, no doubt the latter would cause less social harm at least in the short run. However, mafias persist as many other criminal organizations and syndicates do not. The Colombian government was able to eliminate the Medellin and Cali syndicates. The successor syndicates were comparably effective at smuggling cocaine but posed a much lesser threat to state authority. In contrast, even after a campaign of nearly 50 years by the US Department of Justice, the American Cosa Nostra still operates, even though it is much weakened (Jacobs 2020). Which characteristics of the seven identified above are most important in explaining the persistence of the mafias is unknown, but plausibly it is a combination.

The brief discussion of a range of candidate criminal organizations found more differences than similarities with the five mafias. It may be that it is hard to develop these organizations in modern societies, in which compared with premodern societies there is so much more emphasis on wealth as the single measure of success.

The most important factors that enable mafias to cohere over long periods of time are perhaps those that distinguish them from mere profit-making enterprises. Corporations, even the largest, rarely survive as long as 100 years; there is rapid turnover in the S&P 500, a listing of the 500 largest US firms by capital value.[31] Just as corporations have proven to be quite mortal, purely profit-making criminal syndicates may fail to endure. Money does not breed loyalty. True, the criminal syndicates here considered distinguish themselves from legitimate corporations for their routine and sometimes excessive use of violence. Violence can prevent defections in the short run.

Violence alone, however, does not breed loyalty and cannot substitute for a cultural apparatus engendering a long-term commitment from the members and group legitimacy. It is worth noting that the two Brazilian federations, the most mafia-like of the newer syndicates examined, both had their origins in efforts to improve prison conditions for large numbers of inmates and created elaborate systems of rules and sanctions. It may be that other enduring mafias will only develop in circumstances that create the need for protection against an oppressive, failing, or weak state and when they are able to develop a cultural apparatus capable of legitimizing them vis-à-vis their own members and the surrounding population. We hope that this essay will engender further research on the topic.

REFERENCES

Acosta, Luis J., and Julia S. Cobb. 2019. "Colombian Dissident Rebel Leader Issues New Call to Arms Three Years after Peace Deal." *Reuters* (August 29). https://www.reuters.com/article/us-colombia-peace/colombian-dissident-rebel -leader-issues-new-call-to-arms-three-years-after-peace-deal-idUSKCN1VJ162.
Agence France Press. 2019. "Hells Angels Banned by Dutch Court in Biker Gang Crackdown." *The Guardian* (May 29). https://www.theguardian.com/world/2019 /may/29/hells-angels-banned-by-dutch-court-in-strike-against-biker-gangs.
Albaladejo, Angelika. 2018. "PCC Files Document Gang's Explosive Growth in Brazil and Beyond." *InSight Crime* (June 5). https://www.insightcrime.org/news /analysis/pcc-files-document-gang-explosive-growth-brazil-beyond/.
Allum, Felia. 2016. *The Invisible Camorra: Neapolitan Crime Families across Europe.* Ithaca, NY: Cornell University Press.

[31] A more precise statement is impossible. For a sense of just how difficult it is to measure long-term corporate survival, see the exchange of comments on a blog post (Perry 2016).

Altsean-Burma, Alternative Asean Network in Burma. 2004. *A Failing Grade—Burma's Drug Eradication Efforts*. Bangkok: Altsean.

Anderson, Jon L. 2018. "The Afterlife of Pablo Escobar." *New Yorker* 94(3):50. https://www.newyorker.com/magazine/2018/03/05/the-afterlife-of-pablo-escobar.

Araujo, Marcella. 2019. "Urban Public Works, Drug Trafficking, and Militias: What Are the Consequences of the Interactions between Community Work and Illicit Markets?" *Journal of Illicit Economies and Development* 1(2):164–76.

Arias, Enrique D. 2010. "Drug Cartels: Neither Holy, nor Roman, nor an Empire." In *International Crime and Justice*, edited by Mangai Natarajan. Cambridge: Cambridge University Press.

Arias, Enrique D., and Corinne D. Rodrigues. 2006. "The Myth of Personal Security: Criminal Gangs, Dispute Resolution, and Identity in Rio de Janeiro's Favelas." *Latin American Politics and Society* 48(4):53–81.

Arsovska, Jana. 2015. *Decoding Albanian Organized Crime Culture, Politics, and Globalization*. Los Angeles: University of California Press.

———. 2016. "Strategic Mobsters or Deprived Migrants? Testing the Transplantation and Deprivation Models of Organized Crime in an Effort to Understand Criminal Mobility and Diversity in the United States." *International Migration* 54(2):160–75.

Astorga, Luís. 1999. *Drug Trafficking in Mexico: A First General Assessment*. Paris: MOST Programme, United Nations Educational, Scientific and Cultural Organization.

———. 2012. "México: Organized Crime Politics and Insecurity." In *Traditional Organized Crime in the Modern World: Responses to Socioeconomic Change*, edited by Dina Siegel and Henk van de Bunt. Boston: Springer.

Atuesta, Laura H. 2017. "Narcomessages as a Way to Analyse the Evolution of Organized Crime in Mexico." *Global Crime* 18(2):100–21.

Atuesta, Laura H., and Yocelyn S. Pérez-Dávila. 2018. "Fragmentation and Cooperation: The Evolution of Organized Crime in Mexico." *Trends in Organized Crime* 21(3):235–61.

Ball, Desmond. 1999. "Burma and Drugs: The Regime's Complicity in the Global Drug Trade." Working Paper no. 336. Canberra: Strategic and Defence Studies Centre, Australian National University.

Barker, Thomas. 2014. *Outlaw Motorcycle Gangs as Organized Crime Groups*. Cham: SpringerBriefs in Criminology.

Beittel, June S. 2019. *Mexico: Organized Crime and Drug Trafficking Organizations*. Washington, DC: Congressional Research Service.

Biondi, Karina. 2016. *Sharing this Walk: An Ethnography of Prison Life and the PCC in Brazil*. Chapel Hill: University of North Carolina Press.

BKA (Bundeskriminalamt). 2018. *Lagebild Organisierte Kriminalität Bundesrepublik Deutschland*. Wiesbaden: BKA.

Block, Alan A. 1983. *East Side—West Side: Organizing Crime in New York (1930–1950)*. New Brunswick, NJ: Transaction.

Borkan, Brett. 2010. "Los Rastrojos Gang Infiltrates Colombian Elections." *Colombia Reports* (April 13). https://colombiareports.com/los-rastrojos-gang-infiltrates-colombian-elections/.

Bouchard, Martin. 2020. "Collaboration and Boundaries in Organized Crime: A Network Perspective." In *Organizing Crime: Mafias, Markets, and Networks*, edited by Michael Tonry and Peter Reuter. Chicago: University of Chicago Press.

Bouchard, Martin, and Carlo Morselli. 2014. "Opportunistic Structures of Organized Crime." In *Oxford Handbook of Organized Crime*, edited by Letizia Paoli. New York: Oxford University Press.

Bowden, Mark. 2007. *Killing Pablo: The Hunt for the World's Greatest Outlaw*. New York: Grove Atlantic.

Bunker, Robert J. 2010. "Strategic Threat: Narcos and Narcotics Overview." *Small Wars and Insurgencies* 21(1):8–29.

Bunker, Robert J., and John P. Sullivan. 1998. "Cartel Evolution: Potentials and Consequences." *Transnational Organized Crime* 4(2):55–74.

Calderón, Gabriela, Gustavo Robles, Alberto Díaz-Cayeros, and Beatriz Magaloni. 2015. "The Beheading of Criminal Organizations and the Dynamics of Violence in Mexico." *Journal of Conflict Resolution* 59(8):1455–85.

Calderoni, Francesco. 2010. *Organized Crime Legislation in the European Union: Harmonization and Approximation of Criminal Law, National Legislations and the EU Framework Decision on the Fight against Organized Crime*. Heidelberg: Springer.

Campana, Paolo, and Federico Varese. 2018. "Organized Crime in the United Kingdom: Illegal Governance of Markets and Communities." *British Journal of Criminology* 58(6):1381–1400.

Campbell, Howard. 2014. "Narco-Propaganda in the Mexican 'Drug War': An Anthropological Perspective." *Latin American Perspectives* 41(2):60–77.

Carrigan, Ana. 1996. "An Unlikely Hero: Valdivieso's Crusade against Drug Corruption." *NACLA Report on the Americas* 30(1):6–10.

Catino, Maurizio. 2019. *Mafia Organizations: The Visible Hand of Criminal Enterprise*. Cambridge: Cambridge University Press.

———. 2020. "Italian Organized Crime since 1950." In *Organizing Crime: Mafias, Markets, and Networks*, edited by Michael Tonry and Peter Reuter. Chicago: University of Chicago Press.

Chalk, Peter. 2011. *The Latin American Drug Trade: Scope, Dimensions, Impact, and Response*. Santa Monica, CA: Rand.

Cheloukhine, Serguei. 2008. "The Roots of Russian Organized Crime: From Old-Fashioned Professionals to the Organized Criminal Groups of Today." *Crime Law and Social Change* 50:353–74.

Chew Sánchez, Martha I. 2014. "Paramilitarism and State-Terrorism in Mexico as a Case Study of Shrinking Functions of the Neoliberal State." *Perspectives on Global Development and Technology* 13:176–96.

Clawson, Patrick, and Rensselaer Lee. 1996. *The Andean Cocaine Industry*. New York: St. Martin's Griffin.

Colman, Charlotte, Freja De Middeleer, Antonius Spapens, Stephan Van Nimwegen, Rik Ceulen, Sabine Gerbrands, Letizia Paoli, and Elke Roevens. 2018. *De Grens Voorbij: Belgische en Nederlandse Drugsmarkten in Beweging*. The Hague: Boom.

Commissione Parlamentare Antimafia. 1992. *Audizione del Collaboratore di Giustizia Leonardo Messina*. Rome: Commissione Parlamentare Antimafia

———. 1993. *Relazione sulla camorra*. Doc. XXIII, n. 12, XI legislature. Rome: Camera dei Deputati and Senato della Repubblica.

Congressional Research Service. 2019. *Mexico: Organized Crime and Drug Trafficking Organizations*. Washington, DC: Congressional Research Service.

Correa-Cabrera, Guadalupe. 2017. *Los Zetas Inc. Criminal Corporations, Energy and Civil War in Mexico*. Austin: University of Texas Press.

Corte di Assise Santa Maria Capua Vetere. 2006. "Sentenza contro Abbate Antonio + 129. N. 9/98 R.G. C." June 15.

Corte Suprema di Cassazione. 1987. *Sentenza sul ricorso proposto da Altivalle Sergio ed altri e dal P.G. c Bonavita Luigi ed altri*. Sentenza n. 1683, June 13.

Council of the European Union. 2008. "Council Framework Decision 2008/841/JHA of 24 October 2008 on the Fight against Organised Crime." *Official Journal of the European Union* L300:42–45.

Coutinho, Leonardo. 2019. "The Evolution of the Most Lethal Criminal Organization in Brazil—the PCC." *PRISM* 8(1):56–67.

CSM (Consiglio Superiore della Magistratura). 2020. "Mafie: Camorra." https://www.csm.it/web/csm-internet/aree-tematiche/giurisdizione-e-societa/mafie?redirect=/web/csm-internet/aree-tematiche/giurisdizione-e-societa/mafie&show=true&title=Camorra&show_bcrumb=Camorra.

Davis, Anthony, and Bruce Hawke. 1998. "On the Road to Ruin: Narco-Dollars Lure Burmese Junta toward Heroin Dependency." *Jane's Intelligence Review* March:26–31.

DEA (Drug Enforcement Administration). 2017. *Colombian Cocaine Production Expansion Contributes to Rise in Supply in the United States*. DEA Intelligence Brief. Washington, DC: US Drug Enforcement Administration.

Dias, Camila Nunes, and Fernando Salla. 2013. "Organized Crime in Brazilian Prisons: The Example of the PCC." *International Journal of Criminology and Sociology* 2:397–408.

Dingley, James C. 2012. *The IRA: The Irish Republican Army*. Santa Barbara, CA: Praeger.

DNA (Direzione Nazionale Antimafia e Antiterrorismo). 2017. *Relazione annuale sulle attività svolte dal Procuratore nazionale e dalla Direzione nazionale antimafia e antiterrorismo nonché sulle dinamiche e strategie della criminalità organizzata di tipo mafioso nel periodo 1° luglio 2015–30 giugno 2016*. Prot. 12720/2017/PNA, April 12.

Duncan, Gustavo. 2014. "Drug Trafficking and Political Power: Oligopolies of Coercion in Colombia and Mexico." *Latin American Perspectives* 11(2):18–42.

Durán-Martínez, Angelica. 2017. *The Politics of Drug Violence: Criminals, Cops, and Politicians in Colombia and Mexico*. Oxford: Oxford University Press.

Eccarius-Kelly, Vera. 2012. "Surreptitious Lifelines: A Structural Analysis of the FARC and the PKK." *Terrorism and Political Violence* 24(2):235–58.

Edwards, Adam, and Michael Levi. 2008. "Researching the Organization of Serious Crimes." *Criminology and Criminal Justice* 8:363–88.

European Commission. 1997. "Action Plan to Combat Organized Crime (Adopted by the Council on 28 April 1997)." *Official Journal of the European Communities* C251:1–18.

Europol. 2003. *2003 European Union Organised Crime Report*. Luxembourg: Office for the Official Publications of the European Communities.

———. 2013. *EU Serious and Organised Crime Threat Assessment: SCOTA 2013*. 's-Gravenzande: Deventer.

Felbab-Brown, Vanda. 2009. *The Violent Drug Market in Mexico and Lessons from Colombia*. Washington, DC: Brookings Institution.

———. 2011. *Calderon's Caldron: Lessons from Mexico's Battle against Organized Crime and Drug Trafficking in Tijuana, Ciudad Juárez, and Michoacán*. Washington, DC: Brookings Institution.

———. 2019. *Mexico's Out-of-Control Criminal Market*. Washington, DC: Brookings Institution.

Felson, Marcus. 2009. "The Natural History of Extended Co-Offending." *Trends in Organized Crime* 12(2):159–65.

Florez, Carl P., and Bernadette Boyce. 1990. "Colombian Organized Crime." *Police Studies* 13(2):81–88.

Fuentes, Joseph R. 1999. "Life of a Cell: Managerial Practice and Strategy in Colombian Cocaine Distribution in the United States." PhD dissertation, City University of New York.

Galeotti, Mark. 2012. *Transnational Aspects of Russian Organized Crime*. London: Chatham House.

Garzon, Juan Carlos. 2010. *Mafia and Co*. Washington, DC: Woodrow Wilson Center.

Golz, Michael, and Daniel J. D'Amico. 2018. "Market Concentration in the International Drug Trade." *Journal of Economic Behavior and Organization* 150:28–42.

Grayson, George W. 2010. *La Familia Drug Cartel: Implications for U.S.-Mexican Security*. Carlisle, PA: Strategic Studies Institute. https://www.globalsecurity.org/security/library/report/2010/ssi_grayson.pdf.

Grayson, George W., and Samuel Loga. 2012. *The Executioner's Men: Los Zetas, Rogue Soldiers, Criminal Entrepreneurs, and the Shadow State They Created*. New Brunswick: Transaction.

Guevara, America Y. 2013. "Propaganda in Mexico's Drug War." *Journal of Strategic Security* 6(3):131–51.

Handelman, Stephen. 1995. *Comrade Criminal: Russia's New Mafia*. New Haven, CT: Yale University Press.

Heinle, Kimberly, Octavio Rodríguez Ferreira, and David A. Shirk. 2014. *Drug Violence in Mexico: Data and Analysis through 2013*. San Diego, CA: Justice in Mexico Project.

Hirata, Daniel V., and Carolina C. Grillo. 2019. "Movement and Death: Illicit Drug Markets in the Cities of São Paulo and Rio De Janeiro." *Journal of Illicit Economies and Development* 1(2):122–33.

Human Rights Clinic. 2017. *"Control ... Over the Entire State of Coahuila": An Analysis of Testimonies in Trials against Zeta Members in San Antonio, Austin, and Del Rio, Texas*. Austin: University of Texas Law School.

Hylton, Forrest. 2008. "Medellín: The Peace of the Pacifiers." *NACLA Report on the Americas* 41(1):35–42.

ICG (International Crisis Group). 2007. "Colombia's New Armed Groups." Latin America Report no. 20, May 10. Bogotá: International Crisis Group.

———. 2014. "Corridor of Violence: the Guatemala-Honduras Border." Latin America Report no. 52, June 4. https://d2071andvip0wj.cloudfront.net/corri dor-of-violence-the-guatemala-honduras-border.pdf.

INEGI (El Instituto Nacional de Estadística y Geografía). 2019. "Datos Preliminares Revelan Que en 2018 se Registraron 35 Mil 964 Homicidos." *Comunicado de Prensa* Num. 347/19. Mexico City: INEGI Informa.

InSight Crime. 2011. "Police Arrest Link between Colombia's Rastrojos and the Sinaloa Cartel." *InSight Crime* (January 13). https://www.insightcrime.org /news/analysis/police-arrest-link-between-colombias-rastrojos-and-the-sinaloa -cartel/.

———. 2017. "Rastrojos." *InSight Crime* (February 16). https://www.insightcrime .org/colombia-organized-crime-news/rastrojos-profile/.

———. 2019. "Sinaloa Cartel." *InSight Crime* (March 29). https://www.insightcrime .org/mexico-organized-crime-news/sinaloa-cartel-profile/.

Jacobs, James B. 2020. "The Rise and Fall of Organized Crime in the United States." In *Organizing Crime: Mafias, Markets, and Networks*, edited by Michael Tonry and Peter Reuter. Chicago: University of Chicago Press.

Jones, Nathan P. 2018. "The Strategic Implications of the Cártel de Jalisco Nueva Generación." *Journal of Strategic Security* 11(1):19–42.

Kaplan, Robert D. 1998. "Hoods against Democrats." *Atlantic* (December). https://www.theatlantic.com/magazine/archive/1998/12/hoods-against-democrats /377344/.

Kenney, Michael. 2007. "The Architecture of Drug Trafficking: Network Forms of Organisation in the Colombian Cocaine Trade." *Global Crime* 8(3):233–59.

Kilmer, Beau, Jonathan P. Caulkins, Brittany M. Bond, and Peter Reuter. 2010. *Reducing Drug Trafficking Revenues and Violence in Mexico*. Washington, DC: Rand.

Kleemans, Edward, and Vere von Koppen. 2020. "Organized Crime and Criminal Careers." In *Organizing Crime: Mafias, Markets, and Networks*, edited by Michael Tonry and Peter Reuter. Chicago: University of Chicago Press.

Krauthausen, Ciro. 1997. *Moderne Gewalten: Organisierte Kriminalität in Kolumbien und Italien*. Frankfurt: Campus.

Lacey, Marc. 2008. "Grenade Attack in Mexico Breaks from Deadly Script." *New York Times* (September 25). https://www.nytimes.com/2008/09/25/world/ameri cas/25mexico.html.

LaFree, Gary, Laura Dugan, and Erin Miller. 2015. *Putting Terrorism in Context: Lessons from the Global Terrorism Database*. New York: Routledge.

Lamb, Robert Dale. 2010. "Microdynamics of Illegitimacy and Complex Urban Violence in Medellín, Colombia." PhD dissertation, University of Maryland.

Lee, Renssalaer. 1991. "Colombia's Cocaine Syndicates." *Crime, Law, and Social Change* 16(1):3–39.

———. 2002. "Perverse Effects of Andean Counternarcotics Policy." *Orbis* 46(3):537–54.

Lee, Renssalaer, and Francisco Thoumi. 1999. "The Political-Criminal Nexus in Colombia." *Trends in Organized Crime* 5(2):59–84.

Lessing, Benjamin. 2018. *Making Peace in Drug Wars: Crackdowns and Cartels in Latin America*. Cambridge: Cambridge University Press.

Lessing, Benjamin, and Graham Denyer Willis. 2019. "Legitimacy in Criminal Governance: Managing a Drug Empire from Behind Bars." *American Political Science Review* 113(2):584–606.

Lintner, Bertil. 2002. *Blood Brothers: The Criminal Underworld of Asia*. New York: Palgrave.

———. 2019. *The United Wa State Army and Burma's Peace Process*. Washington, DC: United States Institute of Peace.

Looft, Christopher. 2012. "Mexico Gangs Use Social Networking Sites for Recruitment, Intelligence." *InSight Crime* (May 31). https://www.insightcrime .org/news/brief/mexico-cartels-using-social-networking-sites-for-recruitment -intelligence/.

Marcela Zuñiga, Laura. 2019. "Deadly Riot Shows Paraguay Prisons Unprepared for PCC Onslaught." *InSight Crime* (June 20). https://www.insightcrime.org /news/brief/deadly-riot-paraguay-prisons-unprepared-pcc/.

Maritime Executive. 2016. "Largest Cocaine Bust of Decade on Miami River." *Maritime Executive* (June 2). https://maritime-executive.com/article/largest -merchant-ship-cocaine-bust-of-decade-in-miami.

Massari, Monica, and Vittorio Martone. 2018. *Mafia Violence: Political, Symbolic, and Economic Forms of Violence in Camorra Clans*. New York: Routledge.

McCoy, Alfred W. 1991. *The Politics of Heroin: CIA Complicity in the Global Drug Trade*. Brooklyn, NY: Lawrence Hill.

McDermott, Jeremy. 2015. *The Changing Face of Colombian Organized Crime*. Bogotá: Friedrich-Ebert-Stiftung.

McGovern, Tara A. 2016. "New Armed Groups in Colombia: The Emergence of the BACRIM in the 21st Century." PhD dissertation, George Mason University.

Miguel Cruz, José. 2010. "Central American Maras: From Youth Street Gangs to Transnational Protection Rackets." *Global Crime* 11(4):379–98.

Millard, George H., and Tim Hundleby. 2015. "Organized Crime in Brazil." *Journal of Money Laundering Control* 18(2):234–47.

Milsom, Jeremy. 2005. "The Long Hard Road Out of Drugs: The Case of the Wa." In *Trouble in the Triangle: Opium and Conflict in Burma*, edited by Martin Jelsma, Tom Kramer, and Pietje Vervest. Chiang Mai: Silkworms.

Ministero dell'Interno. 2012. *Relazione Semestrale sull'Attività Svolta e i Risultati Conseguiti dalla Direzione Investigativa Antimafia—gennaio—giugno 2012*. Rome: Ministero dell'Interno.

———. 2017. *Relazione sui programmi di protezione, sulla loro efficacia e sulle modalità generali di applicazione per coloro che collaborano con la giustizia (Secondo semestre 2015 e primo semestre 2016)*. Rome: Camera dei Deputati, Doc. XCI n.8, XVII Legislature.

———. 2020. *Relazione semestrale sull'attività svolta e i risultati conseguiti dalla Direzione Investigativa Antimafia—gennaio-giugno 2019*. Rome: Ministero dell'Interno.

Misse, Michel. 2007. "Illegal Markets, Protection Rackets, and Organized Crime in Rio de Janeiro." *Estudos Avancados* 21(61):139–57.

Monreal Ávila, Ricardo. 2008. "Narcoterrorismo." *Milenio* (September 23). http://lacolumna.wordpress.com/2008/09/23/narcoterrorismo-ricardo-monreal-avila/.

Monzini, Paola. 1999. *Gruppi Criminali a Napoli e Marsiglia: La Delinquenza Organizzata Nella Storia di Due Città: 1820–1990*. Catanzaro: Meridiana libri.

Moors, Hans, and Antonius Spapens. 2017. *Criminele Families in Noord-Brabant*. Appeldoorn: Politie and Wetenschap.

Morgan, W. P. 1960. *Triad Societies in Hong Kong*. Hong Kong: Government Press.

Murray, Joseph, Daniel R. de Castro Cerqueira, and Tulio Kahn. 2013. "Crime and Violence in Brazil: Systematic Review of Time Trends, Prevalence Rates, and Risk Factors." *Aggression and Violent Behavior* 18(5):471–83.

National Drug Intelligence Center. 2008. *National Drug Threat Assessment 2009*. Johnstown, PA: US Department of Justice, National Drug Intelligence Center.

Naylor, Robin. 2003. "Toward a General Theory of Profit-Driven Crimes." *British Journal of Criminology* 43:81–101.

Norman, Susan V. 2018. "*Narcotization* as Security Dilemma: The FARC and Drug Trade in Colombia." *Studies in Conflict and Terrorism* 41(8):638–59.

NPA (National Police Agency). 2018. *Police of Japan 2018*. Tokyo: National Police Agency. https://www.npa.go.jp/english/Police_of_Japan/POJcontents.html.

Nussio, Enzo. 2018. "Ex-Combatants and Violence in Colombia: Are Yesterday's Villains Today's Principal Threat?" *Third World Thematics: A TWQ Journal* 3(1):135–52.

Osorio, Javier. 2015. "The Contagion of Drug Violence Spatiotemporal Dynamics of the Mexican War on Drugs." *Journal of Conflict Resolution* 59(8): 1403–32.

Otis, John. 2014. "The FARC and Colombia's Illegal Drug Trade." Wilson Centre Latin American Program. http://fileserver.idpc.net/library/Otis_FARC DrugTrade2014-ENGLISH%20(1).pdf.

Ownby, David, and Mary F. Somers Heidhues, eds. 1993. *"Secret Societies" Reconsidered: Perspectives on the Social History of Modern South China and Southeast Asia*. Armonk, NY: M. E. Sharpe.

Paoli, Letizia. 2002. "The Paradoxes of Organized Crime." *Crime, Law, and Social Change* 37(1):51–97.

———. 2020. "What Makes Mafias Different?" In *Organizing Crime: Mafias, Markets, and Networks*, edited by Michael Tonry and Peter Reuter. Chicago: University of Chicago Press.

Paoli, Letizia, Victoria Greenfield, and Peter Reuter. 2009. *The World Heroin Market: Can Supply Be Cut?* Oxford: Oxford University Press.

Pardo, Bryce, Jirka Taylor, Jonathan P. Caulkins, Beau Kilmer, Peter Reuter, and Bradley Stein. 2019. *The Future of Fentanyl and Other Synthetic Opioids*. Santa Monica, CA: RAND.

Penglase, Ben. 2008. "The Bastard Child of the Dictatorship: The Comando Vermelho and the Birth of 'Narco-culture' in Rio de Janeiro." *Luso-Brazilian Review* 45(1):118–45.

Perla Diógenes de Aquino, Jania. 2019. "Pioneers: The PCC and Specialization in the Market of Major Robberies." *Journal of Illicit Economies and Development* 1(2):193–203.

Perry, Mark J. 2016. "Fortune 500 Firms 1955 v. 2016: Only 12 Percent Remain, Thanks to the Creative Destruction That Fuels Economic Prosperity." https://www.aei.org/carpe-diem/fortune-500-firms-1955-v-2016-only-12-remain-thanks-to-the-creative-destruction-that-fuels-economic-prosperity/.

Pistone, Joseph D., with the assistance of Richard Woodley. 1988. *Donnie Brasco: My Undercover Life in the Mob*. New York: Dutton.

President's Commission on Organized Crime. 1986. *The Edge: Organized Crime, Business, and Labor Unions. Interim Report*. Washington, DC: US Government Publishing Office.

Ramírez Montañez, Julio C. 2017. "Fifteen Years of Plan Colombia (2001–2016): The Recovery of a Weak State and the Submission of Narcoterrorist Groups?" *Analecta Política* 7(13):315–32.

Ramos da Cruz, Claudio, and David H. Ucko. 2018. "Beyond the *Unidades de Polícia Pacificadora*: Countering Comando Vermelho's Criminal Insurgency." *Small Wars and Insurgencies* 29(1):38–67.

Restrepo, Andrés L., and Álvaro C. Guizado. 2003. "From Smugglers to Warlords: Twentieth Century Colombian Drug Traffickers." *Canadian Journal of Latin American and Caribbean Studies* 28(55–56):249–75.

Reuter, Peter. 2009. "Systemic Violence in Drug Markets." *Crime, Law, and Social Change* 52:275–84.

Reuter, Peter, and Daniel Rico. 2012. "Drug Smuggling Case Study: Los Rastrojos." College Park: University of Maryland. https://spp.umd.edu/research-impact/publications/drug-smuggling-case-study-los-rastrojos.

Romero, Simon. 2011. "In Colombia, New Gold Rush Deepens Old Conflict." *New York Times* (March 3). http://www.nytimes.com/2011/03/04/world/americas/04colombia.html?pagewanted=2&_r=1&hp.

Rossi, Jacques. 1989. *The Gulag Handbook*. New York: Paragon.

Sales, Isaia. 1993. *La Camorra, Le Camorre*. Roma: Editori Riuniti.

Saviano, Roberto. 2008. *Gomorrah: Italy's Other Mafia*. New York: Macmillan.

Schelling, Thomas C. 1971. "What Is the Business of Organized Crime?" *American Scholar* 40:643–52.

Schmid, Alex. 2004. "Terrorism: The Definitional Problem." *Case Western Reserve Journal of International Law* 36(2):371–415.

Schwirtz, Michael. 2008. "Vory v Zakone Has Hallowed Place in Russian Criminal Lore." *International Herald Tribune* (July 29). https://www.nytimes.com/2008/07/29/world/europe/29iht-moscow.4.14865004.html?pagewanted=all&_r=0.

Sciarrone, Rocco. 1998. *Mafie del Nord. Strategie Criminali e Contesti Locali*. Rome: Donzelli.

Seelke, Clare R. 2016. *Gangs in Central America*. Washington, DC: Congressional Research Service.

Sheridan, Mary B. 2020. "More Than 60,000 Mexicans Have Disappeared in the Midst of the Drug War." *Washington Post Blogs* (January 6). https://www

.bostonglobe.com/news/world/2020/01/06/more-than-mexicans-have-been-dis appeared-amid-drug-war-officials-say/EzQRurRKH1DO0OXkTm319O/story .html.

Shinar, Chaim. 2016. "Organized Crime in Russia." *European Review* 24(4):631–40.

Snyder, Richard, and Angélica Durán Martínez. 2009. "Drugs, Violence, and State-Sponsored Protection Rackets in Mexico and Colombia." *Colombia Internacional* 70:61–91.

SOCA, UK Serious and Organised Crime Agency. 2012. "Organised Crime Groups." http://www.soca.gov.uk/threats/organised-crime-groups.

Sokolov, Vsevolod. 2004. "From Guns to Briefcases: The Evolution of Russian Organized Crime." *World Policy Journal* 21(1):68–74.

Spapens, Toine. 2016. "North Brabant: A Brief History of a Hotbed of Organised Crime." In *Illegal Entrepreneurship, Organized Crime and Social Control: Essays in Honor of Dick Hobbs*, edited by Georgios A. Antonopoulos. Cham: Springer.

Thoumi, Francisco E. 2002. "Illegal Drugs in Colombia: From Illegal Economic Boom to Social Crisis." *ANNALS of the American Academy of Political and Social Science* 582(1):102–16.

———. 2012. "Colombian Organized Crime: From Drug Trafficking to Parastatal Bands and Widespread Corruption." In *Traditional Organized Crime in the Modern World: Responses to Socioeconomic Change*, edited by Dina Siegel and Henk van de Bunt. Boston: Springer.

———. 2014. "Organized Crime in Colombia: The Actors Running the Illegal Drug Industry." In *The Oxford Handbook of Organized Crime*, edited by Letizia Paoli. Oxford: Oxford University Press.

Tilly, Charles. 1985. "War Making and State Making as Organized Crime." In *Bringing the State Back In*, edited by Peter B. Evans, Dietrich Rueschemeyer, and Theda Skocpol. Cambridge: Cambridge University Press.

———. 1988. "Foreword." In *The Mafia of a Sicilian Village, 1860–1960: A Study of Violent Peasant Entrepreneurs*, edited by Anton Blok. New York: Polity.

Tolbert, Pamela S., and Richard H. Hall. 2009. *Organizations: Structures, Processes, and Outcomes*. Abingdon: Routledge.

Tops, Pieter, Judith van Valkenhoef, Edward van der Torre, and Luuk van Spijk. 2018. *The Netherlands and Synthetic Drugs: An Inconvenient Truth*. The Hague: Eleven.

Tribunale di Palermo, Ufficio Istruzione Processi Penali. 1985. *Ordinanza-sentenza di rinvio a giudizio nei confronti di Abbate Giovanni + 706*. November 8.

UNODC (United Nations Office on Drugs and Crime). 2017. *Myanmar Opium Survey*. Bangkok: United Nations Office on Drugs and Crime (UNODC), Regional Office for Southeast Asia and the Pacific.

US Department of Justice. 2014. "Motorcycle Gangs." http://www.justice.gov /criminal/ocgs/gangs/motorcycle.html.

US Department of State. 2019. *International Narcotics Control Strategy Report*, vol. 1. Washington, DC: US Department of State, Bureau for International Narcotics and Law Enforcement Affairs.

US Department of Treasury. 2012. "Treasury Sanctions Members of the Camorra." (August 1) https://www.treasury.gov/press-center/press-releases/Pages/tg1666.aspx.

Van de Bunt, Henk G., and Edward R. Kleemans. 2007. *Georganiseerde criminaliteit in Nederland: Derde rapportage op basis van de Monitor Georganiseerde Criminaliteit*. The Hague: Boom.

Van Duyne, Peter C. 1997. "Organized Crime, Corruption, and Power." *Crime, Law, and Social Change* 26:201–38.

Varese, Federico. 2001. *The Russian Mafia: Private Protection in a New Market Economy*. Oxford: Oxford University Press.

———. 2010. "What Is Organized Crime?" In *Organized Crime*, edited by Federico Varese. London: Routledge.

———. 2020. "How Mafias Migrate: Transplantation, Functional Diversification, and Separation." In *Organizing Crime: Mafias, Markets, and Networks*, edited by Michael Tonry and Peter Reuter. Chicago: University of Chicago Press.

Vargas, Ricardo M. 2005. "Drugs and Armed Conflict in Colombia." In *Trouble in the Triangle: Opium and Conflict in Burma*, edited by Martin Jelsma, Tom Kramer, and Pietje Vervest. Chiang Mai: Silkworms.

Venezuela Investigative Unit. 2019. "Massacre on Colombia-Venezuela Border Reveals Rastrojos Civil War." *InSight Crime* (July 2). https://www.insightcrime.org/news/analysis/massacre-colombia-venezuela-border-rastrojos-war/.

Volkov, Vadim. 2014. "The Russian Mafia: The Rise and Extinction." In *Oxford Handbook of Organized Crime*, edited by Letizia Paoli. New York: Oxford University Press.

Von Lampe, Klaus. 2019. "Definitions of Organized Crime." http://www.organized-crime.de/organizedcrimedefinitions.htm.

Von Lampe, Klaus, and Arjan Blokland. 2020. "Outlaw Biker Clubs and Organized Crime." In *Organizing Crime: Mafias, Markets, and Networks*, edited by Michael Tonry and Peter Reuter. Chicago: University of Chicago Press.

Watkins, Ali. 2019. "A Shipping Manifest Said the Container Held Dried Fruit. Inside Was 3,200 Pounds of Cocaine." *New York Times* (March 11). https://www.nytimes.com/2019/03/11/nyregion/cocaine-bust-nyc-newark.html.

Weber, Max. 1978. *Economy and Society: An Outline of Interpretive Sociology*, edited by Guenther Roth and Claus Wittich. Berkeley: University of California Press. (Originally published 1922.)

White House. 2011. *Strategy to Address Transnational Organized Crime: Addressing Converging Threats to National Security*. Washington, DC: White House.

Willis, Graham D. 2017. "Before the Body Count: Homicide Statistics and Everyday Security in Latin America." *Journal of Latin American Studies* 49(1):29–54.

Wolff, Michael J. 2015. "Building Criminal Authority: A Comparative Analysis of Drug Gangs in Rio de Janeiro and Recife." *Latin American Politics and Society* 57(2):21–40.

Xhudo, Gus. 1996. "Men of Purpose: The Growth of the Albanian Criminal Activity." *Frank Cass Journal* 2(1):1–20.

Zdun, Steffen. 2011. "Difficulties Measuring and Controlling Homicide in Rio de Janeiro." *International Journal of Conflict and Violence* 5(1):189–99.
Zhilla, Fabian, and Besfort Lamallari. 2015. "Albanian Criminal Groups." *Trends in Organized Crime* 18:329–47.

Federico Varese

How Mafias Migrate: Transplantation, Functional Diversification, and Separation

ABSTRACT

Many policy makers and some academics believe that mafias move easily between countries and with little difficulty quickly become deeply rooted. The
reality is more complicated. Mafiosi often move away from their home territories because they are forced to do so rather than because they relocate for
strategic reasons; that kind of transplantation abroad tends to be unsuccessful.
Whether transplantation succeeds depends on the presence of mafiosi and
local factors, such as whether markets, construction, or illegal drugs are
booming and poorly regulated. Under some conditions, transplantation
results in wholesale separation between the original organization and the
outpost. Mafiosi abroad often neither plan nor hope to achieve the kinds of
control of territories, industries, and markets they exercise at home but to buy
or sell illegal commodities, thereby engaging in a process of functional diversification.

The movement of Italian mafias from the regions where they are traditionally rooted—Sicily, Calabria, and Campania—to the northern areas
of the country and abroad has been widely discussed (see, e.g., Ciconte

Electronically published June 3, 2020
Federico Varese is a professor of criminology at the University of Oxford and a senior
research fellow at Nuffield College, Oxford. I am grateful to participants in the *Crime and
Justice* meeting on organized crime, Bologna (May 16–18, 2019), for their comments, especially to Francesco Calderoni, Paolo Campana, and Maurizio Catino, who provided additional suggestions and pointed me to relevant sources. Zora Hauser, Francesco Niccolò

1998; Sciarrone 1998; Massari 2001; Forgione 2009; Di Antonio 2010; De Filippo and Moretti 2011; Portanova, Rossi, and Stefanoni 2011; Tizian 2011; Pignatone and Prestipino 2012; Gennari 2013; Pignedoli 2016). Similar phenomena affect other countries. For instance, street gangs such as Mara Salvatrucha, Latin Kings, and Barrio 18 are active across the United States and in Central America. Hong Kong triads are said to be moving to Europe and mainland China, while crime groups from the former Soviet Union are reported to be operating in Western Europe. This trend is of immediate policy concern, and yet it also raises general questions related to the role of local factors in organized crime and the effects of globalization in facilitating serious crime across borders. It is now considered one of the main theoretical issues in the study of organized crime. Since the 2000s a number of significant works on the subject—using a variety of methods including community qualitative studies, comparative historical investigations, descriptive quantitative studies, and hypothesis testing on relatively large data sets—have been published. Understanding of the subject, however, continues to suffer from conceptual confusion, data challenges, and knowledge gaps.

Organized crime is best defined on the basis of the activities of groups, rather than on their organizational structure, contrary to a widely held view. I focus here on the mobility of established criminal groups that, in their territories of origin, control market and territories. I refer to this as governance-type organized crime or usually, for reasons of simplicity, as mafias. The first section of this essay introduces the most important concepts needed to understand mafia mobility: transplantation, functional diversification, and separation. Transplantation refers to mafias' ability to reproduce their capacity to govern some markets or territory far from their places of origin and their main operations. This is a more analytically useful concept than others that appear in the literature such as "stable presence," "settlement," "colonization," "entrenchment," and "hard penetration"; they do not make explicit what the group does in the territory in which it is present. A key distinction needs to be made between transplantation and functional diversification. Mafiosi abroad may engage in activities that do not entail attempts to control markets or territories but rather to buy and sell illegal goods. In the latter case, they engage in functional

Moro, and Dennis Rodgers commented helpfully on an earlier version of this essay. Three anonymous referees also gave detailed comments. Michael Tonry and Peter Reuter helped me clarify my arguments and presentation significantly. This essay draws and expands on work I have published elsewhere (Varese 2001, 2004, 2006, 2010, 2011a, 2012b).

diversification. Under some conditions, the mafia outpost may separate from the "motherland" and become a fully independent new entity.

In Section II, I present two contrasting perspectives on mafia transplantation. According to the Free Movement view, the presence of mafiosi abroad is the product of a rational strategy to colonize new territory, it is a ubiquitous phenomenon, and entrenchment is easy. Such a view tends to suffer from lack of conceptual clarity and of specification of the phenomenon under study and to rely on exaggerated claims. Other scholars have advanced the contrary view, namely, that mafias never move. This I call the No Movement view. While theoretically elegant, this second position cannot explain the limited yet real phenomenon of mafia presence in new places. It assumes that criminal reputations cannot travel across long distances and that the motherland cannot control its agents when they are far away. Criminal reputations do, however, travel across borders, and often the transplanted group is not formed by employees of the motherland. Rather, it is an independent unit using the mafia brand name.

In Section III, I list the main hypotheses that have been advanced to account for mafia transplantation, functional diversification, and separation. Sections IV–VI present the main empirical findings. Concerning transplantation: mafiosi are more likely to find themselves in new territories because of unwanted circumstances rather than because of intentional, rational decisions to colonize new markets and territories. The mere presence of mafiosi as such is not sufficient to predict transplantation. When that presence coincides with particular conditions in the local economy, namely, unregulated expansion in local markets such as construction or drugs, or more generally the inability of the state to provide protection, mafiosi can become entrenched.

Functional diversification is more likely to occur in larger cities and in criminal hubs, and substantial migration from the motherland does not appear to be a necessary precondition. This is in marked contrast to transplantation, which is more likely to succeed in towns and small cities. Several studies report that mafiosi operating abroad were forced out of their places of origin rather being sent by bosses. Finally, separation is comparatively rare, yet it occurred in at least one significant case, that of the Italian American mafia which emerged from Sicilian roots. Such a separation was possible because the outpost grew significantly in power and wealth vis-à-vis to the motherland, and the brand name was easily recognizable.

Section VII outlines conceptual, methodological, and empirical issues that remain unresolved. I emphasize the importance of use of historical comparative methods in qualitative studies of the mafia and the need to identify negative cases. I also discuss the relationships between concepts used in indexes in quantitative studies.

Section VIII outlines emerging research areas and policy implications. Alliances are needed among scholars working on Latin America, the United States, and Europe, as is adoption of compatible frameworks. Policy efforts to control and oppose organized crime must be informed by the key distinction between transplantation and functional diversification and by recognition that certain local markets, such as construction, are more at risk of mafia penetration than are other economic sectors such as import and export of goods.

I. Concepts

I focus on a particular type of criminal organization that seeks to govern markets or territories. I refer to these organizations as governance-type organized crime or, for simplicity, mafias. Since the publication of my study of the Russian mafia (Varese 2001), I have been interested in exploring to what extent mafias operate outside of their traditional territories. In this essay, I return to questions I have addressed elsewhere (esp. Varese 2011*b*) and want to shed further light on transplantation, functional diversification, and separation. In this section, I explain what I mean by these concepts and why I do not use others.

What is organized crime? Despite the variety—and often vagueness—of definitions in official documents and the academic literature, definitions are typically of two types: those that focus on the internal structure of organizations and those that focus on the activities of groups. The first type usually includes a reference to minimum membership ("three or more persons"), the presence of a hierarchical structure, and continuity over time. For instance, according to the United Nations, "'organized criminal group' shall mean a structured group of three or more persons, existing for a period of time and acting in concert with the aim of committing one or more serious crimes or offences established in accordance with this Convention, in order to obtain, directly or indirectly, a financial or other material benefit" (UNODC 2004, art. 2a). For this approach, organized crime is crime that is organized, often highly so. Definitions that emphasize the structure evolved over the twentieth century (Varese 2010). Until the 1960s, organized crime was typically defined as a hierarchical, corporate-like entity. Since the 1970s, organized crime organizations have usually been portrayed as being more flexible, networked, and flat (Catino 2019; Paoli 2020; Reuter and Paoli 2020).

The other type of definition focuses on activities. Several characterizations from the 1960s posit that organized crime groups are illicit enterprises operating in a market producing goods and services, such as gambling, loan-sharking, narcotics, and sexual services (Task Force on Organized Crime 1967, p. 1; Smith 1975, 1978; Edwards and Gill 2002). More recently, Campana and Varese (2018) proposed a framework that distinguishes three sets of illegal activities—production, trade, and governance—each an investment in a different set of resources. In this view, organized crime is not simply crime that is organized, but it is an activity that produces goods and services, including governance (Schelling 1971).[1] The organizational form derives from the activity: for instance, in order to govern, a group must be structured hierarchically with an effective chain of command, invest in violence resources, and have clear membership boundaries. Production of illicit services can, by contrast, be done by small-scale, market-oriented enterprises with minimal organizational structure (Reuter 1983). When law enforcement is weak, such enterprises can grow in size and complexity, just as legitimate counterparts do.

Governance-type organized crime is of particular interest because it undermines the legitimate order. Traditional mafias—Cosa Nostra, the 'Ndrangheta, the Italian American mafia, the Russian mafia, the Japanese yakuza, and the Hong Kong triads—are forms of governance-type organized crime (Varese 2018b; Paoli 2020). Historical clans and federations of the Neapolitan camorra also qualify (Campana 2011b).[2] Groups that normally are classified as gangs, such as Mara Salvatrucha, Latin Kings, and Barrio 18, have also shown an ability to govern both inside and outside prisons. They have expanded across the United States and to Central America (Arana 2005; Cruz 2010), making them a good test for theories of transplantation. The ability to govern in the territory of origin is a

---

[1] Such a perspective excludes some crimes, such as organized theft, sexual harassment, and frauds from the definition of organized crime. For a fuller discussion of these issues, see Varese (2010) and Campana and Varese (2018).

[2] Traditional mafias have developed norms of behavior that are shared across "families." These mafias have memorable initiation ceremonies, similar hierarchical structures, and internal rules, including rules about sex, family life, and relationships among members and with outsiders. These mafias are, in effect, a collection of fairly independent gangs controlling a territory and subscribing to the same rules of behavior. They might fight with each other, but they belong to the same structure. For a fuller discussion of their organizational features, see Catino (2020).

matter of a degree, and to some extent criminal governance coexists with other governance-type institutions. For instance, a group may be able to regulate and control the unlawful distribution only of a given commodity or service, or it may be able to supply protection across several markets, as in the case of traditional mafias (Varese 2010). A recent study by Gordon (2020) on Medellín, Colombia, points to the dynamics of such coexistence.

One implication of this perspective is that governance-type organized crime shares key features with states. Some hybrids exist, such as insurgencies and paramilitary groups. Paramilitary groups in Northern Ireland, Indonesia, Colombia, and Myanmar controlled territories and dispensed highly imperfect forms of justice, while forcing people to pay taxes and protecting illegal trades (Rueda 2009; Peña 2014; Varese 2018*b*, pp. 182, 260). Insurgent groups can be conceptualized as lying on a continuum between governance-type organized crime and states. Yet they also differ. Mafias differ from insurgencies and states insofar as "the set of collective action mechanisms that constrains institutions of governance and makes them accountable to the people" are different (Varese 2010, p. 20). In other words, they are not run as a democracy in which citizens elect their leaders or as a liberal state in which citizens have rights and can appeal to laws that can force the state to reverse its decisions. Such a perspective opens up fruitful theoretical possibilities to give analytical meaning to the expression "mafia state," although this essay is not the place to pursue such a conceptual study.

I refer to governance-type organized crime, or mafias. My choice to focus on this particular kind of crime group is motivated by their significance but also by analytical and practical considerations. As we expand the object of study to groups that engage primarily in predatory crime, theft, or just the sale of illegal goods, the models and potential explanations are bound to differ significantly from those that might account for mafias.[3]

By transplantation, I refer to the ability of a mafia group to supply illegal governance for a substantial period of time to a place outside the territory of origin (Varese 2004, 2006, 2011*b*).[4] Transplantation implies that the mafia is able to provide private protection even in the new territory and not only in the territory of origin. The concept, introduced in 2004, is now widely adopted in the literature. Similar yet arguably less cogent concepts have also been used. Scholars refer to "stable presence"

---

[3] Yet see below remarks on the possible transition of Mexican drug traffickers from trade to governance and production activities.

[4] I use the term governance in this essay as equivalent to criminal protection (Gambetta 1993).

(Calderoni et al. 2016, p. 419), "settlement" (Sciarrone and Storti 2014, p. 45), "colonization" (Forgione 2009, p. 26), "entrenchment" (Armao 2003), and "hard penetration" (Galeotti 2000, p. 38). None of these concepts makes explicit what the group does in the territory in which it is present.[5]

Crime groups might also acquire goods, launder money, and operate in the legal economy. Trading in goods, some of which may be illegal, is analytically different from selling the right to operate in a given market or territory.[6] Campana (2013, p. 318) has suggested that mafias may diversify their activities; in the traditional territory, they govern, while abroad they may buy and sell goods. He calls this "functional diversification," a term that has entered the literature on mafia mobility. Varese (2004, 2011a, 2011b) refers to the search for resources and production inputs that are not available in the territory of origin and need to be bought elsewhere.

"Infiltration" is the expression used by Sciarrone and Storti (2014, p. 45) for instances in which "only certain features of the mafia organizations" are present.[7] Indicators of infiltration include physical presence of individual mafiosi, purely predatory behavior, exploitation of investment opportunities, and more generally engaging in "series of activities, both legal and illegal, that are chiefly economic in nature" (Sciarrone and Storti 2014, p. 54; see also pp. 45, 53). The concept appears to include a range of diverse phenomena, some potentially inconsequential, including the simple presence of a mafioso abroad who might not be engaged in anything at all.[8]

As for involvement in economic activities, it is important to spell out what such involvement entails. Also, it is important to underline that functional diversification differs from the occasional visit abroad. It entails a tangible intention to establish an outpost abroad for the long term, committing resources to such a plan (see Campana 2013, p. 317). Ultimately, the concept of functional diversification expresses that mafia groups might be present abroad with the aim of buying and selling illegal goods and investing in the economy, rather than trying to control markets or territories.

Over time, the mafia group might grow in autonomy and eventually separate from the motherland. Some authors have pointed to this in relation to the separation between the Italian American mafia and the Sicilian

[5] Correctly in my view, Sciarrone (1998) criticizes the use of medical metaphors, such as virus and contagion, to describe to the presence of mafias abroad. See also Spapens (2019).

[6] Kleemans (2007, p. 176) refers to trading in illegal goods and services as "transit crime."

[7] Italian investigators have used the expression "soft presence" (Allum 2014, p. 586).

[8] This appears to be the case of a man convicted of mafia crimes in Italy in the 1990s, who fled to the United Kingdom and lived some 20 years in London, where he appears not to have been involved in any criminal activity (see BBC News 2015).

Cosa Nostra and to the failed attempt of a Lombardy-based 'Ndrangheta group to separate from the Calabria-based organization (Varese 2011*b*, 2012*b*).[9] The key empirical indicator of separation is whether entry in one group gives an automatic right to join the other. For instance, in the case of the Sicilian and Italian American mafias, at some time having gone through the admission ritual in Sicily ceased to be enough to gain entry into American families.

Other concepts such as "transnational organized crime," "power syndicate," and "enterprise syndicate" are of limited value. As the Soviet Union ended, transnational organized crime replaced the menace of communism in some policy circles, argues Woodiwiss (2003). Regardless of the political agenda that might have motivated the use of this construct in Western policy-making circles, transnational organized crime lacks firm analytical grounding. While it is sensible to assume that the term refers to something (activities or people) that at some point crosses borders, it does not specify the constitutive element that makes a group transnational. More specifically, the term does not distinguish between instances of governance and of trade and, thus, has little analytical power to account for how mafias operate across territories. It is also unclear why transnationality per se should be singled out.

Block (1983, p. 129) introduced the concepts "power syndicate" and "enterprise syndicate" in his study of organized crime in New York City. In his succinct and somewhat elusive wording, the "enterprise syndicate ... operates exclusively in the area of illicit enterprises such as prostitution, gambling, bootlegging, and narcotics." As for "power syndicate ... its forte is extortion not enterprise [and it] operates both in the arena of illicit enterprises and the industrial world specifically in labor-management disputes and relations" (p. 129). The conceptual couple has had some influence in the literature,[10] and it may well capture the cases discussed in Block's study. On closer inspection, it does not travel as well as other

---

[9] Allum (2014, pp. 595–97) has suggested that separation is never complete, and relations between the motherland and the outpost are interdependent: activities in foreign countries often relate to the homeland and vice versa (she calls it functional mobility). Sciarrone and Storti (2014, p. 47) introduce the concept of hybridization: "A criminal group ... maintains affinities with the original group but cannot be considered as a direct outgrowth, as it gradually distances itself by adopting an independent model of action and organization." The word hybrid may be misleading, as ultimately the two groups separate and become distinct entities.

[10] This was especially marked in Italy (see, e.g., Catanzaro 1994; Lupo 1996; Balsamo 2006; Asmundo 2011; Sciarrone and Dagnes 2014). For critical discussions of use of the concept, see Santino (2006, pp. 126–28) and Parini (2008).

concepts, such as governance-type organized crime. With "enterprise" it would have been helpful to specify whether the catchall phrase "operates in a market" refers to trading, production activities, or both. Block appears to exclude the possibility that such groups engage in extortion, yet a crime group might well extort illicit businesses. In addition, it has long been established that mafias do not simply engage in extortion but provide forms of governance and criminal protection and are involved in activities well beyond "labor-management disputes and relations" (Varese 2014).

Governance is provided in illegal markets. For instance, US mafia groups ensured that promises between owners of speakeasies and sellers of alcohol were kept in what were known as curb exchanges, places where market actors met and the mafia acted as a governing authority (Critchley 2009, pp. 154–57). To describe this phenomenon, one might say that a "power syndicate" operated in an illegal market but that its forte was protection. Ultimately, the distinction between power and enterprise appears to mirror the distinction between "governance" and "trade," but the concept pair lacks analytical clarity.

II. Two Views on Transplantation

Does transplantation ever occur? Until recently, two views have been prominent. I call them Free Movement and No Movement.[11] The Free Movement view sees mafia presence abroad as easily achieved and ubiquitous, while the No Movement view ignores the limited number of cases in which transplantation has taken place.

A. Free Movement

This position suggests that organized crime migrates easily, because of the spread of globalization and population migration, and that criminal multinational corporations are increasingly unattached to a specific territory. This view is mainly associated with the work of Sterling (1990, 1995), Shelley (1999, 2006, 2019), Castells (2000), Williams (2001), and Naim (2010) and has been influential among policy makers (e.g., United Nations 1994; UNODC 2010). "Crime groups on all continents try to globalize their activities for many of the same reasons as their legitimate counterparts. They seek to exploit valuable international markets," writes

---

[11] I have several times outlined these two views, in particular in Varese (2011*b*, pp. 3, 13–14, 15). I draw on that publication here (see also Varese 2006).

Shelley, director of the Terrorism, Transnational Crime, and Corruption Center at George Mason University (2019, p. 226). Such groups "establish branches around the world to take advantage of attractive labour or raw material markets" (Shelley 2006, p. 43). For Williams, organized crime now "can migrate easily" (2001, p. 71). Castells lists a number of locales where (he posits) well-known mafias have opened outposts, such as Germany for the Sicilian mafia, Galicia for Colombian cartels, and the Netherlands for Chinese triads (2000, p. 201). These and other authors go further to argue that the notions of territorial entrenchment and control are becoming obsolete for a "Global Crime Inc." that "transcends the sovereignty that organizes the modern state system" (Shelley, Picarelli, and Corpora 2003, p. 145). Factors often cited to explain the globalization of criminal activities and the geographic expansion of criminal firms include technological innovation in communications and transportation along with disappearing language barriers (Castells 2000, p. 168; Barak 2001; Shelley 2006, 2019).

Police, judicial authorities, and press reports appear to adopt this view when they write that, for example, the Russian mafia is active in at least 26 foreign countries or that the Calabrese 'Ndrangheta is present in more than 20 (Varese 2011b, pp. 13, 34). After six men were killed outside an Italian restaurant in Duisburg, Germany, in 2007, the Italian Parliamentary Antimafia Commission published a report that claimed that the 'Ndrangheta is a "fluid mafia organization" able to "spread all over the world" following an explicit strategy of criminal colonization (cited in Campana 2011a, p. 208). The former chairman of the Italian Parliamentary Antimafia Commission, in a best-selling book aptly titled *Mafia Export*, argued that bosses intentionally colonize key criminal hubs around the world (Forgione 2009, p. 26). Morselli, Turcotte, and Tenti (2011, p. 166) summarize this viewpoint as follows: "Popular and mainstream depictions of organized crime generally perceive participants to be strategic (or intentional) in their actions. More often, such claims are preceded by the premise that mobility is an effortless task for any group or organization."

B. No Movement

A second view postulates that mafias are closely connected to their territory of origin and rely on a set of network relationships that cannot be reproduced in new settings. Ethnographies of the Sicilian and Italian American mafias published in the 1970s argue that the Cosa Nostra in the

United States emerged because of homegrown conditions, rather than being an Italian export (Ianni 1972; Hess 1973; Blok 1974). In doing so, proponents of this view emphasize the local nature of mafia power. Blok (1974, p. 226) writes that mafiosi's "power domains are locally phrased and it is precisely their control over a distinct locality that enables them to influence higher levels of society as power brokers." When they move to an alien environment, "mafiosi have their wings clipped" (p. 226). Similarly, Ianni writes that "the various *Mafie* in Sicily are engraved on the daily life of the communities in which they live, and they are not for export" (1972, p. 47). The notion that a grand council or central mafia organ sent an advance party to seek new territory across the Atlantic, setting up branch offices in the New World, "is patently absurd" (p. 48).

Writing in the eighties, Peter Reuter underlined the local nature of crime groups. In reference to illegal enterprises specializing in the provision of marijuana and bookmaking services in the United States, Reuter concluded that such groups are "local in scope." In other words, they do "not include branches in more than one metropolitan area" (Reuter 1985, p. 21). Gambetta (1993), in his study of the Sicilian mafia, writes that "not only did the [Sicilian] mafia grow mainly in western Sicily, but, with the exception of Catania, it has remained there to this very day." More generally, the mafia, he adds, "is a difficult industry to export. Not unlike mining, it is heavily dependent on the local environment" (pp. 249, 251).

Similarly, Chu (2000) argues that "Hong Kong triads are localized and they are not international illegal entrepreneurs whose wealth and connections may enable them to migrate to Western countries." Although Hong Kong triads might be involved in international crime, observes Chu, they "are not likely to be the key organisers" (p. 130; see also Finckenauer and Chin 2006, p. 23). Hill reports that the yakuza never "managed to extend their core protective role beyond a native Japanese market" (Hill 2002, p. 53; 2004, p. 112). Weenink and van der Laan (2007) downplay the presence of the Russian mafia in the Netherlands.

Reuter (1985) offered several important theoretical insights into why crime groups, including mafias, routinely fail to expand. Applying key findings from the theory of industrial organization and especially principal-agent models developed in the 1970s in economics (Williamson 1975; Hay and Morris 1979), Reuter noted that distance makes it harder to monitor an employee and ensure that the agent works efficiently and honestly. The agent can misappropriate both tangible and organizational capital from the enterprise by embezzling it and engage in activities not sanctioned by the principal, thereby attracting police attention and endangering the entire organization. In order to escape punishment, the agent might even inform on the bosses back home (Reuter 1985, pp. 21–22). The collection of reliable information on what people do is a vital part of a mafioso's job, but they are likely to find it hard to come by this information in an unfamiliar territory in which they cannot rely on extensive networks of friends and accomplices.

Furthermore, Reuter argued, agents and bosses need to be in touch frequently, thus increasing communication traffic between the two territories. Since face-to-face meetings would be the exception rather than the rule, the likelihood that the police might intercept such communication increases with distance. Finally, reputation is a crucial asset for mafiosi to carry out their jobs. The greater one's reputation for the ability to wield violence is, the less one needs to use it, since victims comply more readily. Reuter wrote that investments in violence, which yield a reputation for being able to deliver on threats, have a higher return when the criminal has contacts, through a continuous chain of other persons, with at least one witness to the violent act. It is more likely that such a chain is broken with distance (Reuter 1985, pp. 21–22, 33). Along similar lines, Gambetta maintained that a reputation for effective violence depends on long-term relationships, cemented within independent networks of kinship, friendship, and ethnicity. It is impossible to reproduce such networks in a new setting (Gambetta 1993, pp. 249–51).

C. The Two Views Reassessed

Studies that endorse the Free Movement view normally suffer from three related problems. First, they do not clearly define the object of study. In the same sweep, they consider crooked oligarchs engaged in tax evasion, illicit businesses, drug cartels, traditional mafias, and even pirates. Second, they do not offer a precise definition of the dependent variable. In other words, they do not specify what the group is doing in the new territory. Often individuals found abroad are taken as evidence that the group has moved. Third, their sources tend to be superficial, including newspaper stories and official reports, rather than in-depth case studies or large-scale quantitative analyses. In sum, it is hard to evaluate these claims. Yet the perspective they present needs to be taken seriously, as it has greatly influenced policy makers and reflects the broader debate on the nature and consequences of globalization, and is consistent with the views of writers who emphasize the deterritorialization of economic power (e.g., Albrow 1996; Bauman 1998; Beck 1999).

The No Movement view is empirically clear and theoretically elegant. Yet there are various reasons to doubt it. Some evidence exists that, under certain conditions, governance-type organized crime groups are capable of operating in distant territories. In his memoirs, Catania mafia boss Antonio Calderone reminisced that, during his time, there were two recognized branches of Sicilian mafia families in central and northern Italy. Another family operated for a while in Tunis, its existence having been recorded since at least the 1930s. "At the time," wrote Calderone, "Tunis was a haven for many mafiosi fleeing Fascism. . . . [There] they had formed a regular family with a representative" (Arlacchi 1993, p. 28; Gambetta 1993, pp. 251, 314).[12] Melchiorre Allegra, a doctor who admitted to belonging to the Sicilian mafia, told authorities in 1937 that the organization had powerful extensions in Tunisia, North America, and Marseilles (Allegra 1962). Sicilian mafiosi operated in the United States, to the point that an organization resembling the Sicilian mafia emerged in some North American cities. Officially sanctioned outposts of the 'Ndrangheta are present in several regions in Northern Italy, such as Piedmont ($n = 11$), Lombardy ($n = 20$), and Emilia-Romagna, where initiation rituals are performed and a degree of control over crucial markets has been observed (Varese 2006; dalla Chiesa and Panzarasa 2012; Ciccarello 2014; Sciarrone and Dagnes 2014; dalla Chiesa and Cabras 2019).[13]

Italian mafiosi appear to be operating outside the country as well. In 1992, 70 Italian mafiosi were serving time in French prisons, 62 *camorristi* were in prison in Spain in 2009, and in 2017 the German Police identified 17 "predominantly Italian" organized crime groups active in Germany (Bundeskriminalamt 2017). The 'Ndrangheta has been found to have a stable presence in Germany, Canada, and Australia (Gratteri and Nicaso 2009, pp. 233–51; Sergi 2015; Calderoni et al. 2016).

Moving beyond Italian groups, at least 30 Taiwanese gangsters lived and worked in Phnom Penh, including the leader of Taiwan Bamboo

---

[12] The presence of the Sicilian mafia has also been documented in Genoa, Liguria, and Northern Italy (La Spina 2013; see also Scaglione and Sciarrone 2014).

[13] The exact number of officially recognized outposts in Emilia-Romagna has not yet been established by investigations. Yet, see Pignedoli (2016) and dalla Chiesa and Cabras (2019) concerning Reggio Emilia.

United, a major triad group (Chin 2003, p. 200). According to reports, a triad boss, Lao Da, was "the main organized crime figure in Vladivostok" (Lintner 2004, p. 93). Xiangu Du, a Chinese national, led a gang in the Russian city of Khabarovsk for four years (1997–2001; He 2003, pp. 201–3). Latino gangs originating from Los Angeles are firmly established in Central America (Arana 2005; Cruz 2010; Varese 2011*b*, p. 191). While the exact nature of their activities and the extent of their presence need to be scrutinized, it seems clear that we are faced with a phenomenon that cannot be dismissed theoretically, and it requires empirical study.

The No Movement view has also been challenged theoretically (Varese 2011*b*, pp. 25–27). First, the reputation for being a menacing criminal organization can travel, thanks to well-meaning newspaper investigations, popular culture, and the media. Even movies and TV series might help advertise a foreign mafia (Varese 2018*b*, pp. 137–57). Colombian cartels quickly became known in the United States for their ruthless methods (Reuter 1995). Members of Los Angeles Latino gangs were easily recognized by their tattoos in El Salvador and Guatemala (Cruz 2010, p. 386). While it takes a long time for a mafia group to collect reliable information, it is plausible that a number of years suffices to create a network of informants. In addition, the information to be collected need not be about complex transactions or numerous locales. It might well be about a local market in the new territory. To the extent that a mafia can count on migration networks in the new locale, some information will be easier to come by. Significant economic investments in the new territory by associates of the incoming mafia can also be a conduit for data gathering. In sum, the collection of information in the new place is not an insurmountable obstacle to transplantation, only a challenge. Finally, it is plausible that agents abroad are harder to monitor.

Yet the hard-to-monitor argument hinges on the assumption that a mafia group is akin to a standard, fully integrated firm. Each mafia family shares norms of behavior and rituals with other families but otherwise has great autonomy in conducting criminal activities. The motherland can devise a simple mechanism to benefit from the outpost, for instance, by asking for a fixed payment every year. Members abroad are not employees of the original organization but instead operate a franchise and may pay a regular fee or offer some other benefits in return for the seal of approval from the motherland. There is evidence that 'Ndrangheta outposts offer tokens of appreciation to the motherland. According to Catanzaro Chief Prosecutor Nicola Gratteri, the outpost "makes offers, sends a thought [meaning a financial payment]" to the coffers of the head of the organization (pers. comm., January 17, 2020).

In sum, there are empirical and theoretical reasons to justify social science studies of mafia transplantation (King, Keohane, and Verba 1994). The design of such research projects must imply variation in the dependent variable, which can take three values: the mafia group might be able to transplant itself, it might fail to do so, or it might engage in activities that differ from what it does in its territory of origin (functional diversification). It would be naive and ultimately wrong to assume that transplantation always occurs whenever it is attempted, although some critics seem to think so. The challenge is to pinpoint the conditions under which it is more likely for each of the three scenarios to occur.

III. Mechanisms of Mafia Transplantation, Functional Diversification, and Separation

In this section, I outline the main hypotheses on transplantation, functional diversification, and separation that have advanced, starting with transplantation.[14]

A. Transplantation

A number of factors have been identified that facilitate transplantation to new territories. They can be divided into two categories: supply and local conditions that generate a demand for mafia services. These dimensions should be analyzed separately. The circumstances that bring mafiosi (the supply) to a new territory, such as generalized migration and mafia migration, differ from local conditions in which organized criminals operate. Their presence may satisfy a local demand for criminal governance, such as the levels of trust and civic engagement, the presence of local protectors, and the presence or absence of new or expanding markets. Some local structural features, such the size of the new locale, might make transplantation easier.

1. *Supply.* Supply can be generated intentionally or unintentionally. Some mafiosi may decide to leave their home territory following a deliberate strategy. The strategic, intentional reasons leading a mafioso to

---

[14] For this section, I draw and expand on Varese (2011*b*, pp. 16–27).

move away may include a search for resources. A legal firm may open a branch abroad in order to acquire workforce, knowledge, the ability to produce innovation, or organizational resources (Zaheer and Manrakhan 2001, p. 670). So might a mafia. The resources sought might include workforce, weapons, hiding places, cameras, bugs, fake passports, and bank accounts. Moving may be a safer and less expensive way to obtain these assets.

Alternatively, the mafia group might want to invest the proceeds of their main activities in other countries. Investments by criminal groups are hidden, done informally through fronts, and often in cash. When disputes arise, resorting to the judicial system is not an option. Furthermore, money laundering and investments in the official economy can involve multiple transactions between agents of the criminal group and entrepreneurs in foreign and inhospitable countries. Businesses can fail, but bosses at home have no way to verify why failures occur. This offers a motivation to send representatives abroad. Finally, a mafia may (as implied by the Free Movement view) decide to expand to a new market or territory if it perceives an absence of local competitors and a good chance of recovering the huge costs involved.

Members of governance-type organized crime groups may be abroad unintentionally. People migrate to look for better living conditions. Every population contains a percentage of criminals, so the larger the number of emigrants, the greater the number of criminals who will enter a new territory. Migration from areas where the percentage of members of governance-type organized crime groups is high makes their transplantation more likely. People migrate to escape wars and natural calamities. Criminals, including those belonging to a mafia, may similarly move to a new territory to avoid being killed in local crime feuds or to avoid arrest by the police. Paradoxically, the more effective police repression is in a high-density mafia territory, the greater the numbers of members who are likely to try to run away. The supply abroad of governance-type organized crime members can thus be the product of intentional decisions or of pressures to relocate. Of course, they would choose where to move, a decision often influenced by the well-known phenomenon of chain migration (MacDonald and MacDonald 1964; Varese 2011*b*, p. 8).

2. *Local Conditions.* Once mafiosi are in a new region, what conditions might allow them to transplant? Robert Putnam, in a ground-breaking study of Italian regional governments, suggested that the level of generalized trust (among people unknown to each other) in the new area could

explain the extent to which mafias become rooted: the lower the level of trust among citizens, the less likely that civil society will be able to organize itself to counter the presence of a mafia group (Putnam 1993). Gambetta (1993) posited that the lower the level of trust among those who break the law, the greater the demand will be for protection services. By guaranteeing pacts and promises, the mafia can facilitate exchanges between criminals who do not trust each other. This implies that mafias are more likely to transplant successfully into places characterized by low levels of trust among both those who respect the law and those who break it.

A demand for criminal governance, the main activity of mafias, may help explain successful transplantation. Such a demand could emerge from sudden development or from rapid expansion of new markets that are not effectively regulated by legitimate authorities. When local authorities cannot define and protect property rights, a need for alternative sources of protection emerges. The less effectively the state can protect its citizens and resolve economic and commercial disputes in legal markets, the greater the search for alternative sources of protection will be. This arises from the state's inability to enforce promises and deals. A second type of demand for protection emerges when legitimate entrepreneurs, dealing in legal commodities, decide to try to sell goods unlawfully, eliminate competition, or organize cartel agreements.

The existence of large illegal markets generates a demand for regulation and protection that cannot be satisfied by official institutions. The mafia can control access to sectors of the economy, offer dispute resolution and protection services, enforce cartel agreements, and reduce competition, thereby penetrating the fabric of the local economy and society. These opportunities are easy to grasp when a supply of individuals trained in the use of violence is present. Such a demand can facilitate both the birth of local groups and the migration of existing ones.

Construction is an economic sector that provides incentives to create cartel agreements: companies compete in a local context, and barriers to entry are relatively low (Reuter 1987; Gambetta and Reuter 1995). Illegal pacts in the construction industry are often formed without mafia involvement when a small number of operators decide to collude and carve up market shares. When the market suddenly expands, however, enforcing cartel agreements and excluding new competitors becomes more difficult without the threat or use of violence.

Companies must, however, compete on the same turf for a gang to exercise effective action. Export-oriented economies, for example, generate less demand for criminal protection: the mafia cannot help exporters penetrate distant markets by putting pressure on another local entrepreneur who exports to a different part of the world.

Other structural features of a new territory, such as its size, can affect the probability of success of transplantation. All else being equal, the smaller the territory or market, the easier it is to control. It is simpler to govern a construction sector with 30 companies than one with 300. If the mafia tries to infiltrate politics, it will have less difficulty in a small electoral district. More votes are needed to influence the election of a mayor in a big city than in a small town. In places where a criminal group or corrupt government officials already provide protection and are entrenched, mafia members from outside will struggle to supplant them.

Other conditions being equal, large electoral districts, large markets, and export-oriented economies make the provision of mafia protection, and therefore transplantation, more difficult. The absence of local protectors makes transplantation easier. Figure 1 summarizes the hypotheses outlined above. Each is in need of empirical testing and highly unlikely to work in isolation.

B. Functional Diversification

Much less work has been done on factors that might predict functional diversification. For this to occur, a supply of mafiosi in the new territory

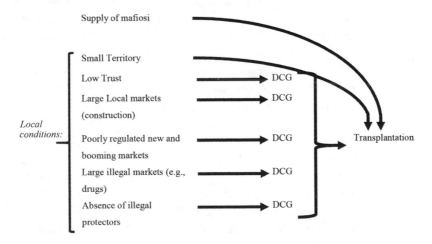

Fig. 1.—Hypotheses for mafia transplantation. Supply of mafiosi is generalized migration and mafiosi migration (intentional/nonintentional). DCG = demand for criminal governance.

is again a background condition that could result from either intentional decisions or forced relocations. Mafiosi might be attracted to a locality to buy certain goods. Equally they might be there as part of a migration trend or to escape turf wars or the police.

Intentional decisions to move might be common, but functional diversification depends not on occasional trips but on establishment of a permanent base. Although counterintuitive, unplanned presence may be common. A second structural factor is the size of the locale. Commodities such as drugs are more likely to be traded in hubs, such as ports, and in large cities than in small towns. For functional diversification, the local market structure should not matter. All that matters is that trading can occur in a relatively secure, anonymous setting, and mafiosi can bring cash in and take goods away. A degree of deregulation of financial markets should also facilitate functional diversification. Moro and Villa (2017, p. 49) suggest that markets with low entry barriers and a prevalence of small and medium firms with limited access to credit will offer more money laundering opportunities to mafiosi who have access to capital and liquidity. Figure 2 summarizes the key hypotheses.

C. Separation

Campana (2013, p. 318) suggests that a foreign outpost involved in acquiring goods and services is more dependent on the motherland than are groups that succeed in transplanting themselves. Thus, we should expect that separation is more likely for groups that have successfully transplanted than for those that developed along the lines of functional

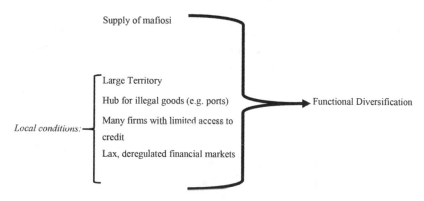

Supply of mafiosi

Local conditions:
Large Territory
Hub for illegal goods (e.g. ports)
Many firms with limited access to credit
Lax, deregulated financial markets

→ Functional Diversification

FIG. 2.—Hypotheses for mafia functional diversification. Supply of mafiosi is generalized migration and mafiosi migration (intentional/nonintentional).

diversification. Additional hypotheses can be suggested. First, for successful separation, the new brand name must be easily recognizable. It might be the same as the original "firm" or something new that resonates with victims. Second, the breakaway outpost must have accumulated enough wealth and influence that it need not fear retaliation from the motherland. In this case, the breakaway unit need not ask permission to use the original brand name. Separation might also occur when the motherland wants to assert greater control over the outpost than its members want, such as imposing deeply disliked bosses or insisting on actions contrary to the interest of the outpost. Finally, separation may result from expulsion (see fig. 3).

Mafia presence in territories far from where the group originated should be viewed as dynamic. Over time, local conditions may dictate a transition from functional diversification to transplantation (Campana and Varese 2018). Mafiosi away from their home territory might start buying goods and involve themselves in money laundering. Eventually they may be able to exploit opportunities to govern local markets such as construction or drugs. However, the difficulties confronting such a transition should not be underestimated. More is required than the presence of mafiosi and investments in the local economy. The more efficient the criminal justice system, the larger the territory, and the greater the presence of local protectors all make the shift from, say, buying drugs to transplantation more difficult.

IV. Empirical Tests: Transplantation

Efforts have been made to test the mechanisms that account for mafia transplantation. Key findings are that the presence of mafiosi abroad appears invariably to be an unintended consequence of other decisions

FIG. 3.—Hypotheses for mafia separation

rather than the product of rational choices to open distant outposts; that significant migration from the home country at some time is necessary but not sufficient for transplantation; that high levels of trust in the new territory do not prevent transplantation; and that dynamics in the local economy, such as a thriving but badly regulated construction market and a small territory, can be decisive.

A. Generalized Migration

In Varese (2011*b*), I presented a series of systematic comparisons between cases that share some similarities but differ as to whether transplantation occurred: the movement of 'Ndrangheta to two towns in Northern Italy, Bardonecchia and Verona; the movement of members of the Russian mafia to Rome and Budapest; and the movement of Cosa Nostra to New York City and Rosario, Argentina. The cases were selected because members of the same mafias of origin attempted to move to territories that shared some theoretically relevant features (naturally, it is next to impossible to find cases that share all features except one in naturally occurring settings; Varese 2019). Migration by itself did not result in transplantation. Similar levels of migration from high-density mafia areas to New York City and Rosario and to cities in central and northern Italy did not invariably lead to long-term mafia entrenchment. A mafia group can satisfy a demand for criminal protection only when migration is combined with the inability of public institutions to govern economic change. Migration from the south to the central Italian region of Tuscany was also substantial (Sciarrone and Dagnes 2014, p. 60), yet no mafia emerged.

Is migration a necessary condition for transplantation? Italian mafia groups appear to exist in places such as Spain that experienced no significant migration from Southern Italy (Sciarrone and Storti 2014, p. 42). Arguably the Italians in Spain are engaged in a process of functional diversification (Allum 2014). However, Sergi (2015) presents data on migration from Calabria to Australia where the 'Ndrangheta, she argues, was able to transplant. Ingrascì (2015, p. 45) notes that organized groups from the Republic of Georgia have been active in the city of Bari, where the largest Georgian immigrant community in Italy lives (see also Varese 2018*b*, p. 70). Significant migration from the home country at some point appears to be necessary but not sufficient for transplantation but is not a condition for functional diversification.

The "policy of forced resettlement" (*soggiorno obbligato*) may have influenced transplantation in Italy; people convicted of mafia crimes were required to reside outside their home regions. Forced resettlement, started in 1956, was premised on the assumptions that organized crime was a product of backward societies and that mafiosi, far from home and immersed in the culture of the northern regions, respectful of the law and marked by a strong civic sense, would abandon their old habits. However misconceived, *soggiorno obbligato* cannot be held responsible for successful transplantation. The 'Ndrangheta was able to transplant in Bardonecchia, in the province of Turin, but failed in other provinces of Piedmont that had received comparable or higher numbers of people sentenced to forced resettlement. The presence of incoming mafiosi does not necessarily lead to long-term transplantation (Varese 2011*b*).

Sciarrone and Dagnes (2014, pp. 55–56) evaluated the effects of migration and forced resettlement on mafia presence in Northern Italy. They found a correlation between mafia groups involved in extortion ("power syndicate") and both migration from the southern mafia regions and forced resettlement in the north. They emphasize, however, that they do not posit mechanical links among migration, forced resettlement, and mafia.

B. Mafiosi's Presence: Unintentional

Varese (2011*b*) was the first published study to focus explicitly on the mechanisms of mafia mobility. In all the cases discussed, mafia members found themselves "abroad" unintentionally. They needed to move because of a court order, law enforcement pressures, or a mafia war. They were not implementing rational long-term strategies to colonize new markets or obtain new products. Their presence in a faraway territory might appear to be a product of globalization, but the primary explanations are state law enforcement pressures, which export the problems to other countries, and internal feuds within mafia organizations. Unlike what might be expected from the Free Movement perspective, I did not find that mafiosi left their territories and opened outposts abroad in order to obtain resources such as labor, intelligence, and specialized equipment.

Other scholars have also concluded that mafia mobility is unintentional. Ethnographers in the 1970s reported that Sicilian mafiosi ended up in the United States because of forces beyond their control. Hess (1973, p. 156) mentioned that, among Sicilian immigrants to the United States, there were mafia members "flee[ing] from the reach of state organs" or who had defied family orders and were seeking refuge in the United States (p. 157).[15] Blok (1974, p. 226) observed that "when not forced by circumstances, mafiosi have little reason to move." Allum (2014) provides an in-depth study of four cases of mobility by members of the Camorra outside of their groups' heartland in and around Naples. They moved to escape either arrests or internal feuds (pp. 587, 588, 590, table 1). She concluded, "Many *camorristi* did not want to leave Naples but were forced to do so. Our findings are similar to those of Varese [2011b, p. 8]" (p. 593). Kleemans and de Boer (2013) describe several instances of Italian mafiosi escaping justice and seeking refuge in the Netherlands.

Arsovska (2014) underscores that hard-core Albanian criminals mentioned in 36 US court cases that she analyzed had not moved of their own volition. Their migration was "not a business choice [but] rather a necessity" (p. 220). Offenders became involved in serious crime after they reached the United States or were "forced to leave their country of origin to escape justice, retaliation, or war. In fact, a number of notorious Albanian organized crime figures were pushed to migrate to escape mafia wars or police repression in their areas of origin" (pp. 220–21). Arsovska (2015), extracting information from court documents, built a database with 254 offenders and 36 variables. She also interviewed 88 ethnic Albanians, 30 of whom had direct knowledge of organized crime. The more direct knowledge of organized crime respondents had, the less they supported the view that Albanian organized crime is exported strategically (p. 166). No respondent who admitted direct contact with Albanian organized crime agreed that organized crime moved strategically to the United States (pp. 166–67, fig. 2).

US Latino gangs known as *maras* provide another transplantation example. In the early 1980s, many Central Americans escaped civil wars by moving to the United States. Thousands came of age in Los Angeles (Cruz 2010, p. 384). Some associated with Latino gangs (Vigil 2010), and police concluded that they were major participants in the 1992 Los Angeles riots (Arana 2005, p. 100). Starting in 1994, California government implemented harsh antigang measures, including stiff prison sentences under the three-strikes law.[16] In 1996, the US Congress authorized

---

[15] I describe other instances of future Italian American organized crime bosses fleeing from Sicily (Varese 2011b, pp. 104–5).

[16] Antigang considerations were not the major reason behind passage of the three-strikes legislation, but it affected gang members (Zimring, Hawkins, and Kamin 2001).

repatriation to their home countries of noncitizens and foreign-born Americans convicted of crimes and sentenced to a year or more in prison. As a result, more than 160,000 people were sent back to Central America and 375,000 more returned voluntarily (Cruz 2010, p. 385). Nearly 50,000 individuals convicted of a variety of crimes were deported to El Salvador, Guatemala, and Honduras (Rodgers and Baird 2015).[17] Many were members of Mara Salvatrucha (commonly known as MS-13), Barrio 18 (also known as 18th Street gang), and Latin Kings. Their presence in Central America was not the result of a "premeditated and centralised process" but an unintended consequence of US deportation policy (Arana 2005, pp. 100–101; Cruz 2010, p. 388). This parallels the flight of Sicilian mafiosi to the United States to escape Benito Mussolini's repression of the mafia beginning in 1925 and led by Prefect Mori (Mori 1933, pp. 151–229).

C. Social Capital/Civicness

Varese (2011*b*) challenged Putnam (1993) and Gambetta (1993), who argued that high levels of trust would prevent mafia from establishing a presence in a new place. I found that a high level of generalized trust and social capital in the population is not sufficient to prevent transplantation. The experience of the town of Bardonecchia, Piedmont, shows that high levels of trust are not sufficient to avoid transplantation and that social capital can remain high despite the existence of a mafia cell. Dagnes et al. (2018, p. 8), in a study of mafia penetration of the construction industry in three northern Italian regions, also observed that economic dynamism, high levels of "civicness," and efficient institutions are not enough to prevent mafia entrenchment. Moro and Villa (2017) tested the effects of interregional variability in civicness on mafia activity in Lombardy, a region with high levels of social capital and wealth. Their findings are consistent with the view that high levels of social capital are not sufficient to prevent mafias' arrival and entrenchment. They also found that higher levels of civicness reduced the probability of mafia presence (p. 54) but reported that "porous sectors" of the economy, such as construction, had a greater effect.

---

[17] Some 180,000 Nicaraguan illegal immigrants were allowed to stay in the United States for political reasons (Rocha 2008). As a consequence, the gang problem in Nicaragua is less severe and local gangs (*pandillas*) survived.

D. Size of the Locale

I found that, all else being equal, smaller administrative units (and related markets) make it easier for mafias to influence politics, sell votes, and establish links with politicians, the press, and even the local priest. In Bardonecchia, a handful of votes (500, according to the local boss boasting in a phone call) was sufficient to determine local elections under a proportional representation system with party list and preference voting (Varese 2011*b*).[18] In a case study of a town near Bardonecchia, Ciccarello (2014, pp. 223, 233–36) reached similar conclusions (see also dalla Chiesa and Panzarasa 2012). Dagnes et al. (2018) studied three cases of mafia penetration of the legal economy in small and medium-sized towns and concluded that small size mattered (p. 8). Sciarrone and Dagnes (2014, pp. 55–56) present preliminary evidence for the entire north of Italy that suggests that a significant number of places where mafia groups have been reported to operate are middle-sized towns with between 10,000 and 50,000 inhabitants, lending support to the view that mafias find it hard to control large metropolitan centers.

E. Demand for Criminal Protection in Local Markets

I found (Varese 2004, 2006, 2011*b*) that a demand for protection that is not met by the legitimate authorities is present in all cases of successful transplantation. The availability of mafiosi and the inability of institutions to govern the economy were key factors in successful transplantation by the 'Ndrangheta in Bardonecchia and by Russian mafias in Hungary.

Not all business sectors are equally attractive to mafiosi. They are more often found in construction, waste disposal, transport, and catering. These sectors have low barriers to entry, are not export oriented, and have low product differentiation. In Bardonecchia, immigrants agreed to work illegally rather than remain unemployed, forgoing union protection and, more generally, state protection. Entrepreneurs employed labor illegally and cheaply and also wanted to restrict competition. A sudden expansion of the construction market to satisfy a boom in demand for holiday homes led to the emergence of a demand for protection against competition. Members of the Mazzaferro 'Ndrangheta clan who had been court-ordered to reside in Bardonecchia began to offer privileged

---

[18] I also found (Varese 2011*b*) that no other mafia group (or state apparatus offering illegal protection) was present in the places where transplantation succeeded.

access to this market to some companies and to manage conflicts between workers and employers.

The centrality of construction is well documented. Dalla Chiesa and Panzarasa (2012) studied a town outside Milan where a group from Calabria was heavily involved in construction. Lodetti (2018) showed how construction and waste removal companies connected to the 'Ndrangheta expelled competitors in the province of Mantua in 2002–17. Ciccarello (2014) showed how expansion of the construction sector in the small town of Leinì, Piedmont, was exploited by an 'Ndrangheta group that worked with the town mayor who in turn benefited from their electoral support. Sciarrone and Dagnes (2014) and Dagnes et al. (2018), in two quantitative studies, found a relationship between construction and mafia presence in northern Italy.

More generally, local markets attract organized crime. Calabrese mafiosi governed the fruit and vegetable market in Melbourne, Australia (Minuti and Nicaso 1994; Sergi 2015). In the southern Italian city of Bari, groups belonging to the Georgian mafia have fought over zones of influence, leading to a high-profile murder in 2012. Investigations and case studies found that Georgian businesses (particularly shipping agencies) in the city paid protection money to Georgian groups to ensure safe passage for their goods through Greece and eventually the Caucasus (Georgian groups appoint a national coordinator in Italy; Ingrascì 2015, pp. 44–45; Varese 2018b, pp. 69–94, 102–3).

Moro and Villa (2017) estimated mafia activities in the populous, rich region of Lombardy, relying on official measures, and constructed a data set that includes information extracted from court cases. They found that total economic activity does not predict mafia presence. Rather, specific features of local markets are correlated to mafia presence. The size of porous economic sectors, such as construction and hospitality, was tightly linked to the mafia presence. Those sectors have low barriers to entry and low diversification (pp. 47, 53). The low barriers generate incentives to close the market through the use of force, as the cases discussed above illustrate.

In two cases of failed mafia transplantation attempts, the local economies relied on exports (Varese 2011b): Verona on furniture exports and Rosario on agricultural exports. There is no benefit from creating cartels in export-oriented sectors of the economy; producers sell in different parts of the world. Producer A and producer B, in competition, might be located at the far ends of the globe. Paradoxically, increased globalization weakens mafias' ability to offer protection to local businesspeople. Sciarrone and Dagnes (2014, pp. 42, 49–51) found a large negative correlation coefficient, statistically significant at the .01 level, between "power syndicates" in nontraditional mafia territories (and in Italy as a whole) and export-oriented local economies.

Piedmont is not a new market economy like some countries in Eastern Europe, but there is an important parallel with the Russian mafia Solntesvskaya's transplantation in Budapest (Varese 2011b). Institutions created in Hungary after the end of the socialist regime were unable to resolve economic conflicts quickly and effectively, thus leaving important sectors of the new market economy without protection, exactly as happened with the immigrant workers of Bardonecchia. People without access to legitimate dispute resolution mechanisms look for nonstate forms of protection. In both Bardonecchia and Budapest, organized crime group members from far away were able to organize and offer services, including dispute resolution and elimination of competitors (Varese 2011b).

Powerful mafia groups emerged in the United States around 1910 as unintended consequences of police reform and grew thanks to Prohibition (Jacobs 2020). Illegal markets such as prostitution, gambling, and late-night drinking had before then been protected by corrupt politicians and police officers. When the mayor of New York launched initiatives against police corruption, illegal markets such as gambling and prostitution and legal markets such as clothing, garbage collection, and construction needed new protectors. In some legal markets, existing operators were happy to turn to an organization able to enforce cartel agreements, exactly as happened later on a smaller scale in Bardonecchia. It was from these origins that the Italian American mafia composed of immigrants from southern Italy evolved (Varese 2011b, pp. 111–20).

When members of Californian Latino gangs arrived in Central America, they found a fertile environment in which to operate. The destination countries were emerging from bitter civil wars, and populations experienced vast social inequalities and exclusion, in a context of rapid urbanization. The demise of dictatorships and the relative opening up to democracy allowed gangs to grow. By the early 1990s, the Mara Salvatrucha and Barrio 18 chapters (clikas) in Salvador had absorbed the local gangs, each controlling a specific neighborhood (Cruz 2010, p. 387). Between 2001 and 2006, governments used harsh measures to fight the growing gang problem, violating human rights and arresting and imprisoning many gang members.

The "harsh hand" (*mano dura*) policy exacerbated the gang problem. Members in detention centers were housed according to their gang affiliation. That allowed members to meet, get to know one another, disseminate information, and coordinate activities. Contrary to the predictions of the No Movement view, the prison system allowed reputations to spread and networks to expand. By 2009, the Salvadoran National Civilian Police estimated that 70 percent of extortion committed in the country was carried out by *maras*. A survey conducted in a sample of deprived neighborhoods in El Salvador, Guatemala, and Honduras reported that around 20 percent of small businesses paid "protection taxes" (Cruz 2010, pp. 382–83). Cruz reported that "in Guatemala, 28 percent of residents of poor communities have to pay taxes to gangs; 34 percent in El Salvador; and 31 percent in Honduras" (p. 383).

The *maras* have not been studied using the framework described in this essay, but they appear to be a case of successful transplantation. It remains unclear, however, to what extent the Central America gangs communicate with their US counterparts and seek permission to open branch offices. Scholars suggest that connections are limited and that there is no single chain of command, but it is likely that such connections have changed over time (Rodgers and Baird 2015; Rodgers, pers. comm., July 5, 2019; see also Ward 2013; for a valuable ethnography on the MS-13, see Martinez D'aubuisson [2015]).

A number of key findings emerge from studies conducted using different data sources and methods. First, mafiosi are likely to be in new territories for reasons other than conscious decisions to transplant. Typical motives include evading the reach of the law, escaping internal feuds, and court decisions. The presence of mafiosi is not by itself sufficient to predict transplantation. However, mafiosi can become entrenched when their presence coincides with unregulated expansions in local markets such as construction or drugs and when local governments are unable to provide protection.

V. Empirical Tests: Functional Diversification

Several authors have tested aspects of functional diversification. Campana (2011*a*, 2011*b*) studied operations in Aberdeen and Amsterdam of the Camorra La Torre clan based in Mondragone, near Naples. He disputes the view that "the La Torre strategically planned to expand their activities abroad, and they successfully managed to 'colonise' new territories."

Rather, "the majority of the clan's affiliates who left Italy were pushed to do so, mainly because of pressure from the law enforcement agencies. However, even if they might not have strategically and rationally decided to leave Italy, it seems that they strategically chose their destination, at least to some extent" (Campana 2011a, pp. 213–14). Members of the group knew people in both places and had family members in Scotland. The decision to move was not strategic even in this instance of functional diversification, but the choice of where to go was not random.

The La Torre clan was present in three countries, Italy, Scotland, and the Netherlands, but did not engage in the same activities in each place. It ran a protection racket in Mondragone, Italy, but did other things in Scotland and Amsterdam. "In Aberdeen, they set up legal companies in the food and catering sector (including two restaurants), in the building sector and in real estate. . . . Amsterdam was a hub devoted to the 'investments' in the illegal economy, mainly drugs and counterfeiting money. There is no evidence of any protection activity in Aberdeen or Amsterdam" (Campana 2011a, p. 213). Kleemans and de Boer (2013) note that Italian mafiosi moved to the Netherlands, where it is relatively easy to hide, in order to avoid arrest. Once there, they became involved in narcotics, rather than in extortion and racketeering.[19] Kleemans and de Boer suggest that Neapolitan camorra members are present in the Netherlands in order to acquire key resources (arms) for the groups back home.

The case of the Russian mafia group Solntesvskaya operating in Rome in the mid-1990s is an instance of functional diversification. They left Russia to avoid an internecine gang war. In Rome they traded in legal and illegal commodities and laundered money arriving from several Russian mafia groups. Investments alone did not result in successful long-term transplantation, as they were unable to identify a demand for protection (Varese 2004, 2011b, 2012a; see also Ingrascì 2015, pp. 40–43; Mazzenzana 2017, pp. 191–93).

Some 'Ndrangheta groups operating in Germany engage in money laundering through legal businesses, such as pizzerias, restaurants, hotels, and drug trafficking. This is the pattern of the group considered responsible for the murder of six people in front of a pizzeria in Duisburg, Germany, on August 15, 2007. Rather than try to govern markets in Germany, the clan was functionally diversifying abroad (Campana 2011a,

---

[19] Gratteri and Nicaso (2009) underscore the importance of the port of Rotterdam as a key narcotics hub for the 'Ndrangheta.

p. 216). Calderoni et al. (2016) showed that some Italian groups have become "entrenched" in Germany, but further work is needed to learn whether they managed successfully to shift from trading to governing.

Allum's (2014) study of members of the Neapolitan Camorra (*camorristi*) in the United Kingdom, Germany, and Spain also found that they did not reproduce the control of local markets and territory that characterizes their presence in the Naples area. Rather, "they travelled to buy goods in one country to sell them in another" (p. 589). The *camorristi* were abroad to undertake "strategic business activities that relate back to the territory of origin in Naples" (p. 594). It remains to be seen whether these individuals moved permanently abroad.

Campana (2013) undertook a quantitative study of the activities of Italian mafias in Europe, using data presented in Forgione (2009). He constructed a data set that includes information on crimes committed in 110 different cities in 22 European Union countries. He found that the groups made investments in legal businesses in the United Kingdom, Germany, France, and Austria and were involved in illegal trades, mainly drug trafficking, in Spain, Portugal, the Netherlands, and Belgium, and in smuggling of counterfeit goods in Eastern Europe. The data are not sufficiently fine-grained to tease out whether Italian groups were exercising a degree of market control in Europe, but references to protection emerged in four cities in Germany (Campana 2013, p. 321). As expected, transplantation is harder to achieve than functional diversification.

Calderoni et al. (2016) extended Campana's (2013) study by considering Italian mafias' presence worldwide, using the analytic technique multiple correspondence analysis. They systematically coded annual reports by two Italian antimafia agencies from 1999 to 2012. The analysis identifies all references in the reports to the Italian mafias in foreign countries. Data include the mafia involved, the country, and the criminal market including drugs, money laundering, and "other" illegal activities. They found that Italian mafias were concentrated in nine countries (the top three were Spain, Germany, and the Netherlands). The drug trade was the most important activity; money laundering and investments in the local economy were less relevant (it is harder to collect information on money laundering than on drugs). The study does not differentiate between trading and governing and the official reports are not sufficiently detailed to specify what these mafias were doing, but the authors were able to distinguish "stable" versus "generic" presence. Canada, Australia, and Germany were the countries in which Italian mafias appeared to be stably present. In these countries, the 'Ndrangheta had created *locali* (officially recognized outposts), equivalent to those in Italy (for qualitative evidence, see Gratteri and Nicaso 2009). The authors concluded that "these cases may fall within the concept of transplantation advanced by Varese [2011*b*, p. 6]" (Calderoni et al. 2016, p. 427).

The key finding of these studies is that substantial migration from the home country does not appear to be a necessary condition for the emergence of functional diversification, which is more likely to occur in larger cities and criminal hubs. This is in marked contrast to transplantation, which is more likely to succeed in towns and small cities. Several studies report that mafiosi operating in foreign markets had been forced out of their home territories, rather than moving to serve as permanent envoys of home country bosses.

VI. Empirical Tests: Separation

Under what conditions can an outpost separate from the motherland? Studies of separation are rare. However, one highly significant example exists: the Italian American mafia. Italian criminal groups with a degree of organization and a leadership structure have existed in New York City since at least 1910: the Morello in East Harlem; the Schiro in Brooklyn; and the D'Aquila, also in Brooklyn. By the late 1920s, two more groups emerged, led by Masseria and Profaci. These groups were the basis for the future "five families" of the Italian American mafia. Between 1910 and 1920, there were three routes into these families. The first was previous membership in a Sicilian *cosca*, a route that remained open as late as 1925. Would-be members carried a letter from Sicily testifying to their position in the *cosca* back home, and any change of family had to be approved by the boss in Sicily. The second was birth in a Sicilian town known to be under the sway of the mafia, where Sicilian mafiosi could vouch for a prospective US member. Third, coming from a well-known mafia family could ease admittance. Dual membership (Sicilian and US) was possible.

By the late 1920s, US families were growing in importance in the eyes of their Sicilian counterparts. For example, when a significant dispute arose between two Palermo mafia factions in 1928 over how to split a payment from a company that had obtained a public contract thanks to the mafia, a US delegation was sent to put an end to the dispute. Around that time, the US groups were becoming autonomous, ending any dependency on the Sicilian homeland. By the end of the "Castellamarese war" in 1931, dual Sicilian and US mafia membership was forbidden, and membership of a Sicilian family was no longer a sufficient qualification to join a US family. Important mafiosi such as Buscetta and Calderone made it clear in the postwar period that the two mafias were separate organizations. When a Sicilian mafioso wanted to join the Montreal family in 1974, he was put on a 5-year probation (Varese 2011b, pp. 120–21; see also Bonanno 1983; Gambetta 1993; Arlacchi 1996; Critchley 2009; Lupo 2015).

A second case worth discussing is the failed attempt of Lombardy-based 'Ndrangheta outposts to separate. Several investigations have shown that the 'Ndrangheta families in Lombardy are not a branch of a large enterprise but autonomous entities that share the same brand name and follow certain basic rules, including obtaining permission from Calabria to create new outposts and appoint bosses. There are approximately 20 such groups in Lombardy alone; most are allied to a particular family based in Calabria. Most members were born in Calabria, although some were born in Lombardy.

Conflicts and misunderstandings between outposts and motherland have been documented since the 1990s. Tensions erupted when Carmelo Novella became the head of the Lombardia, the forum that coordinates families in Lombardy. In 2007–8, Novella attempted to separate from the motherland. The plan envisaged minimal forms of coordination, but creation of new families and appointments would be decided exclusively in Lombardy. The plan was initially well received by other Lombardy families, but Novella made a crucial mistake. Rather than just promoting "independence," he began to interfere in the day-to-day operations and appointments made by local bosses. Their freedom of operation was threatened. All concerned eventually agreed that Novella had to be killed, which happened in July 2008.

The tendency toward the independence of Lombardy did not end with Novella's death. At a meeting of Lombardy-based families on January 20, 2009, it was agreed that the outposts must remain cohesive and interference from the south must be held in check. The new chairman (who is elected every year, indicating a weak figure) indicated that the representative from Calabria was simply "bringing us news from Reggio rather than impos[ing] his laws here" (Varese 2012b, p. xviii). The strict prohibition on interference in the activities of single families was re-emphasized at a subsequent meeting on October 31, 2009 (both meetings were bugged by police). Ultimately, the 'Ndrangheta retains a federal structure, with coordinating forums. Promotions and creation of new outposts must be approved by the center (Varese 2012*b*).

A third case of separation involved individuals who were expelled from the Sicilian mafia at the time of the second mafia war (1981–83) and formed a breakaway group, known as Stidda (Star). At first, some of these individuals were members of a losing faction in the Sicilian mafia; others had been expelled because they married relatives of police officers. The group has been active in southern and eastern Sicily, away from the Sicilian mafia strongholds in the northwestern part of the island. This is not the case of an outpost that lost its official mafia affiliation but suggests that expulsion is another route toward separation. The stiddari's territory does not overlap with that of the Sicilian mafia (Savatteri 2015; Bascietto 2019).

The American Italian mafia experience suggests that sources of income and relative power matter. As income increasingly originates in the new territory, incentives to separate become stronger. They are greater if the new brand name (e.g., "Cosa Nostra") achieves enough of a reputation to be recognized independently of the original brand. The Lombardia case offers some support for the hypothesis. 'Ndrangheta groups there are sufficiently rich and well known to be able to go it alone. Tensions continue to exist, and a delicate balance has to be found if the center wants to retain a degree of control over the outposts. Traditional mafias have not experienced significant instances of separation. This may be due to the flexible nature of relations between outposts and motherland. Outposts pursue their own criminal strategies and interests. Incentives to separate increase only when the motherland interferes with appointments and creation of new families.

VII. Research Challenges

In this section, I address selected conceptual, research design, and data challenges to the study of mafia movements. Functional diversification raised a conceptual challenge. Examples include a diverse range of activities including money laundering in financial centers such as London, creation of shell companies in tax havens such as Panama, and purchase of illegal commodities such as drugs in transportation hubs like Amsterdam and Rotterdam. Functional diversification can also refer to the production of goods and services far from the motherland. These activities are quite different. Factors that might predict one will not necessarily predict others. A way forward is to specify whether the activity undertaken is production or trading and, within trading, to distinguish money laundering from other trading activities.

Qualitative studies of transplantation tend to focus on single successful cases, thus selecting on the dependent variable. This is understandable and not uncommon in political science and traditional ethnography (Varese 2020). Single case studies allow scholars to go beyond judicial data (a common source of evidence in mafia studies) and conduct field interviews and, ideally, extensive field work of the kind undertaken by Whyte in his classic *Street Cornet Society* ([1943]1993). Case study methodology can explore dynamics in depth, identify relevant social mechanisms, and inform the collection of quantitative data (Vaughan 2011). Abell (2009) has argued that narrative case studies can provide paths of causal links, without the need to compare or to generalize. The increasingly popular method of process tracing aims to achieve causality through analytical, temporal description (Bennett and Checkel 2014).

However, case study narratives and process tracing have limitations. First, even atheoretical case studies must describe events, and any description necessarily involves collection and selection of evidence. Valid descriptions need to make selection processes clear. A description can be accurate and valid but uninteresting and ultimately useless.[20] To be useful, it must be oriented toward answering a theoretical question. Explicit theoretical frameworks are necessary to identify an instance as a case of a class of events. Finally, it is doubtful that temporal narratives can achieve causal explanations. The cause of an outcome may not be an immediately preceding event. If so, standard methods must be used to establish causality. In my view, case studies must make selection criteria explicit, including why the particular case was selected, and should be oriented toward testing or building a theory (Panebianco 1991, p. 144; Varese 2019). Choosing cases that appear to deviate from what established theories predict can be extremely valuable to confirm or challenge established results (Eckstein 1975; Thomas 2011).

Efforts to understand why an outcome occurs must consider similar cases in which the outcome of interest did not occur (alternatively, cases

---

[20] Friedman famously observed that it would be descriptively accurate to mention wheat traders' eye colors in a model of the wheat market but irrelevant for predicting price fluctuations (1953, p. 32). Sen (1980) emphasized that description involves selection of evidence and is informed by theory, even if often the theory is hidden.

that appear to differ in many respects but shared the same outcome can be compared). Comparative qualitative historical methodology has been used extensively in sociology and political science (Mahoney 2004) but is nearly absent in the study of mafias.[21]

However, the path to the development of causal statements cannot entirely be solved by adopting this research design. Although controlled experiments in a laboratory allow experimenters to manipulate variables directly, that is impossible and ethically unacceptable in many social studies.

How can we then be sure that outcomes do not depend on factors that are not explicitly accounted for? The best practical solution is to choose cases that are as similar as possible concerning all variables of interest except one but with different outcomes. For instance, among a set of cases transplantation was sometimes successful, but in one it was not. A second challenge relates to negative cases in which the outcome did not occur. How to select such cases? In my work, I follow the possibility principle proposed by Mahoney and Goertz (2004). I regard cases in which the outcome of interest was sought but not realized as "negative." Scholars who adopt this approach can draw on evidence of mafia attempts to transplant in court files, newspaper reports, and the memories of observers and participants.

Quantitative studies also face conceptual and data challenges. One concerns relations between concepts and indexes. The simpler and analytically clearer a concept is, and the less cluttered the index, the easier interpretation of results is likely to be. Sciarrone and Dagnes (2014), for example, created indexes for "enterprise syndicates" and "power syndicates" that are meant to capture mafia presence in different regions in Italy. The first index is meant to capture illicit trades (p. 42), but the indicators include robberies. Robberies are predatory crimes, and it is hard to see why they should be considered "enterprises."[22]

The power syndicate index includes officially recorded mafia-association crimes, asset seizures, and town councils disbanded because of mafia presence.[23] Asset confiscation is a fundamentally ambivalent indicator.

---

[21] Exceptions include Paoli (2000), Varese (2011*b*), and Catino (2019).

[22] In addition, a robbery committed by a mafia group may be an act of intimidation against a reluctant extortion victim rather than a simple crime. Qualitative knowledge is necessary.

[23] Official data contain built-in biases: the judiciary may be more active in confiscating assets and disbanding city administrations in places where the mafia is less powerful, giving

Confiscation can refer to both functional diversification and transplantation. Investments in movable and immovable assets can occur both in places where transplantation has occurred and in places in which only functional diversification is observed.[24] That makes data on confiscated assets difficult to interpret. They should be used with caution and be accompanied by analyses of the types of activity of mafia organizations in each individual territory. More generally, the more indicators included in the index, the harder it is to interpret the results. Good methodological advice is to use indexes sparingly (Apaza 2009).

A special problem arises in studies of mafia movements in Italy that use official data on individuals required by courts to move outside their home territory. These data should include the resettled individuals' province of origin. Individuals required to move may have resided in nontraditional mafia territories. Crucially, not all people forced to resettle were found guilty of mafia-related crimes. For instance, only four of 16 individuals forced to resettle in Verona in February 1974 had been found guilty of mafia-related crimes in the south (Varese 2011*b*, p. 55; see, e.g., *L'Arena di Verona*, February 23, 1974). The data would need to be cleaned qualitatively. It is also not clear to what extent individuals had a degree of choice about their final destinations. If defendants were invited to suggest suitable destinations, forced resettlement would not be an instrumental variable.

Finally, scholars should reflect on the extent to which variables are related to each other. For instance, migration from southern Italy to Germany could be related to crime opportunities in Germany. If so, the key assumption of regression is violated. Multivariate models need to include both migration and economic variables to evaluate the effects of both.

VIII. Emerging Research Agenda and Policy Implications

Mafia transplantation has been more intensively investigated in the past decade than ever before, but much more needs to be done. Some information can improve governments' efforts to control organized crime in

the impression that the mafia is more active there than elsewhere (see, e.g., Calderoni 2011, p. 58).

[24] Calderoni (2011) found that asset confiscations vary significantly with mafia murders, implying that mafias buy assets in their traditional territories.

their territories, but greater attention needs to be paid to unintended consequences.

A. Emerging Research Agenda

A great deal of research has been conducted on mafia movements in Europe. It would be a significant leap forward if scholars working on Asian, Latin American, and American mafias joined forces with European colleagues and adopted comparable frameworks. That could shed light on underexplored subjects such as transitions from trading to governance, interplays between local and incoming crime groups, the significance of a locale's size, and links between social exclusion, weak and corrupt states, and emergence of extralegal governance.

US-based Latino gangs and Mexican cartels offer important targets of research opportunity. What are the links, if any, between *maras* in the United States and Central America? Some research has been conducted, but more is needed. Investigative reports suggest that Mexican cartels have expanded to the United States. The US Justice Department reported that Mexican cartels operate in at least 230 American cities, mainly in California, the Pacific Northwest, and the Eastern US (National Public Radio 2009). Data for 2011 from the National Drug Intelligence Center appear to show a significant reach of Mexican cartels, especially the Sinaloa, in the United States (*Guardian* 2014). These organizations are suppliers and are said to "have a near-monopoly on the distribution of wholesale quantities of drugs in most of the country now" (National Public Radio 2009). These statements need to be substantiated by academic research, but they suggest a possible transition from trading to governance in limited illegal markets. Dulin and Patiño (2020), who have studied the determinants of Mexican cartels' battles over territories within Mexico, found that expansion occurs toward municipalities that are "relatively small in both size and production, with few recorded narcotics offenses" (p. 332). That suggests that Mexican cartels may have become governance-oriented organized crime groups (see also Locks 2014).

A development in Colombia may shed light on neglected dynamics of mafia movements motivated by searches for resources and input goods. Newspaper reports indicate that Mexican cartels are directly engaged in the production and shipping of drugs in Colombia and no longer wait for coca to arrive in Mexico. The son of "El Chapo" Guzman, head of the Sinaloa cartel, was in Medellín for some months in 2016. According to *El Tiempo* (Croda 2018), he opened laboratories for processing coca in the

Medellín area that are capable of producing up to 100 kilos a week. Sinaloa cartel operatives have reportedly bought large plots of land in the Colombian Nariño region in which a quarter of illegal production is concentrated.[25] The Jalisco cartel appears to be operating in Calì, and the Mexican cartel Zetas appears to be present in the Cauca region and in the cities of Suárez and Buenos Aires (Colombia). Since 2016, more than a hundred Mexicans involved in drug trafficking have been arrested in Colombia. According to Fabián Laurence Cárdenas, Director of the Federal Police Antinarcotics Unit in Colombia, "the Mexicans are no longer operating through intermediaries, but want to control production themselves. At a certain point they became concerned that quality was no longer what it used to be, and they lost faith" (Croda 2018).

The dismantling of Pablo Escobar's organization and the Revolutionary Armed Forces of Colombia—People's Army's (FARC) capitulation to the government appear to have enabled outside forces with the necessary resources and infrastructure to become involved in narcotics production in Colombia. Mexicans appear to have brokered a nonaggression agreement, the so-called Rifle Pact, between clans in Medellín. This implies that Mexicans could become regulators of organized crime in Colombia (Varese 2018*a*). It is too early to know. More complex dynamics than exist in Europe may result from combinations of production of illegal goods, incentives to search cross-nationally for input resources, and the limited regulatory capacities of weak states.

B. Policy Implications

Scholars should be cautious in proposing policy implications of their work. Some tentative suggestions emerge. First, the distinction between transplantation and functional diversification is important. One may lead to the other; different strategies are required to fight them.[26]

Migration appears to be a necessary but not a sufficient condition for transplantation. However, a large workforce operating outside the rule of law framework provides opportunities for extralegal forms of governance. Workers who cannot turn to state-sponsored forms of dispute

---

[25] On June 16, 2018, 16 Mexicans and one Ecuadorian, linked to El Chapo's organization, were arrested in the Nariño region with 1,300 kilos of cocaine destined for Mexico (Croda 2018).

[26] This section draws on Varese (2011*a*, pp. 230–31).

settlement might welcome such services, even if they are supplied by criminals. This should not be allowed to happen. If undocumented migrants are present in considerable numbers, authorities should legalize their status, thereby bringing them within the fold of state-provided forms of protection and dispute settlement. Authorities might consider adopting don't ask, don't tell policies concerning the immigration status of workers, in order to lessen their need for illegal forms of governance. An effective justice system will reduce demand for illegal forms of dispute resolution.

Some markets are easier to control than others. Firms that want to enter a new sector of the economy must be able to do so without risking retaliation from incumbents. Violence is an effective way for incumbents to reduce competition in sectors such as construction, waste disposal, and garbage collection that have relatively low barriers to entry. Authorities should ensure easy entry into markets, thereby increasing competition. Simple registration norms, easy resort to legal dispute resolution, and an effective civil law system facilitate easy entry into markets and their smooth functioning. If a sector is already organized as a cartel backed by mafia violence, authorities should consider establishing their own companies to break into the market (see, e.g., Jacobs 1999, pp. 194–96). Such companies would not be easily scared away by incumbents, since they have direct access to police power. Construction especially plays a particular role in the success of mafia transplantation and should be tightly regulated and closely monitored.

The size of a territory matters. All else being equal, it is easier for incoming criminals to control small towns than large cities. How can mafia infiltration in smaller municipalities be prevented? Larger electoral constituencies make it harder to control votes than smaller ones. A party-list proportional representation system with preference voting, to the contrary, makes it easier for mafias to gain influence and control than a first-past-the-post system does. Authorities must recognize the risk of capture of smaller municipalities and be prepared to disband local councils if they become corrupted. Because local authorities often have regulatory power over key elements of the local economy, especially construction, and officials oversee the granting of licenses, their exercises of power must be closely scrutinized. Systems of checks and balances must ensure that permitting and oversight comply with applicable laws. Outside experts should be consulted when key permits are granted. Public offices might be rotated, so that individuals do not serve in a given position for a long period. Routine rotation makes it harder for incumbents to forge long-term ties to individuals who want to influence them.[27]

Finally, American policies in the 1990s were instrumental to transplantation of Los Angeles *maras* to Central America. Mass expulsion of gang members had disastrous consequences: powerful gangs continued to operate in California; emerged in Salvador, Guatemala, and Honduras; and eventually built cross-national albeit loose links. Attempting to get rid of gangs in one place may simply move the problem elsewhere.

Functional diversification should be contrasted with greater attention to financial flows and credit markets. Access to credit is difficult and creates temptations to use illegal sources. Mafias lend money at high interest rates and sometimes use violence to collect. To reduce the spread of illegal lending, authorities should promote medium and small enterprises' access to credit. Offshore areas within Europe should be abolished, and economic sectors in which untraceable transactions are common should be monitored closely, since risks of money laundering are high (Campana 2011*a*; Shaxson 2012; Calderoni et al. 2016; Bullough 2018). Suspicious business practices, such as opening and closing many companies in a short period, should also be closely scrutinized. Monitoring and controls on unexplained wealth are crucial. The fight against functional diversification by mafias within the European Union would be well served by strengthening mechanisms of international cooperation, including the European Arrest Warrant and EuroJust.[28]

Some authors (e.g., Allum 2012) and the European Parliament have recently advocated the introduction throughout Europe of laws criminalizing mafia-type association such as exist in Italy. Such laws authorize stiff sentences for being a member of a mafia group. Laws creating such offenses should be enacted in places in which mafias have been able to transplant. New provisions in a criminal code are, however, only as effective as the criminal justice system is effective, transparent, and fair. In places where corruption or political inference in judicial decision is rife, enactment of new laws can offer no panaceas and be counterproductive.

---

[27] Max Weber famously suggested rotation of office to limit abuses of power. See Gerth and Wright Mills (1970, p. 289).

[28] The European Arrest Warrant laws stipulates that extradition can occur swiftly even if the two countries do not have identical provisions in their criminal laws. On the potential security implication of the United Kingdom leaving the European Union, see Carrera et al. (2018).

Mafia movements across territories is a main theoretical and empirical subject in organized crime research (von Lampe 2012, 2016; Kleemans 2014). Conceptual clarity is improving only slowly. Three phenomena— transplantation, functional diversification, and separation—are central. Mafia transplantation is relatively rare, but it has occurred. Functional diversification encompasses a wide variety of criminal activities—money laundering, offshore creation of firms, buying and selling illegal goods such as drugs and arms, and the production of illegal goods—conducted by mafias outside their traditional territories. This is the area in greatest need of empirically sound and conceptually clear research.

REFERENCES

Abell, Peter. 2009. "A Case for Cases: Comparative Narratives in Sociological Explanation." *Sociological Methods and Research* 38(1):38–70.

Albrow, Martin. 1996. *The Global Age: State and Society beyond Modernity*. London: Polity.

Allegra, Melchiorre. 1962. "Come io, medico, diventai mafioso." *L'Ora*, January 12, 22–23.

Allum, Felia. 2012. "Italian Organised Crime in the UK." *Policing* 6(4):354–59.

———. 2014. "Understanding Criminal Mobility: The Case of the Neapolitan Camorra." *Journal of Modern Italian Studies* 19(5):583–602.

Apaza, Carmen R. 2009. "Measuring Governance and Corruption through the Worldwide Governance Indicators: Critiques, Responses, and Ongoing Scholarly Discussion." *PS: Political Science and Politics* 42(1):139–43.

Arana, Ana. 2005. "How the Street Gangs Took Central America." *Foreign Affairs* 8(3):98–110.

Arlacchi, Pino. 1993. *Men of Dishonor: Inside the Sicilian Mafia; An Account of Antonino Calderone*. New York: Morrow.

———. 1996. *Addio Cosa Nostra: I segreti della mafia nella confessione di Tommaso Buscetta*. Milan: Rizzoli.

Armao, Fabio. 2003. "Why Is Organized Crime So Successful?" In *Organized Crime and the Challenge to Democracy*, edited by Felia Allum and R. Siebert. London: Routledge.

Arsovska, Jana. 2014. "The 'Glocal' Dimension of Albanian Organized Crime: Mafias, Strategic Migration and State Repression." *European Journal on Criminal Policy Research* 20:205–23.

———. 2015. "Strategic Mobsters or Deprived Migrants? Testing the Transplantation and Deprivation Models of Organized Crime in an Effort to Understand Criminal Mobility and Diversity in the United States." *International Migration* 54(2):160–75.

Asmundo, Adam. 2011. "Indicatori e costi della criminalità mafiosa." In *Alleanze nell'ombra*, edited by Rocco Sciarrone. Rome: Donzelli.

Balsamo, Antonio. 2006. "Organised Crime Today: The Evolution of the Sicilian Mafia." *Journal of Money Laundering Control* 9(4):373–78.

Barak, Gregg. 2001. "Crime and Crime Control in an Age of Globalization: A Theoretical Dissection." *Critical Criminology* 10:57–72.

Bascietto, Giuseppe. 2019. *Stidda: L'altra mafia raccontata dal capoclan Claudio Cerbonaro*. Reggio Emilia: Aliberti.

Bauman, Zygmunt. 1998. *Globalization: The Human Consequences*. London: Polity.

BBC News. 2015. "Mafia Boss Domenico Rancadore's Sentence 'expired.'" April 1. https://www.bbc.co.uk/news/uk-england-london-32144720.

Beck, Ulrich. 1999. *What Is Globalization?* London: Polity.

Bennett, Andrew, and Jeffrey T. Checkel, eds. 2014. *Process Tracing: From Metaphor to Analytic Tool*. Cambridge: Cambridge University Press.

Block, Alan. 1983. *East Side, West Side: Organizing Crime in New York, 1930–1950*. London: Transaction.

Blok, Anton. 1974. *The Mafia of a Sicilian Village, 1860–1960*. Oxford: Blackwell.

Bonanno, Joseph. 1983. *A Man of Honour: The Autobiography of Joseph Bonanno*. With Sergio Lalli. New York: Simon & Schuster.

Bullough, Oliver. 2018. *Money Land: Why Thieves and Crooks Now Rule the World and How to Take It Back*. London: Profile.

Bundeskriminalamt. 2017. *Organisierte Kriminalität*. Bundeslagebild. https://www.bka.de/SharedDocs/Downloads/DE/Publikationen/JahresberichteUnd Lagebilder/OrganisierteKriminalitaet/organisierteKriminalitaetBundeslagebild 2017.html.

Calderoni, Francesco. 2011. "Where Is the Mafia in Italy? Measuring the Presence of the Mafia across Italian Provinces." *Global Crime* 12(1):41–69.

Calderoni, Francesco, Giulia Berlusconi, Lorella Garofalo, Luca Giommoni, and Federica Sarno. 2016. "The Italian Mafias in the World: A Systematic Assessment of the Mobility of Criminal Groups." *European Journal of Criminology* 13(4):413–33.

Campana, Paolo. 2011*a*. "Assessing the Movement of Criminal Groups: Some Analytical Remarks." *Global Crime* 12(3):207–17.

———. 2011*b*. "Eavesdropping on the Mob: The Functional Diversification of Mafia Activities across Territories." *European Journal of Criminology* 8(3):213–28.

———. 2013. "Understanding Then Responding to Italian Organized Crime Operations across Territories." *Policing* 7(3):316–25.

Campana, Paolo, and Federico Varese. 2018. "Organized Crime in the United Kingdom: Illegal Governance of Markets and Communities." *British Journal of Criminology* 58(6):1381–400.

Carrera, Sergio, Valsamis Mitsilegas, Marco Stefan, and Fabio Giuffrida. 2018. "Criminal Justice and Police Cooperation between the EU and the UK after Brexit: Towards a Principled and Trust-Based Partnership." CEPS Task Force Reports. https://www.ceps.eu/wp-content/uploads/2018/08/TFR_EU -UK_Cooperation_Brexit_0.pdf.

Castells, Manuel. 2000. *End of Millennium: The Information Age; Economy, Society and Culture*. Oxford: Blackwell.

Catanzaro, Raimondo. 1994. "Violent Social Regulation: Organized Crime in the Italian South." *Social and Legal Studies* 3(2):267–79.

Catino, Maurizio. 2019. *Mafia Organizations: The Visible Hand of Criminal Enterprise*. Cambridge: Cambridge University Press.

———. 2020. "Italian Organized Crime since 1950." In *Organizing Crime: Mafias, Markets, and Networks*, edited by Michael Tonry and Peter Reuter. Chicago: University of Chicago Press.

Chin, Ko-lin. 2003. *Heijin: Organized Crime, Business, and Politics in Taiwan*. Armonk, NY: Sharpe.

Chu, Yiu Kong. 2000. *The Triads as Business*. London: Routledge.

Ciccarello, Elena. 2014. "Politica e 'ndrangheta nel Nord Italia: Il caso di Leinì." *Meridiana* 79:221–41.

Ciconte, Enzo. 1998. *Mafia, Camorra e 'Ndrangheta in Emilia-Romagna*. Rimini: Panozzo Editore.

Critchley, David. 2009. *The Origins of Organized Crime in America: The New York City Mafia, 1891–1931*. London: Routledge.

Croda, Rafael. 2018. "Los narcos mexicanos imponen su ley en Colombia." *El Tiempo*, October 25. https://www.eltiempo.com/justicia/conflicto-y-narcotrafico /presencia-de-carteles-mexicanos-en-colombia-es-un-problema-de-seguridad -nacional-284974.

Cruz, José Miguel. 2010. "Central American *Maras*: From Youth Street Gangs to Transnational Protection Rackets." *Global Crime* 11(4):379–98.

Dagnes, Joselle, Davide Donatiello, Valentina Moiso, Davide Pellegrino, Rocco Sciarrone, and Luca Storti. 2018. "Mafia Infiltration, Public Administration and Local Institutions: A Comparative Study in Northern Italy." *European Journal of Criminology* https://doi.org/10.1177%2F1477370818803050.

Dalla Chiesa, Nando, and Federica Cabras. 2019. *Rosso mafia: La 'ndrangheta a Reggio Emilia*. Milan: Bompiani.

Dalla Chiesa, Nando, and Martina Panzarasa. 2012. *Buccinasco: La 'ndrangheta al Nord*. Turin: Einaudi.

De Filippo, Francesco, and Paolo Moretti. 2011. *Mafia padana: Le infiltrazioni criminali in Nord Italia*. Rome: Editori Internazionali Riuniti.

Di Antonio, Sara. 2010. *Mafia: Le mani sul Nord*. Rome: Aliberti.

Dulin, Adam L., and Jairo Patiño. 2020. "Mexican Cartel Expansion: A Quantitative Examination of Factors Associated with Territorial Claims." *Journal of Crime, Law, and Social Change* 73:315–36.

Eckstein, Harry. 1975. "Case Study and Theory in Political Science." In *The Handbook of Political Science: Strategies of Inquiry*, edited by F. Greenstein and N. Polsby. Reading, MA: Addison-Wesley.

Edwards, Adam, and Peter Gill. 2002. "Crime as Enterprise? The Case of 'Transnational Organised Crime.'" *Crime, Law, and Social Change* 37(3):203–23.

Finckenauer, James O., and Ko-lin Chin. 2006. "Asian Transnational Organized Crime and Its Impact on the United States: Developing a Transnational Crime Agenda." New York: US National Institute of Justice.

Forgione, Francesco. 2009. *Mafia Export: Come 'ndrangheta, Cosa Nostra e Camorra hanno colonizzato il mondo*. Milan: Baldini-Castoldi-Dalai.

Friedman, Milton. 1953. *Essays in Positive Economics*. Chicago: Chicago University Press.

Galeotti, Mark. 2000. "The Russian Mafia: Economic Penetration at Home and Abroad." In *Economic Crime in Russia*, edited by Alena Ledeneva and Marina Kurkchiyan. The Hague: Kluwer Law International.

Gambetta, Diego. 1993. *The Sicilian Mafia*. Cambridge, MA: Harvard University Press.

Gambetta, Diego, and Peter Reuter. 1995. "Conspiracy among the Many: The Mafia in Legitimate Industries." In *The Economics of Organised Crime*, edited by Gianluca Fiorentini and Sam Peltzman. Cambridge: Cambridge University Press.

Gennari, Giuseppe. 2013. *Le fondamenta sulla città*. Milan: Mondadori.

Gerth, Hans, and Charles Wright Mills, eds. 1970. *From Max Weber*. London: Routledge.

Gordon, Jon. 2020. "The Legitimation of Extrajudicial Violence in an Urban Community." *Social Forces* 98(3):1174–95.

Gratteri, Nicola, and Antonio Nicaso. 2009. *Fratelli di sangue*. Milan: Mondadori.

Guardian. 2014. "Mexican Drug Trafficking in the United States: The Sinaloa Cartel's Vast Empire." February 28. https://www.theguardian.com/world/interactive/2014/feb/28/mexican-drug-trafficking-sinaloa-cartel.

Hay, Donald, and Derek Morris. 1979. *Industrial Economics: Theory and Evidence*. Oxford: Oxford University Press.

He, Bingsong, ed. 2003. *Deciphering Mafia-Related Crimes*. [In Chinese.] Beijing: China Procuratorial.

Hess, Henner. 1973. *Mafia and Mafiosi: The Structure of Power*. Lexington, MA: Lexington.

Hill, Peter B. E. 2002. "Tokyo: La rete della yakuza." *Lettera Internazionale* 71:53–55.

———. 2004. "The Changing Face of the Yakuza." *Global Crime* 6(1):97–116.

Ianni, Francis A. J. 1972. *A Family Business: Kinship and Social Control in Organized Crime*. With E. Reuss-Ianni. New York: Russell Sage.

Ingrascì, Ombretta. 2015. "La mafia russa in Italia: Lavori in corso." *Rivista di Studi e Ricerche sulla criminalità organizzata* 1(1):37–55.

Jacobs, James B. 1999. *Gotham Unbound: How New York City Was Liberated from the Grip of Organized Crime*. With Coleen Friel and Robert Raddick. New York: New York University Press.

———. 2020. "US Organized Crime since 1950." In *Organizing Crime: Mafias, Markets, and Networks*, edited by Michael Tonry and Peter Reuter. Chicago: University of Chicago Press.

King, Gary, Robert Keohane, and Sidney Verba. 1994. *Designing Social Inquiry*. Princeton, NJ: Princeton University Press.

Kleemans, Edward R. 2007. "Organized Crime, Transit Crime, and Racketeering." In *Crime and Justice in the Netherlands*, edited by Michael Tonry and Catrien Bijleveld. Chicago: University of Chicago Press.

———. 2014. "Theoretical Perspectives on Organized Crime." In *The Oxford Handbook of Organized Crime*, edited by Letizia Paoli. Oxford: Oxford University Press.

Kleemans, Edward R., and Marcel de Boer. 2013. "Italian Mafia in the Netherlands." *Sicurezza e Scienze Sociali* 1(3):15–29.

La Spina, Antonio, ed. 2013. *I costi dell'illegalità: Una ricerca sul Sestiere della Maddalena a Genova*. Bologna: Mulino.

Lintner, Bertil. 2004. "Chinese Organised Crime." *Global Crime* 6(1):84–96.

Locks, Benjamin. 2014. "Extortion in Mexico: Why Mexico's Pain Won't End with the War on Drugs." *Yale Journal of International Affairs* 10:67–83.

Lodetti, Patrizio. 2018. "'Ndrangheta e impresa mafiosa a Mantova: Le conseguenze sull'economia locale." *Rivista di studi e ricerche sulla criminalità organizzata* 4(1):53–98.

Lupo, Salvatore. 1996. *Storia della mafia: Dalle orgini ai giorni nostri*. Rome: Donzelli.

———. 2015. *The Two Mafias: A Transatlantic History, 1888–2008*. London: Palgrave Macmillan.

MacDonald, John S., and Leatrice D. MacDonald. 1964. "Chain Migration Ethnic Neighborhood Formation and Social Networks." *Milbank Memorial Fund Quarterly* 42(1):82–97.

Mahoney, James. 2004. "Comparative-Historical Methodology." *Annual Review of Sociology* 30:81–101.

Mahoney, James, and Gary Goertz. 2004. "The Possibility Principle: Choosing Negative Cases in Comparative Research." *American Political Science Review* 98(4):653–69.

Martinez D'aubuisson, Juan José. 2015. *Ver, oír y callar: Un año con la Mara Salvatrucha 13*. La Rioja: Pepitas de Calabaza.

Massari, Monica. 2001. "La criminalità mafiosa nell'Italia centro-settentrionale." In *Mafie nostre, mafie loro: Criminalità organizzata italiana e straniera nel Centro-Nord*, edited by S. Becucci and M. Massari. Turin: Edizioni di Comunità.

Mazzenzana, Sarah. 2017. "La criminalità russa: Nota storica sulle origini contemporanee." In *Mafia globale: Le organizzazioni criminali nel mondo*, edited by Nando dalla Chiesa. Milan: Laurana.

Minuti, Diego, and Antonio Nicaso. 1994. `Ndraghete: Le filiali della mafia calabrese*. Vibo Valentia: Monteleone.

Mori, Cesare. 1933. *The Last Struggle with the Mafia*, translated by Orlo Williams. London: Putman. (Originally published as *Con la mafia ai ferri corti*, 1932.)

Moro, Francesco N., and Matteo Villa. 2017. "The New Geography of Mafia Activity: The Case of a Northern Italian Region." *European Sociological Review* 33:46–58.

Morselli Carlo, Matilde Turcotte, and Valentina Tenti. 2011. "The Mobility of Criminal Groups." *Global Crime* 12(3):165–88.

Naim, Moises. 2010. *Illicit: How Smugglers, Traffickers and Copycats Are Hijacking the Global Economy*. New York: Random House.

National Public Radio. 2009. "Cartels Fueling Violence in Mexico Take Root in US." March 25. https://www.npr.org/templates/story/story.php?storyId =102322570&t=1562222624471&t=1562234517653.

Panebianco, A. 1991. "Comparazione e spiegazione." In *La comparazione nelle scienze sociali*, edited by G. Sartori and L. Morlino. Bologna: Mulino.

Paoli, Letizia. 2000. *Fratelli di mafia: Cosa Nostra e 'ndrangheta*. Bologna: Mulino.

———. 2020. "What Do the Five Iconic Mafias Have in Common?" In *Organizing Crime: Mafias, Markets, and Networks*, edited by Michael Tonry and Peter Reuter. Chicago: University of Chicago Press.

Parini, Ercole Giap. 2008. "Myths, Legends, and Affiliation Practices in the Italian Mafioso Imagery: The Local Dimension of Power of a Global Phenomenon." PhD dissertation, University of Calabria.

Peña, Mario Aguilera. 2014. "Las guerrillas marxistas y la pena de muerte a combatientes: Un examen de los delitos capitales y del 'juicio revolucionario.'" *Anuario Colombiano de Historia Social y de la Cultura* 41(1):201–36.

Pignatone, Giuseppe, and Michele Prestipino. 2012. *Il contagio: Come la 'ndrangheta ha infettato l'Italia*. Roma-Bari: Laterza.

Pignedoli, Sabrina. 2016. *Operazione Aemilia*. Reggio Emilia: Imprimatur.

Portanova, Maria, Giampiero Rossi, and Franco Stefanoni. 2011. *Mafia a Milano*. Milan: Melampo.

Putnam, Robert D. 1993. *Making Democracy Work: Civic Traditions in Italy*. Princeton, NJ: Princeton University Press.

Reuter, Peter. 1983. *Disorganized Crime: The Economics of the Invisible Hand*. Cambridge, MA: MIT Press.

———. 1985. *The Organization of Illegal Markets: An Economic Analysis*. Washington, DC: US Department of Justice, National Institute of Justice.

———. 1987. *Rackeetering in Legitimate Industries: A Study in the Economics of Intimidation*. Santa Monica, CA: Rand.

———. 1995. "The Decline of the American Mafia." *Public Interest* 120:89–99.

Reuter, Peter, and Letizia Paoli. 2020. "How Similar Are Modern Criminal Organizations to Traditional Mafias?" In *Organizing Crime: Mafias, Markets, and Networks*, edited by Michael Tonry and Peter Reuter. Chicago: University of Chicago Press.

Rocha, José Luis. 2008. "La Mara 19 tras las huellas de las pandillas políticas." *Envío* 321:26–31.

Rodgers, Dennis, and Adam Baird. 2015. "Understanding Gangs in Contemporary Latin America." In *Handbook of Gangs and Gang Responses*, edited by S. H. Decker and David C. Pyrooz. New York: Wiley.

Rueda, Zenaida. 2009. *Confesiones de una guerrillera*. Bogotá: Editorial Planeta Colombia.

Santino, Umberto. 2006. *Dalla mafia alle mafie: Scienze sociali e crimine organizzato*. Soveria Mannelli: Rubbettino Editore.

Savatteri, Gaetano. 2015. "La Stidda: Mafia nelle terre di zolfo." In *Atlante delle mafie: Storia, economia, società, cultura*, vol. 3, edited by Enzo Ciconte, Francesco Forgione, and Isaia Sales. Soveria Mannelli: Rubbettino.

Scaglione, Attilio, and Rocco Sciarrone. 2014. "Il radicamento in una zona di confine: Gruppi mafiosi nel ponente ligure." In *Mafie del Nord: Strategie criminali e contesti locali*, edited by R. Sciarrone. Rome: Donzelli.

Schelling, Thomas C. 1971. "What Is the Business of Organized Crime." *Journal of Public Law* 20:71–84.

Sciarrone, Rocco. 1998. *Mafie vecchie, mafie nuove*. Rome: Donzelli.

Sciarrone, Rocco, and Joselle Dagnes. 2014. "Geografia degli insiedamenti mafiosi: Fattori di contesto, startegie criminali, e azione antimafia." In *Mafie del Nord: Strategie criminali e contesti locali*, edited by R. Sciarrore. Rome: Donzelli.

Sciarrone, Rocco, and Luca Storti. 2014. "The Territorial Expansion of Mafia-Type Organized Crime: The Case of the Italian Mafia in Germany." *Crime, Law and Social Change* 61(1):37–60.

Sen, Amartya. 1980. "Description as Choice." *Oxford Economic Papers* 32(3):353–69.

Sergi, Anna. 2015. "The Evolution of the Australian 'Ndrangheta: An Historical Perspective." *Australian and New Zealand Journal of Criminology* 48(2):155–74.

Shaxson, Nick. 2012. *Treasure Islands: Tax Havens and the Men Who Stole the World*. London: Vintage.

Shelley, Louise. 1999. "Identifying, Counting, and Categorizing Transnational Criminal Organizations." *Transnational Organized Crime* 5(1):1–18.

———. 2006. "The Globalization of Crime and Terrorism." *e-Journal USA*, February.

———. 2019. "The Globalization of Crime." In *International and Transnational Crime and Justice*, edited by M. Natarajan. Cambridge: Cambridge University Press.

Shelley, Louise, John Picarelli, and Chris Corpora. 2003. "Global Crime Inc." In *Beyond Sovereignty: Issues for a Global Agenda*, edited by Maryann Cusimano Love. Boston: Thomson Wadsworth.

Smith, Dwight C. 1975. *The Mafia Mystique*. New York: Basic.

———. 1978. "Organized Crime and Entrepreneurship." *International Journal of Criminology and Penology* 6(2):161–77.

Spapens, Toine. 2019. "Cerca Trova: The Italian Mafia on Dutch Territory." In *Constructing and Organising Crime in Europe*, edited by Petrus C. van Duyne, Alexey Serdyuk, Georgios A. Antonopoulos, Jackie H. Harvey, and Klaus Von Lampe. Chicago: Eleven International.

Sterling, Claire. 1990. *Octopus: The Long Reach of the International Sicilian Mafia*. London: Norton.

———. 1995. *Crimes without Frontiers: The Worldwide Expansion of Organised Crime and the Pax Mafiosa*. London: Little, Brown.

Task Force on Organized Crime. 1967. *Organized Crime: President's Commission on Law Enforcement and Administration of Justice*. Washington, DC: US Government Printing Office.

Thomas, Gary. 2011. "A Typology for the Case Study in Social Science Following a Review of Definition, Discourse, and Structure." *Qualitative Inquiry* 17(6):511–21.

Tizian, Giovanni. 2011. *Gotica: 'Ndrangheta, mafia e camorra oltrepassano la linea*. Rome: Round Robin.

United Nations. 1994. "Report of the World Ministerial Conference on Organized Transnational Crime." Conference held in Naples, Italy, November 21–

23, 1994, pursuant to General Assembly resolution 48/103 of December 20, 1993. Vienna: United Nations. https://www.imolin.org/imolin/naples.html ?print=yes.

UNODC (United Nations Office on Drugs and Crime). 2004. *United Nations Convention against Transnational Organized Crime and the Protocols Thereto.* Vienna: UNODC. https://www.unodc.org/documents/middleeastandnorthafrica /organised-crime/UNITED_NATIONS_CONVENTION_AGAINST_TRANS NATIONAL_ORGANIZED_CRIME_AND_THE_PROTOCOLS_THERE TO.pdf.

———. 2010. *The Globalization of Crime: A Transnational Organized Crime Threat Assessment.* Vienna: UNODC. https://www.unodc.org/res/cld/bibliography /the-globalization-of-crime-a-transnational-organized-crime-threat-assessment _html/TOCTA_Report_2010_low_res.pdf.

Varese, Federico. 2001. *The Russian Mafia: Private Protection in a New Market Economy.* Oxford: Oxford University Press.

———. 2004. "Mafia Transplantation." In *Creating Social Trust in Post-socialist Transition,* edited by J. Kornai, B. Rothstein, and S. Rose-Ackerman. New York: Palgrave Macmillan.

———. 2006. "How Mafias Migrate: The Case of the 'Ndrangheta in Northern Italy." *Law and Society Review* 40(2):411–44.

———. 2010. "What Is Organized Crime?" In *Organized Crime: Critical Concepts in Criminology,* edited by Federico Varese. New York: Routledge.

———. 2011*a.* "Mafia Movements: A Framework for Understanding the Mobility of Mafia Groups." *Global Crime* 12(3):218–31.

———. 2011*b. Mafias on the Move: How Organized Crime Conquers New Territories.* Princeton, NJ: Princeton University Press.

———. 2012*a.* "How Mafias Take Advantage of Globalization: The Russian Mafia in Italy." *British Journal of Criminology* 52(2):235–53.

———. 2012*b.* "Introduzione all'edizione italiana." In *Mafie in Movimento: Come il crimine organizzato conquista nuovi territori,* edited by Federico Varese. Turin: Einaudi.

———. 2014. "Protection and Extortion." In *The Oxford Handbook of Organized Crime,* edited by Letizia Paoli. Oxford: Oxford University Press.

———. 2018*a.* "Colombia, dimenticare Escobar: I reportage di Repubblica." *Repubblica,* December 28.

———. 2018*b. Mafia Life: Love, Death and Money at the Heart of Organized Crime.* Oxford: Oxford University Press.

———. 2019. "Comparazione e spiegazione: Lo studio delle mafie." In *Lo studio della politica,* edited by R. Mule and S. Ventura. Bologna: Mulino.

———. 2020. "Ethnographies of Organized Crime." In *Oxford Handbook of Ethnographies of Crime and Criminal Justice,* edited by Sandra Bucerius, Kevin Haggerty, and Luca Berardi. Oxford: Oxford University Press.

Vaughan, Diane. 2011. "Analytic Ethnography." In *The Oxford Handbook of Analytical Sociology,* edited by Peter Bearman and Peter Hedström. Oxford: Oxford University Press.

Vigil, James Diego. 2010. *Barrio Gangs: Street Life and Identity in Southern California*. Austin: University of Texas Press.

von Lampe, Klaus. 2012. "Transnational Organized Crime Challenges for Future Research." *Crime, Law, and Social Change* 58(2):179–94.

———. 2016. *Organized Crime: Analysing Illegal Activities, Criminal Structures and Extra-legal Governance*. Los Angeles: Sage.

Ward, Thomas W. 2013. *Gangsters without Borders: An Ethnography of a Salvadoran Street Gang*. New York: Oxford University Press.

Weenink, Anton, and Franca van der Laan. 2007. "The Search for the Russian Mafia: Central and Eastern European Criminals in the Netherlands, 1989–2005." *Trends in Organized Crime* 10(4):57–76.

Whyte, William Foote. 1993. *Street Corner Society: The Social Structure of an Italian Slum*. Chicago: University of Chicago Press. (Originally published 1943.)

Williams, Phil. 2001. "Transnational Criminal Networks." In *Networks and Netwars: The Future of Terror, Crime and Militancy*, edited by Arquilla J. and D. F. Ronfeldt. Washington, DC: Rand.

Williamson, Oliver. 1975. *Markets and Hierarchies*. New York: Free Press.

Woodiwiss, Michael. 2003. "Transnational Organized Crime: The Strange Career of an American Concept." In *Critical Reflections on Transnational Organized Crime, Money Laundering and Corruption*, edited by Margaret E. Beare. Toronto: University of Toronto Press.

Zaheer, Srilata, and Shalini Manrakhan. 2001. "Concentration and Dispersion in Global Industries: Remote Electronic Access and the Location of Economic Activities." *Journal of International Business Studies* 32(4):667–86.

Zimring, Franklin E., Gordon Hawkins, and Sam Kamin. 2001. *Punishment and Democracy: Three Strikes and You're Out in California*. New York: Oxford University Press.

Rossella Selmini

Women in Organized Crime

ABSTRACT

The involvement of women in organized criminal activities such as street
gangs, mafias, and illegal transnational markets, including human trafficking,
human smuggling, and drug trafficking, is an important but understudied
subject. Gendered studies and feminist theories can improve current knowledge and provide important new insights. They can enhance understanding of
women's roles, behavior, motivations, and life stories in all forms of organized
crime and challenge traditional and established ideas about victims, perpetrators, violence, and agency. Women, in all those settings, occupy both passive, subordinate roles and more active, powerful ones. However, ideas that
greater emancipation, labor force participation, and formal equality of women
in our time have fundamentally affected women's involvement in organized
crime have not been validated. Borders between victims and perpetrators are
often blurred. More research is needed on the effects of globalization and
technological change, on the salience of conceptions of masculinity in relation
to organized crime, and on conceptualization of violence in women's personal
lives and criminal actions.

The gender gap became a key issue in criminology in the second half of
the last century. The gap is that women commit fewer of most kinds of
crimes than men do and their offending careers are different, particularly
in relation to violent and more serious crimes (Steffensmeier and Allan
1996; Pitch 2002; Heidensohn and Gelsthorpe 2007, pp. 391–94). The
gap seems even more pronounced in relation to organized crime and
many forms of white-collar crime (Daly 1989).[1] That crime and criminal

Electronically published May 6, 2020
Rossella Selmini is associate professor of criminology, Department of Legal Sciences,
University of Bologna.
[1] Some scholars (Ruggiero 1996; Passas 2000; Vande Walle 2002) argue that the distinction between organized and white-collar crime, considered as forms of economic crime,

organizations are overwhelmingly dominated by men, with women typically playing mostly minor or auxiliary roles, has long attracted criminologists' attention (Adler 1975; Simon 1975; Daly 1989; Simpson 1989).

Women are involved in many forms of organized crime: in street gangs, in mafia organizations, in transnational crime, in adult criminal gangs, and as mules in drug and human trafficking. A Canadian report, one of the few at the country level on the presence and roles of women in organized crime (including some forms of white-collar crime), shows that the number of women convicted of participating in, committing, or instructing[2] some form of organized crime is very low. The majority of women charged and convicted of being involved in organized crime "participated"; only one was involved in commission of a crime (Beare 2010). This report, based on data from 1997 to 2004, seems to confirm the low involvement of women in organized crime and the auxiliary roles they play.

More recent studies, accepting that women's involvement is considerably less than men's, ask new questions and explore new issues. Contemporary research on women in organized crime tries to understand to what extent the apparently substantially lesser involvement of women results from a lack of research, gendered operation of the criminal justice system, or other factors. This includes trying to understand whether women engage in organized crime for the same or different reasons than men and, even if women's involvement is comparatively low, whether and, if so, why their roles and functions are apparently different.

The emergence of feminist criminology and gender studies was fundamental in raising new questions and focusing attention on female delinquency and the gender gap in general and in relation to organized crime. It gave rise to new work that sought to understand why women are

---

has been blurred by globalization and neoliberalism and that comparable issues concerning women's behavior, gender patterns and stereotypes, and concepts of masculinity arise in both. I consider here only organized criminal activities and groups and leave white-collar crime for another day.

[2] The analysis is based on cases of women charged and convicted under the Canadian Criminal Code, which defines organized crime thus: "A 'criminal organization' means a group, however organized, that is composed of three or more persons in or outside Canada and has as one of its main purposes or main activities the facilitation or commission of one or more serious offences that, if committed, would likely result in the direct or indirect receipt of a material benefit, including a financial benefit, by the group or by any of the persons who constitute the group." There are different levels of involvement: participation, commission, and instruction.

traditionally less involved in crime than men and to investigate gendered features of their criminality and their criminal justice system experiences.

The gendered perspective in analyzing female involvement in organized crime raises fundamental issues that I explore in this essay. Are women usually low-level actors, and are they always excluded from leading roles? Should "leading role" be reconceptualized to take gender differences into account? Are women's roles as offenders and victims adequately differentiated? How do broader social, economic, and cultural contexts, including the level of female emancipation in a given society, affect females' participation in organized crime?

These questions have received diverse answers, as I explain below. Controversial issues include the meaning of "playing a leading role," usually understood to imply use of power and sometimes violence; the significance of broader processes of emancipation; and the blurring of boundaries between active, independent agents and victims.

These controversies relate conceptually to questions about what "leading roles" means, what "violence" and "victim" mean, and what methodologies and information are available to study them. Some studies seem to look for women who replicate male roles. Others, taking a gender perspective, look for specific female qualities and attitudes that should reshape conceptualization of what a "leading role" is. Some recent studies using a gendered perspective, for example, challenge the traditional view that women seldom play important roles in organized crime or have only recently become leading figures. Other studies emphasize the need for more nuanced conceptualization of what being a victim means, and for reconceptualization of violence.

History and changes over time matter. Dina Siegel (2014) argues that female participation in organized crime has not suddenly risen. Women have traditionally been important in these organizations, she says, but their roles have only recently gained visibility and become a recurring subject of research. Her and others' recent cross-national and national work shows that women in many different countries during the past century played visible and leading roles in criminal organizations, including in violent activities (e.g., Lavin 2003; Smith 2013).

It is often unclear, however, whether these women, sometimes described in almost heroic ways, really performed powerful roles in criminal organizations such as Italian and Russian mafias, Mexican drug cartels, and Japanese yakuza, and whether they exemplify women acting as independent agents or whether, despite their apparent independence and autonomy, they were controlled by men and subjugated by traditional, masculine, cultural norms and stereotypes. Varese (2017), who discusses women who reached higher positions in Italian, Russian, and Japanese organized crime groups, and others who have studied other organizations offer more complex and nuanced accounts of women in higher roles (e.g., Dino 2007, 2010; Ingrascì 2007*b*, 2014; Siebert 2007, 2010; Campbell 2008; Fleetwood 2014).

Research methodology and sources of information matter. Statistical data, in particular relating to arrests and convictions, do not adequately represent involvement of women in organized crime. However, this is often the primary or only source of information available, particularly concerning women involved in organized crime organizations and illegal markets. A different approach, relying more on qualitative methodologies, including interviews, document and content analyses, and historical research, can shed brighter light. The most interesting contemporary research uses qualitative methods, particularly interviews and life histories, that seem especially informative for efforts to grasp differences and understand motivations. Despite difficulties in getting access to participants in organized crime organizations, these are probably the best methods to use in studying female involvement in organized crime and to study organized crime in general (Rawlinson 2000). Statistical data are not of much use for answering these questions. Reliance primarily on qualitative methods is more likely to enrich understanding of the complexities of women's involvement, the nature of their criminal activities, their links and relationships with men, and their motivations for joining and leaving criminal organizations.

In this essay, I explore the literature on women's involvement in organized crime and discuss key themes. I first summarize debates about criminological theories and concepts and how they might be helpful in understanding female delinquency in general and in organized crime. I emphasize the theoretical importance of feminist perspectives and gendered approaches.

In the next sections, I review the literature and discuss open questions about the involvement of women in criminal organizations, especially in street gangs, Italian mafia groups, and some illegal markets. Work concerning illegal markets mostly focuses on women's roles in human trafficking, smuggling, and drug trafficking. There is of course overlap between criminal organizations and illegal markets. Women in gangs and mafia organizations are involved in the same activities they perform in illegal markets not dominated by those organizations. However, the presence of women in gangs and mafia groups, differently from the presence of women in illegal markets, has been the subject of extensive research that raises important theoretical and empirical issues. It warrants particular attention. In drawing this distinction, I accept a broader, though controversial, definition of organized crime that includes criminal activities performed by groups or networks in a systematic and organized way. In each section, I address several questions. What are the characteristics of female involvement? Why do women engage in organized criminal activities or enter criminal organizations, and how do their criminal careers unfold? What makes their participation in illegal markets or criminal organizations different from men's? How do conceptualizations of a "leading role" and of violence change when women's experiences are taken into account?

I. Conventional Theories of Criminology and Female Offending

Influential criminological theories were long tailored to understand and explain a male phenomenon; little attention was paid to female criminality. Most theories are male-centered, although serious theoretical and empirical efforts have been made in recent decades to incorporate a gender perspective and redress the traditional invisibility of women. Traditional theories may be helpful in understanding the gender gap, but to understand it better and to understand female delinquency, traditional concepts need to be adapted to encompass feminist approaches that take into account the gendered nature of society and power relations in the family and the larger society (e.g., Heidensohn 2006; Heimer and Kruttschnitt 2006; Heidensohn and Gelsthorpe 2007; De Coster, Heimer, and Cumley 2013; Burman and Gelsthorpe 2017).

Giordano, Deines, and Cernkovich (2006), drawing on the Ohio Serious Offenders Study, a long-term follow-up of girls and women, conclude that classical criminological theories need to be revised in ways "that tend to emphasize uniquely gendered processes" (p. 36).[3] This is

---

[3] It is still controversial whether in order to explain female offending we need to develop a new set of independent feminist criminological theories, as proposed by Smart (1976) and Cain (1990) or whether an adaptation or review of theories developed to understand males' violent and antisocial behavior is sufficient (Giordano, Deines, and Cernkovich 2006).

even more necessary in relation to the gender gap in more serious types of crimes, which has been always been wider than in other forms of crime (Steffensmeier and Allan 1996), and in understanding patterns of female involvement. The organizational dimension of organized crime adds new considerations that result from the networks and power relations within which women operate. Hierarchies, roles, and types of functions shape the roles of women in organized crime and in its transnational dimensions. Studies of female offending in general provide useful context, but better understanding of women involvement in organized crime will require development of new concepts and categories, particularly concerning their roles and the types of criminal activities in which they participate.

Broadly speaking, women engage in crime mostly as a result of circumstances they share with men, including poverty, low levels of education, blocked opportunities, unemployment, and troubled family backgrounds. Globalization, and in particular the interconnected processes of depauperization of the global South, migration, changes in family structure, and related crises of gender identity make these circumstances more complex, serious, and widespread (Hagedorn 2005; Moore 2007; Franko Aas 2013). Studies adopting a gender perspective, however, show that those factors may operate differently for males and females, that women suffer more from discrimination because of gender inequalities, and that those criminogenic factors may operate in different ways for women and men. This is true both for individual crime and for organized crime.

In this section, I discuss new insights that build on traditional criminological concepts and new arguments to explain the gender gap or understand female delinquent behavior in a gendered perspective. I focus on more gender-specific studies that are premised more on feminist concepts than on traditional criminological theories. I discuss here concepts and approaches developed to understand the gender gap and female delinquency in general. They offer important insights for efforts to understand women's involvement in organized crime.

Control theories, including those elaborated in Gottfredson and Hirschi (1990) and Hirschi (1969), emphasize internal and external controls and posit that self-control and social bonds restrain people from committing crimes. The gender gap may result from differences in control of women by parents, or more generally by social structure, and by stronger attachment of women to social bonds. Some research has shown a gender-differentiating process of social bonding in which girls are more influenced than boys by some forms of bonds, although the results from empirical research are somewhat inconsistent (De Coster, Heimer, and Cumley 2013, pp. 316–17). The balance of power between parents in a family seems to influence attachment bonds. Power control theory builds on traditional gender-neutral control theories from a gendered perspective, analyzing differences in attachment bonds related to power relations between fathers and mothers, reaching the conclusion that women in patriarchal families are less likely to engage in crime than are women in families with more balanced power relations between parents (Hagan, Simpson, and Gillis 1987).

Differential association is a gender-neutral theory of crime that posits that criminal behavior results from learning experiences. People exposed in social interactions to associations favorable to delinquency and crime are more likely to engage in it, varying with the frequency, intensity, duration, and persistence of associations (Sutherland 1947). Early associations favorable to crime in an intimate context such as the family are the most important for understanding why people engage in criminal behavior. Sutherland claimed that women are less likely to engage in delinquency because socialization processes and stronger controls on their lives make contacts with a delinquent environment less likely. There is empirical evidence supporting this view, summarized by De Coster, Heimer, and Cumley (2013, p. 323), showing that boys are more influenced than girls by peer associations and above all that boys' violent behavior is influenced by association with violent peers. This may explain why women are less involved in violence.

Learning theories have been reinterpreted in a gender perspective by Heimer and De Coster (1999). They showed that girls are not only more controlled than boys are by their parents, but that the learning process itself is gendered. In patriarchal societies, girls are more often acculturated to values of nurturance, passivity, dependence, and weakness than in other societies. Consequently, in thinking about learning processes, we need to consider not only definitions favorable to delinquency but also definitions of gender roles.

Although Ingrascì (2007b) did not set out to test any particular criminological theory, her work on women in Italian mafias refers to the importance of the learning experiences of both men and women growing up in a mafia "clan." Studies of women in Italian mafia groups, as I show below, provide important insights into gendered learning mechanisms and active roles that women play in transmitting criminal values within mafia families.

Strain theory and related ideas about blocked opportunities, relative deprivation, and poverty that conflict with conventional cultural goals are also gender-neutral. The different socializations of men and women concerning the importance of economic success and personal achievement may result in conditions of strain that work differently for women and men (Gilligan 1982; De Coster, Cornell, and Zito 2010). General strain theory, and particularly the work by Broidy and Agnew (1997), suggests that males and females may experience different types of strain and that emotional reaction to strain might be gendered. With the development in mainstream criminology of more gendered approaches, it became clear that women can be affected by the same class-based structural conditions that affect men, and attracted by the same cultural goals, but in different ways (Giordano, Deines, and Cernkovich 2006).

Labeling theory offers another common explanation of the gender gap. Starting from the premise that crime is often a result of a process of criminalization and resulting stigmatization and that deviance and crime are socially constructed, labeling theory posits differences between females and males that result mostly from law enforcement practices that treat women more leniently, aiming to limit, minimize, or avoid their involvement in the criminal justice system (Allen 1987). This approach does not help us understand why women engage in criminal behavior, or their different criminal patterns, but sheds light on women's lesser visibility in crime and differences in criminal justice processes.

The criminal justice system affects women's participation and roles in organized crime in two ways. First, although controversial, out of date, and lacking empirical clear evidence (Heidensohn and Gelsthorpe 2007, p. 399), the argument of "chivalry" by police, prosecutors, and courts toward female offending (Pollak 1961) may help explain why women in crime are often invisible. Second, how particular laws are enforced may affect criminal activity or a criminal organization in ways that sometimes keep women invisible and other times cause them to play more important roles. An example, which I discuss below, occurred when unprecedentedly severe law enforcement measures against Italian mafias in the 1980s and 1990s resulted in women playing more important organizational roles and shrank the traditional gender gap.

Women's greater or lesser visibility in the world of organized crime is thus sometimes a product of officials' decisions whether to report, arrest, and prosecute women and sometimes in legal or law enforcement changes that modify structural needs of criminal organizations. Other studies emphasize that deviant and criminal women, even when treated more leniently, suffer from a double stigmatization (Heidensohn 1996; Pitch 2002) resulting from their gender and their criminal activities. Ingrascì (2007b) provides examples of this double stigma on women in Italian organized crime.

Labeling theory, and related contemporary approaches such as cultural criminology, are useful in exploring other aspects of women's involvement in crime and in organized crime. Examples include the social construction and media representations of female offending, particularly in gangs and organized crime organizations.

II. Emancipation and Gendered Approaches

Studies of women in crime reflect a wide array of approaches that range from adaptations of traditional criminological theories to more explicitly feminist or gendered perspectives that focus on factors that distinctively characterize female behavior and on feminist concepts. Some of these approaches reject the view that women, even when offenders, should be thought of as victims and emphasize women's capacity to behave as active agents, particularly concerning serious violence (Morrissey 2003).

The earliest important theorizing about women and crime was offered by Freda Adler (1975) and Rita J. Simon (1975). Their "emancipation" theory hypothesized that women's lesser criminality resulted from their restricted opportunities in the public sphere rather than from inherent differences between men and women. They predicted that gender gaps would shrink when women participated more actively and independently in the labor market and in the public sphere more generally. Adler expected involvement in violent crime to increase as women became less affected by cultural stereotypes of women's passivity and weakness. Simon focused on the effects of increased economic opportunities available to women in the labor market. Structural equality should mean that differences between genders and gendered behavior would blur and that women would become more involved in property crime.

These early feminist views were soon, and still are, criticized for oversimplifying relationships between women and crime, for their assumption that the causes of male and female offending are the same and develop in the same way, and for lack of supporting empirical evidence (Steffensmeier 1980; Pitch 2002; Heidensohn and Gelsthorpe 2007). The predictions Adler and Simon made proved to be wrong. Subsequent empirical evidence has shown that the gender gap remains remarkably large for both minor crimes such as shoplifting and more serious criminality including involvement in organized and white-collar crime.

Simon and Adler's predictions about criminogenic effects of women's greater emancipation and fuller participation in the labor market also proved to be wrong. The increased presence of women in highly skilled jobs, for example, did not result in significant increases in women's involvement in traditional white-collar crime. Emancipation neither closed the gender gap nor changed existing gendered patterns in the types of crimes women were more and less likely to commit. Women's involvement in crime did not much change following greater emancipation in part because of "institutional sexism in the underworld" (Steffensmeier and Terry 1986, p. 304); illegal markets replicate general patterns of male dominance and gender stratification. This stratification is stronger for activities such as violence that require male "skills" including physical strength and ability to deal with competition, conflict, and organizational complexity.

Official data show some narrowing of the gender gap, but greater social and economic equality of women is not the reason. Women are mostly charged with minor crimes such as drug sales, frauds, and property crimes that are often products of poverty. Continuing inequality is more responsible than increasing equality for increases in female delinquency (Schwartz and Steffensmeier 2008; Beare 2010, p. 10).

Most of the literature on crime by women rejects emancipation theory in favor of gender-specific approaches, but it continues to offer an important frame of reference. Recent studies of women's seemingly more significant roles in Italian mafias, including in financing and administration of businesses and properties, reject emancipation theory but describe greater female emancipation in the whole society as a factor that might explain why some women acquire more significant roles (Siebert 2007; Ingrascì 2007b; Beare 2010).

Much of contemporary feminist criminology has shifted emphasis in efforts to explain the gender gap and differences in male and female delinquency from the effects of emancipation to the influences of patriarchy and gender inequality. This emphasis contributes to efforts to explain sexual and physical abuse in terms of men's power over women in a society that remains fundamentally dominated by patriarchal values. Lesser female delinquency is seen as a reproduction of the marginal roles that women perform in the conventional world. That marginality is said to explain why women are underrepresented in the criminal world and disproportionately engage in minor or powerless forms of delinquency such as shoplifting and prostitution (Messerschmidt 1986).

Ideas about patriarchy, despite a lack of strong supporting empirical evidence, have contributed substantially to the evolution of research on female delinquency and a shift toward "intersectionality" perspectives that combine gender with other significant factors such as class and race.[4] They emphasize the importance of how particular organizational contexts are gendered (Zhang, Chin, and Miller 2007). Taking intersectionality seriously requires willingness to view gender differences as resulting simultaneously from inequality and other structural conditions such as race and class. The intersectionality perspective at the same time enriches and challenges feminist criminology and gendered approaches to female offending, not only for its theoretical complexity but also for feminist criminology's difficulties in locating gender in a multidimensional paradigm (Burman and Gelsthorpe 2017, p. 216).

Chesney-Lind (1989) and Chesney-Lind and Shelden (2004) offered a feminist perspective that focuses on the different effects of patriarchal society on the lives of men and women and on how distinctive female experiences can explain the gender gap and women's delinquency. One important factor is familial sexual and physical abuse; it is often associated with deviant female careers that include misbehavior, transgression, delinquency, and crime. Abuse and violence in the family and later in the criminal milieu are often starting points in sequences of negative factors that explain female involvement in crime generally and in some criminal organizations (Giordano, Deines, and Cernkovich 2006).

Female victimization in violent male-dominated contexts sheds light on why women sometimes engage in offending as self-defense or as a coping strategy (Bottcher 2001). This is important in understanding women's roles in organized forms of crime including gangs and mafia groups, and calls for replacement of traditional rigid distinctions between victims and offenders with more nuanced views.

From the very beginning, a gendered approach to women offending (and victimization) took into consideration how males' experience in crime is shaped by expectations related to masculinity and the social construction

---

[4] Intersectionality theory requires not that women be "added" to a theoretical framework or that gender be treated as a variable in understanding crime, but that gender and gender relations be taken into consideration along with other variables such as class and race. Intersectionality theory asks different questions and challenges conventional theories (Yllö 2005).

of maleness (Cain 1990; Messerschmidt 1993; Connell 1995). This perspective is useful in improving understanding that gender roles are not "a fixed and determined set" (Burman and Gelsthorpe 2017, p. 215), but are part of a changeable process in which both masculinities and femininities are multiple and changeable.

Gendered hypotheses about women's crime have moved away from an emancipatory perspective or from seeing it as a replication or subcategory of male behavior. Women's crime is seen instead as an important phenomenon in itself. In this perspective, female delinquency is "rather a way of being and acting derived from history, long-term psychosocial processes, and the socializing processes that affect women" (Siebert 2007, p. 20). The focus is on how these characteristics shape women's involvement in crime. Contemporary approaches emphasize gendered pathways to offending and, paralleling life-course studies, try to understand how lawbreaking unfolds in women's lives and how much and in what ways this experience is affected by gender dynamics.

A. Criminal Organizations

In this section, I discuss female offending in gangs and mafia groups. There are, of course, other types of criminal organizations, but there is in these two fields a rich, gender-based, and often interdisciplinary literature that has enriched both criminology and gender studies in theory development, empirical variety, and depth. There are different types of gangs and mafia groups. I discuss here stable, long-term gangs and Italian mafia groups.

My focus is on women's roles in these organizations, on their relationships with other members, on their criminal careers within the organization, and on the constraints and opportunities they experience, rather than on specific crimes in which they engage. The range of criminal behavior in these organizations is usually wide and often includes violent and property crimes organized collectively. There is some overlap with issues discussed in relation to illegal markets, given that many women in gangs or mafia groups are involved in drug dealing, human trafficking, and smuggling. Despite a shift in focus from criminal behavior to criminal organizations, the theoretical issues and scholarly controversies discussed above arise.

1. *Gangs.* Most US studies of women's participation in collective delinquency concern gangs. Three patterns emerge. The first is membership in independent female gangs. Second is membership in mixed-gender

gangs that include female sections in predominantly male gangs. Third is the most traditional pattern of females as "auxiliaries" or "appendages" to male members. In this last case, female affiliation often arises from sentimental or kinship relations as girlfriends or sisters (Shelden, Tracy, and Brown 2013, p. 137).

Independent female gangs were first investigated in pioneering work by Ann Campbell (1984, 1990) in New York and by Carl Taylor (1993) in Detroit. They showed that women in female gangs rejected traditional female roles, used force and violence, and developed their own rules and values. They did not simply replicate or imitate male gangs. Taylor (1993, p. 48) claimed that "the gang generally does not differentiate between the sexes" and that women were not discriminated against within the gangs studied.

More recent works try to develop a better understanding of women's roles and convey more nuanced pictures, challenging the images both of powerful female gang members (who are rare) and of girls as appendages (Miller 1998, 2001; Moore and Hagedorn 2001; Vigil 2008).

These studies show that women join, participate in, and leave gangs for some of the same reasons as men, but also for different ones. Like men, women join because of limited legitimate occupational and educational opportunities, or because of neighborhood characteristics and gang exposure (Miller 1998, 2001). However, they also join because of subordination to men and the "powerlessness" of underclass membership (Campbell 1990, p. 173), because of serious family problems and lack of parental supervision, and because of the presence in gangs of boyfriends, siblings, cousins, and friends (Miller 2002).

There are thus some gender-specific reasons why women join gangs. Needs for protection and support may be stronger for girls than for boys; neglect, abuse, and similar family problems play an important role (Moore and Hagedorn 2001). Gangs may seem to be a "safer" space for girls escaping abuse in the family, and a source of identity (Batchelor 2009). Friendships and love relationships are other important motivations. Miller (2002, p. 91), adopting a gender perspective, showed that women felt a sense of empowerment in joining a gang despite the risks of victimization and abuse. Gangs were thought to be refuges from sexual exploitation and abuse, and to offer protection from the harshness of life on the street.

These studies also investigate whether female delinquent activity differs from that of males. Gender roles in conventional society tend to be replicated in gangs. Women in gangs are less involved in criminal activity in general than men, and in violent crime and homicide in particular, but are also less involved in noncriminal activities such as hanging around, drinking, and fighting. A few studies have concluded that there is no great difference between girls and boys in their involvement in minor crime and drug selling, but that criminal activities within the gang are influenced by gender roles expectations (Miller 2002, p. 87).

Similar findings have been reported in the United Kingdom by Batchelor (2009), who shows how violence, both verbal and physical, is committed by girls, particularly against other girls. A history of violence in the family and therefore a high level of toleration of violence, as well as a search for excitement and adrenaline were found in this study of gang girls in the United Kingdom. Violence was not only a way to replicate male behavior, but a consequence of specific contexts and particularly of the ideologies of working-class femininity: "Subordination and agency are simultaneously realized in young women's lives, and thereby demonstrates that there is no such thing as the essential 'gang girl'" (Batchelor 2009, p. 408).

Since female criminality in mixed gender gangs is influenced by perceptions of appropriate male and female roles, serious violence by females is less common (although fighting is a value for girls also), and firearms use is rare. Drug selling is common among girls, although patterns vary between gangs, and women can play very different roles.

Studies of violence by women in gangs tend mostly to discuss replication of male patterns of violence. This is different from studies I discuss below on violence by females in mafia organizations. They typically employ more sophisticated gendered analyses of the diverse ways violence can occur.

The gang literature uniformly shows that joining a gang has more serious consequences for females than for males, because violation of gender norm expectations results in additional social sanctions for women (Moore and Hagedorn 2001). Women are subjected to discrimination and blaming in their own family or community for violation of both behavioral standards and gender stereotypes, particularly in some ethnic groups (Moore 2007; Vigil 2008).

Another reason joining a gang may have more serious consequences for girls than for boys is that what girls expect to be a safer space can become a space of violence and abuse (Miller 1998, 2002). The gang world replicates gender inequality in the larger society and makes women more vulnerable to violence and abuse. Finally, reasons for leaving a gang are different for boys and girls because motherhood plays an important role for girls.[5]

Recent studies that take account of intersectionality explore how gender is interconnected and reshaped by class and race. Vigil (2008) shows that membership by both girls and boys in Chicano gangs in Los Angeles can be explained by "multiple marginality" (combinations of such factors as massive immigration, low employment, poor neighborhoods that affect family structure and stability, school success, deviance, and involvement in crime) but that gender operates as an additional "marginalization factor" for girls.

Latina girls in traditional Mexican families experience stronger gender inequality because of rigid gender stereotypes and patriarchal dynamics. These stereotypes recur in Chicano gangs, and women occupy subordinate status. More independent girls are stigmatized both within and outside the gang. Even girls who are not passive auxiliaries of male gangs and play important, though supportive, roles experience discrimination and moral judgments, especially when they engage in unconventional sexual behavior. Vigil's (2008) studies confirm that girls join gangs for the same reasons that boys do, but that stress in the family has a bigger effect on female gang membership, a history of sexual abuse is more common among female gang members than male gang members, and gang membership is more stigmatizing for females than for males.

The studies on women in gangs prompted a debate between some scholars who saw gang affiliation as liberating for women and others who stressed the "social injury hypothesis" (Joe and Chesnay-Lind 1995; Hagedorn 1998, p. 387). Proponents of the liberation hypothesis start from Adler's (1975) idea that criminal activities can express emancipation and liberation for women and from Taylor's (1993) studies of females in gangs. They assert that girls are not discriminated against in gangs and that joining a gang is a factor in their emancipation. Proponents of the social injury hypothesis stress that joining a gang is not a sign of emancipation because women suffer the same or worse forms of discrimination

---

[5] Hagedorn (1998, p. 388) found that "more than 98 percent of the 176 women who were the founding members of six Milwaukee female gangs left the gangs by the end of their teens. ... Two thirds of the women became teen mothers and more than 90 percent were mothers before their mid-twenties." The literature on desistance of women from gangs and from crime in general is not very well developed.

and sexual victimization in the gang as in the larger society (Hagedorn 1998; Moore 2007; Vigil 2008).

Women with any type of gang affiliation are more at risk than nongang girls of violence, abuse, and dependence, and suffer more from anxiety and depression than do their male counterparts. Initiation rituals and sexual violence seem to be common in a variety of North American gangs, but also in other countries, as Moore's (2007) accounts of biker gangs in New Zealand show.

Some studies embrace ideas from cultural criminology. They emphasize that gangs, redefined as "street organizations," represent a positive form of resistance for members, thereby giving women in gangs a different role. Brotherton and Barrios's (2004) and Brotherton's (2008) studies of the Almighty Latin Kings and Queens (ALKQ) challenge the view that women are "appendages" to men and describe a gendered resistance. "Many woman saw the gang as a resource while they strived both for increased autonomy and to fulfill traditional family obligations in economically distressed and culturally marginalized environments" (Brotherton 2008, p. 64). Women, Brotherton wrote, played important roles in influencing shifts from criminal activities and violence toward more prosocial and communitarian collective action. Even in the ALKQ, however, women were glorified as "the backbone" of the group and framed according to gender stereotypes. Motherhood and female qualities were emphasized, but sexual violence and abuse were not rare.

Similar patterns emerge in many studies of women in organized crime, especially in mafia groups, as I show in the next subsection.

2. *Italian Mafia Groups.* Italian mafias represent a highly specific form of organized crime, deeply embedded in history, tradition, ritual, and distinctive characteristics, and a complex phenomenon that has been the subject of extensive research. The complexity of the main mafia groups is expressed by this definition: "Systems with specific authorities, regimes, and structures, each of these systems interact with its environment, which consists in turn of other subsystems: political, judicial, economic, social, and so on; this interaction is necessary precisely because of the lack of autonomy in the systems themselves, which have no impermeable borders" (Principato 2007, p. 289). All these features shape the extent and characteristics of women's involvement; it has changed across space and over time and varies among the different mafia groups.

Women were long considered to be invisible in Italian mafias. Most recent criminological, historical, anthropological, and gender studies, however, show that women often play important private and public roles that are essential to the organization's survival. Even when not directly involved in criminal activities, they contribute to the cultural transmission and protection of the family and its values (including criminal ones).

We know much more about the roles of women because of research that draws upon information from recent mafia trials and interviews with sentenced women. These sources fueled a new field of research on mafia, including on the roles of women. We know much more now than in earlier times about the internal functioning of mafia groups, and the extent and nature of female participation.

Ingrascì (2007*b*) summarized widely agreed reasons why women became visible in the 1970s. First, changes in the structure, nature, and organization of mafia groups generated shifts toward more entrepreneurial and transnational activities (Savona and Natoli 2007; Catino 2020). Second, broader emancipation and higher levels of education of women in Italy affected women in mafia families.[6] Third, and most important, stronger law enforcement targeting of mafia activities and enactment of harsher laws challenged mafia organizations. Organized crime groups responded by becoming more professional, smaller, more flexible, and less violence-oriented, and the roles of women became more important (Ingrascì 2007*a*, 2007*b*; Savona and Natoli 2007).

Emancipation of women resulted in higher levels of education for women in Italy, including women in mafia families. That is why women in mafia organizations acquired some administrative and financial roles. These roles did not conflict with their subordinate position, however, because they did not challenge traditional male values and because these new roles became necessary to respond to law enforcement pressures that affected male bosses. First, women in mafia families became owners of real estate and bank accounts in order to avoid confiscations under the "Rognoni–La Torre" law that targeted the finances and property of mafia bosses. Second, women began to play more operational and active roles because heightened law enforcement pressures in the 1980s and 1990s resulted in male leaders being arrested or killed or having to flee. There was a shortage of people in leading positions. Women of the family,

---

[6] Varese (2017, p. 122) is more skeptical. He acknowledges that mafias (not only Italian ones) are flexible organizations that can adjust rapidly to changes in the external environment, but observes that their structural embeddedness in sexist societies makes them very slow to accept women's emancipation.

in a culture in which kinship and family are the roots of the organization, could be trusted to represent the absent boss (Siebert 2010, p. 22; Ingrasci 2007*a*, 2007*b*).

That women replaced men who were arrested did not necessarily mean they acquired independent roles. They remained "guardians of the male powers," ready to return to their more invisible world when the rightful owners of those powers returned (Ingrascì 2007*b*, pp. 78–79), and never really occupied or replaced men in powerful positions (Ingrascì 2010; Gribaudi 2010; Siebert 2010). Women, for instance, play active roles in 'Ndrangheta but there are no examples of units or clans in which the leaders were women, or of official affiliation of women through mafia rituals;[7] that remains a male privilege. This, together with women's exclusion from management of violence, allows little possibility of powerful roles (Varese 2017). However, there is evidence of changes across time and space, as I explain in the next subsection.

a. Women in Cosa Nostra, 'Ndrangheta, Camorra, and Sacra Corona Unita. Differences in women's experiences in the main Italian mafia groups relate to differences between the groups. Women affiliated with the Sicilian Cosa Nostra are traditionally considered to be loyal and subordinate wives, daughters, and sisters in the more rural, archaic, ritualistic, and hierarchical structures of Cosa Nostra compared with other mafia groups.

Studies of Calabria's 'Ndrangheta, which shares many organizational features with Cosa Nostra, show that women have become more actively involved in tasks that require skills, education, courage, and independence (Siebert 2007, p. 37; Ingrascì 2007*a*, 2007*b*, 2014). For both exogenous (changes in women's condition in Italian society) and endogenous (changes in the structure of mafia groups) reasons, women in 'Ndrangheta clans acquired significant roles and even some power. Ingrascì (2007*b*) explained how that happened. In the past, they had worked in drug trafficking, in subordinate positions as mules and dealers, and, though rarely, as organizers of drug dealing (as with Maria Serraino, whose story I tell below).

Women seem to play the most important roles in the Camorra (Gribaudi 2010; Allum and Marchi 2018).[8] The Camorra is a network of

---

[7] Women in 'Ndrangheta can cooperate not as official members but in auxiliary roles as "sorelle d'omertà" (Ingrascì 2010, pp. 44–45).

[8] The research was based on analyses of judicial documents and on interviews with 4 of 20 female state witnesses in 2015.

groups with loose affiliation and, at least originally, was an urban phenomenon (Allum 2007; Catino 2020). Other developments and processes
are important: demographic changes (fewer children), the introduction
of maximum-security regimes in prisons for mafia-affiliated prisoners,
and increased seizure and confiscation of assets. A wave of arrests and
convictions during the 1990s opened new roles for women, even if mostly
in subordinate positions. Under the maximum-security prison regimes,
for instance, family visits were less restricted for women. They were more
easily able to have direct contact with imprisoned bosses than were other
mafia members. Camorra also in those years expanded its activities and
became active in drug markets that required more entrepreneurial skills
(Allum and Marchi 2018, p. 363).

Allum (2007, p. 16) concluded that "women in the city clans appear to
have become more active and visible over the last ten years. When a power
vacuum appears, intelligent women take over, they no longer merely defend their men but become active players." It remains unclear, however,
whether this is genuine female emancipation. Gribaudi (2010) claims that
women in Camorra clans have more autonomy that in other Italian mafia
groups and sometimes play active roles and use violence, including homicide, but that this does not necessarily mean that they exercise real power
without male approval. According to Gribaudi, however, things are changing for younger generations, and it is foreseeable that gender and power
relationships may change.

The participation of women in the Sacra Corona Unita has been much
less studied. Its origins are more recent, and other groups' influence, especially 'Ndrangheta and Camorra, is important. Women became more
involved mostly because of the incarceration of many male bosses. The
prison terms of many Sacra Corona Unita leaders were long, but they
continued to rule the organization from inside, using women visitors as
messengers (Massari and Motta 2007).[9] Women in the Sacra Corona
Unita, however, also played more skilled and partly autonomous roles.
Massari and Motta (2007), on the basis of analyses of judicial documents,
describe women acting as money collectors and managing and organizing

---

[9] Massari and Motta (2007, p. 57) describe women's roles as messengers: "Given their
weekly meetings with relatives in prison, members regularly turned to women to deliver
notes for these relatives and were later promptly informed of the results of conversations
or decisions. Similar dynamics were seen during trials, in which women were almost always
present in the audience, profiting from the chance to communicate with their men. In
some cases, these women's homes became meeting places where matters of special interest
were decided and referred later to the jailed family member."

extortion, drug dealing, and cigarette smuggling. They played these roles mostly because of the need to replace an absent clan boss and following the boss's instructions (Massari and Motta 2007, p. 58).

Occasionally women managed more important activities or acted as administrators of sectors of the criminal market. A few acted as consigliere, making decisions about significant issues affecting the group including conflict resolution, vengeance planning, and distribution of roles and power. However, Sacra Corona Unita exhibits the usual mix of tradition and modernity and exemplifies the ambiguous and complex roles that women play in mafia groups.

b. Roles That Women Perform in Mafia Groups: From Private, in the Shade Activities to the "Lady Bosses."   The variety of roles that women perform has been analyzed in great detail, mostly on the basis of judicial materials and interviews with women offenders. Many of these roles are essential to the functioning and survival of the organization but are not necessarily criminal in nature.

Dino (2007, p. 75) distinguishes among social, family, communication, and education roles and shows that women are both victims and perpetrators of "vendetta trasversali," or symbolic instruments used to counteract police control and judicial authorities. Considering these roles, and taking account of social, demographic, geographical, and criminological factors, Dino built a typology of women in mafia organizations: traditional wives who satisfy stereotyped expectations, women who are active participants in the organization, women who show a high degree of independence and autonomy and sometime oppose the mafia clan, women who are companions and lovers, and women who are mafia victims (Dino 2007, p. 76). Ingrascì (2007*b*) offered a narrower distinction between public and private roles and analyzed in depth the few figures who became strategically important in mafia organizations or who opposed mafia values as state witnesses.

Most women play low visibility but fundamental background roles as "the final links in the chain of the criminal organization" (Ingrasci 2007*a*, p. 50). They help maintain the logistical infrastructure of the group, provide services and assistance in the background, and support the social consensus that mafia groups foster.

Women also play more passive and private roles. Analyzing Cosa Nostra and 'Ndrangheta groups, Ingrascì (2007*b*, 2014) described the importance of family. Mothers play the most important role in cultural transmission of mafia values and codes of behavior, a function made especially important by the frequent absence of males. Mothers transmit and sometimes inculcate mafia values and proper gender roles. Pizzini-Gambetta (1999) showed the significant role of women, particularly in the past, in providing emotional support to men, acculturating children into mafia values, and keeping the family functioning within the values and lifestyles of the mafia codes.

Ingrascì (2007*b*, p. 11) argues that these behaviors illustrate successful operation of differential association theory, because value transmission occurs in a private setting over a long period and starts early in life. Not only nurturing and care taking are involved. Mafia values include a culture of violence that women transmit and protect, including the "pedagogy of vendetta" (Ingrascì 2014, p. 65). Women inculcate and reinforce the importance of reacting violently to other clans' attacks. Women keep memories of wrongs alive and routinely perpetuate the narrative of violence and the rituals of "vendetta" (Ingrascì 2007*b*, p. 25; see also Varese 2017, p. 126). Women are thus important figures in the chains of bloody murders that occur in mafia organizations, particularly during clan wars. This role is mostly performed in domestic settings, through conversations with relatives and friends; everyday violence dominates and shapes the lives of these women.

Mafia organizations use arranged and forced marriages to maintain power and control, strengthen networks based on blood ties, enlarge the size of the "cosca," and even celebrate a peace after a conflict among different clans (Ingrascì 2014, p. 67). Women in organized marriages are usually passive objects (Ingrascì 2007*b*, p. 42). A rigid code of honor, based on control and violence, permeates the lives of many women involved in mafia groups; they are controlled not only by their men but also, when the men are absent, by the clan. Many cases of missing women turn out to involve women who were killed for breaking the code of honor (e.g., by committing adultery).

These archaic practices and cultural codes exist alongside other less passive features of women's lives. Participation in criminal activities, sometimes in leading positions, has not been unusual. Occasionally women have been acknowledged as "sorelle d'omertà," a role that is not comparable to that of a male affiliate.[10] In any case, women who reach high positions are

---

[10] That women are not allowed to become formal members of mafia groups (not just Italian ones), a process of ritual initiation, is the main reason why Varese (2017) doubts that women play full roles as active members.

rare. It is questionable whether they really exercise independent agency and power.

Ingrascì (2007*a*, 2007*b*, 2014), Siebert (2007), and Dino (2010) have offered case studies of women who appeared to be true bosses. The most famous is Maria Serraino, whose role was described in detail in witnesses' testimony and in investigative materials related to the Giovine-Serraino 'Ndrangheta clan, analyzed in depth by Ingrascì (2007*a*, 2007*b*). The clan moved from Calabria in the 1960s to a neighborhood of Milan that became its headquarters.[11] Connections with relatives and affiliated clans in Calabria remained active. The clan in Milan established a significant European network that was active mostly in transnational drug trafficking. Maria Serraino appeared not to be acting as a temporary replacement for a missing male but to be involved in decision making and in leading roles at the transnational level, activities for which, including murder, she was sentenced to life imprisonment.

Other women in the clan included her daughter-in-law and her granddaughter, Marisa di Giovine, who grew up in England with an English mother in a nonmafia family but moved to Milan to work with her father. Rita Di Giovine, Maria Serraino's oldest daughter, became a state's witness after she was arrested; it is from her interviews that we learned about her clan and the condition of women in it.

Journalistic accounts made these women visible to a larger public; the press referred to them as the "Mafia rosa" (pink mafia). The sensationalization expresses a traditional way to interpret female delinquency: following an old idea by Lombroso, women who engage in crime are "more criminal" than is normal. Emphasis on these "lady bosses," compared with the stereotype of the invisible, passive wife, exacerbates the dualism through which female crime has often been interpreted (Ingrascì 2007*b*, p. 100). However, even in these cases, women were allowed to play those roles only when they did not challenge traditional mafia values. "The underworld code requires that the woman, even when she shows a clear tal-

---

[11] 'Ndrangheta has spread more in recent decades than other Italian mafia groups into nontraditional mafia areas including northern Italy and elsewhere in Europe. On the mobility of mafia, see Varese (2011) and Calderoni et al. (2016). There is almost no research on how dispersion of Italian mafia groups affected female involvement in criminal activity. For an exception, see Allum (2016). However, there is evidence that internalization of illegal business required a change in the traditional structure of the organizations and contributed to more significant involvement of women in less passive roles.

ent as a leader, is always acting alongside a man" (Ingrascì 2007*b*, p. 71).

c. *Emancipation, Pseudo-Emancipation, or Persistent Inequality?*   The variety of roles women play in mafia groups brings us back to the core issue in analyzing women in organized crime. Are these new roles evidence of real power in criminal organizations and of women's liberation in the underworld, or are traditional gender roles replicated in new, more opaque forms? For sure, the extent and visibility of women in mafia groups have increased as a consequence of greater participation by women and more punitive judicial attitudes (Ingrascì 2014, p. 64).

Maria Serraino highlights ambiguous aspects of the emancipation hypothesis. Interviews with her daughter Rita by Ingrasci (2007*b*) shed light on these powerful female figures. Serraino always needed male approval for her actions and was repeatedly beaten by her husband. Rita was repeatedly raped by her brother beginning when she was nine. Her account confirms that even powerful women in an 'Ndrangheta clan experience everyday violence; that their leadership roles are consequences of crises, not the rule; and that often they were given those roles only because their activities would be less scrutinized by the police than those of men (Ingrascì 2007*a*, p. 51). In the end, even in a mafia group in which women sometimes play apparently remarkable roles, it is difficult to find evidence of meaningful emancipation or liberation.

Ingrascì (2007*a*, p. 52) refers to pseudo-liberation in a world dominated by men and their values. Female power is usually provisional even when women successfully participate in criminal activities such as extortion that involve violence and intimidation (Principato and Dino 1997; Ingrascì 2007*b*).

Other scholars write of "feminization" in the case of Camorra, denying that a real process of internal emancipation is occurring (Zaccaria 2010). Some describe temporary delegation of power, a term first proposed by Principato and Dino (1997) and subsequently used widely in studies of women in mafia groups. Still others remain skeptical about roles women play. Pizzini-Gambetta (2009) and Varese (2017) argue that women in mafia groups never "administer" the use of violence, are always subordinate, and are allowed to participate only because of family ties.

Allum and Marchi (2018, p. 367) argue that use of the word emancipation, even when modified by "pseudo" or "ambiguous," is misleading: "Despite their apparent sentimental independence and professional ascent, a more attentive look at the processes of female involvement in the Camorra reveals some elements that point in the opposite direction, unveiling a deeply rooted male-centered and male-dominated mentality which seems to persist at the heart of the whole criminal system" (p. 368).

Women in Camorra, Allum and Marchi (2018, p. 375) write, despite having seemingly more unconventional lifestyles and despite the extent of their involvement in mafia activities including violence, are involved only as a "reserve army," as "soldiers on standby." The reality is not emancipation but only the use of "human resources for the clan" (p. 377); it is irreconcilable with a liberation hypothesis.

Similarly, Gribaudi (2010), who analyzes the roles of women in Camorra groups, including those who commit homicides and acquire some autonomy, concludes that emancipation is not the right word to describe the conditions of women still in between modernity and tradition. Similarly, Fiandaca (2007, p. 4) asked, "Are we in a real sense dealing here with a form of expressive emancipation in a passage from cultural tradition to modernity? Or is this a form of 'partial,' 'incomplete,' or 'apparent' emancipation characterized by a persistent hybridization between tradition and modernity?" This is a recurring and still open question concerning women in organized criminal organizations. Mafia organizations, their family-based structures, their rigid social control (also on men), and the narrow worlds in which lives are constrained do not justify description of the conditions of these women's lives as "emancipated" (Siebert 2010).

d. Women Who Leave.   Italian law permits remarkably milder sentences for informers and offers a protection program that includes the possibility of starting a new life under a new identity. These have proven to be powerful tools against Italian mafias. Desistance or withdrawal from a mafia group is not easy, however, because of high risks of retaliation. Many state witnesses and relatives of witnesses have been attacked or killed.

Women in mafia organizations sometimes support their partners' decisions to cooperate with the judiciary. Women sometimes play a role in persuading their men to cooperate. Support by wives or partners is essential in helping men deal with challenges and complexities of living a clandestine life (protected by the state) and build a new identity. Brazilian Maria Cristina De Almedia Guimaraes, wife of the well-known former mafia boss Tommaso Buscetta, is an example. Her support was indispensable to his cooperation (Ingrascì 2007b, pp. 140–41).

A remarkable number of women have left their mafia families and become state witnesses. They do so for diverse reasons. Some cooperate not because of a transformative process of redemption but to reaffirm a core mafia value: vengeance. This sometimes happens after a male family member, usually a husband or partner, sometimes a son, has been killed by a rival group. These women express their roles as protectors of the values of the clan and cooperate only to achieve vengeance they cannot otherwise obtain.

Other women, described by Ingrascì (2014) as "agents of change," experience a transformative process that leads them to become state witnesses. Female emancipation, challenges to mafia culture and violence expressed by antimafia associations, and reactions of civil society have helped women leave the clans and enter into protection programs. The numbers are small but are increasing gradually.

This is a difficult process for already vulnerable women. Some, persuaded by family members to stop cooperating and leave the protection program, end up being killed or committing suicide. Only a few women have successfully navigated the cooperation and protection processes and achieved new lives (Ingrascì 2014, p. 76).

Concerns about children provide reasons both to leave the mafias and to remain (Dino 2010), but there are others. Leaving an organized crime group is risky. Many women are unable to accept the risks and use other coping mechanisms and survival techniques within the family to protect themselves and their children.

The decision to cooperate often results from realization of a need to escape the violence and control of the family and the clan. Those cases reflect an emancipatory process associated with an interior change of perspective, often provoked by the killing of a loved one. It is not the wish for vengeance that animates such women, but the need to escape from fear and everyday violence. These women choose innovation over continuity. "Women who collaborate demonstrate their ability to capitalize on the emancipatory influence acknowledged by the whole of society, being agents of change on two levels: one of self-determination and the other of transmission" (Ingrasci 2014, p. 79) of a different model of being a woman.

Emancipation is easier for women who were never seriously involved in their men's criminal activities or whose natal family was not part of a mafia clan (as is true of some women who support their men's decisions to cooperate). Sometimes the decision to cooperate is a first step in a long and risky process that results in true emancipation and initiation of a new life.

Becoming a *pentita* is harder for women than for men. "In a situation marked by dependency, becoming a protagonist demands a special effort, an even greater effort. Acting for oneself in the first person has, in these cases, to be invented from scratch; there are no tradition or cultural models, there are no examples to emulate, no known paths to follow" (Siebert 1996, p. 87). Becoming a state witness is not a normal aspect of desistance from crime but an extreme one. It requires fundamental changes and abandonment of one's identity and implies complex psychological dynamics (Cayli 2016).

These women are often anxious to talk to researchers. Their stories provide incredibly rich source materials.

B. Women in Organized Illegal Markets

Organized crime encompasses a wide variety of criminal behavior engaged in by groups in systematic and more or less structured ways. Definitions and delineations among different criminal activities of organized crime groups have always been difficult to specify, as have borders between legal and illegal markets. Globalization and the spread of neoliberal policies have blurred the traditional "distinction between organized crime groups violating the law and deviating from conformity, and legal business allegedly complying with official rules" (Vande Walle 2002, p. 279). This has contributed to conceptualization of a new organized crime category, transnational crime, which embraces a variety of collective criminal behaviors, sometimes defined as "transit crimes." They include human trafficking, human smuggling, drug trafficking, fraud, and money laundering (Kleemans, Kruisbergen, and Kouwenberg 2014).

The transnational character of much organized crime has helped shed light on roles and functions of women but poses new challenges to traditional and feminist criminological theories. "Today, organized crime is increasingly transnational and the role of women should be analyzed specifically in regard to transnational flows, new markets, products, and clients, and international migrations" (Siegel 2014, p. 57).

A comparative approach, a gender perspective, and a qualitative and interdisciplinary methodology are especially likely to be fruitful in understanding women's involvement in transnational organized crime. Local peculiarities and specific contexts must also be taken into consideration; there are significant differences in women's involvement across countries and cultures.

Although transnational organized crime includes a wide range of criminal enterprises, I discuss women's involvement only in specific illegal markets: human trafficking, smuggling, and drug trafficking. Many studies of the role and presence of women in drug trafficking, however, focus on national markets that operate in an organized way but mostly or only at the local level.

1. *Human Trafficking.* Human trafficking is one of the "fastest growing criminal enterprises" (Blank 2013, p. 55). Women are involved in diverse ways as offenders and as victims, in particular in trafficking for sexual exploitation. Most research on women focuses on them as victims, and only in recent years have their roles as offenders begun to receive attention.

At the international level, and notwithstanding the low reliability of cross-national studies based on national arrest and conviction data, women seem to be involved at higher rates as offenders in human trafficking than in other types of transnational crime (Broad 2015). The United Nations Office on Drugs and Crime (UNODC) reported that women investigated for trafficking in persons, in 2016, were 31 percent, and that 38 percent were convicted (UNODC 2018, p. 35). Numbers are particularly high in the Balkans, above all in Moldova, Romania, Ukraine, and Bosnia and Herzegovina. In some of these countries, Surtees (2008) found that starting from 2004, the majority of recruiters were female; the same was true in African regions. Dutch Prosecution Service data for 2011–15 show that 17 percent of people suspected of human trafficking were women, with higher percentages in some periods and in trafficking for sexual exploitation (Wijkman and Kleemans 2019). The data from these two sources are not comparable for geographical, definitional, and methodological reasons, but they show that women's involvement as human trafficking offenders is substantial.

Trafficking is "viewed as a process, involving recruitment, transportation between countries or within one country, and control in the place of destination" (Blank 2013, p. 58). Women are involved in almost all these stages. They seem to be especially successful in some key activities such as bookkeeping, money laundering, and above all recruiting, which requires persuasive skills, and victims tend to trust women more than men (Surtees 2008, p. 45; Beare 2010, p. 49).

Beare (2010, p. 50), drawing on a Europol report, describes more detailed roles: providing false or counterfeit identity and travel documents; corruption of law enforcement officers or other civil servants; management of "safe houses"; working as pimps; ownership or management of premises or properties where victims are exploited such as bars, nightclubs, brothels, factories, hotels, construction sites, and farms; collection, delivery, and distribution of the profits of trafficking; money laundering; and management of assets and crime proceeds.

These activities vary between countries and with the types of organization involved. Human trafficking provides a wide range of seemingly gender-neutral criminal activities for women, but most studies show that women do not play leading roles. Responsibility for the organization of the criminal enterprises and control of gains mostly remain male business (UNODC 2014, 2016).

National studies show the same results, with a few exceptions I discuss below. Wijkman and Kleemans (2019) mostly confirm that female offenders play low-level roles in the Netherlands (housing victims, controlling victims, exploiting, confiscating documents and passports). However, this could be misleading and result at least partly from defense lawyers' efforts to minimize women's roles in order to increase their chances of acquittal.[12] An earlier, more limited study of female traffickers in the United Kingdom provided somewhat similar results concerning women's involvement at lower levels (Broad 2015).[13] Thus, while human trafficking presents criminal opportunities for women worldwide, more in some areas than in others, it appears to be uncommon for women to acquire leading roles.

This may be different in some places including Ghana, Nigeria, and some parts of the Balkans. Women from Nigeria and Ghana seem to have achieved significant positions in organization and management of prostitution and human trafficking, particularly when they act as "madams" who control the transit process (Siegel and de Blank 2010; Hübschele 2014).

Arsovska and Begum (2014) studied West African and Balkan women involved in a variety of transnational organized crime activities on the basis of a "multicultural feminist perspective." Their findings challenge competing stereotypes of the weak and subordinated victim and the "femme fatale." The multicultural emphasis assumes that places have specific

[12] The study is based on Dutch Prosecution Office files of women over 18 years old who were a suspect and convicted of human trafficking during 1991 to 2016. The files do not give full accounts of individuals' behavior and motivations.

[13] The study relies on quantitative data on females convicted of human trafficking from 2004 to 2008, augmented by a qualitative analysis.

features and peculiarities that include the history of the country or area from which women come. The study, based on existing literature, international reports, and police files, looked at Nigerian and Ghanaian women working as bosses in human trafficking for sexual exploitation and at two groups of Balkan women, one Slavic and one based mostly in Albania and Bosnia.

The Nigerian women were independent agents who possessed substantial autonomy. So did the Slavic Balkan women who were typically of higher social status than the Albanian and Bosnian women who occupied less powerful roles in the same market. Compared with other Balkan countries, Albania and Bosnia have stronger patriarchal cultures and traditional patterns of deeper female subordination. Arsovska and Begum (2014, p. 106) concluded that "it is impossible to utilize one theory of female criminality to explain the variety of trends" and that each analysis needs to be context-specific.

Lo Iacono (2014) studied the mobility of Nigerian women in the Italian sex market and found that roles of victims and perpetrators were intertwined. There was no clear dichotomy. Female Nigerian offenders in human trafficking for sexual exploitation often earlier had been victims.

McCarthy (2019), who studied women in human trafficking in Russia, likewise argues that both a gender perspective and empirical analyses of the context are necessary to overcome traditional stereotypes. She found that female Russian traffickers could be successful as organizers or co-organizers (and not necessarily with male partners) of human trafficking for sex, labor, children, and human organs.

There is scholarly disagreement about the autonomy of women in human trafficking markets, but findings are more consistent about reasons why women become engaged. Most are from deprived backgrounds and became involved through family or kinship networks. Poverty and blocked opportunity seem to be important worldwide, as do kinship networks and previous or current relationships with men involved in the illegal market. Wijkman and Kleemans (2019) summarized motivations: being afraid of male co-offenders' reactions, need and willingness to cooperate with a partner, and becoming an offender in order to cease being a victim. Thus, only some of the reasons for becoming involved in human trafficking are similar for men and women (poverty and blocked opportunities in their country); others are gender-specific.

These studies shed light on an important issue concerning women in organized crime generally: the often blurred boundaries between victims and perpetrators. Women who become perpetrators often have earlier been victims. Becoming a perpetrator sometimes offers escape from being sexually victimized and abused (Broad 2015). Surtees's (2008) study in the Balkans offers further evidence of these intertwined roles for women, showing that some female recruiters were unaware of the risks of exploitation for the recruited women, or were "former or current trafficking victims who were obliged by their traffickers to return home and recruit other women, often under the scrutiny of people working for the trafficker to ensure compliance and prevent escape" (p. 44).

2. *Human Smuggling.* Human trafficking and human smuggling overlap, but neither sexual exploitation nor mafia involvement is normally an element of human smuggling (Campana 2020). Sometimes, however, when smuggled persons are not allowed to move freely on reaching their destinations or when they have financial problems, they become trafficking victims (Blank 2013).

There are fewer studies on female involvement in human smuggling than in human trafficking, even though a pivotal study in the development of a gender perspective on women in organized crime involved smuggling. Following Steffensmeier's (1983) observation that the organizational context is fundamental to understanding women's involvement in organized crime, and adopting a gender perspective that emphasizes the market's organizational structure, Zhang, Chin, and Miller (2007) investigated Chinese human smuggling through 129 interviews, including 23 with participating women.

Particular features of the market facilitated women's involvement and helped them achieve leadership positions. One was that clients tended to rely upon women more than on men because smuggling was not locally viewed as a crime but as a sort of social service. Helping someone migrate was seen as a service to the community, and women were more comfortable providing a service than they might have been doing something seen as antisocial. Community acceptance functioned as a form of neutralization

Other factors affected women's involvement, including Chinese cultural norms that support women's work in the labor market, and increases in divorce rates and women's consequent needs to support themselves, sometimes by illegal means (Shen and Antonopoulos 2016). Family relationships were the most common factor that led women to enter this illegal world, together with needs for money and pursuit of independence and excitement. Shen and Antonopoulos concluded that gender stratification was limited and that women played important roles in a predominantly male illegal activity and were involved in a variety of tasks, and not only in less powerful and more marginal capacities.

Kleemans, Kruisbergen, and Kouwenberg (2014) tested Zhang et al.'s gendered market hypothesis and could not confirm it in other contexts, such as human trafficking for sexual exploitation, fraud, and money laundering. They examined a wider range of criminal activities categorized as organized crime, using files and data from the Dutch Organized Crime Monitor.[14] They found that involvement of women in organized crime activities was more a matter of networks and trust than of blocked opportunities, and was related to complexity and transnationality. Complexity requires more individual skills and individual access. Social embeddedness and "brokerage" (the capacity to serve as "bridges" among isolated networks) may help explain when and under what conditions women play a role.

The hypothesis that particular markets are gender-specific was not confirmed. Women were involved in a variety of activities (mostly low-level but also sometimes in leading positions) and in different markets. Their involvement was more "a question of (individual) capacity and individual access" and was better explained by social embeddedness and brokerage (Kleemans, Kruisbergen, and Kouwenberg 2014, p. 28). A study of Nigerian madams working not in smuggling but in human trafficking for sexual exploitation also showed that brokerage capacity, networks, and relational systems at the transnational level help make women more successful (Mancuso 2014). However, the literature is small and the findings are best described as suggestive. More especially qualitative research is needed.

3. *Drug Trafficking.* Theoretical controversies concerning human trafficking and smuggling recur in studies of the role of women in drug trafficking nationally and transnationally. Most attention centers on women's roles either as leaders with full agency or as support players in a mostly male business. Differently from human trafficking and smuggling, however, there is a fair amount of drug market research based on female offenders' accounts of their experiences.

The reasons women start careers in the drug market are partly the same as men's and partly different. For women from deprived backgrounds, needs for money and access to drugs for personal consumption are

---

[14] Data refer to 247 women investigated for activities, mostly "transit crimes," in organized groups. They constituted 11 percent of all people involved.

important. Beare (2010, p. 57) found that women involved in drug trafficking in Canada were mostly nonwhite, socially marginalized, and in
desperate need of income. Economic needs led them to become involved.
Other reasons are more gender-specific. For instance, Fagan (1994, 1995)
found that drug selling, when it generated enough income, enabled
women to avoid working as prostitutes.

The gender stratification that characterizes organized crime markets
generally tends to be replicated in local and transnational drug trade markets. Most research concludes that women usually play less powerful
roles than men and perform less important activities. Women are often
considered to be unreliable, weak, and unable to deal with the code of
the street.

Women in drug smuggling often work as "mules" and take high risks
for very low rewards (Boyd 2006). They almost never play important organizational roles or make independent decisions, their status is low, and
they are more often a victim than an independent agent (Fagan 1994;
Maher and Daly 1996; Denton and O'Malley 1999). Maher (1997), using
an intersectionality perspective, showed that gender inequality was reproduced in the street drug market, limiting women's opportunities and
placing them in disadvantaged positions compared with men. She also
showed, however, that female lawbreakers were not always passive victims of male domination.

An increasing number of studies show that in some circumstances, and
varying with characteristics of the market, some women perform active
roles in drug trafficking and acquire more leading positions, and not only
because they are friends or partners of men. Not all drug markets are the
same. Denton and O'Malley (1999, p. 528), in a study of female drug
dealers in Melbourne, found that the more fragmented, smaller, and locally based the market, the greater the likelihood that women occupied
leading positions. Other factors associated with women's success included
their reputations, their social networks, support from families and friends,
personal skill, and a "business acumen" (p. 528). Women seemed to suffer
less discrimination in smaller markets in which they operated as capable
agents and where they could use their female resources and skills, not only
to survive, but to acquire some independence. They attract less police attention than do men and can survive better in the illegal world (Denton
and O'Malley 1999; Denton 2001).

Recent studies emphasize that women can play important roles in drug
trafficking criminal organizations. More complex, organized, and trans-

national markets may be more susceptible to greater female involvement in autonomous and independent roles (Siegel 2014). Some women described in the literature acquired legendary auras and apparently dominated illegal drug markets and managed violence. Examples, such as Griselda Blanco ("the cocaine cowgirl"), leader of a successful drug market between Miami and Medellin (Smith 2013), and similar figures in other markets, have been cited to illustrate that women can operate successfully in drug trafficking (Siegel 2014, pp. 54–55; Martín 2015) and should be able to do so in other illegal markets.

Fleetwood's (2014) qualitative study on drug mules provides rich and especially well documented evidence of the independent roles women, under some circumstances, can play in international drug trafficking. This study shows that small, flexible, and temporary groups, based on connections among the people involved, either by kinship, friendship, or ethnic networks, allow women to be active agents and not just passive victims.

Anderson (2005), studying dimensions of women's power in illegal drug markets, proposed a new theoretical framework to help understand their positions. She analyzed four core activities that women routinely perform in drug-dealing organizations (housing and sustenance, purchasing drugs, subsidizing male dependency, and participating in drug sales). She demonstrated that women are sometimes powerful actors in the drug world and that their activities are crucial, although often misunderstood. What is important, she says, is how the roles women play in the organizations are interpreted.

Anderson (2005, pp. 372–73) calls for rejection of the dominant narrative of women as victims and passive actors and urges that "empowerment" (defined as the ability and competence to influence and achieve desired outcomes) and "agency" (defined as the ability to benefit others as well as the self, and in terms of actions that bring about these outcomes) can help give visibility to their roles. This reconceptualization is conceived not only in relations of dominance and control, but also as a "competency and ability to achieve desired ends" that "empowers" women in this context (Anderson 2005, p. 372).

This work raises interesting issues about "supportive roles." A supportive role, in a gendered perspective that gives values to female skills and competencies, is not marginal and could be as powerful as a decision-making position. In any case, supportive roles are fundamental for survival of an organization; without them organizations could not function and survive (Anderson 2005).

Grundetjern and Sandberg (2012), drawing on life stories of convicted female drug dealers, demonstrate that women can use creative strategies and try to "transcend a marginal position" (p. 633).[15] Smartness and female skills can help women obtain successful entrepreneurial roles: "being a woman can even be an advantage" (Grundetjern and Sandberg 2012, p. 623). Even if men dominate this world, women find ways to survive and gain visibility and respect. Strategies for coping with their marginal positions are mostly based on assuming and replicating male values.

Grundetjern and Sandberg (2012) try to find a third alternative that incorporates both the "traditional victim approach and the contemporary empowering approach to female drug dealers" (p. 624). They focus on "street capital," which "points to the importance of early socialization and the practical rationality involved when people start dealing illegal drugs" and "also develops a middle position between individual agency and structural constraints, which is essential to understand the position of female dealers" (p. 625). Street capital is easier for males to accumulate than for females, who need to develop strategies to survive the imbalance.

Holligan and McLean (2019), in a similar study, studied women in a drug market in west Scotland through an intersectionality lens. They emphasize how changes in urban informal economies after postindustrialization affect these practices. They conclude, however, that there is no hope of "liberation" for women in this world and that their subjugation to overarching violent masculinity remains strong. This resembles some findings about the roles of women in gangs.[16]

The most recent literature argues against generalization, in order to avoid stereotypical representations of women in the drug market either as poor victims or as successful operators working in the shadow of powerful male drug dealers. Most important, however, is attention to the context, its history and culture, and roles performed.

Campbell's (2008) study of female drug smugglers on the American-Mexican border sheds light on the roles women play in a market shaped by a deeply patriarchal and violent culture. Even in this context, women play a variety of roles: a few who are freely involved and exercise agency,

[15] Grundetjern and Sandberg (2012, p. 626) single out four strategies: desexualization, violent posture, emotional detachment (self-identification with male values, attitudes, and behaviors), and service-mindedness (a more gender-neutral role of "entrepreneur" or "seller").

[16] As in this case, the study of women in the drug market often relates to women's activities in gangs.

who acquire power and become models for others; middle-level women who succeed but do not experience real empowerment; and women in marginal roles, associated with low-level male smugglers, who are the most victimized. In general, this world is dominated by males; abuse and violence are common, above all for middle- and low-level women. Chances to operate freely and independently are few and occasional (Campbell 2008).

III. Conclusion

Reinterpretations of conventional theories of crime through a gender perspective often describe the female offender as a woman who is "sexually abused by a stepfather or other male relative; runs away from home to escape from the abuse; engages in illegal activities as a survival strategy; comes into contact with other males who either foster or demand further involvement in illegal activities, including prostitution; may self-medicate with drugs and/or alcohol to cope with the abuse and other demoralizing experiences she has encountered on the street, including violence from a male partner" (Giordano, Deines, and Cernkovich 2006, p. 22).

In this essay, I characterize the criminal experience of women in organized crime groups somewhat differently. Some things, such as the common experience of sexual abuse before or while participating in criminal groups, may be the same. This is the most common characteristic of women who participate in organized crime groups, from gangs and drug dealing to human trafficking and mafia groups. Some women enter into criminal groups mostly as a survival strategy. This may be commonplace in drug trafficking and street gangs, but it is not for other forms of organized crime, particularly for women involved in mafia groups because of family connections.

Kinship and love relationships are fundamental to understanding female involvement in organized crime. This seems to be true for human trafficking, smuggling, and participation in street or drug gangs, and it is the rule for involvement in Italian mafia groups. The case of Marisa di Giovine, Maria Serraino's granddaughter, is illuminating. Despite having grown up in England, completely apart from a mafia environment, she chose to return to Italy when she was 18 and to enter the clan run by her grandmother and father (Ingrascì 2007*b*). This shows not only the power of kinship but also how seductive and attractive organized crime's promises of a glamorous and rich life can be.

Siegel (2014) discusses other interesting case studies such as Nigerian "madams" who made money in the sex industry, demonstrated their success in their home communities, and became role models for other women. The allure of easy money, jewels, expensive cars, and other status symbols can lead young women, not differently from young men, to dream of a different and better life. Understanding of how these successful role models are conveyed and how they influence other women's criminal choices can draw on traditional concepts of cultural goals and limited opportunity, but would benefit from insights from cultural criminology and from analyses of the power of representations of crime engagement as a path to a glamorous and exciting life (Siegel 2014, p. 63).

Another understudied subject that requires attention is the relationship between women and violence in organized criminal groups. According to Pizzini-Gambetta (2009, pp. 270–71), "as long as women need to delegate violence I doubt that matriarchy will replace patriarchy in mafia or camorra groups since violence and command cannot be parted in that industry. When competition among Camorra families strikes, weapons count more than networking abilities."

Studies of women in mafia groups show, however, that women sometimes (if temporarily) replace men in leadership roles and achieve the power to command violence and killings. In one case, described by Gribaudi (2010), women belonging to two Camorra clans in conflict organized and carried out a shooting in which four women of the other clan were killed, and one was seriously injured. This is, however, quite unusual. Women exercise their (small) fraction of power differently than men do, and the capacity occasionally to use violence does not necessarily mean real empowerment. Studies of how women in Italian mafia groups perform violence, for instance in keeping the narrative of violence alive and engaging in the "pedagogy of vendetta," demonstrate this gender difference (Ingrascì 2007b, 2014; Varese 2017). Violence, in mafia cultural codes, also means threats and not only real physical violence.

Violence may be less important in other forms of organized crime. Female drug dealers studied by Denton and O'Malley in Melbourne seldom needed to use violence, either because it was unnecessary or because they could be persuasive in other ways.[17] This and similar studies show three important things about relations between women and violence: first, use

---

[17] The same happens for recruiters in human trafficking or smuggling, as the studies I discussed show.

of violence depends on the characteristics of the market; second, women "may operate effectively [in a drug market] without conforming to male-centered visions of what is needed in the business" (Denton and O'Malley 1999, p. 521); and third, women seldom use violence but use other forms of intimidation. This resembles the female Chinese smugglers studied by Zhang and colleagues who avoided violence not because of unwillingness or inability, but because their activity implied different techniques. In short, adopting a gender perspective to understand women's violent behavior in organized crime implies a need to reinterpret violence not only as replication of male behavior but as a product of different socialization processes and of personal experience of victimization.

Another subject that needs fuller investigation is how the condition of being both victims and perpetrators of violence affects women in organized crime. Studies of gangs and drug-dealing groups have explored this in depth, but we need to know more about how growing up in a violent environment affects women's lives, particularly in mafias and in transnational forms of organized crime.

Women in mafia groups, gangs, and illegal drug markets are often exposed to sexual violence and intimate partner abuse. These women, like most of their men, also experience violence in the community, and particularly in communities dominated by mafia groups in which violence permeates everyday life. Few studies[18] have explored how this exposure to violence affects women's violent behavior in organized crime. Findings in other fields, such as Ayuero and Burbano de Lara's (2012) on the "violence in chains" that characterizes the lives of children and adults in deprived Argentinian barrios, offer a useful theoretical framework for conceptualizing violence in more thoughtful ways.

Other issues deserve attention. One concerns desistance from involvement in organized crime. The milieu shapes desistance processes in distinctive ways, because networks (sometime family networks) are involved. Desistance requires not only withdrawal from criminal activities but often breaking a kinship network that may react hostilely or violently, and abandoning a whole life experience. There is a literature that explores female desistance from mafia and gang involvement, but studies of desistance from organized crime (e.g., Bovenkerk 2011) are gender-neutral.

---

[18] Siebert (2007, p. 25) mentions how women experience violence in their surrounding environment and proposes an analogy to living in times of war.

Other important relevant issues are unexplored, unclear, or controversial. The role of globalization processes has been explored only scantily, mostly in studies of human trafficking and smuggling or transnational gangs. How globalization processes affect female offending and whether its influence is gender-neutral or gender-specific remains unclear. Moore (2007), who analyzed women in gangs in the context of globalization processes and in the economic, cultural, and social crisis that globalization provokes, raised interesting theoretical issues, but they were not based on empirical research findings.

We need more case studies, for more countries, and for different kinds of organized crime to understand how globalization affects the experiences of women. For drug trafficking, it would be important to understand how new online markets influence the involvement of women. More broadly, how will this restructuring of illegal markets, which implies moving away from "the code of the street" and its violence, affect female offending.

A related question is how women are affected by movement of mafia groups from their original areas to nontraditional ones. Of the cases I discussed, only Maria Serraino achieved a leading position in a mafia group that moved to northern Italy. Do local conditions in a new area reshape women's participation, or are their roles not influenced by the operational context?

Finally, studies on women in organized crime would benefit from emphasis on masculinity and male values, considering how significant they are in these contexts, and particularly in criminal organizations such as mafia groups and gangs.

Three takeaways: First, the gender perspective on gender relations, gender characteristics of markets, and the distinctiveness of female experience in organized crime have provided critical and fundamental insights. Second, this perspective challenges traditional distinctions between victims and perpetrators and conceptualizations of criminal activity. Concepts of agency and rational choice are challenged. Women's experience in almost all forms of organized crime shows that traditional roles may be blurred; some women are simultaneously victims and perpetrators; modernity and tradition often coexist. The variety of functions women perform shows that they can participate in criminal activities without taking action, simply by supporting and reinforcing background conditions without which the criminal activity cannot survive. Third, the emancipation hypothesis was definitively wrong. Emancipation may help explain why women in organized crime sometimes play more important roles, but gender inequalities tend to be replicated and sometimes amplified for women in criminal organizations. This does not mean that women are only passive and invisible agents. Women can be seen to be performing important roles when a gendered framework of analysis is adopted and when female subjectivity is taken into account.

REFERENCES

Adler, Frida. 1975. *Sisters in Crime. The Rise of the New Female Criminal.* New York: McGraw-Hill.

Allen, Hilary. 1987 *Justice Unbalanced: Gender, Psychiatry and Judicial Decisions.* Milton Keynes: Open University Press.

Allum, Felia. 2016. *The Invisible Camorra: Neapolitan Crime Families across Europe.* Itaca, NY: Cornell University Press.

Allum, Felia. 2007. "Doing It for Themselves or Standing In for Their Men? Women in the Neapolitan Camorra (1950–2003)." In *Women and the Mafia. Female Roles in Organized Crime Structures*, edited by Giovanni Fiandaca. New York: Springer.

Allum, Felia, and Irene Marchi. 2018. "Analyzing the Role of Women in Italian Mafias: The Case of the Neapolitan Camorra." *Qualitative Sociology* 41:361–80.

Anderson, Tammy L. 2005. "Dimensions of Women's Power in the Illicit Drug Economy." *Theoretical Criminology* 9(4):371–400.

Arsovska, Jan, and Popi Begum. 2014. "From West Africa to the Balkans: Exploring Women's Roles in Transnational Organized Crime." *Trends in Organized Crime* 17:89–109.

Ayuero, Javier, and Augustín Burbano de Lara. 2012. "In a Harm's Way at the Urban Margins." *Ethnography* 13(4):531–57.

Batchelor, Jennifer. 2009. "Girls, Gangs and Violence: Assessing the Evidence." *Probation Journal* 56(4):399–414.

Beare, Margaret. 2010. "Women and Organized Crime." Unpublished report. Ottawa, Canada: Research and National Coordination Organized Crime Division, Public Safety.

Blank, Jennifer K. 2013. "Human Trafficking, Migration and Gender: An Interdisciplinary Approach." In *The Other People: Interdisciplinary Perspectives on Migration*, edited by Meg Wilkes Karaker. New York: Palgrave Macmillan.

Bottcher, Jean. 2001. "Social Practices of Gender: How Gender Relates to Delinquency in Everyday Lives of High-Risk Youth." *Criminology* 39:893–932.

Bovenkerk, Frank. 2011. "On Leaving Criminal Organizations." *Crime, Law and Social Change* 55(4):261–76.

Boyd, Susan. 2006. "Representation of Women in the Drug Trade." In *Criminalizing Women: Gender and (In)justice in Neo-liberal Times*, edited by Gillian Balfour and Elizabeth Comack. Black Point, Canada: Fernwood.

Broad, Rose. 2015. "'A Vile and Violent Thing': Female Traffickers and The Criminal Justice Response." *British Journal of Criminology* 55:1058–75.

Broidy, Lisa, and Robert Agnew. 1997. "Gender and Crime: A General Strain Theory Perspective." *Journal of Research in Crime and Delinquency* 34(3):275–306.

Brotherton, David C. 2008. "Beyond Social Reproduction: Bringing Resistance Back in Gang Theory." *Theoretical Criminology* 12(1):55–77.

Brotherton, David C., and Luis Barrios. 2004. *The Almighty Latin King and Queen Nation: Street Politics and the Transformation of a New York Gang*. New York: Columbia University Press.

Burman, Michele, and Loraine Gelsthorpe. 2017. "Feminist Criminology: Inequalities, Powerlessness, and Justice." In *The Oxford Handbook of Criminology*, 6th ed., edited by Alison Libeling, Shadd Maruna, and Leslie McAra. Oxford: Oxford University Press.

Cain, Maureen. 1990. "Towards Transgression: New Directions in Feminist Criminology." *International Journal of The Sociology of Law* 18:1–18.

Calderoni, Francesco, Giulia Berlusconi, Lorella Garofalo, Luca Giommoni, and Federica Sarno. 2016. "The Italian Mafias in the World: A Systematic Assessment of the Mobility of Criminal Groups." *European Journal of Criminology* 13(4):413–33.

Campana, Paolo. 2020. "Human Smuggling: Structure and Mechanisms." In *Organizing Crime: Mafias, Markets, and Networks*, edited by Michael Tonry and Peter Reuter. Chicago: Chicago University Press.

Campbell, Ann. 1984. *The Girls in the Gang*. Cambridge, MA: Basil Blackwell.

———. 1990. "Female Participation in Gangs." In *Gangs in America*, edited by C. Ronald Huff. Newbury Park, CA: Sage.

Campbell, Howard. 2008. "Female Drug Smugglers on the US-Mexico Border: Gender, Crime, and Empowerment." *Anthropological Quarterly* 81(1):233–67.

Catino, Maurizio. 2020. "Italian Organized Crime since 1950." In *Organizing Crime: Mafias, Markets, and Networks*, edited by Michael Tonry and Peter Reuter. Chicago: Chicago University Press.

Cayli, Baris. 2016. "Codes of Commitment to Crime and Resistance: Determining Social and Cultural Factors over the Behaviors of Italian Mafia Women." *Deviant Behavior* 37(1):1–15.

Chesney-Lind, Meda. 1989. "Girls' Crime and Women's Place: Toward a Feminist Model of Female Delinquency." *Crime & Delinquency* 35:5–29.

Chesney-Lind, Meda, and Randall Shelden. 2004. *Girls, Delinquency and Juvenile Justice*. Belmont, CA: Thompson/Wadsworth.

Connell, Raewyn. 1995. *Masculinities*. Cambridge: Polity.

Daly, Kathleen. 1989. "Gender and Varieties of White-Collar Crime." *Criminology* 27(4):769–94.

De Coster, Stacy, and Rena Cornell Zito. 2010. "Gender and General Strain Theory: The Gendering and Emotional Experiences of Expressions." *Journal of Contemporary Criminal Justice* 26:224–45.

De Coster, Stacy, Karen Heimer, and Samantha R. Cumley. 2013. "Gender and Theory of Delinquency." In *The Oxford Handbook of Criminological Theories*, edited by Francis T. Cullen and Pamela Wilcox. Oxford: Oxford University Press.

Denton, Barbara. 2001. *Dealing: Women in the Drug Economy*. Sydney: University of New South Wales Press.

Denton, Barbara, and Pat O'Malley. 1999. "Gender, Trust, and Business: Women Drug Dealers in the Illicit Economy." *British Journal of Criminology* 39(4):513–30.

Dino, Alessandra. 2007. "Symbolic Domination and Active Power: Female Roles in Criminal Organizations." In *Women and the Mafia: Female Roles in Organized Crime Structures*, edited by Giovanni Fiandaca. New York: Springer.

Dino, Alessandra. 2010. "Narrazioni al femminile di Cosa Nostra." In *Donne di Mafia*. Vol. 67, *Meridiana: Rivista di storia e scienze sociali*. Rome: Viella.

Fagan, Jeffrey. 1994. "Women and Drugs Revisited: Female Participation in the Cocaine Economy." *Journal of Drug Issues* 24(2):179–225.

———. 1995. "Women's Careers in Drug Use and Drug Selling." *Current Perspectives on Aging and the Life Cycle* 4:155–90.

Fiandaca, Giovanni. 2007. "Introduction." In *Women in the Mafia: Female Roles in Organized Crime Structures*, edited by Giovanni Fiandaca. New York: Springer.

Fleetwood, Jennifer. 2014. *Drug Mules: Women in the International Cocaine Trade*. London: Palgrave Macmillan.

Franko Aas, Katja. 2013. *Globalization and Crime*. London: Sage.

Gilligan, Carol. 1982. *In a Different Voice: Psychological Theory and Women's Development*. Cambridge, MA: Harvard University Press.

Giordano, Peggy, Jill A. Deines, and Stephen A. Cernkovich. 2006. "In and Out of Crime: A Life Course Perspective on Girls' Delinquency." In *Gender and Crime: Patterns of Victimization and Offending*, edited by Karen Heimer and Candace Kruttschnitt. New York: New York University Press.

Gottfredson, Michael, and Travis Hirschi. 1990. *A General Theory of Crime*. Stanford, CA: Stanford University Press.

Gribaudi, Gabriella. 2010. "Donne di camorra e identità di genere." In *Donne di Mafia*. Vol. 67, *Meridiana: Rivista di storia e scienze sociali*. Rome: Viella.

Grundetjern, Heidi, and Sveinung Sandberg. 2012. "Dealing With a Gendered Economy: Female Drug Dealers and Street Capital." *European Journal of Criminology* 9(6):621–35.

Hagan, John, John Simpson, and A. R. Gillis. 1987. "Class in the Household: A Power-Control Theory of Gender and Delinquency." *American Journal of Sociology* 92(4):788–816.

Hagedorn, John. 1998. "Gang Violence in the Post-Industrial Era." In *Youth Violence*, edited by Michael Tonry. Chicago: Chicago University Press.

Hagedorn, John. 2005. "The Global Impact of Gangs." *Journal of Contemporary Criminal Justice* 21(2):153–59.

Heidensohn, Frances. 1996. *Women and Crime*, 2nd ed. Basingstoke: Macmillan.

———, ed. 2006. *Gender and Justice: New Concepts and Approaches*. Cullompton: Willan.

Heidensohn, Frances, and Lorraine Gelsthorpe. 2007. "Gender and Crime." In *The Oxford Handbook of Criminology*, edited by Mike Maguire, Rod Morgan, and Robert Reiner. Oxford: Oxford University Press.

Heimer, Karen, and Stacy De Coster. 1999. "The Gendering of Violent Delinquency." *Criminology* 37:277–318.

Heimer, Karen, and Candace Kruttschnitt, eds. 2006. *Gender and Crime: Patterns of Victimization and Offending*. New York: New York University Press.

Hirschi, Travis. 1969. *Causes of Delinquency*. Berkeley: California University Press.

Holligan, Chris, and Robert McLean. 2019. "Keeping It in the Family: Intersectionality and 'Class A' Drug Dealing by Females in the West of Scotland." *Societies* 9(22):1–12.

Hübschle, Annette. 2014. "Of Bogus Hunters, Queenpins and Mules: The Varied Roles of Women in Transnational Organized Crime in Southern Africa." *Trends in Organized Crime* 17:31–51.

Kleemans, Edward R., Edwin W. Kruisbergen , and Ruud F. Kouwenberg. 2014. "Women, Brokerage, and Transnational Organized Crime: Empirical Results from the Dutch Organized Crime Monitor." *Trends in Organized Crime* 17:16–30.

Joe, Karen A., and Meda Chesney-Lind. 1995. "'Just Every Mother's Angel': An Analysis of Gender and Ethnic Variations in Youth Gang Membership." *Gender and Society* 9:408–31.

Ingrascì, Ombretta. 2007*a*. "Women in the 'Ndrangheta: The Serraino-Di Giovine Case." In *Women and the Mafia. Female Roles in Organized Crime Structures*, edited by Giovanni Fiandaca. New York: Springer.

———. 2007*b*. *Donne d'onore: Storie di mafia al femminile*. Milan: Bruno Mondadori.

———. 2010. "Donne, 'ndrangheta, 'ndrine. Gli spazi delle donne nelle fonti giudiziarie." In *Donne di Mafia*. Vol. 67, *Meridiana: Rivista di storia e scienze sociali*. Rome: Viella.

———. 2014. "'Ndrangheta Women in Contemporary Italy: Between Change and Continuity." In *The 'Ndrangheta and Sacra Corona Unita: The History, Organization, and Operations of Two Unknown Mafia Groups*, edited by Nicletta Serenata. New York: Springer.

Lavin, Mónica. 2003. "Las Damas del Narco." In *Viento Rojo: Diez Historias del Narco en Mexico*. Mexico City: Plaza Janes.

Lo Iacono, Eva. 2014. "Victims, Sex Workers, and Perpetrators: Gray Areas in the Trafficking of Nigerian Women." *Trends in Organized Crime* 17:110–28.

Maher, Lisa. 1997. *Sexed Work: Gender, Race, and Resistance in a Brooklyn Drug Market*. Oxford: Clarendon.

Maher, Lisa, and Kathleen Daly. 1996. "Women in the Street Level Drug Economy: Continuity or Change." *Criminology* 34(4):465–91.

Mancuso, Marina. 2014. "Not All Madams Have a Central Role: Analysis of a Nigerian Sex Trafficking Network." *Trends in Organized Crime* 17:66–88.

Martín, Yolanda C. 2015. "The 'Queen of Heroin': Gender, Drug Dealing, and Zero-Tolerance Policies in the Dominican Republic." *Dialectical Anthropology* 39(4):443–51.

Massari, Monica, and Cataldo Motta. 2007. "Women in the Sacra Corona Unita." In *Women and the Mafia: Female Roles in Organized Crime Structures*, edited by Giovanni Fiandaca. New York: Springer.

McCarthy, Laureen. 2019. "A Gendered Perspective on Human Trafficking Perpetrators: Evidence from Russia." *Journal of Human Trafficking*. https://doi.org/10.1080/23322705.2019.1571302.

Messerschmidt, James W. 1986. *Capitalism, Patriarchy, and Crime: Toward a Socialist Feminist Criminology*. Totowa, NJ: Rowman & Littlefield.

———. 1993. *Masculinities and Crime: Critique and Reconceptualization of Theory*. Lanham, MD: Rowman & Littlefield.

Miller, Jody. 1998. "Gender and Victimization Risk among Young Women in Gangs." *Journal of Research in Crime and Delinquency* 35(4):429–53.

Miller, Jody. 2001. *One of the Guys: Girls, Gangs, and Gender*. New York: Oxford University Press.

———. 2002. "Young Women in Street Gangs: Risk Factors, Delinquency, and Victimization Risks." In *Responding to Gangs. Evaluation and Research*, edited by Winnie Reed and Scott Decker. National Institute of Justice Report.

Moore, Joan. 2007. "Female Gangs: Gender and Globalization." In *Gangs in the Global City: Alternatives to Traditional Criminology*, edited by John M. Hagedorn. Urbana: University of Illinois Press.

Moore, Joan, and M. John Hagedorn. 2001. "Female Gangs: A Focus on Research." *Juvenile Justice Bulletin*. Washington, DC: US Department of Justice.

Morrissey, Belinda. 2003. *When Women Kill: Questions of Agency and Subjectivity*. London: Routledge.

Passas, Nikos. 2000. "Global Anomie, Dysnomie, and Economic Crimes: Hidden Consequences of Neoliberalism and Globalization in Russia and around the World." *Social Justice* 27(2):16–44.

Pitch, Tamar. 2002. "Le differenze di genere." In *La Criminalità in Italia*, edited by Marzio Barbagli and Uberto Gatti. Bologna: Il Mulino.

Pizzini-Gambetta, Valeria. 1999. "Gender Norms in the Sicilian Mafia 1945–1986." In *Gender and Crime in Modern Europe*, edited by Meg Arnot and Cornelie Usborne. London: Routledge.

Pizzini-Gambetta, Valeria. 2009. "Women in Gomorrah." *Global Crime* 10(3):267–71.

Pollak, Otto. 1961. *The Criminality of Women*. New York: Barnes.

Principato, Teresa. 2007. "The Reasoning behind This Research: An Evaluation of the Results." In *Women and the Mafia: Female Roles in Organized Crime Structures*, edited by Giovanni Fiandaca. New York: Springer.

Principato, Teresa, and Alessandra Dino. 1997. *Mafia Donna: Le vestali del sacro e dell'onore*. Palermo: Flaccovio.

Rawlinson, Patricia. 2000. "Mafia, Methodology, and 'Alien Culture.'" In *Doing Research on Crime and Justice*, edited by Roy D. King Emma Wincup. New York: Oxford University Press.

Ruggiero, Vincenzo. 1996. *Organized and Corporate Crime in Europe: Offers That Can't Be Refused*. Dartmouth: Aldershot.

Savona, Ernesto, and Gioacchino Natoli. 2007. "Women and Other Mafia-Type Criminal Organizations." In *Women and the Mafia: Female Roles in Organized Crime Structures*, edited by Giovanni Fiandaca. New York: Springer.

Schwartz, Jennifer, and Darrell Steffensmeier. 2008. "The Nature of Female Offending: Patterns and Explanation." In *Female Offenders: Critical Perspectives and Effective Interventions*, edited by Ruth T. Zaplin. Boston: Jones & Bartlett.

Shelden, Randall G., Sharon K. Tracy, and William B. Brown. 2013. *Youth Gangs in American Society*. Belmont, CA: Wadsworth.

Shen, Anqi, and Georgios A. Antonopoulos. 2016. "Women in Criminal Markets Activities: Findings from a Study in China." In *Illegal Entrepreneurship, Organized Crime, and Social Control: Essays in Honor of Professor Dick Hobbs*, edited by Georgios A. Antonopoulos. New York: Springer.

Siebert, Renate. 1996. *Secrets of Life and Deaths: Women and the Mafia*. London: Verso.

Siebert, Renate. 2007. "Mafia Women: The Affirmation of a Female Pseudo-Subject—The Case of the 'Ndrangheta." In *Women and the Mafia. Female Roles in Organized Crime Structures*, edited by Giovanni Fiandaca. New York: Springer.

———. 2010. "Tendenze e prospettive." In *Donne di Mafia*. Vol. 67, *Meridiana: Rivista di storia e scienze sociali*. Rome: Viella.

Siegel, Dina. 2014. "Women in Transnational Organized Crime." *Trends in Organized Crime* 17:52–65.

Siegel, Dina, and Sylvia de Blank. 2010. "Women Who Traffick Women: The Role of Women in Human Trafficking Networks; The Dutch Case." *Global Crime* 11(4):436–77.

Simon, Rita J. 1975. *Women and Crime*. Lexington, MA: Lexington Books.

Simpson, Sally. 1989. "Feminist Theory, Crime and Justice." *Criminology* 27(4):605–31.

Smart, Carole. 1976. *Women, Crime and Criminology: A Feminist Critique*. Routledge: London.

Smith, Jennie Erin. 2013. "Cocaine Cowgirl: The Outrageous Life and Mysterious Death of Griselda Blanco, the Godmother of Medellín." https://news.cision.com/byliner/r/byliner-publishes-cocaine-cowgirl–the-outrageous-life-and-mysterious-death-of-griselda-blanco-the-,c9471689.

Steffensmeier, Darrell J. 1980. "Sex Differences in Patterns of Adult Crime, 1965–1978." *Social Forces* 58:1080–108.

———. 1983. "Organization Properties and Sex-Segregation in the Underworld: Building a Sociological Theory of Sex Differences in Crime." *Social Forces* 61(4):1010–32.

Steffensmeier, Darrell J., and Emilie Allan. 1996. "Gender and Crime: Toward a Gendered Theory of Female Offending." *Annual Review of Sociology* 22:459–87.

Steffensmeier, Darrell J., and Robert M. Terry. 1986. "Institutional Sexism in the Underworld: A View from the Inside." *Sociological Inquiry* 56(3):304–23.

Surtees, Rebecca. 2008. "Traffickers and Trafficking in Southern and Eastern Europe: Considering the Other Side of Human Trafficking." *European Journal of Criminology* 5(1):39–68.

Sutherland, Edwin J. 1947. *Principles of Criminology*. Chicago: J. B. Lippincott.

Taylor, Carl S. 1993. *Girls, Gangs, Women and Drugs*. East Lansing: Michigan State University Press.

UNODC (United Nations Office on Drugs and Crime). 2014. *Global Report on Trafficking in Persons*. Vienna: United Nations Publications.

———. 2016. *Global Report on Trafficking in Persons*. Vienna: United Nations Publications.

———. 2018. *Global Report on Trafficking in Persons 2018*. Vienna: United Nations.

Vande Walle, Gudrun. 2002. "'The Collar Makes the Difference': Masculine Criminology and Its Refusal to Recognise Markets as Criminogenic." *Crime, Law and Social Change* 37:277–91.

Varese, Federico. 2011. *Mafie in movimento—Come il crimine organizzato conquista nuovi territori*. Turin: Einaudi.

Varese, Federico. 2017. *Mafia Life: Love, Death, and Making Money at the Heart of Organized Crime*. London: Profile Books.

Vigil, James D. 2008. "Female Gang Members from East Los Angeles." *International Journal of Social Inquiry* 1(1):47–74.

Wijkman, Miriam, and Edward Kleemans. 2019. "Female Offenders of Human Trafficking and Sexual Exploitation." *Crime, Law, and Social Change* 72(1):53–72.

Yllö, Kersti. 2005. "Through a Feminist Lens: Gender, Diversity, and Violence: Extending the Feminist Framework." In *Current Controversy on Family Violence*, edited by Donileen R. Loseke, Richard G. Gelles, and Mary M. Cavanaugh. Thousand Oaks, CA: Sage

Zaccaria, Anna Maria. 2010. "L'emergenza rosa. Dati e suggestioni sulle donne di camorra." In *Donne di Mafia*. Vol. 67, *Meridiana: Rivista di storia e scienze sociali*. Rome: Viella.

Zhang, Sheldon X., Ko-Lin Chin, and Jody Miller. 2007. "Women's Participation in Chinese Transnational Human Smuggling: A Gendered Market Perspective." *Criminology* 45(3):699–733.

Edward Kleemans and Vere van Koppen

Organized Crime and Criminal Careers

ABSTRACT

Widely accepted findings in developmental and life-course criminology cannot be extended to criminal careers of organized crime offenders. While most offenders begin offending at a young age, criminal careers in organized crime are generally characterized by a late onset typically characterized by relatively serious offending. Different patterns exist for different groups, including early starters, adult-onset offenders, and offenders with no previous judicial contacts, but all studies find a significant share of adult-onset offenders. Social relationships, including family, friendship, and work ties, are importantly related to becoming involved in organized crime. Involvement mechanisms are diverse; both conventional and criminal capital are important. Children of organized crime offenders have a high risk of intergenerational continuity of crime. Factors that promote desistance for most offenders, such as employment, sometimes have different meanings for organized crime participants, as some occupations provide criminal opportunities and some work settings foster offender convergence. Widely used concepts such as specialization and desistance are less applicable because of the distinctive nature of organized crime offenses and careers. The most urgent issue for future research is to incorporate the roles of co-offenders into analyses of individual criminal careers.

In 1988, Albert J. Reiss Jr. published an inspiring essay in *Crime and Justice* about co-offending and criminal careers. He concluded that research

Electronically published February 6, 2020

Edward Kleemans is a full professor in criminology and Vere van Koppen is an assistant professor in criminology in the School of Criminology, Faculty of Law, Vrije Universiteit Amsterdam. We thank the editors of this volume, Michael Tonry and Peter Reuter, the participants of the Bologna workshop (May 2019), and two anonymous reviewers for valuable comments on earlier drafts of this essay.

on co-offending "is disproportionately concentrated on juveniles and has focused almost exclusively on documenting how pervasive it is and on speculating on its role in the etiology of delinquency. The etiological questions therefore remain murky, and the consequences of groups for criminal career development remain unexplored. We need, therefore, to devote far more attention to detailed studies of offending careers and to pay special attention to co-offending in those careers, treating each individual's career in terms of its intersections with others" (Reiss 1988, p. 165).

Knowledge about criminal careers has increased significantly since 1988. Primarily through analyzing large longitudinal data sets, the emerging field of developmental and life-course criminology has contributed significantly to our knowledge about the start, continuation, escalation, and ending of criminal careers (e.g., Blumstein et al. 1986; Farrington 2003; Piquero, Farrington, and Blumstein 2003; Blokland, Nagin, and Nieuwbeerta 2005; Jolliffe et al. 2017; Farrington, Lazemian, and Piquero 2019; Weisburd et al. 2020). The building and analysis of large longitudinal data sets were accompanied by major methodological innovations, such as the development of group-based trajectory modeling (Nagin and Land 1993; Nagin 2005; Nagin and Odgers 2010) and the growth and institutionalization of a large research community with its own professional associations and scientific journals. In Lakatos's (1970) terms, developmental and life-course criminology is one of the most successful criminological "research programs" of recent decades and has solved many "scientific puzzles" through sustained and combined research efforts.

Research programs share several basic assumptions and methodologies (e.g., Farrington 2003). This shared focus, however, may sometimes result in implicit disregard of aspects of and theoretical explanations for the phenomena studied. One of the strong points of developmental and life-course criminology, analyses of large longitudinal data sets, may have resulted in a focus primarily on young offenders, high-volume crime, and the individual characteristics of offenders. Older offenders can be studied in longitudinal studies only after passage of considerable time and only if they can be traced and are willing to cooperate with additional data collection sweeps. Follow-up periods, however, typically are short, additional data sweeps are costly, and sample attrition, self-selection, and an (unintended) neglect of adult criminal careers are recurring problems. It is also difficult to include more serious offenders and offenders who start their careers late in life ("adult onset") in these samples. Finally, large longitudinal data sets have serious problems in taking account of the social contexts of crime and of co-offending, as it is difficult enough to keep track of dynamic and stable characteristics of individuals over time. Although some of these characteristics may be related to the wider social context of individuals (e.g., criminal friends, partners, school, or work), each individual is basically treated as an "atom" without further consideration of the "molecules" they are part of or the "chemical reactions" taking place in their social or criminal context.

For research on organized crime, co-offending is the heart of the matter. It is also a defining characteristic. Although there is continuing debate on how organized crime should be defined, many definitions revolve around co-offending and criminal groups (the "who") and criminal activities with serious harm for society (the "what"; e.g., Paoli and Vander Beken 2014; Von Lampe 2016). Many writers agree that at least two or three co-offenders need to cooperate for a prolonged period in some (serious) criminal activities, but there are divergences between wide and narrow definitions. They differ regarding views on the structure of co-offending (from stable, pyramidal organizations to flexible criminal networks with fluid co-offending relationships or even single criminal "entrepreneurs") and on the types of criminal activities that qualify as "organized crime."

Many definitions of organized crime are available (see, e.g., Paoli 2002; Finckenauer 2005; Hagan 2006). Although most contain similar dimensions, including co-offending or groups and activities causing serious harm to society, precise definitions vary. This also applies to the studies discussed in this essay. The United Nations Convention against Transnational Organized Crime defined an organized criminal group as "a structured group of three or more persons, existing for a period of time and acting in concert with the aim of committing one or more serious crimes or offenses, in order to obtain, directly or indirectly, a financial or other material benefit" (United Nations Office on Drugs and Crime 2004, p. 5). Most Dutch studies adopt Fijnaut's definition: organized crime groups "primarily focus on illegal profit, systematically commit crimes that adversely affect society, and are capable of effectively shielding their activities, in particular by being willing to use physical violence or eliminate individuals by way of corruption" (Fijnaut et al. 1998, pp. 26–27). Many studies of Italian and Italian-American mafia groups use narrower definitions, placing more restrictions on the structure of cooperation or types of criminal activities.

When reviewing theoretical and empirical research on organized crime, it is important to remember that the phenomena studied have shifted over time. Studies in the 1960s tended to focus on rural Italian mafia groups and Italian-American mafia families in large cities such as New York (e.g., Cressey 1969). The 1970s and 1980s were marked by the rise of "transnational organized crime," involving large-scale drug trafficking, international fraud, human trafficking, and human smuggling (Kleemans 2014*b*, p. 32). The mafia studies relate primarily to the control of territories or economic sectors by criminal groups; criminal careers, therefore, are often conceptualized within the context of the power and career structures of these criminal organizations. The subject of the more recent work can be characterized as "transit crime" (Kleemans 2007).

The major business of many organized crime groups—particularly in democratic and industrialized Western countries—involves international illegal activities: drug trafficking, smuggling illegal immigrants, human trafficking for sexual exploitation, arms trafficking, trafficking in stolen vehicles, and other transnational illegal activities such as money laundering and tax evasion (e.g., cigarette smuggling and customs fraud). Transit crime involves making money through international illegal trade rather than through protection, extortion, or the abuse of monopoly power ("racketeering"). The structure of cooperation is far more diverse, and offenders often cooperate in smaller groups and in flexible and fluid criminal networks (e.g., Bouchard and Morselli 2014; Bouchard 2020). Co-offenders and criminal networks remain important but are far less restrictive than in careers in criminal organizations that control geographical areas or economic sectors.

Stable, durable criminal organizations such as Sicilian mafia groups, Japanese Yakuza groups, Hong Kong Triads, and Russian mafia groups exist or have existed in recent history (e.g., Gambetta 1993; Paoli 2003; Varese 2011, 2014). However, in many democratic and industrialized Western countries such organizations no longer exist or are the exception rather than the rule. The main reason for this is that illicit markets, often international—often in combination with strong government and effective law enforcement—hinder the emergence of large and stable criminal organizations. Many of the traditional mafias originated during periods before the emergence of large and profitable international illegal markets. The prime example is the boom in international narcotics trade in the 1970s and 1980s.

In addition to stable and durable criminal organizations often involved in racketeering and more flexible criminal networks often involved in transit crime, organized crime scholars also study local illegal markets, involving drugs, prostitution, illegal gambling, and loan-sharking (e.g., Reuter 1983). It can be debated whether all these activities qualify as organized crime in terms of either structures of cooperation or scales of associated harms. Territorial control may be an element of these activities, particularly in relation to local drug markets, and there may be considerable overlap with gang research (e.g., Decker, Melde, and Pyrooz 2013; Pyrooz et al. 2016). These activities are often portrayed in literature from North America as organized crime, but they are often far removed from the core of the organized crime literature. This is true both of structures of cooperation (smaller and more fluid networks) and the scale of activities (in terms of harm, e.g., including lower-level drug dealing and less serious and more local criminal activities).

This essay is structured around the three most important lines of research on criminal careers in organized crime. Their systematic study has increased significantly since the publication of "Criminal Careers and Social Opportunity Structure" (Kleemans and De Poot 2008), which presented quantitative and qualitative analyses of a large population of organized crime offenders active in the Netherlands. Several quantitative studies of larger populations have since been carried out, basically following the primary lines of developmental and life-course studies on high-volume crime (Savona et al. 2017). These studies were mainly carried out in a small number of countries where large data collections were undertaken: the Netherlands, the United Kingdom, Italy, and Australia. The United States has a proud tradition in gang research, mainly highlighting street and prison gangs (e.g., Decker, Melde, and Pyrooz 2013; Pyrooz et al. 2016). Given, however, that the types of offenses and offenders studied in this literature and the literature itself are mostly separate from the organized crime literature, we exclude gang research. More studies based on qualitative research have been published, often based on autobiographies, biographies, and case studies (Savona et al. 2017; Kemp, Zolghadriha, and Gill 2019). Studies of criminal careers in organized crime have produced three lines of new findings.

The first line studies individual sequences of offending in developmental and life-course criminology and applies this approach to organized crime offenders. As is found among general offender populations, organized crime offenders tend to follow various criminal career patterns and include early onset, late-onset, and first-time offenders. In organized crime studies, however, adult-onset offenders are consistently found to be the largest group. Criminal careers in organized crime are generally characterized by a relatively late onset, in the adult years; juveniles are almost absent. This is an important finding. The very phenomenon of adult onset is often debated or denied (e.g., Sohoni et al. 2014), and, more revealingly, it often involves serious criminal activities rather than minor crimes. Organized crime offenders more often have previous judicial contacts than does the general offender population, and those previous contacts are often far more serious. These quantitative studies show that criminal careers in organized crime are very different from those found in the literature on high-volume crime.

A second line of research focuses on how people become involved in organized crime. Many organized crime activities require both criminal and conventional capital. Since organized crime groups depend on a wide variety of capacities, knowledge, and contacts, individual involvement mechanisms are diverse. Family relationships, other social ties, the "social snowball effect," leisure activities and sidelines, and work ties help explain why individuals engage in criminal groups. Some offenders are deliberately recruited by a criminal group because of their criminal or conventional capital; others have more self-initiating roles. Labor market characteristics illustrate this diversity of involvement mechanisms. Italian mafia groups embedded in disadvantaged areas seem to benefit from the ample availability of unemployed and disadvantaged people. For other types of organized crime, employment in particular occupations may provide opportunities for involvement, and work settings may function as "offender convergence settings."

A third line of research deals with concepts from developmental and life-course criminology such as desistance, specialization, life events, and co-offending that are associated with continuity and discontinuity in criminal careers. Such concepts are less easily applicable to organized crime because they are hard to use or have a different meaning for organized crime offenders and their careers. Theories of desistance, for example, predicting that important life events, such as getting married or obtaining a job, will lead to a decrease in offending, do not apply to organized crime; many organized crime careers start only in later adulthood after the typical age of getting married or starting a job. A concept such as specialization is also less appropriate: what is considered a single offense in high-volume crime (such as a burglary or violent offense) is much more limited in time and space than are organized crime activities, which may last for longer periods and be carried out within the context of a criminal group.

This essay follows these three lines of research on criminal careers in organized crime. Section I discusses various pathways in organized crime and highlights the case of adult onset, drawing on studies in the Netherlands, the United Kingdom, Australia, and Italy and recent research on motorcycle gangs. Section II identifies involvement mechanisms and discusses the roles of social ties, life events, intergenerational transmission, and employment. Section III reviews concepts related to continuity and discontinuity that are widely studied within developmental and life-course criminology and applies them to the study of organized crime. Section IV offers conclusions and proposals for future research.

I. Criminal Careers and Adult Onset

What happens to general findings and received wisdom from developmental and life-course criminology when we study different populations of offenders? Two key findings that have been challenged by research into organized crime relate to the well-known age-crime curve and Moffitt's (1993) dual taxonomy. The age-crime curve describes a steep rise in the prevalence of offending in the early teenage years, reaching a peak between ages 15 and 17 and declining over the rest of the life course (Farrington 1986, 2003; Gottfredson and Hirschi 1990, pp. 124–44). Moffitt's taxonomy partitions the aggregate age-crime curve into a large group of people who engage in crime and antisocial behavior during adolescence ("adolescence-limited offenders") and a small group who are antisocial from an early age and remain active in crime and other forms of antisocial behavior throughout their lives ("life-course persistent offenders"). Moffitt's taxonomy exemplifies theories that seek explanations for criminal careers in early life and stable individual differences. She argues that early problem behavior is an indicator that antisocial and criminal behavior is likely to continue later in life. Such "asymmetrical" theories posit that individual differences between offenders exist from the start or are developed early in life and treat adult onset as an anomaly that does not exist or results from measurement error (cf. Sohoni et al. 2014).

Criminal careers studies have found various developmental trajectories of criminal activity over the life course but focus mainly on young offenders and high-volume crime (Piquero 2008; Farrington, Lazemian, and Piquero 2019). Older offenders are largely absent. Research on criminal careers in organized crime, however, contradicts the idea that crimes committed at advanced ages are usually preceded by an adolescent criminal career. Significant groups of adult-onset offenders have been found in many organized crime studies, older offenders comprise a large part of the study population, and very young offenders are largely absent.

These different findings can easily be explained. High-volume crime, such as property and violent crime, is open to everyone and often requires little expertise, skill, planning, or collaboration. Organized crime poses different requirements (Kleemans and De Poot 2008, p. 75). First, social relations are of great importance, as they provide access to suppliers and clients and create a basic level of trust. The relevance of social relations cannot be overstated in a risky, unregulated environment in which the financial stakes are high and that lacks rules and mechanisms that make legal transactions much easier, such as entering into contracts, paying via the official banking system, and reconciling disagreements via mediation or the courts (Reuter 1983). For these reasons, existing social ties are used or illegal business relationships must be built. Not every potential offender has suitable social ties, and building up these relationships takes time and energy.

Second, not all offenders have access to transnational contacts, and some have this kind of access only later in life. Transnational social ties are often salient, as many types of organized crime involve international smuggling: drug trafficking, smuggling illegal immigrants, human trafficking for sexual exploitation, arms trafficking, trafficking in stolen vehicles, and other transnational illegal activities such as money laundering and tax evasion (e.g., cigarette smuggling, European Union fraud).

Third, both collaborations with co-offenders and ties to licit society are important. Criminal activities are often complex, and more co-offenders are required for their successful execution. Contacts with the licit world are important for transport, money transactions, and shielding activities from the authorities. Contacts with co-offenders are thus needed to provide both "criminal capital" and "conventional capital."

Kleemans and De Poot (2008) used the theoretical concept of "social opportunity structure" to describe social ties that provide access to profitable criminal opportunities.[1] Social opportunity structure is unequally

---

[1] The notion of social opportunity structure combines concepts from differential opportunity structure (Cloward and Ohlin 1960), opportunity theory (Clarke and Felson 1993), and social network theory (e.g., Burt 1992; Morselli 2005).

distributed across the population. Some people have social ties that give them direct access to illegal opportunities. Examples include people with transnational contacts that are needed to connect source countries of narcotics to Western consumer markets, and people whose occupations involve mobility, transport, and logistics. Social opportunity structure is unequally distributed across age. Some younger offenders lack necessary social ties, which partly explains why some become involved in organized crime only at later ages. It also explains "late starters," people without any appreciable criminal history or people who switch from legal occupations to organized crime careers.

To describe the general findings regarding criminal careers in organized crime, we have selected from major quantitative studies in the Netherlands, the United Kingdom, Italy, and Australia.[2] Three important methodological considerations warrant preliminary mention. First, all samples are selective and differ concerning why offenders were included. Cullen (2011) argues that criminological research is dominated by adolescents rather than "real," older offenders. Because organized crime often involves criminal activities later in life that can be discovered only if the police investigate them, police priorities to a large extent influence the populations researchers can study. This may also be true for other types of crime (our position), but concerning organized crime, it is a fundamental issue. Investigative agency priorities may have a larger effect on whether specific activities appear in organized crime data sets than in data sets on high-volume crime. There are no convincing reasons, however, why the risk of arrest (mainly for property and violent crime) should differ very much between adolescent offenders, so investigative agency effects should be less important. It makes little sense to try to generalize findings about organized crime careers to larger populations or to take quantitative findings too literally. Large samples, however, even if not generalizable to other populations, often incorporate large numbers of offenders and diverse criminal activities and may focus attention on underexposed phenomena, different types of offenders, and different types of groups.

Second, quantitative methods reduce criminal activities to data points, limiting capacity to take account of contextual information. Organized crime activities, for example, often span longer periods but are still "data

---

[2] In a systematic review of studies of recruitment into organized crime, Savona et al. (2017) distinguished among quantitative studies (12), mixed-method studies (8), and many qualitative ones (often with small sample sizes). They included gang research and focused on recruitment.

points" in a longitudinal data set reflecting criminal careers. Furthermore, criminal activities can be measured in several ways (e.g., incidents, arrests, prosecutions, convictions) in different studies and may have different meanings for different activities.

The third methodological consideration is that it is more important in studies of organized crime careers to focus on qualitative findings than on differences in quantitative findings. The latter may, to a large extent, result from sample and measurement differences. Within these data sets, however, interesting comparisons can be made.

A. Criminal Careers Research in the Netherlands

Large scale work on criminal careers has been done on the Netherlands, the United Kingdom, Australia, and Italy. We examine these literatures in succession. We also discuss work on outlaw motorcycle gangs.

1. *Criminal Careers, Persisters, and Adult Onset.* Twenty years ago, the Dutch minister of justice promised the parliament to report periodically on organized crime in the country. The Organized Crime Monitor, a systematic, large-scale, and ongoing study into the nature of organized crime, is the result. One hundred eighty criminal investigations have been analyzed. Criminal groups (and investigations targeting groups or networks) come in different shapes and sizes. On average in the Netherlands, 10 to 15 offenders work together, but investigations targeting criminal networks of over 100 offenders also exist. Netherlands criminal groups are generally not characterized by a stable, pyramid-shaped organization. Cooperation takes place in more flexible structures that can be characterized as criminal networks with clusters and cliques. Some are dense and operate locally; others are more fluid and operate internationally. While many Dutch criminal groups are involved in production and trafficking of drugs, the Dutch Organized Crime Monitor also includes groups involved in other illegal activities, including human trafficking, weapons smuggling, organized fraud, and money laundering. The main sources of these data are files of closed Dutch police investigations of criminal groups, often spanning 2 or more years, combined with interviews with experts such as public prosecutors and police investigators (Kleemans 2014a). These empirically rich case studies provide qualitative contextual information about offenders' criminal careers. These data were combined with rap sheets from the Dutch Judicial Documentation System on individual characteristics and official judicial records.

The first large-scale study was based on quantitative and qualitative information about 979 offenders involved in 79 different cases that were analyzed in the context of the Dutch Organized Crime Monitor (Kleemans and De Poot 2008). That study described differences with the general offender population, different types of criminal careers (including a substantial number of adult-onset offenders), and various mechanisms through which offenders become involved in organized crime. Two main conclusions stood out. First, juveniles were almost absent; most offenders were in their 30s, 40s, or 50s, or older. Second, a substantial group of adult-onset offenders was present in the data set: these were offenders with no appreciable criminal history who apparently became involved in crime only later in their lives. This finding proved to be robust in follow-up research, on different criminal activities (drugs, fraud, and other activities) and for different roles in criminal groups (leaders, coordinators, and lower-level offenders; Van Koppen et al. 2010). Follow-up studies in other countries, including the United Kingdom, Australia, and Italy, which we discuss below, confirmed the presence of a substantial group of adult-onset offenders in organized crime. This was unexpected because adult onset is considered to be an anomaly in mainstream criminal career research, let alone concerning more serious forms of crime such as organized crime.

Kleemans and De Poot (2008) analyzed the careers of 66 leaders and "nodal" offenders to find out how their careers had developed. This group consisted of 32 adult-onset offenders and 34 with longer careers. A substantial share of leaders were adult-onset offenders who had switched from legal occupations to organized crime. Among the 32 offenders, 19 had backgrounds in legal trade including import and export; 13 had other prior occupations, including the business sector, the construction industry, assembly, hotels and catering, financial services, and government. Kleemans and De Poot identified three types of adult-onset leaders and nodal offenders: people who moved into criminal activities from legal activities (opportunities arising during day-to-day work, particularly in organized fraud cases); people whose career switches from legal to illegal commodities were motivated by the high profits to be made trading in prohibited commodities such as narcotics; and people who seized on criminal opportunities after experiencing significant life events such as financial setbacks and problematic debt situations.

Kleemans and De Poot (2008) also analyzed the criminal careers of 92 "starters," suspects who had no previous judicial contacts and had not "progressed" from high-volume crime to organized crime. Five involvement mechanisms were identified: deliberate recruitment by criminal groups; social ties and the social snowball effect; work ties; leisure activities and sidelines; and life events, including financial setbacks. We return to this topic in Section II.

The quantitative and qualitative research into adult onset and criminal careers provided a compelling case for taking the apparent anomaly of adult onset seriously and for focusing on more than individual differences and long-term risk factors. Kleemans and De Poot (2008) stressed the importance of "social opportunity structure," social ties that provide access to profitable criminal opportunities. As social opportunity structure is unequally distributed across the population and across age, it might also explain involvement, developments, and success in organized crime.

In follow-up research based on the Dutch Organized Crime Monitor, these analyses were extended to larger populations (Van Koppen et al. 2010; Van der Geest, Van Koppen, and Kleemans 2020; Van Koppen et al. 2019). Comparisons have been made with the general offender population (Van Koppen, De Poot, and Blokland 2010). Several studies have found that certain professions provide opportunities for organized crime activities (Kleemans and Van de Bunt 2008) and have focused on the relationship between work and organized crime (Madarie and Kruisbergen 2020; Van der Geest, Van Koppen, and Kleemans 2020; Van Koppen et al. 2019).

2. *Adult Onset and Different Types of Careers.* A follow-up study by Van Koppen et al. (2010) used a larger data set and more qualitative information about different roles in criminal groups and different criminal activities. A semiparametric group model was used to cluster 854 offenders involved in 120 different organized crime cases into groups with similar developmental trajectories. The most important finding relates to the substantial group of adult-onset offenders (40 percent) and a group without any previous criminal records (19 percent). The other groups were early starters (11 percent) and persisters (30 percent). No earlier trajectory study found such a large share of adult-onset offenders. One possible explanation is that particular roles in criminal groups relate to adult-onset offending, for example, lower-level offenders. Another possibility is that particular types of criminal activities account for adult onset. Organized fraud might, for example, be related primarily to adult onset, while drug trafficking might primarily be related to early starters and persisters.

No clear relationship was found, however, between adult-onset offending and particular roles in criminal groups (e.g., leaders, coordinators, lower-level offenders, others) or particular types of criminal activities such as drug trafficking and organized fraud. Closely similar distributions across trajectory groups were found for each type of criminal activity and each type of role. Adult onset characterized offenders in different roles and involved in different types of crimes. These findings turned out to be quite robust. Although the quantitative findings should not be generalized beyond the analyzed cases, within this data set they are very relevant. The neglected case of adult onset turns out to be not an anomaly but to characterize a substantial share of the studied population.

Because this study was based on official records, the dark number problem might explain the substantial share of adult onset. We can never know whether criminal records accurately reflect all criminal behavior of an individual, and an individual who was first arrested as an adult may have committed undetected crimes as a juvenile. It might be argued that organized crime offenders are more successful in avoiding authorities and more often incorrectly identified as an adult-onset offender.

That argument is unconvincing. Adult onset was systematically found across offenders performing different roles from leader to lowest-level actor and across offenders involved in diverse activities from drug trafficking to organized fraud. That adult onset is real is shown by qualitative life histories in which offenders shift from licit careers and licit occupational backgrounds to organized crime (Kleemans and De Poot 2008). Interviews with imprisoned organized crime offenders also confirm the existence and explanations of an adult onset (Van Koppen and De Poot 2013).

Van der Geest, Van Koppen, and Kleemans (2020) recently replicated these findings, using a larger data set of 1,921 individuals from 180 organized crime cases in the Dutch Organized Crime Monitor. The main focus was on socioeconomic factors such as employment and income (which are discussed below). Offending trajectories were described, including, in contrast to the earlier study, minor offenses dealt with by subdistrict judges. In this large sample, organized crime offenders had their first judicial contact on average at age 27. Compared to the traditional age-crime curve (e.g., Gottfredson and Hirschi 1990), offending stayed relatively high and started dropping to a lower level only at age 50.

3. *Differences with the General Offender Population.* To learn how organized crime offenders differ from the general offender population, Van

Koppen, De Poot, and Blokland (2010) analyzed the careers of 746 organized crime offenders included in 120 analyzed cases from the Dutch Organized Crime Monitor. They used an age-matched comparison group from the general offender population, which means that two offender groups with the same age distribution were compared.

An unexpected finding was that many people in both samples had no judicial contacts before adulthood. However, organized crime offenders more often had previous judicial contacts than the general offenders, and those contacts were far more serious. Organized crime offenders thus differed from general offenders in the seriousness of their initial criminal behavior (instead of age of onset, which for both groups was in their mid-20s). The general findings were robust when distinguishing between drug crimes and organized fraud cases. These findings imply that adult onset is not unique to organized crime offenders but is largely overlooked in much research on high-volume crime populations because of data restrictions and heavy reliance on prospective longitudinal studies. A recent systematic review of prospective longitudinal studies suggests that adult onset is present in these data sets but has been largely neglected (Jolliffe et al. 2017).

B. Criminal Careers Research in the United Kingdom

Francis et al. (2013) analyzed the criminal careers of organized crime offenders in the United Kingdom. Their data came not from criminal investigations but from the Police National Computer (PNC) database, a registry of all offenders sanctioned in England and Wales. Because organized crime offenders are not separately identified in the PNC, they selected 4,112 individuals convicted in 2007–10 of offenses "associated with an involvement in organized crime" in terms of crime type, sentence length (a minimum custodial sentence of 3 years), and being sentenced along with at least one co-offender. Francis et al. (2013, p. 15) acknowledge limitations of this complex and indirect selection procedure. The majority of offenders (73 percent) were selected on the basis of a conviction for a drugs-related offense and around 10 percent for having a conviction for a violent offense. Compared with Dutch Organized Crime Monitor data, the sample of "organized crime offenders" is probably more skewed toward high-volume and serious crime. The focus on a minimum custodial sentence of 3 years probably overrepresents recidivists of serious crimes. Similarities in findings for the organized crime offenders and a comparison group of serious crime offenders point in this direction.

The sample was compared to two groups: general offenders and serious crime offenders. The serious crime offenders had received a minimum 3-year custodial sentence between 2007 and 2010 but were not sentenced with a co-offender, and their conviction offense was not among the 185 identified as "likely" or "possibly" related to organized crime. The average age of the organized crime offenders at the time of the conviction for the inclusion offense was 32 years, older than the general offenders but similar to the serious crime offenders. Only 1 percent of organized crime offenders and serious crime offenders were under age 18 at the time of their inclusion offense; this was much lower than for the general offender group (19 percent). Fifty-seven percent of organized crime offenders received their first sanction (court conviction or caution/warning/reprimand) before age 18 and 43 percent at age 18 years or older. Organized crime offenders had more prior sanctions than general offenders (nine compared with three), and serious crime offenders had even more (11).

Analysis of offending frequency by age indicated several routes into organized crime: "Two-thirds of organized crime offenders had offended at a relatively low rate throughout their criminal careers. These included a proportion who had offended very little before adulthood: for example, 1 in 10 did not reach their offending peak until into their 30s and showed no fall in the rate of offending as they got older. Organized crime offenders who followed the more conventional pattern of offending, peaking in late teenage years before rapidly declining, made up less than one in five (18%) of the sample" (Francis et al. 2013, p. 6).

C. Criminal Career Research in Australia

Fuller, Morgan, and Brown (2019) used two intelligence databases (the National Criminal Target List and the National Police Reference System) to create a sample of 2,172 offenders identified by law enforcement as being affiliated with an organized crime group (using a broad definition) and having an Australian criminal history. The majority had their first criminal offense as adults: 25 percent before turning 18, 59 percent at age 20 years or over, 30 percent at age 25 or over, and 10 percent at age 30 years or over. Offending was most common, and remained relatively stable, throughout their 20s and early 30s. Offending frequency gradually increased during this period, as did the seriousness of offenses committed. The findings of a substantial share of adult onset offenders and persistence in offending in the adult years are consistent with the findings from the Netherlands and the United Kingdom. Age at first offense and prevalence of offending varied by crime type. Certain offenses, especially those associated with organized crime, were more common among older offenders (Fuller, Morgan, and Brown 2019, p. 10). For example, those who committed drug offenses tended to be older than those who committed violent or property offenses.

D. *Italian Mafia Groups and Criminal Careers*

Savona et al. (2020) analyzed the criminal careers of Italian mafia members using the unique PROTON Mafia Member data set. It contains information on all individuals who have received final convictions for mafia offenses since the 1980s. The data set includes information on more than 11,000 individuals and 182,000 offenses. The study uses a three-level approach, analyzing the macro-, meso-, and microdimensions of criminal careers. The Italian mafia provides an interesting case for criminal career research, as individual careers are nested within specific mafia families that are part of wider mafia structures (the Sicilian Cosa Nostra, the Neapolitan Camorra, the Calabrian 'Ndrangheta, and the Apulian mafias). These different mafias often have distinctive geographic characteristics and histories.

At the macrolevel, members of the different Italian mafias have different types of criminal trajectories, although significant fractions exhibit late onset and late persistence (Campedelli et al. 2019). At the mesolevel, members of the Sicilian Cosa Nostra, the Neapolitan Camorra, the Calabrian 'Ndrangheta, and the Apulian mafias have very similar patterns, although some distinctive differences emerge. At the microlevel, Italian mafia members commit their first recorded crime, on average, at 25 (median 22). However, entrance into the mafia organization (marked by the first mafia-associated offense) usually occurs later, on average at 34 (median 33). When analyzing differences between individuals with an early or a late entrance into a mafia group (compared to a baseline group), early recruits have fewer years of education and a different criminal profile: they were more versatile in the types of crimes committed before entering the mafia organization and committed less serious offenses (compared to offenders who joined at an "average" age). For late recruits, the opposite pattern was typical (compared to the baseline group).

The authors conclude that violent and versatile offenders with less education tend to enter the mafia groups at younger ages. Offenders are usually recruited by the local mafia group in the province or region of birth.

E. Outlaw Motorcycle Gangs and Criminal Careers

Blokland and Von Lampe (2020) review studies on outlaw motorcycle gangs. Some "motor clubs," particularly in various European countries and Australia, have very high levels of members with criminal records. Some of these clubs or their members are involved in organized crime activities such as drug production, drug trafficking, and extortion. Club activities and other members play significant roles in members' daily lives, raising the questions of whether and how the clubs influence the criminal careers of members. Two recent studies have produced pertinent findings.

Blokland et al. (2019) compared criminal career data of a sample of 601 police-identified Dutch outlaw motorcycle gang members and an age-matched comparison group of 300 non-gang-affiliated motorcycle owners. Dutch outlaw bikers are more often convicted than the average Dutch motorcyclist of minor, more serious, and violent crimes. Criminal careers differed during the juvenile and early adult years, but also—and more so—during the adult years. The results support an "enhancement" hypothesis that combines two effects: selection of crime-prone individuals into motorcycle gangs and facilitation of criminal behavior while there (for a more general review of peer influence and delinquency, see McGloin and Thomas [2019]).

One problem of gang research is that membership is often treated as a binary variable, contrasting those in a gang to those not in a gang, without further differentiation. Such comparisons amplify possible selection effects. A more relevant comparison concerns members of more and less criminal gangs (called "radical" and "conservative" gangs in the motorcycle gangs literature). Van Deuren, Blokland, and Kleemans (2020) used differences in early criminal careers of members of radical and conservative motorcycle gangs to examine their effects on members' adult criminal careers. Using a sample of 2,090 police-identified gang members, they employed quasi-experimental methods (i.e., matching weights) to control for selection bias in order to examine the effect of membership in a radical motorcycle gang on adult crimes, particularly more serious and organized ones. Membership in a radical motorcycle gang was associated with increased offending compared with membership in a conservative one. Members of radical gangs were twice as likely to be involved in organized crimes and were sentenced to prison twice as often. This supports the enhancement hypothesis: gangs select more crime-prone individuals as members, but membership facilitates criminal behavior.

F. Conclusions on Criminal Careers in Organized Crime

Criminal careers in organized crime are different from those that typify the literature on high-volume crime. First, offenders involved in organized crime are generally older, and juveniles are nearly absent. Second, organized crime offenders more often have previous judicial contacts than does the general offender population and for far more serious offenses. Third, criminal careers in organized crime are generally characterized by a relatively late onset (in the adult years); all studies find significant shares of adult-onset offenders. Fourth, criminal career patterns differ for various groups, including early starters, adult-onset offenders, and offenders with no previous judicial contacts. Fifth, differences seem to exist between early starters and adult-onset offenders, particularly regarding education and work as well as criminal profile. Different involvement mechanisms may be at work.

II. Involvement Mechanisms and Recruitment

This section discusses the social embeddedness of organized crime and involvement mechanisms. Specific topics relate to the intergenerational continuity of organized crime and transmission in family structures and the relationship between work and organized crime.

A. Social Embeddedness

Social ties are an essential element in understanding successful involvement in organized crime (Kleemans and Van de Bunt 1999, p. 19). Family and friendship relations and introductions to third parties are important, as they help create a basic level of trust in a risky, unregulated environment. Existing social ties are used or illegal business relationships must be built. Strong social bonds, such as family relationships and marriage, provide a solid basis for trust but may not offer contacts and capabilities that are needed for particular criminal activities. Many organized crime activities need both "criminal capital" and "conventional capital."

Some offenders have strong connections with other offenders (criminal capital) but lack access to people whose conventional jobs, businesses, or specialized knowledge provide access to production locations, storage, (transnational) transport, money transactions, and investments. Many involvement mechanisms relate to social relationships associated with criminal capital or conventional capital.

Kleemans and De Poot (2008) analyzed, in addition to the careers of 66 leaders described earlier, the careers of 92 "starters," offenders who had no prior judicial contacts and who had not "progressed" from high-volume crime to organized crime. They distinguished five involvement mechanisms: deliberate recruitment by criminal groups; social ties and the social snowball effect; work ties; leisure activities and sidelines; and life events, including financial setbacks.

The first mechanism, deliberate recruitment, makes clear that members of existing criminal groups look for potential co-offenders for various reasons. The types of co-offenders needed depend on the nature of the criminal group and the nature of envisaged criminal activities. An organized crime group that produces and transports drugs, for example, may need international truck drivers.

The second mechanism, social ties and the social snowball effect, is a general mechanism with many different, concrete manifestations. It is related to the dynamic nature of many criminal networks and to the transfer of knowledge and contacts. Once individuals become involved in organized crime through social ties, they become less dependent on other people's resources (such as money, knowledge, and contacts) and can attract people from their own social environment (Kleemans and Van de Bunt 1999, p. 33). This social snowball effect differs from traditional views on recruitment, which assume that criminal organizations recruit outsiders to do dirty jobs, who may then climb the organizational ladder by proving their capability. Stable organizations with (some) territorial control exist or have existed in specific areas and periods, so specific circumstances may also influence how people become involved or get "recruited."

The other mechanisms involve kinds of social links that may be forged between potential co-offenders. The third arises in work settings (discussed in Sec. II.C). The fourth relates to leisure activities and locations where people from different social and criminal worlds meet. This may occur in local cafés, shooting clubs, drug outlets, and similar places between people who usually live in different social worlds and do not meet one another in their ordinary daily lives (Kleemans and De Poot 2008, p. 81). The fifth mechanism involves negative life events, such as a financial setback, losing a job, a problematic debt situation, or bankruptcy. This may create or deepen contacts with "generous" moneylenders or "employers."

Savona et al. (2017) produced a systematic review of the social, psychological, and economic factors relating to criminalization and recruitment to organized crime. A practical problem in reviewing these studies is that many focused on the functioning of organized crime groups in general; only some focused on recruitment or on criminal careers of individual offenders. The contexts of these studies vary widely, ranging from mafia groups which control territory to transnational drug trafficking networks and local gangs. Savona and his colleagues nonetheless paint a vivid picture and describe findings for different types of organized crime groups. The main findings relate to social and economic factors; psychological factors play a minor role in their studies. These factors are highly interrelated and sometimes apply more to one type of organized crime group than to others.

The most important factors are consistently shown to be violent attitudes and behavior, criminal background, low economic status, and particular social relations:

> First, violence characterizes OCGs [organized crime groups] activities and is often used to reinforce one's status within the organization. Second, people who turn to OC [organized crime] usually have a significant criminal history and/or a prison background resulting from their proneness to violent and risk-taking behavior. Third, people living in poor and socially disorganized areas experience the lack of access to legitimate means to attain commonly accepted goals. These mechanisms affect individuals' satisfaction and success, promoting the search of illegal alternatives to overcome these difficulties. Fourth, social relations also play a crucial role in the involvement into OCGs. Social proximity and interactions with members of OCGs promote the participation in OC. This includes kinship and other blood ties, allowing to enhance mutual trust and loyalty. (Savona et al. 2017, p. 46)

Savona and his colleagues highlight differences associated with different types of organizations. Many of the studies relate to Italian mafia groups and gangs. They often rely on kinship and blood ties and use initiation rituals to reinforce their group identity. These rituals and cultural factors also apply to some gangs, although we do not think most gangs and their activities qualify as organized crime in terms either of structures of cooperation or the harms their activities cause. For other types of organized crime groups, Savona et al. (2017) stress other factors. Recruitment into drug trafficking organizations is mostly driven by monetary returns. For other types of organization, individuals enter during adulthood "as they develop specialized expertise and social ties with criminals only later in life" (Savona et al. 2017, p. 46).

B. Intergenerational Continuity

Anecdotal evidence from case studies, biographies, and autobiographies shows that the social embeddedness of organized crime has implications for its intergenerational continuity (Savona et al. 2017; Kemp, Zolghadriha, and Gill 2019). Besemer et al. (2017) show in their systematic review and meta-analysis of intergenerational transmission of criminal behavior that a specific focus on organized crime families is often lacking in more general quantitative studies. Several exploratory studies with small samples suggest that children of organized crime offenders are at high risk of intergenerational continuity of involvement (e.g., Sergi 2018; Van Dijk, Kleemans, and Eichelsheim 2019; Spapens and Moors 2019).

Sergi (2018) explored proceedings of the Youth Tribunal of Reggio Calabria in southern Italy aimed at protecting children in families in which one or both parents are investigated for mafia offenses. The study, focusing on sociocultural transmission of 'Ndrangheta culture, shows that the prevention of this transmission has become an essential part of child protection measures. Parental authority can be revoked by the Youth Tribunal. Analysis of case files shows that the tribunal makes explicit connections between parental failures to educate children and the children's risk of becoming involved in deviance and crime.

A recent project in the Netherlands extensively investigated the nature and extent of intergenerational continuity of crime among children of organized crime offenders (Van Dijk, Kleemans, and Eichelsheim 2019). It studied 25 organized crime offenders based in Amsterdam and 48 of their children age 19 or older. Ninety one percent of the 23 sons were known offenders according to police data, 52 percent had committed more than four crimes, and 43 percent had been imprisoned one or more times. Sons had earlier ages of onset than their fathers (sons:

16 years, fathers: 23.5 years). The story with daughters was different. Half had criminal records, primarily for only one minor crime.

A qualitative in-depth analysis was carried out of all members of 14 of the 25 families in police files, justice department files, and child protection service files. Intergenerational transmission seems to be facilitated by mediating risk factors, including the mother's inadequate parenting skills, the father's "notorious" or violent reputation, and deviant social learning. Finally, the results suggest a wider effect of both violence committed outside the house and domestic violence on intergenerational transmission. Violence also appeared in the children's leisure activities (boxing) and in socialization into what is seen as normal behavior. The father's crimes tend to result in a violent reputation for the whole family, which attracted criminal friends and co-offenders for sons and had an adverse effect on child-protection services' access to these families. There seemed to be a "family cycle of multiplying violence and retreating agencies" (Van Dijk, Kleemans, and Eichelsheim 2019, p. 359). Child-protection workers appeared to be hesitant to approach these families and did not use interventions that are normal in less serious cases. The "closed" family systems and use of violence and drugs may be part of a deviant lifestyle and subculture in organized crime families in the Netherlands.

Spapens and Moors (2019) studied seven families in the southern Netherlands that had produced a criminal group leader in at least one generation. The starting point was the generation that produced a criminal leader (based on investigations completed in the second half of the 1990s and the first half of the 2000s); at least three generations were studied. Data were collected from local and regional archives, the population registration database, interviews with practitioners who had been involved with the families, and police files. Most male and female family members in almost every generation had criminal records, but intergenerational transmission of leadership roles had occurred only in two families. Assortative mating appeared to be the explanation: family members selected partners and friends from their own closed and deviant subcultures and seemed to favor those with criminal records. The seven families quickly took advantage of emerging crime markets, particularly the sudden booms in synthetic drug production and indoor cannabis cultivation beginning in the 1990s.

Van Dijk et al. (2019) reported on a large-scale study of intergenerational continuity of crime among children of organized crime offenders, based on a national sample of children of organized crime offenders.

Judicial and police data on 478 convicted organized crime offenders and their children (>16 years) were examined to study offspring's involvement in criminal behavior; factors that might influence that involvement; and the relative risk, compared to a general population comparison group, of intergenerational continuity of offending. Nearly half of the children of organized crime offenders had a criminal record. Sons were significantly more at risk of offending than daughters (59.3 percent vs. 29.8 percent) and committed more serious crimes. The risk of offending seemed to increase strongly with age, which might explain the slightly lower rate of children with criminal records, compared to the pilot study on 25 Amsterdam-based organized crime offenders and their children (of 19 years and older; Van Dijk, Kleemans, and Eichelsheim 2019). Children of female organized crime offenders were at significantly higher risk of offending, compared to children of male organized crime offenders. To examine the relative risk of intergenerational continuity of offending, a comparison was made with a randomly selected group of parents and children from the general population with similar age, gender, and ethnic backgrounds. The results showed that having an organized crime offender as a parent was a strong and significant predictor of offspring offending. Children of convicted organized crime offenders were three times more at risk of criminal behavior in general, and 10 times more at risk of drug-related crime, compared with children in the comparison group. These were higher odds than the odds ratio found by Besemer et al. (2017) in their meta-analysis on intergenerational continuity of general offenses (pooled OR = 2.4).

Children of organized crime offenders seem to be at a higher risk of intergenerational continuity of crime. General explanatory mechanisms include the cycle of deprivation, mediating risk factors (family factors, individual factors, mesofactors), assortative mating, social learning, and self-fulfilling prophecy (police bias; Farrington 2002). The cycle of deprivation does not apply to these children, at least in financial terms; however, deprivation in terms of drug use and other lifestyle characteristics might play a role. As in other studies of intergenerational continuity, mediating risk factors are found on various levels as are social learning and cultural transmission. Van Dijk, Kleemans, and Eichelsheim (2019) suggest that the problematic socialization environment characterized by violent role models, violent conflict resolution styles, and exposure to domestic and other violence may explain the increased relative risk of intergenerational continuity. Processes of assortative mating seem to be strongly present and may be related to the social embeddedness of organized crime activities. Finally, police bias may play a role, as children of organized crime offenders may be more visible and receive more police attention than other children do. By contrast, preventive actions by youth care institutions are hindered by "closed" family systems and their violent reputations.

C. Work

Employment may have diverse effects. Savona et al. (2017) show that mafia groups embedded in disadvantaged areas draw on the ample availability of unemployed and disadvantaged people. For other types of organized crime, employment and particular occupations may provide opportunities for involvement and work settings may function as offender convergence settings (cf. Felson 2006, pp. 98–99). Five studies, based on the Dutch Organized Crime Monitor, have provided interesting insights into the relationship between work and organized crime (Kleemans and Van de Bunt 2008; Van Koppen 2013; Madarie and Kruisbergen 2020; Van der Geest, Van Koppen, and Kleemans 2020; Van Koppen et al. 2019). Research based on police files has also touched on the relationship between work and organized crime (Salinas and Regadera 2016) as have studies based on offender interviews (e.g., Decker and Chapman 2008, pp. 88–113; Van Koppen and De Poot 2013; Wang 2013; May and Bhardwa 2018).

Wang (2013) used information on the criminal careers of 182 incarcerated drug traffickers in the United Kingdom from interviews conducted by the Matrix Knowledge Group (2007). Weak conventional capital (e.g., legitimate employment) seems to be associated with an early onset into trafficking careers. This is triggered by an offer coming from a friend or family member or self-initiation. The level at which offenders entered drug trafficking depended on both criminal capital and conventional capital: "A satisfactory financial situation increases the likelihood of becoming a middle or upper level starter. Legitimate employment is also associated with entry levels, but it is only significant when comparing lower level to middle level starters. However, the content analysis suggests that the type of legitimate jobs might have some impact to facilitate access to higher level positions in the illicit drug trade" (Wang 2013, p. 91).

Kleemans and Van de Bunt (2008) examined the relationship between employment and organized crime, using police files of 1,623 organized crime offenders involved in 120 different investigations. Many organized criminal activities were embedded in work relationships and work settings. Particular professions were frequently encountered. First, professions providing international contacts and international travel may lead to the discovery of opportunities for criminal activities and routine activities that facilitate these opportunities. This may explain the frequent occurrence of people engaged in professions related to mobility, transport, and logistics. Second, individual freedom of movement and autonomy seemed to be important. This might explain the frequent involvement of directors of small businesses, independent professionals, and employees of larger companies and banks who have considerable autonomy. Autonomy and freedom of movement make it easier to combine licit and illicit activities. Third, the social character of some professions may be important, as frequent meetings with different kinds of people present opportunities for finding suitable co-offenders.

Other research based on the Dutch Organized Crime Monitor confirmed that many organized crime offenders owned a business, often one related to their criminal activities. Some offenders started their company with legal intentions but found that the business provided criminal opportunities. Other businesses served only as cover for criminal activities. A business can be used for criminal purposes in three ways: for logistic support (e.g., storage), to legitimize criminal activity (e.g., to cover drug transports), and for money laundering (Van Koppen 2013; Kruisbergen, Kleemans, and Kouwenberg 2015).

Airports provide a prime example of a work setting that can facilitate organized crime activities (Kleemans and Van de Bunt 2008). Madarie and Kruisbergen (2020) analyzed the role of work in logistical nodes, such as airports (11 cases) and ports (5 cases), using information from the Dutch Organized Crime Monitor. Three tactics to smuggle drugs without getting caught were described. First, by evading security checks, for example, by hiding drugs in prepared luggage or people (swallowing balls of drugs or hiding them close to or in their bodies). Second, by completely avoiding security checks, for example, by using contacts with people who—through work privileges—are not subject to them. This can include recruitment of ex-colleagues. Third, by neutralizing security checks, for example, by corrupting police or customs officers.

Social and work-related embeddedness was described in detail. People are approached through social contacts and a social snowball effect occurs. The most frequent occur through family and work relationships.

Involvement of colleagues can be facilitated by a permissive culture that allows offenders to approach potential co-offenders relatively easily. Work-related factors include autonomy, mobility, and similarities between licit and illicit activities (which makes combining them easier). Mobility also stimulates the discovery of new opportunities. Two other work-related factors include social capital and work-specific expertise and skills. These may make particular employees especially attractive to criminal groups. Contacts with employees at logistical nodes are relatively scarce but of great importance for the successful execution of drug smuggling activities.

Interview studies also show that individuals employed in specific sectors, such as logistics or finance, or certain positions (i.e., working independently or unsupervised), are more vulnerable to involvement in organized crime activities (see, e.g., Van Koppen and De Poot 2013; Wang 2013; May and Bhardwa 2018).

The qualitative studies make it clear that relations between work and organized crime should be studied in more depth. Unemployment and lack of income may attract people to illegal activities (the standard view in life-course criminology and in part of the organized crime literature). However, the qualitative studies demonstrate that specific types of employment and specific work settings provide opportunities for illegal activities and for combining licit and illicit activities.

The relationship between work and organized crime has been analyzed in-depth in an analysis of the offending careers of 1,912 offenders in the Dutch Organized Crime Monitor (Van der Geest, Van Koppen, and Kleemans 2020; Van Koppen et al. 2019). A detailed description was provided of the shape and content of offending careers and of the relationship of these offending careers with socioeconomic factors such as employment and income.

Five important conclusions emerged. First, organized crime offenders were, on average, 27 years old at their first judicial contact, and offending remained relatively high until it started dropping at age 50. Second, no effect of employment on crime was found for the total sample, but interesting differences emerged for different roles in criminal organizations. A significant positive effect of employment on offending was found for leaders and coordinators; this is a different pattern than is found in the general literature on employment and offending. Employment increased offending by 31 percent for leaders and 46 percent for coordinators. Employment had a small preventive effect for those in other roles, accounting for a 7 percent reduction in offending. Third, no effect of employment on offending was found for subgroups distinguished by type of organized crime activity. Fourth, trajectory analyses distinguished six groups: high-frequency offenders (3.9 percent), early onset offenders (11.2 percent), mid-onset offenders (9.7 percent), late-onset offenders (12 percent), low-frequency offenders (29.8 percent), and sporadic offenders (33 percent). Fifth, offenders with lower offense frequency trajectories seemed to do better on employment outcomes. No effect of employment on offending was found for any of the trajectory groups.

A study based on the same data set focused, among other things, on the effects on offending of employment, self-employment (having your own business), and employment on the payroll (Van Koppen et al. 2019). Fixed-effects models showed the effects of employment, self-employment, and employment on the payroll. Being employed, in general, was not associated with offending for organized crime offenders. Having your own business, however, was associated with a 30 percent increase in offending for the full sample and a 60 percent increase for leaders.

III. Continuity and Discontinuity

Many questions regarding continuity and discontinuity in criminal careers in organized crime remain unsolved. First, the diversity of criminal career patterns seems to be at odds with the dominant adolescence-limited offenders versus life-course persistent offenders patterns from developmental and life-course criminology and requires further exploration. Second, concepts from the general criminal careers literature, such as "specialization," "escalation," "life events," and "desistance," are hard to use or seem to have different meanings for careers in organized crime. Third, co-offending and the social embeddedness of criminal careers in organized crime are barely understood and difficult to study, particularly for larger populations of offenders and using quantitative research methods. As a result, the role of co-offending "has been one of the most ill-studied of all criminal career dimensions" (Piquero, Farrington, and Blumstein 2007, p. 120). For careers in organized crime, this is also true, even though co-offending is a key issue and an "anomaly" for high-volume crime, the age-co-offending curve tends to decrease after adolescence (Van Mastrigt and Carrington 2019).

The analyses of larger organized crime data sets paint a diverse picture of criminal careers, including early starters and adult-onset offenders, and careers with varying intensity over the life course. Criminal careers often start after adolescence and continue over a long period, if they ever stop (or if offenders get killed). General theories of desistance, which stress important life events (Laub and Sampson 2003), are at odds with the temporal careers and life circumstances of organized crime offenders, who often combine careers in organized crime with work, relationships, and children. Concepts such as "specialization" and "escalation" seem to have little salience when analyzing these criminal careers. Specialization is a murky concept, as it depends on the length of a criminal career, the offense categories used, and the roles in these calculations of data concerning one-shot versus continuous criminal activities. Organized crime offenders commit nonorganized crimes, but many of their crimes are related to organized crime and are committed with co-offenders. To give an example: Is an offender who has committed one burglary, been convicted for one bar fight, and now mainly traffics cocaine from South America to Europe a "generalist" or a "specialist"? And, is an offender involved in trafficking all kinds of drugs from mainland Europe to the United Kingdom a "specialist" or a "generalist"? Finally, it is far from clear whether it is useful to study individual specialization, when organized crime offending by definition requires co-offenders and criminal networks. Criminal groups and collaborations are as, or even more, important than is the individual offender. Efforts to examine specialization by organized crime offenders, despite all these methodological issues, conclude that there is little evidence of specialization (Francis et al. 2013; Fuller, Morgan, and Brown 2019).

Organized crime offenders generally differ from the general offender population in one way: from the onset of their careers they commit more serious offenses. A comparison between Dutch organized crime offenders and the Dutch general offender population, for example, showed that offenders who were ever involved in organized crime were twice as often sentenced to prison following their first judicial contact (Van Koppen, De Poot, and Blokland 2010). Compared with general offenders they spend almost twice as long behind bars.

Many concepts related to criminal careers generally are difficult to apply to organized crime offenders. Analyses of career continuity and discontinuity should therefore rely more on qualitative analyses of offenders' life course than on quantitative analyses of criminal records. Data for qualitative analyses are available from intensive police investigations, statements of defectors, interviews with offenders, biographies, and autobiographies

(Morselli 2005; Savona et al. 2017; Kemp, Zolghadriha, and Gill 2019). Morselli (2005) produced seminal work using a social network perspective. Drawing on two extensive case studies (based on an autobiography and testimony from an FBI informant), he proposed that developments in criminal careers can be explained by deliberate choices people make to invest in particular relationships. He devoted attention to "brokerage" across structural holes in social networks (cf. Burt 1992); people connecting disconnected parts of networks have a "strategic position" that offers diverse strategic and economic benefits.

Challenges in using biographies, autobiographies, and life histories include representativeness and reliability (hereafter we refer to both biographies and autobiographies as "biographies"). These sources may overrepresent exceptional, and long, careers and more talkative informants who sometimes have hidden motives for publishing their stories or their version of the story. And do biographies paint a reliable picture of actual individual behavior and mechanisms in larger criminal networks? In a biography, the individual is the center of the universe; in organized crime, the individual is only one part of the story amid a larger network of interacting offenders. Biographies, interviews, and intensive case studies may nonetheless reveal important theoretical mechanisms that explain the development of careers in organized crime.

Some of these mechanisms resemble patterns described in general reviews of research on involvement mechanisms and recruitment. Others may be specific to organized crime and progression from high-volume crime to more profitable organized crime activities. Strategic investments in relationships, as Morselli (2005) suggested, may be one of these mechanisms. Kleemans and De Poot (2008), using cases from the Dutch Organized Crime Monitor, distinguished four types of "growth mechanisms" in the careers of nodal offenders who progressed from high-volume crime in adolescence to organized crime in adulthood. The first was the versatile but regionally constrained "local hero." For these offenders, versatility is a product of the illicit and licit opportunities local embeddedness provides, but also of the constraints and limited contacts of the local context. The second category involves progression through an increase in scale, often related to specialization, particularly in international drug trafficking. The third relates to progression through financial capital accumulation. Offenders who can accumulate capital become more central players in criminal networks, are able to invest in drug transports (while refraining from hands-on activities), and become "background operators" (by investing in semilegal or legal activities and generating legal income). The fourth relates to expertise, contacts, and network formation. Individuals assume central positions in criminal networks when other offenders and criminal groups need their contacts and expertise. The behavior both of the individual offender and of actors in the wider criminal network are important.

Morselli, Tremblay, and McCarthy (2006) argued that mentors are crucial in finding profitable criminal activities and learning to cope with the risks of a life in crime. The study, based on a survey of adult male offenders held in provincial Quebec prisons, focused not on organized crime but on profitable criminal activities. A substantial proportion of respondents reported that an influential individual, whom they characterized as a mentor, introduced them to a criminal milieu. Morselli, Tremblay, and McCarthy (2006) do not focus on stakes in conformity as an explanation for engaging or not engaging in criminal activities. Instead, they focus on how offenders obtain access to profitable criminal activities and learn to live with the risks of crime. This implies working toward greater, continuous benefits and either reducing risks or learning to live with them. Both adaptations are crucial for a continuing adult career in crime. How individuals, co-offenders, and criminal networks cope with them needs a lot of research effort, as do when, how, and why offenders desist from organized crime.

IV. Conclusion, Discussion, and Future Research

The emerging research on criminal careers in organized crime presents challenges to mainstream developmental and life-course criminology concerning basic assumptions. Large-scale, quantitative studies demonstrate that criminal careers in organized crime are different from those shown in the literature on high-volume crime. Organized crime offenders are generally older, and juveniles are nearly absent. Their careers are generally characterized by a relatively late onset in the adult years, and all studies find a significant share of adult-onset offenders. Finally, different criminal career patterns exist for various groups, including early starters, adult-onset offenders, and offenders with no previous judicial contacts.

Access to profitable criminal opportunities through social relations ("social opportunity structure") is a vital issue in criminal careers research that is often overlooked by focusing primarily on adolescence and high-volume crime and by failing to encompass adult offenders engaged in more profitable organized crimes, white-collar crimes, and cyber-crimes. In terms of social harms and criminal incomes, it is hard to explain why these important crimes fall outside the focus of mainstream developmental and life-course criminology. Practical research problems and principal reliance on large longitudinal studies provide understandable explanations.

The presence of many adult-onset offenders in organized crime challenges the conventional idea that a criminal career, particularly in organized crime, should be preceded by crime in adolescence.Early onset offenders are found in organized crime, but other types of career patterns, including adult- and late-onset offenders, are evident in various countries and data sets we discuss. These groups of offenders cannot be treated as an anomaly but require serious theoretical and empirical attention.

The findings we present apply to various types of organized crime, ranging from locally rooted Italian mafia groups to international transit crime, including smuggling networks. Future research should attempt to find explanations for late-onset offending. Traditional theories explain why young people engage in delinquent and criminal behavior but not why adults—often with a family and a conventional job—participate in serious criminal activities. To study late-onset offenders, longitudinal studies must follow organized crime offenders for considerable periods of time and be able to address recurring problems such as sample attrition and self-selection.

Qualitative research suggests that different involvement mechanisms affect early starters and adult-onset offenders, particularly regarding education and work. Involvement mechanisms include social ties and the social snowball effect, work ties, leisure activities and sidelines, life events (including financial setbacks), and deliberate recruitment by criminal groups. The first mechanism, social ties and the social snowball effect, is a very general mechanism and has various, concrete manifestations, depending on the context. One concerns intergenerational continuity in organized crime: children of organized crime offenders are at much higher risk of intergenerational continuity of crime than is the general population.

Recruitment by criminal groups also depends on the structure of criminal groups and the types of expertise required for specific activities. Savona et al. (2017) demonstrated interesting differences between locally rooted Italian mafia groups and other types of criminal organizations. The mafia groups often rely on kinship and blood ties and use initiation rituals among affiliates to reinforce their group identity. Other factors characterize other types of organized crime groups. Monetary considerations mostly drive recruitment for drug trafficking organizations. For other types of organizations, Savona et al. (2017, p. 46) conclude that individuals enter during adulthood "as they develop specialized expertise and social ties with criminals only later in life."

Employment may also have different effects for involvement in organized crime. Savona et al. (2017) show that mafia groups, embedded in disadvantaged areas, benefit from the ample availability of unemployed and disadvantaged people. For other types of organized crime, employment and particular occupations may provide opportunities for involvement and work settings may function as "offender convergence settings." Qualitative and quantitative studies demonstrate that specific types of employment and specific work settings provide opportunities for illegal activities and for combining licit and illicit activities. Future research should try to unravel the role and context of employment for involvement in different types of crime. It should attend not only to the general effects of employment but also distinguish between various types of occupations and various sectors.

Explanations for crime and for criminal careers are often sought in stakes in conformity. This applies to risk factors and protective factors, which are central in developmental and life-course criminology, but also to standard explanations for why people start, continue, or stop committing high-volume crime, stressing important life events. Important as these life events may be, they operate differently in organized crime careers and the life circumstances of organized crime offenders. Steffensmeier and Ulmer (2005) argue that desistance cannot be explained only by stakes in conformity and that lack of profitable criminal opportunities may also be relevant. Future research should explore how life events relate to organized crime offending in general and to adult-onset organized crime offenders in particular. It should take into account that the timing of crime onset differs from early starters and that it often coincides with an adult life of marriage, family, or work.

Large longitudinal data collections have become increasingly common but mostly target only one part of the total offender population and a specific time span (adolescence and early adulthood; Farrington 2003). They neglect the most serious types of offenders and the most serious forms of crime.

The distinctive patterns that research on criminal careers in organized crime documents should be studied in depth along with other theoretical mechanisms and questions. The fundamental question about early starters in crime should not be how they differ from the general population in terms of risk and protective factors but why and how some of them gain access to profitable criminal opportunities after adolescence and others have unsuccessful criminal careers.

More qualitative studies with larger emphasis on criminal careers in organized crime are needed. Large-scale quantitative studies are based on police records that are by definition selective and influenced by police priorities. Qualitative research could focus on describing and explaining involvement, continuity, and discontinuity of criminal careers through the use of rich police investigation files, testimonies from cooperating witnesses, and offender interviews. Life histories can be reconstructed that include both individual pathways and the social contexts of offending and criminal careers. Selective police priorities should not be viewed as a deficit ("police bias") but as a potential asset. A wealth of knowledge can result from a specific and selective focus on, for example, dominant Italian mafia groups in particular territories or on outlaw motorcycle gangs and their involvement in organized crime activities.

One important question is whether "organized crime" should be used as an "umbrella concept." It could make sense to differentiate between different types of criminal groups (e.g., locally rooted mafia groups involved in racketeering vs. more flexible networks involved in transit crime) and different types of criminal activities.

There may also be many similarities among organized crime groups and participants in diverse other criminal activities. This also applies to parallel phenomena, such as white-collar crime and cybercrime. White-collar crime research addresses adult-onset offenders, various types of careers (including early and late starters), and the importance of work settings (e.g., Weisburd and Waring 2001; Levi 2008; Leeper Piquero and Weisburd 2009; Van Onna 2018). Van Onna (2018), for example, analyzed criminal careers of 644 prosecuted fraudsters and found a large share of adult-onset offenders (78 percent) and diverse career patterns, including "typical criminals" who started early in high-volume crime. Criminal careers of cybercrime offenders may be similar to those in organized crime, as they may also be characterized by a different meaning of employment.

Finally, the most urgent priority for future research on criminal careers in organized crime is to incorporate the role of co-offenders in explaining individual criminal behavior. Co-offending research centers on youths because young people often commit crimes with others (Reiss and Farrington 1991; Lantz and Ruback 2017). Theoretical explanations usually rely on an adolescent context. Criminal careers in organized crime are analyzed almost exclusively by using quantitative data, without taking into account the clustering of offenders within groups. Future work should incorporate co-offending in criminal careers models. Richer qualitative research could also be helpful in explaining the mechanisms through which individuals influence the criminal behavior of others. The thriving field of developmental and life-course criminology can take a next step and respond to Reiss's call by taking co-offending in criminal careers more seriously.

REFERENCES

Besemer, Sytske, Shaikh I. Ahmad, Stephen P. Hinshaw, and David P. Farrington. 2017. "A Systematic Review and Meta-analysis of the Intergenerational Transmission of Criminal Behavior." *Aggression and Violent Behavior* 37:161–78.

Blokland, Arjan A. J., Daniel S. Nagin, and Paul Nieuwbeerta. 2005. "Life Span Offending Trajectories of a Dutch Conviction Cohort." *Criminology* 43:919–54.

Blokland, Arjan, Lonneke Van Hout, Wouter Van der Leest, and Melvin Soudijn. 2019. "Not Your Average Biker; Criminal Careers of Members of Dutch Outlaw Motorcycle Gangs." *Trends in Organized Crime* 22(1):10–33.

Blokland, Arjan, and Klaus Von Lampe. 2020. "Outlaw Biker Clubs and Organized Crime." In *Organizing Crime: Mafias, Markets, and Networks*, edited by Michael Tonry and Peter Reuter. Chicago: University of Chicago Press.

Blumstein, Alfred, Jacqueline Cohen, Jeffrey A. Roth, and Christy A. Visher, eds. 1986. *Criminal Careers and "Career Criminals."* Washington, DC: National Academy.

Bouchard, Martin. 2020. "A Network Perspective on Collaboration and Boundaries in Organized Crime." In *Organizing Crime: Mafias, Markets, and Networks*, edited by Michael Tonry and Peter Reuter. Chicago: University of Chicago Press.

Bouchard, Martin, and Carlo Morselli. 2014. "Opportunistic Structures of Organized Crime." In *Oxford Handbook of Organized Crime*, edited by Letizia Paoli. Oxford: Oxford University Press.

Burt, Ronald S. 1992. *Structural Holes*. Cambridge, MA: Harvard University Press.

Campedelli, Gian Maria, Francesco Calderoni, Tommaso Communale, and Cecilia Meneghini. 2019. "Life-Course Criminal Trajectories of Mafia Members." *Crime and Delinquency* (July). DOI:10.1177/0011128719860834.

Clarke, Ronald V., and Marcus Felson, eds. 1993. *Routine Activity and Rational Choice: Advances in Criminological Theory 5*. New Brunswick, NJ: Transaction.

Cloward, Richard A., and Lloyd E. Ohlin. 1960. *Delinquency and Opportunity: A Theory of Delinquent Gangs*. New York: Free Press.

Cressey, Donald R. 1969. *Theft of the Nation: The Structure and Operations of Organized Crime in America*. New York: Harper & Row.

Cullen, Francis T. 2011. "Beyond Adolescence-Limited Criminology: Choosing Our Future—the American Society of Criminology 2010 Sutherland Address." *Criminology* 49:287–330.

Decker, Scott H., and M. T. Chapman. 2008. *Drug Smugglers on Drug Smuggling: Lessons from the Inside*. Philadelphia: Temple University Press.

Decker, Scott H., Chris Melde, and David C. Pyrooz. 2013. "What Do We Know about Gangs and Gang Members and Where Do We Go from Here?" *Justice Quarterly* 30(3):369–402.

Farrington, David P. 1986. "Age and Crime." In *Crime and Justice: An Annual Review of Research*, vol. 7, edited by Michael Tonry. Chicago: University of Chicago Press.

———. 2002. "Developmental Criminology and Risk-Focused Prevention." In *The Oxford Handbook of Criminology*, edited by Mike Maguire, Rodney Morgan, and Robert Reiner. Oxford: Oxford University Press.

———. 2003. "Developmental and Life-Course Criminology: Key Theoretical and Empirical Issues—the 2002 Sutherland Award Address." *Criminology* 41(2):221–25.

Farrington, David P., Lila Lazcmian, and Alex R. Piquero. 2019. *The Oxford Handbook of Developmental and Life-Course Criminology*. Oxford: Oxford University Press.

Felson, Marcus. 2006. *Crime and Nature*. Thousand Oaks, CA: Sage.

Fijnaut, Cyrille J. C. F., Frank Bovenkerk, Gerben J. N. Bruinsma, and Henk G. Van de Bunt. 1998. *Organised Crime in the Netherlands*. The Hague: Kluwer Law International.

Finckenauer, James O. 2005. "Problems of Definition: What Is Organized Crime?" *Trends in Organized Crime* 8:63–83.

Francis, Brian, Leslie Humphreys, Stuart Kirby, and Keith Soothill. 2013. "Understanding Criminal Careers in Organised Crime." Research Report 74, Department of Mathematics and Statistics and Department of Applied Social Science, Lancaster University.

Fuller, Georgina, Anthony Morgan, and Rick Brown. 2019. "Criminal Histories of Australian Organised Crime Offenders." *Trends and Issues in Criminal Justice* (567). https://aic.gov.au/publications/tandi/tandi567.

Gambetta, Diego. 1993. *The Sicilian Mafia*. Cambridge, MA: Harvard University Press.

Gottfredson, Michael R., and Travis Hirschi. 1990. *A General Theory of Crime*. Stanford, CA: Stanford University Press.

Hagan, Frank E. 2006. "'Organized Crime' and 'Organized Crime': Indeterminate Problems of Definition." *Trends in Organized Crime* 9:127–37.

Jolliffe, Darrick, David P. Farrington, Alex R. Piquero, John F. MacLeod, and Steve Van de Weijer. 2017. "Prevalence of Life-Course-Persistent,

Adolescence-Limited, and Late-Onset Offenders: A Systematic Review of Prospective Longitudinal Studies." *Aggression and Violent Behavior* 33:4–14.

Kemp, Luke, Sanaz Zolghadriha, and Paul Gill. 2019. "Pathways into Organized Crime: Comparing Founders and Joiners." *Trends in Organized Crime* (September). DOI:10.1007/s12117-019-09371-w.

Kleemans, Edward R. 2007. "Organized Crime, Transit Crime, and Racketeering." In *Crime and Justice in the Netherlands*, edited by Michael Tonry and Catrien Bijleveld. Chicago: University of Chicago Press.

———. 2014*a*. "Organized Crime Research: Challenging Assumptions and Informing Policy." In *Applied Police Research: Challenges and Opportunities*, edited by Ella Cockbain and Johannes Knutsson. London: Routledge.

———. 2014*b*. "Theoretical Perspectives on Organized Crime." In *Oxford Handbook of Organized Crime*, edited by Letizia Paoli. Oxford: Oxford University Press.

Kleemans, Edward R., and Christianne J. De Poot. 2008. "Criminal Careers and Social Opportunity Structure." *European Journal of Criminology* 5(1):69–98.

Kleemans, Edward R., and Henk G. Van de Bunt. 1999. "The Social Embeddedness of Organized Crime." *Transnational Organized Crime* 5(1):19–36.

———. 2008. "Organised Crime, Occupations and Opportunity." *Global Crime* 9(3):185–97.

Kruisbergen, Edwin W., Edward R. Kleemans, and Ruud F. Kouwenberg. 2015. "Profitability, Power, or Proximity? Organized Crime Groups Investing Their Money in Legal Economy." *European Journal on Criminal Policy and Research* 21(2):237–56.

Lakatos, Imre. 1970. "Falsification and the Methodology of Scientific Research Programmes." In *Criticism and the Growth of Knowledge*, edited by Imre Lakatos and Alan Musgrave. Cambridge: Cambridge University Press.

Lantz, Brendan, and R. Barry Ruback. 2017. "The Relationship between Co-offending, Age, and Experience Using a Sample of Adult Burglary Offenders." *Journal of Developmental and Life Course Criminology* 3:76–97.

Laub, John, and Robert Sampson. 2003. *Shared Beginnings, Divergent Lives: Delinquent Boys to Age 70*. Cambridge, MA: Harvard University Press.

Leeper Piquero, Nicole, and David Weisburd. 2009. "Developmental Trajectories of White-Collar Crime." In *The Criminology of White-Collar Crime*, edited by Sally S. Simpson and David Weisburd. New York: Springer.

Levi, Michael. 2008. *The Phantom Capitalists: The Organization and Control of Long-Firm Fraud*, rev. ed. London: Routledge.

Madarie, Renushka, and Edwin W. Kruisbergen. 2020. "Traffickers in Transit: Analyzing the Logistics and Involvement Mechanisms of Organized Crime at Logistical Nodes in the Netherlands." In *Understanding Recruitment to Organized Crime and Terrorism*, edited by David Weisburd, Ernesto U. Savona, Badi Hasisi, and Francesco Calderoni. New York: Springer.

Matrix Knowledge Group. 2007. *The Illicit Drug Trade in the United Kingdom*. London: Home Office.

May, Tiggey, and Bina Bhardwa. 2018. *Organised Crime Groups Involved in Fraud*. London: Palgrave Macmillan.

McGloin, Jean M., and Kyle J. Thomas. 2019. "Peer Influence and Delinquency." *Annual Review of Criminology* 2:241–64.

Moffitt, Terrie E. 1993. "Adolescence-Limited and Life-Course-Persistent Antisocial Behavior: A Developmental Taxonomy." *Psychological Review* 100:675–701.

Morselli, Carlo. 2005. *Contacts, Opportunities, and Criminal Enterprise*. Toronto: University of Toronto Press.

Morselli, Carlo, Pierre Tremblay, and Bill McCarthy. 2006. "Mentors and Criminal Achievement." *Criminology* 44(1):17–43.

Nagin, Daniel S. 2005. *Group-Based Modeling of Development*. Cambridge, MA: Harvard University Press.

Nagin, Daniel S., and Kenneth C. Land. 1993. "Age, Criminal Careers, and Population Heterogeneity: Specification and Estimation of a Nonparametric, Mixed Poisson Model. *Criminology* 31(3):327–62.

Nagin, Daniel S., and Candice L. Odgers. 2010. "Group-Based Trajectory Modeling (Nearly) Two Decades Later." *Journal of Quantitative Criminology* 26(4):445–53.

Paoli, Letizia. 2002. "The Paradoxes of Organized Crime." *Crime, Law, and Social Change* 37:51–97.

———. 2003. *Mafia Brotherhoods: Organized Crime, Italian Style*. New York: Oxford University Press.

Paoli, Letizia, and Tom Vander Beken. 2014. "Organized Crime: A Contested Concept." In *Oxford Handbook of Organized Crime*, edited by Letizia Paoli. Oxford: Oxford University Press.

Piquero, Alex R. 2008. "Taking Stock of Developmental Trajectories of Criminal Activity over the Life Course." In *The Long View of Crime: A Synthesis of Longitudinal Research*, edited by Akiva M. Liberman. New York: Springer.

Piquero, Alex R., David P. Farrington, and Alfred Blumstein. 2003. "The Criminal Career Paradigm: Background and Recent Developments." In *Crime and Justice: A Review of Research*, vol. 30, edited by Michael Tonry. Chicago: University of Chicago Press.

———. 2007. *Key Issues in Criminal Career Research: New Analyses of the Cambridge Study in Delinquent Development*. Cambridge: Cambridge University Press.

Pyrooz, David C., Jillian J. Turanovic, Scott H. Decker, and Jun Wu. 2016. "Taking Stock of the Relationship between Gang Membership and Offending: A Meta-analysis." *Criminal Justice and Behavior* 43(3):365–97.

Reiss, Albert J., Jr. 1988. "Co-offending and Criminal Careers." In *Crime and Justice: A Review of Research*, vol. 10, edited by Michael Tonry and Norval Morris. Chicago: University of Chicago Press.

Reiss, Albert J., Jr., and David P. Farrington. 1991. "Advancing Knowledge about Co-offending: Results from a Prospective Longitudinal Study of London Males." *Journal of Criminal Law and Criminology* 82:360–95.

Reuter, Peter. 1983. *Disorganized Crime: Illegal Markets and the Mafia*. Cambridge, MA: MIT Press.

Salinas, Andrea Gimenez, and Sonia Fernandez Regadera. 2016. "Multiple
    Affiliations in Criminal Organizations: Analysis of a Spanish Sample." *Crime,
    Law and Social Change* 65:47–65.
Savona, Ernesto U., Francesco Calderoni, Gian Maria Campedelli, Tommaso
    Comunale, Marco Ferrarini, and Cecilia Meneghini. 2020. "The Criminal
    Careers of Italian Mafia Members." In *Understanding Recruitment to Organized
    Crime and Terrorism*, edited by David Weisburd, Ernesto U. Savona, Badi
    Hasisi, and Francesco Calderoni. New York: Springer.
Savona, Ernesto U., Francesco Calderoni, Elisa Superchi, Tommaso Comunale,
    Gian Maria Campedelli, Martina Marchesi, and Alexander Kamprad. 2017.
    "Systematic Review of the Social, Psychological and Economic Factors Re-
    lating to Criminalisation and Recruitment to OC." In *Report on Factors Relat-
    ing to Organized Crime*. Milan: Università Cattolica del Sacro Cuore.
Sergi, Anna. 2018. "Widening the AntiMafia Net: Child Protection and the
    Socio-Cultural Transmission of Mafia Behaviours in Calabria." *Youth Justice*
    18(2):149–68.
Sohoni, Tracy, Ray Paternoster, Jean Marie McGloin, and Ronet Bachman.
    2014. "'Hen's Teeth and Horse's Toes': The Adult Onset Offender in Crim-
    inology." *Journal of Crime and Justice* 37(2):155–72.
Spapens, Antonius C., and Hans Moors. 2019. "Intergenerational Transmission
    and Organized Crime: A Study of Seven Families in the South of the Neth-
    erlands." *Trends in Organized Crime*. DOI:10.1007/s12117-019-09363-w.
Steffensmeier, Darrell, and Jeffery T. Ulmer. 2005. *Confessions of a Dying Thief:
    Understanding Criminal Careers and Criminal Enterprise*. New Brunswick, NJ:
    Transaction Aldine.
United Nations Office on Drugs and Crime. 2004. *United Nations Convention against
    Transnational Organized Crime and the Protocols Thereto*. New York: United Nations.
    https://www.unodc.org/documents/middleeastandnorthafrica/organised-crime
    /UNITED_NATIONS_CONVENTION_AGAINST_TRANSNATIONAL
    _ORGANIZED_CRIME_AND_THE_PROTOCOLS_THERETO.pdf.
Van der Geest, Victor R., M. Vere Van Koppen, and Edward R. Kleemans. 2020.
    "Delinquent Development, Employment and Income in a Sample of Dutch
    Organized Crime Offenders: Shape, Content, and Correlates of Offending Trajec-
    tories from Age 12 to 65." In *Understanding Recruitment to Organized Crime and
    Terrorism*, edited by David Weisburd, Ernesto U. Savona, Badi Hasisi, and
    Francesco Calderoni. New York: Springer.
Van Deuren, Sjoukje, Arjan A. J. Blokland, and Edward R. Kleemans. 2020. "Es-
    timating the Effect of Gang Membership on Serious and Organized Crimes
    Using Matching Weights." Unpublished manuscript. Amsterdam: Vrije Uni-
    versiteit Amsterdam/NSCR, Faculty of Law.
Van Dijk, Meintje M., Veroni E. Eichelsheim, Edward R. Kleemans, Melvin
    R. J. Soudijn, and Steve Van de Weijer. 2019. "Intergenerational Continuity
    of Crime among Children of Organized Crime Offenders in the Netherlands."
    Journal of Developmental and Life-Course Criminology, forthcoming.
Van Dijk, Meintje M., Edward R. Kleemans, and Veroni E. Eichelsheim. 2019.
    "Children of Organized Crime Offenders: Like Father Like Child? An

Explorative and Qualitative Study into Mechanisms of Intergenerational (Dis) Continuity in Organized Crime Families." *European Journal on Criminal Policy and Research* 25(4):345–63.

Van Koppen, M. Vere. 2013. "Involvement Mechanisms for Organized Crime." *Crime, Law and Social Change* 59(1):1–20.

Van Koppen, M. Vere, and Christianne J. De Poot. 2013. "The Truck Driver Who Bought a Café: Offenders on Their Involvement Mechanisms for Organized Crime." *European Journal of Criminology* 10:74–88.

Van Koppen, M. Vere, Christianne J. De Poot, and Arjan A. J. Blokland. 2010. "Comparing Criminal Careers of Organized Crime Offenders and General Offenders." *European Journal of Criminology* 7(5):356–74.

Van Koppen, M. Vere, Christianne J. De Poot, Edward R. Kleemans, and Paul Nieuwbeerta. 2010. "Criminal Trajectories in Organized Crime." *British Journal of Criminology* 50(1):102–23.

Van Koppen, M. Vere, Victor R. Van der Geest, Edward R. Kleemans, and Edwin W. Kruisbergen. 2019. "Employment and Organized Crime: A Longitudinal Analysis." *European Journal of Criminology*, forthcoming.

Van Mastrigt, Sarah B., and Peter J. Carrington. 2019. "Co-offending." In *The Oxford Handbook of Developmental and Life-Course Criminology*, edited by Lila Kazemian, Alex R. Piquero, and David P. Farrington. Oxford: Oxford University Press.

Van Onna, Joost. 2018. "Blurred Lines: A Study of White-Collar Crime Involvement." PhD dissertation. Vrije Universiteit Amsterdam, Department of Criminal Law and Criminology.

Varese, Federico. 2011. *Mafias on the Move*. Princeton, NJ: Princeton University Press.

———. 2014. "Protection and Extortion." In *Oxford Handbook of Organized Crime*, edited by Letizia Paoli. Oxford: Oxford University Press.

Von Lampe, Klaus. 2016. *Organized Crime: Analyzing Illegal Activities, Criminal Structures, and Extra-legal Governance*. Los Angeles: Sage.

Wang, Wei. 2013. "Conventional Capital, Criminal Capital, and Criminal Careers in Drug Trafficking." PhD dissertation. Simon Fraser University, School of Criminology.

Weisburd, David, Ernesto U. Savona, Badi Hasisi, and Francesco Calderoni, eds. 2020. *Understanding Recruitment to Organized Crime and Terrorism*. New York: Springer.

Weisburd, David, and Elin Waring, with Ellen F. Chayet. 2001. *White-Collar Crime and Criminal Careers*. Cambridge: Cambridge University Press.

Martin Bouchard

Collaboration and Boundaries in Organized Crime: A Network Perspective

ABSTRACT

A network approach helps us better specify and model collaboration among people involved in organized crime. The focus on collaboration raises the boundary specification problem: Where do criminal organizations start, where do they end, and who is involved? Traditional approaches sometimes assume the existence of simple, rigid structures when complexity and fluidity are the norms. A network approach embraces this complexity conceptually and provides methodological guidelines for clarifying boundaries. Boundary specification in organized crime helps solve four puzzles. First, social boundaries: a network approach reduces confusion about social boundaries as criminal entrepreneurs interact with criminals and noncriminals in diverse contexts, only some of them illicit. Second, boundaries of group membership: network data and methods obviate the need for formal membership attributions. Third, ethnic boundaries network analyses reveal that the effective boundaries of criminal organizations are based on social relations, not attributes such as ethnicity. Fourth, recruitment: attending to the larger social environments in which organizations are embedded provides a clearer view of how mechanisms of recruitment cross seemingly rigid boundaries between members and prospective members.

Electronically published May 6, 2020

Martin Bouchard is professor of criminology, Simon Fraser University. He is grateful to the editors, anonymous reviewers, and Evan McCuish, Francesco Calderoni, Chad Whelan, Pierre Tremblay, and Mitch Macdonald for comments and suggestions on earlier drafts.

Social network analysis has transformed conceptualization of crime and delinquency over the past 20 years. Criminological theories centered on social factors can now be tested with better data and measures that provide more sophisticated demonstrations of the mechanisms involved. Social network theory and data have provided novel insights, most notably that better understanding of the structure of networks in which individuals are embedded can improve understanding of the intensity of their involvement in crime (Haynie 2001; Papachristos et al. 2011). Social network analysis has been used effectively in a variety of subfields in criminology, including studies of peer influences on juvenile offenders (e.g., Haynie 2001; Weerman 2011; Young 2011) and research on gang violence (e.g., Papachristos 2009, 2013).

The effects of social network analysis on organized crime research have been substantial. "Organized crime" implies forms of criminality that cannot escape the social, in more ways than one. The word "organized" expresses the idea that individuals form social structures of collaboration in order to generate flows of criminal activity. As with other forms of criminality, with organized crime comes secrecy; the higher stakes involved, and the need for continuity, imply a higher form of secrecy in which trust in associates is crucial. Mechanisms of trust—how it is created and what it achieves—are best understood with network data.

How have social networks affected the study of organized crime? Networks initially provided a useful analogy that allowed scholars and practitioners to describe the tendency for criminal groups to be small, flexible, and horizontal in structure. The network approach, however, has proven to be more than just a convenient conceptual tool. It provides both theory and methods and has stimulated important advances in understanding of organized crime. It allows researchers to model the mechanisms that explain recruitment into criminal organizations, the movement of individuals from inside and outside the organizations, and why collaborations occur with some individuals but not others.

A network approach improves specification and modeling of the nature, fluidity, and context of collaboration and of boundaries in organized crime. My focus in this essay is on a particular aspect of networks and organized crime: boundary specification. I propose that boundary specification, delineation of the real (or imaginary) lines drawn between individuals included in a criminal organization and those excluded, can help solve puzzles of collaboration that traditional, nonnetwork approaches have not solved. It has been argued, for instance, that the boundaries of criminal organizations are blurry and difficult to determine (Papachristos 2006; Bouchard and Konarski 2014); that criminal organizations tend to recruit both within their own ethnicity and increasingly from outside (Kleemans and van de Bunt 1999; Malm, Bichler, and Nash 2011); and that recruitment follows a snowball pattern (Kleemans and van de Bunt 1999), typically occurring through social ties (Savona et al. 2017). Yet, we do not consider the candidates who were available but not selected through the process.

Traditional organized crime research and data are unable to accommodate the inherent fluidity and porous nature of boundaries in organized crime. A network approach accommodates this fluidity in ways that traditional approaches cannot. It allows us to describe the mechanisms of recruitment, for instance, and allows us to make predictions about who might be recruited. A network approach provides a way to map and organize social interactions among organized criminals. It also provides a theoretical framework within which hypotheses can be formulated and tested. The methodological and theoretical features of the network approach are intertwined. Network data illuminate the contours and nature of the collaborative choices available to organized criminals. Network theory helps us formulate hypotheses and models how collaboration is likely to unfold in specific circumstances.

From a policy perspective, understanding of boundaries is central in targeting organized crime. Most countries have laws that make membership in a criminal organization a crime or an aggravating factor in sentencing convicted individuals. Law enforcement agencies have special units that tackle organized crime and priority lists of targeted organizations. Unfortunately for those efforts, the initial step of specifying boundaries is more challenging than it looks. Drawing the contours of criminal organizations is as much art as it is science, and there is no guarantee that the responsible agencies are using optimal tools to determine those boundaries in the first place. There is a lot of work to be done in understanding boundaries and collaboration in organized crime. A network approach, while not without limitations, is especially well-suited for the job.

I focus on aspects of network data that are salient to organized crime; not all network applications make the approach unique or necessary. I focus on subjects concerning which network data offer a particularly powerful approach for improved understanding of organized crime paradoxes or puzzles that network data can at least partially solve. Network analysis and data, of course, are not the only useful approach. For instance, economic theories of organized crime bring a unique set of conceptual and analytical tools that shed light on the dynamics of illegal markets (Reuter 1983; Kleemans 2014). Given the right context, the enterprise model of organized crime makes assumptions about the nature of micro co-offending decisions in criminal conspiracies that overlap nicely with network models of organized crime (Haller 1990). Without context, networks may not be useful, especially in organized crime networks in which status differentiation among network members influences their relations (Calderoni 2012; Varese 2013; Campana 2018).

I am not the first to propose the value of network methods, at least broadly speaking, for criminology as a whole (Morselli 2009; Carrington 2011; Papachristos 2011; Bouchard and Malm 2016; Campana 2016a; Gallupe 2016; Gravel and Tita 2017; Ouellet and Hashimi 2019), or even in organized crime (Sparrow 1991; Kleemans and van de Bunt 1999; Morselli 2005; Bouchard and Morselli 2014). Bouchard and Morselli (2014) argued that a network approach allows us to appreciate how large groups can emerge but not necessarily operate, function, or behave as a large group when crime-to-crime co-offending interactions are considered. They used the term "opportunistic structures" to describe these smaller clusters of individuals working together under the umbrella concept of organized crime.

Yet, despite advances in the use of network analyses in organized crime, and constant growth in the number of scholars adopting network methods, the approach has neither transcended the field nor become a staple in criminology research. One of my aims is thus to demonstrate how networks help us make otherwise impossible advances. A difficulty for efforts to understand collaboration in organized crime is that relationships are multiplex, and networks involve both noncriminals and criminals, sometimes at the same time. Using networks as an organizing principle can help make sense of the various ways in which organized criminals interact and collaborate. When that happens, some of the contradictions that exist in scholarly and law enforcement representations of organized crime can be diminished.

In this essay I discuss four unresolved puzzles of boundary specification in organized crime. First, I consider the social boundary problem, showing how a network approach can reduce confusion as members interact and collaborate with outsiders. Network researchers do not always have access to data extending beyond the criminal network (e.g., co-offender networks), making distinctions between the criminal and the social impossible. Yet, when data on diverse types of interactions are available, a network approach can handle this complexity. Second, I turn to the boundaries of group membership per se, illustrating how the use of network data and methods can obviate the need for formal membership attributions, at least prior to establishing the social structure based on demonstrated social interactions among criminals. Third, I consider the ethnic boundary problem, showing that a tendency for ethnic homophily—the tendency for individuals to connect with others with whom they share characteristics—within criminal organizations does not necessarily make it a suitable descriptor of types of organized crime: the effective boundaries of criminal organizations are first measured by social relations, not attributes like ethnicity. Using relations as a starting point allows us to see the variety of individuals with different ethnic backgrounds in particular organizations. Importantly, a network approach can establish that organizations may be ethnically diverse, but that their members may still display a preference for connections to members of their own ethnic group. Finally, I cover the seemingly rigid boundary that separates current members and outsiders who might be recruited. I show how broadening the view of recruitment to the larger social environment in which the organization and its potential recruits are embedded can provide a clearer view of the mechanisms involved, including recruitment within the organization for specific criminal ventures.

Here is how this essay is organized. Section I provides conceptual background for readers for whom network approaches are a new subject. The network approach is both theory and methods. Any form of organizational structure can be investigated with network data, not only those characterized by horizontal partnerships. Section II, the bulk of the essay, discusses the four boundary specification problems described above. Section III discusses dangers of a network approach: overinterpretation, overcomplexification, and oversimplification. Section IV discusses underdeveloped subjects of which better elucidation may answer remaining puzzles: how and when boundaries form, analyzing organized crime networks over time; variations in cultures of collaboration; age boundaries, collaboration across age groups; and geographical boundaries, analyzing transnational networks. Section V concludes.

I. A Network Approach to Organized Crime:
Conceptual Clarifications

There are key conceptual distinctions that need to be made before we jump into the crux of the argument. First, what does it mean to say that a network approach is both theory and methods? Second, are networks and organizations opposite ends of the organizational spectrum? In other words, can we use networks to study criminal organizations that have clear role and relationship hierarchies?

A. Both Theory and Methods

"Social network analysis" refers to the set of methods used to derive meaning from social interactions (Wasserman and Faust 1994). Network approaches come with distinctive research designs that involve novel ways to generate data (e.g., the use of name generators), to code (e.g., at the dyad rather than the individual level), and a suite of techniques and measures to choose among when describing networks. It is an intellectual world of its own, and easy to get lost in. But social networks are also highly intuitive. We are all embedded in them, and though we vary in our capacity to see, or desire to reflect on, the implications of the structures of our own social networks, network analysis and its methods becomes familiar and rewarding once terminological hurdles are crossed. Many network techniques may be new in a technical sense, but ideas about social networks influencing behavior go back a long way, including Simmel's (1955) important theoretical work on why individuals form groups and how groups (or social circles) interweave in communities of conflicts and affiliations.

Because of the effort required to learn techniques and measures, it is easy to frame social network analysis as a set of methods. These methodological tools are not, however, independent of theoretical underpinnings. Instead, network methods are typically packed with theoretical assumptions, the most fundamental being that social relations influence behavior, attitudes, or both (Knoke and Yang 2008; Borgatti et al. 2009). Social relations are mapped, and locations of individuals in networks are examined because this influence on behavior is assumed to matter. The interdependence of people is fundamental; the actions of one are assumed to affect the actions of others connected to them, sometimes even if this connection is indirect. This interdependence is inconvenient for traditional statistical approaches to crime data, which assume independence of observations. Network approaches embrace interdependence by finding meaning in it (Papachristos 2011). Exponential random graph models (ERGMs), for example, are a type of logistic regression model in which special parameters, such as transitivity (a friend of my friend is also my friend), are included to estimate the effects of interdependence among people, groups, or organizations to explain a network's structure—who connects with whom, and why (Lusher, Koskinen, and Robins 2013).

Part of what makes the network approach also a "theory" is that use of these data cannot be detached from those assumptions. The mere linking of nodes brings to light the main theoretical mechanism of the network approach, namely that a variety of phenomena can be explained by examining the transmission of objects, sentiments, or information from one node to another. It is not, therefore, a single "theory" but a set of assumptions and principles from which theory can be specified. Typically in the social sciences, network data about individuals (how many connections are they brokering) are used to theorize about a nonnetwork outcome (how much money do they make?) (Morselli and Tremblay 2004). Social capital theory, which emphasizes abilities to use social relations to gain advantages, is a common example (Lin, Cook, and Burt 2001). That social capital is theorized or operationalized using networks is important because the theorized mechanism underlying the pursuit of an advantage is assumed to emerge from the transfer of information, knowledge, and sentiment through connections among individuals. Not all individuals are equal in their ability to use their social connections, and those differences may affect the relative advantages they obtain. This is the point of departure of numerous network studies.

This dual role as theory and methods is why I use the term "network approach" in this essay, to encompass the array of roles that networks play in understanding of phenomena such as organized crime. Adopting a network approach implies study of phenomena using network data and using network theory to interpret patterns that are found. Users of those methods do not always realize this. To say, for instance, that a "high betweenness score[1] is indicative of power," or to focus on the measure for making distinctions in data, is tantamount to applying a network theory hypothesis that individuals who score higher matter more than others.

---

[1] Betweenness centrality is a network measure that captures the number of times an individual is found in-between two others, who are otherwise not connected. It is a relatively popular measure among crime network scholars because brokers—a common label for those who score high on this measure—have been shown to be key elements of networks in various illicit contexts, including for disruption purposes (Morselli 2009).

They may have more information, knowledge, or access to resources, or all these desirable attributes at once.[2] It is essential for network scholars to think about the theoretical ramifications of the measures they use in interpreting their findings and to be explicit about the theoretical mechanisms implied in their interpretations.

B. *Networks, Groups, or Organizations?*

There is some confusion concerning whether networks are a distinct organizational form, one that would sit at the lower end of the spectrum of levels of organization (von Lampe 2009; Campana 2016a). In this view, networks describe small, loose "disorganized" partnerships, an organizational arrangement starkly different from hierarchical organizations such as the Italian mafias or outlaw motorcycle groups such as the Hells Angels. This representation of networks as a type of organization may have emerged from a growing realization in empirical studies of organized crime that criminal partnerships are much less formal, rigid, and lasting than was long assumed.[3]

Though it can have value in when terms are clearly defined (e.g., Powell 1990; Podolny and Page 1998; Campana 2016a), this characterization of networks should be resisted. As an approach, network analysis does not discriminate between hierarchies and loose partnerships; networks can describe groupings of any kind. The essential condition is that the grouping involves social interactions among its members. Von Lampe (2003, 2009) aptly summarizes the status of the network approach as generalizable to any type of organization in this way: "The alternative to such a one-dimensional view is to treat networks and organizations as representing distinct structural dimensions while acknowledging that networks and organizations are not empirically independent. Organizations evolve out of and are transcended by networks, just as every organization can be defined as a network because its members are by definition connected through specific ties" (2009, p. 96). I insist on this because it is easy

---

[2] Crime network scholars would benefit from testing the assumption that "brokers do better" more often (Morselli 2010). I suspect that many network brokers ignore their positional advantage and are unsuccessful at obtaining tangible benefits from it. I come back to this idea below when discussing the dangers of overinterpretation.

[3] "Networks as a form of organization" is also a subfield of research in organizational sociology that tries to capture the more informal, trust-based arrangements falling in-between hierarchies and market forms (Powell 1990; Nohria and Eccles 1992; Podolny and Page 1998).

to miss differences in the context of relations for network analyses that do not include contextual information on the nature of ties between individuals. We could wrongly conclude, for instance, that two groups function similarly because they have similar network structures. In some cases, this would be correct. In other cases, however, we would miss that the network effects of hierarchical relations exist only because of the hierarchical context in which they are embedded. In other words, the structure may be the same, but the qualitative nature of ties is different. Ultimately, this highlights a pitfall of network data as a sole source for assessing organizational structure: unless the data include contexts, it may operate at a level that is too abstract to reveal network differences across groups, even when differences exist.

The differences would not be in network structure, but in the mechanisms that allow the network structure to emerge. Statistical methods such as ERGMs can answer questions at the heart of collaborative organized crime structures such as whether a member's ranking, or other attributes such as ethnicity or age, are important drivers of connections in the network (Ouellet, Bouchard, and Hart 2017). These models can examine whether homophily is a driver of connections. For instance, Smith and Papachristos (2016) tested an ERGM on Al Capone's network, finding that ethnic homophily existed in his personal and criminal networks but not in his legitimate network, where homophily was a negative predictor. ERGMs also allow for controlling for behaviors that may exist in any network, criminal or otherwise, such as transitivity, the tendency to become friends with friends of our friends, or to reciprocate ties. That way, confounding network processes can be controlled for, and the results can be assessed at face (statistical) value. We can ask whether rank is a driver of connections, whether some hierarchies behave differently than others, while controlling for other variables like ethnicity and age that might be relevant to these ranks and hierarchies. This allows testing of specific hypotheses related to recruitment, but also to promotion within criminal organizations.

Network data, then, are ideally suited to describe both formal and informal groups. They can also illustrate the different ways in which organizational style influences the nature and structure of social relations (Erickson 1981). The subcultural context in which networks are found is an important source of influence on the structure of social ties, and the nature of collaboration within criminal organizations, ideas I develop further below.

II. Collaborative Ties and the Problem
of Boundary Specification

Criminal "collaboration" refers to individuals working together to produce a criminal outcome. Thus, it excludes scenarios in which two individuals, who otherwise may be "criminals," collaborate in legitimate pursuits. The term *criminal* labels the activity and the context, but not the individuals involved. Collaboration, as I use the term, serves as a generic, umbrella concept[4] that encompasses other terms including collusion, conspiracy, co-offending, or cooperation. Using the term *collaboration* excludes the role of networks in understanding conflicts among criminal organizations. Network data have shown their value in understanding conflicts among street gangs (Papachristos 2009; Descormiers and Morselli 2011; Bichler et al. 2019), but have less often been used to examine patterns in conflicts in other types of groups.

An unintended consequence of adopting a network perspective on collaboration in organized crime is to broaden the view of the unit of analysis. Following the connections among offenders, as a general approach, implies that a diversity of individuals and affiliations in the process will be observed, in contrast to a narrow view of organized crime as represented by mafia families or cartel members in Mexico or Colombia. If criminal organizations go outside their immediate members to collaborate with other criminal entrepreneurs, following connections makes the integration of those outsiders almost unavoidable. This does not mean that the network should be allowed to grow infinitely, until distinctions between organized crime and other criminals disappear entirely. There are numerous qualitatively important differences between the minority of organized criminals and others, including cultural ones (Paoli 2002; Varese 2010) that even a network approach will want to emphasize. Yet, in the end, use of the network approach lets us consider both organized crime and other criminal entrepreneurs as belonging to the same social environment. Because the network of collaborations in organized crime typically includes a diverse range of criminal entrepreneurs, some of whom are independents not affiliated with criminal organizations (Morselli, Paquet-Clouston, and Provost 2017), I use similarly broad lenses to

---

[4] Co-offending, for many, narrowly refers to specific crime events found in police data. Not all collaborative relationships are conspiracies, and, as a specific type of conspiracy, collusive situations are relatively rare when compared with other collaborative behavior in organized crime.

approach the topic. Case studies I discuss and terminology I use reflect this diversity.

Study of collaboration in organized crime necessarily raises the issue of boundary specification.[5] Following collaborative ties among offenders naturally leads to difficulties of characterization: Are all of these contacts part of the criminal organization? Where does the organization stop, and where does it end? In their seminal work on boundary specification, Laumann, Marsden, and Prensky (1983) argued for group boundaries to be approached using a realist strategy, in which boundaries are based on the perspective of members themselves, or a nominalist approach, in which boundaries are specified according to the researcher's analytical framework. The realist strategy is limited to the extent that it requires members to have a shared conception of the group and to be aware of the full extent of the group's composition or operations, relying on the implicit assumption that a natural boundary exists—two conditions that are hard to find in criminal contexts (Ouellet and Bouchard 2018). In contrast, the nominalist approach uses the theoretical questions being examined by the researcher to define group boundaries. The framework favored by Laumann, Marsden, and Prensky (1983) in setting group boundaries is the social network approach. Boundaries, where they exist, should first be set from patterns in social interactions. At the same time, the attributes of individual actors can and should be used to provide context for the interactions in the first place (Ouellet and Bouchard 2018).

In this section, I examine four areas in which a network approach to collaboration in organized crime helps provide a better understanding of boundaries. The first is the difficulty in both social and criminal contexts of determining "membership" in criminal organizations. The second concerns group membership—who is a member, who is an outsider, and how do we tell the difference? The third is ethnic boundaries, whether they exist, and how network data help move away from ethnicity as a type of organized crime. Finally, I discuss recruitment, how and when outsiders cross the initial boundary into the world of organized crime.

A. The Blurred Social and Criminal Boundaries in Organized Crime

Organized criminals do not make it easy for researchers to identify clear boundaries between people involved in their criminal activities and people

---

[5] This paragraph draws from a similar argument on group boundaries in Ouellet and Bouchard (2018) in the context of a terrorist group.

who are material to other parts of their lives. They manage their social and professional lives as we all do, not drawing clear, hard lines between the different spheres of their lives. Individuals from one sphere may intersect with individuals from another: people who met at work may cross paths with other friends and family members; coworkers may become friends; existing friends may be hired in your workplace. Not all coworker conversations involve the personal details of our lives. Not all coworkers are invited to dinner in our homes. Some are; those are not only friends or coworkers, they are both. But not necessarily at the same time; the two roles don't have to occur simultaneously.

Consider two independent criminal entrepreneurs in their mid-30s, Thug and Veteran, each an object of heightened law enforcement attention. Looking at 8 years of police data, Hashimi and Bouchard (2017) found that 50 percent of a network looked like law-abiding citizens. The data included any interactions recorded in police files. Many were not criminal: a speeding ticket, a sobriety test, a surveillance report. Sometimes a frequent accomplice was observed sitting in the backseat of the car, with Thug in the passenger seat, and Thug's wife driving to a local restaurant. Two of the three were otherwise involved in criminal conspiracies, but neither the context nor the behavior was criminal. There is no reason to assume all the participants are members of a criminal group, at least based on only this information.

Penetration of the grey area between criminal and social associations is much easier with a network approach. It acknowledges that relationships have multiple layers. It need not apply a permanent label to individuals, such as whether they are or are not a member of the organization. Its focus on relationships and their context allows the flexibility needed to accommodate complex (or "multiplex") relationships.

Much of the difficulties in disentangling family and criminal ties within Italian mafias, for example, can be illuminated with network data. Paoli (2002) highlighted how elements of Italian culture complicate mafia relations in ways that do not reflect clear-cut boundaries between the criminal and the social. Paoli observed that relationships within Italian families are often mischaracterized. It is a mistake, for example, to assume that most interactions within a particular family involve criminal conspiracies. Leadership does not equate to control (Mastrobuoni and Patacchini 2012). Attendance at events does not imply membership in a criminal organization (Calderoni, Brunetto, and Piccardi 2017). Conflating the family unit with a criminal organization is a mistake; families play cultural roles that cannot, at least from the outside, be easily distinguished from criminal activities (DellaPosta 2017).

A network approach can disentangle family and criminal organization links conceptually and empirically. In network jargon, those relationships are multiplex ties: relations among individuals that are actualized in a variety of contexts. When observed together at a funeral, Al and Nick are friends. When sitting in a café the next day, they may be organizing the next cocaine shipment, making them co-offenders. When they play football that evening, they are teammates. Their relations are multiplex; together, they share three networks: social, criminal, and athletic. The criminal network may be examined by itself, or it may be combined with other networks into a generalized "social network" that includes diverse social interactions. The more network contexts two individuals share, the closer they are assumed to be (Verbrugge 1979).

Network researchers often lack access to more than the criminal network, making distinctions between the criminal and the social impossible. Yet, when data on multiple types of interactions are available, a network approach can easily handle this complexity. Crime and social worlds may be more intertwined in organized crime than in other settings because of the importance of trust (von Lampe 2003; Smith and Papachristos 2016; DellaPosta 2017). Criminal ties can be examined separately from social ties when the aim is to examine collaboration in criminal conspiracies. Both types of ties can be considered together when the aim is to understand the interplay between the social and criminal: How much do organized criminals co-offend with individuals with whom they socialize?

Think back to Thug and Veteran, two individuals who saw themselves as independent criminal entrepreneurs (Hashimi and Bouchard 2017). Their social and criminal worlds were fully intertwined, making it nearly impossible to distinguish where the criminal started or the social stopped. The 101 contacts between them over 8 years of data involved seven recognizable communities or subgroups, which covered 80 percent of the total contacts (20 percent were one-offs or did not involve enough interaction with others to constitute a subgroup). Five of the seven subgroups included mixes of individuals who did and did not have a criminal record; only one group of four individuals qualified as a 100 percent crime clique. All seven subgroups were formed from the accumulation of social interactions; very few explicitly co-offending interactions were recorded.

Thug and Veteran interacted with individuals who were members of criminal organizations. Veteran grew up with four people who became

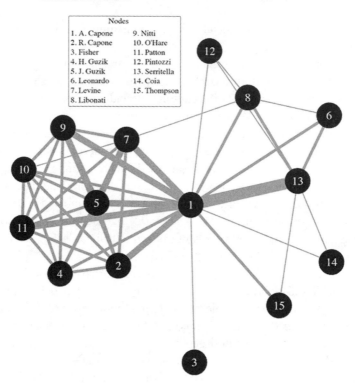

Width of Edge indicates N of Tie Types

Fig. 1a.—Capone's network of close associates. Source: Papachristos and Smith (2014).

members of an outlaw motorcycle gang. They were part of a subgroup of close friends that included Veteran's law-abiding family members. None of those interactions between bikers and family members were criminal in nature, but it would be easy to miss this without data on the contexts of interactions.

Smith and Papachristos's (2016) work on Al Capone's social network provides a clear example of how a network approach can help distinguish between the social and the criminal. They collected rich data on every identifiable individual who could be found to have interacted with Capone during his lifetime and beyond (ca. 1900–1950). They differentiated between social ties with friends, observed to have occurred in purely social contexts; criminal ties observed in the context of actual crimes and conspiracies; and legitimate ties that emerged from interactions in purely legitimate contexts. Figure 1 shows a subset of Capone's network; thicker

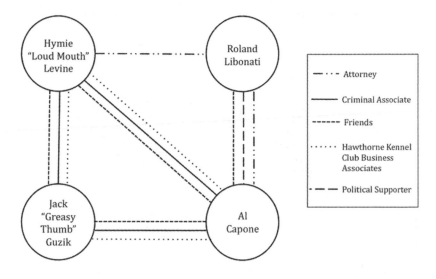

Fig. 1B.—Capone's Hawthorne Kennel Business Club by type of ties. Source: Papachristos and Smith (2014).

lines indicate the number of different types of ties connecting individuals. Relations are not equal, which provides a first layer of understanding about the relative strengths of relationships among people connected to Capone.

Figure 1*b* extracts four nodes from figure 1*a*, Capone (1) and three of his closest criminal associates from the Hawthorne Kennel Business Club, Guzik (5), Levine (7), and Libonati (8). It illustrates variations in contexts in which they interacted. Capone shared a friendship with all three. Libonati and Capone's relationship included political support and legal advice, but never a criminal association. Within the club, only Levine received legal advice from Libonati, but their relationship stopped there. It did not have other layers as did Libonati's with Capone.

A network representation such as is shown in figure 1*a*, which includes all possible types of links between individuals around a crime personality like Capone, appears to indicate that it is of one close-knit criminal group, but it is not. Libonati and others such as Serritella would have to be excluded. The point is that they can be excluded from the criminal group, but included in the more general network representation, because relations were coded, not individuals. With a network approach, relations of particular types can be included or excluded when analyzing networks

(a) Criminal Network   **(b) Personal Network**

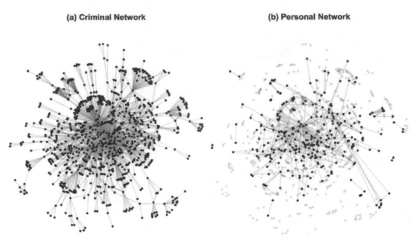

FIG. 1C.—Capone's criminal and personal networks. Source: Smith and Papachristos (2016).

for different purposes. Networks are built from relations between individuals (the lines—or *edges*—we see in networks). Figure 1*c*, which separately shows the larger criminal network (left) and the family and friendship network (right), demonstrates how these two types of links can be examined as the separate networks they are.

Networks that focus solely on criminal ties between individuals, for example, co-offending networks, miss the larger social environments in which criminals are embedded. These other network members are important because they may be candidates for inclusion in a future criminal conspiracy and, even if that never happens, they may influence decisions of members of the organizations and thereby shape network structure (Ouellet and Bouchard 2018). The last point is not trivial. Noncriminals are part of organized criminals' social worlds because they influence decision making; this is crucial in an approach that assumes that social relations are the most important source of influence in human behavior. Crime network scholars do not always take full advantage of the power of network data.

B. A Network Approach to the Boundaries of Group Membership

Although it is tempting to rely on formal membership attribution data to study criminal organizations, the literature on organized crime networks has shown that this can be misleading (Morselli 2009). Law enforcement agencies, in particular, may find it hard to resist the temptation to follow membership data, especially in investigating RICO-like cases. Limiting information to formal members, however, truncates their social worlds unnecessarily. Morselli (2009) showed, for instance, that high-ranking members of Nomads Hells Angels of Montreal were embedded in vast networks of associates of all ranks, including many nonaffiliated individuals who played important brokerage roles. Years before, Morselli and Giguère (2006) showed that legitimate actors played quantitatively and qualitatively important roles in a major drug importation network. Clearly, a broader approach based on social interactions is warranted.

Some criminal organizations like the Hells Angels or the Italian 'Ndrangheta have systems of ranks that make it relatively easy to count their members. There is little need for network data to discover the size of an organization if the number of capos or, in outlaw motorcycle gangs, "full-patched" members can be learned from police investigation techniques and intelligence data analysis. For other types of organization, a majority of criminal groups (Bouchard and Morselli 2014), network data are needed to distinguish members from casual "guests."

For more formal organizations, network data serve a related purpose, notably to understand the relationships across ranks (Morselli 2009; Calderoni 2012). This information is useful for multiple purposes, including prediction of promotions, understanding the structure of cooperation within the organization, and examining recruitment for specific ventures and conspiracies.

An important assumption of a network approach is that patterns of interactions among criminals provide a foundation for determining common membership in a recognizable social grouping. Membership, as I use the term here, involves its least restrictive meaning—belonging to a recognizable group—and does not imply or refer to a formalized membership process. Network data and methods facilitate identification of subgroups within criminal networks based on a clustering of interactions that is denser within the group than outside of it. The distinction between formal membership and informal subgroup membership becomes less salient. People who are assumed to be part of a group are not necessarily people who explicitly say they are members or who committed at least one crime with the group. Instead, members of network-based subgroups have interacted often enough with a set of individuals to belong with those individuals and not others (Laumann, Marsden, and Prensky 1983). In other words, subgroups need to be relatively cohesive to be labeled as such. First consider the social structure shown by interactions among individuals. Formal attributions, if necessary, can wait until that first step is completed.

Ouellet, Bouchard, and Charette (2019) provide a blueprint for using network data on subgroup membership attribution. We extracted subgroups from among a large network of individuals who came into contact with police via arrests and noncriminal police interactions over a 10-year period. The starting point was 261 individuals confirmed to be gang members by use of a combination of police investigation records and ethnographic data. In the spirit of snowball sampling designs, these seeds, their contacts, and the contacts of these contacts made up the full network of 6,604 individuals. Though the 261 seeds were members of so-called Haitian gangs, among the 6,604 connected to them were members of outlaw motorcycle gangs and members of so-called Italian mafia organizations based in Montreal, among others. Subgroups were extracted using a commonly used method in network analysis (the Louvain method; see Blondel et al. 2008) that divides the network into an optimal number of subgroups (communities) based on individuals' patterns of interactions, seeking out local clusters of high interconnectivity. The algorithm first detects subcommunities within the network based on members who have more dense connections with each other than with other members within the network and then proceeds to build a network at the subgroup level, consisting of connections between the subgroups detected in the first step.[6]

Applying this method, we identified 327 subgroups of individuals that averaged 18 members. Importantly, not all individuals in these groups were connected to each other, and not all their connections were found within their assigned Louvain group. This allowed us to examine variations in groups' tendencies to connect within and outside their group, and whether those characteristics were associated with group survival.

To assess survival, we divided the 10-year period in three, so that "survival" implied a stable set of interactions among members for over

---

[6] By comparing the proportion of ties within communities to the proportion of ties between communities, the Louvain algorithm aims to maximize the modularity score, which is equal to zero when there are no within-community ties and equal to one when all ties are within the community, with higher values indicating better fit (Newman and Girvan 2004). Dozens of different classification methods are available in network analysis software. The algorithm for each differs depending on the objectives of the classification.

4 years. Less than 20 percent of the qualified groups were sufficiently stable to be found in at least two periods, and only 6 percent existed for nearly 10 years. Survival was a function of group cohesion, but the relationship was not direct; it was moderated by group size. For small groups, alliances outside the group were key to their survival. The opposite was true for the largest groups: the more alliances outside the organization, the less likely they were to survive. In short, large groups that adopt closed structures are more likely to persist, while survival of small groups depends on less cohesive and more versatile structures. Importantly, none of these hypotheses could have been tested without network data and its capacity to handle, and measure, the complex interplay of connections within and outside criminal groups. Traditional approaches often choose between units of analysis (the "group" or the "individual"). A network approach gets closer to the reality of these groups; their boundaries are bound to be more porous than most nonnetwork analyses can handle.

The lesson learned, and the way forward for organized crime scholars and law enforcement agencies, is to reverse the usual order in which things are done, with a twist. First, establish the social structure of interactions among organized criminals using network data and methods. Second, apply formal membership data on top of the structure uncovered with network data. The twist: the first step requires a relevant starting point, and it could very well be that the optimal starting point requires formal membership data. The networks we analyze capture a portion of something that exists in real life, but they are constructed with partial data (i.e., a biased sample of all interactions that occurred) for research purposes. The process of network construction follows universal, relatively standard, rules of coding, but any such exercise still entails sometimes arbitrary decisions about where to start. Smith and Papachristos (2016) started with Al Capone; Hashimi and Bouchard (2017) with the top two criminal entrepreneurs based on the local police detachment; Calderoni, Brunetto, and Piccardi (2017) with confirmed mafia meeting attendees; others go with all individuals named in organized crime investigations (Morselli 2009; Malm and Bichler 2011; Tenti and Morselli 2014). In all those cases, the relevant starting point was provided in the form of an attribute that may have required qualitative data on membership.

Calderoni and colleagues' (2017) work on the structure of 'Ndrangheta networks exemplifies how that approach may be applied to answer both policy and empirical questions. They analyzed investigative data coming from 574 mafia meetings that, combined, included 256 individuals. Attendance at a meeting was used as the basis for a connection in the network. They used a community detection algorithm similar to that used by Ouellet, Bouchard, and Charette (2019) to extract subgroups from the meeting data. Importantly, membership to these subgroups could be directly compared to known formal membership data from criminal intelligence—groups known as *locali*. The 17 *locali* were structured into seven distinct communities; this means that many members of *locali* had such close and frequent connections that, for all intents and purposes, they belonged to the same *locali*. In short, the geographically and culturally informed distinctions made by mafiosi on *locali* membership only partly matched their network behavior. Arguably, each of the approaches to describing the social structure of the 'Ndrangheta is informative in its own right. Yet, the additional insights provided by network data (which *locali* are close enough to belong to the same community) are hard to overlook.

The study provides one more useful demonstration for my purposes: the identification of mafia bosses from network data. Police data revealed that the 254 individuals who attended meetings included 34 bosses. The networks were not constructed with these bosses used as seeds; instead, all meeting attendees were included. Yet, the formal mafia boss attribution can be applied after the fact to examine whether bosses are positioned differently in the network. Calderoni, Brunetto, and Piccardi (2017) found that the 34 bosses were the brokers in the network. They were not only important within their own communities; they were also the drivers of connections between communities. Many attend local meetings, but only a few select individuals act as representatives of their *locali* outside its geographical boundaries. By combining these patterns, Calderoni and colleagues were able to predict who the bosses were with near-perfect accuracy.

What remains unsolved from pure network-based groupings, as clear-cut as they seem from a data point of view, is whether these boundaries carry meaning for their members. There are at least two situations that could arise. First, group members might disagree with their attributions, pointing out, hypothetically, that their frequent interactions with a set of individuals do not carry sociological meanings associated with group membership. Second, members might not think in terms of group membership at all; they might think of themselves as collaborating with others, sometimes frequently, but disagree that a layer of group membership should be added to these collaborative relationships. Network scholars might argue that group members' perceptions are a matter of awareness, that if they act or "interact" like a group, they can be considered as one. But we should be cautious in interpreting these groupings as material, especially without support from observational or interview data. A boundary may exist in the data, but not in the minds of the individuals involved.

Among Members, Who Is Part of the Core? There are a few boundaries to consider even within criminal organizations. Though a network-based group would be characterized by a higher degree of cohesion within it than outside of it, this group may adopt structures that sometimes vary widely. For example, these structures can be described as varying between centralization (a few individuals responsible for the bulk of connections) and decentralization (connections are more evenly spread), which will affect the relative efficiency of collaboration. Centralized and decentralized structures also affect their vulnerability to disruption (Malm and Bichler 2011; Joffres and Bouchard 2015). Interventions into centralized networks have little effect on peripheral actors who make up the majority of members, but can be devastating if they affect individuals in the center. Conversely, interventions into decentralized networks are more likely to involve individuals with relatively many connections; removal of any one them is unlikely to have large overall effects on the network.

A key boundary within criminal organizations, if one exists, is between the core and peripheral members. The distinction is important to law enforcement agencies that want to disrupt networks. If an organization has a core, and agencies can identify it, targeting the core may affect the organization's capacity to recover.[7] Membership in the core plays a symbolic role; it indicates prestige, achievement of a rank members aspire to, being part of an inner circle with influence over other group members, and authority over organizational decisions.

From a network perspective, a core-periphery structure exists when a handful of members have a high degree of cohesion, while the vast majority of others interact very little, though slightly more often than with members of the core (Borgatti and Everett 2000). If all members display

---

[7] The importance of the core relies on the assumption that its members carry out the most important network functions and are thus difficult to replace. Campana's (2016*b*) analysis of Nigerian human smugglers shows that this is not always true. The most important actors, the least easily replaceable, were madams at the periphery (also see Zhang, Chin, and Miller 2007). Without their recruitment skills, none of the core activities could take place.

high cohesion with other members, or if the core consists of a majority of members, the organization lacks a core-periphery structure. Figure 2 illustrates a simple core-periphery structure in which nodes 1–4 form the core, and the remaining nodes constitute a disconnected periphery. A network approach can improve understanding of whether a criminal organization has a core.

Bouchard and Konarski (2014) used this approach to determine whether a young gang loosely affiliated with the Hells Angels had a core, and whether a police attempt to remove the gang's core had identified the right individuals. Six members whom police targeted were surrounded by 54 others who had at least one connection to the targeted six. The 60 individuals formed a network with a core-periphery structure in which 13 formed a dense core. Five of the targeted six were part of that core, but many were missed, including one with the highest "coreness" score (Bouchard and Konarski 2014). The group survived and became a well-known criminal organization in western Canada.

The existence of a core set of members in a criminal organization indicates a culture of collaboration driven from the center out. Other

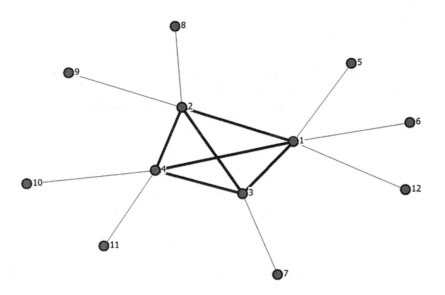

Fig. 2.—A network displaying a simple core-periphery structure. Source: Author.

collaborative structures exist within organized crime, including small-world structures (many highly connected subgroups linked by a few bridging ties, making any actor reachable in only a few steps; Malm and Bichler 2011) and cellular networks distributing illegal commodities across borders (Bruinsma and Bernasco 2004). No matter what the structure, network data allow more precise identification of group boundaries and have some value for understanding collaboration within and across those boundaries. And network blockmodeling techniques (i.e., grouping units based on network equivalence), like core-periphery analyses, allow examination of elements of the structure of organized crime boundaries that are impossible with other techniques.

C. Networks to Investigate the Ethnicity Boundary

Ethnicity-based classifications of organized crime have remained staples of criminal intelligence agencies.[8] Italian-, Asian-, and Mexican-based organizations are found in the classifications of agencies around the world and in textbooks; many add eastern European, African, and Middle Eastern gangs to the mix. These labels may be appropriate when discussing local organized crime phenomena, but not in classifications of types of organized crime.

There is investigative convenience in use of these classification schemes, especially when information is hard to come by. Ethnicity may correlate with distinct illegal market behavior, such as the use of particular smuggling routes or sale of particular drugs. Classification by ethnicity is also compatible with homophily—the tendency of individuals to connect with others similar to them (McPherson, Smith-Lovin, and Cook 2001). Ethnic homophily is a strong driver of connections in social networks, criminal or otherwise (McPherson, Smith-Lovin, and Cook 2001; Hughes 2013; Grund and Densley 2015; Kreager et al. 2017). The notion that these tendencies found in almost any social networks exist in organized crime networks is not, in and of itself, controversial.

The problems raised by use of ethnicity classifications outweigh their benefits (Kleemans and van de Bunt 1999; Bovenkerk, Siegel, and Zaitch

---

[8] For instance, Dubro, Champlain, and McAdam (2019) treat "multiethnic gangs" as a category on its own. Malm et al. (2011) show the lack of predictability of these classifications in matching network behavior, as shall be seen below.

2003; Malm, Bichler, and Nash 2011). Using ethnicity or race as a driver of police priorities creates human rights violations that have no place in the criminal justice system. These classifications can create dangerous oversimplifications in building cases against offenders of a particular ethnicity, regardless of their involvement in organized crime. Belonging to a criminal organization is a common aggravating factor in sentencing in many countries. Ethnicity alone may be used as a justification for targeting individuals, rather than targeting illegal behavior. Ethnicity by itself is a weak basis for distinguishing types of organized crime. Many people in organized crime are involved in supply of commodities in illegal markets. Almost any ethnic group an agency considers targeting is involved in illegal drug and other markets. Use of ethnicity as an overarching classification of organized crime is counterproductive.

A network approach can shed light on ethnicity boundaries and develop theoretically and empirically sophisticated descriptions of the ethnic composition of organizations. Inside the organization, a network approach can examine the association between ethnicity as an attribute and links between individuals who share that attribute. McCuish, Bouchard, and Corrado (2015), for example, describe a sample of 18 individuals taken from a larger criminal group of whom 50 percent were Caucasian, close to 40 percent were Asian, and the rest were Middle Eastern. Members collaborate within and across ethnicities (Tenti and Morselli 2014; Campana 2016b, 2018), even though tendencies for homophily often make collaboration within ethnicity more likely (Grund and Densley 2015).

From a network perspective, the question is not whether gangs and criminal organizations have ethnically varied memberships; they do in places where the general population is diverse. Ethnic composition is more homogenous in mafia families and in organizations such as the Hells Angels, especially if only made men or full-patched members are considered. Compositions vary in diverse ways. To understand the diversity, the effective boundaries of criminal organizations should first be assessed in terms of social relations, not attributes such as ethnicity. Social relations are a starting point for observing the variety of ethnicities in a particular organization. Using ethnicity to chart membership can cause diversity to be overlooked. Organizations may, for example, be ethnically varied, but their members may nonetheless prefer connections to others of their own ethnicity. Those are important subjects, understanding of which can be illuminated using network data and methods.

Some of the most compelling evidence about the role of ethnicity (or, often, nationality) is provided by Paolo Campana. His studies are based on network-specific models called Quadratic Assignment Procedure regression. He investigates whether being from the same ethnicity is associated with network connections. Neither transnational human trafficking networks organizing transport and exploitation from Nigeria to Italy (Campana 2016*b*), nor the migrant smuggling network operating across the Mediterranean (Campana 2018), showed evidence of homophily based on nationality. In the human trafficking network, nationality was a significant negative predictor. Traffickers were more likely to connect with others from different nationalities.

Ethnic collaboration across criminal organizations has also been studied. Malm, Bichler, and Nash (2011) looked at co-offending associations among criminal organizations in British Columbia. Figure 3 shows intelligence data on co-offending among organized crime offenders. The data are aggregated at group level (if an offender from group A co-offends with an offender from group B, groups A and B are assumed to be connected), using intelligence agency categories: outlaw motorcycle gangs

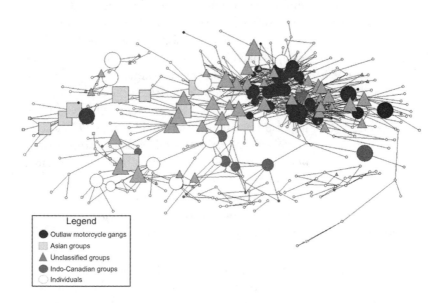

Legend
● Outlaw motorcycle gangs
▪ Asian groups
▲ Unclassified groups
● Indo-Canadian groups
○ Individuals

Fig. 3.—Co-offending between groups in British Columbia, Canada, circa 2007. Source: Malm, Bichler, and Nash (2011).

(dark circles), Asian groups (squares), Indo-Canadian groups (light circles), unclassified groups, and individuals not known to belong to any group (triangles).

Figure 3 shows co-offending connections at the group level. There is a high level of connectivity across groups. Distinct clusters of similar nodes linked together in the same area of the network are not evident. Nodes of different ethnicities are dispersed across the network. The network may display more ethnic homophily than would be expected by chance, but the lack of separate, ethnically homogenous clusters is telling. Groups co-offended within their own group 45–55 percent of the time, revealing significant levels of co-offending across ethnic lines.

These findings may or may not recur elsewhere. British Columbia is known for ethnically diverse criminal groups (McConnell 2015; McCuish, Bouchard, and Corrado 2015). In network terms, British Columbian gangs may show a lesser tendency for ethnic homophily than do gangs in other regions. This suggests a role for culture in shaping social networks. Patterns found in a region will be a product of availability. Individuals in cosmopolitan regions have access to a wider range of potential accomplices of diverse ethnic backgrounds.

There is accumulating evidence that this may be true elsewhere, as Campana's (2016b, 2018) results show. Sarnecki (2001) found many more ethnically mixed dyads than expected in Swedish co-offending data. Tenti and Morselli's (2014) analysis of an investigation of the 'Ndrangheta suggests that even Italian mafias are more diverse than not, especially when the focus is on the illicit activities they undertake and the social organization of those activities. A single investigation of 'Ndrangheta involvement in all levels of illegal drug importation and distribution identifies 242 individuals from at least nine different nationalities. Collaboration across nationalities was the norm, not the exception. Nationality was loosely associated with market level; the Italian groups were more likely to be in import and wholesale roles, effectively making them brokers in the network. This brokerage role meant that the Italian groups were collaborating widely with individuals from diverse backgrounds. Their conclusion:

> The important point that must be retained after these results is that organized crime cannot be restricted to corporate-like and reputed formal criminal organizations and the actions of illegal market participants cannot be framed as formal organizational boundaries. Rather, organized crime . . . is a matter of criminal opportunity and

necessary collaboration. Illegal market participants are not independent from one another—neither exclusive affiliation to specific criminal groups nor ethnic characterisations emerge as important features
in crime. (Tenti and Morselli 2014, p. 39)

The generalizability of these case studies is unclear. There have been
few empirical tests of ethnic collaboration in organized crime networks.
That many of these studies involved transnational rather than local networks played a role in these findings. Others who have adopted broader,
multimarket-level views of networks find greater network diversity, but
also more hierarchy, albeit of a rudimentary kind (Varese 2013).

I draw two conclusions from this literature. First, although there is evidence of both diversity and homophily, generalizations around ethnicity per se are unlikely to be productive. Second, the subject should be investigated with network data, and not on the basis of rigid categories that
assume fixed entities with simple membership rules.

The degree to which criminal organizations collaborate across ethnic
lines can be measured with network data. More precise and potentially
meaningful descriptions of the roles of ethnicity in structuring webs of
conflicts and alliances across groups can be made if collaborative ties
are tracked and followed. Malm, Bichler, and Nash (2011) showed that
use of network analyses facilitated description of both the internal dynamics of criminal organizations and the web of connections between
organizations at the meso level. This offers a significant development
opportunity for the field, especially in understanding conflicts and alliances
across organizations (Papachristos 2009; Descormiers and Morselli 2011;
Bichler et al. 2019).

D. Crossing the Initial Boundary: Recruitment in Organized Crime

A revolution in place-based criminology happened when street segments replaced neighborhoods as the unit of analysis. Crime is concentrated in only some parts of neighborhoods and may not follow the same
trends as in low-crime segments of neighborhoods (Weisburd, Groff,
and Yang 2012). It is common, for example, to observe that one street
segment is experiencing a crime wave even though crime trends are stable
at the neighborhood level.

A network approach can improve understanding of recruitment into
organized crime. If a criminal organization is viewed as a fixed entity

(by analogy to "the neighborhood"), almost every recruitment decision can be attributed to the group as a whole or its leader rather than to the subgroup (the "segment") in which recruitment occurred. For instance, one could say that "Nick was recruited by the organization to run a drug line in the Eastern part of the city." Nick's recruitment, however, is likely to have been both simpler and more complicated than this, depending on how it is understood. The simple view is that Nick is Al's cousin, and Al invited him to join. The complicated view would consider the sequence of events that led to Nick being identified by Al as a potential recruit, the socialization process that acquainted him with other group members, and their opportunities to assess his skill set and trustworthiness; at some point they agreed to make him part of the group. It may, moreover, not have been as simple as Al choosing Nick; Al had also to decide why other potential accomplices were less suitable. Network analyses can situate Nick among the larger pool of potential associates who could have been recruited but were not. With this networked view of recruitment, the mechanisms can be better understood and perhaps better predicted.

Recruitment into organizations like the Sicilian Cosa Nostra or the 'Ndrangheta would not require a network approach if family lineage was a reliable predictor of who is invited and who is not. But as Varese (2018) has shown after examining recruitment and initiation rituals among the yakuza, the triads, and the Russian mafia, this is not necessarily what happens. The 'Ndrangheta and, especially, the Sicilian Cosa Nostra have rules favoring the recruitment of family members; other mafias do not. Those who are recruited come from the larger social network around made men. Potential recruits are observed, sometimes for long periods, before they are invited to join. This facilitates screening out police informants, allows testing of trustworthiness and skills, and helps potential recruits learn the organization's cultural and criminal traditions. Once they become made members, the group becomes their new family. This process occurs among other criminal organizations, such as outlaw motorcycle gangs (Quinn and Forsyth 2011; Blokland and von Lampe 2020). The notion of natal family remains important, but mostly as an analogy and as glue in the social networks assembled as criminal organizations.

A networked view can inform two types of recruitment. The first is the recruitment of individuals invited to join for the first time. The second involves recruitment from within the organization for particular purposes such as a murder conspiracy, a drug-trafficking venture, or to replace a lost member. Both types are driven by common forces, namely, a combination of criminal human capital (an offender's skills) and criminal social capital (an offender's contacts in the organization). Both processes feed on the other (e.g., Coleman 1988); network data are useful in understanding both. For task or role recruitment, it is useful to situate the decision as a search for a suitable accomplice among the larger pool of available associates, using Tremblay's (1993) model. For initial recruitment, it is useful to think of Nick's story above, or many other examples in the literature on recruitment. Savona et al. (2017), in a systematic review, describe a culturally entrenched network process that Kleemans and van de Bunt (1999, p. 11) referred to as a snowball effect. They summed up in this way: "Perhaps this snowball effect is the most important principle of the development of criminal associations: people get in touch with criminal associations through their social relations; as they go along their dependency on the resources of other people (such as money, knowledge and contacts) gradually declines; and finally they generate new criminal associations, which subsequently attract people from their social environment again."

Kleemans and van de Bunt (1999) warned against a view that focuses only on organizations actively recruiting new members; recruitment often occurs organically, as the criminal process unfolds. Often, what we refer to as recruitment is better described as outsiders seeking a role in a particular venture. The extent to which proactive approaches from nonmembers are successful depends on the relative embeddedness of these nonmembers in the organization (are they already connected to one or multiple members?) and the relative importance of the member being approached (does he have influence?). No matter how recruitment unfolds, network mechanisms are at play. The differences in specific mechanisms are a matter of context: who is taking the initiative (the recruiter or the recruited); where is recruitment taking place (the workplace or the neighborhood). Network data accommodate these differences. They are most easily observed in network studies relying on wiretap data: who called whom may reveal the presence of hierarchy in the network, and whether business operations are going according to plan (Morselli 2009).

Most of the evidence on the importance of social networks in recruitment emerges from qualitative social network analysis, in which the role of social ties in recruitment seems ubiquitous. A systematic review of 47 empirical studies of recruitment in organized crime found social ties to be the most important mechanism of entry among the more than 10 factors considered (Savona et al. 2017). Social network data have a major role to play in understanding the mechanics of recruitment. Yet, very few studies of recruitment were designed around social networks. The main blind spot is a sort of sample-selection bias—sampling on the dependent variable. We examine those who have been chosen but learn little of the larger number of individuals who could have been selected but were not.

Having the network of social relations can help figure that out. The decision to recruit a specific individual is a socially embedded decision. We need simultaneously to consider both the recruiter and the recruit's networks. Part of why a specific recruit was selected involves not simply his skills or social capital within the organization, but also the importance of the person who is recruiting or vouching for him in the larger network.

Few published studies of recruitment have used social network data to demonstrate the process, but the importance of social ties is fundamental. A prominent example of a networked view of recruitment is Morselli's (2003) analysis of Sammy Gravano's rise in the Gambino family. Specific contacts, at different times, allowed Gravano entry into the Colombo and then Gambino families, promotion within the Gambinos, and a lengthy criminal career, even considering major rule transgressions. All turning points were driven by key social contacts that mentored and vouched for him, essential for entry and progression within the families. These social mentors differ from technical mentors in that their main function is to affect their proteges' involvement in the social networks, and not necessarily to refine their skill sets (Bouchard and Nguyen 2011). Many mentors serve both purposes. Recruitment into criminal organizations goes through networks. This does not mean that criminal competence is irrelevant. Mentors do not take just anybody under wing; they take on proteges who show promise. Social capital creates human (criminal) capital (Coleman 1988), but the reverse is also true.

Morselli's (2003) analysis reversed the perception that a willingness to use violence to prove loyalty was the main factor in explaining Gravano's rise in the Gambino family. The network came first, abilities developed, and promotion ensued. Violence came last. Gravano's network did not grow linearly with each promotional stage. His core network peaked when he became a capo (underboss) and steadily declined until his indictment as Gambino family underboss in 1990. Initially, the recruit is hierarchically constrained; he relies on the networks of others to climb the hierarchy inside the organization. The recruit crosses the boundaries of the organization based on specific social ties and, if successful, reproduces these network processes at each subsequent promotional stage.

Networked Decisions: Recruitment for Specific Crimes. How do organized criminals decide who to include in a murder conspiracy or a drug-trafficking venture? They look around and find the most suitable partners. Progress on this question was made at the conceptual level, even though data, research designs, and methods existed to support existing theories about cooperation among criminals. The intuition that offenders draw co-offenders from a larger pool of associates predates the explosion of social network analysis in criminology. In 1993, Tremblay published an important essay that laid theoretical and research foundations. He argued that the search for co-offenders is purposeful, social, and rational, but involved trade-offs. Not all suitable co-offenders are trustworthy, and not all trustworthy crime partners are suited for the job. Offenders who can best reconcile these dilemmas were hypothesized to achieve better outcomes.

A network approach makes it possible to visualize the extent and nature of the available co-offenders, and model the likelihood a particular co-offender is selected, based on a combination of network position and potential co-offenders' attributes. Visualization identifies potential candidates, and modeling enhances understanding of selection patterns.

These advantages are not limited to only organized crime studies (McCarthy, Hagan, and Cohen 1998). A network approach can improve understanding of the choices and constraints associated with any decision to cooperate. What is distinctive about organized crime is that most of those decisions are made within the context of an organization, meaning that the pool of suitable candidates may be limited. Decisions about recruitment are bounded. Co-offending decisions are freer outside of criminal organizations, but offenders are subject to many of the same kinds of considerations: Who can do this with me, and whom do I trust to execute well and maintain confidences if caught by the police?

McCuish, Bouchard, and Corrado (2015) studied recruitment decisions in organizing three murders. The group, initially a youth gang, grew into a criminal organization during the 10 years they were followed. Access to official co-offending data during that period was available, which provided complete networks related to all three murders (all led to convictions), but those data could not track social and criminal ties not known to the police. For most crimes, gang members co-offended with people in and outside the gang, but for murder conspiracies, all participants were recruited from the gang leader's inner circle of members. Members were more trustworthy than outsiders; the higher the stakes, the more likely members were to be selected.

Collaborations in organized crime ventures are often based on trust, making some recruitment and co-offending decisions less than optimal (Tremblay 1993). Network data highlight constraints faced by organized criminals and demonstrate individual differences in access to social opportunity structures that characterize organized crime (Morselli 2003; Kleemans and De Poot 2008; Bouchard and Nguyen 2011).

III. Dangers in Interpreting Network Data

Network data are vulnerable to the biases that affect other criminal justice data: incompleteness, recall bias, and overemphasis on some groups at the expense of others (Campana 2016*a*). Campana and Varese (2012), focusing on wiretap data, provide the most comprehensive examination of limitations of illicit network data.

In this section, I discuss limitations of three kinds: overinterpretation, overcomplexification, and oversimplification. Many of these dangers result from lack of contextual data. Network data should normally contain more context information than is possible in traditional quantitative studies.

A. Overinterpretation

When network data are the only or main source of information, it is easy to see more patterns than exist. There is, for example, always a risk of imputing too much intentionality and purpose to observed network patterns. A person may have many connections to others in a criminal network, and link otherwise disconnected individuals, but not take advantage of co-offending possibilities or even recognize them. This may be more common than we know. Researchers seldom ask offenders to describe their self-perceived network position, or their strategies to take advantage of their social networks. Even if individuals are unaware of their network positions and its potential benefits, they are in a position to benefit from their network positions. The potential benefits exist.

Whether they are recognized is another matter entirely. Social capital consists of the ability to use social connections (Lin, Cook, and Burt 2001), not their number or quality. A person could have comparatively few connections but use them exceptionally effectively. Network scholars need to do more to demonstrate that central players are aware of their connections and use them strategically.

A related overinterpretation error is more common: interpreting the whole network while forgetting it was built for particular reasons. The origins of the network always matter, for the same reason they matter in snowball sampling: network composition will be shaped by the seeds from which it grew. The more seeds and the greater their diversity, the more likely we are to understand the characteristics of the population making up the network. Conceptualizing network construction as a sampling process acknowledges that researchers make choices, often arbitrary ones, on whom to include in the network; those choices have implications for interpreting the results. Overinterpretation occurs when scholars interpret the network positions of seeds and nonseeds on the same level. Valid interpretations should always be made on two separate levels—seeds versus nonseeds (e.g., "Among seeds, the most central is. . . . Among nonseeds (i.e., alters), someone who emerges as potentially important is . . ."; Varese 2013; Hashimi and Bouchard 2017).

B. Overcomplexification

Network scholars can become too enthusiastic. Networks can grow almost infinitely. A follow-the-links approach has, in theory, no objective end. In practice, letting networks grow too far away from their seeds confounds analyses. To the extent that the network starting point was well chosen (e.g., a mafia leader, members of a Hells Angels chapter), extending it three or four steps from the original seeds can significantly change its nature. An analysis can begin from an original seed and be extended to include the seed's network, the connections of the seed's connections, and their third-order connections. By the end of the process, the network around the seed could contain 100 or more individuals. The starting point remains relevant; the 100 are known because they are within three steps of the seed. However, the network is no more the seed's than it is the network of any one of the 100 others. Indirect connections diffuse through networks and influence criminal behavior (Papachristos 2011), but interpretations must reflect these complexities.

C. Oversimplification

Oversimplification often results from missing data. All researchers recognize the need to manage missing data problems. With network data, a missing node or link may fundamentally distort characterization of the network (Morselli 2009; Campana and Varese 2012), especially if the network is small. Interpretive errors concerning large networks missing, say, 10 percent of nodes, are less likely than concerning smaller networks in which the 10 percent missing data may be crucial (Burcher and Whelan 2015).

In network analyses, data missing from law enforcement databases can be crucial. Researchers can see, and code for, data concerning people seen by the police, or whom the police think relevant (wives or girlfriends may sometimes be excluded). People who escape police attention do not appear. Some individuals identified in police data are likely not to be central, and are thus unlikely to be picked up in the network analyses. How does someone become visible and central in police data? Typically, by being arrested more often than others who might have been. Those arrested often are not the people at the center of events underlying major crime investigations.

Those issues can be addressed. Multivariate analyses can control for offenders' relative network exposure, net of other important patterns being investigated. The use of data from multiple years often compensates for the effect of including data for some offenders from an atypical year, for instance, years in which they were the targets of major police investigations. Use of multiple data sources can compensate for limitations of any one source. The focus in arrest data on the event and visible co-offending can be offset by adding surveillance data (Rostami and Mondani 2015), if available, or police contact data (Hashimi and Bouchard 2017; Ouellet, Bouchard, and Charette 2019). Criminals, even masterminds, do not fully avoid having police records, even if they are never convicted.

IV. The Future of Research on Networks
and Collaboration in Organized Crime

Network research on organized crime is constantly evolving. Myriad research questions need better answers. I discuss four: how and when boundaries form, variations in cultures of collaborations, age boundaries, geographical boundaries.

A. How and When Boundaries Form

Network data can capture dynamics that exist within criminal organizations, changes in relationships between stable members, and changes in the relative importance of peripheral members who come and go. Network researchers are less interested in changes in the number of members than in the structure of the organization. For example, is it becoming more centralized around a few leaders, as may have been intended during a retrenchment phase, or does the social network of collaborations among members tell a different story?

This approach allows us a chance to draw from network theory to make predictions about survival. Ouellet, Bouchard, and Charette's (2019) study of gang persistence showed that forming alliances outside the organization was key for the survival of the relatively small groups that make up the bulk of organized crime. For large groups, the opposite was true: the more outside alliances, the lower the likelihood of survival. Network descriptions of different criminal organizations may thus facilitate understanding of how they are likely to evolve over time, including their capacity to adapt to disruptions caused by law enforcement (Morselli 2009; Bright, Koskinen, and Malm 2018) and conflicts with other groups (Papachristos 2009; Bichler et al. 2019). Study of illicit networks is largely descriptive and cross-sectional. Work on longitudinal networks has mostly been conducted in the classrooms of hundreds of American high schools. With a few notable exceptions (e.g., Bright, Koskinen, and Malm 2018), the resulting models have rarely been applied to organized crime networks (Ouellet and Hashimi 2019). The opportunity to look into how and when boundaries form is likely to drive the research agendas of many crime and network scholars in the near future.

B. The Emergence of Cultures of Cooperation

Collaboration and group boundaries need fuller study and explanation using network data and methods. That organized criminals collaborate is not mysterious. Christakis's *Blueprint* (2019) shows that collaboration emerges in any society as part of the fabric of human life. However, variations exist in the forms collaboration takes. Some groups form highly centralized networks, with connections passing through only a few individuals, like the core-periphery structures discussed above. Others are more egalitarian; network members have relatively similar numbers of ties to others. Christakis argues that variations are shaped by a combination of the environments in which they are embedded and the cultures of cooperation developed among network members. Consider, for example, the 19 hijackers involved in the 9/11 terrorist plot; their network was long and sparse, with few strong ties within or between different hijackings (Krebs 2002). The stakes were high, and the time required was substantial, making it necessary to keep the conspiracy going for a long time without being detected (Morselli, Giguere, and Petit 2007). This favored a snake-shaped network in which failure of one part of the network would be unlikely to cascade through the rest. Each individual member knew little about the whereabouts of others. The efficiency-security trade-off favored security. Security concerns are associated with sparse networks, efficiency with dense ones (Morselli, Giguere, and Petit 2007).

Criminal organizations have agency in creating cultures that favor more effective collaboration. A cultural environment favoring collaboration is associated with growth and survival of criminal organizations. Organizations that foster environments in which cheating and defections are common are more likely to fail. Just as in the legitimate world, differences in organizations' capacity to establish a culture of cooperation are associated with tangible outcomes, such as longer survival, or high collective achievement (Tremblay, Bouchard, and Petit 2009; Sergi 2016). Ouellet, Bouchard, and Charette (2019) showed that small groups benefit from recruitment; the competency of recruitment decisions, however, is important. Growing in the right way may be crucial to survival of smaller groups.

The preceding observations are hypotheses. There have been few or no empirical demonstrations of the interplay of culture and collaboration in organized crime. It would be challenging to adapt Christakis's (2019) online experiments to real-life organized crime. A way forward would involve combinations of qualitative data on cultures and subcultures with network data on interactions within the subculture (for a brilliant example of concerning gangs, see Tremblay et al. 2016).

C. Age Boundaries

A focus on connections between individuals as a main unit of analysis is bound to pay attention to aspects of organized crime collaborations that are otherwise easily overlooked. Age differences between individuals are one indicator that would benefit from greater attention. Age difference is an indicator of mentorship, an indicator of longer, more successful criminal careers (Morselli, Tremblay, and McCarthy 2006). Scholars interested in criminal trajectories, including whether juvenile delinquency is likely to lead to adult criminality (e.g., Savona et al. 2017; Blokland et al. 2019), should pay attention to relationships between offenders of significantly different ages. Adolescents who interact only with others of the same age are much more likely to desist from crime when they become adults. Having role models, in crime or otherwise, helps frame career paths.

At the organization level, groups that maintain ties to younger people are more likely to survive (Ouellet et al. 2019). The organizational model of the Hells Angels and of other outlaw biker clubs includes establishment of puppet clubs from which future members are recruited (Morselli 2009; Quinn and Forsyth 2011). Similar mentoring functions have been observed in the larger networks of mafia families; they ensure that recruits are properly vetted and that they learn the rules of behavior inside the family (Varese 2018). These cultural and knowledge transfers are inherently social in nature (Sutherland 1937) and best approached with network data. A potential benefit of this approach, at the meso level, is improved understanding of the evolution and demise of criminal organizations. Organizations with healthy stables of potential recruits and a tradition of promotion and cooperation are more likely to survive.

D. Crossing Geographic Boundaries

Network studies of transnational organized crime are not common. Campana (2016b, 2018) constructed transnational networks from major investigative files in a number of countries. Access to files documenting collaborative activities of offenders from multiple countries is often available only in the country whose law enforcement agencies have jurisdiction (e.g., Varese 2013; Tenti and Morselli 2014). These types of studies are important because offenders coordinating cross-border trafficking are often role models, sources of inspiration to other criminals who look up to them (Tremblay and Morselli 2000). They are few in number and hard to detect (Bouchard and Ouellet 2011) and potentially make the most money from crime (Reuter and Haaga 1989; Desroches 2005; Bouchard and Ouellet 2011). Their influence needs to be studied.

This small body of research sets the stage for deeper looks into networks that cross geographical boundaries. The interplay of local connections, and connections that span multiple countries, is poorly understood. Few members of transnational networks are aware of activities and connections beyond the local level. Future research needs to target the drivers of those differences, and whether these networks' transnational nature concerns only select individuals in coordination roles. The implication would be that there is perhaps no transnational organized crime per se; only a few select individuals who broker deals across multiple countries.

V. Conclusion

Morselli (2003) observed that much of the traditional literature on mafia families revolved around networks. From Ianni and Reuss-Ianni's (1972) patron-client relationships to Haller's (1990) fraternity of criminal entrepreneurs, organized crime scholars had difficulty describing the functioning of criminal organizations without emphasizing their social networks. Their frameworks fit within the family of network approaches to crime; they can be enriched by collecting network data. Doing so reveals the mechanisms at play in collaboration among organized criminals. It permits boundaries to be drawn: who is part of the organization and who is not; who is recruited and by whom; and how the organization evolves, reproduces, and survives. Network data clarify the context, for example, of recruitment decisions. Network data are mainly, but not solely, about mapping relations. It is also about understanding why those relations were formed.

How else can alliances across criminal organizations be described accurately? It is indeed challenging to describe the interconnections among cells in a drug distribution chain without referring to networks, or using network terms. The terms "cell," "connection," and even "chain" are the building blocks and foundation of network theory. The leap from thinking of organized crime in terms of network analogies, and consciously applying network data and methods, is not a large one.

Network data by themselves are not enough. A network approach is sometimes possible only when other sources of data and theory are available. Economic approaches are needed to understand market forces that explain involvement in one market but not another. Situational approaches make sense of the decision making involved in establishing an importation route. Subcultural theory aids understanding of the origins and effects of norms on behavior (Kleemans 2014). This volume of *Crime and Justice* is illustrative. Many of the essays discuss similar subjects but use different perspectives. Most refer to work of others that is informed by different perspectives.

I did not discuss other promising areas of research on organized crime that could benefit from network approaches. They can also be used, for instance, to gain insights into conflicts among criminal organizations. Here, the analysis operates in reverse; rather than seek better understanding of collaboration, the aim is to understand noncollaboration—antagonistic relations among organized criminals. The theoretical foundation is the same; conflicts are inherently social acts. Each violent act in a conflict has a history, symbolic meanings, and, because conflicts involve multiple incidents, implications for future incidents. The retaliatory nature of conflicts has an indirect consequence of expanding the social networks in which groups are embedded. A network approach can help understand patterns of conflict that are likely to recur because they are integrated in the identities of the protagonists (Papachristos 2009). Studying alliances and conflicts together makes possible informed predictions about who will win the conflict.

I also did not discuss practical implications of adopting a network approach; they are a selling point for law enforcement agencies contemplating collaborations with academics. Understandably, practitioners have been attracted by the prospect that social network analysis may facilitate the disruption of criminal groups (Bichler and Malm 2015). In principle, those developments are positive; couching target selection decisions for violence reduction in network data is usually an improvement over traditional approaches that often use no systematic data at all.

In practice, policy recommendations stemming from network analyses are only as good as the data used to generate them. Biased data produce biased recommendations. Traditional practices, however, may produce even more harms because of the same biases. Network methods can accentuate biases existing in the data. They can also be used to detect biases. Incorporation of novel methods in law enforcement practice should be accompanied by a concern for transparency, a willingness to independently evaluate performance, and an aim to reduce inequality.

Most of the organized crime literature takes networks for granted. Little is known about why particular individuals rise to their network positions, or what forces cause networks to take one form and not another. Network structures emerge from the interplay of social forces that operate in all social groups. They are at the heart of collaboration in organized crime.

REFERENCES

Bichler, Gisela, and Aili Malm, eds. 2015. *Disrupting Criminal Networks: Network Analysis in Crime Prevention*. Boulder, CO: Lynne Rienner.

Bichler, Gisela, Alexis Norris, Jared R. Dmello, and Jasmin Randle. 2019. "The Impact of Civil Gang Injunctions on Networked Violence between the Bloods and the Crips." *Crime and Delinquency* 65:875–915.

Blokland, Arjan, Lonneke van Hout, Wouter van der Leest, and Melvin Soudijn. 2019. "Not Your Average Biker; Criminal Careers of Members of Dutch Outlaw Motorcycle Gangs." *Trends in Organized Crime* 22:10–33.

Blokland, Arjan, and Klaus von Lampe. 2020. "Outlaw Motorcycle Clubs and Organized Crime." In *Organizing Crime: Mafias, Markets, and Networks*. Vol. 39 of *Crime and Justice: A Review of Research*, edited by Michael Tonry. Chicago: University of Chicago Press.

Blondel, Vincent D., Jean-Loup Guillaume, Renaud Lambiotte, and Etienne Lefebvre. 2008. "Fast Unfolding of Communities in Large Networks." *Journal of Statistical Mechanics: Theory and Experiment* 2008:P10008.

Borgatti, Stephen P., and Martin G. Everett. 2000. "Models of Core/Periphery Structures." *Social Networks* 21:375–95.

Borgatti, Stephen P., Ajay Mehra, Daniel J. Brass, and Giuseppe Labianca. 2009. "Network Analysis in the Social Sciences." *Science* 323:892–95.

Bouchard, Martin, and Aili Malm. 2016. "Social Network Analysis and Its Contribution to Research on Crime and Criminal Justice." In *Oxford Handbooks Online*. New York: Oxford University Press.

Bouchard, Martin, and Richard Konarski. 2014. "Assessing the Core Membership of a Youth Gang from Its Co-offending Network." In *Crime and Networks*, edited by Carlo Morselli. New York: Routledge.

Bouchard, Martin, and Carlo Morselli. 2014. "Opportunistic Structures of Organized Crime." In *Handbook of Organized Crime*, edited by Letizia Paoli. Oxford: Oxford University Press.

Bouchard, Martin, and Holly Nguyen. 2011. "Professional or Amateurs? Revisiting the Notion of Professional Crime in the Context of Cannabis Cultivation." In *World Wide Weed: Global Trends in Cannabis Cultivation and its Control*, edited by Tom Decorte, Gary Potter, and Martin Bouchard. London: Ashgate.

Bouchard, Martin, and Frédéric Ouellet. 2011. "Is Small Beautiful? The Link between Risks and Size in Illegal Drug Markets." *Global Crime* 12:70–86.

Bovenkerk, Frank, Dina Siegel, and Damián Zaitch. 2003. "Organized Crime and Ethnic Reputation Manipulation." *Crime, Law and Social Change* 39:23–38.

Bright, David, Johan Koskinen, and Aili Malm. 2018. "Illicit Network Dynamics: The Formation and Evolution of a Drug Trafficking Network." *Journal of Quantitative Criminology* 35:237–58.

Bruinsma, Gerben, and Wim Bernasco. 2004. "Criminal Groups and Transnational Illegal Markets." *Crime, Law and Social Change* 41:79–94.

Burcher, M., and Chad Whelan. 2015. "Social Network Analysis and Small Group 'Dark' Networks: An Analysis of the London Bombers and the Problem of 'Fuzzy' Boundaries." *Global Crime* 16:104–22.

Calderoni, Francesco. 2012. "The Structure of Drug Trafficking Mafias: The 'Ndrangheta and Cocaine." *Crime, Law and Social Change* 58:321–49.

Calderoni, Francesco, Domenico Brunetto, and Carlo Piccardi. 2017. "Communities in Criminal Networks: A Case Study." *Social Networks* 48:116–25.

Campana, Paolo. 2016a. "Explaining Criminal Networks: Strategies and Potential Pitfalls." *Methodological Innovations* 9. https://doi.org/10.1177/2059799115622748.

———. 2016b. "The Structure of Human Trafficking: Lifting the Bonnet on a Nigerian Transnational Network." *British Journal of Criminology* 56:68–86.

———. 2018. "Out of Africa: The Organization of Migrant Smuggling across the Mediterranean." *European Journal of Criminology* 15:481–502.

Campana, Paolo, and Federico Varese. 2012. "Listening to the Wire: Criteria and Techniques for the Quantitative Analysis of Phone Intercepts." *Trends in Organized Crime* 15(1):13–30.

Carrington, Peter J. 2011. "Crime and Social Network Analysis." In *SAGE Handbook of Social Network Analysis*, edited by John Scott and Peter J. Carrington. Thousand Oaks, CA: Sage.

Christakis, Nicholas A. 2019. *Blueprint: The Evolutionary Origins of a Good Society*. New York: Little, Brown Spark.

Coleman, James S. 1988. "Social Capital in the Creation of Human Capital." *American Journal of Sociology* 94:S95–S120.

DellaPosta, Daniel. 2017. "Network Closure and Integration in the Mid-20th Century American Mafia." *Social Networks* 51:148–57.

Descormiers, Karine, and Carlo Morselli. 2011. "Alliances, Conflicts, and Contradictions in Montreal's Street Gang Landscape." *International Criminal Justice Review* 21:297–314.

Desroches, F. J. 2005. *The Crime That Pays: Drug Trafficking and Organized Crime in Canada*. Toronto: Canadian Scholars' Press.

Dubro, James R., Pierre De Champlain, and William L. MacAdam. 2019. "Organized Crime in Canada." In *The Canadian Encyclopedia*. https://thecanadian encyclopedia.ca/en/article/organized-crime.

Erickson, Bonnie H. 1981. "Secret Societies and Social Structure." *Social Forces* 60:188–210.

Gallupe. Owen. 2016. "Network Analysis." In *The Handbook of Measurement in Criminology and Criminal Justice*, edited by Beth M. Huebner and Timothy S. Bynum. Chichester: Wiley.

Gravel, Jason, and George Tita. 2017. "Network Perspectives on Crime." In *Oxford Research Encyclopedia, Criminology and Criminal Justice*. Oxford: Oxford University Press.

Grund, Thomas U., and James A. Densley. 2015. "Ethnic Homophily and Triad Closure: Mapping Internal Gang Structure Using Exponential Random Graph Models." *Journal of Contemporary Criminal Justice* 31:354–70.

Haller, Mark H. 1990. "Illegal Enterprise: A Theoretical and Historical Interpretation." *Criminology* 28:207–35.

Hashimi, Sadaf, and Martin Bouchard. 2017. "On to the Next One? Using Social Network Data to Inform Police Target Prioritization." *Policing: An International Journal of Police Strategies and Management* 40:768–82.

Haynie, Dana L. 2001. "Delinquent Peers Revisited: Does Network Structure Matter?" *American Journal of Sociology* 106:1013–57.

Hughes, Lorine A. 2013. "Group Cohesiveness, Gang Membership Prestige, and Delinquency and Violence in Chicago 1959–1962." *Criminology* 51:795–832.

Ianni, Francis A. J., and Elizabeth Reuss-Ianni. 1972. *A Family Business: Kinship and Social Control in Organized Crime.* New York: Russell Sage Foundation.

Joffres, Kila, and Martin Bouchard. 2015. "Vulnerabilities in Online Child Exploitation Networks." *Disrupting Criminal Networks: Network Analysis in Crime Prevention* 28:153–75.

Kleemans, Edward R. 2014. "Theoretical Perspectives on Organized Crime." In *Oxford Handbook of Organized Crime*, edited by Letizia Paoli. Oxford: Oxford University Press.

Kleemans, Edward R., and Christianne J. De Poot. 2008. "Criminal Careers in Organized Crime and Social Opportunity Structure." *European Journal of Criminology* 5:69–98.

Kleemans, Edward R., and Henk G. Van de Bunt. 1999. "The Social Embeddedness of Organized Crime." *Transnational Organized Crime* 5:19–36.

Knoke, David, and Song Yang. 2008. *Social Network Analysis*, 2nd ed. Thousand Oaks, CA: Sage.

Kreager, Derek A., Jacob T. N. Young, Dana L. Haynie, Martin Bouchard, David R. Schaefer, and Gary Zajac. 2017. "Where 'Old Heads' Prevail: Inmate Hierarchy in a Men's Prison Unit." *American Sociological Review* 82:685–718.

Krebs, Valdis E. 2002. "Mapping Networks of Terrorist Cells." *Connections* 24:43–52.

Laumann, Edward O., Peter V. Marsden, and David Prensky. 1983. "The Boundary Specification Problem in Network Analysis." In *Applied Network Analysis: A Methodological Introduction*, edited by Linton C. Freeman, Douglas R. White, and A. Kimball Romney. Beverly Hills, CA: Sage.

Lin, Nan, Karen S. Cook, and Ronald S. Burt, eds. 2001. *Social Capital: Theory and Research.* New Brunswick, NJ: Transaction.

Lusher, Dean, Johan Koskinen, and Garry Robins, eds. 2013. *Exponential Random Graph Models for Social Networks: Theory, Methods, and Applications.* Cambridge: Cambridge University Press.

Malm, Aili, and Gisela Bichler. 2011. "Networks of Collaborating Criminals: Assessing the Structural Vulnerability of Drug Markets." *Journal of Research in Crime and Delinquency* 48:271–97.

Malm, Aili, Gisela Bichler, and Rebecca Nash. 2011. "Co–offending between Criminal Enterprise Groups." *Global Crime* 12:112–28.

Mastrobuoni, Giovanni, and Eleonora Patacchini. 2012. "Organized Crime Networks: An Application of Network Analysis Techniques to the American Mafia." *Review of Network Economics* 11(3). https://doi.org/10.1515/1446-9022.1324.

McCarthy, Bill, John Hagan, and Lawrence E. Cohen. 1998. "Uncertainty, Cooperation, and Crime: Understanding the Decision to Co–offend." *Social Forces* 77:155–84.

McConnell, Keiron. 2015. "The Construction of the Gang in British Columbia: Mafioso, Gangster, or Thug? An Examination of the Uniqueness of the BC Gangster Phenomenon." Doctoral thesis, London Metropolitan University.

McCuish, Evan C., Martin Bouchard, and Raymond R. Corrado. 2015. "The Search for Suitable Homicide Co–offenders among Gang Members." *Journal of Contemporary Criminal Justice* 31:319–36.

McPherson, Miller, Lynn Smith-Lovin, and James M. Cook. 2001. "Birds of a Feather: Homophily in Social Networks." *Annual Review of Sociology* 27:415–44.

Morselli, Carlo. 2003. "Career Opportunities and Network-Based Privileges in the Cosa Nostra." *Crime, Law, and Social Change* 39:383–418.

———. 2005. *Contacts, Opportunities, and Criminal Enterprise.* Toronto: University of Toronto Press.

———. 2009. *Inside Criminal Networks.* New York: Springer.

———. 2010. "Assessing Vulnerable and Strategic Positions in a Criminal Network." *Journal of Contemporary Criminal Justice* 26:382–92.

Morselli, Carlo, and Cynthia Giguère. 2006. "Legitimate Strengths in Criminal Networks." *Crime, Law, and Social Change* 45:185–200.

Morselli, Carlo, Cynthia Giguère, and Katia Petit. 2007. "The Efficiency/Security Trade-Off in Criminal Networks." *Social Networks* 29:143–53.

Morselli, Carlo, Masarah Paquet-Clouston, and Chloé Provost. 2017. "The Independent's Edge in an Illegal Drug Distribution Setting: Levitt and Venkatesh Revisited." *Social Networks* 51:118–26.

Morselli, Carlo, and Pierre Tremblay. 2004. "Criminal Achievement, Offender Networks, and the Benefits of Low Self-Control." *Criminology* 42:773–804.

Morselli, Carlo, Pierre Tremblay, and Bill McCarthy. 2006. "Mentors and Criminal Achievement." *Criminology* 44:17–43.

Newman, Mark E. J., and Michelle Girvan. 2004. "Finding and Evaluating Community Structure in Networks." *Physical Review E.* 69:026113.

Nohria, Nitin, and Robert G. Eccles, eds. 1992. *Networks and Organizations: Structure, Form, and Action.* Boston: Harvard Business School Press.

Ouellet, Marie, and Martin Bouchard. 2018. "The 40 Members of the Toronto 18: Group Boundaries and the Analysis of Illicit Networks." *Deviant Behavior* 39:1467–82.

Ouellet, Marie, Martin Bouchard, and Yanick Charette. 2019. "One Gang Dies, Another Gains? The Network Dynamics of Criminal Group Persistence." *Criminology* 57:5–33.

Ouellet, Marie, Martin Bouchard, and Mackenzie Hart. 2017. "Criminal Collaboration and Risk: The Drivers of Al Qaeda's Network Structure before and after 9/11." *Social Networks* 51:171–77.

Ouellet, Marie, and Sadaf Hashimi. 2019. "Criminal Group Dynamics and Network Methods." In *Methods of Criminology and Criminal Justice*, edited by Mathieu Deflem and Derek Silva. Bingley: Emerald.

Paoli, Letizia. 2002. "The Paradoxes of Organized Crime." *Crime, Law, and Social Change* 37:51–97.

Papachristos, Andrew V. 2006. "Social Network Analysis and Gang Research: Theory and Methods." In *Studying Youth Gangs*, edited by James F. Short Jr. and Lorine A. Hughes. Oxford: AltaMira.

———. 2009. "Murder by Structure: Dominance Relations and the Social Structure of Gang Homicide." *American Journal of Sociology* 115:74–128.

———. 2011. "The Coming of A Networked Criminology." In *Measuring Crime and Criminality: Advances in Criminological Theory*, edited by John MacDonald. New Brunswick, NJ: Transaction.

Papachristos, Andrew V., David M. Hureau, and Anthony A. Braga. 2013. "The Corner and the Crew: The Influence of Geography and Social Networks on Gang Violence." *American Sociological Review* 78(3):417–47.

Papachristos, Andrew V., and Chris M. Smith. 2014. "The Embedded and Multiplex Nature of Al Capone." In *Crime and Networks*, edited by Carlo Morselli. New York: Routledge.

Podolny, Joel M., and Karen L. Page. 1998. "Network Forms of Organization." *Annual Review of Sociology* 24:57–76.

Powell, W. W. 1990. "Neither Market Nor Hierarchy: Network Forms of Organization." In *Research in Organizational Behavior*, edited by Barry M. Staw and L. L. Cummings. Greenwich, CT: JAI.

Quinn, James F., and Craig J. Forsyth. 2011. "The Tools, Tactics, and Mentality of Outlaw Biker Wars." *American Journal of Criminal Justice* 36(3):216–30.

Reuter, Peter. 1983. *Disorganized Crime: The Economics of the Visible Hand.* Cambridge, MA: MIT Press.

Reuter, Peter H., and John Haaga. 1989. *The Organization of High-Level Drug Markets.* Santa Monica, CA: RAND.

Rostami, Amir, and Hernan Mondani. 2015. "The Complexity of Crime Network Data: A Case Study of Its Consequences for Crime Control and the Study of Networks." *PloS One* 10:e0119309.

Sarnecki, Jerzy. 2001. *Delinquent Networks: Youth Co-offending in Stockholm.* Cambridge: Cambridge University Press.

Savona, Ernesto, Francesco Calderoni, Elisa Superchi, Tommaso Comunale, Gian Maria Campedelli, Martina Marchesi, and Alexander Kamprad. 2017. "Systematic Review of the Social, Psychological and Economic Factors Relating to Criminalisation and Recruitment to OC." Report on Factors relating to Organized Crime. Milan: Università Cattolica del Sacro Cuore.

Sergi, Anna. 2016. "A Qualitative Reading of the Ecological (Dis)Organisation of Criminal Associations: The Case of the 'Famiglia Basilischi' in Italy." *Trends in Organized Crime* 19:149–74.

Simmel, Georg. 1955. *Conflict and the Web of Group-Affiliations.* Toronto: Free Press. (Originally published in 1922.)

Smith, Chris M., and Andrew V. Papachristos. 2016. "Trust Thy Crooked Neighbor: Multiplexity in Chicago Organized Crime Networks." *American Sociological Review* 81:644–67.

Sparrow, Malcolm K. 1991. "The Application of Network Analysis to Criminal Intelligence: An Assessment of the Prospects." *Social Networks* 13:251–74.

Sutherland, Edwin H. 1937. *The Professional Thief.* Chicago: University of Chicago Press.

Tenti, Valentina, and Carlo Morselli. 2014. "Group Co–offending Networks in Italy's Illegal Drug Trade." *Crime, Law, and Social Change* 62:21–44.

Tremblay, Pierre. 1993. "Searching for Suitable Co–offenders." In *Routine Activity and Rational Choice: Advances in Criminological Theory*, edited by Ronald. V. Clarke and Marcus Felson. New Brunswick, NJ: Transaction.

Tremblay, Pierre, Martin Bouchard, and Sévrine Petit. 2009. "The Size and Influence of a Criminal Organization: A Criminal Achievement Perspective." *Global Crime* 10:24–40.

Tremblay, Pierre, Mathieu Charest, Yanick Charette, and Marc Tremblay-Faulkner. 2016. *Le délinquant affilié : La sous–culture des gangs de rue haïtiens de Montréal.* Montreal: Liber.

Tremblay, Pierre, and Carlo Morselli. 2000. "Patterns in Criminal Achievement: Wilson and Abrahamse Revisited." *Criminology* 38:633–57.

Varese, Federico, ed. 2010. *Organized Crime: Critical Concepts in Criminology.* London: Routledge.

Varese, Federico. 2013. "The Structure and Content of Criminal Connections: The Russian Mafia in Italy." *European Sociological Review* 29:899–909.

———. 2018. *Mafia Life: Love, Death, and Money at the Heart of Organized Crime.* Oxford: Oxford University Press.

Verbrugge, Lois M. 1979. "Multiplexity in Adult Friendships." *Social Forces* 57:1286–309.

Von Lampe, Klaus. 2003. "Criminally Exploitable Ties: A Network Approach to Organized Crime." In *Transnational Organized Crime: Myth, Power, and Profit*, edited by Emilio C. Viano, José Magallanes, and Laurent Bridel. Durham, NC: Carolina Academic.

———. 2009. "Human Capital and Social Capital in Criminal Networks: Introduction to the Special Issue on the 7th Blankensee Colloquium." *Trends in Organized Crime* 12:93–100.

Wasserman, Stanley, and Katherine Faust. 1994. *Social Network Analysis: Methods and Applications.* London: Cambridge University Press.

Weerman, Frank M. 2011. "Delinquent Peers in Context: A Longitudinal Network Analysis of Selection and Influence Effects." *Criminology* 49:253–86.

Weisburd, David, Elizabeth R. Groff, and Sue-Ming Yang. 2012. *The Criminology of Place: Street Segments and Our Understanding of the Crime Problem.* New York: Oxford University Press.

Young, Jacob T. N. 2011. "How Do They 'End Up Together'? A Social Network Analysis of Self-Control, Homophily, and Adolescent Relationships." *Journal of Quantitative Criminology* 27(3):251–73.

Zhang, Sheldon X., Ko-Lin Chin, and Jody Miller. 2007. "Women's Participation in Chinese Transnational Human Smuggling: A Gendered Market Perspective." *Criminology* 45:699–733.

Paolo Campana

Human Smuggling: Structure and Mechanisms

ABSTRACT

Human smuggling is a form of illegal trade in which the commodity is an assisted illegal entry into a country. While this is hardly a new phenomenon, evidence points to increased involvement of smugglers in facilitating these journeys. This has been linked to the hardening of entry policies in developed countries. Smuggling markets tend to possess low barriers to entry and remarkably similar organizational arrangements in all the main smuggling routes in the world: no monopolies and small, localized, and rudimentary hierarchies. There are clear separations between migrant smugglers and their protectors and between migrant smugglers and drug traffickers. The limited empirical evidence suggests that, rather than being involved in other unrelated criminal activities, smugglers often run small-scale legitimate businesses. There is very little evidence of direct involvement of traditional mafia-like organizations. Finally, smugglers, often in competition to attract migrants, have developed diverse strategies to foster transactions, including investing in their reputations, offering warranties, and bringing in third-party escrow services. Recent developments in information technology have facilitated use of social media and the internet.

Human smuggling, also commonly referred to as "migrant smuggling" or "people smuggling," was defined by article 2 of the United Nations Protocol against the Smuggling of Migrants by Land, Sea and Air, adopted

Electronically published May 5, 2020

Paolo Campana is university lecturer in criminology and complex networks at the Institute of Criminology, University of Cambridge. I am most grateful to the editors and two anonymous referees for insightful comments. I am also grateful to the participants in the *Crime and Justice* symposium on organized crime in Bologna in May 2019 and to Andrea Giovannetti for comments on an earlier version of this essay.

by the General Assembly in November 2000, as "the procurement, in order to obtain, directly or indirectly, a financial or other material benefit, of the illegal entry of a person into a State Party of which the person is not a national or a permanent resident." As of May 2019, 112 countries had signed the protocol and made human smuggling a criminal offense. While national legislation differs in how the offense is worded, the UN definition is the gold standard around which all are modeled (Gallagher and David 2014).

Smuggling of migrants between countries for profit in the absence of a legal right to movement is hardly a new phenomenon (Kyle and Koslowski 2011). For instance, in the seventeenth and eighteenth centuries, migration from what is now Germany, and central Europe more generally, to North America was sometimes facilitated by smugglers who operated in ways that anticipate contemporary smuggling stories (Wokeck 1999; O'Reilly 2019). However, while in the past smugglers were mostly needed to exit one's country, contemporary smuggling is mostly concerned with providing illegal entry into a country (with a few exceptions, notably Eritrea and North Korea, and Syria during the civil war). This is reflected in the 2000 UN definition that makes an explicit reference to the absence of "necessary requirements for legal entry into the receiving State" (Article 3, subsection c). Since its adoption, there has been a growth in concern of governments about human smuggling, and all of the major destinations—the United States, Europe, and Australia—have declared a "migration crisis" at some point. The hardening of entry policies in nearly all developed countries has made reliance on smugglers increasingly acute.[1]

Analytically, we can think of human smuggling as a market in which the commodity traded is assisted illegal entry into a country (Bilger et al. 2006; Kleemans 2011; Campana and Varese 2016).[2] Markets, by definition, are characterized by supply and demand. In this instance, migrants constitute the demand side. They are willing to buy a service, illegal entry,

---

[1] See Massey, Durand, and Pren (2016, p. 1576) for an empirical test using US data; see also Ayalew Mengiste (2018, p. 58).

[2] I focus on smuggling understood as assisted illegal entry of migrants, thereby emphasizing activities related to the movement of people (this is in line, alas, with Article 3 and Article 6, subparagraph $1a$ of the UN Protocol). However, the UN Protocol also criminalizes activities "enabling a person who is not a national or a permanent resident to remain in the State concerned without complying with the necessary requirements for legally remaining in the State" (Article 6, subparagraph $1c$). These activities relate to illegal stays rather than to illegal entries and movements and are outside the scope of this essay.

for reasons that include leaving war zones, extreme poverty, economic hardship, and persecution (Robinson and Segrott 2002; Antonopoulos and Winterdyk 2006; Yildiz 2017; Optimity Advisors and Seefar 2018). The demand for smuggling services is satisfied by a number of sellers. In this market, they are characterized as smugglers. Based on their route and ethnicity or nationality, smugglers might be referred to by different names, for instance, *snakeheads* in the case of Chinese smuggling (Chin 1999; Zhang and Chin 2002; Zhang 2008); *coyotes* or *polleros*[3] along the Mexican route to the United States (Izcara Palacios 2014; Sanchez 2015); *muharrib* among Syrians (Achilli 2018, p. 87); *passeur* in West Africa (Maher 2018); and *delaloch* among Amharic-speaking Eritreans and Ethiopians (Ayalew Mengiste 2018, p. 69).

Human smuggling is primarily an offense against a state. When everything goes well, when the smuggler keeps his promise and the migrant safely reaches the destination, the only victim is the state that has seen its borders and its right to exercise control over its territory violated. Human trafficking, by contrast, involves control over a person for the purpose of exploitation and is primarily an offense against an individual (Campana and Varese 2016). An illegal entry into a country may occur, but it is an ancillary element and not a constitutive one. The two terms are often erroneously used interchangeably in the media and public discourse, leading to confusion and hindering our ability to grasp either phenomenon fully and develop effective policies.

However, while there are cases in which a journey started as smuggling and turns into trafficking ("failures of smuggling" as conceptualized in Campana and Varese 2016) or cases in which a trafficker poses as a smuggler to trick a potential victim, by and large the empirical evidence supports the analytical distinction between smuggling and trafficking. Fieldwork has shown that migrants act as buyers of services: they collect information; they choose among possible smugglers; and in some instances they have asset-negotiating power in relation to prices and warranties (Optimity Advisors 2015, p. 36; Maher 2018, p. 40).

Smugglers too behave in ways that suggest a market for services rather than coercive trafficking situations, from price segmentation based on the quality of service (Optimity Advisors 2015, pp. 108–9) to a host of

---

[3] Izcara Palacios (2014, pp. 325–26) notes that *coyote* is more often used and can be traced back to the 1920s; *pollero* is more recent. They are often used interchangeably.

different guarantees. The behavior of the market for smuggling services appears to follow the law of demand and supply. For instance, the price for an "assisted" journey from Greece to Serbia went up from €500 in 2012 to €2,000 (roughly, US$560 to $2,200) mainly due to higher demand and a "slight increase in risk" experienced by smugglers (Optimity Advisors 2015, p. 43). In other instances, an increase in supply brought prices down, as in Libya in 2015 (Kingsley 2015).

This is not to say that migrants may not face risky situations and violence or, indeed, that smugglers always act reliably and honestly. According to the Missing Migrant Project of the International Organization for Migration (IOM), at least 3,318 migrants lost their lives worldwide in 2019.[4] Since the records began in 2014, a total of at least 34,477 migrant fatalities have been recorded by IOM, with 2016 being the deadliest (8,070 fatalities). The yearly average between 2014 and 2019 was 5,746. The Mediterranean route constantly ranks as the deadliest; it accounted for 64 percent of all fatalities in 2016. This is likely the result of both heightened risk due to the sea crossing, and improved data collection (data on fatalities in the Libyan desert are arguably of lesser quality). The number of deaths recorded by IOM at the US-Mexico border was 2,336 from 2014 to 2019, with a yearly average of 389 (442 in 2018, the deadliest year on record).

IOM also provides estimates of the mortality rate per attempted crossing for the entire Mediterranean sector: this includes sea arrivals in Spain, Italy, Cyprus, and Greece, land arrivals in Spain, and interceptions by the Tunisian National Guard and the Turkish and the Libyan coast guards. The death rates were 1.4 percent for 2018 and 0.7 percent for 2017.

Besides risking death, migrants may also face exploitation while en route. Using a postdeportation survey conducted in Mexico with 655 migrants who used the services of smugglers and were apprehended by US authorities, Slack and Martinez (2018, p. 153) documented 42 instances of people held by coyotes, often following a steep increase in the originally agreed fee, or by individuals posing as smugglers.[5] This translates into a 6 percent chance of being exploited. Of 1,602 people who arrived in

---

[4] Data from https://missingmigrants.iom.int/.

[5] Slack and Martinez (2018, pp. 159–60) used data from the second wave of the Migrant Border Crossing Study. The sampling frame included individuals 18 years of age or older who were apprehended by any US authority and repatriated to Mexico. Participants were randomly selected using a spatial sampling technique and interviewed face-to-face (response rate 94 percent).

Italy from Libya and were interviewed by IOM in 2017, 36 percent said they had been forced to work or perform activities against their will (Brian 2017, p. 9; it is not specified whether this happened at the hands of smugglers or other actors).

The complexity of the phenomenon, and often its contradictions, emerges neatly from the postdeportation survey in Mexico; 75 percent of migrants reported being satisfied with the services provided by the smugglers (Slack and Martinez 2018, p. 153).[6] In interviews with migrants along one of the most perilous migrant routes from Ethiopia to Europe crossing through Sudan and the Libyan desert, smugglers were "repeatedly described as supportive and protective by migrants. *Delaloch* are consistently described as saviors," thus refuting "perceptions of smugglers as exploitative or violent" (Ayalew Mengiste 2018, p. 71). Achilli (2018) paints a similar picture of smuggling across the Eastern Mediterranean. A Syrian refugee described smugglers as "neither good nor evil. You pay for a service and you get what you pay for" (quoted in Achilli 2018, p. 83).

Exploitation is often a consequence of the undocumented status of a migrant rather than a direct consequence of smugglers' action (Campana and Varese 2016; Achilli 2018, p. 79). The cost of smuggling services can place migrants in debt, making them vulnerable to accept exploitative working conditions during or after the journey and potentially leading to labor, sexual, or criminal exploitation. When analyzing such cases, it is crucial to tease out the exact role a smuggler played—and whether he or she was directly involved in the exploitation.

This essay proceeds as follows. The first section discusses issues related to the measurement of human smuggling and offers an assessment of two major routes, into the European Union and the United States, for which we have the best evidence base. Section II surveys what is known about the organization of smuggling activities in relation to a number of international routes. Section III discusses relationships between human smuggling and other illegal activities, particularly drug trafficking and protection. Section IV looks at the ways smugglers foster transactions in the smuggling market and overcome the acute trust problem that characterizes such markets. Section V presents a brief assessment of

---

[6] Smugglers can also be at the receiving end of violence, including one murder documented by Slack and Martinez (2018) in which migrants decapitated their smuggler with a machete.

TABLE 1

Human Smuggling: A Summary of the Evidence

Smuggling markets show remarkably similar features throughout the world.
Such markets generally involve little violence among smugglers.
Smuggling groups are usually small and generally composed of individuals who are not
    otherwise criminal.
There is little overlap between drug and human smuggling.
There is little or limited mafia-type organized crime direct involvement in human
    smuggling.
There is an important, and often neglected, distinction between smugglers and protectors.
The market for smuggling services possesses many features normally associated with legal
    markets, including competition and the importance of reputation and trust, and it relies
    on well-developed financing traditions.

---

policy responses. Section VI concludes (see table 1 for a summary of the evidence).

I. Assessing the Extent of Human Smuggling

Empirical knowledge about human smuggling, despite the existence of a commonly agreed legal definition of the phenomenon, is, to put it mildly, very patchy. There is no global estimate of the extent of human smuggling. Only a minority of countries regularly produce statistics on it (McAuliffe and Laczko 2016, p. 10). Reliable statistics are difficult to compile for a number of reasons. Human smuggling is illegal; both smugglers and migrants have strong incentive not to leave traces. Similarly, states may have an incentive not to collect or divulge such data if, for instance, they believe that migrants are only passing through their territory. Transit countries may have an incentive to allow an efficient underground smuggling system rather than risk becoming a bottleneck in a longer smuggling route. Some states may simply lack the capacity and resources to collect data on smuggling. This is particularly true of states with weak institutions and porous borders. Furthermore, some states may decide not to make such data publicly available for political and security reasons. Australia, for instance, introduced restrictions on release of information following the launch of a military-led antismuggling operation in 2013 (Gallagher and McAuliffe 2016, p. 223).

Some countries report aggregate data on irregular migration rather than on human smuggling. However, not all irregular migration involves the assistance of a smuggler; people can cross borders alone or can enter a county legally and overstay the terms of their visa. Migrants regularly living in a country at the time of the data collection following a regularization process may have used the service of a smuggler in the past. In other cases, the number of asylum applications may be used as a proxy for smuggling. However, not all asylum seekers necessarily used a smuggler to reach the country where the application has been lodged, nor have all smuggled individuals necessarily lodged an asylum application.

The official data available on human smuggling tend to be produced by law enforcement agencies, particularly border control agencies, and usually record detected illegal border crossings (IBCs) and come with a number of limitations. Statistics normally refer to crossings rather than individuals. If the smuggling process extends across multiple countries, there is a risk of double-counting the same individuals. Equally, in case of multiple interceptions, the same individual may be counted multiple times. Official statistics can also underrepresent the phenomenon since they do not include undetected crossings and migrants. This makes it difficult, for example, to take into account instances in which a journey resulted in deaths.[7] Furthermore, not all illegal border crossings are necessarily made with the assistance of a smuggler, and there is variation in the use of smugglers depending on the route. Finally, statistics may be influenced by changes in the level of policing rather than by changes in human smuggling. Notwithstanding their limitations, however, law enforcement statistics often constitute the best and sometimes the only data source available.

There are large differences in the ability of law enforcement authorities, and in the ability of states more generally, to collect data on illegal border crossings and in their willingness to make the data public. It is best therefore to resist the temptation to attempt to make global estimates of human smuggling. Individual routes or even subroutes are preferable as a macro unit of analysis. At present, our best evidence base relates to routes into the European Union and the United States.

A. Smuggling into the European Union

European Union (EU) member states have over time increased their coordinated law enforcement response to human smuggling, including through establishment of a dedicated Anti-Smuggling Centre within Europol (2017) and a common Border and Coast Guard Agency (Frontex).

---

[7] Some ad hoc projects, such as the Missing Migrant Project of the International Organization for Migration, try to address this issue; https://missingmigrants.iom.int/.

Table 2 presents yearly illegal border crossings into the EU detected since 2010 in relation to the three major routes[8] of entry: the Western Mediterranean Route from North Africa to Spain; the Central Mediterranean Route from North Africa to Italy and Malta; and the Eastern Mediterranean Route mostly from Turkey to Greece.[9]

How many of these IBCs have involved smugglers? It is safe to assume that journeys that include a sea crossing have likely been facilitated by smugglers. In 2017, 93 percent of IBCs on the Western Mediterranean Route, 82 percent on the Eastern Mediterranean, and 100 percent on the Central Mediterranean involved a sea crossing (Frontex 2018, p. 43). The following year, 98 percent of IBCs on the Western Mediterranean Route, 60 percent on the Eastern Mediterranean, and all the Central Mediterranean ones involved crossing a sea (Frontex 2019, p. 43). Land crossings can be made with or without a smuggler, but given heightened border controls, a conservative estimate is that two-thirds of crossings were made with the assistance of a smuggler. Averaging across the 2 years, over 98 percent of Western Mediterranean crossings can be attributed to smugglers; over 90 percent of Eastern Mediterranean crossings; and all of the Central Mediterranean ones.

Frontex also provides figures on the number of "facilitators" identified in any given year. These figures need to be taken with extreme caution as they conflate people with different roles in facilitating irregular entry into the EU, including those involved in production of counterfeit documents, and are likely grossly to underestimate the number of smugglers operating outside the EU. According to Frontex (2018, p. 46; 2019, p. 44), the number of facilitators has hovered around ten thousand for the last 5 years: 10,234 (2014); 12,023 (2015); 12,621 (2016); 10,246 (2017); and 10,642 (2018).

B. Smuggling into the United States

The US Department of Homeland Security (DHS) produces annual reports on a number of metrics related to illegal entry of migrants ("aliens" in US statutory language). Table 3 presents the number of apprehensions, or illegal border crossings, detected by law enforcement authorities at the

---

[8] The remaining routes in the European Union record negligible figures. For example, in 2018, 1,084 illegal border crossings were recorded for the entire Eastern Borders Route, 1,051 for the West African Route (from Senegal to Canary Islands, Spain), and zero for the Black Sea Route (Frontex 2019, p. 16).

[9] Perhaps better described as the "Aegean Route."

TABLE 2
Illegal Border Crossings into the European Union, 2010–18 (Major Routes)

	2010	2011	2012	2013	2014	2015	2016	2017	2018
Eastern Med.	55,688	57,025	37,224	24,799	50,834	885,386	182,277	42,305	56,561
Central Med.	4,450	64,261	15,151	45,298	170,664	153,946	181,376	118,962	23,485
Western Med.	5,003	8,448	6,397	6,838	7,842	7,164	9,990	23,143	57,034
Total	65,141	129,734	58,772	76,935	229,340	1,046,496	373,643	184,410	137,080

SOURCE.—Frontex (various years).

TABLE 3

US Southwest Border Apprehension by Sector, FY 2007–17

	Big Bend, TX	Del Rio, TX	El Centro, CA	El Paso, TX	Laredo, TX	Rio Grande Valley, TX	San Diego, CA	Tucson, AZ	Yuma, AZ	Total
FY2007	5,536	22,920	55,883	75,464	56,714	73,430	152,460	378,239	37,992	858,638
FY2008	5,391	20,761	40,961	30,312	43,668	75,473	162,390	317,696	8,363	705,015
FY2009	6,360	17,082	33,521	14,999	40,569	60,989	118,721	241,673	6,951	540,865
FY2010	5,288	14,694	32,562	12,251	35,287	59,766	68,565	212,202	7,116	447,731
FY2011	4,036	16,144	30,191	10,345	36,053	59,243	42,447	123,285	5,833	327,577
FY2012	3,964	21,720	23,916	9,678	44,872	97,762	28,461	120,000	6,500	356,873
FY2013	3,684	23,510	16,306	11,154	50,749	154,453	27,496	120,939	6,106	414,397
FY2014	4,096	24,255	14,511	12,339	44,049	256,393	29,911	87,915	5,902	479,371
FY2015	5,031	19,013	12,820	14,495	35,888	147,257	26,290	63,397	7,142	331,333
FY2016	6,366	23,078	19,448	25,634	36,562	186,830	31,891	64,891	14,170	408,970
FY2017	6,002	13,476	18,633	25,193	25,460	137,562	26,086	38,657	12,847	303,916

SOURCE.—DHS (2019, p. 121).

southwest border between the US and Mexico spanning Texas, New Mexico, Arizona, and California during the last 10 fiscal years available. Similarly to Frontex, these data are event-based and not person-based, meaning they do not represent a count of unique individuals apprehended at the border (DHS 2018, p. 18).

How many IBCs involved smugglers? DHS (2019) provides estimates based on surveys with apprehended migrants conducted by the Office for Migration Statistics and the US Border Patrol. The Office for Migration Statistics also estimates a constant increase in the rate of smuggler usage: from 40–50 percent in the 1970s to 95 percent in 2006 (DHS 2018, p. 48). Similarly, US Border Patrol interviews have been estimated to show a smuggler "usage rate" between 80 and 95 percent among migrants apprehended in 2015, in clear contrast to the situation before 2001 when "relatively few illegal border crossers hired a smuggler" (DHS 2018, p. 48). Data from the Mexican Migration Project at Princeton University point to a similar level of smuggler involvement (close to 90 percent in 2017: Sanchez 2018, p. 153).

Over the years, the composition of the nationality of migrants has changed substantially with a constant decline of migrants holding Mexican citizenship (table 4). In fiscal year (FY) 2008 migrants with Mexican citizenship constituted 93 percent of the total; this fell to 46 percent in FY 2016 (see also DHS 2018, p. 146).

Overall, the yearly trends for the EU point to an ability of smuggling markets to expand quickly and to a considerable degree, most likely following increases in demand (Campana 2017). IBCs on the Eastern Mediterranean Route increased by 1,641 percent between 2014 and 2015 and on the Central Mediterranean Route by 99 percent between 2012 and 2013 and 277 percent in 2013–14. Between 2010 and 2011, the increase on the Central Route was 1,344 percent (Campana 2017).

Data from the United States suggest greater stability, perhaps an indication of a more mature market. Occasionally, however, same sectors experience steep increases (e.g., the Rio Grande Valley, Texas, where the number of crossings increased 4.3 times between 2011 and 2014). These rates of increase suggest that barriers to entry and levels of resources required for an actor successfully to enter the market, or for an existing actor to expand operations, are probably low.[10] Empirical evidence from

[10] See Campana (2017) for further discussion.

TABLE 4

US Southwest Border Apprehensions by Citizenship, FY 2008–16

Country	2008	2009	2010	2011	2012	2013	2014	2015	2016
Mexico	653,035	495,582	396,819	280,580	262,341	265,409	226,711	186,017	190,760
El Salvador	12,133	11,181	13,123	10,368	21,903	36,957	66,419	43,392	71,848
Guatemala	15,143	14,125	16,831	17,582	34,453	54,143	80,473	56,691	74,601
Honduras	18,110	13,344	12,231	11,270	30,349	46,448	90,968	33,445	52,952
All other	6,584	6,633	8,727	7,777	7,827	11,440	14,740	11,788	18,709
Total	705,005	540,865	447,731	327,577	356,873	414,397	479,371	331,333	408,870

Source.—DHS (2018, p. 46).

China, Turkey, Mexico, and Niger supports this observation (Zhang and Chin 2002; Spener 2009; Campana 2017; Demir, Sever, and Kahya 2017; Brachet 2018).

II. The Structure of Human Smuggling

How are smuggling activities organized? To answer this question, I turn to the evidence available in relation to some of the main smuggling routes.

A. Organizational Arrangements along Four Main Routes

I discuss four main routes: from China into the US and Europe, across the US border with Mexico, into Europe via Turkey and Greece, and into southern Europe from Africa.

1. *Chinese Smuggling into the US and Europe.* Early works by criminologists on human smuggling investigated the structure of smuggling operations between China and the United States in the late 1990s. Ko-lin Chin and Sheldon Zhang, both independently and jointly, have provided insight into Chinese-American smuggling operations based on interviews with individuals directly involved in smuggling migrants (Chin 1999; Zhang and Chin 2002; Zhang 2008). They noted that Chinese human smuggling organizations differ in their structure from the traditional triads, as they "are made up of decentralized associations of criminals of diverse backgrounds, and the relationships among core members are mostly horizontal" (Zhang and Chin 2002, p. 759; see also Chin 1999).

Interactions tend to take place within small groups, with each group focused on a specific set of tasks (Zhang 2008, p. 145). Zhang and Chin describe the network of smugglers as a "task force, committed to one task or one operation at a time—that is, to deliver their clients to their destiny and get paid" (Zhang and Chin 2002, p. 750). These task forces tend to be small with a core group of generally three or four individuals brought together purely by business arrangements. Chin (1999, p. 41) observed that smuggling of Chinese migrants was carried out by groups "working independently, each with its own organization, connections, methods and routes. ... No one of these groups, however, dominates or monopolizes the lucrative trade" (Zhang and Chin 2002, p. 750). Smugglers often have a history of previous social interactions, for example thorough family networks or business dealings. Speaking the same Chinese dialects or growing up in the same place were found to be conducive to establishing smuggling partnerships (Zhang and Chin 2002, p. 750).

More recently, Soudijn (2006) looked at the Netherlands experience. He conducted an analysis of police files combined with field interviews with members of the Chinese community and police officers and identified organizational arrangements similar to those described a decade before in relation to the United States. Crucially, he noted that "no evidence was found of a central organization controlling any (let alone all) smuggling operations, either from the Netherlands or from abroad" (Soudijn 2006, p. 127). He maintained that the level of coordination among different groups operating at different stages was minimal, and rejected the "chain" metaphor often used to describe Chinese smuggling operations.

2. *Smuggling across the US-Mexican Border.* Spener (2009, p. 150) carried out an in-depth study of smuggling across the Texas border and concluded that there was no evidence of monopolization of the market by a single group or small set of groups. Further, he noted that, overall, the level of sophistication of the *coyotes* in the 2000s was not "especially greater" than the "organized bands of coyotes" operating in the 1920s (Spener 2009, p. 152). Similarly, Izcara Palacios (2014) found no evidence of smugglers using violence against other smugglers in order to monopolize the market. Sanchez (2015, p. 44) found no evidence of "the existence of a single, centralized, power providing operational or logical support in any of the smuggling groups identified."

3. *Smuggling into Europe via Turkey and Greece.* Içduygu and Toktas (2002) explored organizational arrangements underpinning the illegal movement of Iraqi and Iranian migrants. They described the smuggling operations as "a loosely cast network, consisting of hundreds of independent smaller units which cooperate along the way" (p. 46). They found no evidence of any "godfather-like" figure. Human smuggling was not characterized by "international, centralized organizations" but by "smaller, local and flexible organizations" (p. 46). Each organization operated independently, as "a small part of a larger chain" with no centralized oversight (p. 47). In some cases, smugglers might hand over migrants directly to another independent smuggler after a border crossing. These arrangements seem to have remained largely unchanged over the years (Içduygu 2018, p. 33).

Evidence of similar arrangements can be found concerning Afghani and Pakistani migrants (Koser 2008; Aksel et al. 2015, pp. 19–24). Based on interviews with convicted Turkish-based smugglers, Demir, Sever, and Kahya (2017, p. 384) note the absence of an "international umbrella organization" with "branches in several countries." Smuggling is instead based on groups that "communicate and cooperate . . . horizontally" across the different stages of the process (p. 384). Rather than being similar to a mafia-type organization, these small groups are "loosely connected" with limited if any internal hierarchy (p. 385). Smugglers rarely used violence and did not carry guns. This is confirmed by Achilli (2018, p. 85) in his work on the movement of Syrian migrants. Smuggling along the Eastern Mediterranean corridor, crossing from Turkey into Greece and then onward across the Balkans, "mostly consist[s] of a system of flexible and independent organizations that enter into partnerships with one another for short periods."

4. *Smuggling into Europe from Africa.* Activities along the smuggling route from the Horn of Africa to Europe via Libya and Italy appear to be segmented and carried out by localized and rudimentary hierarchies. Empirical evidence from Campana (2018), based on quantitative analysis of data manually extracted from court files, demonstrates that smugglers are largely independent and autonomous in their decisions, with indicators of competition among them.

Figure 1 shows the first formal representation of a network of smugglers. It depicts the connections among smugglers operating along the Central Mediterranean Route (migrants are excluded from the analysis).

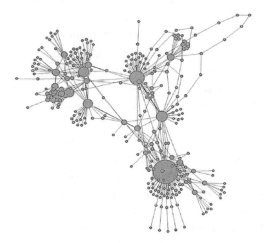

Fig. 1.—Network of contacts among smugglers operating along the Central Mediterranean Route (Horn of Africa to Europe via Libya). Note: Size of the nodes indicates degree centrality. Source: Campana (2018, p. 489).

It is based on real world contacts captured in phone wiretaps, testimony, and other forensic evidence. Each node in the figure represents an individual, and its size points to that individual's importance in the network measured by the number of connections (ties) each person has established (degree centrality).

Individuals have different levels of centrality, with a small number of higher centrality actors. Contacts tend to cluster around those actors, suggesting the presence of rudimentary hierarchies. Small hierarchies can be identified at all stages of the smuggling route, and their reach tends to remain local. Additionally, there is no evidence of a single hierarchical organization, but rather a collection of independent actors. Even in networks involved in the supply of a truly transnational commodity, namely the movement of people from the Horn of Africa to northern Europe, the local dimension plays an important role. The odds of connection between smugglers are almost seven times higher if they are both involved in the same stage of the journey (Campana 2018).

There are strong indications of competition—a "far cry from the idea that smuggling markets are characterized by the presence of kingpins who can exert monopolistic control over a certain route" (Campana 2018, p. 493). Work on segments of the route supports the same conclusions. Ayalew Mengiste (2018, p. 69) describes a similar segmentation of the process with smugglers specializing in moving migrants from Eritrea to Ethiopia or Sudan and then either connecting them with another smuggler or leaving them free themselves to look for other smugglers who can facilitate the rest of the journey, and points out that Eritrean migration should not be "reduced to" kidnappings for ransom or trafficking for organ harvesting, but rather understood as "a local and transnational, community-based, proximity-oriented phenomenon dependent on specific entanglements of social and smuggling networks" (p. 71).

Arrangements along the West African route appear to follow a similar pattern. Brachet (2018, p. 29) maintains that what are often defined as transnational networks in Niger are "rather fragmented and uncoordinated chains of actors." He notes that "there are no transnational criminal networks in Agadez but rather small-scale low-investment activities" (p. 29). A senior smuggler interviewed in Agadez by Raineri (2018, p. 69) explained that they "mainly work on the basis of occasional agreements, including part-time. Anyone can be a smuggler for some time; you just bring your own car, and then leave with no fear of reprisals whatsoever." Competition appears to be rife in Agadez, bringing down prices (Raineri 2018, p. 72).

Molenaar (2017) observed a growth of "travel agencies" from 15 in 2007 to 70 in 2013.

All the migration flows discussed show a striking similarity in organization. This is further observed in a review prepared for the European Commission in which Optimity Advisors (2015, p. 48) note that "for all the routes [in the EU] studied, migrant smuggling operations appear to be organised along a primarily horizontal structure of intermediaries that interface with each other." While at first glance this might suggest hierarchical, top-down organizations, a closer look "reveals that even the larger networks, which span over several regions, are often organised around only one or two main actors who control bigger or smaller networks competing or cooperating with each other, and rely on the involvement of a range of additional actors who provide specific services" (p. 48). Smugglers are not tied to specific groups.

While there are striking similarities between routes, there are also differences in the degree of sophistication of smuggling operations. One main factor that affects the relative complexity of smuggling operations is the degree of difficulty in providing the service or making a journey. Some difficulties are the consequence of natural elements: organizing a sea crossing across the Mediterranean requires greater resources and more specialized skills than crossing land borders in a valley. Others are the consequence of heightened border controls or conflicts.

B. Internal Organization

Hierarchies tend to be rudimentary, almost nonexistent, but not all smugglers are equal. Some have more prestige, autonomy, and resources. These main actors are often referred to as "organizers" (Bilger, Hofmann, and Jandl 2006; Soudijn 2006; Optimity Advisors 2015; UNODC 2018; Campana 2018). Bilger, Hofmann, and Jandl (2006, p. 78) describe the organizer as a person who "controls the whole process." However, while organizers by definition need to possess some degree of control over both processes and other people's activity, the reach of their control can easily be overstated, particularly when relying on evidence collected from migrants who themselves might not have had direct contact with the organizers (e.g., Bilger, Hofmann, and Jandl 2006, p. 78). I (Campana 2018, p. 488) define organizers as "individuals who give orders but do not receive them; they are in a position to make pivotal decisions regarding smuggling operations." While some possess international connections, their ability to exert direct control is normally limited to a specific stage, for example within the sea crossing in the Mediterranean or within the journey from Sicily to a destination in continental Italy.[11]

The available evidence reveals some signs of specialization among smugglers, including drivers, brokers, fake document providers, people running and surveilling safe houses, and money collectors (İçduygu and Toktas 2002; Zhang and Chin 2002; Campana 2018; UNODC 2018). Zhang and Chin (2002, pp. 751–54) describe Chinese smuggling as characterized by "little hierarchical differentiation" but with a "well developed" division of labor. Smuggling across the Eastern Mediterranean has similar characteristics: "even though these groups generally lacked centralized and hierarchical structures, a number of roles could be identified within the organizations" (Achilli 2018, p. 15). A host of roles besides the organizers were identified, ranging from boat owners to cashiers, drivers, lookouts, and bodyguards.

Are smuggling groups organized along ethnic lines or shared nationality? Fragmented evidence suggests that the answer is often yes. This is the case for the Chinese smuggling organizations studied by Zhang and Chin (2002) and Soudijn (2006). Based on 51 German court proceedings, Neske (2006) observed that higher level smugglers tend to share the same ethnicity (often also with the migrants).

While the core of an organization may be ethnically homogeneous, coordination is likely to extend to individuals of different ethnicities or nationalities. This is the case, for instance, with local fixers (Neske 2006). This resembles my (Campana 2018) description of a smuggling ring operating between the Horn of Africa and Scandinavia via Libya and Italy. Of 28 smugglers based in Italy for whom reliable information about their nationality was available, 18 were Eritreans, 7 were Ethiopians, and one each was from Ghana, Ivory Coast, and Guinea (the smuggled migrants were overwhelmingly Eritreans). A similar pattern emerged in an Albanian ring operating between Belgium and the United Kingdom (Myria 2018, pp. 105–6).

Soudijn (2006, p. 46) offers further evidence: of 178 individuals identified by the Dutch authorities in Chinese smuggling cases between 1996

---

[11] That not all smugglers are equal also emerges from Zhang and Chin (2002, p. 748) on Chinese human smuggling: "Those who invested most in smuggling operations were also the ones to make the most money, whereas many others were merely playing auxiliary roles by recruiting clients and making referral fees."

and 2003, 108 were from mainland China, 12 from Hong Kong, and 2 from Taiwan. Chinese nationals were by far the most numerous, but they had established working relationships with individuals of 12 other nationalities, of which the largest group not surprisingly were 20 Dutch nationals.

Why do smugglers prefer working with people from the same ethnicity? Ethnic background per se is not what matters. Ethnicity (or nationality) is a proxy for shared language, facility in establishing contacts and checking reputations, and a strategy to minimize risk and uncertainty (Zhang and Chin 2002).[12]

Finally, how can we explain the ability of small unsophisticated smuggling organizations to move large numbers of migrants? The answer lies in the nature of the service rendered; by and large it does not appear to require large investments in resources and capital. The story of a small ring moving migrants in a van across the US-Mexican border illustrates this well. The ring consisted of five people: three men in Austin, Texas, and two collaborators in Mexico, one at the border and one working as a recruiter in the state of Zacatecas (Spener 2009). One smuggler reported that between 10 and 12 migrants were driven across the border on each trip. He estimated making around 30 trips in 12 months, charging each migrant $1,200 (Spener 2009, pp. 153–54).

Spener (2009) conservatively estimates that 600 migrants were smuggled per year with revenues in excess of $780,000. This story shows that increasing the number of migrants substantially would not require a large investment. Addition of a second van and a couple more drivers could have at least doubled the number of migrants transported, with neither resource difficult to come by. The relative simplicity of the modus operandi explains why smugglers can adapt quickly to changing circumstances such as a sudden increase in demand. The low level of resources required suggests that a large number of competing groups may have been in operation at the same time. This matches with the experience of a US federal judge who had seen "hundreds, if not thousands, of 'alien smuggling' defendants in his courtroom over the years" (Spener 2009, p. 154).

III. Is Smuggling a Specialized Activity?

The empirical evidence on the sociodemographic characteristics of smugglers is very limited. Studies that have attempted to offer quantitative

---

[12] More generally, see Kleemans and van de Bunt (2003) on the importance of social ties.

profiles of smugglers often rely on small convenience samples. Demir, Sever, and Kahya (2017) carried out 54 face-to-face interviews with convicted smugglers who were arrested and sentenced in Turkey. All interviewees were male, with an average age of 36 years; 52 percent identified themselves as Kurdish and 32 percent as Turkish. Half had a primary school qualification, 22 percent a secondary school diploma, and 20 percent a high school diploma (Demir, Sever, and Kahya 2017, p. 378). Of 292 individuals I analyzed in Campana (2018), who were operating between the Horn of Africa and Scandinavia via Libya and Italy, 277 (95 percent) were male. Migrant smuggling seems mostly to be a male-dominated business (Optimity Advisors 2015, p. 52).

Individuals with a position of responsibility in smuggling into Europe tend to be age 35 or older; aides and guides tend to be younger, between 18 and 25 (Optimity Advisors 2015, p. 52). Many sources indicate that smugglers tend to have other legitimate occupations. Of smugglers interviewed by Demir, Sever, and Kahya (2017, p. 319), 91 percent cited another legitimate occupation, and only one described smuggling as his main activity. Similarly, Chinese smugglers interviewed by Zhang and Chin (2002, p. 758) did not consider smuggling their main livelihood. They engaged in a host of legitimate business activities. They were small business owners, handymen, taxi drivers, fruit stand owners, fast food restaurant owners, housewives, massage parlor owners, police officers, and government officials. Eritrean smugglers tend to be soldiers or people who work and live in border areas and have experience crossing borders, sometimes as a result of trading activities (Ayalew Mengiste 2018, p. 68).

While many smugglers run legitimate activities, most are not involved in illegal activities other than smuggling. The majority of smugglers interviewed by Demir, Sever, and Kahya (2017, p. 379) had no criminal background (38 percent) or had been involved only in smuggling (31 percent). Only one was classified as related to a mafia-type organization, and three were connected to drug trafficking (5 percent). These findings are in line with the analysis of 174 smugglers arrested in Istanbul between 2007 and 2013 by Icli, Sever, and Sever (2015). Forty-five percent did not have a criminal record, and 23 percent had been involved only in smuggling. Six (3 percent) had been involved in narcotics. Similarly, Stone-Cadena and Alvarez Velasco (2018, p. 205) found no evidence of "any involvement of transnational organized crime" in human smuggling out of Ecuador.

Smugglers do not seem to engage in violence against fellow smugglers. Of the 28 Italian-based smugglers I identified (Campana 2018), none were involved in violence against any other smuggler in the network. Similarly, Zhang and Chin (2002) concluded that violence among smugglers was rare. They suggested that violence might carry negative consequences particularly concerning the desire "to build and maintain a trustworthy image" (p. 756). Violence does not appear to be a valuable resource, and smugglers prefer to convey an image of themselves as service providers, as travel agents for people who cannot enlist the services of a legal one (as in the case of smugglers interviewed by Achilli [2018] in the Eastern Mediterranean). The Mexican smugglers described by Sanchez (2018) were mostly marginalized ordinary citizens who entered the market in "an attempt to supplement their incomes rather than driven by criminal intention" (p. 149).

I now turn to first discuss the relationship between the smuggling of people and trafficking of drugs and then the often overlooked relationship between smugglers and protectors.

A. Human Smuggling and Drug Trafficking

To what extent are drug trafficking organizations involved in the smuggling of migrants? And vice versa? Chin (1999) explored this in relation to heroin smuggling from Southeast Asia and found little evidence that smugglers were involved in drug trafficking, contrary to claims by US authorities. Of 300 migrants he interviewed, only one reported being asked by smugglers to carry two bags of opium (from the Golden Triangle to Bangkok; Chin 1999). No drugs were seen on board vessels by those who left China by sea (Chin 1999, p. 35).

What about the Mexican-US route, a major route for both drug trafficking and migrant smuggling? This is a place where there is a sizable demand for smuggling services and where sophisticated drug trafficking organizations operate. Yet, there is little evidence of a mélange of smuggling of drugs and migrants.

Spener (2009) reviewed 197 cases of "alien smuggling" prosecuted in the federal courthouse in Laredo, Texas, in the early 2000s and found only one case in which drugs had been seized (47 pounds of marijuana). Only 10–15 percent of defendants had previous convictions for drug felonies, often for simple possession and not for sale or distribution (it is not uncommon for smugglers to use cocaine or marijuana during difficult crossings). Qualitative evidence from a host of informants, including migrants, smugglers, human rights activists, US attorneys, probation officers, public defendants, judges, and law enforcement officials indicated almost unanimously that drug trafficking and human smuggling at the end of the 1990s and in the early 2000s were "generally separate businesses" (Spener 2009, pp. 155–56). Overall, "it did not appear that drug-moving and people-moving were necessarily carried out by a single organization" (p. 157).

This separation seems to have persisted over the years. According to Izcara Palacios (2014, p. 324), the empirical evidence on ties between migrant smuggling and drug trafficking is "scarce." His interviews with 85 smugglers suggest a clear separation between migrant smuggling and drug trafficking in the mind of smugglers themselves. As one smuggler put it, "either you're a *pollero* and carry people, or you're a drug dealer and carry drugs. Over there you can't do both things at once" (p. 336).

This does not mean that coyotes do not sometimes switch from migrant smuggling to drug trafficking. Spener found evidence of men who used to work as smugglers and then joined a drug trafficking organization, mainly due to the prospect of higher earnings. Good smugglers make for good recruits for drug trafficking organizations, as they possess knowledge of routes and trails. However, when smugglers decide to join a drug trafficking organization, they "leave *coyotaje*" and "cut ties with the social world" outside the drug trafficking organization (Izcara Palacios 2014, p. 331). Migrants and drugs do "not typically appear to be transported and housed in the same places at the same times" (Spener 2009, p. 157). Some segments of routes may be entirely off-limits to migrants as "drug traffickers prefer to keep migrants out of drug trafficking routes, most likely to avoid unwanted attention from law enforcement" (Sanchez and Zhang 2018, p. 142).

In recent years, there have been increasing numbers of reports of migrants carrying backpacks with drugs across the US-Mexico border. However, Sanchez and Zhang (2018) argue that this should not be interpreted as a sign of a convergence between human smuggling and drug trafficking operations. Migrants' testimonies indicate that "the decision to carry drugs often was a personal, complex choice, rather than the result of coercion" (p. 143). It was more a consequence of lack of financial resources "to cover basic needs like room or board, or having run out of money after traveling vast distances and no longer able to afford smuggling fees, [that] some migrants opted to assist drug traffickers in exchange for financial compensation or transportation within the United States" (p. 143).

Working with drug traffickers can mean improved travel conditions for migrants and access to faster routes that are inaccessible to smugglers. Traffickers and smugglers seem to offer separate, somewhat competitive travel options. Sanchez and Zhang (2018) point out that "our data also show that migrants were able to decline, along some corridors and in some instances, collaborations with criminal actors with no repercussion. Among our respondents, for example, no one reported having faced retaliation as a result of his or her unwillingness to work or travel with drug traffickers" (p. 147). The claim that human smuggling and drug trafficking organizations have converged along the Mexican corridor remains unconvincing.

B. Protectors and Smugglers

The relationship between smugglers and protectors is crucial—yet it is often misunderstood or overlooked. In their works on the Italian-American mafia, Schelling (1971) and Reuter (1983, 1985) pointed to a separation between individuals specialized in protection (governance) and other illegal actors. That separation exists in human smuggling.

Zhang and Chin (2002) found no clear evidence of "a connection between human smugglers and traditional Chinese crime groups in the United States or elsewhere." Of 90 individuals interviewed, only three claimed to be members of traditional criminal organizations and none was participating in smuggling "on behalf of their gangs" (p. 747). The majority "took efforts not to entangle themselves with street gangs or other crime groups in the Chinese community. However, this does not mean that none of the smugglers have access to gangs when the situation calls for it" (p. 747). Smuggling, they argue, is separate from traditional Chinese criminal societies such as triads, tongs, and street gangs that are normally involved in racketeering. Members of such organizations can participate in the trade, but typically they do it on their own, independently.

I (Campana 2018) analyzed an active smuggling route cutting across Sicily—an island with a long-standing mafia presence. There was no evidence of any involvement of the Sicilian mafia in smuggling in Sicily or elsewhere, despite the island being a key point in the smuggling route. I identified no payments of protection money to the Sicilian mafia.

Smugglers can enlist the services of protectors if needed, for instance to recover a debt. This emerges neatly from the testimony of a Chinese smuggler based in the United States: "If a client fails to live up to her end of the agreement, I will have to ask her to return the money. I don't worry a bit about not getting my money back. I have someone who is a Vietnamese gang member and I will ask him to pay her a visit. . . . I believe she will pay me quickly. But I don't like to use these debt collectors. They charge 50 percent of the collected money" (quoted in Zhang and Chin 2002, p. 747).

I found an equally clear separation between smugglers and protectors in Libya where militia members played the role of protector. A statistical analysis of interactions within a smuggling ring demonstrated that smugglers are more likely to coordinate with fellow smugglers than with other militia members (Campana 2018, p. 490; odds ratio $= 6.3, p < .001$). This does not, however, imply complete separation as cross-role interactions did take place, mostly in the form of smugglers paying bribes to militia members in order to be able to operate.

Payment of protection fees to local militias has also been documented by journalists. Reporting from Libya, Kirkpatrick (2015) estimated fees. In 2015, smugglers paid $100 or more at each local militia checkpoint for each truck carrying 15–20 migrants; permission to use a secure departure point could cost as much as $20,000 a month. Militias were not normally directly involved in human smuggling but charged smugglers a fee for the right to operate in the territory they controlled (Micallef 2017, p. 32). The practice continued until mid-2017 when, under pressure from European countries, militias stopped, or considerably reduced, protecting smugglers (Micallef 2017, p. 9; Lewis and Scherer 2017).

Together with implementation of a coast guard under direct control of the Tripoli-based government, the switch in the militias' attitude toward smuggling is thought to have largely contributed to the large decline in sea crossings from Libya (down 80.2 percent between 2017 and 2018, with a further decrease in 2019; see table 2). In some instances, as in Niger, official authorities levy protection fees on smugglers (Brachet 2012, p. 100). Local police officers levy arbitrary taxes at checkpoints ranging from 500 CFA, slightly less than one US dollar, to a few thousand (around US$10; Brachet 2012, p. 102). Based on field observations between 2003 and 2008, Brachet estimated the annual revenues generated at between 861 million CFA and 3.5 billion CFA ($1.5 to $6 million).

There is ample evidence of protection fees imposed by Mexican drug trafficking organizations that have control over a territory. The protection money, known as *el piso* or *derechos de piso*, is "a one-time toll to access specific parts of the migrant trail under the control of a DTO [Drug

Trafficking Organization]. The payment of *piso* entitled migrants and their guides to, in theory, travel without fear" (Sanchez and Zhang 2018, p. 141; Sanchez 2018, p. 154; Izcara Palacios 2014, p. 3). As in Libya, protectors do not seem to be directly involved in smuggling. Of 85 Mexican smugglers interviewed by Izcara Palacios (2014, p. 333), 96 percent claimed that drug cartels were not directly involved in smuggling (three indicated otherwise, but one was relying on hearsay and a second was unable to provide details). Rather than being involved directly in smuggling migrants, organized crime groups levy a tax on the right to smuggle migrants across territory they control. The separation between smugglers and protections emerges neatly from the words of migrants:

> *Margot:* Along the border, the ones who govern all that are the, the ... how are those called?

> *Leslie:* La mafia.

> *Margot:* La mafia?

> *Leslie:* Yes, you only pay [la mafia] when you arrive with the coyote [to a specific point].

> *Margot:* Yes, [the smuggler] gives [the fee] to the mafia

> (Sanchez 2018, p. 141).

Leutert (2018) indicates that organized crime groups, such as the Gulf cartels and the remaining factions of the Zeta cartels, tax the movement of people and goods, particularly in the state of Tamaulipas, "the failure of a smuggler to pay the proper fee for migrants to cross a TCO's [transnational criminal organization] territory might also lead to the migrants being kidnapped" (p. 19). In some cases, drug trafficking organizations might deliberately leave intimidating signs on the route, such as burned or flipped cars, as a warning to those who don't pay the fee (Sanchez and Zhang 2018, p. 142). In testimonies collected by Sanchez and Zhang (2018), the threat of violence was sufficient for smugglers to comply with the protectors' requests.

Organized crime groups involved in protection might recruit former smugglers to help them levy the protection tax because of their knowledge of the routes, their ability to detect other smugglers and identify those who had not paid up, and, their ability to "know how to gain their [migrants'] trust and distinguish between those with money and those without" (Izcara Palacios 2014, p. 332).

This separation between smugglers and protectors is often neglected in public discourse. In some cases, including Mexico, there is an oft-repeated mantra that "cartels are entering" the smuggling business. However, there are two problems with this. First, the word "entering" is vague and does not indicate whether cartels are directly involved in smuggling or are taxing smugglers. Second, media descriptions are often superficial. In a case discussed in Spener (2009, p. 159), English-language news sources such as the *Associated Press* and the *San Antonio Express* news "wrote reports suggesting the direct involvement of the cartel in transporting people." The Mexico City–based newspaper *La Jornada* "indicated that the cartel's arrested leaders were involved only in charging *coyotes* the *derecho de piso* in Reynosa, formerly paid as bribes to local law enforcement authorities" (p. 159). The two scenarios are radically different.[13]

IV. Smuggling Mechanisms: Reputation and Warranties

Smugglers often operate in an environment in which multiple organizations are active (Campana 2017; Achilli 2018). These organizations may compete to attract migrants (Campana 2018). Migrants look for clues about the quality and the reliability of the service rendered by smugglers, trying to avoid cheaters and unscrupulous operators. A survey of undocumented migrants deported to six Mexican cities showed that the main qualities migrants value in smugglers are "trustworthiness, honesty, comportment, and treatment" (Slack and Martinez 2018, p. 152). Building trust, therefore, is of extreme importance (Sanchez 2018, p. 151, on Mexico). However, smugglers operate in a context of illegality in almost all parts of the world.

As of April 2019, 112 states had ratified the UN Protocol against the Smuggling of Migrants (UN 2000) that makes smuggling a criminal

---

[13] The relationship between smugglers and kidnappers is often misunderstood. I found (Campana 2018) a clear separation between smugglers and kidnappers operating across the Libyan desert. This separation also emerges neatly from the words of a former Eritrean smuggler: "We often travel at night. But the hyenas and Rashida kidnappers are active at night. You must know how and when to move to safe routes. A single mistake may lead all of us to a disaster: imprisonment, death or kidnapping by kidney harvesters or ransom in the Egyptian desert" (quoted in Ayalew Mengiste 2018, p. 68).

offense. This condition of illegality has consequences for how the market operates. It prevents establishment of formal enforcement mechanisms to solve disputes, ensure compliance, and enforce contracts (Reuter 1983, chap. 5; Reuter 1985; Campana and Varese 2013). Furthermore, illegality directly affects the availability and quality of information available. Sellers may find it difficult and costly to advertise their products and services (Reuter 1983, 1985; Gambetta 2009; Campana and Varese 2013). Buyers may find it more difficult to collect reliable information about the services offered (Reuter 1985; Campana and Varese 2013). Moreover, illegality makes it difficult to track individuals, which is further exacerbated by the potentially higher-than-average mobility of people involved in irregular migration.

In many ways, the smuggling market resembles the market for second-hand cars studied by George Akerlof (1970). Like car sellers, smugglers (sellers) possess more information about the quality of their products than migrants (buyers) do, and it is very difficult for buyers to distinguish between reliable smugglers and cheaters. Were all smugglers equally reliable, the problem of asymmetric information would be irrelevant. However, much like car sales, the smuggling market includes sellers with varying degrees of trustworthiness and some outright cheaters and impostors (see Slack and Martinez 2018, p. 170). There have been documented instances of individuals posing as smugglers in bus terminals and areas around international bridges in Mexican border towns in order to swindle migrants or lead them to isolated places and then assault and rob them (Spener 2009, p. 155).

The problem of asymmetric information is intensified by the potentially severe consequences migrants face if they pick a dishonest smuggler.[14] The trust problem is, thus, a crucial dimension of human smuggling. The importance of trust in supporting transactions in general is well documented (Gambetta 1988; Coleman 1990; Yamagishi and Yamagishi 1994), including and in contexts in which contracts cannot be drafted or enforced (Reuters 1985; Gambetta 1993; Campana and Varese 2013). Smugglers themselves have described their work as "a business that requires

---

[14] Cheaters and impostors are more likely to abuse migrants than bona fide smugglers: "A close reading of several Tamaulipas newspapers in the late 1990s indicated that some of the abuses that were attributed to coyotes were committed by people posing as coyotes who never had any intention of transporting their victims to a U.S. destination" (Spener 2009, p. 155).

trust" (Achilli 2018, p. 89; see also van Liempt 2007, p. 171). How, then, do they try to solve that problem?

A. Reputation

One way to address the trust problem and achieve a competitive advantage is to invest in one's reputation. Reuter (1983, 1985) stressed the importance of reputation in contexts characterized by illegality. Human smuggling is no exception. A reputation for reliability and competence is a vital aspect of a smuggler's identity (Bilger, Hofmann, and Jandl 2006). Smugglers go to great lengths to build a good reputation.

Chin (1999) has documented instances in Chinese smuggling of top-level smugglers who have contributed money to their hometowns and made generous donations to improve local infrastructures. The importance of a good reputation is highlighted by migrants who have been smuggled: "Big snakeheads are mainly wealthy business owners. That's why people trust them. . . . Big snakeheads *have got to have* a good reputation" (quoted in Chin 1999, p. 30, emphasis added).[15] Things have not changed over the years. In their report for the European Commission, Optimity Advisors (2015, p. 45) pointed out that in "places with high competition . . ., smugglers care about their reputation" (also see Bilger, Hofmann, and Jandl 2006). In a phone call wiretapped by Italian authorities, a smuggler claimed to have paid "compensation" to families of victims of a deadly shipwreck in the Mediterranean: "[Yusef] continues saying that his fellow countrymen trusted him, and he is extremely sorry for what happened; contrary to other organizers, he had personally notified the families who have lost somebody in the shipwreck, and he had even sent 5000 dollars to his village and to the village named 'Adi Hargets' for the relatives of the victims from these areas" (police summary of the conversation, quoted in Campana 2018, p. 495). A reputation for being efficient and reliable becomes more important as the market becomes more competitive. In another wiretapped conversation, the same smuggler expressed concern about his competitors being able to offer a better service to the migrants: "Yusef asks Samuel if there is any news. Samuel replies that he has been there [in the Reception Center] for 28 days, and two of

---

[15] Most of Chin's respondents viewed "big snakeheads as smart and capable business people with power, wealth, good reputation, and connections" (Chin 1999, p. 32), but not all had good reputations. Some were described as "selfish, untrustworthy people who cared nothing for the needs and feeling of their customers" (Chin 199, p. 31).

Muhammad's boats have arrived in the last two days. Yusef then complains, asking why the guy isn't sending 'ours' . . . while the others keep sending people" (police summary of the conversation, quoted in Campana 2018, p. 495).[16]

Evidence from the Mexican route paints a similar picture. In a situation in which there is no monopoly of a single smuggler or group of smugglers, migrants normally choose a smuggler based on his or her reputation for "being competent and trustworthy or at least . . . less incompetent and less untrustworthy than other coyotes" (Spener 2009, pp. 73, 173). Besides causing a loss of potential customers, a bad reputation can increase the risk of apprehension; smugglers known to abuse and extort migrants appeared more likely to be targeted by law enforcement, as they were more likely to be reported by their "dissatisfied" customers (Spener 2009, p. 173).[17]

Smugglers may use competitors' bad reputations to gain a competitive advantage. This has been documented on the southern Mexican border where Mexican smugglers stress their nationality vis-à-vis Central American competitors in order to benefit from "the bad reputation of their Central American counterparts, and do their best to maintain the tensions around this imaginary" (Guevara Gonzalez 2018, p. 184).

A good reputation is a valuable asset, but protecting it can pose challenges. Reuter (1985) highlighted difficulties in monitoring members when an illegal organization grows in size and expands its reach. These difficulties arise for smugglers. Spener (2009, p. 175) observed that when

[16] The same smuggler was aware of the importance of collective reputations. In another phone wiretap, he suggested that his interlocutor should talk to a smuggler "who has embarked some people against their relatives' will" as such behavior will hurt "everybody" (Campana 2018, p. 495). He gave the example of "a group of people who share the same house whose bathroom is dirty, and it reflects badly on everybody, not just on the person who has made the bathroom dirty" (police summary of the conversation, quoted in Campana 2018, p. 495).

[17] Smugglers can also be held hostage by migrants to make sure they will honor their promises by collecting compromising information that can be used against them (Gambetta 2009; Campana and Varese 2013; see Schelling [1960, 2006] on hostage-taking as a strategy to ensure commitment). A Syrian migrant who had successfully reached the United Kingdom pointed to use of this strategy following an unsuccessful attempt to cross the Aegean Sea: "We had the number of the smuggler and called him and told him this happened with us and the boat was broken and we didn't tell the police about you and because of that we want a new trip or we will return to the police. You are this person and one of the men said that 'I have a photo of you. I took a photo of you. Believe me I will publish the photo if you don't bring us another boat and we also have children and women with us so behave with us' and he [the smuggler] said 'okay, okay, tomorrow I will get you a new boat and will send you on a new trip'" (Campana and Gelsthorpe 2019).

participants in smuggling operations "were separated from one another geographically, did not engage in frequent and intense face-to-face inter-actions with one another, and specialized in activities at only one point along the chain, it could be difficult for participants to be very confident about precisely how their collaborators were behaving when they were not physically with them." A costly solution is to maintain close monitor-ing throughout the whole journey, for example, by having a trusted per-son travel with the migrants. Cases have been documented of smugglers using this strategy within organizations operating between San Luis Potosí in Central Mexico and Atlanta (Spener 2009, p. 175). However, as risks of detection and imprisonment increase, this solution can quickly become too costly. Smugglers may decide to segment their business and provide ser-vices only over a shorter, well-defined leg of the journey.

Reputations associated with illegal activities tend not to travel easily (Reuter 1985). It is not surprising that smugglers and migrants tend to come from the same place, as this shared background helps information travel more easily and increases the cost of cheating. This emerges neatly from the story of Abu Hamza, the Syrian head of a smuggling organiza-tion in Turkey composed of around 30 people (Achilli 2018). Formerly the owner of a jewelry shop in his village, he had the economic and social capital to open a smuggling enterprise. Despite operating out of Turkey, most of his customers and associates came from Abu Hamza's village in Syria. A similar pattern can be detected in smuggling by Somalis and Afghanis. Majidi (2018, p. 106) observes that the "choice of a smuggler starts within the community." Smugglers are often known directly by the migrant or indirectly through relatives and friends. Migrants have an incen-tive to choose smugglers they know; likewise, smugglers have a similar in-centive so they can locate the family of the migrants if needed, for instance to collect payments. The further migrants travel from home, the "ties that bind and protect migrants in their journeys become more and more ten-uous" (Majidi 2018, p. 98) and expose them to greater risk.

The importance of the community of origin has been demonstrated also in Ecuadorian smuggling. Stone-Cadena and Alvarez Velasco (2018) report that indigenous people normally choose indigenous smugglers be-cause "the community itself would have greater leverage over the actions of coyotes because of their membership in the community, therefore en-suring the safety and protection of migrants traveling under their watch" (p. 202). There is an expectation that "indigenous coyotes would be more accountable to their communities, as the ties were stronger than with mestizos, especially if the coyote resided in the same village or province in which he recruited clients" (p. 202). During their fieldwork in indigenous communities, Stone-Cadena and Alvarez Velasco found that information on a smuggler's behavior was routinely fed back to the local community.[18]

Communities, word-of-mouth, and personal referrals remain the main conduit of information.[19] Over the years, however, smugglers have started using opportunities offered by social media and the internet more generally to promote their businesses and reputations (Optimity Advisors 2015, p. 37; Roberts 2017). Dekker et al. (2018) show that 80 percent of 51 Syrian refugees they interviewed in the Netherlands consulted social networking sites such as Facebook and LinkedIn before migrating.[20] While technology enables circulation of information to wider audiences, it recast the trust problem in new ways. Roberts (2017) looked at 10 Arabic-speaking Facebook groups in which smuggling services were advertised and discussed. In the online environment, smugglers developed new strategies to boost their reputations and build trust. For instance, they would post pictures of themselves at the end of a successful trip or share videos received from migrants they had successfully smuggled to indicate reliability. A particularly powerful strategy is to post screenshots of conversations, generally on WhatsApp or Telegram, between the smuggler and his clients while en route. This is done to build an image of themselves as reliable, caring, and polite (Roberts 2017, pp. 21–23).

Social media also offer a platform to exchange feedback on smugglers, much like well-known online platforms such as eBay operate. Migrants can consult online feedback to check a smuggler's credentials. Roberts (2017) identified instances in Facebook groups of both positive and negative feedback for named smugglers. In some cases, smugglers replied to criticisms and tried to redress the situation (Roberts 2017, pp. 40–46).[21] Interviews

---

[18] Shared ethnicity, language, and, ever more, birthplace help smugglers solve their internal monitoring problems. Zhang and Chin (2002, p. 762) observe that in Chinese smuggling the "enforcement of contracts and assignments relies heavily on informal social control sustained through a cultural environment that promotes shared expectations and understanding of the tasks at hand" and that "familial relations, speaking the same dialect, or sharing the same ancestral townships" reinforce this informal social control.

[19] See, e.g., Optimity Advisors and Seefar (2018) concerning West African migrants.

[20] Of 655 migrants in Slack and Martinez's sample (2018, p. 162), 53 percent were referred to the smuggler by someone they knew, 11 percent knew the smuggler before the crossing attempt, and 36 percent had no prior ties.

[21] Tech-savvy migrants are more likely to take advantage of online platforms and thereby decrease their risk of victimization along the journey. The opposite is true for migrants

with Arab-speaking migrants confirm the existence of online rating systems and suggest that in some instances migrants checked such reviews with those who posted them (Campana and Gelsthorpe 2019).

B. Warranties, Payments, and Escrow Services

Another strategy smugglers have developed is to offer warranties. One type is "multiple-attempts" insurance: if a journey is not successful, migrants will be able to repeat it at no additional cost. Akerlof (1970) identified warranties as a strategy that good sellers might adopt to differentiate themselves from bad ones (as only good sellers would be able to afford offering such warranties). Similarly, smugglers might give migrants the right to reattempt a crossing for free if they fail to reach their agreed destinations. These insurance policies might cover both organizational failures and interceptions by law enforcement authorities.

Optimity Advisors (2015, p. 46) indicate that when "an advance payment has been agreed, the contract often entails clauses indicating the number of attempts (including a supply of fresh documents if needed)." This practice has been commonly reported along the Eastern Mediterranean route. However, it occurs elsewhere. A similar arrangement is in place for the route from Ecuador to Mexico and the United States; smugglers give migrants three chances to make the journey (Álvarez Velasco 2018, p. 179). Similarly, at the southern Mexican border "some facilitators offered border crossing packages that included multiple crossing attempts. If the migrant was detained by immigration authorities, robbed along the way, or extorted by drug trafficking organizations, becoming unable to complete the journey, he or she could contact the facilitator afterwards to use his or her additional travel 'credits'" (Guevara Gonzalez 2018, pp. 186–87). There is evidence of a three-attempt guarantee to Afghani and Pakistani migrants in relation to crossings from Pakistan to Iran (Aksel et al. 2015, p. 20). Interviews with Arab-speaking migrants smuggled into Greece and the United Kingdom have highlighted situations in which smugglers have honored multiattempt contracts (Campana and Gelsthorpe 2019).

Payment arrangements can also be designed in a way that offers warranties about the reliability of a given smuggler. One is to split the payment

---

coming from rural areas or with lower educational levels. This disadvantage has been highlighted concerning migrants coming from rural areas in Pakistan, Ethiopia, and Nigeria (Optimity Advisers 2015, p. 37).

into two parts: a deposit before departure and the rest upon successful arrival; Optimity Advisors (2015) provide examples in relation to smuggling into Europe. The deposit offers a two-way warranty: it gives assurances to the migrant and also to the smuggler. A nonrefundable deposit commits a migrant to buy the service from that smuggler. This protects the smuggler from a migrant switching to a competitor while increasing smugglers' incentives to deliver on their promises. Smugglers might be more inclined to offer this type of arrangement the more competitive the market is.

Chinese smuggling is striking because of the high sums at stake. Smugglers have responded by developing relatively sophisticated financial arrangements. In the late 1990s, when the average smuggling fee was $27,745, migrants were typically required to make a down payment of $1,000 (Chin 1999, p. 37). In some cases, the trust problem was so acute that even this was not paid in advance, but only when the journey had started: "Once I got on the ship, I turned over my identification card to the little snakeheads and they went to my home, collected the $1,000, and returned the identification card to my family" (quoted in Chin 1999, p. 37). Informal contracts were drawn detailing rules and obligations, as the largest part of the payment had to be collected at some stage after arrival. "One chilling aspect of these contracts is the understanding by both parties that the smugglers can hold their clients hostage if the clients, upon arrival in America, do not come up with the smuggling fee" (p. 37). Arrangements of this kind create large monitoring costs for the smugglers, as the fee might not be paid in full for long periods.

The US Department for Homeland Security found evidence of similar arrangements along the US-Mexico route. Until the end of the 2000s, smugglers charged initial fees as low as $100, and $1,000–$3,000 upon arrival at the destination. These prices have increased to $1,200 for the initial stage and $8,000 at the destination (DHS 2018, p. 48).

More generally, requiring only a partial advance payment raises the problem of how to be sure the rest will be paid at journey's end. In close-knit communities, it may be possible to monitor people over long periods, but in most cases smugglers face an almost impossible challenge. Activities are fragmented, and smugglers are normally involved only in one segment of a much longer journey. From the evidence available on the structure of smuggling operations, it is extremely difficult and costly for a Turkish- or Libyan-based smuggler to monitor migrants once they disembark in Italy or Greece and to collect the remaining sums.

Escrow services offer a solution. An escrow service is an arrangement in which a third party receives the agreed sum and disburses it only when conditions agreed to by the seller and the buyer are met. For smuggling, this is when a migrant has reached the agreed destination. Normally, the system works like this: the migrant receives a code when the agreed sum of money is paid to a third party; when the journey is completed, the migrant communicates the code to the smuggler or the third party, and the sum is released. Provided that the third party is trusted by both smuggler and migrant, the system increases the migrant's confidence and offers the smuggler a guarantee that the full amount is available and obtainable (with conditions).

The use of escrow services was documented in the early 2000s in relation to Iraqi smugglers operating along the Turkish route into Europe (Içduygu and Toktas 2002, p. 48). The practice has continued along the Turkey-Greece route (Triandafyllidou and Maroukis 2012, chaps. 5 and 6). It happens elsewhere. There is evidence of Somali migrants using "financial facilitators" who act as escrow services (Majidi 2018, p. 107).[22] *Hawalader*, the operators of the *hawala* financial network, might also double as escrow services.[23] The network is commonly used by migrants from the Horn of Africa, the Middle East, and Central and South Asia (particularly Afghanistan and Pakistan; Optimity Advisors 2015, p. 47). Legal nonbanking systems such as Western Union or MoneyGram are also reported to be used (Optimity Advisors 2015, p. 47).

International nonbanking systems have a crucial desirable quality; they allow for separation between the place where the smuggling service is rendered and the place where the payment is made (and the money kept). This emerged clearly with Eritrean smugglers operating in Libya whom I described (Campana 2018, p. 493). The service was often sought and agreed in Libya, but the payment was made into a deposit held by a *hawalader* based in Israel. This is mutually convenient because it decreases risks for both smugglers and migrants; migrants need not carry large sums of cash while traveling, and smugglers need not possess large amounts of money in unsafe areas such as Libya. The international reach of a

---

[22] There is evidence that, when competition is intense, smugglers may have to accept a full payment only upon successful completion of the journey and without the guarantee of a "financial facilitator" (Majidi 2018, p. 111).

[23] *Hawala* is an informal money transfer system; it is comparable to nonbanking financial institutions such as Western Union or MoneyGram; see Varese (2016).

hawala network allows for the money being paid on behalf of the migrant at very little cost by relatives living in the country of origin or in a diaspora community.[24]

V. Assessing the Policy Response

A few studies have looked at the effects of policy changes on the dynamics of human smuggling. Quantitative assessments of policy responses are rare. While some have looked at changes in legislation on the decision to migrate irregularly (Bazzi et al. 2018), the effects of heightened border controls on decisions to enlist the services of a smuggler have been rarely measured. One exception is a study by Massey, Durand, and Pren (2016, p. 1565) using data on border crossings collected by the Mexican Migration Project: 151,785 Mexican individuals were surveyed in 23,851 households and then matched with data on US border patrol expenditures and information on social and socioeconomic conditions in Mexico and the United States. They found that the rapid increase in border enforcement that began in 1986 had no effect on the likelihood of initiating undocumented migration; displaced migrant routes from safer crossing locations to much riskier places, such as the Sonoran Desert; increased the likelihood that migrants enlist the service of a smuggler; and only modestly increased the likelihood of apprehension. Making the journey riskier and costlier changed the dynamics of migration. Migrants who needed to hire a smuggler were unlikely ever to return to their home country. A traditional pattern of circular migration morphed into one-way migration due to the change in incentives. The probability of returning to Mexico fell from 0.48 in 1980 to zero in 2010, with some significant yearly fluctuations (Massey, Durand, and Pren 2016, p. 1590).

Massey, Durand, and Pren concluded, the "militarization [of the US border] failed to reduce undocumented entry but paradoxically did reduce the rate of return migration to increase the net rate of unauthorized

---

[24] There is variation across nationalities in how payments are collected. There have been cases among Afghani migrants in which full payment was made in advance by giving property or other assets to a principal smuggler who took on the responsibility to finance the migrant's journey to the final destination (Içduygu and Toktas 2002, p. 48). It is unclear what type of warranties the principal smuggler offers apart from, perhaps, being embedded in the same community as the migrant's family. This arrangement potentially increases migrants' vulnerability as they become fully dependent on the principal smuggler concerning routes taken and means of transportation chosen (Içduygu and Toktas 2002, p. 48).

migration and increase undocumented population growth [in the United States]" (p. 1592). They estimated that the undocumented Mexican population in the United States would have been 31 percent lower than the recorded 2010 level if the border patrol budget had remained at the 1986 level (p. 1593). They concluded that the increase in enforcement made crossing the border more expensive because of increased prices for smuggling services.[25] Crossing through arduous points, such as the Sonoran Desert, would add $116 per trip (p. 1577). An increase in smuggling fees over time was also reported by the US Department of Homeland Security; this covaries with the increase in apprehensions (DHS 2018, p. 48).

Europe has recently experienced a large increase in illegal border crossings and responded with a mix of different policies. To stem flows on the Eastern Mediterranean Route, the European Union signed an agreement with Turkey that increased patrolling on the Turkish coast and introduced disincentives for those found to have crossed illegally. A preliminary assessment suggests a marked decrease in illegal border crossings across the Eastern Mediterranean (fig. 2).

The agreement took effect at the end of the first quarter (Q1) of 2016. There was a sharp decline in arrivals in the following quarter compared with the previous quarter (−94.2 percent) and the second quarter of 2015 (−87.1 percent). On average, between the second quarter of 2016 and the first quarter of 2017, there was a 95 percent year-on-year decrease. From 2017 on, the level of crossings is in line with pre-2015 data (not shown). To assess the extent to which these patterns are attributable to the policy change or to changes in demand for smuggling services caused by the intensity of the conflict in Syria will require further analysis.

The Central Mediterranean presents more complex and challenging problems. Between October 2013 and July 2017, the priority was to rescue vessels and migrants by means of vast search-and-rescue operations conducted by states and NGOs in a context of relaxed border controls. This began to change in July 2017 when restrictions to NGO-led operations were introduced (ANSA 2017). It accelerated in June 2018 when a new right-wing government in Italy adopted a "closed ports" policy (BBC 2018). The collapse of that government in August 2018 led to a new, more

---

[25] They estimated an increase of $732 in crossing costs for each point increase in the log of Border Patrol budget; this translates into an implied increase of $507 when the Border Patrol budget is doubled: Massey, Durand, and Pren (2016, p. 1577).

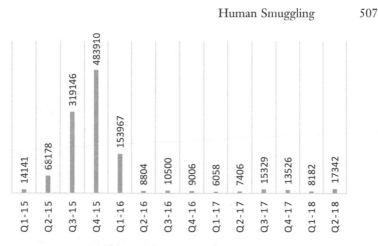

Fig. 2.—Illegal Border Crossings across the Eastern Mediterranean (Q1 2015–Q2 2018). Source: Elaboration on Frontex, Quarterly Risk Assessments.

left-leaning executive in September 2019, which softened Italy's stance (Tondo 2019).

Data from the Italian Ministry of Interior suggest that the hardened policy is consistent with a decrease in the number of individuals arriving in Italy (fig. 3). However, this preliminary assessment does not take into account changes in demand for smuggling services. In addition, there have been changes at other stages along the migration route, especially in Libya, where militias stopped protecting smugglers, and in Niger, where the government outlawed many of the operators who had supplied assisted migration services under pressure from the European Union (Brachet 2018; Raineri 2018).

Amenta, Di Betta, and Ferrara (2016) used official data on monthly illegal sea crossings into Italy between January 2011 and March 2016 to assess the effect of rescue operations on migrant smuggling. They found that military rescue operations at sea increased the number of people crossing and the likelihood of success of migrants' journeys. Their model controls for conflicts both in the migrants' countries of origin and in Libya, GDP per capita of the migrants' countries of origin, weather conditions at sea, and reported deaths at sea. Rescue operations are estimated to have added an extra 4,130 departures per month. Deiana, Maheshri, and Mastrobuoni (2019, p. 22) looked at the period 2009–17 and also found increases in illegal border crossings in periods when rescue operations were in place.

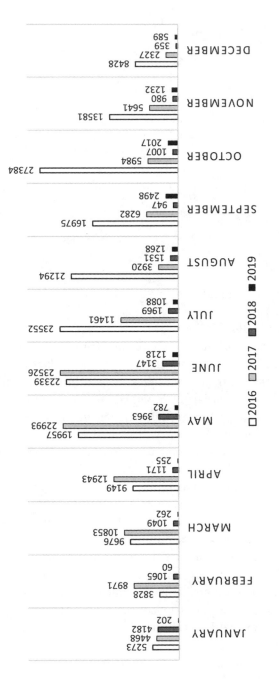

Fig. 3.—Monthly boat landings identified in Italy, January 2016–December 2019. Source: Elaboration on Italian Ministry of Interior.

What about the effect of rescue operations on risks for migrants? EPSC (2017, p. 2) offers estimates of the number of migrants who died or went missing in the Central Mediterranean in 2011–16. In 2011–12, the 2 years before the launch of the first large-scale rescue operation, *Mare Nostrum* (October 2013), an average of 1,052 individuals per year died or went missing. In 2014–16, that increased to 3,536 per year. This was due mainly to the increased number of departures. In relative terms, the mortality risk fell following the launch of rescue operations. In 2011, the risk of deaths and missing migrants combined was 29 per 1,000 individuals who successfully crossed the Mediterranean. In 2012, it was 21. After launch of the rescue operations, this fell to 18 in both 2014 and 2015.[26]

A very preliminary assessment suggests that rescue operations have been successful in relative terms in saving lives, but have not decreased the absolute number of deaths. More sophisticated models are certainly needed, but these are not so straightforward to specify.[27]

The Mediterranean rescue operations highlight risks of unintended consequences of well-intentioned policies. The evidence for 2016 is illustrative. This was the year when budgets, assets, and areas of operation of EU rescue operations were massively expanded (EPSC 2017, pp. 2–3). In addition, in 2016 the largest number of active NGO rescue vessels (9) were in operation, and they were operating closer to the Libyan coast than ever before (sometimes within Libyan territorial waters; EPSC 2017, p. 6, fig. 7). In the same year, the number of migrants who died or went missing at sea reached its highest level during 2011–16, and the mortality risk rose to 25 per 1,000 (in line with pre-2013 levels). This is likely to have been the consequence of a change in smugglers' modus operandi.

There is evidence that smugglers started to provide migrants with satellite phones, GPS, and one or more emergency contacts after the launch of large-scale rescue operations, and instructed them to make direct contact with the Italian or Maltese authorities or merchant ships in order to be rescued (Optimity Advisor 2015, p. 39). Smugglers also decreased the sizes of the boats they used as the expected length of the journey decreased when rescue teams began to operate closer to the Libyan territorial

[26] For 2013, the mortality risk is 15 per 1,000 successful crossings, and the absolute number of deaths and missing migrants is 644 (EPSC 2017, p. 2).

[27] See Deiana, Maheshri, and Mastrobuoni (2019, p. 37) for a more sophisticated approach and their warning about difficulties in attributing causality; see also Steinhilper and Gruijters (2018, p. 526).

waters (Altai Consulting 2015, p. 91; EPSC 2017).[28] There is evidence that smugglers switched from sturdier, more expensive fishing boats and decommissioned commercial vessels to cheaper, more dangerous, rubber dinghies (EPSC 2017, p. 7). Finally, smugglers decided not to board or pilot the boats, but let migrants take command (EPSC 2017, p. 7). Overall, this evidence shows that smugglers can quickly adapt to policy changes. This in turn can generate unintended and pernicious consequences.

Policies to tackle smuggling pose moral dilemmas. They often imply difficult trade-offs between protecting the right of a state to control the movement of people across its borders and curbing illegal markets while at the same time protecting the lives and welfare of migrants and individuals' rights to seek asylum. Rescue operations at sea are likely to reduce mortality rates while increasing the number of individuals crossing and the size of the smuggling markets, ultimately increasing the profit for smugglers (Amenta, Di Betta, and Ferrara 2016). Heightened border controls are likely to increase apprehension rates but also to exacerbate dangers and risks faced by migrants (Slack and Martinez 2018, p. 171). More patrolling will increase prices paid by migrants but decrease the quality of the smuggling services rendered. Slack and Martinez (2018) observed that smugglers in Mexico were less willing to walk with migrants for fear of arrest and harsh penalties and, as a consequence, that migrants were more likely to get lost and die while crossing treacherous areas. Similarly, smugglers operating across the Mediterranean responded to the increased likelihood of detection and conviction by not boarding the boats and training migrants how to make the voyage on their own (Optimity Advisors 2015). Stopping treacherous crossings across the desert or the Mediterranean may involve restricting the right of people to move on land, as in Niger, or people's rights to make asylum claims in a safe country.

My focus has been on the relationship between border controls and smuggling operations. More work is also needed to understand the effects of broader changes in migration policies on demand for smuggling services, for example, on availability of safe and legal migration channels and on opportunities for economic development in countries of origin. These

---

[28] There is further evidence of smugglers responding strategically to changes. When the crossing from Calais, France, to Dover, United Kingdom, became decreasingly viable due to heightened controls, some smugglers switched to Hoek van Holland in the Netherlands (Optimity Advisors 2015, p. 33).

policies affect smuggling operations by increasing or decreasing demand and thus can offer alternative ways to curb human smuggling, but they are outside the scope of this essay.

VI. Looking Forward

I have surveyed current knowledge about human smuggling, a trade in which the commodity traded is an assisted illegal entry into a country. Empirical knowledge remains patchy. There is no global estimate of the extent of smuggling, and only a tiny minority of countries produce useful statistics.

Even so, some findings stand out. Similar organizational arrangements appear to characterize the main smuggling routes. Human smuggling is not a monopolized business. This is true for all the routes analyzed, including smuggling out of China, assisted irregular movements into Europe via Turkey and North Africa, and across the US-Mexico border. The smuggling market is populated by "decentralized associations of criminals" (Chinese smuggling: Zhang and Chin 2002, p. 759), "small, local and flexible organizations" (across Turkey: Icduygu and Toktas 2002, p. 46), and "localized and rather rudimentary hierarchies" (into Europe from North Africa: Campana 2018). The markets and organizations are a far cry from the sophisticated, hierarchical mafia model.

What explains the remarkable similarities in so many, and such different, settings? And what explains the features we observe? The answer to both questions lies in the nature of human smuggling. Four characteristics appear important, and they are not context-specific. First, smuggling services can be supplied without large investments in capital and resources: individuals and small-scale enterprises can afford to be in this business if the investment needed is low. Second, there are limited economies of scale to be achieved; smuggling is a low technology and labor-intensive business. Third, the high cost of monitoring agents and migrants over long distances creates strong incentives for smuggling organizations to remain localized. Finally, it is likely that smugglers possess short time horizons. No evidence is available on smugglers' careers; steep fluctuations in the flows suggest that smuggling may not be a long-term occupation. This resonates with the limited evidence on smugglers' backgrounds: except for involvement in smuggling, they tend to run legitimate businesses.

Smugglers are not typically involved in other criminal activities. They more closely resemble legitimate small-scale entrepreneurs than hardened criminals trading in diverse illegal commodities. Evidence concerning US-Mexico routes, important for both migrant smuggling and drug trafficking, strongly suggests that the two markets are almost entirely separate in terms of both participants and, often, routes.

Finally, there is very little evidence of involvement of traditional mafia-like organizations. In some areas, including Mexico, Libya, and Niger, smugglers must pay protection fees in order to operate. In Mexico, this *derecho de piso* is paid to local drug trafficking organizations. In Niger it is paid to local police officers. In Libya, it was imposed by local militias until mid-2017 when militias appeared to have switched from protecting smugglers to stopping them. There is a clear separation between smugglers and protectors, much as Schelling (1971) and Reuter (1983, 1985) predicted.

Why traditional mafia-like organizations seem not to be directly involved remains a puzzle. I offer here a list of possible explanations. First, mafias possess resources, including especially access to violence, that are of little use in human smuggling (violence among smugglers is very limited). Second, they tend to lack crucial resources such as ability to speak the same languages as migrants and capacity to build positive reputations among would-be migrants and their communities. Both are key factors in smuggling markets. As a consequence, traditional mafias may be at a considerable disadvantage in tapping into the demand for smuggling services.

Mafias in any case tend to be "heavily dependent on the local environment" (Gambetta 1993, p. 251) and to show little territorial flexibility. Smugglers by contrast may need to move their operations, by choice or because of external pressure, and require more territorial flexibility (Campana 2017). However, relocating even to a nearby city can be difficult for a mafia organization (Paoli 2020).[29]

Human smuggling, like many legal markets, appears to involve competition in attracting customers. However, smugglers cannot establish formal mechanisms to solve disputes, ensure compliance, and enforce contracts, and they suffer from acute information asymmetries. Smugglers have devised strategies to overcome the trust problem and foster transactions, including investing in a positive reputation. Smugglers may go to great lengths to build and protect their reputations, including paying

---

[29] Local factors can also be at play. In Sicily, smuggling agreements are sometimes made inside reception centers, which are under around-the-clock police surveillance; this is a difficult environment for mafias to operate in.

compensation in case of incidents and investing in their image. Reputation has been shown to play a key role at the community level and for some routes in the online presence of smugglers. Reputations do not travel easily (Reuter 1985). It is not surprising that smugglers and migrants tend to share the same ethnic background and often the same place of origin.

Recent developments in information technology have led smugglers to use social media and the internet to advertise their services and build their reputations. They have also sought to build confidence by developing "multiple attempts" warranties and providing escrow services of credible third parties entrusted with holding payments due smugglers until migrants safely reach their destinations.

This is not to deny that migrants often face risky situations and violence or that some smugglers are unreliable and dishonest. According to IOM, 5,579 migrants lost their lives on average each year between 2014 and 2019. Many more are likely to have been victims of abuse or exploitation: 6 percent of 655 migrants surveyed in Mexico said they were held by smugglers following a steep increase in the originally agreed fee or by individuals posing as smugglers. Of 1,602 migrants interviewed in Italy by IOM, one in three who crossed through Libya reported being forced to work or do things against their will. In any case, the cost of smuggling services can place migrants in debt and make them vulnerable to having to accept exploitative working conditions during or after the journey.

A handful of studies have looked at the effects of policy changes. The scant evidence suggests that increases in enforcement at the US-Mexico border led to an increase in the use of smugglers and a shift toward use of riskier routes, and modestly increased chances of apprehension. Smugglers appear to have responded to increased patrolling by increasing their fees (Massey, Durand, and Pren 2016). Preliminary evidence from Europe suggests that hardening of policies toward illegal movement is consistent with a decrease in the number of people crossing the sea to reach Italy and Greece.

Rescue operations in the Mediterranean pose difficult moral dilemmas. They appear both to increase the number of people successfully reaching Italy (and increase smugglers' earnings) and to reduce the mortality risk at sea (but not the absolute number of fatalities). Overall, the evidence suggests that heightened border controls increase apprehension rates and prices (thus potentially reducing demand) but decrease the quality of the services rendered by smugglers and exacerbate dangers and risks migrants face. This generates a difficult trade-off between minimizing harm to migrants and enforcing the rights of states to set and enforce immigration rules.

Three subjects warrant much greater attention. First, more work on smugglers' profiles is needed, including about their backgrounds, sociodemographic characteristics, and criminal records. Evidence on smugglers' criminal careers is almost nonexistent.

Second, more should be done to study changes in smuggling markets. Unanswered questions abound. Very little is known about movement of smugglers and their responses to changes in policies and in demand. What is the extent of displacement effects caused by policy changes? What is the geographical extent of smugglers' movement if they need to relocate? What are the difficulties in relocating a smuggling business? Equally, very little is known about smugglers' behavior in response to decreases in the market size. What happened to the smugglers based in Libya after their market shrank? Why do smugglers appear not to resort to violence to keep out competitors, particularly in dwindling markets? Why more generally are smuggling markets characterized by low levels of violence?

Finally, more should be learned about interactions between smugglers and migrants, particularly concerning migrants' decision making, information seeking, and concerns about smugglers' reputations. Large-scale quantitative surveys of migrants could provide much-needed insights into interactions between the demand and supply sides of smuggling markets.

REFERENCES

Achilli, Luigi. 2018. "The 'Good' Smuggler: The Ethics and Morals of Human Smuggling among Syrians." *Annals of the American Academy of Political and Social Sciences* 676(1):77–96.
Akerlof, George A., 1970. "The Market for 'Lemons': Quality Uncertainty and the Market Mechanism." *Quarterly Journal of Economics* 84(3):488–500.
Aksel, Damla B., Angeliki Dimitriadi, Maegan Hendow, Ahmet İçduygu, Aysem Biriz Karacay, Michaela Maroufof, and Jenny Andersson-Pucher. 2015. *Study on Smuggling of Migrants. Case Study 3: Pakistan–Turkey–Greece*. Brussels: European Commission.

Altai Consulting. 2015. *Migration Trends across the Mediterranean: Connecting the Dots*. Cairo: IOM Middle East and North Africa Regional Office.

Álvarez Velasco, Soledad. 2018. "Ecuador." In *Migrant Smuggling Data and Research: A Global Review of the Emerging Evidence Base*, vol. 2, edited by Anna Triandafyllidou and Marie McAuliffe. Geneva: IOM.

Amenta, Carlo, Paolo Di Betta, and Calogero G. Ferrara. 2016. "A Subsidized Tragedy: A Program Evaluation Approach for the Patrolling of the Mediterranean Sea." Working Paper. Department of Economics, University of Palermo.

ANSA. 2017. "Minniti Says Debate on NGO Code Over." *ANSA Press Agency*, July 26.

Antonopoulos, Georgios A., and John Winterdyk. 2006. "The Smuggling of Migrants in Greece: An Examination of Its Social Organization." *European Journal of Criminology* 3(4):439–61.

Ayalew Mengiste, Tekaling. 2018. "Refugee Protections from Below: Smuggling in the Eritrea-Ethiopia Context." *Annals of the American Academy of Political and Social Sciences* 676(1):57–76.

Bazzi, Samuel, Sarah Burns, Gordon Hanson, Bryan Roberts, and John Whitley. 2018. *Deterring Illegal Entry: Migrant Sanctions and Recidivism in Border Apprehensions*. NBER Working Paper no. 25100. Cambridge, MA: NBER

BBC. 2018. "Italy's Matteo Salvini Shuts Ports to Migrant Rescue Ship." *BBC News*, June 11.

Bilger, Veronika, Martin Hofmann, and Michael Jandl. 2006. "Human Smuggling as a Transnational Service Industry: Evidence from Austria." *International Migration* 44(4):59–93.

Brachet, Julien. 2012. "From One Stage to the Next: Transit and Transport in (Trans) Saharan Migrations." In *African Migrations Research: Innovative Methods and Methodologies*, edited by Mohamed Berriane and Hein de Haas. Trenton, NJ: Africa World.

———. 2018. "Manufacturing Smugglers: From Irregular to Clandestine Mobility in Sahara." *Annals of the American Academy of Political and Social Science* 676(1):16–35.

Brian, Tara. 2017. "The Middle East and North Africa." In *Fatal Journeys: Improving Data on Missing Migrants*, vol. 3, part 2, edited by Frank Laczko, Ann Singleton, and Julia Black. Geneva: International Organisation for Migration.

Campana, Paolo. 2017. "The Market for Human Smuggling into Europe: A Macro Perspective." *Policing* 11(4):448–56.

———. 2018. "Out of Africa: The Organization of Migrant Smuggling across the Mediterranean." *European Journal of Criminology*, https://doi.org/10.1177%2F1477370817749179.

Campana, Paolo, and Loraine Gelsthorpe. 2019. "Choosing a Migrant Smuggler: Decision Making under Conditions of Uncertainty." Working paper, Institute of Criminology, University of Cambridge.

Campana, Paolo, and Federico Varese. 2013. "Cooperation in Criminal Organizations: Kinship and Violence as Credible Commitments." *Rationality and Society* 25(3):263–89.

———. 2016. "Exploitation in Human Trafficking and Smuggling." *European Journal on Criminal Policy and Research* 22(1):89–105.

Chin, Ko-lin. 1999. *Smuggled Chinese: Clandestine Immigration to the United States.* Philadelphia: Temple University Press.

Coleman, James S. 1990. *Foundations of Social Theory.* Cambridge, MA: Harvard University Press.

Deiana, Claudio, Vikram Maheshri, and Giovanni Mastrobuoni. 2019. "Migration at Sea: Unintended Consequences of Search and Rescue Operations." SSRN Working Paper, https://vmaheshri.github.io/publication/migrants/.

Dekker, Rianne, Godfried Engbersen, Jeanine Klaver, and Hanna Vonk. 2018. "Smart Refugees: How Syrian Asylum Migrants Use Social Media Information in Migration Decision-Making." *Social Media+Society*, https://doi.org/10.1177%2F2056305118764439.

Demir, Oguzhan O., Murat Sever, and Yavuz Kahya. 2017. "The Social Organisation of Migrant Smugglers in Turkey: Roles and Functions." *European Journal of Criminal Policy Research* 23:371–91.

DHS (Department of Homeland Security). 2018. *Border Security Metrics Report: Fiscal Year 2017.* Washington: Department of Homeland Security.

———. 2019. *Border Security Metrics Report: Fiscal Year 2018.* Washington, DC: Department of Homeland Security.

EPSC (European Political Strategy Centre). 2017. *Irregular Migration via the Central Mediterranean.* Brussels: European Political Strategy Centre / European Commission.

Frontex. 2018. *Risk Analysis for 2018.* Warsaw: Frontex.

———. 2019. *Risk Analysis for 2019.* Warsaw: Frontex.

Gallagher, Anne, and Fiona David. 2014. *The International Law of Migrant Smuggling.* Cambridge: Cambridge University Press.

Gallagher, Anne, and Marie McAuliffe. 2016. "South-East Asia and Australia." In *Migrant Smuggling Data and Research: A Global Review of the Emerging Evidence Base*, edited by Marie McAuliffe and Frank Laczko. Geneva: International Organization for Migration.

Gambetta, Diego, ed. 1988. *Trust: Making and Breaking Cooperative Relations.* Oxford: Basil Blackwell.

Gambetta, Diego. 1993. *The Sicilian Mafia.* Cambridge, MA: Harvard University Press.

———. 2009. *Codes of the Underworld: How Criminals Communicate.* Princeton, NJ: Princeton University Press.

Guevara González, Yaatsil. 2018. "Navigating with Coyotes: Pathways of Central American Migrants in Mexico's Southern Borders." *Annals of the American Academy of Political and Social Sciences* 676(1):174–93.

İçduygu, Ahmet. 2018. "Middle East." In *Migrant Smuggling Data and Research: A Global Review of the Emerging Evidence Base*, vol. 2, edited by Anna Triandafyllidou and Marie McAuliffe. Geneva: International Organization for Migration.

İçduygu, Ahmet, and Sule Toktas. 2002. "How Do Smuggling and Trafficking Operate via Irregular Border Crossings in the Middle East? Evidence from Fieldwork in Turkey." *International Migration* 40(6):25–54.

Icli, Tülin Günşen, Hanifi Sever, and Muhammed Sever. 2015. "A Survey Study on the Profile of Human Smugglers in Turkey." *Advances in Applied Sociology* 5(1):1–12.

Izcara Palacios, Simon Pedro. 2014. "Coyotaje and Drugs: Two Different Businesses." *Bulletin of Latin American Research* 34(3):324–39.

Kleemans, Edward R. 2011. "Human Smuggling and Human Trafficking." In *Oxford Handbook on Crime and Public Policy*, edited by Michael Tonry. New York: Oxford University Press.

Kleemans, Edward R., and Henk van de Bunt. 2003. "The Social Organisation of Human Trafficking." In *Global Organized Crime: Studies of Organized Crime*, edited by Dina Siegel, Henk van de Bunt, and Damián Zaitch. Dordrecht: Springer.

Kingsley, Patrick. 2015. "Libya's People Smugglers: Inside the Trade That Sells Refugees Hopes of a Better Life." *The Guardian*, April 24.

Kirkpatrick, David D. 2015. "Before Dangers at Sea, African Migrants Face Perils of a Lawless Libya." *New York Times*, April 27.

Koser, Khalid. 2008. "Why Migrant Smuggling Pays." *International Migration* 46(2):3–26.

Kyle, David, and Rey Koslowski, eds. 2011. *Global Human Smuggling: Comparative Perspectives*. Baltimore: Johns Hopkins University Press.

Leutert, Stephanie. 2018. "Organized Crime and Central American Migration in Mexico." Policy research project report, Robert Strauss Centre, University of Texas at Austin.

Lewis, Aidan, and Steve Scherer. 2017. "Exclusive: Armed Group Stopping Migrants Boats Leaving Libya." *Reuters*, August 21.

Maher, Stephanie. 2018. "Out of West Africa: Human Smuggling as a Social Enterprise." *Annals of the American Academy of Political and Social Sciences* 676(1):36–56.

Majidi, Nassim. 2018. "Community Dimensions of Smuggling: The Case of Afghanistan and Somalia." *Annals of the American Academy of Political and Social Sciences* 676(1):97–113.

Massey, Douglas S., Jorge Durand, and Karen A. Pren. 2016. "Why Border Enforcement Backfired." *American Journal of Sociology* 121(5):1557–1600.

McAuliffe, Marie, and Frank Laczko. 2016. "Report Overview." In *Migrant Smuggling Data and Research: A Global Review of the Emerging Evidence Base*, edited by Marie McAuliffe and Frank Laczko. Geneva: International Organization for Migration.

Micallef, Mark. 2017. *The Human Conveyor Belt: Trends in Human Trafficking and Smuggling in Post-revolution Libya*. Geneva: Global Initiative against Transnational Organized Crime.

Molenaar, Fransje. 2017. *Irregular Migration and Human Smuggling Networks in Niger*. The Hague: Clingendael Institute.

Myria. 2018. *Annual Report Trafficking and Smuggling of Human Beings*. Brussels: Federal Migration Centre.

Neske, Matthias. 2006. "Human Smuggling to and through Germany." *International Migration* 44(4):121–63.

Optimity Advisors. 2015. *A Study on Smuggling of Migrants*. Final report. Brussels: European Commission.

Optimity Advisors and Seefar. 2018. *How West African Migrants Engage with Migration Information En-Route to Europe*. Brussels: European Commission.

O'Reilly, William. 2019. "Selling Souls: Trafficking German Migrants, Europe and America, 1648–1780." Working paper, Department of History, University of Cambridge.

Paoli, Letizia. 2020. "What Makes Mafias Different?" In *Organizing Crime: Mafias, Markets, and Networks*, edited by Michael Tonry and Peter Reuter. Chicago: University of Chicago Press.

Raineri, Luca. 2018. "Human Smuggling across Niger: State-Sponsored Protection Rackets and Contradictory Security Imperatives." *Journal of Modern African Studies* 56(1):63–86.

Reuter, Peter. 1983. *Disorganised Crime: The Economics of the Visible Hand*. Cambridge, MA: MIT Press.

———. 1985. *The Organization of Illegal Markets: An Economic Analysis*. Washington, DC: National Institute for Justice.

Roberts, Zoe. 2017. "Information Exchange between Smugglers and Migrants: An Analysis of Online Interactions in Facebook Groups." MPhil dissertation, Institute of Criminology, University of Cambridge.

Robinson, Vaughan, and Jeremy Segrott. 2002. *Understanding the Decision-Making of Asylum Seekers*. Research study 243. London: Home Office.

Sanchez, Gabriella E. 2015. *Human Smuggling and Border Crossing*. Abingdon: Routledge.

———. 2018. "Mexico." In *Migrant Smuggling Data and Research: A Global Review of the Emerging Evidence Base*, vol. 2, edited by Anna Triandafyllidou and Marie McAuliffe. Geneva: International Organization for Migration.

Sanchez, Gabriella E., and Sheldon X. Zhang. 2018. "Rumors, Encounters, Collaborations, and Survival: The Migrant Smuggling-Drug Trafficking Nexus in the US Southwest." *Annals of the American Academy of Political and Social Sciences* 676(1):135–51.

Schelling, Thomas C. 1960. *The Strategy of Conflict*. Cambridge, MA: Harvard University Press.

———. 1971. "What Is the Business of Organized Crime." *Journal of Public Law* 20:71–84.

———. 2006. *Strategies of Commitments and Other Essays*. Cambridge, MA: Harvard University Press.

Slack, Jeremy, and Daniel E. Martínez. 2018. "What Makes a Good Human Smuggler? The Difference between Satisfaction with and Recommendation of Coyotes on the US-Mexico Border." *Annals of the American Academy of Political and Social Sciences* 676(1):152–73.

Soudijn, Melvin R. J. 2006. *Chinese Human Smuggling in Transit*. Leiden: Netherlands Institute for the Study of Crime and Law Enforcement (NSCR).

Spener, David. 2009. *Clandestine Crossings: Migrants and Coyotes on the Texas-Mexico Border*. New York: Cornell University Press.

Steinhilper, Elias, and Rob J. Gruijters. 2018. "A Contested Crisis: Policy Narratives and Empirical Evidence on Border Deaths in the Mediterranean." *Sociology* 52(3):515–33.

Stone-Cadena, Victoria, and Soledad Álvarez Velasco. 2018. "Historicizing Mobility: *Coyoterismo* in the Indigenous Ecuadorian Migration Industry." *Annals of the American Academy of Political and Social Sciences* 676(1):194–211.

Tondo, Lorenzo. 2019. "Italy's New Government Says Migrants Can Disembark from Rescue Boat." *The Guardian*, September 14.

Triandafyllidou, Anna, and Thanos Maroukis. 2012. *Migrant Smuggling: Irregular migration from Asia and Africa to Europe*. Basingstoke: Palgrave Macmillan.

UN (United Nations). 2000. *Protocol against the Smuggling of Migrants by Land, Sea and Air, Supplementing the United Nations Convention against Transnational Organised Crime*. New York: United Nations.

UNODC (United Nations Office on Drugs and Crime). 2018. *Global Study on Smuggling of Migrants*. Vienna: United Nations Office on Drugs and Crime.

Van Liempt, Ilse. 2007. *Navigating Borders: Inside Perspectives on the Process of Human Smuggling into the Netherlands*. Amsterdam: Amsterdam University Press.

Varese, Federico. 2016. "Underground Banking and Corruption." In *Greed, Corruption, and the Modern State: Essays in Political Economy*, edited by Susan Rose-Ackerman and Paul Lagunes. Cheltenham: Edward Elgar.

Wokeck, Marianne S. 1999. *Trade in Strangers: The Beginnings of Mass Migration to North America*. University Park: Pennsylvania State University Press.

Yamagishi, Toshio, and Midori Yamagishi. 1994. "Trust and Commitment in the United States and Japan." *Motivation and Emotion* 18(2):129–66.

Yildiz, Ayselin. 2017. *Perception of "Smuggling Business" and Decision Making Processes of Migrants*. Ankara: International Organization for Migration.

Zhang, Sheldon X. 2008. *Chinese Human Smuggling Organizations: Families, Social Networks, and Cultural Imperatives*. Stanford, CA: Stanford University Press.

Zhang, Sheldon X., and Ko-lin Chin. 2002. "Enter the Dragon: Inside Chinese Human Smuggling Organisations." *Criminology* 40(4):737–68.

Klaus von Lampe and Arjan Blokland

Outlaw Motorcycle Clubs and Organized Crime

ABSTRACT

Outlaw motorcycle clubs have spread across the globe. Their members have been associated with serious crime, and law enforcement often perceives them to be a form of organized crime. Outlaw bikers are disproportionately engaged in crime, but the role of the club itself in these crimes remains unclear. Three scenarios describe possible relations between clubs and the crimes of their members. In the "bad apple" scenario, members individually engage in crime; club membership may offer advantages in enabling and facilitating offending. In the "club within a club" scenario, members engage in crimes separate from the club, but because of the number of members involved, including high-ranking members, the club itself appears to be taking part. The club can be said to function as a criminal organization only when the formal organizational chain of command takes part in organization of the crime, lower level members regard senior members' leadership in the crime as legitimate, and the crime is generally understood as "club business." All three scenarios may play out simultaneously within one club with regard to different crimes.

Fact and fiction interweave concerning the origins, evolution, and practices of outlaw motorcycle clubs. What Mario Puzo's (1969) acclaimed novel *The Godfather* and Francis Ford Coppola's follow-up film trilogy did for public and mafiosi perceptions of the mafia, Hunter S. Thompson's

Electronically published June 3, 2020

Klaus von Lampe is professor of criminology at the Berlin School of Economics and Law. Arjan Blokland is professor of criminology and criminal justice at Leiden University, Obel Foundation visiting professor at Aalborg University, and senior researcher at the Netherlands Institute for the Study of Crime and Law Enforcement. We are grateful for valuable comments on earlier drafts from the editors, two anonymous reviewers, and participants in the May 16–18, 2019, *Crime and Justice* conference in Bologna on organized crime.

(1966) book *Hell's Angels* and ensuing biker exploitation films did for out-law motorcycle clubs (Seate 2000; Stanfield 2018). Together they inspired working-class youths around the globe to establish outlaw motorcycle clubs (Perlman 2007). The "outlaw" label originally meant only that clubs were not affiliated with the American Motorcyclist Association (AMA). However, the movies depicting bikers as modern-day frontiersmen, often battling a corrupt system, gave added significance to the "outlaw" label (Dulaney 2006; Sánchez-Jankowski 2018). The stylized version of reality the films provided led youths to aspire to live up to the Hollywood biker image. While Hollywood bikers like Peter Fonda and Jack Nicholson, sometimes literally, got away with murder on the big screen, many outlaw bikers' deviant behavior got them into trouble with the law in real life.[1]

In the half century since publication of Thompson's book, law en-forcement agencies in many countries have come to see outlaw biker clubs as public security threats, and outlaw bikers have repeatedly been associated with serious crimes, including murder, drug trafficking, and extortion (e.g., Interpol 1984; Organized Crime Consulting Committee 1986; Europol 2005; Australian Crime Commission 2012). As a result, law enforcement, politicians, and the media usually refer to them as out-law motorcycle "gangs." The term gang, however, evokes a plethora of meanings (Hallsworth and Young 2008), including some that are intrin-sically linked to urban North America and may not readily apply to Eu-ropean and other contexts (van Gemert and Weerman 2015). Finally, use of the term gang tends to create a false dichotomy between good and bad motorcycle clubs (Roks and Van Ruitenburg 2018). Hence, following others' lead (e.g., Quinn and Koch 2003; Veno 2009), we use "club" as a more neutral and less prejudicial term. This acknowledges that outlaw motorcycle clubs are clubs in the narrow sense of the word, often officially registered associations, and that there appear to be great variations in criminal involvement among outlaw biker clubs and among different branches of the same club (Quinn and Koch 2003; Barker and Human 2009; Lauchs and Staines 2019).

---

[1] Some writers further differentiate between outlaw clubs and 1 percent or one-percenter clubs (Wethern and Colnett 2004; Dulaney 2006). Both are unaffiliated with the AMA. The latter are said to have promoted club membership from a mere hobby into an all-encompassing lifestyle, including the antiestablishment attitude associated with be-ing an "outlaw." In the academic literature, the terms outlaw motorcycle clubs and 1 per-cent clubs are sometimes used interchangeably to refer to 1 percent clubs (e.g., Barker 2015).

Academic interest in outlaw biker clubs, especially when compared with street gangs and organized crime groups such as the Italian and American mafias, has been scant and leaves fundamental questions unanswered (Bain and Lauchs 2017). In this essay, we ask what can be learned if outlaw motorcycle clubs are approached through the lens of organized crime research. From an organized crime perspective, outlaw biker clubs are an interesting object of study for several reasons; they are highly visible, formal organizations and their members, unlike in stereotypical organized crime groups, have not traditionally come from minority backgrounds (Barker 2007). Our interest, broadly speaking, is in where outlaw bikers fit in discussions of the organization of crimes and criminals. The question is not simply, "Are outlaw biker clubs a form of organized crime?" That would do justice neither to the complexity of the outlaw biker phenomenon nor to the complexity of the concept of organized crime.

We focus on two main themes. One is the criminality of outlaw bikers, a subject around which much of the pertinent empirical research is centered. The second concerns the functions of outlaw motorcycle clubs as organizational entities in relation to crimes committed by their members. This is as much a conceptual as an empirical question, one on which the need for further research is most urgent. We address other issues concerning outlaw biker clubs only in passing or not at all. These include the links between outlaw bikers and other criminal groups such as mafia associations, street gangs, and prison gangs; overlaps between the outlaw biker subculture and political groups such as right-wing extremists; and outlaw biker clubs acting as proxies of the state (Abadinsky 2013; Barker 2015; Klement 2019; Zabyelina 2019; Harris 2020).

The essay is divided into three sections. Section I provides a brief overview of the outlaw biker phenomenon and how it is perceived by law enforcement agencies. In Section II, we review what is known about the involvement of members of outlaw biker clubs in various types of crimes. We propose a typology of biker crime, distinguishing among lifestyle crimes, entrepreneurial crimes, and symbolic crimes. These crimes are diversely motivated; their organization involves distinctive requirements and constraints that influence different ways they typically relate to a club's formal organization. In Section III, we distinguish three different scenarios in which the criminal behavior of outlaw bikers is or can be related to the club. These scenarios can play out separately or simultaneously for different crimes within the same club or chapter. We employ a situational perspective, thus rejecting a simple one-dimensional conception of outlaw motorcycle clubs as criminal organizations.

I. Outlaw Motorcycle Clubs

The origins of the outlaw biker subculture are usually traced to adrenaline-craving World War II veterans who, having survived the horrors of war, clung to their military machines in an effort to retain some of the thrill of their fighting tours (Yates 1999; Reynolds 2000; McBee 2015). These blue-collar men, socialized into the masculine brotherhood of the army, are said not to have felt at home in the middle-class motorcycle clubs sanctioned by the AMA and, as a consequence, established their own clubs (Dulaney 2006; Barker 2015). Lurid club names, such as the Booze Fighters and the Pissed Off Bastards of Bloomington (POBOB), bespoke their antiestablishment attitudes (Wood 2003). In a notorious incident in Hollister, California, on July 4, 1947, over 500 non-AMA-affiliated bikers are reported to have crashed the annual AMA-organized Gypsy Tour, behaving drunk and disorderly and solidifying the image of non-AMA, or "outlaw," clubs as antisocial and a menace to society (Fuglsang 2001; Veno 2007, 2009; Barker 2015).[2] The subsequent media storm would likely long ago have been forgotten, if reports of this and similar incidents had not inspired the first movie to bring the biker subculture to the screen, Laslo Benedek's film *The Wild One*, starring a young Marlon Brando as the leader of an outlaw biker club called the Black Rebels Motorcycle Club (Austin, Gagne, and Orend 2010).[3] It was loosely based on historical events, and Brando's adversary in the film, Lee Marvin, allegedly modeled his character on "Wino" Willy Forkner, an infamous member of the Booze Fighters and an active participant in the Hollister incident (Barker 2007). *The Wild One* was sedate by today's standards, but controversy surrounded it. It was banned in the United Kingdom, which enhanced Brando's rebel image and enlarged the movies' influence on youth culture throughout the Western world (Farrant 2016).

---

[2] Female bikers and biker clubs were present in Hollister (e.g., the Tracy Gear Jammers), but gendered media accounts helped forge the outlaw biker as a deviant male identity (Hoiland 2018).

[3] Most notably, disturbances in Riverside, California, during the Memorial Day Weekend Gypsy Tour of 1948 that reportedly involved over 1,000 motorcyclists and led to the death of a woman associated with one of the male bikers (Reynolds 2000).

A. Hells Angels

In 1948, former POBOB Motorcycle Club member Otto Friedli established an outlaw motorcycle club in Fontana, California, that would become the most iconic of all, the Hells Angels Motorcycle Club (HAMC) (Barker 2018). Named after a 1930 war movie and numerous World War II bomber squadrons that used the name, several unrelated clubs calling themselves "Hells Angels" became active in California during this time. Largely through the efforts of future HAMC president Ralph "Sonny" Barger, these clubs merged in the mid-1950s and adopted uniform attire, organizational structure, and admission criteria (Barger 2001). The original Hells Angels were recognizable by their sleeveless denim vests, which had an embroidered club logo—a winged skull wearing a pilot's cap—as a center patch on the back, together with an arched top rocker stating the club's name, and an arched bottom rocker naming the city, or sometimes the state, where the club was chartered. The HAMC issued written regulations that governed the weekly meeting of charter members, specified procedures for acceptance of new members, and set out general rules of "good conduct" such as "no fighting among club members" and "no using dope during a meeting" (Barger 2001). The rules required ownership of a motorcycle, attesting to the motorcycle being "the dominant symbol of subcultural commitment" (Wolf 1991, p. 85).

The Californian Hells Angels' notoriety rose quickly after publication of Thompson's acclaimed journalistic account *Hell's Angels*. The unexpected success of the 1966 movie *The Wild Angels*, starring members of the Venice, California, HAMC charter as supporting actors to Peter Fonda and Nancy Sinatra, all but transformed the HAMC from local to international celebrities (Perlman 2007). The Californian Hells Angels advised on and starred in other biker films including *Hells Angels on Wheels* (1969) with Jack Nicholson. International biker magazines such as *Easyriders*, available from 1970 onward, did the rest (Fuglsang 2002).

The Hells Angels' media image drew attention from young bike-riding toughs around the globe who adopted the imagery of their US role models. The Californian Hells Angels began to accept local clubs outside California as official HAMC chapters. Already by 1961 the HAMC had an officially recognized chapter in Auckland, New Zealand; the first Australian charter in Sydney followed in 1968 (Veno 2009; Lauchs 2019b). In 1969 the first European chapter was set up in the United Kingdom. Other European countries, including Switzerland in 1970, Germany in

1973, and the Netherlands in 1978, soon followed. In retrospect, the HAMC's expansion appears not to have been strategically planned but often to have been initiated by local biker groups, in some cases using the name "Hells Angels" and wanting recognition by the Californian HAMC (e.g., Schutten, Vugts, and Middelburg 2004). In April 2019 the Hells Angels website showed an HAMC presence in 58 countries on five continents.[4]

B. Chicago Outlaws

Other US-based clubs were organized, both regionally and internationally. Among them were the Chicago Outlaws, whose roots go back to the McCook Outlaws of Cook County, Illinois, established as early as 1936. In 1954, the Chicago Outlaws adopted leather jackets as official club dress and a logo depicting a skull and two crossed pistons, affectionately referred to as "Charlie," which closely resembled the logo of Brando's fictional motorcycle club in *The Wild One*. In 1964, several local clubs merged under the name Outlaw Nation, with Chicago designated as the mother chapter. In 1977, perhaps not coincidentally the year the HAMC opened its first Canadian chapter, the Canadian outlaw motorcycle club Satan's Choice joined the Outlaws in a so-called patch-over, becoming the first non-US Outlaws chapter. The Outlaws had no presence abroad until 1993 when a French chapter was established; a Norwegian chapter was set up in 1995. Other European clubs followed, some of which had used the Outlaw name for decades. The Outlaws Motorcycle Club website at the time of writing showed chapters in 28 countries.[5]

C. Bandidos

The Bandidos Motorcycle Club was established in San Leon, Texas, in 1966 during the height of the Hollywood biker craze. International chapters were established in Australia in 1983 and France in 1989. Together with the Hells Angels, Outlaws, the US-confined Pagans Motorcycle Club, the Mongols, and the Sons of Silence, the Bandidos are among the major US outlaw motorcycle clubs (Barker 2015). Global expansion, however, can have downsides. According to the Bandidos website, the US mother chapter, unhappy with growing "differences of opinion with

---

[4] See http://hells-angels.com/world.

[5] See http://www.outlawsmcworld.com.

regard to club values and definitions," decided in 2007 to sever all ties with Bandidos chapters outside the United States. The US Bandidos redesigned its signature "Fat Mexican" logo to underline its independence. European, Asian, and Australian chapters have continued to use the older version. At the time of writing, the US Bandidos website coexisted with the "official Bandidos website."[6] The latter was redesigned as the Bandidos Motorcycle Club Worldwide website, showing chapters in 32 countries, including the United States.[7]

D. Other Countries' Clubs

The popularity of the outlaw biker subculture, and the dominance of the Hells Angels, led clubs elsewhere in the world to (re)cast themselves into the HAMC mold (McNab 2013; Silverstone and Crane 2017). Many adopted similar signature clothing and logos, bylaws and regulations, and organizational structure. More than 5,000 distinct clubs have been formed in the history of the outlaw motorcycle subculture, most outside North America, including 50 percent in Europe, 18 percent in Latin America, 6 percent in East Asia, 5 percent in Australia and New Zealand, 2 percent in the Middle East and North Africa, and 1 percent in South Africa (Lauchs 2019b). Some domestic clubs later patched over to one of the internationally active US clubs; others stuck to their original colors. The major US clubs, especially the Hells Angels, provided the prototype on which other outlaw clubs pattern themselves. The US clubs however do not, or no longer, dominate the outlaw biker scene in many places outside the United States and Canada, in sheer numbers or in influence. Some indigenous clubs, such as Australia's Rebels Motorcycle Club and the Netherlands's Satudarah Motorcycle Club, have begun establishing chapters in the United States. The Hells Angels, however, retain their mythical status (Veno 2009; Barker 2015).

E. Organizational Structure

The Californian Hells Angels provided a template for outlaw bikers in appearance and behavior. They also provided a blueprint for the organizational structures of outlaw biker clubs, which almost always use the

---

[6] See https://www.bandidosmcunitedstates.com.

[7] See https://www.bandidosmc.com. The Dutch weekly *Panorama* reported something similar about the Mongols Motorcycle Club, which expanded internationally but disestablished many of its European chapters in 2017 (de Hoogh 2017).

same or similar names to define certain command positions (Abadinsky 2013; Barker 2015). Figure 1 depicts the formal structure typical for outlaw motorcycle clubs from which there are few fundamental deviations.

The club is organized in local units called charters or chapters. Each chapter has to have a physical location where it holds club meetings. Most often these locations are clubhouses that are "a central part of biker life" (Veno 2009, p. 94) and demonstrate the club's vitality and persistence. Some are heavily fortified to safeguard members from attacks by rival gangs and from law enforcement actions (Wolf 1991).

One chapter typically acts as the "mother chapter." This position may be permanently held by the founding chapter, or may alternate between different chapters over shorter or longer intervals. Orders regarding club business flow from the mother chapter to the local chapters (Wolf 1991). However, binding decisions transcending individual chapters may also be made at regional, national, or international meetings (Barker 2015).

A special position is held by so-called nomads, elite members who are not part of a local chapter and who may be organized in special nomad chapters. Their increased mobility allows them to function as rapid response teams for the club, which gives them an elevated status (Veno 2009; Barker 2015; Ahlsdorf 2017).

The local chapters widely follow the same model (McGuire 1987; Mallory 2012; Abadinsky 2013). They are commonly headed by a president, formally the highest rank, and a vice president who is second in

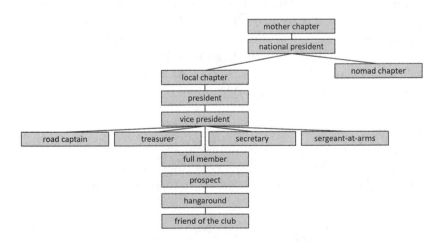

Fig. 1.—Formal structure typical for outlaw motorcycle clubs

rank. The mother chapter provides the club's national president. Below the vice president are a number of officer ranks more or less horizontally differentiated by function. These include the road captain, treasurer, secretary, and sergeant-at-arms. Patches typically worn on the front of the individual's biker vest identify its wearer's rank. The road captain is responsible for organizing the logistics of runs or ride outs. The treasurer is responsible for financial administration, including collecting membership dues and managing the "defense fund" from which financial support is given to members facing criminal charges or doing prison time. The secretary organizes and take notes during obligatory weekly and incidental meetings of full members, commonly referred to as church meetings. While the other board functions are primarily bureaucratic, the sergeant-at-arms is responsible for internal discipline and enforcement of club rules. He is also responsible for meting out punishment to members who are found disobedient. His authority to use force against fellow members places him somewhat closer in the hierarchy to the president and vice president. Together with the president and vice president, the road captain, treasurer, secretary, and sergeant-at-arms form the chapter's board (Abadinsky 2013; Barker 2015; Ahlsdorf 2017). An exceptional case is the Finks Motorcycle Club in Australia, which has either only one formal position, the sergeant-at-arms, according to one source (Veno 2009), or three, the sergeant-at-arms, treasurer, and secretary, according to another (Lauchs 2019a).

Each chapter has a number of full members, recognizable by a vest with both the top and bottom rocker and the center patch depicting the club's logo. Although members take orders from chapter board members, the board's power is limited by a system of direct democracy, usually a show of hands, by which decisions about club business are made. All members have an equal say. For most decisions, the majority rules, although some may require a qualified majority or unanimity (Veno 2009; Ahlsdorf 2017). The legitimacy of the board's decisions depends heavily on whether they are considered to benefit the club, rather than individual board members. Board members thus constantly face the danger of being degraded or, like other members, being expelled, in good or bad standing, by a vote of the members. "Big" Willem van Boxtel, longtime national president of the Dutch Hells Angels, for example, was voted out in bad standing after allegedly remaining silent about a plan to liquidate an associate of the Amsterdam chapter on club grounds (Schutten, Vugts, and Middelburg 2004; Burgwal 2012).

People who aspire to full membership typically go through an elaborate initiation phase. On the outskirts of the club are "hangarounds" and "friends of the club," although some clubs do not distinguish between the two. To become a friend, a person needs one or more members to vouch for him. The sponsors act as mentors throughout the initiation period and usually afterward as well. Friends may need to be accepted by majority vote during a church meeting (Wolf 1991; Barker 2015). This ritual repeats itself when friends are promoted to become hangarounds and hangarounds are promoted to prospect status. The prospect status, which may last from a few weeks to several years, is solidified by wearing a biker vest with just the bottom rocker. The prospect is not yet a full member but enjoys recognition for making it to the semifinals. Prospects may be present during church meetings but do not vote. Like individuals, entire chapters can obtain prospect status, for instance when chapters of native clubs want or are invited or pressured to patch over to a larger local or international club (Wolf 1991; Veno 2009; Barker 2015).

The lengthy initiation phase serves practical and symbolic functions. Practically, from the perspective of wannabes, it provides a first feel of the outlaw biker lifestyle and an opportunity to evaluate whether the lifestyle fits their aspirations. It also allows existing members to size up potential brothers. Symbolically, the initiation phase functions primarily to detach prospective members from their civilian ties and to transform the individual's principal identity to that of outlaw biker. Full membership requires members to place club concerns over private concerns at all times (Wolf 1991; Veno 2009).

Sometimes violent initiation rites, obligatory participation in social events, and cultivated animosity with rival groups serve to strengthen the ritualistic kinship ties and maintain the extreme level of brotherly altruism expected between members (Wolf 1991). An important drawback of all-encompassing ritual kinship is that it limits the pool of potential members to people already socialized into at least some of the core values that dominate the outlaw biker psyche (see Paoli 2003).

Many outlaw motorcycle clubs have formalized the requirements for joining the club, and the procedures that govern the club's functioning and decision-making, in a set of written rules and regulations. In some clubs, including the Hells Angels and the Bandidos, they are referred to as bylaws (Barger 2001; Caine 2009). Other clubs, such as the Pagans, refer to club rules. The Outlaws refer to the "national constitution" that governs the behavior of all Outlaw members in the United States (Mallory 2012). The Mongols' website shows the five "commandments" applicable to members of the Mongols nation worldwide.[8]

The written rules may describe requirements for becoming a member and define procedural steps to be taken during the process. The Bandidos bylaws, for example, state that individual members must own at least a 750 cc Harley-Davidson or facsimile, should have their motorcycle fully functioning for at least 335 days per year, and pay monthly membership dues of $25. New chapters are to pay "a one-time donation of $1,000" to the national treasury. Membership requirements usually reflect the exclusivity of the club. Many rules aim to safeguard the club against infiltration by members considered "inferior" because they are not genuine bikers or are law enforcement personnel, and thereby protect the club's reputation.

The bylaws often refer to how decisions on club matters are made, denoting, for example, in which body votes are cast, who is allowed to vote, how individual votes are weighed, and the size of the majority needed for a decision to be accepted. Finally, the written rules list dos and don'ts for members. The Mongols' commandments, for example, include "A Mongol never steals from another Mongol," "A Mongol never causes another Mongol to get arrested in any shape, way, or form," and "A Mongol never uses his patch for personal gain."

Some bylaws specify penalties for transgression of the rules. Transgression of the Hells Angels bylaws, for instance, may result in a monetary fine, an "ass-whipping," "possible loss of patch," or "automatic kickout from club" (Wolf 1991, p. 355). In general, members' obligations reflect the core values of the ritualistic biker brotherhood and efforts to safeguard club members from outside interference. Some rules are meant to prevent members from behaving in ways that can have negative consequences for the club. An example is the infamous "no drug burns" rule in the Hells Angels bylaws that sought to protect the club from retaliation by disenfranchised business partners in a member's or members' illicit enterprise (Barger 2001).

Finally, many of the bigger clubs have puppet or support clubs. Many are motorcycle clubs themselves that officially affiliate with a bigger club—for example, by pledging their support on their website. Support clubs

[8] See https://www.mongolsmc.com/about.

provide a pool from which outlaw motorcycle clubs can select potential members or, many times, a group of individuals who have a prospect—however distant—of possible membership and are willing to work hard to satisfy the whims of the outlaw bikers. According to law enforcement officials, this may include dirty work that reduces the risk of full members being implicated in crimes. Finally, support club membership may augment the club's ranks in periods of intergang rivalry and violence (Barker 2017). The Hells Angels in Denmark, for example, established AK81, an acronym for "Always Ready," with the "8" and "1" referring to the eighth and first letter in the alphabet: "H"ells "A"ngels. Members of AK81 are not required to ride a motorcycle or wear a biker vest, and their appearance is more like that of a street gang (Klement 2016*a*).

F. Law Enforcement Perceptions

During the 1950s and early 1960s, outlaw motorcycle clubs were seen primarily as a public menace, known mostly for drunken and disorderly behavior. Local law enforcement agencies, increasingly aware of criminal involvement of outlaw bikers, launched undercover operations during the 1970s. Using findings of local operations, the FBI targeted Sonny Barger and the Oakland Hells Angels as a criminal organization under the federal Racketeer Influenced and Corrupt Organizations Act (RICO) enacted in 1970 to provide tools for use against organized crime groups. In the subsequent trial that ended in 1980, Barger was acquitted as the jury found no proof that the crimes committed were part of club policy. Since then, numerous Hells Angels and members of other outlaw biker clubs have been successfully prosecuted under RICO, partly for involvement in profit-making crimes such as drug trafficking and partly for violent acts against rival biker groups.

For many years, prosecutors failed to establish that an outlaw motorcycle club or chapter as such qualified as a criminal enterprise (Lauchs, Bain, and Bell 2015). This has changed only recently. For example, in 2018 a jury found that the Mongols constituted a criminal enterprise responsible for murder, narcotics trafficking, and drug transactions (Department of Justice 2019).

Despite the early failures of RICO prosecutions, outlaw motorcycle clubs came to be viewed in the United States as an organized crime threat akin to the Italian-American mafia and other criminal groups organized along ethnic lines. Adding outlaw bikers with their white Anglo-Saxon background to the category of "non-traditional organized crime" (President's

Commission on Organized Crime 1983) may have been a convenient way to diffuse allegations of ethnic bias in conceptualization of organized crime.

Other countries' perceptions of outlaw bikers also shifted from public nuisance to organized crime threat. Typically, interclub violence galvanized law enforcement agencies to adopt a repressive approach to outlaw motorcycle clubs. As early as the 1970s, Australia, Canada, Denmark, and other countries experienced violent clashes between rival biker groups that left several bikers dead or wounded (Cherry 2005; Langton 2010; Katz 2011; McNab 2013). New levels of alarm were reached when biker violence took tolls among innocent bystanders, particularly the "Canadian Biker War" between the Rock Machine and the Hells Angels that lasted from 1994 until 2001 and resulted in 160 murders, including an 11-year-old boy. The "Great Nordic Biker War" between Hells Angels and Bandidos resulted in 11 bikers' deaths in Denmark, Finland, Norway, and Sweden between 1994 and 1997 in addition to the death of one bystander and the maiming of several others in bomb attacks (Barker 2015). In countries in which biker violence reaches these levels, outlaw motorcycle clubs tend to symbolize organized crime (Morselli 2009; Katz 2011; Korsell and Larsson 2011).

In other countries, law enforcement perceptions have followed different paths. In Germany, for example, it was not interclub violence but alleged involvement in forced prostitution and extortion that prompted the first determined government response to outlaw bikers. In 1983 the first German charter of the Hells Angels, located in Hamburg, was rescinded and several of its members were put on trial (Geurtjens, Nelen, and Vanderhallen 2018).

The Netherlands did not experience excessive interclub violence, in large part because of the Hells Angels' dominance of the Dutch bikers scene. In the absence of official policies on organized crime, handling of outlaw bikers changed from regulated tolerance during the 1970s and early 1980s to laissez-faire during the late 1980s and 1990s. Not until 2000 did Dutch authorities adopt a more repressive stance, especially toward the Hells Angels (Blokland, Soudijn, and Teng 2014; Geurtjens, Nelen, and Vanderhallen 2018). By that time, outlaw motorcycle clubs had a prominent place on international law enforcement agendas.

In 1991, following a Danish initiative, Interpol launched "Project Rockers," centered on the creation of a network of police experts on outlaw motorcycle clubs. By 1999, 27 countries tied by the presence of the

Hells Angels, including 21 from Europe, the United States, Canada, Brazil, South Africa, Australia, and New Zealand, participated (Smith 1998; Bjorngaard 1999; Barker 2015). In 1996, the nascent European police agency Europol launched its own biker-related project, "Operation Monitor," under the aegis of the Danish National Police. It sought to collect and exchange intelligence on outlaw motorcycle clubs with a special focus on drug trafficking. "Operation Monitor" prompted member states to look more closely at their domestic outlaw biker scenes (Heitmüller 2014).

The overall picture from a law enforcement perspective mainly evolved along two lines. First, in many countries outlaw biker violence reached a point at which it could no longer be described as merely rebellious, especially when innocent bystanders began to fall victim to biker warfare. Second, outlaw bikers increasingly engaged in more organized types of crime, leading law enforcement agencies increasingly to perceive them as internationally operating criminal organizations.

II. Outlaw Bikers and (Organized) Crimes

The contention that outlaw motorcycle clubs have evolved into criminal organizations has two basic implications: that their members are systematically engaged in criminal activities, and that the clubs play a key role in their members' criminal conduct. We examine both suggestions, starting with the criminal involvement of outlaw bikers. First, however, we clarify what types of crimes are at issue.

A. Types of Biker Crime

It is a truism that not all crimes are the same. There are differences not only in their seriousness, however defined, but also categorical differences concerning, for example, the nature of victimization when there is an identifiable victim, and the meaning and function that criminal acts have for perpetrators. A differentiated understanding of criminal activities, as opposed to a broad-brush concept of crime, is important in the study of criminal organizations because of interconnectedness and interdependencies between what organizations do and how they are structured. According to one view, for example, criminal structures need to be viewed primarily as "emergent properties" of criminal behavior (Cornish and Clarke 2002, p. 52).

Accordingly, we begin discussion of outlaw motorcycle clubs in the context of organized crime by differentiating among types of crime members commit, before considering to what extent and in what ways their crimes can meaningfully be attributed to the clubs.

Official and journalistic accounts often refer indiscriminately to any kind of criminal involvement as evidence of the criminal nature of biker clubs. Academic writings take a more nuanced approach. Quinn and Koch (2003), for example, offer a "rough division" of biker crime into four categories along two dimensions, the level of planning and preparation and the underlying purpose of criminal conduct. By differentiating among spontaneous and planned expressive acts, short-term instrumental acts, and ongoing instrumental enterprises, they allow for gradations between more or less "organized" crimes and emphasize differences between "acts of violence and hedonism" driven by impulses and emotions and entrepreneurial behavior oriented toward material gain (Quinn and Koch 2003, p. 295).

Similarly, Lauchs, Bain, and Bell (2015) distinguish "organized crime associated" offenses for profit and "barbarian culture" offenses. Barbarian culture offenses "match the traditional notion of an outsider subculture that acts in a manner unacceptable to society" and include traffic offenses, drunk and disorderly behavior, and minor drug offenses (p. 27). Planned aggressive acts not associated with crimes for profit are also viewed as barbarian.

The Quinn and Koch (2003) typology and the distinction between "organized crime associated" and "barbarian culture" offenses are valuable but do not sufficiently capture the different ways in which members' criminal conduct may pertain to the biker subculture and to biker clubs as organizational entities. Cognizant of the inconvenience associated with the addition of another classification scheme, we nonetheless opt for a tripartite distinction of outlaw biker crimes centered on their purposes and meanings. Distinguishing proximal from distal goals, and economic from symbolic goals, we arrive at the following typology:

Lifestyle crimes: criminal acts associated with behaviors that constitute prominent elements of the outlaw biker subculture.

Symbolic crimes: criminal acts that feed into the status and reputation of the individual member, chapter, or club.

Entrepreneurial crimes: criminal acts committed for profit that benefit the individual member, chapter, or club.

Lifestyle crimes are typically related to riding and partying as key elements of the outlaw biker subculture. Emblematic examples include traffic violations and minor drug offenses associated with recreational use of illegal substances. Impulsive predatory crimes such as stealing spare parts of parked motorcycles, or robbing passersby for gas money, are also regarded as lifestyle crimes as they do little to enhance the financial standing of the individual member or the club. To the extent that outlaw bikers' sexual morality, which tends to conceive of women as property of individual bikers or of the club as a whole (Hopper and Moore 1990; Wolf 1991), clashes with mainstream norms, some sexual offenses such as statutory rape can also be classified as lifestyle crimes. So can some acts of violence prevalent among outlaw bikers, such as domestic violence, that do little to increase the perpetrator's status within the subculture (Smith 2002).

Symbolic crimes have the potential to affect the subcultural standing of those involved. Often, although not necessarily, they are acts of violence. Symbolic crimes typically result from honor contests that provide bikers opportunity to boost their status and reputation at others' expense. Symbolic crimes thus serve a more distant goal that goes beyond the offending situation. Especially violence directed toward socially close individuals has the potential to result in symbolic resources (Gould 2003; Gravel et al. 2018). Nonviolent symbolic crimes, for instance, could include breaking and entering to steal rival clubs' paraphernalia, or damaging a rival club's property by setting fire to their clubhouse. Symbolic crimes also include planned expressive acts of violence toward rival peers (Klement 2019). Within the hypermasculine outlaw biker world, lifestyle crimes such as spontaneous bar brawls can quickly acquire symbolic meaning. Should an individual biker be the losing party, retaliation is likely, often with help from a number of brothers, providing symbolic relevance to any further violent encounters (Quinn and Koch 2003).

Finally, entrepreneurial crimes potentially yield material profit. Like symbolic crimes, the aims of entrepreneurial crimes are often not immediate, which distinguishes them from lifestyle crimes. Entrepreneurial crimes can be predatory, simply costly to the victim, or market based, with illegal goods or services provided for an agreed-on price. Entrepreneurial crimes include criminal acts committed in preparation for making a criminal profit, such as manufacture of illegal drugs. Entrepreneurial crimes can be nonviolent or violent (e.g., extortion); their key aim is to enhance the material position of the individual member or club.

As with symbolic and lifestyle crimes, there is a clear link between entrepreneurial crimes and lifestyle crimes in that the biker lifestyle encourages some entrepreneurial crimes and not others. Being a frequent patron of nightclubs and shabby bars is more likely to incite drug dealing and forced prostitution than bankruptcy fraud or insider trading.

A miscellaneous "other" category remains that cannot be linked to the biker subculture. This includes such crimes as downloading child pornography from the internet, which is neither entrepreneurial nor symbolic and does not spring from subcultural biker behaviors or values.

Lifestyle crimes are a justifiable cause for societal concern, but for students of organized crime, bikers' involvement in ongoing profit-making crimes and excessive symbolic violence are more relevant. Profit-making crimes, when successfully perpetrated, yield material gains larger than can be instantly used or spent, creating a need for outlets for illicit goods and ways to launder illicit proceeds. Whether one or a few members, cliques, or entire chapters are involved is an empirical question rather than a defining characteristic. This is also true of symbolic crimes. Given that although individual and club reputations are highly intertwined, the honor contested is often perceived to be the club's and to require participation of many if not all members. Symbolic crimes range from spontaneous to planned but often require at least some coordination.

B. Extent of Criminal Involvement of Outlaw Motorcycle Club Members

There is substantial evidence that members of outlaw motorcycle clubs are more extensively involved in crime than are members of other motorcycle clubs or of the general population. This is not surprising. Criminal tendencies and records are not a disadvantage to people who aspire to membership in an outlaw club; to the contrary, they are usually an advantage. The clubs themselves, by bringing together criminally active people and by engaging in lifestyle and symbolic crimes, make criminal involvement more likely.

1. *Crime Prevalence.* Surprisingly few studies have systematically charted the level and scope of criminal activities of outlaw motorcycle club members. Table 1 shows studies that have used law enforcement data to examine the prevalence of criminal involvement among members of outlaw motorcycle clubs and, less often, of members of their support or puppet clubs.

Canadian research covering 63 clubs active in Quebec during 1973–88 found that 70 percent of 1,530 outlaw bikers in the sample had a

TABLE 1

Studies That Have Used Law Enforcement Data to Examine the Prevalence of Criminal Involvement among Members of Outlaw Motorcycle Clubs

Source	Country	Sample Size	Club(s)	Criminal Involvement (%)	Measure of Criminal Involvement
OMC members:					
Tremblay et al. 1989	Canada	1,530	HAMC	70	Conviction
Barker 2015	Canada	249	HAMC	82	Conviction
BRÅ 1999	Sweden	100	HAMC, BMC	75	Conviction
Rostami and Mondani 2019	Sweden	1,142	HAMC	97	Suspicion
Klement 2016a	Denmark	307	HAMC, BMC, NNMC	96	Conviction
Klement 2016b	Denmark	396	HAMC, BMC, NNMC	92	Conviction
Blokland et al. 2019	Netherlands	601	Multiple	82	Conviction
Blokland, Van der Leest, and Soudijn 2019	Netherlands	1,617	Multiple	86	Conviction
Houghton 2014	Australia	...	Multiple	47	Conviction
Lauchs 2019a	Australia	64	Finks	100	Conviction
Support club members:					
Rostami and Mondani 2019	Sweden	1,866	RDMC, RWC	95	Suspicion
Klement 2016b	Denmark	554	HAMC, BMC, NNMC puppet clubs	87	Conviction
Blokland et al. 2019	Netherlands	473	Multiple	78	Conviction

NOTE.—OMC = Outlaw Motorcycle Club; HAMC = Hells Angels Motorcycle Club; BMC = Bandidos Motorcycle Club; NNMC = No Name Motorcycle Club (Danish indigenous club); RDMC = Red Devils Motorcycle Club; RWC = Red and White Crew.

criminal record (Tremblay et al. 1989). Law enforcement data eclectically published during a more recent period of intensified intergang rivalry among Canadian outlaw biker clubs suggest even higher percentages (cited in Barker 2015, pp. 148–49).

Criminal justice contacts are also prevalent among Scandinavian outlaw motorcycle club members. A Swedish study of 80 Hells Angels and 20 Bandidos found that three-quarters had been convicted at least once (BRÅ 1999). Rostami and Mondani (2019), in a network study of the Swedish Hells Angels, found that 97 percent of members in their sample had been officially registered as a crime suspect. In a series of publications, Klement and colleagues (Klement, Kyvsgaard, and Pedersen 2011; Klement and Pedersen 2013; Klement 2016a, 2016b) report on criminal careers of people identified as Danish outlaw bikers in the Police Intelligence Database (PID). More than one in 10 had been convicted at least once before being registered as outlaw bikers in the PID.

One of us, with colleagues, has studied the criminal careers of people officially registered by law enforcement personnel in the Netherlands as outlaw bikers (Blokland, Soudijn, and Teng 2014; Blokland, Van der Leest, and Soudijn 2018, 2019; Blokland et al. 2019). These studies used conviction data to reconstruct the juvenile and adult criminal careers of outlaw motorcycle club and support club members. Guilty verdicts, prosecutorial fines, and prosecutorial waivers for policy reasons were counted as "convictions"; acquittals and prosecutorial waivers for technical reasons were disregarded. The first study found that 82 percent of 601 outlaw bikers reported to be affiliated with an outlaw biker club between 2008 and 2013 were convicted at least once between age 12 and mid-2013. These individuals, who included full members, prospects, and hangarounds, were 44 years of age on average when convicted. A follow-up study found that nearly 86 percent of 1,617 registered outlaw motorcycle club members in the sample were convicted at least once between 2010 and 2015 (Blokland, Van der Leest, and Soudijn 2019).

Finally, of all known outlaw motorcycle club members in Queensland, Australia, 47 percent had a criminal record for one or more serious offenses (excluding traffic offenses and petty crime; Houghton 2014). A recent study on Australia's Gold Coast Finks Motorcycle Club found that all members had committed traffic offenses and many had committed minor drug offenses (Lauchs 2019a).

Crime prevalence also appears to be high among members of support or puppet clubs. Rostami and Mondani (2019) found that 95 percent of police-identified Swedish members of the Hells Angels' support clubs the Red Devils and Red and White Crew had been suspected of a crime. Klement (2016*b*) found that 87 percent of 554 Danish puppet and support club members had been convicted at least once. Blokland, Van der Leest, and Soudijn (2019) found a slightly lower prevalence (78 percent) among Dutch support club members.

Caution is needed, however, when drawing conclusions from studies using samples of police-identified outlaw bikers, as they may suffer from sampling bias. Criminally active outlaw bikers are more likely to end up in the sample than are their law-abiding brethren; this will inflate the percentage of convicted outlaw motorcycle club members. The extent to which selective sampling distorts findings depends on the conviction rate among outlaw bikers not included in the sample, and the extent to which the sample includes the total outlaw biker population. Assuming different hypothetical conviction rates among unidentified outlaw bikers and different levels of population coverage, Blokland, Van der Leest, and Soudijn (2019) estimated that the "true" conviction rate among members of Dutch outlaw motorcycle clubs is likely to be between 56 and 86 percent. Because the crime prevalence in an age-matched random sample of 300 Dutch male motorcycle owners who were not known to the police as outlaw bikers was a little over 32 percent, it is safe to conclude that criminal involvement among outlaw bikers in the Netherlands is higher than in the general male population.

2. *Crime Frequency.*   Crime prevalence indicated by the presence or absence of a criminal record is a crude measure of criminal involvement. Individuals with a single conviction and others with many each count as one and contribute equally to the prevalence rate. Information on the frequency of convictions of outlaw bikers enriches the picture.

Studies differ in the length and nature of the period examined in ways that may affect the frequency of offending recorded. The database used in the Blokland and colleagues studies (Blokland, Van der Leest, and Soudijn 2019; Blokland et al. 2019), for example, includes both club membership years and preceding years. Percentages reported by Klement (2016*a*, 2016*b*) in contrast pertain primarily to the period before becoming an outlaw biker (defined as before registration in the PID).

Criminal careers studies of the general offender population usually find conviction frequency highly skewed to the left: most offenders have only a few convictions, but a small minority accumulate many. This pattern characterized non-outlaw bikers in the Dutch studies, as the first pane in figure 2 shows. In contrast, the distribution of conviction frequency in both Dutch outlaw biker samples (second and third panes) is far more equal and even skewed to the right; more than one in four were convicted 10 or more times. The fourth pane in figure 2 shows the distribution of conviction frequency in the Danish biker sample (although differences between the Danish and Dutch studies make the data not fully comparable). Offending frequency among Danish bikers has a more pronounced rightward skew, meaning that the majority have extensive criminal records. Similar comparative patterns were found for Dutch and Danish support and puppet club members.

Additional research on criminal career dimensions of outlaw bikers before, during, and after club membership is clearly needed. Existing evidence suggests that outlaw bikers disproportionately engage in crime compared to the general population and do so at higher than average rates.

3. *Crime Mix.* Crime mix refers to the nature of the offenses committed. Organized crime researchers are likely to be most interested in entrepreneurial crimes and symbolic interclub violence. Arrest or conviction data, however, usually distinguish between different kinds of offenses only by reference to criminal code sections. This does not distinguish the various kinds of outlaw biker crimes as we have conceptualized them. Broad categories such as "assault," for example, include behavior ranging from domestic violence and barroom skirmishes to preplanned interclub clashes. These data do, however, show that outlaw bikers' criminal involvement extends well beyond lifestyle crimes.

A 2015 National Alliance of Gang Investigators Associations survey asked respondents about outlaw bikers' involvement in various types of crime. Outlaw bikers were reported to be most often engaged in assaults and weapons possession (in over 50 jurisdictions) and threats and intimidation (over 40 jurisdictions); this may reflect the outlaw biker subculture's hypermasculine nature and likely pertains to both lifestyle and symbolic violence. Outlaw bikers were also reported to be involved in street-level drug dealing (over 40 jurisdictions) and large-scale manufacture and distribution of narcotics (both in over 20 jurisdictions). Respondents from more than 10 jurisdictions reported bikers' involvement in money laundering (Federal Bureau of Investigation 2015).

These findings are broadly consistent with findings of a similar 2003 survey of 1,061 US law enforcement agencies (cited by Barker 2015, pp. 94–95). Ninety percent of the agencies reported outlaw bikers in

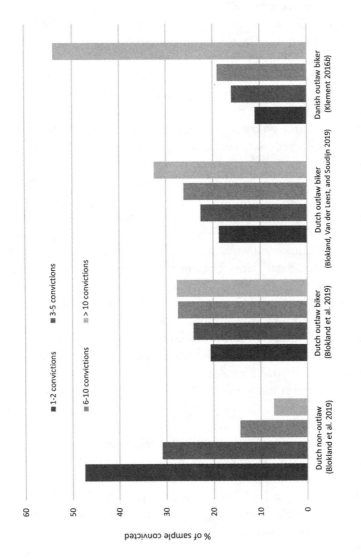

FIG. 2.—Distribution of conviction frequency, Danish and Dutch studies

their respective jurisdictions frequently or occasionally engaged in distributing narcotics, and 76 percent reported frequent or occasional involvement in manufacture of narcotics. More than half reported frequent or occasional involvement in money laundering. The criminal repertoire of outlaw bikers in the United States thus encompasses lifestyle and symbolic crimes and entrepreneurial crimes aimed at making and concealing criminal profit.

Only a few other studies have reported on outlaw bikers' criminal involvement. Of crimes of the population of outlaw bikers registered between 1984 and 1988 in Quebec province, 25 percent were property crimes, 8 percent were violent offenses, and 28 percent involved narcotics (Alain 2003). Klement (2016a) found that 69 percent of members of the Danish Hells Angels, Bandidos, and No Name Motorcycle Club known to the police were convicted at least once of a violent offense. Fifty-nine percent were convicted of drug possessions, often pertaining to the individual's own use and thus most likely reflect lifestyle crime. Thirty-four percent were convicted of sale or trafficking of narcotics, both entrepreneurial offenses. Of support club members' narcotics offenses, 49 percent were for possession and 22 percent were for sale or trafficking.

Blokland, Van der Leest, and Soudijn (2019) found that 85.2 percent of the outlaw bikers in their sample were convicted of a traffic offense at least once. Over half (56.7 percent) were convicted of at least one violent offense and more than a third (34.6 percent) at least once of a drug offense. Under Dutch prosecutorial policy, possession of a small amount of drugs for personal use is tolerated, which means convictions for drug offenses signify entrepreneurial crimes. Other entrepreneurial crimes (referred to as "organized crimes"), of which 11.7 percent of the sample were convicted, included extortion, money laundering, and human trafficking. Percentages for support club members were largely comparable, though they were less often convicted of violent (49.7 percent), drug (25.7 percent), and "organized" crimes (7.8 percent).

Blokland and David (2016), in an analysis of 40 crimes mentioned in 27 court files pertaining to Dutch outlaw motorcycle club members between 1999 and 2017, found that 80 percent involved entrepreneurial crimes. In one described instance of symbolic violence, "twenty to thirty" members of a Dutch indigenous outlaw motorcycle club raided the clubhouse of a non-outlaw club located in their territory and, threatening arson, forced its abandonment.

Geurtjens (2019) used the Quinn and Koch (2003) crimes typology in a study of 185 news articles from local newspapers in the Meuse Rhine Euroregion (parts of Belgium, Germany, and the Netherlands) pertaining to the four largest outlaw biker clubs in the area (Hells Angels, Bandidos, Satudarah, and Outlaws). Twenty-four percent of 85 criminal incidents could be categorized as "spontaneous expressive acts," 22 percent as "planned aggressive acts," and 39 percent as pertaining to "ongoing instrumental enterprises." Barker and Human (2009) in a similar study of newspaper articles concluded that half of all crimes between 1980 and 2005 concerning the four big US outlaw motorcycle clubs—Hells Angels, Outlaws, Bandidos, and Pagans—concerned ongoing instrumental enterprises.

Finally, Australian data analyzed by Goldsworthy and McGillivray (2017) indicate that 4,323 criminal charges between April 2008 and April 2014 resulting in guilty verdicts involved Queensland members of outlaw motorcycle clubs. The charges included 595 counts of drug possession (14 percent of all charges) and 285 counts of committing public nuisance (nearly 7 percent); both can be categorized as lifestyle crimes. Entrepreneurial crimes made up only about 2 percent of the guilty verdicts, including 102 counts of producing, trafficking in, or supplying drugs. Another Queensland study limited its scope to serious crimes, excluding lifestyle crimes such as traffic offenses and minor drug possession. Through the end of 2016, 112 members of outlaw motorcycle clubs received guilty verdicts. Fifty (45 percent) received a prison sentence for violent crimes, 29 (26 percent) for drug offenses, 11 (10 percent) for firearms offenses, and 14 (13 percent) for other crimes (Lauchs and Staines 2019).

III. Outlaw Motorcycle Clubs and (Organized) Crimes

Participation of members of an outlaw motorcycle club in criminal activities, including ongoing organized crimes, does not necessarily make the club a criminal organization. Indiscriminate law enforcement use of such terms as "criminal organization," "organized crime group," or "crime syndicate" concerning outlaw motorcycle clubs masks fundamental and ongoing conceptual debates. These debates, which center on the importance of analytically separating groups as organizational entities from their members as individuals, also occur in relation to mafia groups

(Anderson 1979; Haller 1992; Paoli 2003) and street gangs (Decker, Bynum, and Weisel 1998; Densley 2012, 2014).

A. Street Gangs, Organized Crime Groups, and Outlaw Motorcycle Clubs

Law enforcement agencies commonly refer to outlaw motorcycle clubs as outlaw motorcycle gangs to denote that they are criminal organizations, not "clubs." What gang scholars consider to be a gang, however, is different from what organized crime scholars consider to be an organized crime group (Roks and Van Ruitenburg 2018). As a first step toward a better understanding of how outlaw motorcycle clubs relate to both gangs and organized crime groups, building on Decker and Pyrooz (2015) we compare these two kinds of groups along two defining dimensions: structure and activity.

Gangs have been defined as "any durable, street-oriented youth group, whose involvement in illegal activity is part of its group identity" (Klein and Maxson 2006, p. 4). Other definitions exist (Ball and Curry [1995] and Curry [2015] provide overviews), including elements such as "a general lack of discipline that characterizes the control that gangs have over gang members" (Decker and Pyrooz 2014, p. 282). The dominant view is that many street gangs are diffuse aggregations of individuals and lack an obvious hierarchical structure, clearly defined leadership, levels of membership, membership roles and obligations, and precise gang boundaries. Leadership appears to be highly situational, membership requirements to be transitory, and membership to be blurry at best, both to law enforcement and to self-acclaimed gang members. Most gangs do not hold regular meetings, have written rules of conduct, or manage to enforce significant levels of discipline on members. The young ages of many gang members may contribute to this. Exceptions to this common image, however, exist. Some gangs have more rational, instrumental structures and operate in many ways that resemble legitimate corporations (e.g., Venkatesh and Levitt 2000).

Organized crime researchers have reached a similar consensus. The once prevailing image of organized crime groups was of pyramidal structured enterprises in which each individual is allocated a clear set of tasks and responsibilities. That has given way to a more fluid and dynamic conception in which criminals cooperate in loose, situationally defined networks that allow them to adapt to continuously changing opportunities and constraints in the criminal markets in which they operate (e.g.,

Bruinsma and Bernasco 2004; Bouchard and Morselli 2014). As with gangs, exceptions exist. Some criminal businesses have features that mirror legitimate corporations (von Lampe 2016a). People engaged in organized crime organization are typically older than street gang members (Kleemans and de Poot 2008).

The main difference between street gangs and organized crime groups therefore lies not so much in how they are positioned on the organizational continuum but rather in their activities (Decker and Pyrooz 2015, p. 298). Constructing and maintaining the collective identity of the gang is key for gang members and is reflected in the types of crimes they typically commit. Turf is often central to a gang's identity and much of the violence gang members commit is motivated by perceived violations of actual or symbolic turf boundaries by members of other gangs. As a result, intergang violence is common even in the absence of feared or real infringements of criminal markets. To optimally serve its symbolic purpose, violence is often committed in public and features excessive displays of power. A drive-by shooting may not be as accurate as a coordinated assassination, but in symbolic violence, the statement is what counts.

In contrast, organized crime groups, understood in terms of illegal enterprises, tend to seek economic rather than symbolic goals; the main driver of collaboration is to maximize illegal profit from predatory crime or provision of illegal goods and services. Violence may occur but is usually instrumental to achievement of economic goals—for example, to overcome resisting victims, intimidate potential witnesses and informants, or deal with criminal competition. Even in organized crime groups such as mafia associations that function as mutual aid societies and territorially based underworld governments, use of symbolic violence is limited and largely confined to phases of organizational disarray (Catino 2014; Lupo 2015). Violence has high costs. Excessive use attracts unwanted law enforcement attention, which is bad for illicit business. Avoidance of violence seems to characterize organized crime groups (von Lampe 2016a).

Figure 3 summarizes conventional wisdom concerning similarities and differences between street gangs and organized crime groups along a structural organizational dimension that runs from informal-diffused (disorganized) to instrumental-rational (organized), and a goal orientation dimension that runs from symbolic to economic. Groups on the informal-diffused end of the continuum lack a clear hierarchy, formal meetings are rare or nonexistent, and codes of conduct are limited to secrecy and loyalty (Decker and Curry 2000; Morselli 2009). Groups

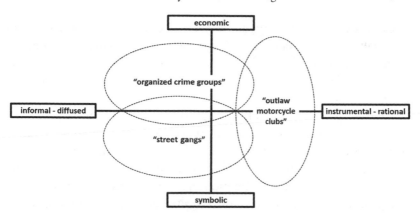

FIG. 3.—Similarities and differences between street gangs and organized crime groups

at the instrumental-rational end of the continuum have a vertical structure, coordinated actions, and clearly demarcated boundaries. Symbolic goals or functions include peer affiliation, friendship, revenge, and turf. Criminal groups on the economic end of these dimensions seem to care less about symbolism and more about making money (Decker and Pyrooz 2015).

Both street gangs and organized crime groups appear to gravitate toward the informal-diffused end of the structural dimension, with the exception of mafia associations. They have a formalized structure and display some level of vertical differentiation, at least with respect to individual mafia families (Catino 2014). Outlaw motorcycle clubs, like mafia associations, tend to present themselves as strongly hierarchical organizations with clearly described membership obligations and strictly defined boundaries. Some are registered legal entities and have copyrighted their colors and patches to prevent unauthorized use. The Hells Angels have gone to court to challenge unauthorized use of their name and logo (Kuldova 2017).

Outlaw motorcycle gangs are associated with both entrepreneurial and symbolic crimes. Outlaw bikers have been convicted for profitable illicit activities such as narcotics production and distribution and trafficking in guns and humans but are also known for extremely violent public displays of intergang rivalry that appear motivated by honor and revenge rather than by potential revenues. Their goals thus run the full spectrum from purely symbolic to purely economic.

Compared to street gangs and organized crime groups, outlaw biker clubs fall on the instrumental-rational end of the organizational continuum. Their criminal behavior seems to transcend the divide between symbolic and entrepreneurial more than either street gangs or organized crime groups.

Figure 3 provides a useful starting point to understand how outlaw motorcycle clubs compare to street gangs and organized crime groups, but it is based on generalizations that call for more refined examination. First, implicit to positioning the three types of groups along the organizational dimension is the assumption that group structure is always and unequivocally linked to members' criminal activities. Second, placing entrepreneurial and symbolic crimes on opposite sides of a continuum may imply that particular types of crime are mutually exclusive in a group's criminal repertoire. Both these implications are premature.

B. Crime and Its Relation to the Club as an Organizational Entity

Closely linked to the criminal involvement of outlaw bikers is the question of how their crimes relate to clubs and chapters as organizational entities. There are different notions about this. Veno (2009, p. 179), for example, argues that profit-making crime—namely, drug crimes—cannot be ascribed to clubs or chapters as a whole: "The members do it, but it's not a club-organized thing." Sometimes, outlaw biker clubs are portrayed as supporting criminal activities without direct involvement— for example, by providing a network of trusted contacts (Quinn and Koch 2003) and an intimidating reputation (Wolf 1991, p. 127; Quinn and Forsyth 2011), or providing a forum for resolution of conflicts (Piano 2017).

A symbiotic relationship is sometimes assumed to exist between the profit-making illegal activities of individual members and the club as a whole. Quinn and Forsyth (2011) argue that clubs largely rely on their members to raise funds without asking too many questions and may provide seed-money loans for criminal businesses. Sometimes, outlaw biker clubs or chapters are considered to be directly involved in the sense that a club "directly supervises the organized criminality of its members" (Quinn and Forsyth 2011, p. 228). Barker and Human (2009) suggest that there is a continuum of clubs and chapters, including some in which only a few members engage in serious criminal activities, some composed of small groups of criminally active members who operate with or without tacit approval of the club as a whole, and some that function "as gangs oriented toward criminal profit" (p. 175; see also Barker 2015; Lauchs, Bain, and Bell 2015).

C. A Situational Approach

We adopt a situational approach. By this we mean that how crime relates to the club or chapter as an organizational entity may differ for different types of crime and may differ even for one type of crime from one occasion to the next. Rather than conclude that crime is "not a club-organized thing" or that some clubs function as "gangs," we believe that crime may be completely separate from the club or chapter on one occasion, while being club business the next, depending on the particular circumstances. Below we examine three analytically distinct scenarios of links between outlaw motorcycle clubs and crime (fig. 4; see also von Lampe 2019). Given the paucity of valid data, we use these scenarios primarily as heuristic devices rather than as a classificatory scheme to organize known cases.

The first scenario, "bad apples," acknowledges that there may be only limited overlap between outlaw motorcycle clubs and the activities of criminally active members. For example, it is well established that gang members, and outlaw bikers, often cooperate with co-offenders outside the gang (Morselli 2009; Bouchard and Konarski 2013). In the "bad apple" scenario, individual members engage in criminal activities as independent operators on their

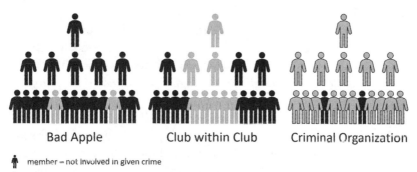

    Bad Apple   **Club within Club**   **Criminal Organization**

member – not involved in given crime

member – involved in given crime independent from club

member – involved in given crime on behalf of club

FIG. 4.—Scenarios of links between outlaw motorcycle clubs and crime

own, with other club members, or with nonmembers. In these cases, club members are essentially autonomous in their decisions to commit a given crime and in their choices regarding the specifics of the crime. Outlaw motorcycle clubs sometimes characterize members implicated in criminal conduct as bad apples, insisting that having criminals among their members is not unique to outlaw biker clubs and that members commit crimes on their own, as a private matter (see Veno 2009, p. 62; Barker 2015, p. 44).

The second scenario we will discuss, "club within a club," is similar to the bad apple scenario in that members commit crimes on their own account. However, the situation is different in that most if not all members, and especially the club or chapter leadership, are involved. A large overlap exists between the formal club structure and a parallel structure engaged in crime; from the outside it may appear that the club as a club is committing these crimes. Importantly, however, relations and interactions within the parallel structure do not follow the same logic as the formal club structure. For example, authority derived from formal positions in the club hierarchy may not carry over to decisions with respect to criminal activity. This scenario is neither purely hypothetical (see, e.g., Morselli 2009) nor does it apply exclusively to outlaw motorcycle clubs. Gang researchers have observed that drugs are sometimes distributed through the ranks from gang leaders to lower level members but that "drug sales are fundamentally an individual or small-group activity, not coordinated by the collective gang. The gang instead provides the reputational and criminogenic resources to sustain the enterprise" (Densley 2014, p. 533).

In the third scenario, "criminal organizations," outlaw motorcycle clubs, or their chapters, engage in criminal activities as organizational entities. scenario corresponds to the law enforcement agency claim that outlaw motorcycle clubs have morphed into "highly structured criminal organizations" (Federal Bureau of Investigation 2009, p. 8). The decision to commit a crime is made collectively through the established decision-making mechanism, club resources are invested, and individuals directly involved act on behalf, and in the interest, of the club. Not all members are necessarily involved, but if crime is considered to be club business it can be assumed to be backed by the entire membership.

These three scenarios could play out simultaneously within a given outlaw motorcycle club or chapter. Depending on the situation, members may act as independent operators, or as members of a criminal organization. This may apply to crimes for profit as well as symbolic crimes and lifestyle crimes. For example, several club members may commit a rape on club premises. This could be viewed as a bad apple scenario in which the perpetrators take advantage of the relative safety of the club environment, trusting fellow members not to talk to the police. Within the same club or chapter there may also be a large group of members, including senior members, who run an extortion racket using the power of the patch to intimidate victims, which would fit the club within a club scenario. Finally, the club or chapter may decide to dismantle a newly formed rival club by forcefully seizing its club colors. This fits the club as criminal organization scenario.

1. *The Bad Apple Scenario.* The bad apple scenario reflects how outlaw motorcycle clubs were initially portrayed. In the absence of evidence to the contrary, it likely remains the predominant pattern with crimes being committed by members in "a freelance fashion" (Monterosso 2018, p. 691). The scarce empirical research provides little evidence one way or the other. However, co-offending data suggest that most biker crime is individual crime, assuming that more than one member will likely be involved when a club acts as an organizational entity. Existing research shows that outlaw bikers who commit crimes tend to operate as lone offenders or to co-offend with nonmembers rather than in groups of fellow outlaw bikers. Blokland and David (2016), analyzing 27 criminal cases involving members of outlaw motorcycle clubs as suspects, found that more than one outlaw biker was implicated in only one-third of the cases. Rostami and Mondani (2019), with samples of thousands of cases, examined Swedish co-offending data for members of the Hells Angels and two support clubs. Only a small fraction of collaborations involved members of the same group. Among Hells Angels, only 13.2 percent of co-offending ties were to another Hells Angels member. Of those intragroup ties, 74 percent connected members of the same chapter (Rostami and Mondani 2019, p. 45).

In the bad apple scenario, by definition, outlaw motorcycle clubs as such do not commit crimes. This does not imply, however, that they play no role. Quite to the contrary, outlaw motorcycle clubs by their very nature may in a number of ways influence and promote the criminal conduct of their members. This is most relevant to the bad apple scenario but also applies to the other two scenarios.

Outlaw motorcycle clubs provide members a social environment that is tolerant of and often sympathetic toward criminal conduct, even when

criminal involvement is limited and individual criminal conduct is neither implicitly nor explicitly encouraged by the club as such. In part, this
is a function of the people outlaw biker clubs tend to attract and recruit.
Law enforcement data since at least the mid-1960s have consistently
shown that disproportionately high shares of outlaw bikers have criminal
records. Research has found some support for the selection hypothesis
that outlaw motorcycle clubs prefer to recruit criminally inclined individuals (Thornberry et al. 1993; Klement 2016*b*; Blokland et al. 2019).
Ethnographic research shows that violence is an integral part of the outlaw biker subculture within the larger context of the "saloon society milieu" (Quinn 2001, p. 390). Accordingly, proven ability and willingness
to use violence, regardless of its legality, can be a key criterion for acceptance as a member (Wolf 1991; Veno 2009).

   There are conflicting accounts about whether clubs require prospective
members to commit a crime, possibly even murder (Marsden and Sher
2007). Where this practice reportedly exists, it is thought to be aimed at
preventing infiltration by undercover police officers (Lavigne 1989; Veno
2009). Regardless of the truth of these claims, outlaw motorcycle clubs, including the more "conservative" and less criminally oriented, appear generally to be intent on refusing entry to current or former police officers
(Wolf 1991; Barker 2015). In contrast, a criminal background is not an exclusion criterion. The historically high share of convicted offenders among
outlaw bikers is reflected in outlaw bikers' self-perceptions (Barger 2001,
p. 124: "most of us were card-carrying felons") and in norms and practices
adopted to cope with this situation. For example, jail time is one of the few
excuses recognized by club bylaws for not complying with duties such as
maintaining a roadworthy motorcycle or attending club meetings (Wolf
1991; Veno 2009; Abadinsky 2013).

   The effects of selecting criminally inclined individuals are reinforced
by a process that Wolf (1991, p. 100) has described as "an expected norm"
of a probationary period for new members: the "disaffiliation" from social
ties outside of the club. This means that affiliation goes hand in hand with
weakening of bonds to conventional society and thereby weakening
mechanisms of informal social control (Sampson and Laub 1997). However, while disaffiliation may affect friendship networks and possibly intimate partnerships, it does not necessarily lead to new members giving up
employment or entrepreneurship in the legal economy (Wolf 1991;
Barger 2001).

Outlaw motorcycle clubs do not generally hold members accountable for involvement in criminal activities, and, accordingly, there is no loss in formal or informal status connected with being implicated in a crime. The prevailing rationale seems to be that an outlaw biker "can do anything he wants to do" (Spurgeon 2011, p. 319) as long as he does not violate norms of the outlaw biker subculture or specific rules of his club (Veno 2009; Quinn and Forsyth 2011). For example, many outlaw biker clubs have traditionally banned use but not sale of intravenous drugs (Wolf 1991). According to a former high-ranking member of the Outlaws motorcycle club, the rule was "What a man did on his own time was his own business" (Spurgeon 2011, p. 319).

Rules against drug dealing seem to exist only to the extent that there could be negative repercussions for the club, such as the "no drug burns" rule of the Hells Angels that forbids members ripping off partners in drug deals (Barger 2001, p. 46). In a similar vein, the Edmonton chapter of the Rebels forbade members to wear their club colors or any other club symbols when selling drugs (Wolf 1991, p. 268).

It would be a rare occurrence for an outlaw biker to be expelled for a crime he has committed. In one such exceptional case mentioned by Barker (2015), a member of the Bandidos was forced out after having killed a popular former boxing champion. Another, mostly unwritten, outlaw biker rule forbids cooperation with law enforcement and disclosure of club-related information to outsiders and specifically to the media (Wolf 1991; Veno 2009; Barker 2015).

As a consequence, outlaw bikers who prepare or carry out criminal activities can rely on others not to divulge incriminating information. In turn, all members regardless of their criminal inclination subject themselves to the real possibility that they will have to remain silent about crimes of other members, and that "their silence and inaction gives tacit support and increases the likelihood that criminal behavior will continue and progress" (Barker 2015, p. 101).

Outlaw motorcycle clubs may also support the criminal conduct of members in more direct ways as a by-product of features of their normative and institutional framework—namely, those concerning group cohesion and mutual aid. Clubs may provide funds to members in need, which may include members using these funds as investment capital for illegal activities (Quinn and Forsyth 2011), or clubs putting up money to post bail or pay retainers for lawyers (Barger 2001; Veno 2009).

In a more comprehensive way, outlaw motorcycle clubs are based on the notion of ritual brotherhood. As Veno (2009, p. 88) explains, "When members call each other 'brother' they actually mean it. For many, the club becomes their family, particularly if they've come from dysfunctional homes." A key facet of the notion of brotherhood is an obligation to lend mutual assistance in a system of interpersonal reciprocity that encompasses a wide range of spheres from sharing motorcycle parts to providing emotional support in crises, but also includes providing shelter to fellow members who are fugitives from the law (Wolf 1991). Encapsulated in the system of mutual assistance is the principle of mutual protection: "All members of the club will support a fellow member when threatened" (Wolf 1991, p. 98). The rule is supposed to apply "under any circumstances" (Wolf 1991, p. 127) and "no matter what the cause" (Barger 2001, p. 67; see also Quinn and Koch 2003). While members face repercussions internally if they abuse the outlaw biker code of honor for personal interests, externally the rule establishes a protective shield in that nonmembers are discouraged from taking action against members (Wolf 1991). When members engage in illegal activities on their own, they remain under the protection of fellow club members, be it against predatory criminals or against disloyal business partners.

The generalized expectation that an outlaw biker can count on unquestioned support from fellow club members, along with the outlaw bikers' reputation for violence, feeds into what is called the "power of the patch" (Smith 1990; Wolf 1991; Barker 2015; Lauchs, Bain, and Bell 2015). The term refers to the intimidating and fear-instilling effect of wearing the colors of an outlaw motorcycle club; what Barker (2015, p. 11) calls "intimidation by reputation." The power of the patch means that criminally inclined outlaw bikers not only operate behind a protective shield but possess intimidation capital that they can use as an asset in criminal activities—for example, to intimidate victims or witnesses (Wolf 1991; Barker 2015) or law enforcement officials (Gomez del Prado 2011).

Blokland and David (2016) report that outlaw bikers appearing as suspects in criminal cases they analyzed regularly referred to their membership in an outlaw motorcycle club to emphasize numerical and physical dominance over their victims. In this respect, essentially everything outlaw motorcycle clubs and individual outlaw bikers do that strengthens the power of the patch facilitates and benefits their criminal conducts. This includes symbolic crime—namely, violence in interclub

conflicts—and aggressive and violent behavior more generally. Importantly, following an argument Marcus Felson (2006) has made with respect to street gangs, the power of the patch could be bolstered by members
of other clubs and even by nonaffiliated bikers so long as the public and
the media do not differentiate between clubs or categories of bikers.

A further crime-promoting effect of belonging to an outlaw motorcycle club could be that formation of criminal network ties is facilitated.
Outlaw motorcycle clubs, with their high proportions of criminally inclined members, inevitably function as offender convergence settings
where potential partners in crime meet and socialize (Felson 2003;
Kleemans and De Poot 2008). In addition, selective recruiting and em-
phases on mutual loyalty and support should provide a basis for trust
even between members who are not in regular face-to-face contact
(Paoli 2003). This may be particularly significant given the wide geographical reach of intraclub ties in large international clubs with chapters in various countries and continents. A high-ranking Hells Angel
and FBI informant reported that members of the UK Hells Angels
sought to import cocaine from Brazil and, when they could not find a
supplier, asked members of the Rio de Janeiro chapter to find one for
them (Lavigne 1997).

For some of the same reasons that bring outlaw bikers together, outsiders may view them as desirable partners in crime. Membership in an
outlaw motorcycle club implies qualities such as adherence to a code of
silence and willingness to use violence that are commonly valued in the
underworld. Outlaw bikers may also be attractive crime partners because
of the power of the patch—for example, to collect loansharking debts:
"The bikers are recruited because of their 'tough-guy' image and because
they are close-mouthed and will not talk when apprehended by police"
(Pennsylvania Crime Commission 1991, p. 201; see also Wolf 1991). At
the same time, they seem accessible because of their visibility. They are
reportedly often contacted by outsiders who assume that outlaw motorcycle clubs sell drugs (Veno 2009).

The bad apple scenario illuminates characteristics that outlaw motorcycle clubs share with some organized crime groups, such as the southern
Italian mafia associations, Chinese triads, and Japanese yakuza, all of
which are associational criminal structures (von Lampe 2016a, 2016b).
Francis Ianni (1975), in his seminal study of criminal networks in New
York, distinguished "two forms of behavioral organizations" that he
called "associational networks" (p. 293) and "entrepreneurial networks"

(p. 307). Entrepreneurial networks exist to profit from crime. Associational networks foster mutual trust among criminals, promote a basic criminal code of conduct, and shape criminal reputations (Ianni 1975).

Patricia Adler (1985, p. 63), observing drug smugglers and wholesalers in Southern California, similarly distinguished business structures in the form of partnerships, groups, and supplier-customer relations from "friendship networks" consisting of "social affiliations," some having "business overtones," and "a larger circle of acquaintances which was composed of dealers and smugglers the individual knew socially, yet with whom he or she had no business dealings." Mark H. Haller (1992), examining the Philadelphia family of the Italian-American Cosa Nostra, offered essentially the same distinction. He concluded that the mafia family served three functions: as a fraternal order fostering "male bonding and social prestige for members," as a businessmen's association through which "members make useful business contacts, learn about business opportunities, and perform mutual favors for fellow members and their associates," and as an association that sets and enforces rules among members similar to lawyers' self-governance in bar associations (Haller 1992, pp. 2–4).

Hartmann and von Lampe (2008) provided another example of an associational criminal structure with parallels to outlaw motorcycle clubs. They studied the German underworld of the 1920s and 1930s, focusing on the Ringvereine that were originally officially chartered mutual aid associations of ex-convicts. The Ringvereine had an active club life with regular meetings, excursions, and social events, including lavish funeral processions for deceased members. Legal expenses were paid from club coffers, as was support for members and their families during times of imprisonment. Pins, rings, and other club insignia made members recognizable to outsiders. This made it easy for members to make use of the Ringvereine's reputational value.

Organizations with associational criminal structures tend to have four basic features that also characterize outlaw motorcycle clubs: bonding, communication, mutual support, and a code of conduct. From friendship networks of drug traffickers to mafia organizations, associational criminal structures create and reinforce affectionate bonds that give members a sense of belonging and convey exclusivity and elitism, which can translate into enhanced social status. Solidarity and cohesion among members facilitate relatively safe communication of criminally relevant information, and the internal system of mutual assistance and support facilitates access to resources for commission of crimes and for mitigating risks of arrest and incarceration. Finally, outlaw motorcycle clubs fit the mold in that they express a normative consensus in the absence of applicable and binding social norms that regulate deviant and criminal behavior, thereby increasing predictability and reducing uncertainty in interactions among criminals (von Lampe 2016*b*).

Associational criminal structures vary on some dimensions, including their degree of illegality, their visibility, and their formalization and organizational complexity. In all of these respects, outlaw motorcycle clubs are at one end of the continuum. Importantly, the clubs have noncriminal origins and, unless they have been banned by the authorities, typically are registered legal associations. In this respect they resemble Chinese triads and the Ringvereine, which started out as mutual aid societies of migrant workers in China and of ex-convicts in Germany, respectively, and sometimes retained this status while engaging in criminal activities (Chu 2000; Hartmann and von Lampe 2008).

Another variation exists with respect to visibility. Most associational criminal structures are secretive; affiliation may become apparent only after close observation (Hobbs 1989). Some, however, are easily recognizable through tattoos, such as the post-Soviet fraternity of the thieves-in-law (Cheloukhine and Haberfeld 2011); pins, such as with the Ringvereine; or clothing, as with some street gangs (Decker, Katz, and Webb 2008). All in this respect resemble outlaw biker clubs.

2. *Clubs within Clubs.* In the bad apple scenario, some members are involved in a particular criminal activity, but most are not. This is a fairly strong indication that a distinction should be made between what members do as individuals and what clubs do as clubs. In the club within a club scenario, things are far less obvious. From a distance it may appear that the club is organizing and carrying out crimes. On closer inspection, the criminal operation is parallel to but separate from the club.

Classification of outlaw motorcycle clubs as criminal organizations is often a matter of degree, hinging on the proportion of members involved in criminal activity (Wolf 1991). From this perspective, the club within a club scenario might seem to involve hair splitting. However, if outlaw motorcycle clubs are to be the units of analysis, the focus should be on a particular club as an "extra-individual entity" (Ahrne 1990, p. 37), defined by structures, procedures, and resources, and capable of agency. Whether crimes involving members can meaningfully be attributed to the club depends on the roles these structures, procedures, and resources play. The entire membership, including the leadership, could commit crimes collectively without qualifying as a case of a club as a criminal organization so long as the crimes occur outside of the functioning of the club as such.

Lack of pertinent research makes it difficult to offer concrete examples of the club within a club scenario. Law enforcement, journalists, and autobiographical accounts typically lack the level of detail necessary to determine into which of our three scenarios a given case falls. Hells Angels involvement in the illegal drug trade in Quebec in the late 1990s may exemplify the club within a club scenario. Extensive investigations over several years implicated dozens of Hells Angels members, especially in its elite Nomad chapter, together with members of a support club and numerous nonmembers. The Nomads and the support club were alleged to exist solely to commit crimes for profit (Morselli 2009). Network analysis of surveillance data revealed, however, that the structure of the drug trafficking network only partly mirrored the formal structure of the Hells Angels. The 12 members of the Nomad chapter were not the most central players in the overall scheme, and some lower ranking participants (including Nomad prospects and support club members) held more influential positions in the trafficking network than did most of the Nomads (Morselli 2009, 2010).

The Pagans motorcycle club (PMC) of the 1970s and 1980s offers another possible example. At the time PMC had its strongest presence in Pennsylvania. Investigations showed that Pagans members and associates, including senior members, were involved in drug trafficking, mostly of methamphetamine and phencyclidine (PCP). In 1984, 22 PMC members and associates, including the president, vice president, sergeant-at-arms, and eight other members of the mother club were indicted for various drug-related offenses. The indictments alleged that the defendants used "the structure and organization of the PMC to organize, facilitate and control the manufacture and distribution of controlled substances both within the PMC and outside of it" (United States Attorney for the Eastern District of Pennsylvania 1984, p. 21819). This appears to be an example of an outlaw motorcycle club functioning as a criminal organization, but a more in-depth analysis by the Pennsylvania Crime Commission (1991) suggests that it better fits the club within the club scenario.

The Pennsylvania Crime Commission described the typical pattern as involving an outside supplier who provides drugs to a member of the mother club who in turn provides the drugs to chapter presidents in the relevant geographical areas. The local club presidents divide the drugs among their members for further distribution through their respective associates. According to the Pennsylvania Crime Commission, the mother club's members are not collectively and directly involved in selling drugs. Instead, they grant permission to networks within the club to distribute drugs and, in turn, profit through tribute or kickbacks by which mother club members receive a percentage of the profits. The commission stresses that the "formal structure of the outlaw club … is not necessarily the same as its economic structure, which tends to be fairly decentralized. Income-gathering activities frequently involve small, operationally independent units—small work groups or partnerships among members which may also include nonmember associates" (Pennsylvania Crime Commission 1991, p. 194).

The club within the club scenario could be quite common. There have been many failed attempts by law enforcement authorities to establish that a particular club, or chapter, qualifies as a criminal enterprise under RICO laws in the United States (Quinn 2001, pp. 386–87; Lauchs, Bain, and Bell 2015, pp. 71, 79). There is also reason to believe that clubs, for purposes of self-preservation, make conscious efforts to separate the formal club structure from criminal conduct (Quinn 2001). For example, in a Hells Angels meeting that was secretly taped by an FBI informant, Ralph "Sonny" Barger declared, "We got to get one thing straight with everybody: what goes on in this room is one hundred percent legal. We don't talk about illegal things here. Because if you're doing anything illegal, I don't want to know about it 'cause it's not club business" (Lavigne 1997, pp. 197–98).

From a theoretical perspective, outlaw motorcycle clubs may be ill-suited to operate as criminal businesses given their formalized structure and public exposure. It is often said in the organized crime literature that criminal organizations tend to "have relatively simple structures" (Southerland and Potter 1993, p. 254) and that illegal businesses tend to be "localized, fragmented, ephemeral, and undiversified" (Reuter 1983, p. 131). The underlying rationale is that illegality imposes constraints on organizational sophistication, growth, and visibility, at least when laws are strictly enforced (Paoli, Greenfield, and Reuter 2009, pp. 204–6). From this angle, conducting illegal businesses through an outlaw motorcycle club is counterintuitive. Arthur Veno (2009, p. 173) observed, "If you're going to commit serious crime you don't brand yourself outlaws, wear the most provocative clothes you can muster, and break every society norm (and most road rules) you can."

3. *Clubs as Criminal Organizations*.   The likely frequency of the club within the club phenomenon does not rule out the possibility that outlaw motorcycle clubs at times function as criminal organizations. Factors specific to particular clubs might offset some of the constraints of illegality. Even if outlaw motorcycle clubs are ill-suited to functioning as criminal organizations for profit-making crime, they may be involved in other types of crime.

The club as criminal organization view of outlaw motorcycle clubs appears to be widely shared among law enforcement officials and journalists. The academic literature is much more cautious. Some authors, however, argue that some outlaw biker clubs, or chapters of some clubs, fall into this category (see, e.g., Wolf 1991; Barker 2015). Remarkably, the standards that arguably make this classification appropriate have received scant attention. The reasons for classifying an outlaw motorcycle club as a criminal organization usually remain implicit.

Barker emphasizes the degree to which the membership is involved in criminal activities. He highlights two dimensions: "the extent of the members' involvement in organized crime" and "whether the club's officers and leaders are involved in the planning and execution of these criminal activities" (Barker 2015, p. 73). Under these circumstances, Barker suggests, the criminally oriented leadership and majority of members can take advantage of the traditional outlaw biker club structure and procedures to recruit trusted accomplices and insulate senior members from prosecution (Barker 2015, p. 102; Australian Crime Commission, citation in Lauchs, Bain, and Bell 2015, p. 71).

Lauchs and colleagues hint at two different constellations: a biker club or chapter directing crime "through the mechanisms of . . . a hierarchy," which could mean that the formal club structure doubles as a business or that illegal business activity is delegated to individual members or third parties, and "through loose networks of members working with their associates," which suggests that the club or chapter as an organizational entity has no direct involvement and merely provides social or cultural context for the conduct of individual members (Lauchs, Bain, and Bell 2015, p. 26). In a further elaboration of the first notion, Lauchs (2019*a*, p. 292) specifies that a club could be considered a criminal organization when senior members use "their authority within the club to direct criminal activity by other members and associates," which signals that "the club has serious criminal activity as its goal."

Other criteria could be considered. One might ask whether club resources are used, whether the risk of loss is borne by the club or by individual members, or whether in members' understanding criminal activities are legitimated by and an expression of "what the club stands for." A litmus test would be to ask by what logic orders are given and followed, and what happens if orders are not followed or if members act in ways detrimental to successful completion of a criminal project. Will they be reprimanded for violating the club's norms and values or for violating contractual obligations?

By default, the analysis centers on the formal authority structure of the club that combines elements of participatory and representative democracy. Some decisions are made by the membership as a whole, some by the elected leadership that may be half of a chapter's members, and some by individual elected office holders who have power to direct and discipline members within certain limits and within defined areas of responsibility (Wolf 1991).

As Letizia Paoli (2003, p. 44) has observed of the Sicilian mafia, outlaw motorcycle clubs may experience a shift "toward a patrimonial form of domination" in which leaders surround themselves with loyal followers who provide a permanent basis of power. Assertion of power might be somewhat limited by tradition, but formal mechanisms of legitimization and control would be devalued. Outlaw motorcycle clubs have experienced violent internal power struggles (Edwards 2012) and subtler schemes to control chapters, such as by buying votes (Veno 2009). In these cases, attention has to be paid not to formal structures but to how the club's decision-making mechanisms relate to criminal activities of members.

When these standards are used, it is not easy to find undisputable examples of outlaw motorcycle clubs operating as criminal organizations. Limited empirical research and lack of sufficiently detailed journalistic and law enforcement accounts make the search for illustrative cases difficult. Drawing on Wolf's (1991) ethnographic research, we have identified at least two incidents that seem to fit the club as criminal organization scenario. Both involve symbolic crimes. The Edmonton chapter of the Rebels engaged in a violent confrontation with a unit of paratroopers stationed nearby who frequented a bar the Rebels had adopted as their club bar. Plans of action were drawn up initially by the members present at the bar and subsequently at a formal club meeting.

Wolf (1991) details a comparable event arising from a rivalry between outlaw motorcycle clubs in which a Rebels chapter acted as an organizational unit in committing violent crimes. An out-of-town outlaw motorcycle club established an Edmonton chapter. This prompted the officers of the Rebels club to meet with the officers of an allied biker club and devise a plan of action. The Rebels and their allies stormed a meeting of the rival club, assaulted those present, and confiscated their club colors. These were burned on the spot except for one jacket that was put on display in the Rebels clubhouse.

Another, peculiar, case of crime-for-profit that seems attributable to an outlaw motorcycle club is described in the autobiography of a former leading member of the Outlaws. To raise funds to cover mounting legal bills, the club had butane lighters imprinted with the slogan "Support Your Local Outlaws." When it learned that lighters supplied by a Canadian business could only be sold at a loss after paying import duties, the Outlaws decided to smuggle the lighters into the United States (Spurgeon 2011). This case shows an outlaw motorcycle club willing to commit crimes for profit, of course, but it does not really fit the image of a business structure geared toward the provision of illegal goods and services.

A more classic case of crime for profit involves a triple murder, which received massive media attention, of members of the Dutch Nomads chapter of the Hells Angels. The story was reconstructed from wiretap information and witness testimonies (Schutten, Vugts, and Middelburg 2004; Van den Heuvel and Huisjes 2009). This case illustrates a complex situational interplay among the different scenarios. The president of the Dutch Hells Angels Nomads chapter and a local drug dealer apparently arranged a shipment of nearly 300 kilograms of cocaine from the Dutch Antilles to the Netherlands. The cocaine was provided by a Colombian cartel. Allegedly, the president and two fellow Nomads stole the cocaine with no intention of remunerating the Colombian cartel. This would fit the club within a club scenario and involve an entrepreneurial crime that evolved from market-based to predatory.

According to law enforcement, the 14 remaining Nomads, fearing indiscriminate retaliation by the Colombian cartel, killed the president and his collaborators in the Hells Angels clubhouse during a church meeting and dumped their bodies in a nearby canal. Eighteen bullets from three different guns were recovered from the three bodies. All three had been shot through their right hands, suggesting punishment for the "drug burn." In the legal aftermath, all 14 Nomads members present at the church meeting refused to testify. All were initially convicted of manslaughter by the district court but were later acquitted by the court of appeals. The court did not doubt the prosecutor's narrative of events but concluded that it could not be proven who had fired the fatal shots. Accepting the prosecutor's account, the president and his henchmen fell victim to internal discipline carried out in accordance with club rules (Schutten, Vugts, and Middelburg 2004; Van den Heuvel and Huisjes 2009). Theft of the drugs exposed fellow members to the vengeance of a conned business partner. That had ramifications at the club level and resulted in club action to protect its interests.

Yet another link between crimes for profit and outlaw motorcycle gangs was found in an analysis of 183 interviews with "relatively successful adult offenders" conducted by undergraduate students of the University of Montreal between 1996 and 2007 (Tremblay, Bouchard, and Petit 2009, p. 28). Tremblay, Bouchard, and Petit (2009) provide evidence that the Hells Angels dominated the drug trade in Quebec. They estimate that nearly 50 percent of the cocaine dealing jobs and 25 percent of the workforce in the cannabis cultivation industry in the province were under the influence of the Hells Angels; these drug market participants directly or indirectly depended on the Hells Angels to sell or obtain drug supplies. According to Tremblay and colleagues, the Hells Angels functioned "as a chamber of commerce" with "about 100 affiliated or 'franchised' entrepreneurs who share the same trademark, logo or banner" and who "are themselves relatively autonomous entrepreneurs seeking partners to conduct business" (Tremblay, Bouchard, and Petit 2009, pp. 34–35).

The empirical biker literature, however, lacks studies of entrepreneurial biker gangs that resemble the corporate street gang described by Venkatesh and Levitt (2000). Local sets of a Chicago-based gang organized drug dealing with a staff of paid members who received fixed salaries. The local sets operated under the supervision of a central leadership board, which controlled procurement of drugs from sanctioned suppliers and regularly collected a franchise payment of a percentage of illicit profits. Recruitment and promotion were based on economic performance, and failure to meet economic goals was treated as a group transgression. Venkatesh and Levitt characterize this business model as the outcome of a process by which the gang lost its original character and its ideology of a social-support network rooted in ritual kinship.

Their interpretation of the underlying dynamics of gang evolution resembles a narrative of outlaw bikers whose interests shift from motorcycles to illicit profit making that has been a common thread since the
1970s in debates about outlaw motorcycle gangs (see Nossen 1975).

D. Intersecting the Biker Crime Typology with the Three Scenarios

We approach the subject of biker clubs functioning as criminal organizations broadly, rather than focus on the narrow question of whether
outlaw motorcycle clubs function as illegal businesses in markets for illegal goods and services. In this section, we discuss the roles of clubs and
chapters in lifestyle, symbolic, and entrepreneurial crimes and examine
the roles outlaw motorcycle clubs play in governance of illegal markets
and criminal milieus. This differentiated approach appears warranted
because different types of crimes may have different meanings and implications for the clubs and place different demands on the clubs' structure and resources.

Lifestyle crimes include, for example, receiving stolen goods for club
purposes such as holding parties or outfitting the clubhouse. These types
of crimes are directly related to the outlaw biker subculture and to the
club's core social and cultural functions. Club participation in these activities, as clubs, evokes the broader pattern of kinds of deviant and criminal behavior among members that fit the bad apple or club within a club
scenarios.

Symbolic crimes carried out by outlaw motorcycle clubs are typically
discussed in relation to interclub conflicts within the outlaw biker subculture (e.g., Morselli, Tanguay, and Labalette 2008; Klement 2019).
However, there can also be instances when clubs seek to enhance their
status and reputation in the wider saloon society. This is exemplified by
the anecdote reported about actions of the Edmonton Rebels against a
paratroopers unit for control of their club bar. A view commonly expressed in the academic literature is that violent confrontations between
clubs are inherent in the outlaw biker subculture and are not necessarily
related to competition in, or control over, illegal markets (Wolf 1991;
Veno 2009; Quinn and Forsyth 2011; Grundvall 2018).

Wolf (1991) argues that interclub rivalries can be explained by four
drivers that are all tied to territoriality. The first is personal pride that
patch holders feel about belonging to the dominant club in an area.
The second is group power. Wolf proposes that the club with the greatest

territorial status will attract the best recruits and be better positioned in interactions with clubs in other territories. The third is the desire to reduce uncertainty in relations between the biker subculture and the host society. By controlling the number of outlaw biker clubs and the behavior of outlaw bikers in its territory, a dominant club can reduce risks of conflict and police harassment. Wolf observes that ordinary citizens tend not to differentiate between biker clubs so that actions of one club affect all outlaw bikers in the area. The fourth driver, securing profits from drug dealing, prostitution, and extortion, is central in journalistic and law enforcement interpretations of biker violence but according to Wolf and other scholars characterizes only some clubs.

On Wolf's argument, symbolic crimes, especially against rival clubs, are in outlaw motorcycle clubs' perceived self-interest. That these crimes happen should be no surprise. This does not rule out the possibility, however, that individual members and cliques within a club sometimes take matters into their own hands.

We discuss links between entrepreneurial crimes and outlaw motorcycle clubs in relation to the bad apple and club within a club scenarios. We caution against hasty assumptions that clubs, or chapters, function as profit-making illegal businesses given that constraints of illegality tend to favor small, fragmented, and inconspicuous structures. A profit orientation is not traditionally an element of the outlaw biker subculture. A shift toward a business model would cause "ideological confusion" (Venkatesh and Levitt 2000, p. 444) about the club's purposes that would likely be exacerbated by a shift in recruitment emphasis from "righteous bikers" to entrepreneurs.

The regulatory function Tremblay, Bouchard, and Petit (2009) ascribe to Hells Angels in the Quebec drug trade is a more likely scenario. By allowing drug dealers to operate under their trademark, outlaw motorcycle clubs extend the protective and intimidating effect of the power of the patch to a wider circle of non–patch holders, thereby lowering their costs of operation and increasing costs for nonaffiliated market participants who lack alternative backing. To the extent that an outlaw motorcycle club is the only provider of franchised protection, it resembles mafia groups that siphon off a share of the profits generated in illegal or legal markets under mafia control (Schelling 1971; Reuter 1983; Gambetta 1993). Some of the same considerations that make outlaw motorcycle clubs ill-suited to function as illegal businesses may facilitate assumption of a governance function within the underworld.

Outlaw motorcycle clubs have a military potential based on their numbers, who include the members and associates of a given chapter but potentially the entire outlaw motorcycle club. Established clubs tend to be embedded in criminal milieus, which gives them capability to collect intelligence on those who might defy and challenge their power. Their hierarchical structure facilitates processing of intelligence and coordinated responses to challenges. Importantly, they possess a characteristic most underworld competitors lack: recognizability. Groups that seek to provide protection need to advertise their existence and their services and to build and maintain a reputation for effective use of violence (Gambetta 1993). Outlaw motorcycle clubs are visible and distinguishable, which provides a clearer reference point for reputation than clandestine criminal groups can easily achieve. They can easily detect imposters and take drastic measures against unauthorized nonmembers who display club symbols (see, e.g., Christie 2016). In addition, they have established rules and standards for recruitment of new members and leadership succession, which facilitates maintenance of a collective identity and reputation despite fluctuations in membership and generational change (Gambetta 2009).

There is, however, reason to believe that outlaw motorcycle groups' capacity to gain underworld control is limited. To establish dominance, they may have to engage in violent confrontations with less conspicuous groups. Their high visibility and the fixed locations of their clubhouses put them in a distinct disadvantage; they offer much easier targets for attack than do their nonbiker opponents.

A number of propositions have been offered about the extent and nature of links between outlaw biker clubs and organized crime. The main emphasis is on crime for profit. It is frequently said that such connections need not exist for all outlaw biker clubs. Some clubs, and some chapters, may not be at all involved in serious crime. Even within a club or a chapter that is notorious for serious criminal involvement, some members may not participate (Wolf 1991; Quinn and Koch 2003; Barker 2015).

One common theme in the academic debate is that outlaw bikers fall into two groups: criminally oriented "entrepreneurs" and "purists" who pursue a deviant lifestyle centered on motorcycling (Quinn and Forsyth 2011, p. 217). Quinn and Koch (2003, p. 283) describe a "continuum of behavioral orientations" and caution that "each club, chapter, and situation is unique and dynamic and requires specific examination."

There is no scholarly consensus about the dynamics of relationships between various orientations. One view is that there are shifts back and forth and the criminal orientation tends to become dominant in times of intense interclub rivalries when illegal profits are needed to cover the costs of gang warfare (Quinn 2001; Barker and Human 2009). Another view is that there is a general trend toward increasing criminal involvement. Veno (2009) suggests that police repression has had a negative selection effect and motivated law-abiding members to quit, thus empowering members with a criminal orientation to shape clubs' and chapters' character.

Piano (2017, 2018), drawing on the economic theory of clubs, interprets organizational changes since the 1970s as indicators of a general transformation of outlaw motorcycle clubs into criminal enterprises. The formation of overarching hierarchical structures, he argues, typically with a mother chapter at the top, has occurred in response to increasing involvement of bikers in the underground economy. At the same time, traditional means of producing group cohesion and loyalty—namely, sacrifice and stigma—may have lost out to economic incentives.

From another perspective, purists and entrepreneurs depend on each other: purists rely on funds generated by entrepreneurs, who in turn depend on "purists" to maintain the cohesion and reputation of the traditional outlaw biker fraternity (Quinn and Forsyth 2011, p. 217; see also Lauchs, Bain, and Bell 2015).

IV. Conclusion

Figure 3 depicted the conventional wisdom about the relative position of outlaw motorcycle clubs, street gangs, and organized crime groups in a two-dimensional space defined by the level of organizational structure and the aims of group members' crimes. Outlaw motorcycle clubs may be more structured as organizational entities than are street gangs or organized crime groups, but this does not mean that the organization of club members' criminal behavior follows the hierarchical logic of the club itself. Links between outlaw motorcycle clubs and crime can be manifold, varying with the degree to which criminal activities and structures overlap with club activities and structures and with the degree of involvement in lifestyle, symbolic, and entrepreneurial crimes. Only under the club as a criminal organization scenario do criminal activities and organizational structure overlap completely. The other scenarios make less use of the organizational structure of the club. Criminal activities under the bad apple scenario fall furthest to the diffused end of the spectrum, as figure 5 shows.

At present, we have no basis for gauging the relative empirical importance of the various constellations. This would require in-depth analyses of a large number of well-documented cases involving a representative sample of outlaw motorcycle clubs. We conclude, however, contrary to conventional media and law enforcement agency portrayals, that motorcycle clubs functioning as illegal businesses in the pursuit of illicit profits is an unlikely scenario. The assumption that biker clubs or chapters operate as criminal organizations is most plausible when criminal activities are closely related to the self-perception and the nature of outlaw motorcycle clubs. This is the case with lifestyle and symbolic crimes, particularly in violent conflicts between biker clubs. Outlaw motorcycle clubs are, however, comparatively well-situated to acquire positions of power in the underworld—for example, in establishing protection systems for illegal drug market entrepreneurs.

Even when outlaw motorcycle clubs as such do not commit crimes, they can contribute to the commission of crimes because of their recruitment of criminally inclined individuals, their deviant subcultures including a code of silence, and the intimidating and protective effects of the power of the patch. In this respect, they have more in common with mafia associations than Hollywood appeal. Like mafias, they provide their

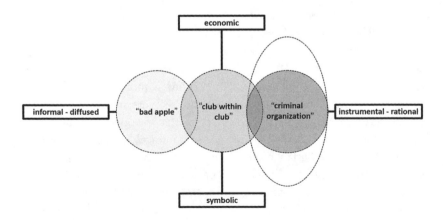

FIG. 5.—Spectrum of organizational structure

members a ritualized sense of brotherhood and protection in the absence of legal recourse. Unlike mafias, however, outlaw motorcycle clubs in most countries seem to lack extensive upperworld alliances; this limits their criminal potential outside the nightlife economy. Outlaw motorcycle clubs' territorial control, when it exists, tends to be limited to the biker subculture and in most countries does not encompass the underworld as a whole or legitimate economic sectors. Despite some mafia-like characteristics, outlaw motorcycle clubs should not routinely be categorized as criminal organizations. Careful case-by-case analyses are needed of the different roles they potentially play in the criminal activities of their members.

Our conclusions have policy and research implications. We endorse Quinn and Koch's (2003) observation that each biker club and each situation needs to be examined separately. Assessments require a differentiated approach that accounts for differences in the prevalence and nature of the crimes committed by bikers, and clubs' and chapters' different roles in relation to these crimes. There is, for example, no clear link between the level of criminal involvement of individual bikers and the degree to which a particular club or chapter can meaningfully be characterized as a criminal organization. Ignoring this can easily lead to excessive or misdirected measures. At the same time, the claim that biker crime is just a matter of bad apples neither withstands empirical scrutiny nor acknowledges that outlaw biker clubs by their very nature can support and shape criminal conduct—for example, through the power of the patch. Policies such as restrictions on public display of club symbols thus can potentially be appropriate crime-reducing measures (Bjørgo 2019), even involving clubs that have no links to crime except through bad apples.

Our most important conclusion is the need for further research. We need better understanding of the inner workings of outlaw biker clubs, of mechanisms and dynamics in the development of individual clubs and chapters, and of the overall outlaw biker subculture. Comparatively little is known about the world of outlaw bikers. The best evidence so far comes from ethnographic research and quantitative analyses of law enforcement data. Both approaches face structural obstacles. Ethnographers must deal with a difficult-to-reach population and with research funding that often imposes strict timetables that are fundamentally at odds with the imperatives and uncertainties of field research. Analysis of law enforcement data depends on the willingness of state agencies to allow access to data. Not surprisingly, quantitative studies typically come from countries that are prominent in organized crime research because their law enforcement communities are generally more research friendly. There is a need for case studies of criminally involved biker clubs, based on interviews with bikers and comprehensive analyses of police intelligence, that can better illuminate the inner workings of outlaw motorcycle gangs in relation to their members' crimes.

REFERENCES

Abadinsky, Howard. 2013. *Organized Crime*. Belmont, CA: Wadsworth.

Adler, Patricia A. 1985. *Wheeling and Dealing: An Ethnography of an Upper-Level Drug Dealing and Smuggling Community*. New York: Columbia University Press.

Ahlsdorf, Michael. 2017. *Alles über Rocker: Die Gesetze, die Geschichte, die Maschinen*. 5th ed. Mannheim: Huber Verlag.

Ahrne, Göran. 1990. *Agency and Organization: Towards an Organizational Theory of Society*. London: Sage.

Alain, Marc. 2003. "Les bandes de motards au Québec: La distinction entre crime organisé et criminels organisés." In *Traité de criminology empirique*, 3rd ed., edited by M. Le Blanc, M. Ouimet, and D. Szabo. Montreal: Les Presses de l'Université de Montréal.

Anderson, Annelise G. 1979. *The Business of Organized Crime: A Cosa Nostra Family*. Stanford, CA: Hoover Institution.

Austin, D. Mark, Patricia Gagne, and Angela Orend. 2010. "Commodification and Popular Imagery of the Biker in American Culture." *Journal of Popular Culture* 43(5):942–63.

Australian Crime Commission. 2012. *Assessment of Organized Crime in Australia, 2011–2012*. Canberra: Australian Crime Commission.

Bain, Andy, and Mark Lauchs, eds. 2017. *Understanding the Outlaw Motorcycle Gangs*. Durham, NC: Carolina Academic Press.

Ball, Richard A., and G. David Curry. 1995. "The Logic of Definition in Criminology: Purposes and Methods for Defining Gangs." *Criminology* 33(2):225–45.

Barger, Ralph "Sonny." 2001. *Hells Angel: The Life and Times of Sonny Barger and the Hells Angels Motorcycle Club*. London: Fourth Estate.

Barker, Thomas. 2007. *Biker Gangs and Organized Crime*. Waltham, MA: Anderson.

———. 2015. *Biker Gangs and Transnational Organized Crime*. Waltham, MA: Anderson.

———. 2017. "Motorcycle Clubs or Criminal Gangs on Wheels." In *Understanding the Outlaw Motorcycle Gangs*, edited by Andy Bain and Mark Lauchs. Durham, NC: Carolina Academic Press.

————. 2018. *The Outlaw Legacy of Violence*. New York: Routledge.

Barker, Thomas, and Kelly M. Human. 2009. "Crimes of the Big Four Motorcycle Gangs." *Journal of Criminal Justice* 37(2):174–79.

Bjørgo, Tore. 2019. "Preventing Organised Crime Originating from Outlaw Motorcycle Clubs." *Trends in Organized Crime* 22(1):84–122.

Bjorngaard, Wenche. 1999. "Le projet Rockers: Les bandes de motards hors-la-loi." *Revue Internationale de Police Criminelle*, nos. 474–75, 23–24.

Blokland, Arjan, and Jeanot David. 2016. "Outlawbikers voor de rechter: Een analyse van rechterlijke uitspraken in de periode 1999–2015." *Tijdschrift voor Criminologie* 58(3):42–64.

Blokland, Arjan, Melvin Soudijn, and Eric Teng. 2014. "'We zijn geen padvinders' Een verkennend onderzoek naar de criminele carrières van leden van 1 percent-motorclubs." *Tijdschrift voor Criminologie* 56(3):1–28.

Blokland, Arjan, Wouter Van der Leest, and Melvin Soudijn. 2018. *Profielen van Nederlandse outlawbikers en Nederlandse outlawbikerclubs*. Apeldoorn: Politie & Wetenschap.

————. 2019. "Officially Registered Criminal Careers of Members of Dutch Outlaw Motorcycle Gangs and Their Support Clubs." *Deviant Behavior*. https://doi.org/10.1080/01639625.2019.1619422.

Blokland, Arjan, Lonneke Van Hout, Wouter Van der Leest, and Melvin Soudijn. 2019. "Not Your Average Biker; Criminal Careers of Members of Dutch Outlaw Motorcycle Gangs." *Trends in Organized Crime* 22(1):10–33.

Bouchard, Martin, and Richard Konarski. 2013. "Assessing the Core Membership of a Youth Gang from Its Co-offending Network." In *Crime and Networks: Criminology and Justice Series*, edited by Carlo Morselli. New York: Routledge.

Bouchard, Martin, and Carlo Morselli. 2014. "Opportunistic Structures of Organized Crime." In *The Oxford Handbook of Organized Crime*, edited by Letizia Paoli. New York: Oxford University Press.

BRÅ. 1999. *Mc-Brott: BRÅ-rappport 1999:6*. Stockholm: Brottsförebyggande rådet.

Bruinsma, Gerben, and Wim Bernasco. 2004. "Criminal Groups and Transnational Illegal Markets: A More Detailed Examination on the Basis of Social Network Theory." *Crime, Law, and Social Change* 41(1):79–94.

Burgwal, Leo. 2012. *Hells Angels in de Lage Landen*. Hoofddorp: Sanoma Media BV.

Caine, Alex. 2009. *The Fat Mexican: The Bloody Rise of the Bandidos Motorcycle Club*. Toronto: Random House.

Catino, Maurizio. 2014. "How Do Mafias Organize? Conflict and Violence in Three Mafia Organizations." *European Journal of Sociology* 55(2):177–220.

Cheloukhine, Serguei, and Maria R. Haberfeld. 2011. *Russian Organized Corruption Networks and Their International Trajectories*. New York: Springer.

Cherry, Paul. 2005. *The Biker Trials: Bringing Down the Hells Angels*. Toronto: ECW Press.

Christie, George. 2016. *Exile on Front Street: My Life as a Hells Angel . . . and Beyond*. New York: Thomas Dunne.

Chu, Yiu Kong. 2000. *The Triads as Business*. London: Routledge.

Cornish, Derek, and Ronald V. Clarke. 2002. "Analyzing Organized Crimes." In *Rational Choice and Criminal Behavior: Recent Research and Future Challenges*, edited by Alex R. Piquero and Stephen G. Tibbetts. New York: Routledge.

Curry, G. David. 2015. "The Logic of Defining Gangs Revisited." In *The Handbook of Gangs*, edited by S. H. Decker and D. C. Pyrooz. Malden, MA: Wiley.

Decker, Scott H., Tim Bynum, and Deborah Weisel. 1998. "A Tale of Two Cities: Gangs as Organized Crime Groups." *Justice Quarterly* 15(3):395–425.

Decker, Scott H., and G. David Curry. 2000. "Addressing a Key Feature of Gang Membership: Measuring the Involvement of Young Members." *Journal of Criminal Justice* 28(6):473–82.

Decker, Scott H., Charles M. Katz, and Vincent J. Webb. 2008. "Understanding the Black Box of Gang Organization: Implications for Involvement in Violent Crime, Drug Sales, and Violent Victimization." *Crime and Delinquency* 54(1):153–72.

Decker, Scott H., and David C. Pyrooz. 2014. "Gangs: Another Form of Organized Crime?" In *The Oxford Handbook of Organized Crime*, edited by Letizia Paoli. New York: Oxford University Press.

———. 2015. "Street Gangs, Terrorists, Drug Smugglers, and Organized Crime: What's the Difference?" In *The Handbook of Gangs*, edited by S. H. Decker and D. C. Pyrooz. Malden, MA: Wiley.

De Hoogh, Michael. 2017. "Afgezet in bad standing, de vrees van elk motorclublid." *Panorama*, no. 2, January 11–18, 2017.

Densley, James A. 2012. "The Organisation of London's Street Gangs." *Global Crime* 13(1):42–64.

———. 2014. "It's Gang Life, but Not as We Know It: The Evolution of Gang Business." *Crime and Delinquency* 60(4):517–46.

Department of Justice. 2019. "Federal Jury Orders Mongols Motorcycle Gang to Forfeit Logos," January 11. https://www.justice.gov/usao-cdca/pr/federal-jury-orders-mongols-motorcycle-gang-forfeit-logos.

Dulaney, William L. 2006. "Over the Edge and into the Abyss: The Communication of Organizational Identity in an Outlaw Motorcycle Club." PhD dissertation, Florida State University.

Edwards, Peter. 2012. *The Bandido Massacre: A True Story of Bikers, Brotherhood and Betrayal*. Toronto: Harper Perennial.

Europol. 2005. *EU Organized Crime Report*. The Hague: Europol.

Farrant, Finola. 2016. *Crime, Prisons, and Viscous Culture: Adventures in Criminalized Identities*. London: Palgrave Macmillan.

Federal Bureau of Investigation. 2009. *National Gang Threat Assessment 2009*. Washington, DC: National Gang Intelligence Center.

———. 2015. *National Gang Report 2015*. Washington, DC: National Gang Intelligence Center.

Felson, Marcus. 2003. "The Process of Co-offending." In *Crime Prevention Studies*, vol. 16, edited by M. J. Smith and D. B. Cornish. Monsey, NY: Criminal Justice Press.

———. 2006. *Crime and Nature*. Thousand Oaks, CA: Sage.

Fuglsang, Ross S. 2001. "Framing the Motorcycle Outlaw." In *Framing Public Life: Perspectives on Media and Our Understanding of the Social World*, edited by Stephen D. Reese, Oscar H. Gandy Jr., and August E. Grant. New York: Routledge.

———. 2002. "'The Meek Don't Win': Easyriders and the Construction of Biker Community." Paper submitted to the Midwest Popular Culture Association annual conference, October 4–6, Milwaukee.

Gambetta, Diego. 1993. *The Sicilian Mafia: The Business of Private Protection*. Cambridge, MA: Harvard University Press.

———. 2009. *Codes of the Underworld: How Criminals Communicate*. Princeton, NJ: Princeton University Press.

Geurtjens, Kim. 2019. "Busting Outlaw Bikers: The Media Representation of Outlaw Motorcycle Gangs and Law Enforcement in the Meuse Rhine Euregion." SSRN. https://doi.org/10.2139/ssrn.3418513.

Geurtjens, Kim, Hans Nelen, and Miet Vanderhallen. 2018. "From Bikers to Gangsters: On the Development of and the Public Response to Outlaw Biker Clubs in Germany, the Netherlands, and Belgium." In *Outlaw Motorcycle Clubs and Street Gangs: Scheming Legality, Resisting Criminalization*, edited by Tereza Kuldova and Martín Sánchez-Jankowski. Cham: Palgrave Macmillan.

Goldsworthy, Terry, and Laura McGillivray. 2017. "An Examination of Outlaw Motorcycle Gangs and Their Involvement in the Illicit Drug Market and the Effectiveness of Anti-association Legislative Responses." *International Journal of Drug Policy* 41(1):110–17.

Gomez del Prado, Grégory. 2011. "Outlaw Motorcycle Gangs' Attempted Intimidation of Quebec's Police Forces." *Police Practice and Research: An International Journal* 12(1):66–80.

Gould, Roger V. 2003. *Collision of Wills: How Ambiguity of Social Rank Breeds Conflict*. Chicago: University of Chicago Press.

Gravel, Jason, Blake Allison, Jenny West-Fagan, Michael McBride, and George E. Tita. 2018. "Birds of a Feather Fight Together: Status-Enhancing Violence, Social Distance and the Emergence of Homogenous Gangs." *Journal of Quantitative Criminology* 34(1):189–219.

Grundvall, Stig. 2018. "Inside the Brotherhood: Some Theoretical Aspects of Group Dynamics in Biker Clubs." In *Outlaw Motorcycle Clubs and Street Gangs: Scheming Legality, Resisting Criminalization*, edited by Tereza Kuldova and Martín Sánchez-Jankowski. Cham: Palgrave Macmillan.

Haller, Mark H. 1992. "Bureaucracy and the Mafia: An Alternative View." *Journal of Contemporary Criminal Justice* 8(1):1–10.

Hallsworth, Simon, and Tara Young. 2008. "Gang Talk and Gang Talkers: A Critique." *Crime Media Culture* 4(2):175–95.

Harris, Kira. 2020. "Russia's Fifth Column: The Influence of the Night Wolves Motorcycle Club." *Studies in Conflict and Terrorism* 43(4). https://doi.org/10.1080/1057610X.2018.1455373.

Hartmann, Arthur, and Klaus von Lampe. 2008. "The German Underworld and the Ringvereine from the 1890s through the 1950s." *Global Crime* 9(1–2):108–35.

Heitmüller, Ulrike. 2014. "Die Rolle der IT im Kampf gegen Kriminalität." *C't Online*, June 13. https://www.heise.de/ct/artikel/Die-Rolle-der-IT-im-Kampf -gegen-Kriminalitaet-2219502.html.

Hobbs, Dick. 1989. *Doing the Business: Entrepreneurship, the Working Class, and Detectives in the East End of London*. Oxford: Oxford University Press.

Hoiland, Sarah L. 2018. "'Impromptu Fiesta' or 'Havoc in Hollister': A Seventy-Year Retrospective." *International Journal of Motorcycle Studies* 14. https:// motorcyclestudies.org/volume-14-2018/impromptu-fiesta-or-havoc-in-hollister -a-seventy-year-retrospective-sarah-l-hoiland.

Hopper, Columbus B., and Johnny Moore. 1990. "Women in Outlaw Motorcycle Gangs." *Journal of Contemporary Ethnography* 18(4):363–87.

Houghton, Des. 2014. "Queensland's Outlaw Motorcycle Gang Members Are Overwhelming Criminals with Serious Convictions." *Courier Mail*, May 2. http://www.couriermail.com.au/news/queensland/queenslands-outlaw-motor cycle-gang-members-are-overwhelming-criminals-with-serious-convictions /story-fnihsrf2-1226903844876.

Ianni, Francis A. J. 1975. *Black Mafia: Ethnic Succession in Organized Crime*. New York: Simon & Schuster.

Interpol. 1984. *Motorcycle Gangs*. Lyon: ICPO Interpol General Secretariat.

Katz, Karen. 2011. "The Enemy Within: The Outlaw Motorcycle Gang Moral Panic." *American Journal of Criminal Justice* 36(3):231–49.

Kleemans, Edward R., and Christianne J. de Poot. 2008. "Criminal Careers in Organized Crime and Social Opportunity Structure." *European Journal of Criminology* 5(1):69–98.

Klein, Malcolm W., and Cheryl L. Maxson. 2006. *Street Gang Patterns and Policies*. New York: Oxford University Press.

Klement, Christian. 2016*a*. "Crime Prevalence and Frequency among Danish Outlaw Bikers." *Journal of Scandinavian Studies in Criminology and Crime Prevention* 17(2):131–49.

———. 2016*b*. "Outlaw Biker Affiliations and Criminal Involvement." *European Journal of Criminology* 13(4):453–72.

———. 2019. "Outlaw Biker Violence and Retaliation." *PLoS ONE* 14(5): e0216109.

Klement, Christian, Britta Kyvsgaard, and Maria L. Pedersen. 2011. *Rockere, bander og risikofactorer*. Copenhagen: Danish Ministry of Justice.

Klement, Christian, and Maria L. Pedersen. 2013. *Rockere og bandemedlemmers kriminelle karrierer og netværk i ungdommen*. Copenhagen: Danish Ministry of Justice.

Korsell, Lars, and Paul Larsson. 2011. "Organized Crime the Nordic Way." In *Crime and Justice in Scandinavia*, edited by Michael Tonry and Tapio Lappi-Seppälä. Chicago: University of Chicago Press.

Kuldova, Tereza. 2017. "Hells Angels™ Motorcycle Corporation in the Fashion Business: Interrogating the Fetishism of the Trademark Law." *Journal of Design History* 30(4):389–407.

Langton, Jerry. 2010. *Showdown: How the Outlaws, Hells Angels, and Cops Fought for Control of the Streets*. Mississauga: Wiley.

Lauchs, Mark. 2019a. "Are Outlaw Motorcycle Gangs Organized Crime Groups? An Analysis of the Finks MC." *Deviant Behavior* 40(3):287–300.

———. 2019b. "A Global Survey of Outlaw Motorcycle Gang Formation." *Deviant Behavior*. https://doi.org/10.1080/01639625.2019.1630217.

Lauchs, Mark, Andy Bain, and Peter Bell. 2015. *Outlaw Motorcycle Gangs*. New York: Palgrave Macmillan.

Lauchs, Mark, and Zoe Staines. 2019. "An Analysis of Outlaw Motorcycle Gang Crime: Are Bikers Organised Criminals?" *Global Crime* 20(2):69–89.

Lavigne, Yves. 1989. *Hells Angels: "Three Can Keep a Secret If Two Are Dead."* New York: Kensington.

———. 1997. *Hells Angels: Into the Abyss*. New York: Harper.

Lupo, Salvatore. 2015. *The Two Mafias: A Transatlantic History, 1888–2008*. New York: Palgrave Macmillan.

Mallory, Stephen. 2012. *Understanding Organized Crime*. Burlington, MA: Jones & Bartlett.

Marsden, William, and Julian Sher. 2007. *Angels of Death: Inside the Biker's Empire of Crime*. Toronto: Vintage Canada.

McBee, Randy D. 2015. *Born to Be Wild: The Rise of the American Motorcyclists*. Chapel Hill: University of North Carolina Press.

McGuire, Phillip C. 1987. "Outlaw Motorcycle Gangs: Organized Crime on Wheels (Part I)." *National Sheriff* 37(2):68–75.

McNab, Duncan. 2013. *Outlaw Bikers in Australia: The Real Story*. Sydney: Pan Macmillan.

Monterosso, Stephen. 2018. "From Bikers to Savvy Criminals: Outlaw Motorcycle Gangs in Australia; Implications for Legislators and Law Enforcement." *Crime, Law, and Social Change* 69(5):681–701.

Morselli, Carlo. 2009. "Hells Angels in Springtime." *Trends in Organized Crime* 12(2):145–58.

———. 2010. "Assessing Vulnerable and Strategic Positions in a Criminal Network." *Journal of Contemporary Criminal Justice* 26(4):382–92.

Morselli, Carlo, Dave Tanguay, and Anne-Marie Labalette. 2008. "Criminal Conflicts and Collective Violence: Biker-Related Account Settlements in Quebec, 1994–2001." In *Organized Crime: Culture, Markets, and Policies*, edited by Dina Siegel and Hans Nelen. New York: Springer.

Nossen, Richard. 1975. *Report of the National Conference on Organized Crime, October 1–4, 1975, Washington, Part 3*. Washington, DC: Law Enforcement Assistance Administration.

Organized Crime Consulting Committee. 1986. *Report of the Organized Crime Consulting Committee*. Columbus: Ohio Attorney General.

Paoli, Letizia. 2003. *Mafia Brotherhoods: Organized Crime, Italian Style*. New York: Oxford University Press.

Paoli, Letizia, Victoria A. Greenfield, and Peter Reuter. 2009. *The World Heroin Market: Can Supply Be Cut?* New York: Oxford University Press.

Pennsylvania Crime Commission. 1991. *Organized Crime in Pennsylvania: A Decade of Change*. Conshohocken: Pennsylvania Crime Commission.

Perlman, Allison. 2007. "The Brief Ride of the Biker Movie." *International Journal of Motorcycle Studies* 3. https://web.archive.org/web/20180424011040/http://ijms.nova.edu/March2007/IJMS_Artcl.Perlman.html.

Piano, Enzio. 2017. "Free Riders: The Economics and Organization of Outlaw Motorcycle Gangs." *Public Choice* 171(3):283–301.

———. 2018. "Outlaw and Economics: Biker Gangs and Club Goods." *Rationality and Society* 30(3):350–76.

President's Commission on Organized Crime. 1983. *Organized Crime: Federal Law Enforcement Perspective; Record of Hearing I, November 29, 1983.* Washington, DC: US Government Printing Office.

Puzo, Mario. 1969. *The Godfather.* New York: G. P. Putnam's Sons.

Quinn, James F. 2001. "Angels, Bandidos, Outlaws, and Pagans: The Evolution of Organized Crime among the Big Four 1 Percent Motorcycle Clubs." *Deviant Behavior* 22(4):379–99.

Quinn, James F., and Craig J. Forsyth. 2011. "The Tools, Tactics and Mentality of Outlaw Biker Wars." *American Journal of Criminal Justice* 36(3):216–30.

Quinn, James, and D. Shane Koch. 2003. "The Nature of Criminality within One-Percent Motorcycle Clubs." *Deviant Behavior* 24(3):281–305.

Reuter, Peter. 1983. *Disorganized Crime: The Economics of the Visible Hand.* Cambridge, MA: MIT Press.

Reynolds, Tom. 2000. *Wild Ride: How Outlaw Motorcycle Myth Conquered America.* New York: TV Books.

Roks, Robby, and Teun Van Ruitenburg. 2018. "Dutch Gang Talk: A Reflection on the Use of the Gang Label in the Netherlands." In *Outlaw Motorcycle Clubs and Street Gangs: Scheming Legality, Resisting Criminalization*, edited by Tereza Kuldova and Martín Sánchez-Jankowski. Cham: Palgrave Macmillan.

Rostami, Amir, and Hernan Mondani. 2019. "Organizing on Two Wheels: Uncovering the Organizational Patterns of Hells Angels MC in Sweden." *Trends in Organized Crime* 22(1):34–50.

Sampson, Robert J., and John H. Laub. 1997. "A Life-Course Theory of Cumulative Disadvantage and the Stability of Delinquency." In *Developmental Theories of Crime and Delinquency*, edited by T. Thornberry. Piscataway, NJ: Transaction.

Sánchez-Jankowski, Martín. 2018. "Gangs, Culture, and Society in the United States." In *Outlaw Motorcycle Clubs and Street Gangs: Scheming Legality, Resisting Criminalization*, edited by Tereza Kuldova and Martín Sánchez-Jankowski. Cham: Palgrave Macmillan.

Schelling, Thomas C. 1971. "What Is the Business of Organized Crime?" *Journal of Public Law* 20(1):69–82.

Schutten, Henk, Paul Vugts, and Bart Middelburg. 2004. *Hells Angels in opmars: Motorclub of misdaadbende?* Utrecht: Monitor.

Seate, Mike. 2000. *Two Wheels on Two Reels: A History of Biker Movies.* North Conway, NH: Whitehorse.

Silverstone, Dan, and Philip Crane. 2017. "Mapping and Conceptualizing Organized Motorcycle Gangs: The British, German, and Spanish Experience." In

Understanding the Outlaw Motorcycle Gangs, edited by Andy Bain and Mark Lauchs. Durham, NC: Carolina Academic.

Smith, Bruno W. 1998. "Interpol's 'Project Rockers' Helps Disrupt Outlaw Motorcycle Gangs." *Police Chief* 65(9):54–56.

Smith, Doris Jean. 1990. *Reference Groups and Ritualistic Behavior: A Cultural Perspective on Addiction*. San Bernadino, CA: CSUSB ScholarWorks.

Smith, Richard C. 2002. "Dangerous Motorcycle Gangs: A Facet of Organized Crime in the Mid-Atlantic Region." *Journal of Gang Research* 9(4):33–44.

Southerland, Mittie, and Gary W. Potter. 1993. "Applying Organization Theory to Organized Crime." *Journal of Contemporary Criminal Justice* 9(3):251–67.

Spurgeon, David Charles. 2011. *Bikin' and Brotherhood: My Journey*. Nashville: Nelson.

Stanfield, Peter. 2018. *Hoodlum Movies: Seriality and the Outlaw Biker Film Cycle, 1966–1972*. New Brunswick, NJ: Rutgers University Press.

Thompson, Hunter S. 1966. *Hell's Angels: The Strange and Terrible Saga of the Outlaw Motorcycle Gangs*. New York: Random House.

Thornberry, Terence P., Marvin D. Krohn, Alan J. Lizotte, and Deborah Chard-Wierschem. 1993. "The Role of Juvenile Gangs in Facilitating Delinquent Behavior." *Journal of Research in Crime and Delinquency* 30(1):55–87.

Tremblay, Pierre, Martin Bouchard, and Sevrine Petit. 2009. "The Size and Influence of a Criminal Organization: A Criminal Achievement Perspective." *Global Crime* 10(1):24–40.

Tremblay, Pierre, Sylvie Laisne, Gilbert Cordeau, Angela Shewshuck, and Brain MacLean. 1989. "Carrieres criminelles collectives: Evolution d'une population delinquante (groups de motards)." *Criminologie* 22(2):65–94.

United States Attorney for the Eastern District of Pennsylvania. 1984. "Press Release." *Congressional Record-Senate*, August 1, p. 21819.

Van den Heuvel, John, and Bert Huisjes. 2009. *De Gevallen Engel. Een Man tegen de Hells Angels*. Utrecht: House of Knowledge.

van Gemert, Frank, and Frank Weerman. 2015. "Understanding European Gangs." In *The Handbook of Gangs*, edited by S. H. Decker and D. C. Pyrooz. Malden, MA: Wiley.

Venkatesh, Sudhir Alladi, and Steven D. Levitt. 2000. "'Are We a Family or a Business?' History and Disjuncture in the Urban American Street Gang." *Theory and Society* 29(4):427–62.

Veno, Arthur. 2007. *The Mammoth Book of Bikers*. London: Robinson.

———. 2009. *The Brotherhoods: Inside the Outlaw Motorcycle Clubs*. Crows Nest: Allen & Unwin.

von Lampe, Klaus. 2016a. *Organized Crime. Analyzing Illegal Activities, Criminal Structures, and Extra-legal Governance*. Thousand Oaks, CA: Sage.

———. 2016b. "The Ties That Bind: A Taxonomy of Associational Criminal Structures." In *Illegal Entrepreneurship, Organized Crime, and Social Control: Essays in Honor of Professor Dick Hobbs*, edited by G. A. Antonopoulos. Cham: Springer.

————. 2019. "Public Nuisance, Public Enemy, Public Servant? Introduction to the Special Issue on Outlaw Bikers in Europe." *Trends in Organized Crime* 22(1):1–9.

Wethern, George, and Vincent Colnett. 2004. *A Wayward Angel*. Lanham, MD: Rowman & Littlefield.

Wolf, Daniel. 1991. *The Rebels: A Brotherhood of Outlaw Bikers*. Toronto: University of Toronto Press.

Wood, John. 2003. "Hells Angels and the Illusion of the Counterculture." *Journal of Popular Culture* 37(2):336–51.

Yates, Brock. 1999. *Outlaw Machine: Harley-Davidson and the Search for the American Soul*. New York: Broadway Books.

Zabyelina, Yuliya. 2019. "Russia's Night Wolves Motorcycle Club: From 1 Percenters to Political Activists." *Trends in Organized Crime* 22(1):51–65.

Mike Levi and Melvin Soudijn

Understanding the Laundering of Organized Crime Money

ABSTRACT

Four conditions influence the complexity of organized crime money laundering. First are diverse types of crime and forms in which proceeds are generated, including the type of payment, the visibility of crimes to victims or authorities, and the lapse before financial investigation occurs (if it does). Second, the amount of individual net profits causes differences between criminals who have no use for laundering, who self-launder, and who need assistance from third parties. Third are the offender's goals and preferences in spending and investing crime proceeds. Investments are often close to home or country; some opt to wield power, but much is freely spent on a hedonistic lifestyle. Fourth, expected and actual levels of scrutiny and intervention of the anti–money laundering regime influence saving and reinvestment decisions and some arrests and confiscations, but there is no clear cause-and-effect relationship. The four conditions can intertwine in numerous ways. When conditions necessitate or stimulate more complex laundering schemes, this is reflected not only in techniques but also in social networks that emerge or are preconditions. Complex cases often depend on the assistance of professionals, outsiders to the criminal's usual circle, who are hired to solve particular financial and jurisdictional bottlenecks.

Money laundering can be carried out in many ways, ranging from simple to complex, with numerous variations in laundering costs, and includes a

Electronically published March 6, 2020

Michael Levi is professor of criminology in the School of Social Sciences, Cardiff University. He is grateful for support from the UK Economic and Social Research Council's Transnational Organised Crime Research. Melvin Soudijn is a senior researcher, National

wide range of participants, from elite professionals to homeless addicts acting as "front people" for business and property holdings (Reuter and Kleiman 1986; Levi and Reuter 2006; Caulkins and Reuter 2010). To make sense of this diversity, money laundering is commonly explained as a way of hiding the proceeds of crime so that the authorities cannot take it back, and so that offenders can use it to enjoy a more affluent life-style and legitimize themselves and their assets.

Hiding money from the authorities is not something new or recent. From the US Prohibition era to the 1960s, long before the criminaliza-tion of money laundering, Al Capone and Meyer Lansky (and doubtless, others) tried to hide their crime proceeds and distanced their public assets and wealth from the behaviors that gave rise to them in order to reduce their tax payments and criminal vulnerabilities. Especially since the 1980s, when "following the money" and restricting criminals' access to the fruits of their crimes became significant elements of international policy aimed at transnational organized crime, hiding the proceeds of crime evolved into a continuous cat-and-mouse game with the authorities. It is there-fore fair to assume that the more controls over the origins of money that are erected, the greater the need for concealment from licit society. But then again, not every criminal goes to the same lengths to set up trusts and offshore companies to obscure the background of their wealth. So what drives this difference?

One obvious explanation is the volume of profits from crime relative to laundering costs. Setting up trusts and using offshore companies require registration and consultancy fees. A professional advisor is often needed as well. Expenditures can quickly rise to thousands of euros or dollars that eat into the criminal profit. If the criminal profit was small to begin with, efforts at concealment become pointless and cost-inefficient. However, it would be wrong to imagine that, at a certain financial profit point, every criminal of note reaches out to international law firms for offshore financial services, such as the morally and now economically bankrupt Panamanian-based law firm Mossack Fonseca & Co.[1] That simply has not been proven in any literature on money laundering. Likewise, many differences crop

---

Police of the Netherlands, and a research fellow of the Netherlands Institute for the Study of Crime and Law Enforcement. We are grateful to Peter Reuter, Michael Tonry, and anonymous referees for their comments.

[1] For more background information on the type of dubious services and clients Mossack Fonseca & Co. provided, see https://www.icij.org/investigations/panama-papers.

up when comparing criminals involved in organized crime, who supposedly make more money than ordinary street criminals. Most spend large amounts of cash on a hedonistic lifestyle, use a basic loan-back construction in which crime money is supposedly "lent" by a close relative, or start a fictitious turnover scheme in which illegal profits are commingled with the turnover of a legitimate business. Only a few take the Panamanian route, so to speak, and set up complex money laundering schemes.

This leaves us with a puzzle. We know that organized crime activities are for a large part carried out with the goal of making a financial profit. These illicit proceeds in turn intertwine with the structures and everyday life of licit society: spending for leisure activities, buying or investing in real estate, setting up businesses, and corrupting the authorities. But what are the conditions that influence the level of complexity of money laundering, and to a lesser extent its patterns, in relation to organized crime?

The answer to this question is the topic of this essay. In Section I, we go deeper into the concept of money laundering, which we explore using two different approaches, an economic and a legal one. Both have pros and cons.

In Section II, we construct a conceptual framework of factors that affect the need for, and use of, money laundering schemes by criminals involved in organized crime. Each factor is illustrated with several examples. Our analytical framework finds its roots in crime scripting and situational crime prevention; that is to say, we view certain conditions as having known effects on the incidence and forms of money laundering. In Section III, we move from technical complexity to social complexity by including the need for outside help provided by professional money launderers. We conclude with a general discussion that raises as yet unanswered questions about the effects of measures on both laundering and crimes committed by the loosely denotated and still controversial concept "organized crime." One final preliminary observation: some readers will notice that most of the literature and examples that we use come from the Global North, especially Europe. This is because European research on money laundering, compared with other parts of the world, has been able to make systematic use of court files or to gain access to police investigations in regard to organized crime. This makes for a detailed reality that is absent from money laundering research that solely focuses on legal aspects, international frameworks, or normative policy recommendations using evidence bases whose analytical or empirical weaknesses are seldom acknowledged.

I. Background

The literature on money laundering generally can be divided into two different types of approach, an economic approach and a legal one. Each has strengths and weaknesses.

In the economic approach, the focus lies on how the criminal money ends up in the legal economy. This is usually explained by use of a three-stage model that has been promoted by US agencies since the 1980s and subsequently integrated into international agencies' and anti–money laundering (AML) training cultures: placement, layering, and integration (e.g., Schott 2003; Dean, Fahsing, and Gottschalk 2010).

Placement is the introduction of criminal proceeds into the financial system. This can be done, for example, by depositing cash or transferring money via money remittance bureau to foreign or domestic bank accounts, thus transforming cash into banked assets. Layering is creating a distance between the unlawful origins of the money in order to give it the appearance of legitimacy, for example, by using loan backs ("borrowing" your own money against the security of funds already deposited in a foreign personal or business account), fictitious turnover schemes (commingling illegal profits with the turnover of a legitimate business), front companies, shell corporations, and other financial constructions. This leads to the final phase, integration, in which the disguised criminal proceeds are spent or invested in the legal economy at home or abroad. Note that for some international offenders, there can be a split national affiliation between countries of residence and of origin, so whether investment of proceeds is at "home or abroad" is not always self-evident.

Others have added to this model by including a preliminary stage that precedes placement. This could happen, for instance, when cash is physically smuggled abroad, or exchanged for other currencies before it is deposited into the financial system.

Although the three-phase model is widely used, it can be criticized for several shortcomings. We point out five types of "flaws" that sometimes make the model less of a proper fit to reality.

First, not all three phases need to come into play. When financial fraud, for instance, results in the fraudulent transfer of legitimate money into the criminal's (often nominee or fake identity) accounts, the proceeds of crime are already in the financial system. They therefore do not need to be "placed." Placement and layering can also be skipped when cash is used to purchase assets directly, though if they are purchased in a third-party name, this might be viewed as layering.

Second, the model suggests there is a sequential "law" in which criminal money always ends up integrated in the legal system. In reality, however, criminal money does not always need to be laundered and integrated (Soudijn 2016). Though organized crime may be primarily about generating money, it seems to be taken for granted that many organized criminals are not also in business to have a "good time," but are all committed to a Protestant-ethic aim of saving and of integration into respectability. To put it differently, a chaotic lifestyle of leisure consumption that revolves around casinos, nightclubs, and brothels can be paid for in cash. This is a form of integration, but it is not usually what policy makers might have in mind, and it does not fit the model of threatening the virtue of the licit world of finance and economy.

Third, the origins of cash (or of cryptocurrencies) do not matter in the criminal underworld in which illicit transactions abound. Especially in an organized crime (or paramilitary) context in which many people have regularly to be paid maintenance "wages," the proceeds of crime can directly be used to pay off accomplices or to invest in new criminal ventures, such as the financing of a new shipment of cocaine. Van Duyne (2002) refers to an "aquarium economy," an underground environment in which fishy criminal money keeps circling around and never enters the legal system. Besides, criminal cash sometimes gets taken out of both the illegal and legal economy altogether. House searches of organized criminals occasionally turn up hundreds of thousands or even millions of dollars or euros that are apparently stashed away for a rainy day behind false walls, hidden floorboards, or in the attic or under the bed. We do not know to what extent hoarding is an artefact of the need to avoid real or feared anti-money laundering controls or whether such offenders would have kept the money close even absent any such controls. For example, they might be concerned about the need for a quick getaway with their crime proceeds, whether from the authorities or from rival criminals.

A fourth criticism of the three-phase model is that it was developed in the early 1980s for the fight against drug smuggling and thereby overemphasizes the role of cash. At that time, principally all drug sales were made in cash, not touching the financial system. However, other crimes such as many fraud schemes, or the use of technological financial innovations like cryptocurrencies, completely sidestep the use of cash, which in any case is in decline as a proportion of transactions, especially in the Global North (Riccardi and Levi 2018) but also in the Global South, with the rise of electronic payments systems and mobile phone banking, such as the m-Pesa in East Africa.[2] Use of cash is also avoided by trade-based money laundering (TBML), the process of disguising and moving value through the use of legitimate transactions in physical goods or in services, often by electronic manipulation of value (FATF 2006, 2008; APG 2012).[3]

Fifth, the model also runs the risk of "ingenuity fallacy"; the situation is imagined to be more complex than it really is (Felson and Boba 2010). This is observable when the model is explained with the use of complex money laundering cases. Accompanying illustrations feature the offices of banks or trust agencies, shares, yachts, or private jets based in luxurious offshore tax havens. This gives the impression that money laundering is a very complicated matter, routinely carried out by professionals from the financial service industry and therefore best handled by investigators with a degree in accountancy. In reality, most money laundering investigations carried out by tax authorities or police investigators are quite straightforward and do not necessarily involve financial specialists. We are not arguing that these complex cases are fictitious; our concern is that they distort the perception of the phenomenon by ignoring the large number of simpler cases.

A final criticism of the three-phase model is that it fails to capture evolution in the workings of AML practices. The US Presidential Commission on Organized Crime (1986) merely recommended pursuit of criminal money "as a powerful lever" to attack its somewhat narrow vision of organized crime, without going into any more detail; meanwhile, the criminalization of money laundering has since resulted in a global system of similar, functionally equivalent legislation and institutions not envisaged in the original analytical model, which was aimed at the domestic US financial system.[4] This is not a normative criticism, but the reshaping

[2] See also https://fas.org/sgp/crs/misc/R45716.pdf. Cryptocurrencies can be spent only in outlets that will accept them, which at the time of writing is a quite limited range. Cryptocurrencies are therefore often exchanged for fiat currencies or cash in a later stage of the money laundering operation. The proportion of illicit market purchases that are laundered in cryptocurrencies is unknown but, though rising, unlikely to be dominant for some time.

[3] Sometimes these trades are fictitious, which means that in principle their existence can be falsified after financial and documentary investigation. Given scarce resources, such investigations are unlikely to happen in practice unless they are an accompaniment to major frauds.

[4] Functional equivalence is an OECD Anti-Bribery Convention concept that focuses attention on the work that rules do rather than on their form: so countries are not required to *criminalize* corporate responsibility if civil or administrative mechanisms exert similar control effects. Current AML laws are based on the 1988 UN Convention against the

of the control process is an object of study in its own right, for criminologists and sociolegal and international relations scholars.

This leads us to the second approach to money laundering, the legal one. International legal standards—whose importance and harmonizing influence have been growing this century, due to the efforts of the Financial Action Task Force (FATF), created in 1989, and corollary developments in regions such as the EU—construct money laundering generally as:[5]

1. The conversion or transfer of property, knowing that such property is derived from criminal activity or from an act of participation in such activity, for the purpose of concealing or disguising the illicit origin of the property or of assisting any person who is involved in the commission of such activity to evade the legal consequences of his action.
2. The concealment or disguise of the true nature, source, location, disposition, movement, rights with respect to, or ownership of property, knowing that such property is derived from criminal activity or from an act of participation in such activity.
3. The acquisition, possession, or use of property, knowing, at the time of receipt, that such property was derived from criminal activity or from an act of participation in such activity.

In other words, depending on the particularities of the jurisdiction's legislation, a person is guilty of money laundering if he or she knowingly receives, possesses, or uses money (or other properties) generated by any criminal activity, or if he or she actually did suspect or even reasonably could have suspected the money's criminal origins.[6] Furthermore, persons who participate in, associate to commit, attempt to commit, and aid, abet, facilitate, and counsel on money laundering matters can also be prosecuted.

Illicit Traffic in Narcotic Drugs and Psychoactive Substances (the Vienna Convention); the 2000 UN Convention on Transnational Organized Crime (the Palermo Convention); FATF recommendations (2013, 2018); and five (and rising) EU Directives commencing in 1991 (e.g., 91/308EC; 2001/97/EC).

[5] Following S.3(1)(a) of the Vienna Convention and European Council Directive 91/308/EEC of 10 June 1991 on prevention of the use of the financial system for the purpose of money laundering.

[6] Although some countries debate whether the proceeds of foreign tax evasion should also fall under this provision, and others such as the UK have legislated to make it so, making due diligence tasks for customers challenging for regulated persons and institutions.

The offense of laundering does not rely on whether the actions effectively legitimize the funds or were intended to do so.

Based on this broad legal outline of money laundering, a global system for a risk-based approach became institutional practice (Halliday, Levi, and Reuter 2014; Nance 2018). This resulted in ever more standardized scrutiny according to compliance regulations, extensive Customer Due Diligence and Know Your Customer procedures, alertness and Enhanced Due Diligence for Politically Exposed Persons (public officials and their families, both domestically and elsewhere in the world), and the filing of Suspicious Activity Reports (SARs; in some jurisdictions called Suspicious Transaction Reports [STRs], and in Australia, Suspicious Matter Reports).

The enormous reach of the legal definition—stretching from the transnational 'Ndrangheta to burglars putting proceeds of crime into their bank account in their own name—makes it unhelpful as a coherent category of activity. It is for this reason we opt to approach money laundering from an economic perspective, that is, how does money derived from organized crime activities interact with the legal economy? However, we also put the three-phase model aside because of its many drawbacks. Instead, influenced by crime scripts and routine activities models, we keep a careful eye for the conditions that influence the level of complexity and patterns of money laundering, in relation to organized crime.

II. Conceptual Framework

We join the framers of the United Nations Convention against Transnational Organized Crime 2000 and national legislators in sidestepping the problem of defining organized crime with any serious clarity. For our purposes, it is not relevant whether criminal funds are derived from South American cartels smuggling drugs, mafia members extorting business owners, white-collar criminals committing planned frauds or tax crimes, or major corporations involved with grand corruption or environmental crimes. All of these sources of crime proceeds can sometimes involve committing "organized crime" offenses when they are carried out with multiple persons over longer periods of time, though the latter crimes are only sometimes undertaken by "organized crime" groups in the sense of "full-time criminal bodies" as conventionally understood in media, police, and political parlance. Besides, the very considerable rise of fraud—especially online fraud—as a mode of crime commission in contemporary societies has muddied the classical distinction between organized and white-collar crime. Readers should fit the particulars of what they deem organized crime cases into our framework, bearing in mind that strong images of respectable business or professional firms can disarm "suspiciousness" of transactions and erect conscious or unconscious barriers to police and other investigations. Nevertheless, in practice, our examples are taken from activities and personnel that we suspect most people would regard as "organized crime."[7]

It is a mistake to associate money laundering only with the *criminal* law risks to offenders. Though purchasers of illegal commodities are not victims in the same sense that blackmail and fraud victims are, victims of "organized crime" and third parties with legal standing (including governments and bodies such as the Stolen Asset Recovery Initiative [StAR][8]) may pursue civil litigation against suspected offenders without needing to overcome mutual legal assistance difficulties (including prosecutorial resistance in the home countries of kleptocrats), and with adjudication based on criteria slightly lower than the criminal law burden of proof in a criminal court. Taking into account civil litigation and regulatory risks as well as prosecution, laundering needs only to be as sophisticated and complex as the control process forces it to be. To allow for this diversity in money laundering needs, we take as our point of departure a general crime script and routine activities perspective.

Crime scripting is a research tool that is used for detailed, sequential analyses of specific and precisely defined crime events or criminal activities. To develop a crime script, the crime itself is thoroughly deconstructed and reduced to its individual components or scenes (Cornish

---

[7] This is a nontrivial issue. In some countries, the links between politics, business, and suppliers of criminal services are close, and ideas about criminals subverting polities require refinement. Current allegations about EU countries, whether early members such as Italy, or more recent ones such as Bulgaria, Hungary, Malta, and Romania, illustrate how controversial and empirically contested such constructions of "organized crime" as "outsiders" can be, even in advanced economies with supposedly equivalent systems of governance. For a "strong" perspective on these threats, see Shelley (2014, 2018). In a study for the European Parliament, Levi (2013) calculates very different costs of organized crime in Europe, depending on whether the construct is one of mafia-type groups only, or of this plus the much looser networks that comply with the low threshold of EU and UN criteria for organized crime. This essay does not require the resolution of this issue, but denotation issues are difficult to escape.

[8] StAR is a partnership between the World Bank Group and the United Nations Office on Drugs and Crime that supports international efforts to end safe havens for corrupt funds. The UK has much-heralded civil Unexplained Wealth Orders that permit alleged proceeds of corruption abroad to be frozen and forfeited, but there were only four cases (involving many accounts) from 2018 to the end of 2019. See https://fcpablog.com/2019/11/20/uks-new-freeze-and-seize-powers-upheld-in-moldovan-money-laundering-case/.

1994). Each individual component has its own characteristics, which in turn can provide insights into how the crime comes together. Thus, an illegal drugs manufacturer and trafficker has to be able to accomplish the stages of obtaining precursor chemicals, making the drugs, finding markets, and transporting the goods. These insights are important because crime scripting is intended for developing a hands-on approach to crime. An accurate script makes it possible to develop interventions that diminish or prevent criminal opportunities or incentives (Felson 2004).

A preventative approach in which crime scripts are used has its history in theories about routine activities "theory," problem-oriented policing, and situational crime prevention. The latter has established a systematic body of work, which shows that crime prevention is achieved by keeping motivated offenders away from suitable targets at specific times and spaces or by increasing the presence of "capable guardians." For a mental road map, various types of crime interventions are arranged across a five-pronged approach: increasing the effort, increasing the risks, reducing the rewards, reducing provocation, and removing excuses (Felson and Clarke 1998; Bullock, Clarke, and Tilley 2010; Tilley and Sidebottom 2017).

A straightforward application to organized crime and money laundering, however, turns out to be more complicated, especially in relation to guardianship (Von Lampe 2011; Kleemans and Soudijn 2017). While the presence of others who might stop the crime or report offenders has strong discouraging effects on ordinary crimes, in a money laundering context, guardians such as bankers, lawyers, and auditors may simply be hurdles that must be overcome by sidestepping the particular individuals or disarming potential suspicions. Some whom we would term "money guardians" may be knowingly and willingly corrupt, some may be coerced into helping, and others may be innocent. However, even innocent potential guardians in financial settings are not primarily on the lookout for signs of misconduct, since their raison d'être and profit lie in serving their clients. Except for customers coming in with large cash-filled bags marked "swag," or people known (during the account take-on process required by AML regulations) to have modest jobs and backgrounds suddenly transacting in anomalously large sums or volumes, it is often not obvious whether requests for service are legitimate or criminal. In countries that include lawyers and accountants in money laundering reporting requirements, even if the professionals are suspicious, some may be concerned primarily about whether *they* will be punished for breaching their duties rather than whether there is reasonable suspicion that a crime has been committed by a current or potential client.

This is not to say that it is impossible to use crime scripts and situational prevention techniques in relation to organized crimes. Even organized crimes can and need to be reduced into smaller subsections. For instance, human trafficking can contain subsections on recruitment, travel, housing, and accommodation of the victims. Likewise, a crime script of synthetic drug trafficking could start early in the chain with the procurement of essential precursors needed much later (Chiu, Leclerc, and Townsley 2011; Vijlbrief 2012).

This slight detour about crime scripts brings us back to our main point. All crimes for economic gain that generate more profit than can be spent or readily stored physically require a separate crime script on how the financing and proceeds of crime are handled. After all, the leading, though not the only, motive for carrying out organized crime activities is to make a profit. How such laundering is carried out depends on local circumstances and changes from crime to crime, from criminal group to criminal group, and from country to country. Writing the generic money laundering crime script therefore is not empirically or theoretically defensible (though see Gilmour [2014] for an attempt). Even so, there are several conditions that affect the level of complexity of money laundering in relation to organized crime in the broadest sense:

1. *Type of crime*, particularly whether primarily cash-generating or generating electronic funds;
2. *Revenue* shows differences between criminals who have no use for money laundering, those who self-launder, and those who need help with laundering;
3. *Offender's goals*, such as individual needs and preferences in regard to financial or other returns from criminal investments;
4. *Anti–money laundering regime*, such as expected and actual levels of scrutiny and intervention.

A. Type of Crime

The first factor in our framework is in what type of crimes the organized crime group is involved. As explained below, different types of crime have different financial aspects, including the type of payment, the need to pay people extraterritorially, the visibility of the crimes to victims or to the authorities, and the elapsed time before financial investigation occurs (if it ever does).

Whether criminal proceeds come in cash, electronic form (including cryptocurrencies), or barter changes the approach route to the possible money laundering process. When the proceeds are in cash, for example, the average AML regime will impose some constraints on spending and investment habits. In high-income, OECD (Organisation for Economic Co-operation and Development) economies, especially in expensive areas, a house, for instance, nowadays is rarely bought with cash.[9] Criminal cash therefore needs to be converted to electronic form, after which it can be transferred.[10]

Some types of crime generate benefits only in the form of cryptocurrencies. For instance, the trade on the dark web in restricted medicines, drugs, stolen credit cards, or ransomware schemes are all paid for with cryptocurrencies. This has its own advantages in regard to concealment, but also has its own detours for conversion into the ownership of our hypothetical house (Kruisbergen et al. 2019). Fraud offenses, by contrast, normally generate proceeds of crime that are already in the financial system and are thus more easily moved around to finance a purchase, for example via a mortgage backed by offshore assets that are proceeds of crime, to make the purchase look less suspicious.

Long-term nonfungible investments like houses may have to withstand serious investigation at some stage over lengthy periods if they are not to risk confiscation. Rigged bids for public works are even better, in that the contracts are paid by the government and thus generate a paper trail that seems above suspicion: the nonperformance or inferior performance of the contract is not routinely visible, especially if quality inspectors are paid off.

---

[9] Although exceptions exist. For instance, in the US in 2015, 53 percent of all Miami-Dade home (and 90 percent of new home) sales were made with cash—double the national average (McPherson 2017). In Canada, large proportions of real estate (and luxury cars in British Columbia and Ontario) were purchased for cash; see https://www.macleans.ca/economy/realestateeconomy/b-c-s-money-laundering-crisis-goes-national/.

[10] Although buying a house without any mortgage at all can by itself raise questions. The average homeowner borrows money from a bank to finance the purchase of real estate, unless they can show or plausibly claim that they are buying from the proceeds of a previous sale or an inheritance. European lawyers and notaries would normally ask for the source of funds and be expected to check on what they are told, though all may not investigate with equal diligence or forensic skill.

Different types of crime have differences in their visibility to others as crime. Some crimes, such as the trade in child online sexual exploitation, are completely and clearly illegal from beginning to end though the consumption and production of the images are concealed. Other crimes take place in grey areas. VAT (value-added tax) fraud, for example, usually becomes a crime only after the fraudulent filing of incorrect tax returns, unless there is forensic evidence of planning before the attempt is completed. Forcing women into prostitution is human trafficking, but when the sex work takes place openly in legal brothels or red light districts, customers and municipal auditors are not always aware, and may not want to know or care, that the labor is involuntary. Furthermore, when legal work is partly supplemented by illegal labor, for example in high cash-flow businesses such as bars and restaurants, it becomes easier to commingle legal and illegal money. As a result, it becomes less clear which part of generated profits is legal and which is criminal.

Another problem is that different jurisdictions hold different interpretations about certain types of "crime."[11] Tax crimes (not tax avoidance) constitute a good example. Declaring a false tax return results in a financial profit for the fraudster, namely the amount due not paid. Because tax evasion is a criminal offense in many jurisdictions, an increasing number of countries argue that any willfully unpaid taxes are the proceeds of crime and thereby are equated to money laundering. The FATF formally separately includes fraud and tax "crimes" on direct or indirect taxes in its list of predicate crimes. When unpaid taxes are moved abroad, this can become a problem for the prosecution when the receiving country does not consider tax evasion a crime and therefore is unwilling to exchange

[11] According to the FATF (https://www.fatf-gafi.org/glossary/d-i/), *designated categories of offenses* means: participation in an organized criminal group and racketeering; terrorism, including terrorist financing; trafficking in human beings and migrant smuggling; sexual exploitation, including sexual exploitation of children; illicit trafficking in narcotic drugs and psychotropic substances; illicit arms trafficking; illicit trafficking in stolen and other goods; corruption and bribery; fraud; counterfeiting currency; counterfeiting and piracy of products; environmental crime; murder, grievous bodily injury; kidnapping, illegal restraint and hostage-taking; robbery or theft; smuggling (including in relation to customs and excise duties and taxes); tax crimes (related to direct taxes and indirect taxes); extortion; forgery; piracy; and insider trading and market manipulation. When deciding on the range of offenses to be covered as predicate offenses under each of the categories listed above, each country may decide, in accordance with its domestic law, how it will define those offenses and the nature of any particular elements of those offenses that make them serious offenses.

information that is needed to prosecute these offenders.[12] However, parallel routine tax information exchange has become more common due to political pressure on "secrecy havens." It can also be difficult for bankers and lawyers to form a suspicion as to whether deposited funds are the proceeds of foreign tax evasion: a predicate crime in the UK, for example, but not everywhere.

Different types of crime also result in differences in the frequency with which criminal proceeds are generated. Some crimes generate a continuous flow of daily or monthly illicit proceeds, whereas others are one-time events that follow no discernible pattern. Take for example the difference between forced prostitution and wholesale cocaine trafficking. A Dutch investigation into human trafficking found that prostitutes were forced to earn a daily minimum of at least 1,000 euros, six days a week. Other organized crimes that continuously bring in money are loan sharking and protection money. Conversely, a cocaine smuggler who organized the shipment of hundreds of kilos of cocaine needed weeks of preparation to arrange fake cargo, shipping manifestos, and other paperwork. When all was arranged, he had to wait another couple of weeks for the transatlantic freighter to dock in the harbor, offload his cargo, and unpack it in a warehouse in order to sell the cocaine for a profit of 3,000–5,000 euros a kilo.

The difference between receiving numerous small sums regularly, and tens or even hundreds of thousands of euros intermittently and irregularly, leads to different money laundering dynamics. Small amounts of cash can be commingled with, say, the daily turnover of a bar. But to launder a single large sum of money needs better planning in order not to raise suspicion. Of course, the money can also be commingled with the turnover of a bar or tattoo or beauty parlor, but it would need discipline and much more planning, and one bar or restaurant might not be enough to plausibly account for the turnover level if investigated by law enforcement.

In some countries, drug trafficking generates vast volumes of cash that need to be laundered. According to FinCEN (2005), over $120 million

---

[12] Switzerland considered the fraudulent filing of accounts in Switzerland as a crime, but not the "evasion" of taxes without active falsification: since 2016, "serious tax crimes" in both direct and indirect taxation have become predicate offenses for money laundering. Switzerland defines tax fraud leading to tax evasion of more than CHF300,000 in a year as a serious tax crime. Assisting foreign tax evasion remains legal unless it involves forging documents and similar complicities.

from illicit drug sales in the US were smuggled in bulk into Mexico over 3 years for the Arellano-Felix "gang," which were then brought back into the US by declaring the currency in the name of the currency exchange houses in Mexico, therefore concealing the illicit origin of the funds. The currency was deposited into US bank accounts held in the name of the currency exchange companies. Maybe to make the money trail harder to follow, money from these accounts was wire transferred to bank accounts around the world, after which the trail went cold or was not publicly pursued.

B. Revenue

The second factor in our general framework is the amount of revenue organized crime generates and, more importantly, the net profit of individual crime members. Both lack dependable estimations.

Revenues are important as a component in a claim to official attention, but they tend to receive little attention in claims of effectiveness of controls. While official documents concerning money laundering or organized crime often confidently mention the scale of global or national money laundering (e.g., according to the UNODC, 2.7 percent of global GDP)—what van Duyne and Levi (2005) term "facts by repetition"—academic experts are more reserved.

This cautious attitude is not mere academic pedantry but because all methods used to estimate the size and scale of the criminal economy and money laundering have serious flaws (Reuter 2013; van Duyne, Harvey, and Gelemerova 2019). Furthermore, just as in the licit economy, there is economic inequality and wealth concentration among organized criminals (van Duyne and De Miranda 1999; UNODC 2011). Many have subsistence or immediate lifestyle incomes, and others get sums so large that even if they are highly hedonistic, they would find it difficult to spend and are forced to save and launder. The extent to which they need or want to do so is highly dependent on the position of the individual in the organized crime network. In general, the crime boss or leading organizer will make more than key personnel ("lieutenants") or outside experts (professional money launderers), who in turn will make more than interchangeable accomplices (couriers and transporters, local "enforcers," straw men). It is therefore likely that organized crime is typically characterized by a highly unequal distribution of wealth, but valid numbers are not available. In transnational activities, questions are seldom asked about who in which countries takes the predominant share of profits from crime.[13]

Generally, a distinction can be made between persons who have little use for money laundering, those who self-launder, and those who need help in doing so (Malm and Bichler 2013). The first two groups are generally considered very large compared with the third. Levitt and Venkatesh (2000) found that most drug dealers who worked at street level earned just above minimum wage and would have been better off *financially* serving hamburgers at a fast-food restaurant. A telltale sign was that most foot soldiers also held part-time jobs in the legitimate economy. Likewise, as shown by Reuter et al. (1990), approximately two-thirds of Washington, DC, drug dealers reported being legitimately employed at the time of their arrest. This suggests that their illegal profits were supplements to licit earnings. Only a few gang leaders were able to earn high economic returns (Venkatesh 2008).[14] For this reason, global or national estimates about crime revenues are—apart from their methodological errors—unsuitable for our framework. Without a sense of the number of participants who share the criminal profits, and the apportionment of these profits, it is not clear what meaning or value estimates of total sums laundered have, beyond showing that this is a "very big problem."

Because of lack of dependable statistics on criminal revenue, let alone their aggregate profits, net of costs including corruption, we have to make do with other sources such as official proceeds of crime confiscation, case studies, and interviews, although none are really satisfactory.

In an ideal administrative world, confiscation of legal assets in criminal cases signals what an individual can be proven to have gained in illicit proceeds.[15] A database of confiscation cases paired with type of offenses could thus inform us of the total illicit amount and the type of asset. However,

---

[13] There is no criminological equivalent of the Gini country inequality measure in economics.

[14] Levitt and Venkatesh (2000) explained the involvement of street-level dealers as playing the long game, hoping to be able to rise someday to the top and finally earn a large illegal income. But perhaps it sometimes may just be that criminals are around in their environment, and involvement in crime offers some degree of social conformity and a feeling that they are more important than they would otherwise be in the licit precariat economy. The *Homo economicus* model neglects the pleasure that people derive from crime (Katz 1988; Levi 2008) and also from exercising power and taking risks in licit business.

[15] Though some regimes allow for this to be done on civil burdens of proof, others by reversing the burden of proof postconviction in relation to the sources of income, and others still require in practice the linking of confiscated assets to proven crimes.

as a Transcrime (Savona and Riccardi 2015) research project on the portfolio of organized crime in Europe showed, this is easier said than done. First, there is a wide range of confiscation regimes in different states. Some assets are eligible for confiscation in one country, whereas it is impossible to recover the same assets (or data about them) in another. Second, most countries do not adequately record confiscation. This makes it impossible to produce solid statistical analyses.

There is also substantial attrition between court orders and confiscation. When Kruisbergen, Kleemans, and Kouwenberg (2016) examined 102 Dutch cases in detail, the initial public prosecutor's claims totaled €61,928,210, but this was reduced to €27,463,899 (44 percent) at the end of the court procedure, of which only €11,325,036 (41 percent, or 18 percent of the original claims) was eventually collected. There are similar findings in Australia and the UK (Goldsmith, Gray, and Smith 2016; Chaikin 2018; Levi 2018; see also Sittlington and Harvey 2018).

Another way of establishing the amount of revenue and individual net profits is to study individual offenders and their money laundering habits by analyzing their court or police files. However, gaining access to this kind of material can be quite hard, and in some countries even impossible. Furthermore, many police investigations lack financial details. The reason is that most investigations on crimes that are organized are focused on the predicate crimes. Generally, as soon as a shipment of cocaine is intercepted, a protection racket is dismantled, or human trafficking is stopped and the perpetrators are arrested, the investigation is considered to be a success. In turn, evidence of the predicate crimes is enough to obtain a conviction. Because financial information on money laundering will seldom, depending on the country and other evidence available, add substantially to the length of the prison sentence, it is simply not needed in court. Or worse, including charges of money laundering could delay the entire prosecution when assets need to be traced abroad via slow international mutual legal assistance requests. Conversely, when an investigation starts from a money laundering angle, the predicate crimes may not be needed (depending on both law and judicial interpretation). It is rare for the two (predicate crime and financial data) to come together.

Insights can also be gained by approaching organized crime participants themselves. However, organized criminals who launder money are difficult to reach. They are unlikely to fill in questionnaires or respond en masse to fieldworkers: talking about money is much more dangerous than talking about past misdeeds that have been punished already, are past their statute of limitation period, or are impossible to prove because of lack of evidence. Criminal money, and the way it was laundered, however, is almost indefinitely subject to confiscation. Talking about riches might also attract unwanted attention from criminal predators. That is not to say that it is impossible to carry out interviews about criminal money, but generally this will be because of good rapport between subject and researcher and reveal little about the overall picture unless the interviewee is a central or nodal figure.

A notable exception is the Matrix Knowledge Group (2007). Researchers were able to talk to 222 drug offenders in UK prisons about drug markets and financial profits. It turned out that their money laundering methods were generally not sophisticated. However, the researchers note that this may reflect self-selection. "Dealers with more sophisticated money laundering approaches may have been reluctant to volunteer" (Matrix Knowledge Group 2007, p. 40). Alternatively, such dealers might more rarely have been caught!

A replication in the Netherlands encountered the same problems (Unger et al. 2018). Although the study was much smaller ($N = 25$ with a response rate of 56 percent), the information gleaned was not illuminating. Most had hardly any experience with complicated money laundering methods. Tellingly, an advocacy group of ex-prisoners did not want to cooperate with the interviewers because talking about money was "not done," and fear of confiscation would preclude any meaningful talks. Trying to get a university project on board that worked with former tax frauds also led to nothing (Unger et al. 2018). Several attempts were made to interview the ex-offenders but were not successful. This led to the conclusion that fear of asset confiscation prevented talks about money and spending habits. Interviewing lawyers also led to nothing. They were not "inclined" to talk (one would guess in the abstract) about the financial position of their clients. Interviews with bank employees also elicited no information. Banks had no legal mandate or permission, for fear of criminal liability for "tipping off," to divulge how suspected criminals spent their money; their focus, which may have shifted due to changes in public-private cooperation in the UK, was largely on cash that criminals tried to put in their accounts.

Finally, a focus group study by Sittlington (2014) of ex-offenders from Northern Ireland largely confirmed other studies' findings about high spending by offenders and prosecutors going after low-hanging fruit and being reluctant to prosecute stand-alone laundering cases. The special circumstances of strong paramilitary influences in Ireland differ from those in many other countries, though the Irish peace process may have led not so much to less organized crime but to the replacement of the collective paramilitary fund with largely personal benefits.

C. Goals

The third factor in our general framework is what organized criminals seek to accomplish with their criminal proceeds. Because interviewing organized criminals about their illegal income proved not very fruitful, we should look at how they spend their money and try to infer goals from behavior (see also Fernández Steinko 2012).

Several studies show that, like average personal budgets, criminal expenses can be sorted in the usual categories, albeit with some over-the-top spending habits (van Duyne 2003; Matrix Knowledge Group 2007). There are small daily household expenses for food like groceries, variable payments for utility bills, clothing, and hobbies, next to fixed costs like insurance, car leases, rents or mortgages, and larger outlays such as buying a new car or a house or setting up a company (or for that matter, financing new criminal activities). Some studies (van Duyne 2013; Savona, and Riccardi 2015) have looked at official confiscation records and describe a plethora of cars, motorcycles, boats, houses, jewelry, electronic appliances, fur coats, and the incidental antique work.[16] However, it may have been these very items of conspicuous consumption that drew the attention of the authorities and financial investigators to the criminals in the first place.

What criminals seek to accomplish with these expenditures has been less often investigated. The goal of some is not hard to deduce. Reinvesting in criminal endeavors or financing large sums of money in a conflict

[16] The literature on money laundering can sometimes overemphasize the role of antiquities and art. Occasionally, a crime boss turns out to be a fond collector of expensive paintings and the like. However, art that merely hangs on a wall is not money laundering in an operational sense, though it may count as hiding the proceeds of crime in a legal sense. Only when it is bought with the intention to sell it on in the licit economy does it serve a money laundering function. Furthermore, certain types of white-collar crime offenders (corporate fraudsters, oligarchs, or corrupt public officials) move in different social circles than do most drug dealers and pimps. A house decorated with expensive art may be part of the former group's self-image (and sometimes even a reflection of their taste); the latter group is more likely to be fond of stills from The Godfather (Van Duyne, Louwe, and Soudijn 2014). Nevertheless, small high-value products are appreciated in the event of a need for a quick getaway or forced sale.

with other organized groups (Krakowski and Zubiria 2019) is carried out with the objective of generating future profits, or even survival. Daily household expenditures are motivated by wanting more comfortable living conditions. But lifestyle expenditures, for example, can have complex motives. The criminal who dines out every evening, runs up large casino losses, and spends large sums on gaudy jewelry might do it to satisfy his personal needs, perhaps fill an emotional void, but might also want to project the image of a successful "made man" (BRÅ 2014). Many ordinary bourgeois citizens might avoid such a brash person, but in the criminal environment, flamboyance can deliver the message that here is somebody willing to do extralegal business and who is successful at it. Flashy cars and expensive front row tables at public boxing matches or private boxes at soccer matches can send the same message.[17]

Another way of examining goals of criminal expenditures is to look at larger ones. They can indicate longer-term strategies. Take for example a Dutch study into 1,196 individual investments of convicted organized crime offenders (Kruisbergen, Kleemans, and Kouwenberg 2014). The study distinguished between investments that could fall under a standard economic approach and a criminal infiltration approach.

The standard economic approach, summarized as "profitability," stresses the similarity between organized crime offenders and legal entrepreneurs; both are assumed to make investments based on the aspiration for good economic returns. A difference might be that criminal investments involve additional costs because they need to circumvent the AML regime. This might make it more attractive to invest in opportunities with smaller returns, but lower risks of detection. This in turn is affected by perceptions of invulnerability to official action, which vary over time and place.[18]

Investments that fall under the criminal infiltration approach are summarized as "power" in that organized criminals seek to gain power or

---

[17] We know less about how female organized criminals or launderers behave in equivalent circumstances.

[18] Farfán-Méndez (2019) hypothesizes that drug trafficking organizations with hierarchical structures—understood as structures that process information and acquire knowledge—prefer risk-averse methods, whereas wheel networks tend to use risk-tolerant procedures for laundering money. However, as the author notes, "additional data are needed in order to continue to evaluate the hypothesis" (Farfán-Méndez 2019, p. 308), and we are somewhat skeptical of the evidence base for this to date. It is unclear whether money laundering strategies are decided at the level of the whole drug trafficking organization, or by the individual leader (and as such reflect his psychological preferences), who coincidentally may or may not have proper access to money laundering advisers.

influence in the legal economy. This is also one of the risks the FATF warns about. Criminals might use their profits to acquire control over segments of the local or, especially in smaller jurisdictions, national economy through strategic investments or bribes. A deep angst about money laundering corrupting the integrity of banking and financial services drives much of the AML regime, at least rhetorically.

The Dutch study (Kruisbergen, Kleemans, and Kouwenberg 2014) showed that investments were often made in real estate, for several reasons. First, criminals need a place to live. Second, real estate is generally a safe investment over the long term. Third, prices are not always transparent and can thus be used to launder money, supplementing the official price with money under the counter. Finally, ownership can often be concealed through the use of legal entities. As far as was known, criminals invested on a smaller scale in commercial properties, likely in order to facilitate their criminal enterprises. Investments in legal businesses were largely in the retail and commercial sectors. About half of these companies were used to support "transit crime" activities like drug smuggling. This could be in the form of logistical support (storage or transport), and legitimizing or concealing criminal activity. For instance, a cleaning company could order chemicals used for the production of synthetic drugs, or a fruit or flowers company could order a container from South America in which cocaine was smuggled.

Fernández Steinko (2012) found similar types of investments in Spain. To the extent that such businesses are used for criminal purposes, they are not successful laundering vehicles, though they may provide decent cover for offending unless investigated intensively. Companies could also function as money laundering vehicles, absorbing cash money, hiding ownership, or providing bogus salaries. A pilot study in Italy, the Netherlands, Slovenia, Sweden, and the UK on the infiltration of organized crime in legitimate business developed a model to help understand the type of business at risk (Savona and Berlusconi 2015). Risk (or attractiveness) factors include low level of technology, small company size, low barriers to entry, and weak or developing regulation (Savona and Berlusconi 2015).[19] Establishing or taking over a legitimate company is also part of many fraud-related schemes (Berlusconi 2016).

---

[19] A follow-up study developed a more advanced risk model based solely on firms confiscated from Italian organized crime from 1983 to 2016 (Savona and Riccardi 2018).

However, investments in real estate and commercial properties in the Dutch study (Kruisbergen, Kleemans, and Kouwenberg 2014) did not properly fit the profitability or power approach. Although real estate generally appreciates in value over the long term, hardly any known criminals were building up portfolios in real estate. Properties were mostly used in their immediate day-to-day lives and not leased or rented out. The investments were also not geared to touch the legal financial world in any significant way or to control specific segments of society. This prompted the researchers to come up with another theory, the social opportunity structure, a symbiosis of social network theory and opportunities theory.

Social ties and trust direct a criminal's opportunities for carrying out criminal business and also apply to their choices for investing the proceeds of crime (van Duyne and Levi 2005; BRÅ 2014). Organized criminals whom we know about want to stay close to their investments from a physical and social point of view. They invested in their original home country or their country of residence and seldom held financial assets in areas in which they were not personally involved. These are styled "proximity" investments (Kruisbergen, Kleemans, and Kouwenberg 2014). Savona and Riccardi (2018) mention investments that are culturally close to the organized crime group, such as bikers investing in tattoo shops.

That is not to say that profitability or power never come into play, or that proximity precludes any use of power. Offenders who are not involved solely in transit crime but focus on racketeering could spend more on "power." Organized crime groups in several European countries invest in the construction business and allied areas that entail "more capillary infiltration of the local political, business, and social community" (Savona and Riccardi 2015, p. 157). Sometimes, real investments in property and in the services sector (such as security) offer a route to exploiting and extending local power and deter police intervention.[20] Ponce (2019) recounts how drug trafficking organizations in Mexico illegally finance campaigns of politicians. Organized crime groups in Albania are also reported to invest part of their criminal proceeds in the cultivation of politicians (Global Initiative 2018). Apparently, around the 2017 parliamentary

---

[20] Sometimes other pressures and social objectives—for example, preparing and running a successful Olympic Games or World Cup—may deflect police interventions or give corrupt leaders an excuse for not doing so. This has even been alleged of the "failure" to pursue some London organized criminals prior to the 2012 London Olympics (Gillard 2019).

election in Albania, there was such a large influx of drug money used to influence politics that it affected the exchange rate of the lek (Global Initiative 2018). Many other countries have analogous scandals, not all of them as dramatic as in Mexico or Albania.

Although the criminal investments in the Dutch studies were relatively small on a national level and were not aimed to take over or monopolize segments of business, the local level should also be taken into consideration. Here it was found that some criminals knowingly *and* unknowingly wielded some influence. For example, a local municipality was not eager to target a certain cannabis grower because the legal side of his commercial business employed dozens of people who would otherwise end up on social security (Soudijn and Akse 2012). Some criminals sponsored local football clubs, which in turn enabled these clubs to attract better players (with extra cash paid under the counter). Better players translated to winning more matches and generating more interest in the club. This in turn led to cozy relationships between the football club's managers and sponsors, with representatives from the local government. These things can create an aura of power and untouchability around the offender and their entourage. More generally, a sports club of any kind also offers a relatively safe space where criminal and licit business can be mixed without looking out of place or inherently suspicious.

Bruinsma, Ceulen, and Spapens (2018) reported that a third of Dutch municipalities have encountered "philanthropic" criminals. Case samples showed sponsorship of sports clubs, events, and fundraising activities, and setting up of charities. Some criminals even acted as "informal mayors" in their neighborhoods (see also Campana and Varese 2018). Outlaw motorcycle gangs explicitly used philanthropic activities like visiting children's hospitals and distributing stuffed animals to improve their images (Kuldova 2018).

Philanthropic activities occur in many other parts of the world, albeit on a larger scale. Pablo Escobar is still locally revered for giving money to the poor and stepping in where the authorities had withdrawn (both money and reputation laundering). Italian mafia groups and the yakuza (and some officially designated terrorist groups, e.g., in Pakistan) have been reported to help with relief efforts. These efforts cost little money and need no laundering but generate immense local goodwill while shaming the national government (Kuldova 2018), thus enhancing the comparative legitimacy and "collective efficacy" of the crime group. For white collar criminals, there are other benefits, such as large tax deductions for charitable contributions.[21]

Another mixture of power and proximity sometimes occurs when criminals from ethnic minorities establish business or religious societies within their own communities (Soudijn and Akse 2012). Sometimes they are able to portray themselves as successful and generous businesspeople, which leads to higher standing within the community or even to dealing with the government as a community representative.[22] It is often unclear to what extent ethnic societies are aware of the criminal origins of their affluent members.

In short, although organized criminals' motivations may be more varied than a simple *Homo economicus* model would predict (notably obtaining social standing), achievement of their goals often involves activities that violate money laundering legislation.

D. *The Anti–Money Laundering Regime*

The final component in our framework is the way in which the anti–money laundering (AML) regime is locally carried out. Since 1986, when the US Presidential Commission on Organized Crime recommended a follow-the-money strategy, a plethora of general regulatory and criminal justice measures have been developed to prevent and deter an ever-broadening range of criminals from using the financial system to hide the proceeds of crimes or to finance terrorism or weapons of mass destruction. An important driver of the AML regime is the intergovernmental FATF. This task force, which describes itself on its website as a "policy-making body," has developed a set of "recommendations" (originally in 1990, revised in 1996, 2001, 2003, and 2012) that have become the international standard for combatting money laundering.[23]

The AML regime is in essence one gigantic global and local exercise in attempted situational crime prevention, with most staffing and expenditure costs falling upon the private sector.[24] To use situational crime prevention

[21] Struggles over the acceptance or rejection of philanthropic offers, and past donations by shamed or questionable-background wealthy donors to the prestigious arts and culture bodies and elite universities, is too broad a subject for us to address in this essay.

[22] In a different era, mobster Joseph Colombo (1923–1978) established the Italian-American Civil Rights League to protest stereotypical depictions of Italians as being members of the mafia. At its height, it had a following of over 40,000 people.

[23] See https://www.fatf-gafi.org/about.

[24] The validity of data on compliance costs is difficult to test; they vary over time and place as a function of regulatory risks, but an estimate for AML costs for financial institutions in

parlance, the obligation of banks and other sectors to report unusual or suspicious transactions aims to "increase the effort" by enhancing the level of surveillance applied to commercial transactions. Compulsory measures to report all cash deposits, money transfers, or payments above a certain financial amount[25] are illustrative. Specifically accredited individuals or teams within banks who are allowed to vet certain financial transactions and reject or "de-risk" individual or business customers can be called "access control" operators. All these measures set rules and require training and thus by themselves raise the awareness or remove excuses of those involved.

This is what Garland (1996) termed "responsibilisation," the shifting of the burden of crime control onto the private sector, though Garland wrote about this in relation to mundane crimes. Reporting entities and their employees (e.g., bankers and lawyers) are required to identify their customers and to record and report suspicious (or suspected) transactions and all transactions with high-value dealers in cash above a legally fixed minimum, at risk of prosecution and regulatory sanctions.[26]

Failure to conduct checks or make reports to the national Financial Intelligence Unit (FIU) if suspicions have been aroused results sometimes in large fines, especially if rule breaking can be shown to be intentional or systemic (which may not be desired because of the collateral damage to the bank or to the banking system).[27] To give a few examples, Wachovia

---

North America is $31.5 billion in 2018 (https://risk.lexisnexis.com/insights-resources/research/2019-true-cost-of-aml-compliance-study-for-united-states-and-canada). An earlier study found it to be $28 billion in six countries in Asia (https://www.lexisnexis.com/risk/intl/en/resources/research/true-cost-of-aml-compliance-apac-survey-report.pdf), and another found that average AML compliance costs per financial institution in several continental European countries range from US$17.2 million in Switzerland to US$23.9 million in Germany, totaling an estimated $83.5 billion in Europe (LexisNexis 2017). The businesses regulated by the UK Financial Conduct Authority (FCA 2018) employ at least 11,000 full-time equivalent staff specifically for money laundering and financial crime issues, with a salary bill alone of £650 million per year. These costs do not have to be paid out of taxation directly, but they do have to be paid from the profits of regulated firms.

[25] This minimum varies between countries. In Australia, for example, it is zero at the time of writing.

[26] One of the earliest examples are Italian authorities who noticed in the late 1970s that proceeds of bank robberies funded the activities of the Brigate Rosse; subsequently, Italian banks were required to report large cash deposits. There have been periodic attempts to reduce the variable limits on cash payments in the EU; see Riccardi and Levi (2018).

[27] No breakdown exists of regulatory penalties into "organized crime" and other cases. Penalties are activity measures, not indicators of effectiveness (or the opposite). In our view, AML effectiveness should not be seen in simple binary terms. Penalties imposed in any one year are affected by (sometimes lengthy and multinational) regulatory or criminal

Bank settled in 2010 for US$160 million to resolve allegations that its weak internal controls allowed Mexican cartels to launder millions of dollars' worth of drug proceeds. HSBC Holdings, PLC, agreed in 2012 to pay US$1.9 billion after admitting laundering drug money for Mexican and Colombian drug cartels. Citigroup in 2017 agreed to pay US$97.4 million in a settlement after admitting to criminal violations by willfully failing to maintain an effective AML system. Dutch ING Bank accepted and paid a settlement for €775 million agreed by the Netherlands Public Prosecution Service in 2019 for not acting properly as a gatekeeper to the financial system. According to the settlement agreement, ING had set up their internal compliance system for monitoring transactions in such a way that only a limited number of money laundering signals were generated. Australia's Commonwealth Bank of Australia paid the Australian authorities US$430 million when large numbers of organized criminals exploited the failure to link large frequent (53,750 in total) cash deposits into the bank's "Intelligent Deposit Machines" to its AML system. At the end of 2019, heavy penalties were threatened for Westpac in Australia for 23 million reporting violations, which included some unreported wire transfers in relation to, for example, child sex trafficking in the Philippines.

Fines should be seen in the context of overall profits and of profits from the sorts of activities that were neglected. However, these heavy nominal fines not only pressure the bank to be more compliant but also aim to send a powerful signal to other banks to improve or at least spend more money on their AML departments. Formal regulatory measures have been globally accepted, after initial resistance, by most sections of the private sector (with the exception of the legal profession in some countries, such as Australia, Canada, and the US, which have successfully resisted the legal obligation to report suspicions to FIUs) and have become part of a transnational legal order (Halliday, Levi, and Reuter 2019); these measures aim to universalize controls and create a level playing field against organized criminals.

An important development in flagging suspicious or suspect[28] transactions is the use of big data. Banks, for example, automatically check each

---

investigations into conduct that may have occurred years previously. Fifty-eight AML penalties were handed down globally in 2019, totaling US$8.14 billion, double the amount, and nearly double the value, of penalties handed out in 2018, when 29 fines of $4.27 billion were imposed (https://www.encompasscorporation.com/blog/encompass-aml-penalty-analysis-2019/).

[28] Because "suspicious" implies that there is something in the transaction that reveals something inherently suspicious/criminal, whereas "suspected" simply signals that a cognitive judgment has been made by the observer (Gold and Levi 1994; Levi and Reuter 2006).

financial transaction with a multitude of algorithms for divergent behavior. These algorithms are often bought from third-party companies. The use of big data seems well suited to counter money laundering. First, an enormous amount of financial data is generated by the clients, customers, and citizens of private, semiprivate, and public parties. Just think about the number of transactions that banks, money transfer companies, insurers, land/property registration agencies, chambers of commerce, and tax authorities, to name a few, process on a daily basis. Second, financial data are relatively straightforward, easy to code, and have long been digitalized. A specific monetary value in a specific period is transferred or belongs, or appears to belong, to a certain person or organization. Third, because financial transactions are essential for the functioning of society, great pains are taken to avoid errors. Transactions, therefore, match between different partners or systems, and unique identifiers are in place. This makes it relatively easy to combine financial data from different parties, which is one of the preconditions of big data analyses.

Some of the monitoring measures clearly deflect and perhaps even prevent crimes altogether, including frauds against the banking system and other forms of organized crime. Data about this are very seldom available. In the UK, the Nationwide Building Society—the largest, with 15 million customers—closes down 12,000 accounts a year, half of them for suspected "money muling" activities in which genuine accounts are used to push through domestic or foreign proceeds of crime transactions. The mid-sized Santander Bank—with 14 million accounts—alone closes down some 10,800 UK accounts annually because of suspected money muling activity.[29] In 2017, in the UK, 1.15 million account-opening attempts were rejected for financial crime-related reasons.[30] Prima facie, this might suggest that the system is quite good at prevention, though one cannot deduce from these data how many (ill-defined) financial crimes are not prevented from account-opening in the UK (and this proportion may be wildly different elsewhere in the world, where such data are not collected or are unavailable).

[29] Economic Crime—Anti–money laundering supervision and sanctions implementation, Treasury Select Committee HC 2010, Q.692, http://data.parliament.uk/WrittenEvidence/CommitteeEvidence.svc/EvidenceDocument/Treasury/Economic%20Crime/Oral/96630.html.

[30] Economic Crime—Anti–money laundering supervision and sanctions implementation, Treasury Select Committee HC 2010, Q.695, http://data.parliament.uk/Written Evidence/CommitteeEvidence.svc/EvidenceDocument/Treasury/Economic%20Crime/Oral/96630.html.

Garland was identifying a trend in relation to ordinary crimes. However, this trend has turned out to have been an extraordinarily ambitious attempt to impose responsibilities on a uniform global scale. In the US, the reporting entities filed more than 3 million SARs in 2017, against only 150,000 in 1996. In Europe, 1.5 million SARs were filed in 2017 across the then-28 EU member states, almost double the number in 2006. The UK, the Netherlands, Italy, Latvia, and Poland are the top five SAR issuers in Europe. Does this mean that the UK is more effective than the Netherlands, or twice as effective as Italy but nowhere close to the US? Clearly not. In all of these countries (plus Denmark, Estonia, Malta, and Sweden) there have been massive money laundering scandals, connected both to organized crime and to other sorts of offenders such as Russian, African, Middle Eastern, and eastern European oligarchs. Furthermore, it is often not possible to deduce what proportion of SARs relate to organized crime, however defined, or indeed of correctly reported transactions that relate to any type of crime. How would we expect bankers, lawyers, and high-value dealers to know for certain that their clients were criminals or that the transactions were proceeds of crime in general or of particular crimes? The system circumvents this by requiring them to have systems in place, not to know for certain. Nor do we know the number or proportion of transactions that actually related to crimes but that were *not* suspected or, that if suspected, were not reported to the national FIUs, or were investigated only after being reported.[31]

There are many gaps in reporting, both legislatively (e.g., lawyers in many jurisdictions are not obliged to file their suspicions) and in practice. For instance, two reports on casino gambling, real estate, luxury vehicle sales, and horse racing in British Columbia (German 2018, 2019) show widespread evasion of controls in Canada, which only shortly before had been highly praised by FATF for the effectiveness of its controls.[32]

In theory, a stringent AML regime makes it more necessary than a lax one to take serious steps to hide the criminal origins of assets. In reality, it

---

[31] Europol (2017) reports that only 10 percent of suspicious activity reports are further investigated after collection, a figure that is unchanged since 2006. However, even if one accepts that figure as accurate, it understates somewhat the potential value of the data contained in these reports, irrespective of whether further investigations are triggered. It also raises questions about the value of FIUs demanding an ever-increasing number of SARs from professionals, whose lack of follow-up is sometimes deflected by FIU complaints about their low quality; see NCA (2019).

[32] See also Amicelle and Iafolla (2018) for some insights into financial services sector perspectives there and elsewhere.

depends how the AML regime is actually put into practice. Some, arguably most, regimes simply do not have the manpower or resources to go after every indication of money laundering. Hülsse (2008) drew attention to "paper compliance" that camouflaged nontargeting of certain types of laundering. For instance, the lack of due diligence requirements by Companies House in the UK, the official register of companies and corporations, has been a significant weakness,[33] albeit one shared by other business registers in the EU and elsewhere.

An experimental study in which potential intentionally dubious customers approached financial intermediaries around the world by email has shown that AML rules are applied less stringently in the UK and, especially, the US, compared with more stigmatized "secrecy havens" such as the British Virgin Islands and Belize, at least to approaches from strangers (Findley, Nielson, and Sharman 2014). To the extent that this is true in practice, it may reflect the differential external pressure that such jurisdictions are under to comply with procedures, including the role of FATF as a political instrument of the Great Powers. A case in point is the race to the bottom spearheaded by financial secrecy and trust laws in South Dakota and Delaware.[34] Money in a South Dakotan trust fund is almost impossible to reach by the authorities because of its protected secrecy status. Furthermore, while well over a hundred countries in the world signed up to the global agreement "Common Reporting Standard," an agreement put in place in order to exchange information on the assets of each other's citizens abroad, the US failed to do so.

How an AML regime is put into practice is also dependent on the level of corruption. Effective monitoring is thereby dependent on the weakest link. Corrupting a guardian of the financial system such as a bank employee helps the criminal to circumvent the measures that the guardian is meant to enforce. Perceptions of corruption can also be important in deterring people from making SARs if they think that clients will get to hear about them from the authorities by leaks, whether in developed or less-developed economies. This applies both to wealthy elites who are or, if identified correctly, should be categorized by regulations as

---

[33] See Transparency International UK (2017) and NCA (2018, p. 38). BEIS (2019) has made some reform proposals in a public consultation aimed at improving levels of vigilance at Companies House and the companies' register. Time will tell whether any postconsultation changes have significant impact.

[34] See https://www.theguardian.com/world/2019/nov/14/the-great-american-tax-haven-why-the-super-rich-love-south-dakota-trust-laws.

Politically Exposed Persons (PEPs), and to other organized criminals who may be suspected of having strong connections to the authorities. In kleptocratic regimes, including some post-Soviet ones but also mafia-influenced countries such as Italy, the concentration of influence and power shapes both law enforcement and business opportunities such as the award of government contracts.

Too much corruption, however, can be unsafe for criminal investments in the long run (Unger, Rawlings et al. 2006; Unger, Ferwerda et al. 2018). Corrupt regimes are unstable and unreliable and are therefore not safe to trust. The more money an organized criminal or corrupt bureaucrat has to lose, the more important it is to get at least a significant amount of it out of the country into financial safe havens.

Initiatives that rank AML effectiveness per country quickly fall short when the data are scrutinized. For instance, the FATF uses a complex system called "Mutual Evaluation Reports" (MERs). The MERs are a kind of lengthy peer review of member states on the level of compliance with its numerous recommendations that, since 2013, have included both technical compliance and an attempt at effectiveness judgments. However, as van Duyne, Harvey, and Gelemerova (2019) noticed, some MERs report the number of investigations, and others report cases solved or only the number of prosecutions; terms have no fixed meaning; statistical management was seriously lacking in many countries; and there is little or no disclosure (and possibly little actual knowledge) of the public- and private-sector cost of carrying out the domestic AML regime. This makes cross-country comparison infeasible, and makes assessment for many single countries difficult.

Nevertheless, countries are ranked according to four scores ranging from Compliant, Largely Compliant, Partially Compliant, or Noncompliant. Although these scores are more subjective than based on statistical processing of data, countries that score especially badly can suffer economic sanctions (also see Sharman 2011; Halliday, Levi, and Reuter 2014; Platt 2015). After criticism, in 2013, of putting too much emphasis on measuring formal legislative and institutional arrangements, the FATF sought to update the MER process but still struggles to work out what data and measures are both relevant and possible (Levi, Reuter, and Halliday 2018). Indeed in late 2019, just prior to its planned visit to Australia, the FATF suspended its follow-up process pending a review of the MER process as a whole.

Another attempt to measure the risk of money laundering around the world is the AML Index that is published by the Basel Institute of Governance. The ranking is based on 14 indicators that include, among others, MERs, the Transparency International Corruption Perception Index, and press freedom (Basel Institute 2018). Notwithstanding glaring weaknesses like Companies House checks on registrations, the AML Index gives the United Kingdom a good score and places it above the United States, Germany, and Japan. But then again, according to this index Dominica, Latvia, and Bulgaria score even better. Here we can see the impact of giving equal weight to countries' MER. Some countries were arguably very strictly evaluated by teams from the International Monetary Fund, while others are evaluated less critically (though perhaps with more procedural legitimacy) by neighboring countries (Halliday, Levi, and Reuter 2014). There is ongoing debate about the appropriate role in National Risk Assessments or MERs of local knowledge (or beliefs) in assessing risks, for example, in informal communities in Africa.

III. Professional Money Launderers and the Supply of Money Laundering Services

There are reams of articles about the legal and technical components of the AML and compliance processes and an increasing amount of material on their international relations components. FATF has been a successful policy entrepreneur. Sociological analysis of the cultures in which compliance operates has been weaker and focused largely on the banking and money remittance systems. Investigative journalism and nongovernmental organization activism have yielded considerable insights into "high end" relations between Global North bankers, oligarchs, and corrupt politicians (Shaxson 2011; Posner 2015; Enrich 2017; Obermayer and Obermaier 2017; Bullough 2018) and, however hard to test their veracity,[35] financial sector memoirs add some insights (Birkenfeld 2016; Kimelman 2017). "Organized crime" in the conventional sense cannot necessarily be recognized in these accounts because it is not clear whether

---

[35] Some cultural criminologists might not accept the relevance or importance of testing veracity. Though a perspective does not have to be shared by others or be "accurate" to be genuinely held, even those who believe that "offender accounts" are important ought to worry about verification problems for "facts" about offending. This is a broad dispute, for which this essay is not the right place.

the labeling process makes bankers' and lawyers' treatment of organized crime funds different and plausibly more rigorous, whether from morality or from pragmatism, in defending themselves and the institution against large fines, risks of prosecution, and reputational damage. Others have studied the role of creative compliance in the interaction between tax evasion and tax planning (McBarnet and Whelan 1999). How professionals now respond to drug merchants and human traffickers bearing cash is less well understood, other than via iconic cases such as HSBC and other publicized banking violations that lie outside conventional criminological discourses.

In other words, we know more about major corporate misconduct cases and their links to culture from sociological and media studies of the financial crisis (e.g., Tett 2010; Luyendijk 2015) than we do about the demimonde or underworld aspects of laundering. This is important because routine activities models require their setting in ordinary interactions and elite commercial law firms, and bankers are as remote from these routines as they are from neighborhood law firms, local retail banks, and money service businesses.

We know little about the supply side of money laundering services (besides criminal and regulatory cases, media exposé cases, and mystery shopping research). Generally speaking, variability exists among offenders in the need for laundering services, and in the resources that different sorts of offenders bring to the table that enable them to dispose of the proportion of illicit income they wish to conserve (Horgby, Särnqvist, and Korsell 2015). Some criminals have the necessary expertise to launder their own illegal profits, whether they be small or large. This is called self-laundering. It is difficult to delineate where particular financial thresholds lie at which a person decides to self-launder or not. It depends on the type of crime, the amount involved, offenders' goals, and the AML regime. Criminals who can execute complicated fraud schemes are likely to be able to self-launder their criminal profits, even if these are quite substantial. Criminals who derive their income from directing drug sales in the street will probably find themselves at a loss when it comes to setting up a complicated international company structure. But as we discussed above, the need for money laundering also depends on the goals to which the criminal money is to be applied and to the rigor of the AML regime. If a criminal wants only to buy a new gold chain at the local jeweler, a simple story about the money being a birthday present might be enough. However, if he wanted to buy a new yacht, a better story and a plausible, if false, paper trail are probably needed. Then again, had the offender lived in a region without an adequate AML regime (or a corrupted or intimidated private or public-sector guardian), a story would not be needed at all.

If self-laundering is not an option, the laundering can be outsourced to facilitators, also known as financial enablers or professional money launderers (PMLs). These are people who, as experts in their field, are contracted with by the criminal to solve particular financial bottlenecks (Kleemans, Brienen, and Van de Bunt 2002; Kruisbergen, Van de Bunt, and Kleemans 2012). A PML is thus not just anyone who assists in money laundering, but somebody who provides an essential service to offenders who want to be able to develop crimes at scale. This is an important distinction from so-called front men or straw men. Such people are useful in many a money laundering scheme, but they are merely signatories to property deeds, vehicle registrations, or company documents. They have no say in the planning or execution of the money laundering scheme itself. In contrast to PMLs, they are easily replaceable. Some front people are random addicts recruited on the street, in prison, or in seedy bars who earn a couple of hundred euros at most. Others are found closer to home, including friends, significant others, and family members (sometimes allegedly without their knowledge).[36] Sometimes, knowingly, unknowingly, or willfully blind, students or fraud victims are recruited personally or via social media as "money mules" to run financial transfers through their legitimately opened bank accounts.[37] They are sometimes told lies about acting for marketing firms or about trouble opening new accounts.

How often PMLs come into play is not clear and depends on local circumstances. Some studies estimate quite low numbers. Analyzing 52 Dutch money laundering convictions involving over €450,000, van Duyne (2003) found only two cases in which PMLs were involved. Based on an analysis of 129 Canadian organized crime networks during 2004–2006, Malm and Bichler (2013) estimated that only 8 percent of drug-market launderers could be classified as PMLs. Reuter and Truman (2004) found that

[36] A study of confiscated firms that belonged to Italian mafia-type organized crime groups showed that female ownership was about 50 percent higher than the national average (Savona and Riccardi 2018). Using spouses and girlfriends as straw women has the advantage of providing them with a seemingly legitimate income (Soudijn 2010).

[37] See https://www.cifas.org.uk/newsroom/new-data-reveals-stark-increase-young-people-acting-money-mules; https://www.europol.europa.eu/newsroom/news/over-1500-money-mules-identified-in-worldwide-money-laundering-sting; https://www.bbc.co.uk/news/uk-england-45797603.

16 percent of people in prison for laundering drug money had no other drug involvement. Other estimates are unsupported.

Though there is no reason why the proportions of PMLs should be similar over time and place, such differences may be attributable in part to how police investigations are carried out (Soudijn 2016). That in itself is influenced by the extent to which money laundering is or is not prioritized by judicial authorities and by their experience in dealing with ambitious and sometimes costly cases when budgets are constrained, either encouraging or discouraging them from taking on similar cases. Van Duyne's low figure can be partly explained by his inclusion of a period when AML legislation was not yet in place in the Netherlands. Another factor influencing investigations is the existence of self-laundering offenses. In some jurisdictions, self-laundering is not a prosecutable offense, which means that criminals are usually targeted through traditional complicity and offenses (and related investigative tools).

Even when money laundering legislation is in place, PMLs can still be overlooked during police, customs, or other law enforcement investigations. This often happens when the focus lies solely on predicate crimes such as large-scale drug smuggling. Considerable efforts are made to intercept or confiscate the smuggled drugs, and when this goal is reached, the case is often deemed a success and closed. In about half of the cases in a Dutch study of 31 case files on large-scale cocaine smugglers (smuggling hundreds of kilos of cocaine on average), one or more PMLs were involved (Soudijn 2014). This high score not coincidentally could be traced back to about half of the cases in which the investigators had also been actively looking for PMLs and had dedicated resources to do this from the earliest planning stages. Levi and Osofsky (1995) noted that financial investigators in the United Kingdom were often brought in at the tail end of investigations for asset recovery rather than being mainstreamed; that is often still the case (Levi 2018). It is therefore likely that the percentage of PMLs in nonfraudulent organized crime activities that generate large-scale profits (over €350,000) could be closer to 100 percent. Forensically, if PMLs are harder to convict, their relative absence in conviction-based data sets is understandable.

A. Classifying PMLs

PMLs can be classified in different ways. Malm and Bichler (2013) point out that there is a difference between PMLs who serve multiple criminal clients, and (in their terms) opportunistic launderers who work exclusively for one person. These latter cases often involve a relationship based on friendship or kinship. From a disruption perspective, little is known about how difficult it is to replace a PML if one is disabled by enforcement, retirement, or assassination.

Another way to classify PMLs is by profession. Several studies mention lawyers, accountants, notaries, real estate agents, and even stockbrokers (Malm and Bichler 2013). In other words, PMLs are mostly active in professions that require some qualifications, or at least have their own professional status. Middleton and Levi (2005, 2015) discuss mainly lawyers who launder the proceeds of their own crimes such as fraud, but also those who launder the proceeds of other people's crimes after mutual attraction through vice or blackmail. They also note that changes in ethical legal culture, financial pressures from commercial deterioration, and ownership of law firms may increase money laundering opportunities and needs. Benson (2018, 2020) analyzed 20 cases between 2002 and 2013 in which lawyers or accountants were convicted of money laundering. The cases demonstrated considerable variation in the actions and behaviors of lawyers that can be considered to facilitate money laundering, and for which professionals can be convicted. These variations related to the purpose of the transactions, the level of financial benefit gained by the professional, and the nature of their relationship with the predicate offender. Acting in the purchase or sale of residential property and moving money through their firm's client account were the most common means by which lawyers were involved with criminal funds. However, the cases also included lawyers who wrote to a bank to try to unfreeze an account; paid bail for a client using what were considered to be the proceeds of crime; transferred ownership of hotels belonging to a client; written a series of profit and loss figures on the back of a letter; and witnessed an email, allowed the use of headed stationery, and provided legal advice for a mortgage fraudster. Four lawyers were involved knowingly and intentionally, but in the majority of cases, there was no evidence of a deliberate decision to offend or of dishonesty on the part of the lawyer. Money laundering enablers therefore are not a homogenous phenomenon, and we should distinguish between professional money laundering and laundering by people with professional status. The culpability of the latter set is heavily disputed by their professional bodies, who regard "professional enablers" as a derogatory term to discredit the legitimacy of both their profession and their arguments against regulation (first author interviews in the United Kingdom, 2016–2019).[38]

Not all PMLs are regulated or qualified professionals. There are several reasons for this. First, some describe themselves using loose terms like *tax adviser* or *financial consultant* that need no formal financial training or regulatory permit to practice. Second, some PMLs originally had a background as a lawyer or notary but had been disqualified because of fraudulent activities. They can no longer act as licensed lawyers or notaries but continue to advise criminals on how to launder their financial gains, even though some of their activities may require involvement by licensed professionals who may or may not be knowing parties to the transactions. Third, a group of PMLs have carved out a financial niche by wiring or physically smuggling large amounts of cash through banking networks (underground, as they held no permit), although greater attention to transaction volumes of customers and "de-risking" (i.e., account closing) may inhibit such efforts over time.

A differentiation can also be made between PMLs whose activities are cash-based and circumvent the legal economy, those who create a false paper trail in the legal economy, and those who solely focus on cryptocurrencies (Soudijn 2019). The last category provides outlets for exchanging fiat currencies into new, virtual coins or vice versa. Exchanging cryptocurrencies by itself is not a criminal offense; however, by deliberately targeting conspicuous clients (and charging a premium compared to normal exchangers), they become part of a money laundering scheme. Or rather, they become money launderers. The premium price charged, if proven to the satisfaction of the court, can be evidence that they knew that the proceeds were illicit.

Because financial investigations in the Netherlands of large-scale cocaine smuggling groups often involved underground bankers, increasing knowledge has been gained about this subgroup. It became apparent that PMLs of this type were largely structured along ethnic lines (Soudijn 2016). Criminal cash that virtually traveled across corresponding accounts often was found in specific Indian, Pakistani, and Afghani networks. Collectively, they are known as *hawala* networks (Jost and Sandhu 2003; Maimbo 2003).[39] Bulk cash smuggling was organized around Colombian,

---

[38] Google and other web platforms that take money for advertising fraudulent companies are also enablers according to the same logic.

[39] The term *hawala* has Arabic roots and means exchange. For more linguistic detail, see Martin (2009).

Mexican, Venezuelan, Chinese, Lebanese, and Israeli networks.[40] In other parts of the world, underground banking is mentioned, for example, in relation to Somalian, Vietnamese, and Tamil communities, although it is less clear how they transported money from organized crime (El Qorchi, Maimbo, and Wilson 2003; Cheran and Aiken 2005; Hernandez-Coss 2005).

Although the structure of each underground banking group had a clear ethnic background, it was observed that they worked together when it was to their advantage and did not discriminate against clients from other nationalities. The underground bankers in the Dutch study not only transferred money but also functioned as escrow accounts, exchanged smaller for larger dominations (and vice versa), changed currencies, and even held criminal savings.[41]

General classification of PMLs can also be made according to the activities or services they provide. The FATF (2018) mentions a number of such specialized services: consulting and advising, registering and maintaining companies or other legal entities, serving as nominees for companies and accounts, providing false documentation, commingling legal and illegal proceeds, placing and moving illicit cash, purchasing assets, obtaining financing, identifying investment opportunities, indirectly purchasing and holding assets, orchestrating lawsuits, and recruiting and managing money mules. This script analysis does not tell us about which actors play multiple or single roles.

Another way to look at the services provided by PMLs is to focus on their specific roles. The FATF (2018) distinguishes eight, although this list should not be considered exhaustive: leading and controlling; introducing and promoting; maintaining infrastructure (e.g., a money mule herder, a person who oversees the deployment of the people who are hired only to transfer or smuggle illicit money); managing documents; managing transportation; investing or purchasing assets; collecting illicit funds; and transmitting funds. PMLs can perform more than one role. The feasibility of using these roles for research or analysis has not been tested.

---

[40] These networks can also use virtual smuggling networks. For example, the NCA (2019) reports about a form of Chinese underground banking called "daigou," which partly makes use of Chinese student accounts.

[41] Passas (1999, 2003) coined the term "Informal Value Transfer Systems" (IVTS) as an alternative to underground banking to emphasize that they provide no services other than the transfer of money. In hindsight, the term IVTS itself is too narrow, as some underground bankers did and do carry out more activities than informally transferring money.

B. Criminal Careers of PMLs

It is a common law-enforcement trope that some close-knit organized groups, for example, those based on religion or race, send younger relatives to study law or accountancy who are subsequently employed by the criminal family as money launderers. But this requires a longevity of vision and commitment to long-term criminality that may be uncommon. It may take many years before a lawyer or accountant is in a position to help an organized crime group, and supervision arrangements within a firm may inhibit the scale of their assistance.

Although little attention has been devoted specifically to PMLs, life-course research shows that criminal facilitators, in general, frequently seem to move lateral entry into organized crime late in their career (Kleemans and De Poot 2008). They come into contact with crime at a later stage in their lives. This "adult onset" does not conform to the stereotypical age-crime curve observed elsewhere in criminological research (Kleemans and Van Koppen 2020). This curve describes a rise in offending during adolescence, followed by a strong and steady decline over the rest of the life course. PMLs are also often different from life-course persistent offenders in that they do not typically engage in antisocial behavior from an early age and remain criminally active later in life. On the contrary, criminal facilitators are generally found to have become criminally active only in their thirties, forties, or later. At that stage of life, they skip the petty crime convictions that make up the typical age-crime career but quickly accumulate a criminal record in relation to organized crime offenses.

One difference between early and late onset is that the usual offender has somewhat limited low self-control due to his young age, and the types of crime typically included in their criminal records are open to anyone. Petty crime, rowdy behavior, and other sorts of public nuisance do not need special skills and planning. Organized crime offenses, by contrast, are not open to anyone but require the necessary contacts (both licit and illicit), trust, and skills (Kleemans and De Poot 2008). That is not to say, however, that the typical organized crime offender is a late starter. Some are born into the right (wrong) kind of family and learn by doing and by example at an early age.

For criminal facilitators, including PMLs, this is generally not the case. They generally became involved in organized crime activities through social ties at later stages in life, albeit by different paths. The connection often happens by chance. Living in the same neighborhood, having mutual friends or encounters in the work place, or enjoying the same hobbies and vices lead to meetings across different walks of life that would not have happened otherwise.

Life events are another type of chance that stands out. These events are life-changing occurrences, often related to financial setbacks like becoming bankrupt or losing a job. For instance, a financial setback can prompt one person to seek out a moneylender and thus become entangled with the criminal underworld. Another person with gambling debts may hear through his social circle about a grey market for currency trading and be asked to become involved. A normally crime-inhibiting life event like marriage can lead to crime when it is into a criminal family and leads to involvement in a father-in-law's illegal business.

One caveat about the late onset of PMLs is that such a conclusion is based primarily on research in relation to Dutch transit-oriented organized crime. It is not automatically applicable to countries with other types of organized crime (and other amounts of revenue, other goals of crime money, and other AML regimes).

C. The Principal-Agency Problem

The financial proceeds of organized crime can be entrusted to a PML to launder when needed. Criminal and launderer come into contact with each other because of a criminal's deliberate search or a chance encounter (e.g., at sporting or vice venues). This launches the PML's criminal career. The question of trust remains puzzling. Why do criminals trust a new acquaintance, perhaps one with financial problems that tempt them into offering criminal services, to do a proper job and not defraud or betray them? How are potential conflicts and tensions resolved?

This type of problem can be approached from the perspective of "principal-agency theory" as developed in the business and management literature (Jensen and Meckling 1976; Ross 1976; Eisenhardt 1989; Kiser 1999). The principal is the party that wants a job done on their behalf, and the agent is the party that is contracted. In the case of money laundering, the criminal who needs money laundered would be called the principal, and the PML the agent.[42]

Principal-agency theory tries to find solutions to so-called agency problems, real and potential conflicts that arise from transactional arrangements.

---

[42] Money laundering agency problems are usually placed in the licit economy. For example, the FIU or a regulator is the principal, and banks which should file SARs become the agents (Araujo 2010; Takáts 2011).

There are two types of agency problems. The first occurs when goals and interests of the agent and principal diverge.

The second occurs when the principal finds it difficult or expensive to verify whether the agent is behaving appropriately (Eisenhardt 1989). In the case of money laundering, this has a circular logic. The PML is hired because of the criminal's lack of money laundering expertise. But how, then, can the principal be sure that the PML is doing an adequate job? Agents might also misrepresent their abilities. Having imperfect knowledge of the action of an agent is called information asymmetry.

In the case of money laundering or any criminal business, there are other challenges not found in legitimate businesses (e.g., the absence of a legal contract enforcement mechanism, the risk of interference from law enforcement, and risks of violence from competitors or the principal). All of these uncertainties and risks increase the potential for disputes and conflicts. To counter agency problems, various mechanisms can be devised to align the interests of the agent with those of the principal. These also fall into two general categories: monitoring and the use of incentives and disincentives.

With monitoring, the principal tries to close the gap of any information asymmetry. A complete closure would mean following the agent every step of the way, but that would cost enormous time and energy. Moreover, when two or more agents are involved, close monitoring becomes logistically impossible. In the legal business world, the principal must rely on such techniques as filing of reports, standardization of tasks, and use of supervisors. In the illegal business world, such solutions are hardly feasible because they leave paper trails. Therefore, a more commonly observed way to solve the agency problem in the illegal business world is through use of financial incentives and physical disincentives.

Financial incentives can be substantial. For instance, a study on the physical smuggling of money made from high-volume cocaine trafficking, using business records of the smugglers themselves, showed that it cost between 10 and 17 percent to transport money from Europe to South America (Soudijn and Reuter 2016). This is considerably more expensive than the 2–4 percent identified in earlier US work for crossing the Mexican border (Farfán-Méndez 2019). For instance, a Colombian underground banker who received one million euros in the Netherlands could charge 12 percent and thus need to deliver only €880,000. But it was also noted that the high prices of the smuggling agents were also partly insurance. If the money was intercepted or lost, the principal was guaranteed delivery at the expense of the agent. Another example of financial incentives can be found in the exchange rates of bitcoins stemming from criminal activities. Less scrupulous exchangers who exchanged bitcoins for cash (or vice versa) offered their services for 7–15 percent to criminals, way above going market rates of 0.25–0.30 percent (Visser 2017). Given the risks of fraud by those running bitcoin exchanges, this could have been both insurance and a technological skills premium.

Agents are also kept in line by disincentives like cuts, fines, or the threat and use of violence. Although money laundering is not usually connected to violence, there are more than enough examples of violent outcomes. Meyer Lansky lived to the age of 81, but others were not so lucky. In 1982, the corrupt banker Roberto Calvi, also called God's banker because of his close ties to the Vatican and his role in its *Banco Ambrosiano*, was found hanging under a bridge in London, with bricks in his pockets, attributed initially by the City of London police to suicide. No doubt coincidentally [*sic*], his secretary Grazielle Corracher fell from a window to her death on the same day. According to public prosecutors in Rome, Calvi was punished by the mafia for substantial losses when his bank went under.

A Dutch money laundering report estimated that one PML a year is killed in the Netherlands and more are wounded (Soudijn 2017). This is a high number for a country with a very low homicide rate. Although violence surrounding money laundering is rare compared to violence surrounding narcotics trafficking, the stakes are just as high—or higher. When money is lost or badly managed, the predicate crimes have been committed for nothing. Patience and understanding can run short and generate further violence or criminal inefficiencies linked to loss of trust and friendship (if any).

When criminal money is successfully laundered and invested in real estate, it is no longer immediately available. This is not always appreciated, sometimes with fatal results, by criminals who become cash-strapped or simply mistrustful. When PMLs are killed (or die from natural causes or accidents), there may be genuine problems for survivors and principals in gaining access to the funds and knowing what belongs to whom in mixed assets. Furthermore, entering the world of money laundering later in life also brings its own dangers. People lacking the street-smarts that most organized criminals possess sometimes become victims of their new environment. They can fall prey to intimidation, and when word gets out that they are handling large amounts of cash, they can become the target of extortion and robberies by rival criminal groups.

IV. Discussion

We set out in this essay to determine the conditions that influence the level of complexity of money laundering in relation to organized crime. This immediately posed the difficulty of defining money laundering. It was resolved pragmatically by focusing not on a (country-variable) legal definition of money laundering but on an economic one: how money derived from organized crime activities interacts with the legal economy. That is not to say that legal definitions are an unimportant object of study. A legal angle can reflect the changes in the politics of lawmaking and monitoring, or the constraints they do or do not pose to criminal, civil, and administrative justice. Evolving legislation has significant effects on mutual legal assistance and extradition because of this (in EU terminology) "approximation" of laws and regulation. Although the number of incoming and outgoing mutual legal assistance requests are usually set out in MERs (as they are a performance indicator for cooperation), their importance in bringing offenders to justice or in reducing organized crime remains underanalyzed, despite rhetorical use of the term *effectiveness*.

Another difficulty in preparing this essay was to differentiate the laundering of organized crime funds from other sources of criminal income, which include tax evasion, grand corruption, and the financing of terrorism. All of these behaviors can involve committing organized crime offenses or at least offenses that are highly organized. In the end, we followed the traditional framework of organized crime, criminal activities carried out with multiple persons over longer periods, rather than focusing on corporations which commit crimes to raise their sales or profits in the context of otherwise lawful activities, or kleptocrats who may receive or extort bribes from overseas corporations and domestic sources. This reflects no judgment about the relative harms of those criminal activities but simply retains consistency with the organized crime theme.

In our framework, we distinguished four important factors (type of crime, revenue, goals, and AML regime) that influence the level of complexity of money laundering in relation to organized crime. The sequence is of no great importance because the four conditions can intertwine in numerous ways. For instance, large illicit proceeds are easier to launder, and hence less complex, when the AML regime has limited coverage or is corruptible. These proceeds of crime might even come about because of corruption, which makes it easier to defraud the state or international bodies such as the EU or overseas aid agencies, or can be reinvested in the political process when all or part of the goal is development of "power."

Depending on the circumstances of the four factors put forward in our framework, money laundering can be carried out in more or less complex ways. Recognizing that this needs further specification, we suggest four categories: no need for laundering, and laundering methods of low, medium, and high complexity. Each level carries several implications for official response.

In the first category, money laundering methods are not needed. Criminal money can be spent in cash in the legal economy without attracting attention and repercussions of the authorities. There are differences in such circumstances across countries. Country A might have lower thresholds in place for buying goods for cash compared to country B. Consequently, investigating such cases should not be too difficult, and could be handled by any local police unit, provided adequate AML laws are in place.

In the second category, only low levels of complexity are needed. Again, the circumstances can vary by country. Drug traffickers in South America and human trafficking gangs in Europe might both have very low levels of laundering complexity. But whereas drug traffickers can circumvent AML regimes because of corruption of banking and criminal justice, human traffickers may not make enough money to necessitate evasion of AML rules beyond cross-border smuggling and can go about just purchasing property in home countries that do not rigorously scrutinize the origins of funds for such purposes. Investigating low levels of complexity again should not tax investigative powers too highly (although corruption is a risk).

In the third category, money laundering becomes harder to detect. The laundering scheme will not be obvious at first glance but will collapse quickly if critically examined. A drug trafficker can commingle illegal proceeds in the daily turnover of an auto repair shop or a restaurant or beauty parlor, but if almost no customers show up, it is not a very robust scheme if investigated competently and reasonably promptly.

Finally, some laundering operations are highly complex and necessitate dedicated investigative teams and accountants which can detect the ultimate beneficial ownership of holdings and trusts. Such cases are often related with fraud offenses but could also be the legacy of having overlooked financial assets of organized crime figures in previous years or even generations. Another aspect of these complex cases is that professional money launderers may be involved.

Studies reveal no obvious pattern to what criminals do with the proceeds of crime, even once they have indulged their hedonistic appetites. We continue to think that each individual offender, network, or crime group begins with its own capabilities to launder, and some actively or adventitiously search for co-offenders who can help them, whether voluntarily or as part of an extortionate relationship. Some of these succeed; others fail. We do not know how hard it is to find another professional launderer, but probably it is not extremely difficult in most countries. In jurisdictions where offenders have cynical views about the morality of bankers and lawyers, they will be more inclined to ask them to help, especially if the professionals are from their communities, are known to have vices or financial weaknesses, and may be more amenable to pressure and temptation which may take place after grooming over time. In jurisdictions where such professionals are ethically schooled and have reporting requirements that are significantly policed, and where there are relatively few economic pressures, most such requests are likely to be turned down. Such differential association models are difficult to test, and the data are too weak and anecdotal to enable general inferences to be made. There is no reason why the involvement of professionals in money laundering should be constant over place and time: to that extent, universal statements are likely to be overgeneralizations.

It is possible that law enforcement professionals' efforts and their resources have not been strong enough, including the reluctance of enforcement agencies to shift their patterns of intelligence development and interventions in directions recommended by FATF and "follow the money" advocates. This will be an ongoing debate. General trends in the anonymization of money, including the decline of cash (for example, in jurisdictions like Sweden) and the rise of cryptocurrencies, will affect the attractiveness of some crimes and the ease of laundering. But, skepticism should be exercised about the hype that surrounds some of these trends, which need to be related in detail to the forms of crime. Cryptocurrencies have undoubtedly become more popular as a sales medium and laundering mechanism, but their proportion of proceeds or profits from crimes not perpetrated on the Internet is likely to be modest for some years to come.

Perhaps it is too ambitious to aim to affect all organized crime rather than particular communities, criminal organizations, or particular forms of criminal activity. The weight of satisfying public expectations can easily descend into populist policing, a concern of libertarians and scholars who object to "Policing for Profit" (Baumer 2008; Worrall and Kovandzic 2008; Carpenter et al. 2015; Holcomb et al. 2018) and brush aside the economic and social costs of AML, which are less visible to the public and to politicians. The visible face of AML consists of egregious failures of bank reporting of transactions connected to drug, human, or endangered wildlife trafficking. The successes are seldom trumpeted, to protect reporting bodies and people. But AML and proceeds-of-crime freezing and confiscation are ways to show that something is being done to stop at least some offenders from enjoying the fruits of their crimes. That is a nontrivial social function whose effects on offending and on society itself merit evaluation.

REFERENCES

Amicelle, Anthony, and Vanessa Iafolla. 2018. "Suspicion-in-the-Making: Surveillance and Denunciation in Financial Policing." *British Journal of Criminology* 58(4):845–63.
APG (Asia/Pacific Group). 2012. *APG Typology Report on Trade Based Money Laundering*. Sydney: Asia/Pacific Group on Money Laundering.
Araujo, Ricardo A. 2010. "An Evolutionary Game Theory Approach to Combat Money Laundering." *Journal of Money Laundering Control* 13(1):70–78.
Basel Institute on Governance. 2018. *Basel AML Index 2018 Report*. Basel: Basel Institute on Governance.
Baumer, Eric P. 2008. "Evaluating the Balance Sheet of Asset Forfeiture Laws: Toward Evidence-Based Policy Assessments." *Criminology and Public Policy* 7:245–55.
BEIS (Business, Energy, and Industrial Strategy). 2019. *Corporate Transparency and Register Reform*. London: Department for Business, Energy and Industrial Strategy. https://www.gov.uk/government/consultations/corporate-transparency -and-register-reform.
Benson, Katie. 2018. "Money Laundering, Anti-Money Laundering and the Legal Profession." In *The Palgrave Handbook of Criminal and Terrorism Financing Law*, edited by Colin King, Clive Walker, and Jimmy Gurulé. Cham: Palgrave Macmillan.
———. 2020. *Lawyers and the Proceeds of Crime: The Facilitation of Money Laundering and Its Control*. New York: Routledge.
Berlusconi, Giulia. 2016. "Organized Criminals and the Legal Economy." In *Organised Crime in European Businesses*, edited by Ernesto U. Savona, Michele Riccardi, and Giulia Berlusconi. London: Routledge.

Birkenfeld, Bradley C. 2016. *Lucifer's Banker: The Untold Story of How I Destroyed Swiss Bank Secrecy*. Austin: Greenleaf Book Press.

BRÅ (Brottsförebyggande rådet). 2014. *Follow the Money: An Anthology on Asset-Oriented Law Enforcement*. Stockholm: BRÅ.

Bruinsma, Monique, Rik Ceulen, and Antoine Spapens. 2018. *Ondermijning door criminele 'weldoeners': Inventariserend onderzoek*. Den Haag: SDU, Den Haag.

Bullock, Karen, Ron V. Clarke, and Nick Tilley, eds. 2010. *Situational Prevention of Organised Crimes*. Devon: Willan.

Bullough, Oliver. 2018. *Moneyland: Why Thieves and Crooks Now Rule the World and How to Take It Back*. London: Profile.

Campana, Paolo, and Federico Varese. 2018. "Organized Crime in the United Kingdom: Illegal Governance of Markets and Communities." *British Journal of Criminology* 58(6):1381–1400.

Carpenter, Dick M., II, Lisa Knepper, Angela C. Erickson, and Jennifer McDonald. 2015. *Policing for Profit: The Abuse of Civil Asset Forfeiture*, 2nd ed. Arlington, VA, https://ij.org/report/policing-for-profit/.

Caulkins, Jonathan P., and Peter Reuter. 2010. "How Drug Enforcement Affects Drug Prices." In *Crime and Justice: A Review of Research*, vol. 9, edited by Michael Tonry. Chicago: University of Chicago Press.

Chaikin, David. 2018. "A Critical Analysis of the Effectiveness of Anti-Money Laundering Measures with Reference to Australia." In *The Palgrave Handbook of Criminal and Terrorism Financing Law*, edited by Colin King, Clive Walker, and Jimmy Gurulé. Cham: Palgrave Macmillan.

Cheran, Rudhramoorthy, and Sharryn Aiken. 2005. "The Impact of International Informal Banking on Canada: A Case Study of Tamil Transnational Money Transfer (Undiyal)." Working Paper. Ottawa: Law Commission of Canada.

Chiu, Yi-Ning, Benoit Leclerc, and Michael Townsley. 2011. "Crime Script Analysis of Drug Manufacturing in Clandestine Laboratories: Implications for Prevention." *British Journal of Criminology* 51(2):355–74.

Cornish, Derek B. 1994. "The Procedural Analysis of Offending and Its Relevance for Situational Prevention." In *Crime Prevention Studies*, edited by Ron V. Clarke. Monsey, NJ: Criminal Justice Press.

Dean, Geoff, Ivar Fahsing, and Peter Gottschalk. 2010. *Organized Crime: Policing Illegal Business Entrepreneurialism*. Oxford: Oxford University Press.

Eisenhardt, Kathleen M. 1989. "Agency Theory: An Assessment and Review." *Academy of Management Review* 14(1):57–74.

El Qorchi, Mohammed, Samuel M. Maimbo, and John F. Wilson. 2003. *Informal Funds Transfer Systems: An Analysis of the Informal Hawala System*. Washington, DC: International Monetary Fund.

Enrich, David. 2017. *The Spider Network: The Wild Story of a Math Genius, a Gang of Backstabbing Bankers, and One of the Greatest Scams in Financial History*. New York: Custom House.

Europol (European Union Agency for Law Enforcement Cooperation). 2017. *From Suspicion to Action: Converting Financial Intelligence into Greater Operational Impact*. Luxembourg: Europol.

Farfán-Méndez, Cecilia. 2019. "The Structure of Drug Trafficking Organizations and Money Laundering Practices: A Risk Appetite Hypothesis." *Journal of Illicit Economies and Development* 1(3):294–311.

FATF (Financial Action Task Force). 2006. *Trade Based Money Laundering*. Paris: Financial Action Task Force.

———. 2008. *Best Practices Paper on Trade Based Money Laundering*. Paris: Financial Action Task Force.

———. 2013. *National Money Laundering and Terrorist Financing Risk Assessment*. Paris: Financial Action Task Force.

———. 2018. *Professional Money Laundering*. Paris: Financial Action Task Force.

FCA (Financial Conduct Authority). 2018. *Financial Crime: Analysis of Firms' Data*. London: Financial Conduct Authority. https://www.fca.org.uk/publication /research/financial-crime-analysis-firms-data.pdf.

Felson, Marcus. 2004. *Crime and Everyday Life: Insights and Implications for Society*, 2nd ed. Thousand Oaks, CA: Pine Forge.

Felson, Marcus, and Rachel L. Boba. 2010. *Crime and Everyday Life*, 4th ed. Thousand Oaks, CA: SAGE.

Felson, Marcus, and Ron V. Clarke. 1998. *Opportunity Makes the Thief: Practical Theory for Crime Prevention*. London: Police Research Series.

Fernández Steinko, A. 2012. "Financial Channels of Money Laundering in Spain." *British Journal of Criminology* 52(5):908–31.

FinCEN. 2005. *Annual Report*. https://www.fincen.gov/sites/default/files/shared /annual_report_fy2005.pdf.

Findley, Michael G., Daniel L. Nielson, and Jason C. Sharman. 2014. *Global Shell Games: Experiments in Transnational Relations, Crime, and Terrorism*. New York: Cambridge University Press.

Garland, David. 1996. "The Limits of the Sovereign State: Strategies of Crime Control in Contemporary Society." *British Journal of Criminology* 36(4):445–71.

German, Peter. 2018. *Dirty Money: An Independent Review of Money Laundering in Lower Mainland Casinos Conducted for the Attorney General of British Columbia*. Vancouver: Peter German and Associates. https://news.gov.bc.ca/files/Gaming _Final_Report.pdf.

———. 2019. *Dirty Money—Part 2: Turning the Tide—An Independent Review of Money Laundering in B.C. Real Estate, Luxury Vehicle Sales, and Horse Racing*. Vancouver: Peter German and Associates. https://icclr.org/wp-content/uploads /2019/06/Dirty_Money_Report_Part_2.pdf?x21689.

Gillard, Michael. 2019. *Legacy: Gangsters, Corruption, and the London Olympics*. London: Bloomsbury.

Gilmour, Nicholas. 2014. "Understanding Money Laundering. A Crime Script Approach." *European Review of Organized Crime* 1(2):35–56.

Global Initiative. 2018. *The Political Economy of Organized Crime in Albania and Its Links to the United Kingdom*. Geneva: Global Initiative against Transnational Organized Crime.

Gold, Michael, and Michael Levi. 1994. *Money-Laundering in the UK: An Appraisal of Suspicion-Based Reporting*. London: Police Foundation.

Goldsmith, Andrew, David Gray, and Russell G. Smith. 2016. "Criminal Asset Recovery in Australia." In *Dirty Assets*, edited by Colin King and Clive Walker. London: Routledge.

Halliday, Terrence, Michael Levi, and Peter Reuter. 2014. *Global Surveillance of Dirty Money: Assessing Assessments of Regimes to Control Money-Laundering and Combat the Financing of Terrorism.* Chicago: American Bar Foundation. http://www.lexglobal.org/files/Report_Global%20Surveillance%20of%20Dirty %20Money%201.30.2014.pdf.

———. 2019. "Anti-Money Laundering: An Inquiry into a Disciplinary Transnational Legal Order." *Journal of International, Transnational, and Comparative Law* 4:1–25.

Hernandez-Coss, Raul. 2005. "The US-Mexico Remittance Corridor: Lessons on Shifting from Informal to Formal Transfer Systems." World Bank Working Paper no. 47. Washington, DC: World Bank.

Holcomb, Jefferson E., Marian R. Williams, William D. Hicks, Tomislav V. Kovandzic, and Michele Bisaccia Meitl. 2018. "Civil Asset Forfeiture Laws and Equitable Sharing Activity by the Police." *Criminology and Public Policy* 17(1):101–27.

Horgby, Anna, Daniel Särnqvist, and Lars Korsell. 2015. *Money Laundering and Other Forms of Money Management. Criminal, Undeclared, and Murky Money in the Legal Economy.* Stockholm: Swedish National Council for Crime Prevention.

Hülsse, Rainer. 2008. "Even Clubs Can't Do without Legitimacy: Why the Anti–Money Laundering Blacklist Was Suspended." *Regulation and Governance* 2(4):459–79.

Jensen, Michael C., and William H. Meckling. 1976. "Theory of the Firm: Managerial Behavior, Agency Costs and Ownership Structure." *Journal of Financial Economics* 3(4):305–60.

Jost, Patrick M., and Singh H. Sandhu. 2003. *The Hawala Alternative Remittance System and Its Role in Money Laundering.* Lyon: Interpol.

Katz, Jack. 1988. *Seductions of Crime: The Moral and Sensual Attractions of Doing Evil.* New York: Basic.

Kimelman, Michael. 2017. *Confessions of a Wall Street Insider: A Cautionary Tale of Rats, Feds, and Banksters.* New York: Skyhorse.

Kiser, Edgar. 1999. "Comparing Varieties of Agency Theory in Economics, Political Science, and Sociology: An Illustration from State Policy Implementation." *Sociological Theory* 17(2):146–70.

Kleemans, Edward R., Marion E. I. Brienen, and Henk G. van de Bunt. 2002. *Georganiseerde criminaliteit in Nederland: Tweede rapportage op basis van de WODC–monitor.* Den Haag: WODC.

Kleemans, Edward R., and Christianne J. De Poot. 2008. "Criminal Careers in Organized Crime and Social Opportunity Structure." *European Journal of Criminology* 5:69–98.

Kleemans, Edward R., and Melvin R. J. Soudijn. 2017. "Organised Crime." In *Handbook of Crime Prevention and Community Safety*, edited by Nick Tilley and Aiden Sidebottom. Abingdon, VA: Routledge.

Kleemans, Edward, and Vere van Koppen. 2020. "Organized Crime and Criminal Careers." In *Organizing Crime: Mafias, Markets, and Networks*, edited by Michael Tonry. Chicago: University of Chicago Press.

Krakowski, Krzysztof, and Gladys Zubiría. 2019. "Accounting for Turbulence in the Colombian Underworld." *Trends in Organized Crime* 22:166–86.

Kruisbergen, Edwin W., Edward R. Kleemans, and Ruud F. Kouwenberg. 2014. "Profitability, Power, or Proximity? Organized Crime Offenders Investing Their Money in Legal Economy." *European Journal on Criminal Policy and Research* 21(2):237–56.

———. 2016. "Explaining Attrition: Investigating and Confiscating the Profits of Organized Crime." *European Journal of Criminology* 13(6):677–95.

Kruisbergen, Edwin W., Eric R. Leukfeldt, Edward R. Kleemans, and Robert A. Roks. 2019. "Money Talks: Money Laundering Choices of Organized Crime Offenders in a Digital Age." *Journal of Crime and Justice* 5:569–81.

Kruisbergen, Edwin W., Henk G. van de Bunt, and Edward R. Kleemans. 2012. *Fourth Report of the Organized Crime Monitor: Summary*. Den Haag: Boom Lemma.

Kuldova, Tereza. 2018. "When Elites and Outlaws Do Philanthropy: On the Limits of Private Vices for Public Benefit." *Trends in Organized Crime* 21(3):295–309.

Levi, Michael. 2008. *The Phantom Capitalists: the Organisation and Control of Long-Firm Fraud*, 2nd ed. Andover: Ashgate.

———. 2013. "Drug Law Enforcement and Financial Investigation Strategies." Modernising Drug Law Enforcement, Report 5. London: International Drug Policy Consortium. https://www.tni.org/files/MDLE-5-drug-law-enforcement-financial-investigation-strategies.pdf.

———. 2018. "Reflections on Proceeds of Crime: A New Code for Confiscation?" In *Criminal Law Reform Now*, edited by John Child and Anthony Duff. Oxford: Hart.

Levi, Michael, and Lisa Osofsky. 1995. "Investigating, Seizing, and Confiscating the Proceeds of Crime." Crime Detection and Prevention Series Paper 61. London: Home Office.

Levi, Michael, and Peter Reuter. 2006. "Money Laundering." In *Crime and Justice: A Review of Research*, vol. 34, edited by Michael Tonry. Chicago: University of Chicago Press.

Levi, Michael, Peter Reuter, and Terrence Halliday. 2018. "Can the AML/CTF System Be Evaluated without Better Data?" *Crime, Law, and Social Change* 69(2):307–28.

Levitt, Steven, and Sudhir Venkatesh. 2000. "An Economic Analysis of a Drug Selling Gang's Finances." *Quarterly Journal of Economics* 115(3):755–89.

LexisNexis. 2017. *The True Cost of Anti-Money Laundering Compliance*. European ed. LexisNexis Risk Solutions. https://risk.lexisnexis.com/global/-/media/files/corporations%20and%20non%20profits/research/true%20cost%20of%20aml%20compliance%20europe%20survey%20report%20pdf.pdf.

Luyendijk, Joris. 2015. *Swimming with Sharks: My Journey into the World of the Bankers*. London: Guardian Faber.

Maimbo, Samuel M. 2003. "The Money Exchange Dealer of Kabul: A Study of the Hawala System in Afghanistan." Report. Washington, DC: World Bank.

Malm, Aili, and Gisela Bichler. 2013. "Using Friends for Money: The Positional Importance of Money Launderers in Organized Crime." *Trends in Organized Crime* 16(4):365–81.

Martin, Martina. 2009. "Hundi/Hawala: The Problem of Definition." *Modern Asian Studies* 43(4):909–37.

Matrix Knowledge Group. 2007. *The Illicit Drug Trade in the United Kingdom*, 2nd ed. London: Home Office.

McBarnet, Doreen, and Chris Whelan. 1999. *Creative Accounting and the Cross-Eyed Javelin Thrower*. Chichester: John Wiley.

McPherson, Gary. 2017. "Floating on Sea of Funny Money: An Analysis of Money Laundering through Miami Real Estate and the Federal Government's Attempt to Stop It." *University of Miami Business Law Review* 26:159–90.

Middleton, David. J., and Michael Levi. 2005. "The Role of Solicitors in Facilitating 'Organized Crime': Situational Crime Opportunities and Their Regulation." *Crime, Law, and Social Change* 42:123–61.

———. 2015. "Let Sleeping Lawyers Lie: Organized Crime, Lawyers and the Regulation of Legal Services." *British Journal of Criminology* 55(4):647–68.

Nance, Mark T. 2018. "The Regime That FATF Built: An Introduction to the Financial Action Task Force." *Crime, Law, and Social Change* 69(2):109–29.

NCA (National Crime Agency). 2018. *National Strategic Assessment of Serious and Organised Crime 2018*. London: National Crime Agency.

———. 2019. *Chinese Underground Banking and "Daigou."* London: National Crime Agency.

Obermayer, Bastian, and Frederik Obermaier. 2017. *The Panama Papers: Breaking the Story of How the Rich and Powerful Hide Their Money*. London: OneWorld.

Passas, Nikos. 1999. *Informal Value Transfer Systems and Criminal Organizations: A Study into So-Called Underground Banking Networks*. Den Haag: WODC.

———. 2003. *Informal Value Transfer Systems, Terrorism, and Money Laundering: A Report to the National Institute of Justice*. Den Haag: WODC.

Platt, Stephen. 2015. *Criminal Capital: How the Finance Industry Facilitates Crime*. London: Palgrave.

Ponce, Aldo F. 2019. "Violence and Electoral Competition: Criminal Organizations and Municipal Candidates in Mexico." *Trends in Organized Crime* 22(2):231–54.

Posner, Gerald. 2015. *God's Bankers: A History of Money and Power at the Vatican*. New York: Simon & Schuster.

Reuter, Peter. 2013. "Are Estimates of the Volume of Money Laundering Either Feasible or Useful?" In *Research Handbook on Money Laundering*, edited by Brigitte Unger and Daan van der Linde. Cheltenham: Edward Elgar.

Reuter, Peter, and Mark A. R. Kleiman. 1986. "Risks and Prices: An Economic Analysis of Drug Enforcement." In *Crime and Justice: A Review of Research*, vol. 7, edited by Michael Tonry and Norval Morris. Chicago: University of Chicago Press.

Reuter, Peter, Robert J. MacCoun, Patrick Murphy, Allan Abrahamse, and Barbara Simon. 1990. *Money from Crime: A Study of the Economics of Drug Dealing in Washington, DC*. Santa Monica, CA: RAND. https://www.rand.org/pubs/reports/R3894.html.

Reuter, Peter, and Edwin M. Truman. 2004. *Chasing Dirty Money: The Fight against Money Laundering*. Washington, DC: Institute for International Economics.

Riccardi, Michele, and Michael Levi. 2018. "Cash, Crime, and Anti-Money Laundering." In *The Palgrave Handbook of Criminal and Terrorism Financing Law*, edited by Colin King, Clive Walker, and Jimmy Gurulé. Cham: Palgrave Macmillan.

Ross, Stephen A. 1976. "The Economic Theory of Agency: The Principal's Problem." *American Economic Association* 63(2):134–39.

Savona, Ernesto U., and Giulia Berlusconi. 2015. *Organized Crime Infiltration of Legitimate Businesses in Europe: A Pilot Project in Five European Countries*. Trento: Transcrime–Università degli Studi di Trento.

Savona, Ernesto U., and Michele Riccardi, eds. 2015. *From Illegal Markets to Legitimate Businesses: The Portfolio of Organised Crime in Europe. Final Report of Project OCP—Organised Crime Portfolio*. Trento: Transcrime–Università degli Studi di Trento.

———. 2018. *Mapping the Risk of Serious and Organised Crime Infiltration in European Businesses: Final Report of the MORE Project*. Milano: Transcrime–Università Cattolica del Sacro Cuore.

Schott, Paul. 2003. *Reference Guide to Anti-Money Laundering and Combating the Financing of Terrorism*. London: World Bank.

Sharman, Jason C. 2011. *The Money Laundry*. Ithaca, NY: Cornell University Press.

Shaxson, Nicholas. 2011. *Treasure Islands: Tax Havens and the Men Who Stole the World*. London: Bodley Head.

Shelley, Louise. 2014. *Dirty Entanglements: Corruption, Crime, and Terrorism*. New York: Cambridge University Press.

———. 2018. *Dark Commerce: How a New Illicit Economy Is Threatening Our Future*. Princeton, NJ: Princeton University Press.

Sittlington, Samuel, and Jackie Harvey. 2018. "Prevention of Money Laundering and the Role of Asset Recovery." *Crime, Law and Social Change* 70(4):421–41.

Sittlington, Samuel B. Kerr. 2014. "What Are the Factors That Influence the Effectiveness of Anti-Money Laundering Policy Implementation in the UK? Exploring Money Laundering Crime and Policy." Unpublished PhD thesis, Newcastle Business School, Northumbria University.

Soudijn, Melvin R. J. 2010. "Wives, Girlfriends and Money Laundering." *Journal of Money Laundering Control* 13(4):405–16.

———. 2014. "Using Strangers for Money: A Discussion on Money-Launderers in Organized Crime." *Trends in Organized Crime* 17(3):199–217.

———. 2016. "Rethinking Money Laundering and Drug Trafficking: Some Implications for Investigators, Policy Makers and Researchers." *Journal of Money Laundering Control* 19(3):298–310.

————. 2017. *Witwassen: Criminaliteitsbeeldanalyse 2014*. Driebergen: Landelijke Eenheid.

————. 2019. "Using Police Reports to Monitor Money Laundering Developments: Continuity and Change in 12 Years of Dutch Money Laundering Crime Pattern Analyses." *European Journal on Criminal Policy and Research* 25(1):83–97.

Soudijn, Melvin R. J., and Theo Akse. 2012. *Witwassen: Criminaliteitsbeeldanalyse 2012*. Driebergen: Korps landelijke politiediensten–Dienst Nationale Recherche.

Soudijn, Melvin R. J., and Peter Reuter. 2016. "Cash and Carry: The High Cost of Currency Smuggling in the Drug Trade." *Crime, Law, and Social Change* 66(3):271–90.

Takáts, Előd. 2011. "A Theory of 'Crying Wolf': The Economics of Money Laundering Enforcement." *Journal of Law, Economics, and Organization* 27(1):32–78.

Tett, Gillian. 2010. *Fool's Gold: How Unrestrained Greed Corrupted a Dream, Shattered Global Markets, and Unleashed a Catastrophe*. London: Abacus.

Tilley, Nicholas, and Aiden Sidebottom. 2017. *Handbook of Crime Prevention and Community Safety*. London: Routledge.

Transparency International UK. 2017. *Hiding in Plain Sight: How UK Companies Are Used to Launder Corrupt Wealth*. London: Transparency International UK.

Unger, Brigitte, Joras Ferwerda, Ian Koetsier, Bojken Gjoleka, Alexander van Saase, Brigitte Slot, and Linette de Swart. 2018. *DeAard en omvang van criminele bestedingen*. Utrecht: Universiteit Utrecht. Summary: https://www.wodc.nl/binaries/2790_Summary_tcm28-354715.pdf.

Unger, Brigitte, Greg Rawlings, Madalina Busuioc, Joras Ferwerda, Melissa Siegel, Wouter de Kruijf, and Kristen Wokke. 2006. *The Amounts and the Effects of Money Laundering*. Den Haag: Ministerie van Financiën.

UNODC (United Nations Office on Drugs and Crime). 2011. "Estimating Illicit Financial Flows Resulting from Drug Trafficking and Other Transnational Organized Crime." Research report. Vienna: UNODC.

US Presidential Commission on Organized Crime. 1986. *The Cash Connection: Organized Crime, Financial Institutions, and Money Laundering*. Washington, DC: US Government Printing Office.

van Duyne, Petrus C. 2002. "Money-Laundering: Pavlov's Dog and Beyond." *Howard Journal of Criminal Justice* 37(4):359–74.

van Duyne, Petrus C. 2003. "Money Laundering Policy: Fears and Facts." In *Criminal Finances and Organising Crime in Europe*, edited by Petrus van Duyne, Klaus von Lampe, and James L. Newell. Nijmegen: Wolf Legal.

————. 2013. "Crime-Money and Financial Conduct." In *Research Handbook on Money Laundering*, edited by Brigitte Unger and Daan van der Linde. Cheltenham: Edward Elgar.

van Duyne, Petrus C., and Hervey de Miranda. 1999. "The Emperor's Cloths of Disclosure: Hot Money and Suspect Disclosures." *Crime, Law, and Social Change* 31(3):245–71.

van Duyne, Petrus C., Jackie H. Harvey, and Liliya Y. Gelemerova. 2019. *The Critical Handbook of Money Laundering: Policy, Analysis and Myths*. London: Palgrave.

van Duyne, Petrus C., and Michael Levi. 2005. *Drugs and Money: Managing the Drug Trade and Crime-Money in Europe*. London: Routledge.

van Duyne, Petrus C., Lena Louwe, and Melvin R. J. Soudijn. 2014. "Money, Art, and Laundering: Coming to Grips with the Risks." In *Cultural Property Crime: An Overview and Analysis of Contemporary Perspectives and Trends*, edited by Joris D. Kila and Marc Balcells. Leiden: Brill.

Venkatesh, Sudhir. 2008. *Gang Leader for a Day: A Rogue Sociologist Crosses the Line*. London: Penguin.

Vijlbrief, Matthijs F. J. 2012. "Looking for Displacement Effects: Exploring the Case of Ecstasy and Amphetamine in the Netherlands." *Trends in Organized Crime* 15(2–3):198–214.

Visser, S. 2017. "Nieuwe witwastypologieën in de strijd tegen witwassen met virtuele betaalmiddelen." *Tijdschrift voor Bijzonder Strafrecht en Handhaving* 4(4):217–23.

Von Lampe, Klaus. 2011. "The Application of the Framework of Situational Crime Prevention to "Organized Crime."" *Criminology and Criminal Justice* 11(2):145–63.

Worrall, John L., and Tomislav V. Kovandzic. 2008. "Is Policing for Profit? Answers from Asset Forfeiture." *Criminology and Public Policy* 7(2):219–44.

Index